THE FIRST ANGELINOS

THE FIRST ANGELINOS

The Gabrielino Indians of Los Angeles

By

William McCawley

A Malki Museum Press/Ballena Press Cooperative Publication

Editors

Malki Museum Press: Harry Lawton
Ballena Press: Sylvia Brakke Vane

Library of Congress Cataloging-in-Publication Data

McCawley, William, 1952-
  The First Angelinos: the Gabrielino Indians of Los Angeles / by William McCawley.

    p. cm.
"A Malki Museum Press/Ballena Press cooperative publication."
Includes biographical references and index.
ISBN 0-9651016-1-4 (cloth : alk. paper) : $49.95
ISBN 0-9651016-0-6 (pb : alk. paper) : $34.95

1. Gabrielino Indians. 2. Gabrielino language.
E99.G15M34 1996
979.4'9--dc20   95-43042
                                                                                     CIP

Orders: Malki Museum Press, Morongo Indian Reservation, 11-795 Fields Road, Banning, CA 92220
                or
        Ballena Press Publishers' Services, P.O. Box 2510, Novato, CA 94948.

Printed in the United States of America.

To my sons Michael and Jonathan

In the west beyond pimǘ'ŋa [Santa Catalina Island] there is a land which rises as a sierra from the sea with pines, fruits and flowers. That county is called 'erḙ́spat, and the Captain of that county is šEhḚ́vajt. He cares for all and tolerates no evil. . . . Those who do not believe šEhḚ́vajt, he punishes. God made both worlds. They are connected. The one there is connected and balanced with the one here.

- José Zalvidea

TABLE OF CONTENTS

FIGURES

MAPS

ACKNOWLEDGMENTS

This book was created over a long period of time with several lengthy interruptions; it is therefore impossible to remember and acknowledge everyone who contributed to its successful completion. I apologize to anyone whose name I may have inadvertently omitted.

The editorial boards of Malki Museum Press and Ballena Press were unwavering in their support of my work and for this I am deeply grateful. In this regard, I should especially like to thank Katherine Saubel, Lowell Bean, Harry Lawton, and Sylvia Vane for their devotion to the project.

Many individuals contributed their time and their labor to the endeavor. Lowell Bean has been not only an editor, but also a teacher, a mentor, and a friend. Keith Dixon's editorial work was crucial to the success of this book. Michael Lerch and Dee Schroth of Malki Museum Press, and Susan Cole, Heather Singleton and Sylvia Vane of Ballena Press worked hard to prepare the manuscript for press; without their efforts *The First Angelinos* could not have been published.

I thank those individuals and institutions who assisted my research by providing photographs and reference materials, by making artifact collections available, by providing access to archaeological sites, and by sharing their ideas and suggestions: Lynn Bailey, Eloise Barter, Kathleen T. Baxter, Lowell Bean, Tom Blackburn, Sally Bond, Dot Brovarny, Ed Castillo, Keith Dixon, Bob Edberg, Bill Frank, Roberta Greenwood, Margaret Hardin, Michael Hart, Robert Jackson, John Johnson, Chester King, Ed Krupp, Michael Lerch, Bill Mason, Patricia Moore, Pam Munro, Sheila O'Neil, Steve O'Neil, William M. Roberts, John W. Robinson, Charles Rozaire, Richard Smith, Steve Schwartz, Jacquelyn Sundstrand, Jan Timbrook, Kris and Jean Van Tatenhove, Mary Wolfskill, and Andrew Yatsko.

The Bancroft Library, University of California, Berkeley
The Bowers Museum
California Historical Society, Title Insurance and Trust Photo Collection
California State University, Dominguez Hills, Special Collections and Archives
California State University, Long Beach, Department of Anthropology
Catalina Island Museum
Channel Islands National Park
Field Museum of Natural History
Grace Hudson Museum and The Sun House
Henry E. Huntington Library
Library of Congress
Lowie Museum of Anthropology (now the Phoebe Hearst Museum of Anthropology), University of California, Berkeley
National Anthropological Archives, Smithsonian Institution
National Archives and Records Administration, Cartographic and Architectural Branch
Natural History Museum of Los Angeles
National Museum of the American Indian, Smithsonian Institution
Natural Resources Office, Naval Air Station North Island, San Diego
Natural Resources Office, Naval Air Weapons Station, Point Mugu
Peabody Museum of Archaeology and Ethnology
Santa Barbara Mission Archive Library
Santa Barbara Natural History Museum
Southwest Museum
Sunny Slope Water Company

The idea for this book came from the late California archaeologist Frank Fenenga. Originally I had planned only a magazine article; Frank encouraged me to think in grander terms.

Although I did not have the pleasure of meeting the late Travis Hudson, I felt his influence and drew inspiration from his work.

The success of a project like this depends upon the support of many family members, friends and loved ones; I am deeply grateful for their encouragement and their patience.

William McCawley

INTRODUCTION

by Lowell John Bean

This book, *The First Angelinos*, by William McCawley, provides a state of the art introduction to Gabrielino culture and history. Ever since it was published in 1962, Bernice Johnston's *California's Gabrielino Indians* has been the reference of choice with respect to the Gabrielino (*Tongva*), who occupied the Los Angeles area when the Spanish arrived in 1769. Johnston's book was enthusiastically welcomed by both the public and scholars. Although meant for the general public, and therefore not fully referenced, it dealt in considerable detail with a people who have been and are the subject of much inquiry, a people at that time thought to have become extinct without notable information about them having been recorded. This well-written, fully cited, and more comprehensive volume by William McCawley will receive accolades from the public and the scholarly community as an even more fully realized study of the Gabrielino than Johnston's.

The book by Johnston was a marked improvement on its predecessors in part because she had access to at least some of the notes from John Peabody Harrington's "early Gabrielino informants" (1962:iv). Indeed, Harrington wrote the preface to the book. In the ensuing 30 years, Harrington's vast body of notes has been organized and made available on microfilm, and has provided McCawley with much more detailed information than was available to Johnston. He has benefitted not only from Harrington's notes themselves, but also from secondary sources derived from Harrington's notes. These include Blackburn's *December's Child;* Blackburn and Hudson's *The Material Culture of the Chumash Interaction Sphere* (5 volumes); Hudson, Timbrook, and Rempe's *Tomol;* and others.

In addition to Harrington's superb notes on the various aspects of Gabrielino culture, McCawley made use of those of C. Hart Merriam. Merriam interviewed southern California Indians at even earlier dates than Harrington, and, like Harrington, left an abundance of unpublished material. It is a peculiar fact of California Indian studies that these two scholars, who were somewhat outside the mainstream of California Indian students, have lately contributed so significantly to our knowledge. They did not initially publish as much of the data they collected in the various anthropological journals as others did, but, being indefatigable collectors, assembled far more information than most.

McCawley carefully studied the ethnographic literature on other southern California Indian groups, especially those with whom the Gabrielino maintained trade and ceremonial relationships, and made full use of publications regarding California Indians that appeared in anthropological series published by the University of California, Berkeley (UCB), such as the University of California Publications in American Archaeology and Ethnology; the Anthropological Record Series, and the like. These were, in the first half of the twentieth century, the principal venues for the presentation of scholarly anthropological research. They were edited and managed by Alfred L. Kroeber and his various colleagues. Apparently, professional differences and personal enmities precluded Harrington and Merriam from publishing much in the various UCB series, Harrington's *Culture Element* volume being a rare exception. It was Robert Heizer, a student of Kroeber's, who finally recognized the value of Merriam's material, and arranged for its publication. The efforts of archivists at The Bancroft Library at UCB, the Library of Congress, the National Anthropological Archives at the Smithsonian Institution in Washington, D.C., and other similar institutions are to be commended for maintaining such materials for all who are interested in the culture and history of California Indians.

Mr. McCawley has diligently incorporated and made available a great many data not previously reviewed in detail, e.g., the data available in the "gray literature" of cultural resource management studies, the extensive notes accompanying museum collections of Gabrielino material culture, and archaeological research done in the past several decades—a formidable body of work in comparison with that available to previous writers. We have many to thank for the emergence of these materials in recent years, and the changes in the anthropological discipline that have made them useful. As new demands have been placed on the anthropological and historical discipline by Indian communities—as consultants in legal and procedural matters, such as the various Claims cases, federal recognition applications, and cultural resource studies—more precise accounts of Native American history have emerged. Many new works have also resulted because of the new scholarly interests that have developed in the past several decades, e.g., interests in the processes of socio-cultural development, the nature and function of enmity-amity systems, and the nature of political organizations (past and historic). These are only a few of the many issues related to an understanding of the various levels of cultural complexity that Californians achieved prior to and after European contact. The reasons for environmental and cultural changes, and explanations of how these cultures persisted, adopted and changed over time have added an extraordinary new body of research, all of which influences contemporary views of the Gabrielino and others.

The discipline has also been blessed by a vigorous renewed interest in historical resources and processes regarding Indian cultures, resulting in the sophisticated uses of the Spanish mission records, so well exemplified in the works of scholars like John Johnson, Randall Milliken, Robert Jackson and others. New demographic and sociological data are available for analysis, and scholars have a more sophisticated capacity to see the ways in which European institutions impacted California Indians demographically, socio-politically, culturally, medically, and philosophically, and how California Indian people effected the cultural, political and economic development of Europeans.

McCawley's discussion of economic centers, boundaries, ritual systems, religious beliefs, leadership, power, astronomy, calendars, magical flight, class structures, and other subjects fit well into current research that is revealing greater societal complexity, greater intercultural participation, and the many contributions of Indians to the development of the southern California cultural historical dynamics. His study permits us to understand why the Gabrielino developed in the ways they did, their relationships to neighboring groups, and their persistence as a culturally identifiable group. It makes possible a better comparative analysis of cultural development in this area, an area complex environmentally, historically, and linguistically.

It provides an opportunity for non-Indian and Indian scholars studying southern California to compare one group's cultural ways with another's—a task that will help explain much about the region as a whole. Mr. McCawley would be the first to agree that his work, the result of many years of careful research, is not the last word. He has plans for more work, and other scholars will join him. There are a number of avenues of research that may be of value to pursue.

Such further research will benefit from other contemporary studies. There is greater detail available from early Hispanic period accounts than when Johnston and earlier writers considered Gabrielino history. Not only are more archival resources available on the Spanish-Mexican period, but several scholars have examined the nature of the period in detail; e.g., Mason, Phillips, Forbes, Pitts, Rawls, and Hurtado. They have elicited important insights into the intercultural and historical processes of the area, especially the very real effects of such institutions as the ranchos, missions, pueblos, different legal systems, and the effects of diseases over the centuries upon California Indians.

A review of prehistory of the Los Angeles area, derived from the extraordinary new data available from the archaeological record, which has grown so much in the last several decades, would be a most welcome companion piece to this volume. Scholars should be able to interpret materials from this archaeological record, fit what they learn into the broader theoretical systems that have emerged in recent years of discourse and coordinate it with linguistic, historical and ethnographic data.

Another avenue of research that new resources would enrich would be a study of the impact of neighboring southern California cultures on one another after contact with the missions. Indian people moved into neighboring territories as these were depleted by removals to the missions—the Luiseños, Cahuillas, and Serranos apparently moved into territory the Gabrielinos had occupied. In other instances, people from these groups worked on mission ranches in various capacities. There they learned new ideas and incorporated new materials into their own culture, borrowing some from the Spanish and some from the neighbors with whom they came in contact.

Data from the various sources now available to scholars can be interpreted from a broader perspective of a regional area composed of several cultures that shared much with one another yet were each quite different. Southern California can be viewed as a special laboratory—a region largely related in the historical past but deriving from several distinctly different cultural groups—for the study of cultural development and exchange, ethnicity maintenance and its processes. For example, the economic system that had developed in southern California, previously barely mentioned, is now understood to have been dependent on extraordinary interconnections reaching across the whole of southern California, Baja, and into Arizona.

Publication of *The First Angelinos* comes at an opportune moment, since in recent years many of the descendants of the Gabrielino people have made themselves known, as have many others once thought to be culturally extinct, and have become active in the regeneration of their identity. Before that, they were, to outsiders and non-Indians, and even to many other southern California Indians, quite invisible. When the author and his associates met with a group in San Gabriel in 1978-79 in order to discover if there were a viable group of people with Gabrielino identity who could be consulted about their feelings and reactions to the development of a transmission line passing through their territory, they were pleasantly surprised to enter a room full of people who acknowledged a Gabrielino cultural background and recognized a common cause. A sad fact of the meeting was that the last Gabrielino speaker, who was there, we were told, was unable to hear or speak.

The First Angelinos will have different meanings to different people. It will serve as a basic textbook and/or reference on the Gabrielino in college classrooms belonging to departments of anthropology, history, and ethnic studies. It will be a rewarding book for anyone with an interest in Native Americans or in American history to read. It will grace many a coffee table. It will, it is to be hoped, inspire numerous scholars to further study. For those Gabrielino peoples seeking federal recognition it will be a cornerstone in establishing their very legitimate claims. Most important of all, it may provide youngsters who have a Gabrielino heritage with knowledge about their ancestors and enhance their pride in their heritage.

Plate 1. A Gabrielino home. Traditional Gabrielino houses had a circular floor plan and were constructed in a dome shape; according to historical accounts the largest of these structures could house fifty people. This is a detail from a painting of Mission San Gabriel completed by Ferdinand Deppe in 1832 (see Plate 4).

Plate 2. A pictograph, or rock painting, from the Cave of the Whales on San Nicolas Island. The figures are executed in black pigment and may represent killer whales. The cave was once extensively decorated with petroglyphs (rock carvings) depicting sharks, fish, and various geometric forms; unfortunately the naturally damp conditions within the cave have caused the deterioration of much of this artwork.

Plate 3. Pictographs from the Winter Solstice Site at Burro Flats. The brilliant rock paintings, executed in red and white against a black background, decorate the interior of a shallow rock shelter. At the time of the winter solstice, the paintings in this rock shelter are illuminated by a narrow shaft of sunlight.

Santa Barbara Mission Archive Library. Author's photograph.

Plate 4. A painting of Mission San Gabriel completed in 1832 by Ferdinand Deppe. In the lower right corner of the painting is a traditional Gabrielino home (see Plate 1); to the left of the mission are the rows of adobe houses occupied by the neophytes (Christianized Indians).

CHAPTER 1

INTRODUCING THE GABRIELINO INDIANS

T he crowded landscape of Los Angeles holds an ancient story. It is the story of the brave and resourceful Indian peoples who once inhabited the spacious valleys and plains of Los Angeles and Orange counties in southern California; of daring seafarers who travelled the open sea in wooden canoes to trade with their kinsmen dwelling on the Channel Islands; of skillful hunters clad in deerskin costumes who roamed the valleys and hills in search of their prey; of powerful shamans who transformed themselves at will into bears and wolves, and an all-knowing, all-powerful creator-god who established the rules by which life was to be lived. It is a story of tragedy and great courage, and an Indian people decimated by disease, prejudice, and poverty, struggling to survive in a new and often unfriendly world. It is the story of the Gabrielino Indians.

Who were the Gabrielino, where did they come from, and how did they live? This book answers these questions and provides a detailed survey of these fascinating people and their culture. The Gabrielino were not the first people to inhabit the Los Angeles area; they were heirs to a non-European cultural tradition that had evolved over thousands of years. It is in recognition of this heritage that they will be referred to as the First Angelinos.

In addition to serving as an introduction and general survey, this book is intended to fill a long-standing need for a reference and resource guide to the Gabrielino and their culture. For this reason, source materials are cited in the preferred style of anthropological publications. Microfilm citations list the author, date of publication, reel (R) and frame (F). Unless otherwise noted, bracketed comments within a quoted section are by William McCawley. Italicized words were italicized in the quoted original. A detailed bibliography appears at the end of the book.

The present work employs a large number of Gabrielino names and terms that will be unfamiliar to most readers. Because Gabrielino was a language that did not have a standardized written alphabet, Gabrielino words have been recorded in various ways by different researchers. The present volume employs a standardized orthography developed by Pamela Munro, Professor of Linguistics at the University of California at Los Angeles. Direct quotations retain the original linguistic spellings to preserve the flavor of the source materials.

In general, the pronunciation of Gabrielino words follows a number of basic rules. Vowels are pronounced as in Spanish. The letters *ch* are pronounced as in *ch*urch; *hw* is like English *wh* in *wh*ich (not witch); *hy* is like the sound that comes before the oo sound in English *h*ue; *kw* is like English *qu* in *qu*ail; *η* is like the sound at the end of si*ng*; *sh* is roughly as in *sh*ip; *x* is like a Spanish *j* or a German or Scottish *ch* (as in Ba*ch*); *nk* is pronounced like *ngk*, as in English ba*nk*.

Gabrielino words have one vowel that is long and stressed, and in the present orthography this vowel is doubled: aa, ee, ii, oo, uu. The language does not have any words that begin with a vowel; rather, such words have a glottal stop (') at the beginning. A glottal stop is the catch in your throat between the two vowels of a word like "uh-oh." The sounds of our letters *b* and *d* appear only in Gabrielino words borrowed from Spanish (Munro n.d.).

A full appreciation of the Gabrielino and their place in the history of Los Angeles requires an understanding of the way in which information derived from varied sources must be blended to recreate a picture of this lost world. Only by making use of the patient, painstaking efforts of historians, archaeologists, and anthropologists can this story be told.

It is a tale that begins long before Europeans arrived in the New World.

THE EARLIEST PEOPLE

Thousands of years before Columbus came to this continent, Los Angeles and the surrounding region were occupied by Indian peoples descended from the ancient hunters who first crossed from Asia into North America via the Bering Strait. The date of the earliest local occupation remains uncertain; however, a growing body of data in the form of radiocarbon dates from archaeological sites on the Channel Islands demonstrates that a fully maritime-adapted, seafaring culture existed in southern California at least ten thousand years ago. San Clemente Island was occupied by 7,785 B.C., and humans had reached San Nicolas Island by 6,210 B.C. On the mainland, discoveries at Rancho La Brea and the recovery of ancient stone tools at Malaga Cove on Santa Monica Bay, suggest a long history of occupation for the region (Wallace 1955:188-190; Willey 1966:365; Raab and Yatsko 1990:18-19; Salls 1990b).

Sometime prior to 6000 B.C., the lifestyle of the early peoples living in the Los Angeles area changed significantly. Hunting, which was previously the primary food-gathering activity on the mainland, became less important, while a greater reliance was placed upon the gathering of wild seeds and plant foods. The maritime-adapted peoples living along the coast also appear to have turned to terrestrial food resources, perhaps in response to the silting of the coastal estuaries that were vital to their economy. During this period plant foods were prepared by grinding on stone platforms known as "metates," using handstones referred to as "manos." As a result archaeologists sometimes refer to this cultural period as the "Millingstone Period," "Millingstone Horizon," or "Food Collecting Period."

Whether the change in food gathering preferences represents the arrival of new peoples or the gradual cultural evolution of the earlier hunting peoples in response to environmental change is unclear; however, similar developments were occurring throughout much of California at approximately the same time. The Los Angeles-Santa Monica Mountain region was home to one group of Millingstone peoples whose archaeological remains are known as the "Topanga Culture" (Wallace 1955:191-193, 1978:28-30; Elsasser 1978:55; Raab and Yatsko 1990:19).

By approximately 3,000 B.C., the people of the Millingstone Period had developed a more sophisticated food gathering economy that combined the benefits of hunting and the collecting of wild plants and seeds. Fishing, sea mammal hunting and shellfish gathering became important activities for the Indians living near the coast and on the Channel Islands. Important archaeological sites dating from this period include the Big Tujunga Site at Big Tujunga Wash in the San Fernando Valley and Little Harbor on Santa Catalina Island. Archaeologically speaking, this period of diversified food gathering is sometimes called the "Intermediate Period," "Intermediate Horizon" or "Diversified Subsistence Period." (Wallace 1955:193-194, 1978:30; Elsasser 1978:55).

THE UTO-AZTECANS

Sometime during the Millingstone or Intermediate periods new peoples began entering southern California. Anthropologists refer to these people as Uto-Aztecans because they spoke a language belonging to the Uto-Aztecan linguistic stock that once extended across the Great Basin region of Utah, Nevada, and California (in older literature the term Shoshonean is used instead of Uto-Aztecan, although the people are the same). Traveling from the Great Basin, perhaps to escape drought or food shortage, the Uto-Aztecans entered and occupied southern California from the desert to the coast, absorbing or displacing the earlier population of Hokan-speaking peoples.

The date of the Uto-Aztecan arrival in southern California is an issue of great interest to archaeologists. The time span of this migration is uncertain; however, it most likely occurred in a number of successive waves over a lengthy period. Some would place this event prior to 2000 B.C., while others prefer a relatively late date of A.D. 700. Linguistic evidence suggests a date of A.D. 1-500 (Kroeber 1925:574-580; Koerper 1979). Regardless, the Uto-Aztecans were present in southern California during the final phase of prehistory, which is commonly referred to as the "Late Period" or "Late Horizon" and is thought to have commenced around A.D. 1-500.

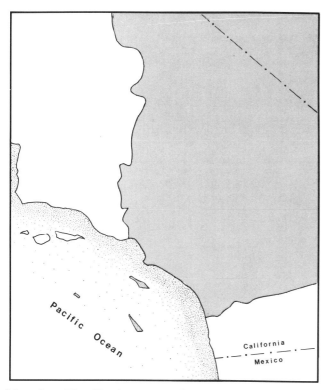

Map 1. The Uto-Aztecan territory (shaded) in southern California; this territory included the southern Channel Islands. Unless otherwise noted, all maps were prepared by author.

The Late Period saw a number of important economic and cultural developments, including increased use of the bow and arrow, the concentration of larger populations in settlements and communities, and the growth of regional subcultures (Wallace 1955:195-199; Moratto 1984:159). By the time Cabrillo arrived in coastal California waters in A.D. 1542, the Indian peoples of southern California had developed a number of these regional subcultures. Among these were several groups of Uto-Aztecan Indians, each speaking a different language and residing within its own geographical territory.

THE GABRIELINO

One of the most impressive of the Uto-Aztecan groups, the Gabrielino, occupied much of present-day Los Angeles and Orange counties. Their name derives from the incorporation of many of their people into Mission San Gabriel during the eighteenth century. For similar reasons the Indians who inhabited the valley surrounding the San Fernando Mission are often called the Fernandeño, although culturally the Gabrielino and the Fernandeño appear to have been so

closely related that the distinction is unnecessary. Throughout the present volume the term Gabrielino will be used when describing cultural traits common to both groups. The term Fernandeño will be reserved to describe geographical or cultural features specific to those Gabrielino dwelling in the San Fernando Valley.

The early Indian inhabitants of the Los Angeles region remain shadowy figures known only from their archaeological remains. In contrast, the Gabrielino are revealed by the ethnographic and ethnohistorical records as a people of material wealth and cultural sophistication. They inhabited a vast tract of some of the most fertile and productive land in California, and prior to contact with Europeans their population may have grown to more than 5,000 people living in 50 to 100 towns and settlements on the mainland and on the southern Channel Islands. Their territory stretched from Topanga Canyon in the northwest, to the base of Mount Wilson in the north, to the San Bernardino vicinity in the east, and to the Aliso Creek vicinity near El Toro Road in the southeast, encompassing in all more than 2,500 square miles (Kroeber 1925:621; Strong 1929:8; Shinn 1941:65-68; Bean and Smith 1978).

In addition to this mainland territory, the Gabrielino occupied three of the Channel Islands lying off the coast of southern California, Santa Catalina, San Clemente, and San Nicolas, and also made excursions to Santa Barbara Island. They maintained a maritime trade network using large canoes of carefully shaped and fitted wooden planks, and were proficient sailors, traveling primarily during the summer months when the sea was calm, not hesitating to make the 60 mile journey to lonely San Nicolas Island (Swartz 1960; Bean and Smith 1978; Hudson 1981). The prestige and political strength of the Gabrielino were enhanced by impressive achievements in pre-industrial technology and economics, as well as religion and oral literature. Culturally, the Gabrielino have been described as the "wealthiest and most thoughtful of all the Shoshoneans of the State" (Kroeber 1925:621).

HISTORICAL ACCOUNTS

Information about this fascinating Indian group has been gathered from a wide variety of sources over a period of more than four centuries. The earliest accounts were written during the 1500s and 1600s by Spanish seafarers exploring the California coast. The last historical accounts were completed after the United States had taken control of California in the mid-1800s.

THE CABRILLO EXPEDITION, 1542

The first Europeans of record to observe the Gabrielino were the seafarers who accompanied Juan Rodríguez Cabrillo up the California coast in the sixteenth century. Cabrillo may have been searching for the mouth of a large, navigable river known as the Río de la Señora. This legendary waterway, also known as the Northwest Passage or Strait of Anian, was believed to provide a convenient route across North America (Bolton 1908:3-4; Wagner 1929:73-74, 1941:9). The search for the Río de la Señora led Cabrillo and his crew to the Channel Islands and their inhabitants. It was perhaps at Avalon Harbor, on the island of Santa Catalina, that Europeans first encountered the Gabrielino in October of 1542.

> At nightfall they were close to some islands which are about seven leagues from the mainland, and as the wind died out they could not reach them that night. Saturday, the 7th, at daybreak, they reached them, and named them "San Salvador" [Santa Catalina] and "Vitoria" [San Clemente]. They anchored at one and went ashore with the ship's boat to see if there were any people there. As the boat was nearing land a great number of Indians came out of the bushes and grass, shouting, dancing, and making signs to come ashore. As from the boats they saw the women fleeing, they made signs to them not to fear; so shortly they became assured and put their bows and arrows on the ground. Launching into the water a fine canoe containing eight or ten Indians, they came out to the ships. These were given some beads and presents with which they were well pleased, and shortly went back. The Spaniards afterwards went ashore and both the Indian men and women and everybody felt very secure. Here an old Indian made signs to them that men like the Spaniards, wearing clothes and having beards, were going around on the mainland. They remained at this island only until midday (Wagner 1929:85).

The following day the Spaniards sailed across the channel and into a sheltered body of water which they named the "Bay of Smokes," commonly believed to be San Pedro Bay. The smoke from Gabrielino fires

may have inspired this colorful name. These fires may have been set as signals inviting the explorers to land; another possibility is that they were grass fires set during seasonal rabbit hunts (see Chapter 7). The Spaniards took aboard some Indians who had rowed out to meet them, and from them they learned that parties of Spaniards were also exploring the interior regions of the mainland. The Indians near San Diego had told a similar story, and the persistence of these reports is noteworthy. They probably stemmed from accounts of Spanish explorations along the Colorado River that were brought to the coast by Indian traders (Wagner 1929:332-334, notes 56, 72-74; 1941:17).

Following their encounter with the Gabrielino, the explorers sailed northward, continuing as far as Monterey Bay before turning back. They spent December and the better part of January at one of the islands, now believed to have been Santa Catalina. Here, on January 3, 1543, Cabrillo died of an infection suffered as the result of a broken limb (Wagner 1941:20, 55; Kelsey 1986:157-159).

THE SEBASTIAN VIZCAINO EXPEDITION, 1602

Fifty years elapsed between Cabrillo's expedition and the next recorded contact between the Gabrielino and Europeans in 1602. In that year a seafaring expedition led by Sebastián Vizcaíno was searching for a northern harbor that could be used by Spanish galleons returning from Manila (Wagner 1929:154, 173-174). While sailing north along the California coast the expedition stopped at Santa Catalina, probably landing at Avalon (Wagner 1929:235, Map 26, 401, note 133). The Gabrielino welcomed them warmly and "began to raise smokes on the beach, and when they saw they had anchored, the women, children, and old men began to shout and make demonstrations of joy in proof of their happiness. They came running to the beach to receive the guests who were arriving" (Wagner 1929:236). The islanders made a very favorable impression on the explorers. The men were described as "well built and robust" while the women were "well featured and well built, of good countenance and eyes and modest in their looks and behavior. The boys and girls are white and blond, and all are affable and smiling" (Wagner 1929:236, 237).

Later explorers would also note that the Gabrielino seemed lighter-skinned than the Indians farther to the south. The Gabrielino were fascinated by the Spaniards' exotic clothing and European-style implements and were "very light-fingered and clever, and in stealing anything and in putting it in safety [they] are ingenious" (Wagner 1929:237, 239).

Detailed accounts of this voyage were written by the expedition leader Sebastián Vizcaíno and Father Antonio de la Ascensión. In his journal Father Antonio reports seeing "well-made canoes of boards fastened together," noting that "some of these canoes were so large that they would hold more than twenty people," although "in the small ones there are ordinarily three when they go fishing, two men with their paddles . . . one in the stern and the other in the bow, and a boy between to throw out such water as the canoe might make" (Wagner 1929:236). Also noteworthy were articles of Gabrielino fishing equipment, especially a "harpoon made of fishbone," and "vessels and pitchers in which they keep water" which were "made of reeds." The islanders had "many dogs of medium size and of good appearance like our spotted retrievers, only they do not bark, but howl like coyotes." The islanders maintained a thriving trade with the mainlanders in which roots shaped "something like small potatoes" were an important commodity (Wagner 1929:236-237).

Other important observations made by the Spanish in 1602 describe Gabrielino religious practices. Near Isthmus Cove on Santa Catalina the Spaniards observed a "place of worship or temple where the natives perform their sacrifices and adorations." According to Father Antonio it

> was a large flat patio and in one part of it, where they had what we would call an altar, there was a great circle all surrounded with feathers of various colors and shapes, which must come from the birds they sacrifice. Inside the circle there was a figure like a devil painted in various colors, in the way the Indians of New Spain are accustomed to paint them. At the sides of this were the sun and the moon. When the soldiers reached this place, inside the circle there were two large crows larger than ordinary ones, which flew away when they saw strangers, and alighted on some near-by rocks. One of the soldiers, seeing their size, aimed at them with his harquebus [matchlock rifle], and discharging it, killed them both. When the Indians saw this they began to weep and display great emotion. In my opinion, the Devil talked to them through these crows, because all the men and women held them in great respect and fear (Wagner 1929:237).

More than three centuries have elapsed since these early voyages of exploration, yet the accounts remain as fascinating as ever. The next recorded contact between the Gabrielino and Europeans occurred more than 150 years later.

THE PORTOLA EXPEDITION, 1769

In the late 1700s the Spanish, concerned about English and Russian incursions on the west coast, decided to establish Alta California as a buffer state to protect their holdings in New Spain. The colonization of Alta California by the Spanish Crown began in 1769 with an expedition led by Gaspar de Portolá. Accompanied by the Franciscan Padre Junípero Serra, Portolá established frontier outposts at San Diego and Monterey, crossing the Gabrielino territory three times within a period of 12 months (Johnston 1962:116).

Portolá's party was the first recorded land expedition to explore Alta California, and it foreshadowed unimaginable changes for the Gabrielino, changes that would forever alter Indian cultural traditions that had evolved over more than a millennium. Three members of the expedition maintained journals in which they recorded their observations: the expedition's leader Gaspar de Portolá, Miguel Costansó, and Father Juan Crespí. These journals record the hardships of the expedition and describe the Indian towns and settlements the explorers passed on their way to Monterey. The terrain was rugged and choked with brush, but the Indians were friendly and welcoming. Father Crespí repeatedly remarked upon the generosity of these people. In one case, "the Indians from a village in the valley came to visit us. They came without arms, and with a friendliness unequalled; they made us presents of their poor seeds" (Bolton 1927:138). On another occasion the Spaniards pitched camp near "a populous village of Indians, who received us with great friendliness. Fifty-two of them came to the camp, and their chief told us by signs which we understood very well that we must come to live with them; that they would make houses for us, and provide us with food" (Bolton 1927:141).

It seems apparent from Father Crespí's journal that the explorers' visit during late July and early August coincided with a period of heightened ritual activity. A great deal of food was available at each town, and festivals were underway (Bolton 1927:143). It is also clear that the Gabrielino regarded the Spanish visitation as a very special event. The expedition coincided with a period of extraordinarily frequent earthquakes, which undoubtedly increased the awe, and perhaps apprehension, felt by the Indians (Bolton 1927:142).

FATHER JUAN VIZCAINO'S ACCOUNT, 1769

While Portolá's party made its way northward, two supply ships, the *San Carlos* and the *San Antonio*, sailed up the coast from Baja California destined for San Diego. Because of faulty navigational information, the *San Antonio* sailed far north of San Diego. When the error was discovered, the ship had already reached the vicinity of the northern Channel Islands (Woodward 1959).

The *San Antonio*'s navigational problems have proven a windfall to students of the Gabrielino. A log maintained by a Franciscan priest aboard the ship, Father Juan Vizcaíno (not to be confused with Sebastián Vizcaíno, the leader of the 1602 expedition), contains important observations on the Gabrielino, especially those dwelling on the islands. The Spanish seafarers engaged in a vigorous trade with the islanders, and in return for several articles of European-style clothing they received "two robes made of twisted skins . . . made of alternating black and brown strips of otter fur," and "stones which they seem to value highly, such as rock crystal, and mineral stones containing lots of lead" (Vizcaíno 1959:12, 14). One small party of Gabrielino brought "as a sign of peace, a stick about a yard long, with a tassel of black feathers and some tufts of fiber of the color of coconut husk, tied to the pole like a flag" (Vizcaíno 1959:13). Father Juan made observations regarding the Gabrielino canoes and fishing techniques that verified and expanded the information provided by earlier explorers (Vizcaíno 1959:16).

PEDRO FAGE'S ACCOUNT, 1775

One of the leading members of Portolá's 1769 expedition, a soldier by the name of Pedro Fages, served as Commandante of the new Spanish territory of Alta California from 1770 to 1774 (Priestley 1937:x). In 1775, Fages wrote an account of California and its peoples based largely on his observations made during the 1769 expedition and subsequent explorations. Fages noted that the Gabrielino were "fair, have light hair, and are good looking" and he noted that "they have their rafts of reeds on which to go out to sea, and by means of these the Indians of

the plain of San Gabriel communicate with the islanders of San Clemente and Santa Barbara" (Priestly 1937:ix; Fages 1937:21, 23).

THE JOSE LONGINOS MARTINEZ ACCOUNT, 1792

Another early account was written in 1792 by a naturalist, José Longinos Martínez. Although Martínez devoted most of his attention to the Chumash Indians living northwest of the Gabrielino, he provides an interesting description of the trading practices of the Catalina islanders. Martínez

> sent an Indian . . . to gather . . . all the products of that island. . . . The chief . . . sent me everything which to his way of thinking was valuable in the dominions of his island. This came to two sealskins, two sea-otter skins, several strings of abalones (auriculares) and limpets (patelas), one of the small stones of silver and lead . . . and several others of quartz, sardonyx, and jasper (Martínez 1938:52-53).

WILLIAM SHALER'S ACCOUNT, 1805

In 1805 William Shaler, a Yankee sea captain engaged in the fur trade, visited Santa Catalina Island. According to Shaler these Indians, as well as the inhabitants of the other Channel Islands and the mainland coast opposite them, were quite special, being "a handsome people, remarkably sprightly, courteous, and intelligent, and display great ingenuity in all their arts" (Shaler 1935:56). Shaler, being a seafarer, made his own observations of the plank canoes, which were

> of small pine boards, sewed together in a very curious manner; these are generally capable of carrying from six to fourteen people, and are in form not unlike a whale boat; they are managed with paddles, and go with surprising velocity; they besides make a great variety of curious and useful articles of wicker work, and excellent pots and mortars of stone (Shaler 1935:56).

THE *INTERROGATORIOS* OF 1812-1813

The colonization of Alta California that began in 1769 with the Portolá Expedition continued into the following century. Gradually missions were established from San Diego to the San Francisco region, and Indians were converted to Catholicism and relocated to the new settlements. Within the Gabrielino territory two missions were founded, Mission San

Gabriel, established in 1771, and Mission San Fernando Rey, established in 1797.

Despite the close contact between the missionaries and the Indians, for the most part the Spanish remained ignorant of the peoples and cultures they had absorbed, unable to comprehend lifestyles that they could not reconcile with their own Christian beliefs. To overcome this failing, and to help the government administer the new territory, a systematic investigation of the Indians of California was undertaken. The *Interrogatorios* of 1812-1813 were the first attempt to systematically record data on the Indians of California and their cultures. The investigation consisted of 36 questions sent to each mission in Alta California. Responses were received from 18 missions, three of which had resident Gabrielino populations— Mission San Gabriel, Mission San Fernando, and Mission San Juan Capistrano. The responses were prepared during a 20-month period from December 31, 1813, to August 11, 1815 (Geiger 1976:1).

The *Interrogatorios* explored many different facets of California Indian culture, including marriage customs, worship of the sun and moon, the use of fermented drinks, and burial customs. Although the *Interrogatorios* were intended to be an administrative document, many of the questions seem to be academic in nature (Meighan 1976b:3). As a result, the survey is an invaluable source of information for students of California Indian cultures.

FATHER GERONIMO BOSCANA'S ACCOUNT, 1822

One of the Franciscan missionaries who prepared answers to the *Interrogatorios*, Father Gerónimo Boscana, went on to complete the first in-depth study of a California Indian culture. Father Boscana's book describes the Indians of Mission San Juan Capistrano, many of whom were Gabrielino, and there is no question but that a large part of the information gathered by the priest is of Gabrielino origin (Kroeber 1925:636-637, 644; Hudson and Blackburn 1978:241).

Father Boscana's book, originally titled *Historical Account of the Belief, Usages, Customs and Extravagancies of the Indians of this Mission of San Juan Capistrano Called the Acagchemem Tribe* is commonly referred to by the abbreviated title *Chinigchinich*. *Chinigchinich* (or *Chengiichngech* as it will be spelled in this book) was the pre-Christian deity worshipped by the Indians living at Mission San Juan Capistrano. Much of Boscana's book is devoted

to describing the rituals and beliefs associated with this supernatural being.

The value of Boscana's book was clearly recognized by the California anthropologist Alfred L. Kroeber, who called it "easily the most intensive and best written account of the customs and religion of any group of California Indians in the mission days" (Kroeber 1925:636). It is especially surprising that such a sympathetic and insightful study was written by a Spanish Catholic missionary who, at least officially, could only deride many of the beliefs and practices he witnessed as "superstitions of a ridiculous and most extravagant nature" (Boscana 1933:61). A few biographical facts about this remarkable missionary-ethnologist are worthy of note.

Father Boscana was born on the island of Majorca off the coast of Spain on May 23, 1776, and took the habit of the Franciscan Order on August 4, 1792. He arrived in Mexico in 1803. Boscana served at Soledad Mission in 1806, at Mission La Purísima from 1806 to 1812, Mission San Luis Rey in 1812 and 1813, and at Mission San Juan Capistrano from 1814 to 1826. He was then transferred to Mission San Gabriel and was buried at the same mission following his death on July 5, 1831 (Harrington 1933:103-105, note 6; see also Cottrell 1985 regarding Father Boscana's service at San Juan Capistrano).

An interesting description of Father Boscana was provided by Mrs. Eulalia Perez, a resident at San Gabriel from 1821 until her death in 1877. According to Mrs. Perez, "Padre Boscana was a small fat man of fair complexion. . . . He was a great user of snuff. He was very affectionate and good, only he seemed to me a little bit wrong in his mind. When the attack was on him nobody spoke to him, for it seemed he was angry at everybody, even at himself" (Sánchez 1929).

Father Boscana reported that the sources of his information were "three aged Indians, the youngest of whom was over seventy years of age. They knew all the secrets, for two of them were *capitanes* [chiefs], and the other a *pul* [shaman], who were well instructed in the mysteries." Father Boscana used "gifts, endearments, and kindness" to learn "their secrets with their explanations" and be allowed to witness "the ceremonies which they performed" (Boscana 1933:17-18).

Boscana wrote *Chinigchinich* during the years of his residence at Mission San Juan Capistrano, completing his work around 1822; he prepared at least two, and possibly three copies. The first reference to Boscana's work appears in a French book, *Exploration du territoire de l'Orégon, des Californies, et de la mer Vermeille, exécutée pendant les années 1840, 1841 et 1842* by Eugène Duflot de Mofras, published in 1844 in Paris (Wilbur 1937). As the title of his book suggests, de Mofras visited California between 1840 and 1842, and it was during this visit that he acquired a copy of Boscana's work. The current location of the de Mofras copy is unknown (Bright 1978:iii).

A copy of Boscana's manuscript was discovered by an American writer, Alfred Robinson, among the mission documents held by his father-in-law, Captain José Antonio de la Guerra y Noriega of Santa Barbara, who was the Syndic, or custodian, of the mission properties. Robinson published Boscana's work in 1846 as part of his book *Life in California During a Residence of Several Years in That Territory.* Robinson's work was reprinted by Alexander Taylor in eleven issues of the *California Farmer and Journal of Useful Sciences* in 1861. In 1933 Robinson's version of *Chinigchinich* was reprinted with extensive ethnological notes by the anthropologist J. P. Harrington (Harrington 1933:106, note 7, 240; Heizer 1976; Bright 1978:iii).

Another copy of *Chinigchinich* was brought forward by Harrington in 1934. Harrington discovered this manuscript in the Bibliothèque Nationale in Paris, that institution apparently having acquired it in 1884 from a Frenchman named Alphonse Pinart. Pinart was an associate of León de Cessac, another Frenchman who did extensive anthropological research along the coast of California in the late nineteenth century, and it may have been de Cessac who originally acquired the manuscript from Santa Barbara Mission in 1873 (Bright 1978:iii-iv).

The Boscana manuscripts present an intriguing puzzle. The locations of the de Mofras and Robinson copies are unknown, and in fact, it is unclear whether these represent two copies and the de Cessac-Pinart a third, or whether the de Mofras copy is one and the same as either the Robinson or the de Cessac-Pinart manuscripts (Heizer 1976). Hopefully, the mystery will one day be solved by the rediscovery of one or more of these valuable documents.

Father Boscana's study remains a unique and valuable account of Indian life, one that is especially important because it is based upon firsthand observations made while the Indian cultures of southern California were still intact. *Chinigchinich* offers a wealth of detail on the daily lives of the Indians of San Juan Capistrano and a thoughtful review of their religious beliefs and practices. Indeed, the study of the Gabrielino would be much the poorer were it not for Father Boscana's remarkable account.

HUGO REID'S ACCOUNT, 1852

Thirty years after the completion of *Chinigchinich* a second landmark study of the Gabrielino was written by Hugo Reid, a Scotsman who settled in California and married the daughter of the chief of the Gabrielino town of *Comicranga*, a woman by the name of Victoria (Dakin 1939; Heizer 1968:1-2). As a result of this marriage, Reid had a unique opportunity to learn about the Gabrielino firsthand from his wife and her family.

The Gabrielino world had changed a great deal since Boscana's time. Diseases brought to California by the Spaniards and other Europeans had decimated the Indian population, while the political and economic disruption the Indian communities had suffered as a result of the colonization of Alta California led to the abandonment of many traditional Gabrielino towns and settlements. The mission system, which in many ways contributed to the decline of the Gabrielino culture, became the target of relentless opposition from the newly established government of Mexico, that state having achieved independence from Spain in 1821. The properties of the California missions were seized by the Mexican government in the 1830s as part of the Secularization Acts, supposedly to be distributed to Indians resident at the missions, but actually (in most cases) sold to private citizens. The outcome of this period of turmoil was a massive migration of Gabrielino away from their traditional homeland, many resettling as far north as Monterey (Reid 1852:100).

Reid documented these changes, as well as a great deal of information about the Gabrielino in pre-mission times, in a series of 22 "Letters" to the *Los Angeles Star* newspaper. Reid's Letters were published in weekly installments in the *Star* beginning with the February 21, 1852, issue. A later version, published in 1885, included additional notes and illustrations by W. F. Hoffman (Hoffman 1885, n.d.; Heizer 1968:3-4; LaLone 1980:55).

Although Reid did not identify the sources of his information, it is likely that much of it came from his wife's family. Two other possible consultants are mentioned in his Letters. The first was an old woman who resided in San Gabriel in 1852. Her name was Bona and she spoke the "court language," that is, the language of the Gabrielino elite. The second was Canoa, "a captain [chief] and . . . a great wizard [shaman]" who was living at San Fernando (Reid 1852:14, 27). Both of these people were members of the Gabrielino ruling class and therefore well-informed about Gabrielino history and culture.

Reid may have hoped that publication of his Letters would earn for him an appointment as a federal Indian agent, for his fortunes had declined following the American takeover of California in 1847, and he was eventually forced to sell most of the property that he and Victoria had acquired. The appointment of such a sympathetic and insightful agent could have benefitted the Gabrielino and the other Indians of southern California greatly. Unfortunately, this opportunity passed with Reid's death on December 12, 1852. Victoria Reid died 16 years later in 1868, a victim of smallpox, and was buried at Mission San Gabriel (King 1899; Harrington 1986:R104 F006).

At the time of his death Reid left uncompleted an English-Indian language manual for the Indians of southern California (Dakin 1939:196). Although these vocabularies were reportedly sent to the library of Santa Clara College after his passing (Hayes 1929:102), the author of the present volume has been unable to locate them. Manuscript copies of Reid's original Letters are archived at the Natural History Museum of Los Angeles County; other Reid papers and correspondence can be found at the Huntington Library in San Marino.

GABRIELINO LIFESTYLES

Using the information preserved in the historical accounts of the early explorers, Father Boscana, and Reid, and supplementing them with modern ethnohistoric and archaeological studies, one can present a detailed survey of the Gabrielino and their culture. In the simplest terms the Gabrielino can be described as a southern California Indian people practicing a hunter-gatherer lifestyle and living in communities with populations ranging from 50 to 200 or more individuals.

Although the basic lifestyle of the Gabrielinos' was that of hunter-gatherers, the wealth of food and natural resources in the Gabrielino homeland, coupled with their strategic location between the Chumash Indians to the northwest and the other Uto-Aztecan Indians to the south and east, allowed them to build a complex society of significant economic power and cultural influence. The Gabrielino homeland became a cultural melting pot in which the Uto-Aztecan tradition met and fused with the vigorous maritime-oriented culture of the coastal Chumash to create a society of immense vitality and creativity. As a result, the Gabrielino are regarded as having been one of the most materially rich and culturally influential Indian groups of southern California (Kroeber 1925:621; Bean and Smith 1978:538).

The Gabrielino territory encompassed important economic centers, such as the community of *Nájquqar* located at Isthmus Cove on Santa Catalina Island, and a revered religious and ceremonial center, *Povuu'nga*, located on what later became Rancho Los Alamitos (Reid 1852:8-9; Boscana 1933:32; Harrington 1933:148, note 77). Gabrielino shamans were held in such high esteem that they were believed to live at least 200 years and were thought capable of bending trees with their great strength (Roberts 1933:4).

The name Gabrielino, originally spelled Gabrileños, came into use around 1876 to describe the Indians living in the Los Angeles area at the time of Spanish colonization in 1769. This name, of which Gabrieleños is another spelling, arose from the incorporation of many of these Indians into Mission San Gabriel, and it has been retained for convenience by most subsequent writers and researchers. The Indians dwelling in the San Fernando Valley received the name Fernandeños due to their incorporation into Mission San Fernando, although there is little question but that they, too, were Gabrielino (Bean and Smith 1978: 538, 548).

Whether or not the Gabrielino had a general name for themselves is unclear. Although Reid stated that they did not, later researchers reported the names *Tong-vá* and *Tobikhar* as having been used by these Indians to describe themselves. *Tong-vá* was the term used by the Gabrielino living near Tejón; however, two Gabrielino consultants working with anthropologist Harrington reported that "*tōŋwe*" was a ranchería in the San Gabriel area. The word *Tobikhar*, which means "settlers" and may have been derived from *Tobohar* or *tovaar*, the Gabrielino name for the earth, was used by those living in the San Gabriel region

(Reid 1852:9; Merriam 1955:77-86, n.d.b; Heizer 1968:105, note 1; Harrington 1986:R104 F490).

The Gabrielino of the Los Angeles area called themselves *Komiivet*, from the word *komii*, meaning "east," and were so-called by the Fernandeño. In return, the Gabrielino called the Fernandeño *Pasheekwarom*, from *pasheekwnga*, the name of the Indian community once located at San Fernando. Related Gabrielino names may include *pasheekvetam* and *pavaashekwar* (Bean and Smith 1978:548; Harrington 1986:R104 F216, R106 F62).

Yet another name that has been reported for the Gabrielino is *Kizh* or *Kij*, perhaps derived from the word meaning "houses." However, one Harrington consultant reported that the name *Kizh* applied specifically to the Gabrielino living in the vicinity of Whittier Narrows (Kroeber 1907:140-141; Heizer 1968:105, note 1; Harrington 1986:R102 F26, R129 F345).

At a local level the Gabrielino seemed to have described themselves with reference to their home communities by adding the syllable "vit," "bit," or "pet" to the end of the town name. Thus *Kaweengavit* indicated an individual who resided in the town of *Kaweenga* (Harrington cited in Johnston 1962:10). During historic times the Gabrielino seem to have adopted the name *Pepii'maris* to describe themselves, although properly speaking the term refers only to the inhabitants of Santa Catalina, which the Gabrielino knew as *Pemuu* or *Pemuu'nga* (Kroeber 1925:634; Harrington 1986:R102 F24,25). Today some Gabrielino have chosen to be known as the Tong-vā.

SOCIAL ORGANIZATION

Much of the Gabrielinos' success can be attributed to their sophisticated social structure which allowed them to exercise a surprising degree of control over their economy. At the lower end of the social structure, each family belonged to a lineage group which was headed by a chief known as a *tomyaar*. Generally, each community consisted of one or more lineage groups, although some communities may have had a broader political authority over other settlements as well (for example, see the discussion of *'Ahwiinga* in Chapter 3).

Lineages participated in a system of "ritual congregations" that promoted and regulated inter-

actions among the members (see Bean 1972a:151 for a discussion of ritual congregations among a neighboring Indian group, the Cahuilla). *Tomyaars* formed alliances which they often cemented by marriage, and these frequently extended across language boundaries to unite the Gabrielino with other Indian groups. Extensive networks of trade and ritual exchange are reported to have linked the Gabrielino with the Cahuilla, Chumash, Serrano, and Luiseño (Bean 1972a:123; Bean and Smith 1978:547).

Professional groups also appear to have formed organizations that drew together members from separate lineages. Gabrielino shamans were members of the *'antap*, a prestigious and powerful ritual association dominated by the Chumash, and also possessed a similar organization of their own, the *yovaarekam* (Hudson and Underhay 1978:30; Hudson and Blackburn 1978:231, 246). Among the Chumash, skilled artisans such as canoe builders and bowl-makers were organized into guilds; such organizations probably existed among the Gabrielino as well (Blackburn 1975:10).

TECHNOLOGY AND RELIGION

The wealth and economic strength of the Gabrielino were reflected in their technology and in the richness and quality of the items used by them in everyday life. They were highly skilled craftsmen who made use of raw materials obtained either locally or through trade, and their creations often show a thoughtful blend of beauty and practicality. Cooking utensils and other items of soapstone were decorated with delicately incised geometric or abstract designs, while objects made of bone or wood were often decorated with shell inlay set in asphaltum. Baskets and other woven items displayed geometric designs done in warm shades of brown using naturally-occurring color variations in rushes and other plant materials. Bolder designs were created by dyeing the rushes black.

Perhaps the most significant contribution the Gabrielino made to the Indian cultures of southern California was the system of beliefs and rituals associated with the creator-god *Chengiichngech*. The data presently available suggest that this religion developed among the Gabrielino, originating at the town of *Povuu'nga* near Alamitos Bay and later spreading southward to the Luiseño, Cupeño, and

Kumeyaay (sometimes known as the Diegueño) (Kroeber 1925:621-622; Bean and Smith 1978:547-548). The *Chengiichngech* religion remained prominent among the Indians of southern California long after the introduction of Christianity.

LANGUAGE AND LITERATURE

The Gabrielino are believed to have spoken several regional dialects of the same Uto-Aztecan language (Geiger and Meighan 1976:19, answers from Missions San Gabriel and San Fernando; Kroeber 1925:621; Harrington 1962:viii). Reid provided a pronunciation guide for the Gabrielino, observing that the language had "a great many liquid sounds" with gutturals "so softened down as to become quite agreeable to the ear." In the same Letter, Reid produced a vocabulary of Gabrielino words. A similar work based on a document from Mission San Gabriel has also been published (Woodward 1944:145-149).

Gabrielino vocabularies have been recorded by Horatio Hale (1846), Johann Buschmann (1855), Alexander Taylor (1860a), Oscar Loew (Gatschet 1879), Henry Henshaw (n.d.), and Alfred Kroeber (1907; 1909). Gabrielino vocabularies located by the author among the C. Hart Merriam papers at The Bancroft Library are included as Appendices I and II of the present volume (Merriam n.d.c); only one of these vocabularies has been previously published (Merriam 1979). The Taylor and Loew vocabularies are reproduced as Appendices III and IV; and the Hale and Henshaw vocabularies, as Appendices V and VI. Information on Gabrielino vocabularies can also be found throughout the Gabrielino and Fernandeño field-notes of Harrington (1986).

The Gabrielino created an extensive and imaginative oral literature consisting of legends, myths, songs, and historical accounts. Specially-trained bards and storytellers preserved this literature by memorizing it word for word. Surviving from this literature are stories about Coyote, the constellation known today as the Pleiades, and the creation of the world. Other Gabrielino stories tell of fearsome wars waged by Gabrielino shamans using their supernatural powers. One lengthy narrative that explores the themes of greed, vengeance, love, and eternal life offers ample testimony to the fertile imagination of Gabrielino storytellers.

PHYSICAL ATTRIBUTES AND DRESS

Physically, the Gabrielino were a robust, handsome, brown-skinned people, although comments by Father Antonio de la Ascensión and Pedro Fages suggest that they were lighter in complexion and hair than their Uto-Aztecan neighbors to the south (Wagner 1929:236-237; Fages 1937:21). Surviving photographs taken near the turn of the century show them to be full-faced, with strong features. The men tended to be bearded, although more traditionally whiskers were plucked using tweezers made from clamshells (Harrington 1942: 15-16, items 493, 495). Prior to the adoption of European and American dress and grooming habits, Gabrielino men and women wore their hair long, even below the shoulders. Hair was parted in the middle and worn loose, or with one braid down the back that might be tied with a woven band decorated with shell beads. Sometimes both men and women wore their hair doubled back or tied on top and held in place with hairpins of bone or wood. Women wore bangs, which they kept trimmed by singeing (Harrington 1942:15-16, 18, items 488, 492, 507, 587, 588; Hudson and Blackburn 1985:76-85, 176, 339-345).

Cleanliness and hygiene were important aspects of Gabrielino life, and many followed the custom of bathing each day before dawn. In fact, it was *Chengiichngech* himself who commanded that a bath must be taken daily (DuBois 1908:83; Harrington 1933:168, note 141; 1986:R105 F685). The Gabrielino made frequent use of sweathouses in which a dry sauna was used; afterwards they rinsed in a nearby pool (Geiger and Meighan 1976:72-73, answers from Missions San Gabriel and San Fernando; Kroeber 1925:628).

Prior to missionization, Gabrielino men and children typically went naked (Harrington 1942:19, items 665-666). Women wore skirts made from rabbit skins, tule, plant fiber, or the bark of cottonwood or willow trees, while women of the elite social class wore skirts of buckskin or sea-otter pelts. These skirts usually consisted of a front and back flap and were worn with a belt. Often they were decorated with beads or fringes. The women of San Nicolas Island wore dresses of bird skins (Reid 1852:23-24; Nidever 1937:84; Woodward 1957:264; Hudson and Blackburn 1985:27-39).

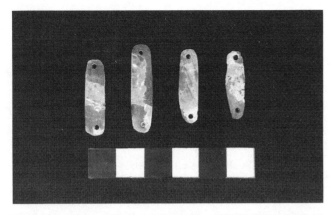

Natural History Museum of Los Angeles County Nos. A4616-M-4E-1, A4616-M-4E-6, A4616-M-4E-13, A4616-M-4E-17

Fig. 1. Ornaments attached to earrings or sewn on clothing were made by carefully shaping and drilling abalone shell. The scale is in centimeters. Photograph by author.

Catalina Island Museum No. G-258

Fig. 3. Small soapstone box containing limpet shell beads. The beads may have been strung on a cord for a necklace. Photograph by author.

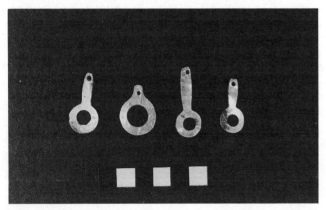

Catalina Island Museum No. G-201 (all)

Fig. 2. Another type of abalone shell decoration that may have been attached to earrings or sewn on clothing. Photograph by author.

Catalina Island Museum No. G-61 (all)

Fig. 4. Pendants or necklace ornaments made from pieces of soapstone that have been shaped and drilled. Photograph by author.

Men sometimes wore cloaks made from animal skins, although this custom may have depended upon the social status of the individual. Cloaks were held on the shoulders by tieing together opposite corners, or joining the edges with shell fasteners or pins of wood or bone (Boscana 1933:56; Harrington 1942:19, item 629; Hudson and Blackburn 1985:43-54). The Gabrielino normally went barefoot, although sandals of hide, grass, or yucca fiber were worn when traveling over rough ground (Harrington 1942:19, item 660; Hudson and Blackburn 1985:94-99).

Although daily dress was simple and sparse, personal and ritual body adornment was often quite elaborate. Both men and women commonly pierced their earlobes with a cactus thorn or a needle made from the yucca plant, and wore ear ornaments. Women wore large and elaborate earrings manufac-

tured from shell and feathers (Reid 1852:24; Harrington 1942:16, item 512; Hudson and Blackburn 1985:234-236). Men, too, had their ears pierced so that they could wear small tubes of cane in which they carried tobacco. Although Reid (1852:24) stated that "rings or ornaments of any kind were never attached to the nose" others have reported that the Gabrielino wore wooden rods through the nasal septum. *Tomyaars* and shamans sometimes wore hawk feathers through their nasal septums (Harrington 1942: 16, item 538, 1986:R106 F152; Hudson and Blackburn 1985:239-242).

Necklaces and bracelets might consist of strings of beads made from stone or shell. Flowers, when in season, were worn extensively by women and children. During historic times, necklaces of glass beads obtained through trade with Europeans became popular

(Reid 1852:24; Harrington 1942:16, items 525-527, 530, 531; Hudson and Blackburn 1985:251-253, 258-292, 297-304).

Other forms of personal ornamentation included tattooing and face and body painting. Tattoos, which were worn by both men and women, consisted of vertical lines on the chin, traverse bars upon the cheeks, or both. Property marks, which were cut into trees or posts to indicate ownership, were used by landowners as personal tattoos (Heizer 1968:114, note 29). The Gabrielino are reported to have tattooed their foreheads, while the Fernandeño tattooed lines on their chins and circles on their cheeks (Harrington 1942:16, items 516, 521; Hudson and Blackburn 1985:324-327). According to Father Boscana (1933:48), "girls were tattooed in their infancy, from their eyebrows down to their breasts, and some from the chin only, covering the arms entirely in both cases. The execution of this was not generally carried out until they reached their tenth year, and varied in the application and style."

Tattooing was accomplished by pricking the skin with a cactus thorn and rubbing charcoal made from the mescal plant (*Yucca whipplei*) into the wound to produce a permanent blue design. Another method employed pads soaked in a dye made from charcoal mixed with juice squeezed from green nightshade leaves. The pads were tied over the sores until they healed, leaving a permanent blue color (Boscana 1933:48; Hudson and Blackburn 1985:325-326). One of Harrington's informants reported that "Untan la quijada [they smeared the jaw] with the pounded leaves of this [nightshade] & de ay lo pican [pricked it]. And se mura verde despues [it looks green afterwards]" (Harrington 1986:R105 F313).

Reid provided some information on body painting, noting that it varied according to the occasion and individual taste. Red ochre, he observed, was commonly used by women both as a rouge and a sunscreen (Reid 1852:38). Red, white, and black were the colors commonly used in ritual body painting, although blue might be used as well, and paint was applied using fingers or a stick (Harrington 1942:18, items 611, 613, 615, 619, 621; see also Hudson and Blackburn 1985:313-323).

EARLY ETHNOGRAPHIC RESEARCH

The Gabrielino population continued to decline in the years following the 1852 publication of Reid's Letters, due largely to disease, assimilation into the Mexican population, and migration away from the Los Angeles area. Perhaps as a result of this decline, little new research on the Gabrielino or their culture was conducted prior to the turn of the century. An exception to this concerns Indian vocabularies. The earliest Gabrielino vocabularies were prepared by the missionaries to aid their efforts to proselytize the Indians (see Woodward 1944). Later in the 1800s, European and American researchers compiled linguistic data from the Gabrielino and other Indian groups for comparative vocabularies. The major contributions from this period are outlined below.

HORATIO HALE, 1846

In 1846, Horatio Hale published a vocabulary that included many words collected from the "Kizh" of San Gabriel between 1838 and 1842 (Hale 1846). Hale may have thought that *Kizh* was a general name that applied to the Indians living near San Gabriel; however, subsequent research by Harrington suggests that this name applied specifically to those Gabrielino living near Whittier Narrows (see Chapter 3).

JOHANN KARL EDUARD BUSCHMANN, 1855

In 1855, Johann Buschmann published linguistic data that he had collected from the Indians living near San Gabriel and San Juan Capistrano missions (Buschmann 1855). Buschmann also used the term *Kizh* for the Indians living near San Gabriel; however, he may have been following Hale in this regard.

ALEXANDER TAYLOR, 1860

In November, 1856, Alexander S. Taylor collected Gabrielino linguistic and ethnographic data from a consultant by the name of Juan de Polloma, who was described as being about 60 years of age. Taylor's vocabulary was published as part of his "Indianology of California" series in the *California Farmer and Journal of Useful Arts*, Vol. XIII, No. 12, May 11, 1860 (Taylor 1860a, n.d.; Heizer 1968:4).

OSCAR LOEW, 1875

In 1875, Dr. Oscar Loew visited the San Gabriel Mission region and collected vocabularies from "two old men" who still spoke the Gabrielino language. One of these consultants was a *tomyaar* by the name of Fernando Quinto who was between 90 and 100 years of age. Loew's vocabularies were published by Albert Gatschet in 1879 in volume 7 of the *Report Upon United States Geographical Surveys West of the One Hundredth Meridian* (Gatschet 1879:475; see also Harrington 1986:R105 F504).

H. W. HENSHAW, 1884

In 1884, H. W. Henshaw collected a Gabrielino vocabulary from "a very old . . . Indian . . . living in an Indian rancheria near the town of Banning. He formerly lived at the San Gabriel Mission." The consultant's wife and children spoke Serrano, and his granddaughter, a schoolgirl, acted as interpreter (Henshaw n.d.).

TWENTIETH CENTURY ETHNOGRAPHIC RESEARCH

The establishment in 1901 of the Department and Museum of Anthropology at the University of California, Berkeley signalled the start of a new era of inquiry into the state's rapidly disappearing Indian cultures. Five researchers in particular made significant contributions to the study of the Gabrielino during the early years of the twentieth century: J. P. Harrington of the Bureau of American Ethnology; J. W. Hudson, who was collecting data for the Field Museum of Chicago; A. L. Kroeber and W. D. Strong of the University of California; and C. H. Merriam, a privately funded researcher.

JOHN P. HARRINGTON

John P. Harrington was unquestionably the most productive Gabrielino researcher of the twentieth century. Harrington has been extolled as a tireless field researcher who was single-mindedly devoted to the preservation of the rapidly disappearing Indian cultures of California and other states. His fieldnotes on file at the National Anthropological Archives at the Smithsonian Institution include data on many Indian cultures and reportedly fill 1000 boxes; another million pages of data may be stored at other locations (Walsh 1976:13).

Harrington produced an annotated version of Father Boscana's *Chinigchinich* in 1933; the following year he published a previously unknown version of *Chinigchinich* based upon a manuscript which he had located in the Bibliothèque Nationale in Paris (Harrington 1934; see Bright 1978).

According to Harrington's notes, during the years 1914 to 1933 he worked with 11 Gabrielino consultants and four Fernandeño consultants. Among the most prominent of these were José de los Santos Juncos, José Zalvidea, Felicitas Serrano Montaño, Jesús Jauro, Juan and Juana Meléndrez, and Setimo López (Harrington 1986:R105 F695; Mills and Brickfield 1986:67-76). The information gathered by Harrington was summarized in *Culture Element Distributions: XIX*, published by the University of California in 1942. Harrington's Smithsonian fieldnotes have been published on microfilm and are widely available to researchers (Harrington 1986).

J. W. HUDSON

In 1901, J. W. Hudson interviewed Mrs. James Rosemyre, a Gabrielino consultant who was living at Tejón. Mrs. Rosemyre provided J. W. Hudson with a Gabrielino vocabulary and some ethnographic data. These records, as well as other notes and papers dealing with J. W. Hudson's research, are on file at the Grace Hudson Museum and the Sun House, the City of Ukiah, California (Vane and Bean 1990:108; J. W. Hudson n.d.).

ALFRED L. KROEBER

Alfred L. Kroeber's leadership in promoting California anthropology as an academic discipline was of enormous benefit to the study of Indian cultures throughout the state. Kroeber served the Department and Museum of Anthropology at Berkeley for 45 years, and his *Handbook of the Indians of California*, published in 1925, was the first complete survey of the Indian cultures of the state. In addition, Kroeber's analysis of Boscana's *Chinigchinich*, published in 1959, highlights a number of important differences between the existing manuscripts (Kroeber 1959).

Kroeber worked with two Gabrielino consultants around 1907-1909: José Zalvidea (whom Kroeber knew by the names José Varojo and José Sevaldeo); and Rosario, who was born at San Fernando (Kroeber 1907:70, 1909:251). Kroeber's papers and fieldnotes are on file at The Bancroft Library, University of California, Berkeley.

C. HART MERRIAM

C. Hart Merriam conducted field research among the Gabrielino in the early 1900s. He worked with two important Gabrielino consultants: Mrs. James Rosemyre, who was interviewed around 1903 and provided valuable data on the Gabrielino Mourning Ceremony; and José Zalvidea, a consultant who also worked with Kroeber and Harrington (Merriam 1955:84, n.d.a, n.d.b, n.d.c). Merriam also produced a number of fine portrait photographs of California Indians; his portraits of Mrs. Rosemyre and José Zalvidea appear in the present volume.

Merriam was one of the earliest researchers to work with the mission registers. Under Merriam's guidance, research assistant Stella R. Clemence compiled a listing of village names from the registers of 12 California missions; information from the San Fernando, San Gabriel, and San Juan Capistrano registers was compiled during 1920. Data contained in these listings includes the number of Indians baptized from each village by year; there is also some anecdotal information (Merriam 1968).

Merriam's papers and notebooks are on file at The Bancroft Library, University of California, Berkeley and at the Library of Congress in Washington D. C. (Merriam n.d.a, n.d.b, n.d.c).

WILLIAM DUNCAN STRONG

William Duncan Strong conducted important field research among several Uto-Aztecan-speaking Indian groups of southern California during the 1920s. Although he did not specifically work with any Gabrielino consultants, Strong's research with neighboring Uto-Aztecan-speaking groups such as the Luiseño, Serrano, and Cahuilla provides comparative data that help fill many of the present gaps in the Gabrielino record.

The results of Strong's research have been published in *Aboriginal Society in Southern California* (Strong 1929). This book remains a standard reference in the study of southern California Uto-Aztecan-speaking Indian peoples.

GABRIELINO CONSULTANTS

The research conducted by J. W. Hudson, Kroeber, Harrington and Merriam would not have been possible without the cooperation of a handful of Gabrielino consultants who generously gave of their information and time. Some of these individuals, such as José de los Santos Juncos and José Zalvidea, were elderly people who remembered life during the Mission Period. Much of the information they provided was learned from parents and family members who remembered details of Gabrielino life before European colonization began in 1771.

The following section describes some of the better-known Gabrielino consultants; other consultants will be introduced in the text as appropriate.

JESUS JAURO

Jesús Jauro worked with Harrington in 1932 and again a year later in 1933. At the time of the second series of interviews he was 90 years of age. Juaro is reported to have been one of the last Gabrielino speakers; during his work with Harrington in 1933 he recorded more than 50 Indian songs. He died in 1934 (Mills and Brickfield 1986:68, 71).

JOSE DE LOS SANTOS JUNCOS

José de los Santos Juncos worked with Harrington between 1914 and 1916, and in December, 1918. He provided a wealth of information on Gabrielino place-names, culture, local history, and vocabulary; he also reported on several Gabrielino songs. His real name was reportedly Santos Salas; the Harrington notes most frequently refer to him as "Kewen," "Kuhn," or simply "K" (Mills and Brickfield 1986:71; Harrington 1986:R105 F495, 614).

Santos Juncos was of Juaneño descent. The Juaneño were Indians who lived in the vicinity of Mission San Juan Capistrano; many of the Juaneño entered the mission and became Christians, although Gabrielinos also formed a significant portion of the Indian population at Mission San Juan Capistrano. Harrington reported that Santos Juncos'

father was José Engenio Juncos born at S.J.C. [San Juan Capistrano]. Inf's [informant's] mother was Maria Valediana, b. [born] at S.J.C. Both parents were of S.J.C. descent. inf's mother was about 4 ft. high when the great earthquake occurred [the 1812 earthquake which destroyed the church at San

Juan Capistrano] (Harrington 1986:R102 F710,741; R105 F559).

According to Harrington, Santos Juncos's father and mother were both shamans and Santos Juncos himself would have followed in this tradition had his parents not intervened. Harrington wrote that

> when K. [Kuhn or Kewen] was a boy he used to have nightmares & it was said he would be [a] big person. He would have, if his parents had not pierced his ears. His father was a hechicero [sorcerer] & his mother was a little bit hechicera. They took a big batéa [basketry tray] . . . and they medically treated him & extracted from his heart . . . the espuma of the tSåtSŋitSam [literally the foam or froth of *Chengiichngech*, who was the creator-god of the Gabrielino] (Harrington 1986:R105 F561).

Although he was of Juaneño descent, the information provided by Santos Juncos primarily concerned the Gabrielino. According to Harrington Santos Juncos "was never much among the J. Inds. [Juaneño Indians]" (Harrington 1986:R104 F23).

There appears to be conflicting information concerning Santos Juncos' date of birth. Harrington reported that he "was born at L.A. . . . in 1820;" however, Harrington also noted that "when Ams. [Americans] arrived [during the late 1840s?]. . . [he] was 20 yrs. old." An obituary in the Los Angeles Times for February 10, 1921, reports that Santos Juncos "was born at the old [San Gabriel] mission in 1815" (*Los Angeles Times* 1921; Harrington 1986:R104 F23).

During part of his adult life Santos Juncos worked for a Los Angeles lawyer known as Colonel Kewen; because of his obvious intelligence and his association with the lawyer he received the nickname Kewen. Harrington wrote that Santos Juncos was "the last Ind. of aqui [here]. . . . he worked for [Kewen] . . . & like . . . [Kewen] he talked much" (*Los Angeles Times* 1921; Mills and Brickfield 1986:68; Harrington 1986:R105 F614). Santos Juncos also resided for a time with the family of Benjamin (don Benito) Wilson. He worked on various sheep ranches in southern California and "once wandered and worked as a sheepshearer on S. [Santa] Cruz Island." According to Santos Juncos, his sister kept company with the famous bandit Joaquín Murrieta (Harrington 1986:R104 F23, R105 F560).

The last 40 years of Santos Juncos' life were spent at Mission San Gabriel. He remained in good health until the very end, dying peacefully in his sleep on February 9, 1921. He was buried in the mission cemetery (*Los Angeles Times* 1921).

SETIMO LOPEZ

Setimo López, a Fernandeño consultant, worked for Harrington around 1916. During his interviews with Harrington he provided ethnographic data as well as information on San Fernando Valley placenames. Setimo had a half-brother by the name of Martin Violin (Harrington 1986:R106 F070; Mills and Brickfield 1986:75).

JUAN AND JUANA MELENDREZ

Juan Meléndrez and his wife, Juana Meléndrez, worked with Harrington around 1916. Juan was the son of Maria Encarnacion Chohuya (also known as Espiritu) and the grandson of Odón, a Fernandeño *tomyaar*. In 1845, Odón along with two other Indians named Urbano and Manuel had received the grant of El Escorpión; this tract of former mission land was located in the western San Fernando Valley. Juan's wife, Juana, was from San Gabriel and spoke Gabrielino (Harrington 1986:R106 F81, 111; Mills and Brickfield 1986:75).

National Anthropological Archives, Smithsonian Institution

Fig. 5. Photograph of Felicitas Serrano Montaño, a Gabrielino consultant who worked with Harrington.

FELICITAS SERRANO MONTANO

Felicitas Serrano Montaño worked with Harrington from 1916 to 1918, providing linguistic and ethnographic data on the Gabrielino. At that time she was living in San Bernardino with her husband, a Mexican by the name of Nasario Montaño.

Felicitas Montaño was the eldest of 13 children born to Luisa Serrano, a Gabrielino Indian, and Belardo Serrano, a Serrano Indian. She reported to Harrington that "her [Felicitas' mother's] . . . ancestors came from the islands—but Fel's [Felicitas'] mother herself was not born on the isla" (Harrington 1986:R102 F485, R104 F006, 048, 096, 315, 507, R105 F688; Mills and Brickfield 1986:68-70).

FERNANDO QUINTO

Fernando Quinto was interviewed by Oscar Loew in 1875, at which time he was described as "a nonagenarian [between 90 and 100 years old] chief" who appeared to be near death. Quinto provided Gabrielino linguistic data which were used in a comparative vocabulary prepared by Albert Gatschet (Gatschet 1879:475).

According to Harrington, Quinto had two daughters, Celedonia and Martina (Harrington 1986:R102 F842, 059, R105 F504).

MRS. JAMES ROSEMYRE

Mrs. James Rosemyre was interviewed by J. W. Hudson in 1901, and by Merriam in Bakersfield in 1903 and 1905. She provided important linguistic and ethnographic data, including a detailed description of the Gabrielino Mourning Ceremony (Merriam 1955:84-86; J. W. Hudson n.d.).

Although Rosemyre was born near present Tehachapi, she spent her childhood at Mission San Gabriel. Her father was a Serrano Indian and her mother was Gabrielino; Rosemyre reportedly spoke both languages. Her maiden name was Narcisa Higuera.

Rosemyre was married to James "Jimmy" Rosemyre and lived at Tejón Canyon; her husband ran the commissary and general store on Rancho El Tejón (Latta 1976:177, 179). A portrait of Mrs. Rosemyre and her six children appears in Latta (1976:140). According to Harrington, she died in Bakersfield around 1912 (Harrington 1986:R105 F580).

Courtesy, The Bancroft Library Y/24a/P2

Fig. 6. Photograph of Mrs. James Rosemyre, a Gabrielino consultant who worked with Merriam and J. W. Hudson. Photograph by Merriam in 1903.

MANUEL SANTOS

Manuel Santos worked with Harrington around 1918 and provided linguistic and placename data. He is described by Harrington as a Fernandeño consultant, although there are other data to suggest that he was Serrano (Harrington 1986:R105 F636; Mills and Brickfield 1986:68, 72).

JOSE MARIA ZALVIDEA

José Zalvidea worked with a number of researchers including Kroeber, Merriam, and Harrington. Zalvidea was living at Highland in San Bernardino County when he was interviewed by Kroeber; at that time Zalvidea was in poor health and "so feeble that it was only possible to question him for a short time." Merriam interviewed and photographed Zalvidea at the San Manuel Indian Reservation near San Bernardino. According to Merriam, Zalvidea could not speak Gabrielino, and "his talk is mainly *Mar'-ring-i-yum* 'Serrano' with a sprinkling of

Fig. 7. Photograph of José Zalvidea, a Gabrielino consultant who worked with Kroeber, Harrington, and Merriam. Photograph by Merriam.

Cahuilla." Harrington worked with Zalvidea from 1914 to 1917. Zalvidea is identified by a bewildering array of names which include: José Varojo, José Verrujas, Guorojos, José Sevaldeo, and Joe *San-wu-dā'-yah*. Some of these may be variant spellings of his lineage name (Kroeber 1907:70; 1909:251; Mills and Brickfield 1986:69-71; Merriam n.d.c).

Zalvidea was one of the most informative Gabrielino consultants. His family (on his father's side) was of the *worómmoyam* lineage; according to Zalvidea the lineage name refers to his grandfather and "is . . . not a placename. . . . It means they came without a blanket or anything." Zalvidea reported that his father was born and lived on Santa Catalina Island, although he himself was raised in the San Gabriel Valley; Zalvidea also reported that he had ancestors who were from the coast near Santa Monica and Topanga. His mother's name was Nolberta, and he had several brothers: Luis (his older brother); Pedro (a younger brother); José, who lived in

Oklahoma; and Pete, who had died by the time of the Harrington interviews (ca. 1914-1917). José Zalvidea also had a sister who had died at San Gabriel sometime prior to his interviews with Harrington (Kroeber 1907:70; Harrington 1986:R102 F25, 114, 378, 654, R103 F415, 449, R105 F467; Merriam n.d.c).

The data provided by Zalvidea have a special significance because of family ties that appear to link him with two Gabrielino Indians mentioned by Reid in 1852. As noted above, Reid described a Gabrielino *tomyaar* (and shaman) named Canoa who was from Santa Catalina Island; according to Zalvidea, Canoa was his relative on his father's side. Zalvidea reported to Harrington that "Josefa, [was the] daughter of old kano'º [Canoa], [and] lives at Colton. Kano'º was a Santa Catalina Indian" and "Josefa . . . is a relative of Z. . . . on Z's father's side. . . . the rancho of Josefa was kíηkiηa and 'atàvjaηa [*Kiinkenga* and *'Aataveanga* were Gabrielino communities located on the Palos Verdes peninsula]." Harrington went on to note that "Cristóbela of S. G. [San Gabriel] was Z's sobrina [niece]. . . . She has Josefa, daughter of old kano'º . . . . Kano'º is Ind. of pimuu'ηa [Indian of *Pemuu'nga* or Catalina]" (Reid 1852:27; Harrington 1986:R102 F658, R103 F41).

Another Gabrielino mentioned by Reid was a woman by the name of Bona who resided at San Gabriel. According to Harrington, "Bona is Z's [Zalvidea's] paternal grandmother's elder sister. She died very old" (Harrington 1986:R103 F41).

Was José Zalvidea aware of Reid's research? Perhaps, although Harrington noted only that "Z. [Zalvidea] knew Reid. Vitoria was Reid's wife" (Harrington 1986:R102 F659). Nonetheless, it seems quite possible that José Zalvidea may have obtained some of his information from the same sources consulted by Reid during the mid-1800s.

ARCHAEOLOGICAL STUDIES

The information gathered by ethnographers and historians is complemented and enhanced by data gained from the excavation of Gabrielino archaeological sites. These excavations have been carried out over the last 100 years, and although the early work was conducted under less than scientific standards, important data have been gleaned from this archaeological research.

Much of the early excavation was done by relic hunters and avid professional collectors known as "antiquarians." The primary goal of the antiquarians was the gathering of artifacts for display in their homes and in museums, and this unfortunately encouraged the wholesale destruction of archaeological sites with a great loss of supporting data. The scientific value of the subsequent artifact collections is compromised by the lack of firm site data and the carelessness with which the excavations were conducted. In many cases these problems have made it difficult or impossible to reliably date sites and artifacts to the correct prehistoric period. In contrast, modern archaeology employs far more precise techniques to gather a wide range of information that furthers our understanding of a site's use, date of occupation, and cultural significance.

PAUL SCHUMACHER

One of the earliest individuals to collect artifacts along the Pacific coast was Paul Schumacher. During the late 1870s, Schumacher worked for both the Smithsonian Institution and the Peabody Museum of Harvard University, conducting extensive excavations on the Channel Islands and the mainland. During the summer and fall of 1877, Schumacher was excavating Indian cemeteries on Santa Catalina and is reported to have collected 24 cases of artifacts. In April, 1878, he spent several weeks digging on Rancho los Cerritos before returning to Catalina again later that year (Splitter 1956:122-123; Grant 1978:525). One of Schumacher's most important achievements was the identification of the extensive Indian soapstone quarries on Santa Catalina and their importance in the prehistoric trade network of southern California (Schumacher 1878b). A partial catalog of artifacts collected by Schumacher was published in 1904 in the *Bulletin of the Southern California Academy of Sciences* (Williamson 1904).

LEON de CESSAC

Also active during the years 1877 to 1879 was León de Cessac, previously mentioned in connection with the *Chinigchinich* manuscript published by Harrington in 1934. León de Cessac conducted excavations at numerous locations along the California coast as well as San Nicolas Island. The Cessac Collection now resides in the Musée de l'Homme in Paris (see Reichlen and Heizer 1963).

F. M. PALMER

The largest collection of Gabrielino artifacts assembled during the early twentieth century was reportedly owned by Dr. F. M. Palmer, a dentist and amateur collector who was an associate of Paul Schumacher. Palmer's artifact collection was assembled during the years 1877 to 1895 and is said to have exceeded both the Smithsonian and the Peabody Museum collections in completeness and rarity of finds. Although Palmer collected from a number of counties including Los Angeles, San Bernardino, Santa Barbara, and Ventura, he reported that his most fruitful digging was on the Channel Islands and on the mainland coast, especially between Santa Monica and Redondo Beach. Several lists of artifacts in the Palmer Collection have been published, and for a time the collection was on display at the Los Angeles Chamber of Commerce. It was reportedly donated to the Southwest Museum (Williamson 1904; Palmer 1905; Splitter 1956:124-126).

RALPH GLIDDEN

Ralph Glidden was an antiquarian who worked for the Museum of the American Indian when it was associated with the Heye Foundation of New York; he collected extensively on Santa Catalina, San Nicolas, and San Miguel islands in the early 1920s. Glidden's work has been sharply criticized because, like other collectors of his generation, he bought, sold, and traded artifacts, thereby making it difficult for modern researchers to verify the original site locations of many items (Wlodarski 1978, 1979b:57-59, 1982:8-10). Nevertheless, some significant research has been conducted using mortuary data collected by Glidden (Decker 1969). The Glidden Collection, much of which is housed in the Catalina Island Museum in Avalon, remains one of the most extensive collections of Gabrielino artifacts in southern California. As such it represents an irreplaceable cultural treasure.

OTHER EARLY 1900s COLLECTORS

Several other collectors were active during the early years of the twentieth century. Among these early amateurs and antiquarians were Arthur Sanger, whose collection of materials from the Channel Islands now is in the Museum of the American Indian, Smithsonian Institution; C. F. Holder, who wrote a number of popular books promoting southern California early in this century; and W. Murbarger, who excavated on San Clemente Island for the Bowers Museum of Santa Ana (Holder 1910; Murbarger 1947; Zahniser 1981:2.13-2.19). Unfortunately, little or no documentation exists for most of this early work.

WPA EXCAVATIONS

During the depression years of the 1930s, a number of archaeological excavations were carried out in Orange County under the auspices of the State Emergency Relief Administration and the Works Progress Administration. A total of 24 sites was excavated and reported upon during a five-year period from 1935 to 1940, including important sites located in the Santa Ana Mountains, on the coastal plain overlooking the Santa Ana River, and at Goff's Island near Laguna Beach. A number of these reports, as well as an interesting summary titled "A Study of Primitive Man in Orange County" by J. W. Winterbourne and Mrs. G. E. Ashby, the project supervisors, have been published in the *Pacific Coast Archaeological Society Quarterly* (Chace 1965:6-101, 1966:15; Ashby and Winterbourne 1966; Winterbourne 1967, 1968a, 1968b, 1968c, 1969; Hudson 1969; see also Mead 1969 for a critique of the WPA excavation techniques). Other notable archaeological projects undertaken during these years include fieldwork on San Nicolas Island in 1926 and the excavation of Big Dog Cave on San Clemente Island in 1939, both conducted by the Natural History Museum of Los Angeles County, and the excavation of the Malaga Cove site on Santa Monica Bay in 1936 and 1937 by the University of Southern California (Woodward 1941; Walker 1952:27-69; Bryan 1970a).

MODERN ARCHAEOLOGICAL RESEARCH

Today archaeological work on the Gabrielino continues, although the focus has shifted from artifact collection to a more thorough and precise collection and analysis of data. Technological improvements during the last several decades have resulted in more complete data recovery. Valuable information on settlement patterns, subsistence strategies, and prehistoric technology is being obtained through careful investigations carried out by colleges, universities, museums, and private institutions.

POPULAR ACCOUNTS

The first broad synthesis of historical, ethnographic, and archaeological data on the Gabrielino was published by Bernice Johnston in 1962. Johnston's book *California's Gabrielino Indians* incorporated Harrington's fieldnotes, and brought together valuable information on the Gabrielino and their culture. Written in a lively narrative style, *California's Gabrielino Indians* filled a long-standing void in the literature of the California Indians and has done much to promote public awareness and understanding of the Gabrielino and their history.

An annotated bibliography of the published literature on the Gabrielino has been prepared by LaLone (1980).

A number of fictionalized accounts of the Gabrielino have also been written. Two accounts worthy of note are *Yamino Kwiti* by Donna Preble (1940), and *Island of the Blue Dolphins* by Scott O'Dell (1960). *Island of the Blue Dolphins* is based upon the life of Juana María, a Gabrielino woman who was marooned on San Nicolas Island for 18 years until her rescue in 1853.

SUMMARY

The date of the earliest local occupation by Indian peoples remains uncertain; however, archaeological data indicates that a fully maritime-adapted, seafaring culture existed in southern California at least ten thousand years ago. San Clemente Island was occupied by 7,785 B.C., and humans had reached San Nicolas Island by 6,210 B.C.

Sometime prior to 6,000 B.C., the lifestyle of the early peoples living in the Los Angeles region changed significantly. Hunting became less significant and a greater reliance was placed on the gathering of wild seeds and plant foods. Whether this change was brought about by environmental factors or the arrival of new peoples remains unclear. However, by 3,000 B.C. a more sophisticated food gathering economy had evolved which incorporated both hunting and the gathering of seeds and plant foods.

An event of major significance in southern California prehistory was the arrival of Uto-Aztecan-speaking peoples from the Great Basin. The date of this migration, which probably occurred in successive waves over a lengthy period of time, is uncertain. It may have occurred prior to 2,000 B.C. or as late as A.D. 700. Also uncertain are the reasons for this gradual migration into California. Environmental change or food shortages may have been contributing causes.

The final phase of prehistory in southern California, known as the Late Period, commenced sometime around A.D. 1-500. A number of important developments occurred during the Late Period; these included the concentration of larger populations in communities and the development of regional subcultures. A number of these regional subcultures evolved among Uto-Aztecan-speaking groups, each of which had its own language and resided within its own geographical territory.

One of the most interesting of these Uto-Aztecan groups was the Gabrielino. The Gabrielino occupied much of modern Los Angeles and Orange counties, including the southern Channel Islands of Santa Catalina, San Clemente, San Nicolas, and Santa Barbara. They spoke several regional dialects of their own Uto-Aztecan language, and their population may have exceeded 5,000 people living in 50 to 100 communities and settlements. Gabrielino society was organized into lineages, each under the leadership of its own *tomyaar* (chief); Gabrielino communities were occupied by one or more lineages. In turn, lineages were organized into a system of confederations or "ritual congregations" that regulated social, political, and economic interactions among the groups.

The Gabrielino practiced a hunting-gathering economy. In addition, communities located on the islands and on the mainland coast were fully maritime-adapted; canoes made from wooden planks allowed seafarers to engage in deep-sea fishing and conduct trading ventures that linked the mainland and the islands. The Gabrielino also had a highly developed religious system centered on the worship of the creator-god *Chengiichngech*.

Information on the Gabrielino has been gathered from a wide variety of historical, ethnographic, and archaeological sources. The earliest descriptions of the Gabrielino were recorded in 1542 by members of the Cabrillo Expedition. The most important historical accounts of the Gabrielino were written by Father Gerónimo Boscana, around 1822, and by Reid in 1852. Father Boscana was a Spanish missionary stationed at San Gabriel and San Juan Capistrano missions. Reid, a Scotchman, was married to a Gabrielino woman named Victoria who was the daughter of a local *tomyaar*.

During the 1900s, important ethnographic investigations were conducted by a number of researchers, including Harrington, J. W. Hudson, Kroeber, Merriam, and Strong. Important Gabrielino consultants in this research include Jesús Jauro, José de los Santos Juncos, Setimo López, Juan and Juana Meléndrez, Felicitas Serrano Montaño, Fernando Quinto, Mrs. James Rosemyre, Manuel Santos, and José Maria Zalvidea.

Research on the Gabrielino continues, and each discovery adds to our knowledge of this intriguing people. The story of the Gabrielino as told in the following pages is a multifaceted account of a vigorous, innovative people and the society they created. The setting for this story is the territory that today comprises Los Angeles and Orange counties. The valleys, prairies, foothills and islands of this land were home to the Gabrielino. Here the story of the First Angelinos unfolds.

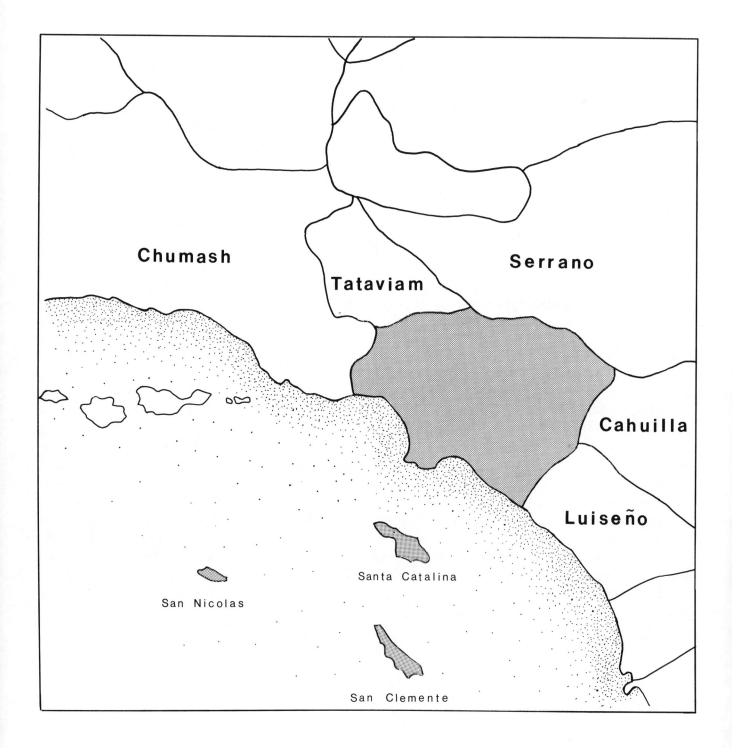

Map 2. The Gabrielino territory (shaded) and neighboring Indian groups. Tiny Santa Barbara Island (which lies west of Santa Catalina and northeast of San Nicolas) is not shown; the Gabrielino visited Santa Barbara Island but did not occupy the island.

CHAPTER 2

HEARTH AND HOMELAND

The Indians of southern California shared a sophisticated hunter-gatherer lifestyle with both the Uto-Aztecan and non-Uto-Aztecan peoples of this region. Interaction among them was common, frequently extending across language barriers, and included intermarriage as well as political alliances and trade networks. In fact, the continuity of culture among the Indians of southern California was so notable that anthropologist W. D. Strong described it as "a liquid medium that flowed more or less evenly from group to group, thinning out more and more the farther each cultural influence extended from its source" (Strong 1929:145-146).

The cultural similarities between the Indian peoples of southern California, as well as the strong interplay among them, must be taken into account when defining the territories occupied by individual language groups such as the Gabrielino. Boundaries between groups are characterized by broad frontiers of shared influence in which bilingualism, intermarriage, and a blending of cultural characteristics is evident.

Examples of such cultural blending can be found along the fringes of the Gabrielino territory. The Gabrielino living in the San Fernando Valley reportedly spoke Ventureño, a Chumash dialect, as well as Fernandeño, and mission records indicate that many of the occupants of *Topaa'nga*, a Gabrielino community located near the Gabrielino-Chumash border, had Chumash names. The Chumash community of *Maliwu*, which bequeathed its name to the modern community of Malibu, not only contained Gabrielino occupants but was ruled by a Gabrielino chief named Saplay from Catalina Island. Decorated stone bowls recovered from archaeological remains in the Malibu area also display a blending of Chumash and Gabrielino artistic motifs (Brown 1967:8, 45; Lee 1981:16,37; Harrington 1986:R106 F81).

The eastern border of the Gabrielino territory was a region of shared influence with the Juaneño, a subgroup of the Luiseño Indians speaking a distinct regional dialect. Temescal Valley, located east of the Santa Ana Mountains between Corona and Elsinore, is believed to have been simultaneously occupied by both the Gabrielino and Juaneño. In addition, Juaneño hunting and gathering expeditions may have ranged as far north as the Santa Ana River, well within the territory traditionally attributed to the Gabrielino (Kroeber 1907:144; O'Neil 1988).

GABRIELINO TERRITORY

The territory of the Gabrielino included the watersheds of the Los Angeles, San Gabriel, Río Hondo, and Santa Ana rivers, an area which encompasses all of the Los Angeles basin. The approximate boundaries of this territory can be defined using the data presently available; however, future research will undoubtedly refine these estimates. In the west the boundary between the Gabrielino and the Chumash fell somewhere between Malibu and Topanga creeks, while in the north the Gabrielino territory stretched to the base of the San Gabriel Mountains. In the east the boundary between the Gabrielino and the Serrano and Cahuilla Indians can be defined by an imaginary line from Mount San Antonio, popularly known as Mount Baldy, eastward perhaps as far as the San Bernardino vicinity, then southward to Monument Peak and Santiago Peak in the Santa Ana Mountains. In the southeast the boundary between the Gabrielino and the Luiseño fell somewhere between Newport Bay and Aliso Creek (Kroeber 1925:621; Bean and Smith 1978:538, figure 1; O'Neil 1988).

Reid (1852:8-9) reported that San Bernardino lay within Serrano territory. However, George Shinn, an early resident of San Bernardino County who was

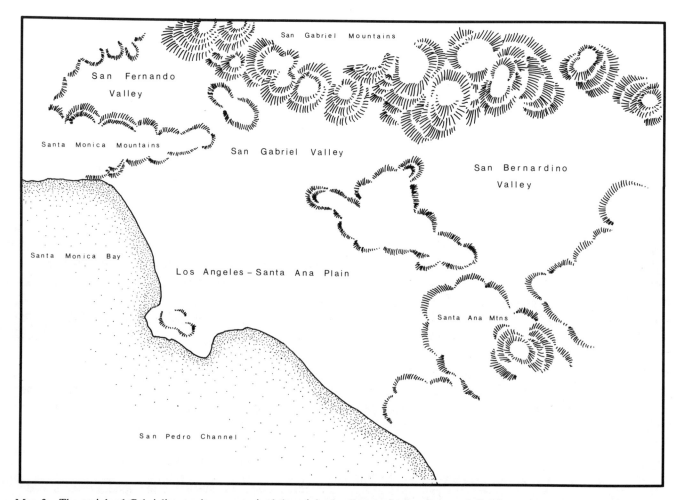

Map 3. The mainland Gabrielino territory comprised three inland valleys and a broad coastal plain.

familiar with the local Indian settlements, suggested that "the sites of San Bernardino, San Manuel, Redlands, Crafton, and the fertile land along the Santa Ana river southeast of Colton had originally been occupied by people who spoke the San Gabriel language" (Shinn 1941:66; see also Strong 1929:8-9). The Gabrielino also occupied the southern Channel Islands of Santa Catalina, San Clemente, and San Nicolas. Santa Barbara Island appears to have been occupied by them only on a temporary and periodic basis (Swartz 1960; Bean and Smith 1978:538; Hudson 1981:193-194).

The total area of the Gabrielino mainland territory exceeded 1,500 square miles. Most of this territory lies below 1,000 feet in elevation and consists of a lengthy coastal plain and several broad inland valleys. For the purposes of the discussion that follows, these will be designated the San Fernando Valley, the San Gabriel Valley, the San Bernardino Valley, and the Los Angeles—Santa Ana Plain.

The climate of this region is Warm Mediterranean, meaning that it is similar to that found in countries adjacent to the Mediterranean Sea.   During the twentieth century, average annual precipitation has been less than 15 inches, although in the higher mountain regions 40 inches is not unusual. During Gabrielino times, the land was well-watered by three major river systems and numerous streams and tributaries, many of which ran throughout the year. In addition, prior to cattle and sheep ranching there was much less runoff, which resulted in a higher water table and more ground water.   The predominant vegetation comprised grass and coastal sagebrush in valley bottoms and chaparral at higher elevations. At least eight distinct habitats, or ecological zones, existed within this territory, including Saltmarsh-Estuary, Freshwater Marsh, Grassland-Herbland, Southern Oak Woodland, Riparian Woodland, Chaparral, Coastal Sage Scrub, and Beach and Coastal Strand (Dixon 1974:40-43; Bean and Smith 1978:539).

POPULATION ESTIMATES

Estimates of the total Gabrielino population are limited by the available data; however, previously published estimates suggest a population in A.D. 1770 that exceeded 5,000 (Bean and Smith 1978:540). These estimates can be substantiated by ethnographic and historic data. Reid identified 28 Gabrielino communities, two of which were located on Santa Catalina and San Clemente islands, and reported that "there were a great many more villages than the above, probably some forty" (Reid 1852:7-8). Reid's observation is corroborated by the settlements that can be identified from mission records and the research of Kroeber and Harrington. More than 50 Gabrielino placenames have been associated with communities occupied around the time of Spanish colonization, although some of these may have been of minimal size.

Estimates of the average population size of the Gabrielino communities must be based primarily upon the accounts of the early explorers, which indicate that mainland community populations ranged from 50 to 150 inhabitants at the time of European contact, with 100 perhaps being a reasonable average (Smith and Teggart 1909; Teggart 1911). Mission records indicate that by 1797 most communities in the San Fernando Valley contained somewhat less than 100 inhabitants (Forbes 1966:139); however, this is almost 30 years after European contact, and populations had undoubtedly been reduced by disease and emigration. Using the above data, if approximately 55 Gabrielino communities were simultaneously occupied, with the average community population at about 100, a total estimated population in excess of 5,000 is easily justified.

Two important points must be noted with regard to these population estimates, which may be conservative. First, some Gabrielino communities may have contained more than 150 inhabitants. For example, when the Sebastián Vizcaíno expedition visited Isthmus Cove on Santa Catalina Island in 1602 the explorers were met by more than 300 Indians (Bolton 1908:85). Similarly, when the Portolá Expedition visited a community in the San Fernando Valley in 1769 they were met by 205 men, women, and children (Teggart 1911:24-25). Second, unrecorded epidemics of European diseases may have decreased the Indian population of southern California. Pablo Tac, a Luiseño Indian from Mission San Luis

Rey, reported that one such epidemic reduced the population of the neighboring Luiseño from 5,000 to 3,000 (Tac 1952). Similar early epidemics may have affected the Gabrielino population as well.

SETTLEMENT PATTERNS

A Gabrielino community consisted of one or more lineages, each comprising several related nuclear families (Harrington 1942:32, items 1238, 1241, 1261, 1263). Inland communities maintained permanent geographical territories or usage areas which, according to studies of the inland Luiseño, probably averaged 30 square miles (White 1963:117; but see Oxendine 1983:44 for a critique of White's territorial analysis of the Luiseño); these territories are sometimes referred to by the Spanish term, ranchería. It is unclear whether this pattern also held in certain regions that were particularly rich in food resources, such as the coastal areas. Within its territory, or ranchería, each community maintained a primary settlement as well as a variety of hunting and gathering areas, ritual sites, and other special use locations. These subsidiary sites might be periodically occupied while a special activity, such as acorn gathering, was under way; once that activity was completed the population would return to the main settlement. For purposes of the following discussion, the term community will refer to the primary settlement and the population that resided at that location.

ENVIRONMENTAL FACTORS INFLUENCING SETTLEMENT

The mainland Gabrielino preferred certain locations within their vast homeland as sites for their primary settlements. Among the most important factors affecting this preference were the existence of a stable food supply and a reliable source of water, as well as a measure of protection against flooding. Studies of the neighboring Luiseño and Chumash Indians indicate that large, permanent communities typically developed near the interfaces of several environmental zones or habitats. Such locations offered a greater variety of food resources and helped ensure against famines brought about by drought, pestilence, or seasonal fluctuations in the availability of wild crops (White 1963:116-117; Landberg 1965:111-112; Oxendine 1983).

An examination of the distribution of known Gabrielino communities suggests a similar pattern. Permanent settlements appear for the most part to have been situated near the intersection of two or more environmental zones. Three geographical areas appear to have been especially favored, namely, the prairie-foothill transition zone ringing the interior plains, elevated locations near major watercourses, and coastal sites near sheltered bays and inlets.

The distribution of known Gabrielino communities also suggests considerable regional variation in the density of settlement. In some regions, such as the San Fernando Valley or the San Bernardino Valley, communities appear to have been rather widely distributed. Other regions, such as the San Gabriel Valley or the Palos Verdes Peninsula, may have been more densely populated.

Although caution must be exercised when drawing conclusions from the limited data available, it appears that variations in population probably resulted from a combination of social, economic, and environmental factors. Studies of the neighboring Luiseño and Chumash suggest that the economic patterns of inland, coastal, and Channel Island groups were different, and that the coastal and Channel Island groups placed a much greater reliance upon marine food resources than did the interior groups (White 1963:121-122; Landberg 1965:107-118; see also Oxendine 1983:44). This is substantiated by Reid's observation regarding the Gabrielino that "fish, whales, seals, sea-otters, and shellfish, formed the principal subsistence of the immediate coast-range of Lodges and Islands" (Reid 1852:22), and the report of the missionaries at San Fernando that "those on the coast are fond of every species of fish especially the whale" (Geiger and Meighan 1976:85, answer from Mission San Fernando).

Another important factor in the economies of the coastal and island Gabrielino was the development of a vigorous maritime trade based in large part upon the plank canoe and the exchange of Catalina soapstone for mainland goods (Kroeber 1925:629). Other cultural distinctions between inland and coastal groups were noted by Father Boscana, who studied the Indian population residing at San Juan Capistrano, which included both Gabrielino and Juaneño peoples. When discussing the oral literature of these people, the Franciscan priest observed that "the Indians of this particular location . . . account for the creation of the

world in one way, and those of the interior . . . in another" (Boscana 1933:27).

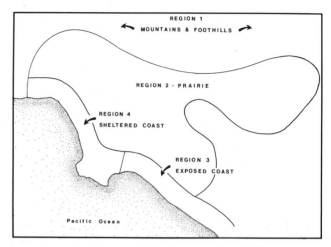

Map 4. The mainland Gabrielino territory can be divided into four geographical regions. This map is based on Hudson (1971).

GEOGRAPHICAL REGIONS

The mainland Gabrielino territory can be divided into four geographical regions, each of which offered a distinctive variety of resources (see Hudson 1971). The first region comprised the interior mountains and adjacent foothills, including the Santa Ana, San Gabriel, and Santa Monica ranges. Distinctive food resources available within this region included numerous small animals, deer, acorns, sage, and piñon nuts. The second geographical region included the prairies flanking the interior mountains, an area that included the San Fernando, San Gabriel, and San Bernardino valleys, and a greater portion of the Los Angeles—Santa Ana Plain. Significant food resources found within this region included acorns, sage, yucca, deer, numerous small rodents, cactus fruit, and a variety of plants, animals, and birds associated with the freshwater marshes.

The third geographical region was the exposed coastal strip extending from San Pedro south to Newport Bay. Food resources found within this region included shellfish, rays, sharks, and fish that are available near coastal inlets. The fourth region was the sheltered coastal strip from San Pedro north to Topanga Canyon. Food resources within this region included shellfish, sharks, rays, fish of many species (including pelagic, i.e., deep-water fish), sea mammals, and sea birds.

SETTLEMENT AND SUBSISTENCE PATTERNS
WITHIN THE REGIONS

At the present time the most complete model of Gabrielino settlement and subsistence strategies suggests three broad patterns of cultural adaptation (see Hudson 1971). The first settlement and subsistence pattern prevailed in the interior mountains, where primary settlements were located in the lower reaches of canyons that offered protection against cold weather. During spring and summer, individual family units dispersed to seasonal camps to gather bulbs, roots, and seeds, while in the fall these families moved to oak groves to gather acorns.

The second settlement and subsistence pattern prevailed among the communities located on the inland prairies. During the winter these communities divided into family units that migrated to shellfish-gathering camps located along the exposed coast south of San Pedro. Few, if any, primary settlements are thought to have been located along the exposed coast, probably because much of the area was low-lying marshland subject to winter flooding. A region of higher elevation extending from the Newport Bay area southward may have been an exception (see Howard 1977).

The third settlement and subsistence pattern was found among the communities scattered along the sheltered coastal strip extending northward from San Pedro. During the winter, when storms and rough seas made fishing impossible, the occupants of these communities dispersed to inland camps where they hunted and gathered acorns, seeds, berries, and roots.

Although this model does not encompass the entire range of variation in Gabrielino settlement and subsistence patterns, it does provide a broad framework for the integration of future research. The testing and refining of this model is an important focus of archaeological research in the Gabrielino homeland (see Ross 1970; Howard 1977; Koerper 1981; Craib 1982; Wlodarski et al. 1985).

COMMUNITY ORGANIZATION

The primary settlement was the heart of Gabrielino political and spiritual life. Larger primary settlements functioned as political, legal, and administrative centers; some, such as *Povuu'nga* on Alamitos Bay, served as ritual centers. Other settlements may have provided a focal point for regional trade activities. For example, *Nájquqar* on Santa Catalina Island may

have provided a central depot for the trade in soapstone.

Gabrielino settlements were organized along a regular pattern, although smaller communities might lack some of the features of the larger population centers. In the middle of the settlement was an unroofed religious structure known as the *yovaar*; surrounding the *yovaar* were the homes of the chief and the elite members of Gabrielino society, and beyond them were the houses owned by other members of the community. Adjacent to the settlements were large cleared areas which were used as playing fields for races and games. Sweat huts were commonly located near streams or pools of water which were used for rinsing, while the special huts occupied by women during menstruation were located near the outskirts of the settlement.

RELIGIOUS STRUCTURES

The center of each community was occupied by an unroofed sacred enclosure known as the *yovaar* (Reid 1852: 21; Bean and Smith 1978:542; Hudson and Blackburn 1986:56-60). The earliest description of a Gabrielino *yovaar* was recorded by Father Antonio de la Ascensión in 1602 (Wagner 1929:237). According to Father Antonio it was a

> place of worship or temple where the natives perform their sacrifices and adorations. . . . This was a large flat patio and in one part of it, where they had what we would call an altar, there was a great circle all surrounded with feathers of various colors and shapes, which must come from the birds they sacrifice. Inside the circle there was a figure like a devil painted in various colors. . . . At the sides of this were the sun and the moon.

Generally the *yovaar* consisted of an open, level courtyard surrounded by a brushwork fence. Father Boscana observed that the enclosure was "four or five yards in circumference, not exactly round, but inclining to an oval" (Boscana 1933:37); Reid (1852:21) described the surrounding fence as "circular and formed of short stakes, with twigs of willow entwined basket fashion, to the height of three feet." José de los Santos Juncos, a Gabrielino consultant who worked with Harrington, reported that the enclosure was round, 50 feet in diameter, with a fence of tule mats eight feet high (Harrington 1986:R104 F007, R125 F367; see also Harrington 1933:135-138, note 55; Hudson and Blackburn 1986:56-60). Poles with feathered streamers were sometimes erected in the four cardinal directions (Reid 1852:41; Hudson and Blackburn 1986:63).

A shallow trench divided the interior of the *yovaar* in half, and in each half stood a small, circular enclosure. One of these, which was made of woven reeds and stood six feet in height, may have served as a storage area for the ritual implements owned by the lineage. The second enclosure was lower, perhaps less than a foot in height, and made of wooden stakes pounded into the ground. Sheltered within this fence of stakes was a figure representing *Chengiichngech*, the spiritual being and creator-god of the Gabrielino (Boscana 1933:37).

The *Chengiichngech* figure consisted of the skin of a coyote, or sometimes a mountain lion, which was stuffed with bird's feathers, the horns of deer, lion's claws, beaks and talons from hawks and crows, and other objects sacred to the god. Arrows were inserted through the animal's mouth with the feathers protruding. The figure was draped with a feather cloak and was supported on a wooden framework (Boscana 1933:37). Harrington's Luiseño consultant José Olivas Albañez drew a rough sketch of the *Chengiichngech* figure. The drawing depicted it as an animal skin stretched across a small wooden fence; the fence consisted of two vertical posts set into the ground a short distance apart which supported three horizontal crosspieces. Hanging from this fence was the skin of an animal; the animal's front legs were outstretched and the rear legs dangled near the ground (Harrington 1986: R125 F490).

In later years following missionization and the spread of Christianity, the design of the *yovaar* seems to have been modified. A brushwork fence was still erected, but the *Chengiichngech* figure was no longer represented. Rather, in the center of the clearing was a hearth consisting of a firepit surrounded by two or three pot-rest stones (Harrington 1933:136; 1986: R125 F367).

The construction of the *yovaar* was ordered by *Chengiichngech* to provide a place "where they might pay to him adoration, offer up sacrifices, and have religious worship" (Boscana 1933:29). In comparing religious architecture from cultures throughout the world, Mircea Eliade (a historian of religion) found that ritual structures often symbolize the universe (Eliade 1957:36-37, 42-47). For the Gabrielino, the *yovaar* represented a sacred space where communi-

cation between the secular and supernatural worlds was possible. To enter the *yovaar* was to experience the sacred and be in contact with *Chengiichngech*, and for this reason admittance was strictly regulated. Reid (1852:21) observed that "the only ones admitted into the church, were the seers and captains, the adult male dancers, the boys training for that purpose, and the female singers. But on funeral occasions the near relatives of the deceased were allowed to enter." Father Boscana (1933:38) corroborated this information:

> Very great was their veneration for the . . . temple, and they were extremely careful not to commit the most trivial act of irreverence within. No one was permitted to enter it on their feast days but the chief, the *puplem*, and elders. The remainder of the people remained outside of the stakes. The younger class did not dare to approach even the entrance. Profound silence was observed generally throughout the assembly . . .

Other structures of religious purpose that might be located within a community included a second enclosure, which was maintained for "rehearsing in and teaching children . . . to dance and gesticulate" (Reid 1852:21).

COMMUNITY STRUCTURES

Outside the brushwork wall of the *yovaar* lay the dome-shaped reed houses of the community's occupants. The placement of a home within a community, its size, and the quality of its construction, were determined by the wealth and social status of the owner. The *tomyaar* and other wealthy members of the elite class had the privilege of building their homes near the center of the community and contiguous to the *yovaar*. In addition to being near the sacred enclosure, this location provided greater protection in times of war. The large and imposing homes of the *tomyaar* and other Gabrielino elite probably housed several related families. Beyond lay the smaller homes of the commoners; poor members of the community occupied simple lean-to structures or windbreaks near the outskirts of the settlement, seeking shelter elsewhere during inclement weather (Boscana 1933:37; Hudson and Blackburn 1983:351).

HOUSES

On the mainland, Gabrielino houses were "made of sticks, covered in around with flag mats worked or platted [the term flag refers to plants with long, sword-shaped leaves]" (Reid 1852:9), but on the islands and the mainland coast whale ribs might be substituted for wooden posts, while sea lion hides could be used as a covering in place of rushes (Schumacher 1876:21; Kroeber 1925:634; Harrington 1986:R102 F852; Raab and Yatsko 1990:15). The Gabrielino living on San Clemente Island as well as those near Newport Bay and in the Santa Ana Mountains, may have followed the Luiseño practice of building semi-subterranean houses by first digging a two-foot deep hole the diameter of the house and then erecting the wood and rush structure over it; semi-subterranean houses were reportedly easier to keep warm (Sparkman 1908:212-213; Kroeber 1925:654; McKusick and Warren 1959:120; Ross 1970:84; Hafner 1971:9). Gabrielino houses averaged from 12 to 35 feet in diameter, although some were as large as 50 feet in diameter. While visiting Santa Catalina Island in 1602 Father Antonio de la Ascensión observed "houses made like cabins" which were covered with "a mat of rushes very closely woven . . . which they set up on some great upright forked poles. They are so spacious that each will hold fifty people" (Wagner 1929:237; see also McKusick and Warren 1959:120; Winterbourne 1967:13; Hudson and Blackburn 1983:323-339; Meighan 1983:165; Rogers 1993:20).

The Gabrielino house was durable, earthquake-proof, and easily repaired. The steep pitch of the tall, dome-shaped roof aided runoff and helped keep the interior dry during heavy rains, while the walls of thatch and matting allowed air to circulate and remain fresh. A smoke hole with a removable cover at the apex of the dome also helped keep the interior fresh. A hearth located in the center of the floor provided heat and warmth, and tule mats covered the doorway, which was carefully placed to avoid cold drafts from the north wind (Harrington 1942:10, items 212, 219). Following missionization, the Gabrielino and other southern California Indians continued to build houses using traditional materials and techniques, although the circular floor plan and dome-shaped roof were abandoned in favor of square structures with gabled roofs. One American who visited these homes made of reeds and willows reported that the houses were "proof against rain and were warm and comfortable" (Rose 1959:55).

March was the preferred month for house building, for at that time of year the willow bark was fresh and green and could be readily made into cord. Once a level area was chosen for the house it was cleared of brush and rocks and a tall pole erected. A long string was attached to the pole, and using this the builder scratched a large circle into the ground. Post holes were dug a step apart along the circumference of the circle, and poles of sycamore or willow were erected. These poles had previously been cut or burned down, then trimmed with flint knives; the lower ends were charred in a flame to retard rotting (Harrington 1942:10, item 205; Hudson and Blackburn 1983:325-328).

When all the peripheral poles were erected, each was bent and lashed to the pole opposite to form a dome-shaped framework for the walls and roof. This framework was strengthened with horizontal crosspieces lashed with willow cord and then covered with a layer of tule mats. A layer of thatching six to twelve inches thick consisting of wild alfalfa, fern, or carrizo was then added and held in place by another set of crosspieces. A smoke hole which could be covered in adverse weather was built into the apex of the roof (Harrington 1942:10, item 206; Hudson and Blackburn 1983:325).

The Gabrielino home was finished with great care. The doorway was framed with bundles of tule lashed to the wooden uprights, while the door itself consisted of tule mats. Inside the doorway a trench caught runoff which might enter during a storm. The floor was of earth sprinkled with water and pounded hard with stones, and a hearth was located in the center (Hudson and Blackburn 1983:329-330).

HOUSE FURNISHINGS

The interior of a large home was comfortably furnished. Tule mats covered the dirt floor, and rugs and blankets of rabbit, bear, and sea-otter hides gave added comfort. Some of these blankets consisted of hide strips woven on a string weft, while Reid noted that "their covering at night consisted of rabbit skins, cut square and sewed together in the form of a bedspread" (Reid 1852:24; also Bolton 1908:85; Harrington 1942:23, items 861, 862; Hudson and Blackburn 1983:375, 385-388).

In the center of the floor a ring of cobbles outlined

the hearth, and within this ring vessels of soapstone sat above the flames on three pot-rest stones, much as a teakettle or saucepan might be left to simmer on a stove.   José de los Santos Juncos reported to Harrington that "Indians made fire by firesticks or by striking rocks together, but made it seldom. They got a big log to burning and had fire night and day" (Harrington 1942:25, items 929, 930; Hudson and Blackburn 1983:355-360; Harrington 1986:R102 F759). Stone mortars as well as jars and bowls of soapstone and wood sat near the hearth within easy reach of the cook.

Sleeping areas could be screened for privacy with reed mats. Bedding was made from matting and sometimes was supported on bedsteads of forked willow poles driven into the ground. Pedro Fages, speaking of the Chumash Indians, described similar beds as "built up high on bedsteads of heavy sticks; a reed mat serves as a mattress, and four others as curtains, forming a bedroom. Beneath the bedsteads are the beds of the little Indians, commodiously arranged" (Fages 1937:48; also Harrington 1942:10, item 228; Hudson and Blackburn 1983:372-374). Harrington's Juaneño consultant Anastacia de Majel described the construction of a Juaneño bedstead. First, they "cut 4 horcones [forked supports], one clavado [exactly] at each corner. [They] then put 4 stout poles, for edges of bedstead, & then got sauz or sauco [willow or elder], both have tough bark to use as barkstrips, & inf. [informant] knows just how to lash these poles to the crotches; then put on slats, & soft stuff on top" (Harrington 1986:R128 F682).

Stools were made from whale vertebrae, and infants were safely supported in cradleboards padded with hides and furs. These cradleboards consisted of an inverted, U-shaped wooden framework strengthened with crosspieces. A belt of hide or vegetable fiber was used to hold the infant in place (Harrington 1942:10, item 230; Hudson and Blackburn 1982:316-327, 1983:369-370).

Baskets in a variety of shapes and sizes were used in the Gabrielino home, some for food preparation, others for storage; basketry trays of various sizes were used as well. Water was stored in large-necked water bottles made from twined reeds. These bottles, which may have stood as high as three feet, were plastered with asphaltum for waterproofing and were kept in most houses. Small-necked globular trinket baskets were used for storage of small items, and trash was collected in large, open-twined wastebaskets. Hooks and pegs lashed to the framework of the walls provided convenient places to hang a variety of items used in everyday life, such as bows, arrow quivers, brooms, fire-drills, and hide bags (Hudson and Blackburn 1983).

OTHER STRUCTURES

Adjacent to many of the houses were windbreaks made of vertical poles covered with rush mats; these windbreaks provided convenient open-air kitchens for food preparation and cooking. Near each of the houses were large, coiled granary baskets used for storing acorns and chía seeds. These granaries sat on raised platforms made from sticks lashed together and supported on wooden poles driven into the ground. Mats or baskets served as lids, and sometimes the granaries were coated with asphaltum for waterproofing. During foul weather the granary baskets were moved indoors (Winterbourne 1967:15; Hudson and Blackburn 1983; Harrington 1986:R102 F501).

Semi-subterranean sweathouses with earthen roofs were also a regular feature of Gabrielino communities. These sweathouses were used primarily by the men both for ritual purposes, such as preparing for a hunt, and for hygiene. Small semi-circular sweathouses had roofs of wooden poles set into the ground and covered with soil, although sometimes a small sweathouse was built into an earthen bank. A dry sauna was used to heat the interior, and because there was no smoke hole the fire was built near the doorway. A nearby pool was used for rinsing. Like the Chumash, the Gabrielino probably also had larger, ceremonial sweathouses consisting of hemispherical, earth-covered domes 12 feet or so in diameter. A small door placed in the apex of the roof doubled as a smoke hole, and a ladder consisting of a notched wooden pole led down into the interior (Kroeber 1925:628; Harrington 1942:9, 11, items 180, 246; Geiger and Meighan 1976:72-73, answer from Mission San Gabriel; Hudson and Blackburn 1986:33-43).

Adjacent to the primary settlements were large, level clearings used as playing fields for races and games of hoop-and-pole or shinny. Among the Chumash, these fields were often surrounded by low fences of poles and mats or interwoven brush (Geiger and Meighan 1976:58, answer from Mission San Fernando; Hudson and Blackburn 1986:48-49).

California Historical Society-TICOR Photo Collection, University of Southern California Library, No. 4690
Fig. 8. Gabrielino sweathuts were similar to this Luiseño sweathut on the Soboba Indian Reservation photographed around 1885.

Burial grounds were an important element of every community. The exact location of Gabrielino cemeteries in regard to the communities is unclear; they may have been situated outside, but near, the primary settlements, as were Chumash and Kitanemuk graveyards (Harrington 1942:37). The Gabrielino marked graves with baskets, or with gravestones comprising a sandstone slab decorated with etched figures commemorating the deceased (Merriam 1955:85; Heizer 1968:104, 123, note 66). A missionary at San Fernando may have been describing a Fernandeño cemetery with funeral poles when he wrote that "in their race-courses they make large circles in the center of which they raise a pole covered with bundles of feathers from the crow and which is adorned with beads" (Geiger and Meighan 1976:58, answer from Mission San Fernando).

LOCATING SETTLEMENTS

As noted above, the Gabrielino may have occupied 50 or more communities at the time of European contact. Information on Gabrielino placenames is found in a number of sources. Gabrielino community names are found in the registers of births, marriages, and deaths from Missions San Gabriel, San Fernando, and San Juan Capistrano, and data from these registers has been compiled by a number of individuals (Sugranes 1909; Engelhardt 1922, 1927a, 1927b; Merriam 1968; Muñoz 1982; O'Neil 1988, n.d.; King 1993; Temple n.d.a, n.d.b). Community name and locational data have also been published by Reid (1852), Alexander Taylor (1860a), and Kroeber (1907, 1909, 1925). A compilation of Gabrielino and Fernandeño placenames and locations by J. R. Swanton (1953) seems based primarily on previously published sources. Original data from Indian consultants is also presented in the published works of Harrington (1933, 1986). Much of

Harrington's placename data was incorporated in *California's Gabrielino Indians* (Johnston 1962); however, new information from Harrington's notes is presented in Chapters 3, 4, and 5 of the present volume.

A number of factors must be considered when mapping the locations of Gabrielino settlements. The anthropologist A. L. Kroeber (1925:616) summarized the situation quite well when he commented:

> The Indians of this region, Serrano, Gabrielino, and Luiseño, have long had relations to the old ranchos or land grants, by which chiefly the country was known and designated until the Americans began to dot it with towns. The Indians kept in use . . . native names for these grants. Some were the designations of the principal village on the grant, others of the particular spot on which the ranch headquarters were erected, still others of camp sites, or hills, or various natural features.

Kroeber went on to point out that with the passing of the villages the Indians "think in terms of Spanish grants or American towns." Writing around 1917, the anthropologist concluded that the opportunity to prepare a true map of village locations "passed away 50 years ago" (Kroeber 1925:616; Heizer 1978b:8).

More than 75 years have passed since Kroeber wrote these words, and the task facing the modern researcher attempting to map the Gabrielino homeland has grown even more formidable. Massive urban development has changed the landscape so thoroughly that the researcher must rely primarily on archival sources, including early maps. Unfortunately, little or no locational information is presently available for many of the communities named in the mission registers; as if to further confuse the issue, some of the settlements listed in the registers appear to be variant spellings of the same names.

Surprisingly, archaeological research is of limited value in identifying the locations of even the largest Indian communities of southern California. More than a century of disturbance by antiquarians and relic hunters has destroyed or heavily damaged most of the archaeological sites in the area. Tragically, only a fraction of the sites that once existed in this region have been preserved; fewer still were adequately investigated prior to their destruction.

The difficulties outlined above are limiting factors in the present volume as well. In most cases, the historic and ethnohistoric data presently available make it possible to locate major Gabrielino communities within the boundaries of early Spanish grants or Mexican Period ranchos. It should be noted, however, that some of the larger grants and ranchos encompassed thousands of acres. In a few cases, the ethnographic data collected by Harrington suggest more precise locations. Occasionally, archaeological data have confirmed the accuracy of these locations. Wherever possible, the author of the present volume has attempted to resolve discrepancies in the data and correlate Gabrielino placenames with modern landmarks. Unfortunately, for many sites this is not possible given the data currently available. In these cases, it was deemed best to present the relevent historical and ethnohistorical data and make it available to researchers. Future studies will refine the locations of these and other communities and provide a clearer and more complete picture of the Gabrielino homeland.

SUMMARY

The Indians of southern California, including the Gabrielino, practiced a hunter-gatherer lifestyle. Interaction was common among these Indian groups and included intermarriage, political alliances, and trade networks. As a result, boundaries between groups were characterized by broad frontiers of shared influence in which bilingualism, intermarriage, and a blending of cultural characteristics is evident.

The total area held by the Gabrielino exceeded 1,500 square miles and included the watersheds of the Los Angeles, San Gabriel, Santa Ana, and Río Hondo rivers. The Gabrielino also occupied or held Santa Catalina, San Clemente, San Nicolas, and Santa Barbara islands. Within this territory were more than 50 settlements or communities, with populations that ranged from 50 to 150 people. The total Gabrielino population probably exceeded 5,000; however, it is unclear whether early, unrecorded epidemics of European diseases affected the population size.

Each Gabrielino community consisted of one or more lineages which maintained a permanent geographical territory. On the basis of studies of the inland Luiseño, these territories, or rancherías, are estimated to have included 30 square miles. Within each territory there was a primary settlement as well as a variety of hunting and gathering areas, ritual sites, and special use locations. The term community, as it is used in the present volume, applies to both the primary settlement and the population residing at that settlement. Gabrielino communities were typically located at the interface of several environmental zones. The ideal community (primary settlement) location offered a nearby source of fresh water, protection against flooding, and access to a variety of food resources throughout the year.

At the present time, three Gabrielino settlement and subsistence patterns have been identified. The first pattern applied to the interior mountain regions, where primary settlements were located in the lower reaches of canyons which offered protection against cold weather. During summer, families traveled to seasonal camps to gather bulbs, roots, and seeds; in the fall they traveled to oak groves to gather acorns. The second pattern prevailed among communities which were located on the inland prairies. During the winter these communities divided into family units and traveled to shellfish-gathering camps located along the coast south of San Pedro. The third settlement and subsistence pattern was found among communities located along the coast north of San Pedro. During the winter, the occupants of these communities dispersed to inland camps to hunt and gather plant foods.

A Gabrielino community typically contained a variety of religious, residential, and recreational structures. In the larger communities, a *yovaar*, or sacred enclosure, was located near the center of the settlement. Surrounding the *yovaar* were the houses owned by the *tomyaar* and other members of the Gabrielino elite class. Some of these elite homes may

have reached 50 feet in diameter and housed several related families. Furnishings included wooden bedsteads, floor mats, stools of whale vertebrae, and baskets of various shapes and sizes. Windbreaks located adjacent to the houses provided open-air cooking areas. Surrounding the *yovaar* and the homes of the elite were smaller houses occupied by the rest of the community. Other features found in the settlements included sweathouses, level clearings used as playing fields, and cemeteries.

The task of locating the Gabrielino communities is made difficult by the early incorporation of the Gabrielino population into the Spanish missions and ranchos. The massive urbanization which has characterized much of Los Angeles and Orange counties has also complicated the task, forcing the researcher to rely primarily on historic and ethno-historic sources of information.

The Gabrielino communities and settlements are discussed in detail in the following three chapters, which are organized by geographical region. The discussion begins in Chapter 3 with the mainland communities situated in the San Fernando, San Gabriel, and San Bernardino valleys. Chapter 4, which focuses on the coastal communities located on the Los Angeles—Santa Ana Plain, is presented in two sections: the first deals with the inland communities, the second with the communities located on or near the seacoast. Finally, Chapter 5 covers the Channel Islands of Santa Catalina, San Clemente, San Nicolas, and Santa Barbara, reviewing the placename and settlement data for each of these unique island worlds.

CHAPTER 3

THE PEOPLE OF THE INLAND VALLEYS

The northern region of the Gabrielino territory comprises three broad inland prairies known as the San Fernando, San Gabriel, and San Bernardino valleys. Together these valleys constitute half of the total Gabrielino territory; individually, each forms a distinctive geographical and environmental subregion within the homeland of the First Angelinos.

THE SIMI AND SAN FERNANDO VALLEYS

The San Fernando Valley comprises 160 square miles of prairie bounded on the north and west by the San Gabriel and Santa Susana mountains, on the south by the Santa Monica Mountains and Cahuenga Peak, and on the east by the Verdugo Mountains. Valley floor elevations range from 500 feet above sea level in the southeast to 1,000 feet above sea level in the west. Several foothill passes located along the southeastern edge of the valley provide access to the San Gabriel Valley.

Although the Gabrielino may have ranged beyond the San Fernando Valley (Shiner 1949), the available evidence indicates that primary settlements were restricted to the valley itself. Harrington's consultant Setimo López reported that "the V. [Ventureño] held Simi and Tapo" and "Tapo is an old Indian place, too. The name means ablon [perhaps abalon (abalone), a reference to shell or limestone deposits?] in F. [Fernandeño]" (Harrington 1986:R106 F39, 72). During the Spanish and Mexican periods Tapo was a rancho owned by José de la Guerra y Noriega; the rancho was famous for its wine and brandies (Thompson and West 1883:390; Sheridan 1926:1.168; both references cited in Librado et al. 1979:174). The name *Tapo* survives in Tapo Canyon, located along the northern edge of Simi Valley.

Ten Gabrielino communities located in the San Fernando Valley will be discussed in the following section including: *'Atavsanga, Siutcanga, Pasheeknga, 'Achooykomenga, Pakooynga, Tohuunga, Muuhonga, Wiqanga, Kaweenga,* and *Haahamonga.* Each of these communities appears to have been located in the prairie-foothill transition zone.

WESTERN SAN FERNANDO VALLEY

The western region of the San Fernando Valley is rich in Gabrielino heritage. Here was located the 1,110-acre Mexican land grant known as Rancho El Escorpión (Beck and Haase 1974, Map 37). According to information provided by one of Harrington's consultants, Sétimo López, it was called ". . . Rancho del Escurpión because there was an animal there, very big . . . like [a] culebra [snake] but very grueso, grande [thick, large], but escurpion has legs . . . [and it] lived in the cave at Escurpion and passed from one side to the other side through the cave" (Harrington 1986:R106 F053).

Harrington wrote:

> the canyon that comes down from the west and passes just south of Bell's [Charlie Bell, the owner of Rancho El Escorpión at that time] barns and houses starts up by Burro Flat . . . . I do not know the name of the canyon . . . and so will call it here Los Escurpiones canyon. . . . One mile or maybe a mile and half up this Escurpiones canyon above Bell's house is a flat with a grove of encinos [oaks] on it—where Indian rancheria used to be. Farther on up (about five miles from Bell's house I believe Bell said) is a place where the creek runs over flat rocks. . . . The flat rock where the water runs over it is full of mortar pits—[it] is a bedrock mortar. . . . Old Indians told Bell that the women used to pound up acorns in these holes . . . (Harrington 1986:R106 F117).

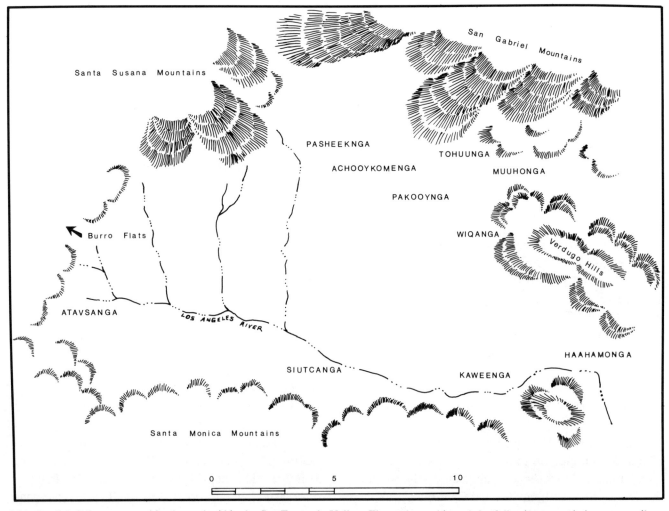

Map 5. Gabrielino communities located within the San Fernando Valley. The scale on this and the following maps is in statute miles.

Sétimo López reported that the Fernandeño called the rancho *'Atavsanga*. According to López "it was the ranch of Charley Bell. . . . This is the V. [Ventureño] name too" (Harrington 1986:R106 F101). King (1993:19-21) gives the Ventureño name as *Huwam*.

Castle Peak was an important Gabrielino landmark in this region. According to Sétimo López, Castle Peak was known as "Kas'élewun," a name which he translated as "lengua," or "tongue"; the name *Kas'élewun* is Ventureño. A bead shrine was reportedly located atop the peak (Harrington 1986:R106 F101, 117; Romani et al. 1988:110).

Juan Meléndrez remembered the names of three caves located near Castle Peak: the Cave of *Munits*; the Cueva de los Chuchos or "Cave of the Dogs"; and the Cueva de las Pulgas or "Cave of the Fleas." In Gabrielino mythology *Munits* was a sorcerer who died when his belly was ripped open by Sparrow Hawk. According to Meléndrez, *Munits*

lay down on top of the Escurpion Peak above the cave . . . to sun himself. The gavilan [Sparrow Hawk] thereupon arrived and kept diving about above munits as munits lay there. [M]units kept telling the gavilan to come to him, that he wanted the gavilan to give him one of his wing feathers . . . to put in . . . [his] nose as a nosestick . . . . The gavilan, however, in one of his dartings ribbed [ripped] munits's belly open thereby sacar-ing [taking out] . . . some of munits's tripas [intestines]. . . . Thus munits perished (Harrington 1986:R106 F152).

Harrington noted that the mouth of the cave "was formerly not very large and has now largely caved in. This mouth faces Moore canyon" (Harrington 1986:R106 F152). According to Harrington, the Cueva de los Chuchos was "a few hundred yards upstr. [upstream] from Charlie Bell's house and on the Calabasas ward side of the canyon." A cave was supposed to link the Cueva de los Chuchos and the Cave of *Munits*. The Cueva de las Pulgas was located opposite the Cueva de los Chuchos in the same canyon (Harrington 1986:R106 F152).

According to José Zalvidea, *Totoonga* was another Gabrielino community situated within the boundaries of El Escorpión, the name *Totoonga* being derived from *Totaa*, meaning "stone," and probably referring to ". . . rocks way up on the mountain there. There was little land there. They saw them when they descended" (Harrington 1986:R102 F438). However, there is conflicting information regarding the location of this community. On another occasion Zalvidea noted that "tŏtaŋa, Piedregal near San José [perhaps Rancho San José at Pomona]" and "tŏtavit means pedregal [stony ground]" (Harrington 1986:R102 F302); the San Gabriel Mission registers placed "Totábit en el rio de Sta. Anna [*Totoonga* on the Santa Ana River]" (Merriam 1968:120). Perhaps the name *Totoonga* applied to two serparate locations, a community located in the eastern portion of the Gabrielino territory and a geographical placename in the San Fernando Valley. Zalvidea reported that the inhabitants of *Totoonga* were wiped out by an epidemic, noting that "they had smallpox there. They vaccinated and [but?] they all died" (Harrington 1986:R102 F438).

Two miles southeast of *Kas'élewun* was an old adobe ranch house set amongst a "group of oak trees" in a "corner of hills." Sétimo López gave the Fernandeño name of this location as "kwaru [*Kwaa'ronga*]" which he translated as "El Zapo [El Sapo]," or "the Toad"; *Kwaa'ronga* was also known as "el Aguage de los Guares [the water-hole of the Guares]" (Harrington 1986:R106 F102, 191). Merriam gives *kwar'-ro* as Gabrielino for frog (Merriam n.d.c).

North of El Escorpión was the "luna hill," the southernmost of two hills located east of Chatsworth Reservoir. The luna hill received its name from a large, buff-colored boulder six feet tall and seven feet in diameter, which was situated about three-fourths of the distance from the crest of the hill. It was

> the only stone on the hillside, and . . . it face[d] San Fernando and was a landmark discernable from the San Fernando vicinity when one looked across the valley Escorpion ward . . . luna was the name both of the stone itself and of the whole hill or in fact group of hills where it was situated. . . . The stone was shaped like a semicircle lying on the flat side of the semicircle, the stone being flat [and] its surface being inclined at an angle of

perhaps 45° to vertical. Its surface is weathered with a sort of marks or spots which might be likened to the spots on the moon—these spots are partly formed by lichen growth (Harrington 1986:106 F151).

The northernmost of the two hills near Chatsworth Reservoir was known as the "loma de los Judios," or "hill of the Jews." According to Meléndrez there was a ravine that scarred the southern face of the hill, and at one time there was a cave that opened onto the ravine. Inside the cave lived the Judios, and

> people used to go there to consult or solicit magical aid from the Judios. Melendrez and the other boys were warned to avoid and fear the place, but nevertheless Melendrez and other boys went there once and tossed a stone into the mouth of the cave, whereupon sulphur-like fumes came out of the cave. Two years ago [around 1914?] Melendrez visited the quebradura [ravine] but found that the cave had entirely fallen in or disappeared . . . (Harrington 1986:R106 F151).

Juan Meléndrez, who accompanied Harrington in 1916 on a visit to various sites in the San Fernando Valley, reported that an old road or trail once ran from San Fernando across the valley floor "in an absolutely straight line" to the luna hill. The road was

> so straight that at one point where a nopalera [prickly pear cactus] was in the line, it cut directly through the nopalera so as not to make any deflection . . . the old Indians made that road straight as an arrow. It ran from San Fernando straight toward the luna hill, and on arriving there passed through the portezuela [opening or pass], with the luna hills to the left or Calabasas ward and the loma de los Judios to the right or Las Pilitas ward (Harrington 1986:R106 F151).

Meléndrez reported to Harrington that a ranchería, or Indian community, existed near Chatsworth Reservoir. "Meléndrez v'd [volunteered] . . . that one long rancheria extended from where we were [probably northwest of Chatsworth Reservoir] a couple of miles to the Triunfo ward [southwestward] of where we were and that fragments of shell, etc., are picked up in this whole stretch." According to Harrington, Meléndrez implied that "the name of that rancheria was El Escurpion de las Salinas" and that "there are two Escurpiones: El Escurpion Viejo (Charlie Bell's ranch) and El Escurpion de las Salinas." Harrington also noted that an "old Indian cemetery and place that was like a god to the Indians (cemetery and said place like a god are one and the same place) was up on top of the mountain immediately back of where we were (Conejo ward) [westward]" (Harrington 1986:R106 F152).

The "place that was like a god to the Indians" may refer to a complex of ritual sites located west of Chatsworth Reservoir at Burro Flats. There are two impressive ritual sites located at Burro Flats; the first is associated with the summer solstice, the second with the winter solstice. There are also a number of related midden and rock art sites. The Summer Solstice Site comprises a number of natural and artificial rock features aligned so that for several days around the date of the solstice the shadow cast by a tall boulder falls directly across a bedrock mortar, or "grinder-hole," worn into a rock outcropping a few feet away.

The Winter Solstice Site at Burro Flats is impressive not only for its ritual associations, but also for its striking beauty. This site, which consists of a small rock shelter decorated with vivid pictographs (rock paintings) executed in red and white upon a black background, is the best known example of Gabrielino-Chumash rock art. A special feature of this shelter is a naturally-formed notch along the upper edge of the opening. For several days around the time of the winter solstice a slender triangle of sunlight formed by this notch illuminates a series of concentric circles painted on the rock wall. Like the Summer Solstice Site, the rock shelter at Burro Flats was most likely used during seasonal rituals. These rituals, as well as the Burro Flats Site itself, will be explored in greater detail in Chapter 8 (Benson 1980; Edberg 1985; Romani et al. 1985; Romani et al. 1988; see also Sanburg et al. 1978).

'Ashaawnga, a Gabrielino placename that referred to the "sierra del águila" or "eagle mountain," was also located at the western edge of the San Fernando Valley. Harrington offered that the site was near "Las Calabazas," an old name that he associated with present-day Chatsworth. According to José Zalvidea the eagle rock was "on top of the mountain . . . black like an eagle seated with folded wings." José de los Santos Juncos observed that "there was no Indian village there. Robbers used to kill many people there." According to Gabrielino legend, Sparrow Hawk, one of the mythical "first people," climbed the hills near 'Ashaawnga and turned to stone after his

wife's death (Harrington 1986:R102 F395, 397, 410-411, R106 F233-240).

ENCINO

According to Sétimo López, the Gabrielino community of *Siutcanga* was located at El Encino (Harrington 1986:R106 F31, 96, 98). El Encino refers to Rancho El Encino, a 4,461 acre tract granted to three ex-mission Indians named Ramón, Francisco, and Roque (Robinson 1952:33-34; Cowan 1956:34; Beck and Haase 1974).

In August, 1769, the members of the Portolá Expedition crossed the San Fernando Valley. On August 5th, the explorers halted close to a very large pool of water; nearby was "a populous Indian village" whose inhabitants were "very good-natured and peaceful. They offered us their seeds in trays or baskets of rushes." The Gabrielino visited the explorers "in such numbers that . . . we counted as many as two hundred and five, including men, women, and children" (Teggart 1911:23-25). The historian Herbert Eugene Bolton identified the camping place as "near Encino," and it is possible that the settlement that the Spaniards observed was *Siutcanga* (Bolton 1927:151; see also Brown 1967:8).

In 1984 and 1985, archaeological excavations near the intersection of Ventura and Balboa boulevards in the city of Encino revealed evidence of a Gabrielino community that may have been *Siutcanga*. The community lay on the bank of an ancient stream bed and included a cemetery in which both human and animal burials were interred. Radiocarbon dating established that this site was occupied by a succession of Indian peoples beginning as early as 5000 B.C. Tragically, much of this invaluable site was destroyed by redevelopment; only a fraction remains preserved under a protective layer of landfill (R. Mason 1986; Whitney-DeSautels 1986).

SAN FERNANDO

The Gabrielino community of *Pasheeknga*, located near the site where Mission San Fernando was established in 1797, was reportedly the most populous community in the San Fernando Valley. The community of *'Achooykomenga* was situated nearby, although the exact location is uncertain (Taylor 1860a; Engelhardt 1927b:10; Harrington 1986:R102 F424). According to a note in the San Fernando baptismal register *'Achooykomenga* was the "ra. in cuyo sitio esta fundata la mision [rancheria in whose place the mission is founded]" (Merriam 1968:93).

Sétimo López reported that "tsiwájana . . . is a meadow above the represo [dam] (the represo is sikwáŋa [*Shikwaanga*])" and that "sikwáŋa" was "Lopez's place (reservoir). It means una cosa verde [a green thing]." Sétimo López explained that "Geronimo Lopez owned the land over there (by huhuj) and where the reservoir (represo) is now (a mile sw of the mission)." According to this consultant "the Gerenimo [Geronimo] Lopez ranch = sikwáŋa. [It] belonged to José Miguel, an old Indian. His son died and another son they carried to the isla and therefore the old man went crazy and his wife Rafaela sold the ranch to a woman of the Feliz family and she sold 20 acres to Geronimo Lopez" (Harrington 1986:R106 F30, 41, 96, 100, 114). The represo was a masonry dam built to supply water to Mission San Fernando; it was completed at the end of 1808. An aqueduct one-half a league in length (approximately one and one-half miles) was constructed in 1811. Sétimo López may have confused his directions, for the remains of this dam are approximately one mile northeast (not southwest) of the mission (Engelhardt 1927a:21; Webb 1952:77).

The name *huhuj*, also mentioned by Sétimo López in the material quoted above, apparently refers to "a little gap in the hills. . . . It is wsw of the Mission. A foot and horseback trail ascended this gap and descended on the other side" (Harrington 1986:R106 F99, 113).

According to José Zalvidea, a mesa with live oaks located west of San Fernando was known as *'Ahikanga*. "A San Fernando Indian once told an American who had a ranch there that he did not want him to live there because it was the land of the wind. Bad wind would fall upon the place. The American said the wind would not hurt him. But later a terrible whirlwind came and tore down the American's house" (Harrington 1986:R102 F395). The name *'Ahikanga* comes from *'ahikan*, "wind" (Gatschet 1879:439).

Another Gabrielino consultant, José de los Santos Juncos, told Harrington that a shrine was located in the hills "where a woman named La Paloma lived, back of San Fernando." This shrine was near "a cave of the wind. Wind made [a] buzzing sound there all of the time. Used to throw abalorio [shell beads] there and leave a sick man there for a while and thus treat him" (Harrington 1986:R102 F833). Santos

Juncos also told of a place "near S.[San] Fernando, by Cuesta de S.[Santa] Susana. . . . Virgin Mary was there on a mule—left mule's footprints on [a] rock, for rocks used to be soft like mud. . . . She was washing the infant's clothes there. And there was a poisonous yerba [herb] there and she changed it to yerba santa" (Harrington 1986:R102 F754).

San Fernando Mission registers list a community or settlement of *Pakooynga*, from which the name of the city of Pacoima is most likely derived (Merriam 1968:98; Kroeber 1925:896). According to Sétimo López, the name means "la entrada [the entrance]" (Harrington 1986:R106 F005, 056).

BIG AND LITTLE TUJUNGA CANYONS

Two important Gabrielino communities, *Tohuunga* and *Muuhonga*, were located along the northern edge of the San Fernando Valley at the base of the San Gabriel Mountains. According to Sétimo López the Gabrielino also held the mountains above these communities (Harrington 1986:R106 F66). José Zalvidea placed the community of *Tohuunga* "near San Fernando;" the archaeological site of LAn-167 near the mouth of Little Tujunga Canyon is the probable location of this community (Ruby 1966; Forbes 1966; Harrington 1986:R102 F435).

The name *Tohuunga* is derived from *tuxuu'*, meaning "old woman," and perhaps refers to "a rock shaped like an old woman" in Little Tujunga Canyon (Harrington 1986:R102 F435, R106 F41). Martín Feliz, another Harrington consultant, learned from the Fernandeño woman named Espíritu (the mother of Harrington consultant Juan Meléndrez) that an old name for Tujunga Canyon was "La Reina," or "The Queen," perhaps in reference to Mary, the mother of Jesus. This name was bestowed upon the canyon because "the queen came in [the] form of a whale & petrified at the mouth of that canyon, as a red rock 25 ft. long, which can be seen by going to Sunland" (Harrington 1986:R106 F164). Feliz also reported that an old Indian cemetery was located at the mouth of Tujunga Canyon (Harrington 1986:R106 F178).

During the spring of 1991 the author visited Little Tujunga Canyon in the company of archaeologist Steven Schwartz and his wife Audrey. Several years earlier they had identified a natural rock feature in a cliff-face matching the location and description of *tuxuu'* as reported by Sétimo López. According to this consultant "There was a rock shaped like an old woman. . . . She was in [a] sitting position" (Harrington 1986:R106 F41). As we watched the play of sunlight on the distant southern face of the rocky cliff the form of *tuxuu'* appeared, becoming more evident as the day progressed and the shadows lengthened. She was crouched on her knees in a sitting position, just as López had described her.

José Zalvidea located the community of *Muuhonga* "about two and a half miles from San Fernando, farther up the canyon from San Fernando." Zalvidea related a story about *Muuhonga* in which "all the fish and animals of the sea" were invited to a fiesta where they were murdered by their hosts. The victims were shot with arrows, and "there are rocks at Muhŭ'ηa which resemble people with heads bent forward as if shot." Only turtledove escaped by making a tremendous leap, landing on Santa Catalina Island. Turtledove "felt so badly that he began to cry, and that is why he is crying yet" (Harrington 1986:R102 F416).

Zalvidea translated the name *Muuhonga* as "tiraron jarazos [they shoot arrows]." However, José de los Santos Juncos noted that the Gabrielino word *muhu* means owl, suggesting that a more likely translation of *Muuhonga* is "Place of the Owl" (Harrington 1986:R102 F416, 418).

Sétimo López noted that "Lopez canyon is the next one west of Little Tejunga canyon. [An] old rancheria and cemetery [were] on [the] mesa at its mouth. . . . inf. [informant] forgets the Indian name" (Harrington 1986:R106 F136).

VERDUGO HILLS

The Gabrielino community of *Wiqanga* was located in Cañada de las Tunas (tuna cactus, *Opuntia* sp.) at the west end of the Verdugo Hills. Sétimo López, commenting on the placename *Vijabit* listed in the San Fernando Mission registers, remarked "wiqár = espina [thorn]. . . . wiqáηa is the Cañada de las Tunas in Span. [Spanish]. Means cañada de las espinas in F. [It is an] old name" (Harrington 1986:R106 F059).

EASTERN SAN FERNANDO VALLEY

According to José Zalvidea, the Gabrielino community of *Kaweenga* was located at "Cahuenga"; this location was corroborated by José de los Santos Juncos and Manuel Santos. Cahuenga refers to Rancho Cahuenga, granted in 1846 to Luis Arenas. It was located at the present day site of Universal City. The name of the Mexican Period rancho was undoubtedly derived from the earlier Gabrielino placename, *Kaweenga*, which José Zalvidea reported to mean "la sierra [the mountain]" (Cowan 1956:21; Harrington 1986:R102 F400, 405). The name survives in Cahuenga Peak.

Reid reported that the community of *Haahamonga* was located on Rancho de los Verdugos (Reid 1852:8); Rancho de los Verdugos is most likely a reference to Rancho San Rafael, also known as La Zanja, granted to José María Verdugo in 1784. This rancho included portions of present-day Glendale, Eagle Rock, and Burbank, and was known at various times as Hahaonuput, Arroyo Hondo, Zanja, and San Rafael (Gudde 1949:292; Cowan 1956:87). The name Hahaonuput was very likely derived from the Gabrielino name *Haahamonga*.

José Zalvidea reported the name *Haahamonga* to mean "walking, they seated themselves" (Harrington 1986:R102 F439).

SAN GABRIEL VALLEY

East of the San Fernando Valley and across the Cahuenga Pass lies the San Gabriel Valley. The San Gabriel Valley comprises 200 square miles of prairie land surrounded in large part by mountains and foothills. The San Gabriel Mountains border the valley on the north, the San José Hills on the east, and the Puente Hills on the south. West of the valley are the San Rafael Hills and Cahuenga Peak, while in the southwest lies the broad prairie land of the Los Angeles—Santa Ana Plain. Elevations in the San Gabriel Valley range from 300 feet above sea level in the southern regions to 1,000 feet above sea level along the base of the San Gabriel Mountains in the north.

SAN GABRIEL MOUNTAINS

Two Gabrielino names have been recorded for the San Gabriel Mountains, formerly known as the "Sierra Madre." One of Harrington's consultants gave the name as "qajt [*xaayy*]," meaning "la sierra," or "the mountain." José Zalvidea, however, reported that the San Gabriel range was known as "Hifàkupa." According to Zalvidea the name *Hifàkupa* means "está parado la sierra de antes [literally, the former mountain is standing]" (Harrington 1986:R102 F327, 449).

However, Kroeber associated the name "Hisakupa" with a Serrano placename near Big Bear Lake in the San Bernardino Mountains (Kroeber 1925:Plate 57). Mrs. James Rosemyre reported to Merriam that the Gabrielino name for the San Gabriel Mountains was "Ah-sook'-să-vit" (Merriam n.d.c; see also Appendix I of the present volume), which is probably derived from *'Ashuukshanga*, a Gabrielino community located near the mouth of the San Gabriel River canyon.

José de los Santos Juncos reported that the San Gabriels "were uninhabited in Indian times. . . . There were many bears there" (Harrington 1986:R102 F16, R104 F008); however, a number of archaeological sites once existed in the San Gabriel River canyon. The canyon was also part of an important trade route that crossed the mountains to reach the Mohave Desert. Other routes reportedly led through Millard and Little Santa Anita canyons (Robinson 1977:13-14, 1983:10-11).

Nine important Gabrielino communities located within the broad expanse of the San Gabriel Valley will be discussed in the following section. Five of these appear to have been located on or near major watercourses associated with the Río Hondo including: *Shevaanga, Sonaanga, Sheshiikwanonga, 'Akuuronga*, and *'Aluupkenga*. The remaining four appear to have been located within the prairie-foothill transition zone including: *'Ashuukshanga, Weniinga, 'Ahwiinga*, and *Pemookanga*.

PASADENA

Several Gabrielino placenames have been recorded for the northwestern regions of the San Gabriel Valley. The Arroyo Seco lies east of the San Rafael Hills near Altadena and Pasadena. According to Harrington's consultant Manuel Santos, the Arroyo Seco was known to the Gabrielino as "M₃ˀˀkat," a name meaning "'rocky' or something like that" (Harrington 1986:R102 F187). Manuel Santos reported the name "Punítavjat" for Pasadena (Harrington 1986:R102 F231, R105 F636), although according to José Zalvidea, "no people lived at Pasadena in Indian times. It was puro llano [pure prairie]" (Harrington 1986:R102 F213).

SAN GABRIEL, SAN MARINO

Four important Gabrielino communities located in the San Gabriel vicinity were *Shevaanga, Sonaanga*,

Sheshiikwanonga, and *'Akuuronga*. These four communities were situated in a fertile, well-watered region that was eventually chosen as the permanent site of Mission San Gabriel. Reid noted that prior to the mission's founding the site was "a complete forest of oaks, with considerable underwood." Nearby in the "hollow nearest to the Mission . . . was a complete thicket, formed of sycamores, cotton-wood, larch, ash and willows; besides, brambles, nettles, palma cristi, wild roses and wild grape-vines lent a hand to make it impassable, except were [where] footpaths had rendered entrance to its barriers" (Reid 1852:72-73).

The close proximity of these settlements to one another suggests that there may have been important political, economic, and ritual ties between the communities. The Indians of this region also shared a regional dialect which the priests at San Gabriel called "*Simbanga.*" Kroeber associated *Simbanga* with the community of "Siba," that is, *Shevaanga* (Kroeber 1925:621; Geiger and Meighan 1976:19, answer from Mission San Gabriel).

According to historical and ethnographic data, *Shevaanga* was located near the present site of Mission San Gabriel. Reid (1852:7) reported that the community was at San Gabriel. One of Harrington's consultants, perhaps José Zalvidea, reported "sivápet," a variant name for *Shevaanga*, as the name "not of San Gabriel but of a place near San Gabriel—a barranco [ravine] near where the old Los Angeles road crossed the river" (Harrington 1986:R102 F834). He also noted that "šivápit means 'piedras [stones],' . . . [and] refers to the whole locality around San Gabriel, or to a place a little beyond the mission." Another consultant, Manuel Santos, reported that the name means "flint" (Harrington 1986:R102 F266, 267).

Two other Gabrielino placenames are also associated with the immediate San Gabriel locality, although it is unclear whether they are variant names for *Shevaanga* or separate communities or settlements. Alexander Taylor (1860a) reported that "the site of the Mission was called *Toviscanga*, and near by was a large rancheria." In fact, the name *Toviscanga* was penned by Father Junípero Serra on the title page of the Book of Confirmations at Mission San Gabriel (Johnston 1962:142). Kroeber, working with the Taylor information as well as data provided by a Luiseño consultant, suggested that the names *Tuvasak* as well as "Siba-" and "Toviska-" all referred to San Gabriel (Kroeber 1907:143-144, 1925:621). José

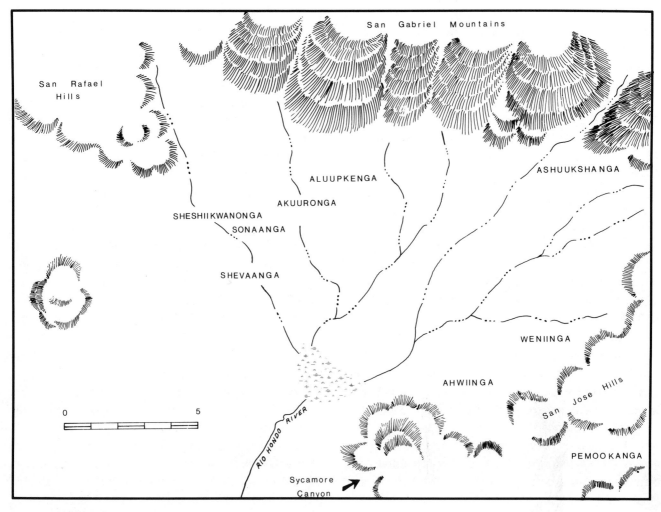

Map 6. Gabrielino communities located within the San Gabriel Valley.

Zalvidea reported to Harrington that the name means "tierra blanca" and that "there used to be white earth there. . . . [T]here is now no white earth there. . . . tȯviska'ηa is an old man" (Harrington 1986:R102 F304).

The other recorded placename for the San Gabriel vicinity is *Tōηwe*. Jesús Jauro, a Luiseño consultant for Harrington, reported that "Tōηwe . . . may be a ranchería, a name of S. Gabriel locality." Jesús "used to hear his mother saying to'oηve of a person talking . . . Gabrielino" (Harrington 1986:R104 F490). Adán Castillo, a Luiseño consultant who worked for Harrington, reported that in "R. [the Reyano dialect of Luiseño] pom-to'ηva wd [would] mean where the people used to grind their seeds on the rocks. R. po-to'ηva, where he or she grinds. tcam-to'ηva, our grindery. The noun has to have some possessional prefixed" (Harrington 1986:R105

F426). Merriam reported that the Gabrielino living in the Tejón region near Bakersfield at the turn of the century referred to themselves as *Tong-va* (Merriam 1955:77).

According to José Zalvidea, "'apåtšijan is a place where the water entered for San Gabriel" and "the pear orchard [at San Gabriel] was located a little this side of the place called 'apåtšijan." It was "the lake by San Gabriel. The name means 'cienega'" (Harrington 1986:R102 F070).

Reid (1852:7) placed *'Akuuronga* near "the presa," a stone dam built to serve Mission San Gabriel. The dam, which is still standing, is located between present La Presa Street and San Gabriel Boulevard on the north side of Huntington Drive. José Zalvidea reported that "'akurangna, where there is much wood (fire wood)" was "the Indian name of La Presa" (Harrington 1986:R102 F63, R104 F42). Indians lived at or near *'Akuuronga* until the 1870s or later. The "*rancheria*" was a small community of 12 to 15 Indian and Mexican families employed by the Sunny Slope Vineyards. According to L. J. Rose, Jr., who was born in 1862, and spent many childhood hours at the *rancheria*, the settlement was about five acres in extent. The homes were built of tules gathered from a nearby swamp, although the traditional dome-shaped Gabrielino house design was abandoned in favor of square buildings with gabled roofs (Rose 1959:55).

According to Reid (1852:7) the Gabrielino community of *Sonaanga* was on "Mr. White's Farm," Michael White being an early settler in the area. Harrington visited la presa and White's Farm between 1914 and 1918 in the company of José de los Santos Juncos. Harrington wrote that "from La Presa we drove South Pasadena ward a few blocks where we reached the site of the old ranch of Miguel Blanco, alias Miguel White. He was an American, but was married to a Spanish California woman whose surname before marriage was Reyes." Harrington gave the location of the ranch as "a quarter of a mile or so South Pasadena ward [west] . . . of La Presa." Harrington also prepared sketch maps of both locations (Harrington 1986:R104 F41-43).

Reid located the community of *Sheshiikwanonga* where the priests at Mission San Gabriel planted a pear orchard (Reid 1852:7). The mission pear orchard was the "Huerta de Peras [orchard of pears]" or " La Huerta Cuatín [Orchard of Cuatín]," a grant of 128 acres made to Reid's wife Victoria in 1830 following the secularization of Mission San Gabriel (Cowan 1956:31). The meaning of Cuatín is at present unclear; Hanna (1946:78) suggests it is based on an Indian word, while Gudde (1949:84) suggests it is derived from the Spanish word for twin, which is cuate.

Harrington visited the site of the Huerta de Peras between 1914 and 1918, accompanied by José de los Santos Juncos and a second consultant named Thomas Cooper. Harrington noted that Santos Juncos "had no trouble in locating the Huerta de Peras . . . as in the orange grove between the hill on which the [Henry E.] Huntington residence stands and the highway where we were [probably Huntington Drive; the Huntington residence is in the community of San Marino]." According to Harrington, Thomas Cooper who had

lived at this spot [near the Huerta de Peras] since 1862, . . . went on foot with me. . . . Mr. Cooper spent at least an hour in carefully pointing out the borders of the old Huerta de Peras. . . . The Huerta de Peras was a long strip, probably nowhere over 100 yards wide, extending in a diagonal direction as regards the way the present roads of the neighborhood are laid out. . . . The trees were still standing when Mr. Cooper . . . saw the place and must then have been some 75 years old. Both he and Santos knew the various kinds of pears which grew in this country. . . . There were peras de San Juan, so called because they ripen very early . . . by San Juan's day, [and] peras de vergamóte, which one could not eat except when they were just ripe because they puckered the mouth so. . . . Mr. Cooper described the soil of the Huerta de Peras as a black adobe, very good for horticulture. . . . Santos said that the Huerta de Peras was also called La Huerta Cuatín. He gave no information as to why it was called thus (Harrington 1986:R104 F43-44).

Harrington drew a sketch map of the boundaries of the pear orchard, locating it south of the Henry E. Huntington residence (Harrington 1986:R104 F033).

WHITTIER NARROWS

In the region now occupied by the Whittier Narrows Dam and Flood Control Basin, the confluence of the Río Hondo and San Gabriel rivers once formed a great marshland that bordered the northern slopes of the Puente Hills. Nearby was Misión Vieja, the first site of Mission San Gabriel; sometime around 1774 it was moved to its present location in San Gabriel (Johnston 1962:129; see Harrington 1986:R104 F36 for a sketch map of the Misión Vieja site).

According to Harrington's consultant Raimundo Yorba, the Gabrielino living in the Whittier Narrows area referred to themselves as *Kichireños*. According to Yorba "his mother was half San Grabielino Indian. She was what they called a Kichireño, one of a bunch of people that lived at that place just this side of San Gabriel which is known as the Mision Vieja. Kichireño is not a placename, but a tribename, the name of a kind of people" (Harrington 1986:R129 F345).

Reid (1852:7) reported that *'Iisanchanga* lay near Misión Vieja; José Zalvidea concurred and offered that the name means "wolves, deriving it from *'īsawt*, wolf," although Harrington noted that the etymology was "not clear" (Harrington 1986:R102 F135). Although early historical accounts mention a

Gabrielino community near Misión Vieja, it is curious that *'Iisanchanga* does not appear as a recognizable name in the mission registers. Perhaps *'Iisanchanga* was a small settlement consisting of a few families, or simply a geographical placename (O'Neil n.d.). In this regard it is noteworthy that Manuel Santos gave a somewhat similar word, "¦ sutkava'ª," as the Indian name for Pomona (Harrington 1986:R105 F636).

The community of *Wiichinga* was also located in the Whittier Narrows area. According to mission records compiled by Merriam it was a "ra, que esta al oriente de esta Mision en un llano cerrado de agua por todos lados [ranchería, that is to the east of this Mission on a plain closed by water on all sides]." This may have been a small settlement rather than a large community. The mission records compiled by Merriam note only one entry; it was recorded in 1771 and was the first baptism performed at the mission (Merriam 1968:117).

ARCADIA, SIERRA MADRE

Reid (1852:8) reported that the Gabrielino community of *'Aluupkenga* was located on the grounds of his own Rancho Santa Anita, a grant of three square leagues (about 20 square miles; a Spanish league was 2.63 miles) that includes the cities of Arcadia and Sierra Madre (Webb 1952:9, note 7; Cowan 1977:90). José Zalvidea reported that *'Aluupkenga* was at Santa Anita, "'where a little water is drunk' as when one drinks only a little, as when one drinks hot soup. . . . " He reported that the name means "the wind enters to the heart as when it is a little hot and you inhale wind a little to cool off" (Harrington 1986:R102 F59-60).

The name *Ahapchingas*, recorded by Alexander Taylor (1860a) may refer to the community of *'Aluupkenga*. According to Taylor a "clan or rancheria" named the "Ahapchingas" was located "between Los Angeles and San Juan Capistrano," and were "enemies of the Gabrielenos or those of San Gabriel" (Taylor 1860a, n.d.; see also Heizer 1941b).

AZUSA

The community of *'Ashuukshanga* lay a short distance south of the mouth of San Gabriel River canyon. Manuel Santos reported that the "name means poco vuelta [little turn]," and that "the real place is by the bend in the canyon" (Harrington 1986:R102 F77). According to José Zalvidea,

however, the name *'Ashuukshanga*, which survives in the modern city name of Azusa, "comes from 'asŭk, 'his grandmother.' It means 'su abuela la tierra' [his grandmother the earth]." Zalvidea suggested that "the grandmother must have turned to stone. There were people everywhere that turned to stone" (Harrington 1986:R102 F75). Kroeber offered yet another translation of this placename, suggesting that it may have meant "skunk place" (Kroeber 1925:895).

North of *'Ashuukshanga* lies San Gabriel River canyon, which was the terminus of an important trade route leading from the San Gabriel Valley to the Mohave Desert. José de los Santos Juncos reported that "in Azusa [San Gabriel] Canyon there is a big painted rock with a hole through it" (Harrington 1986:R102 F75), and "there back of Azusa [is] the great cave; red painted, [it] must have been excavated. It must have been the home of some captain [chief]" (Harrington 1986:R102 F206).

A large boulder decorated with pictographs was once located 30 yards north of the San Gabriel River in Azusa Canyon; it has been given the archaeological site designation LAn-164. The rock paintings on this boulder include both geometric and naturalistic design elements executed in red; these pictographs may have been retouched during the 1930s. Another nearby boulder with yellow pictographs was designated Lan-163. These paintings, which were first published by Hoffman in 1886, may have been done as part of a Gabrielino puberty ritual (Hoffman 1886; Sanburg 1972; see also Robinson 1983:10-11).

José Zalvidea reported the placename "šišú'vit" as "San Antonio, a place two miles from Azusa." According to Zalvidea the spot was known by this name because "there was a devil woman there who used to live there and this devil woman had a child which was not her own. The gopher told the child to run away, far away, and so the child was freed from the power of the devil woman" (Harrington 1986:R102 F265). The Gabrielino word for devil is *shiisho* (Harrington 1986:R103 F31; Munro n.d.).

According to Manuel Santos, "Wihåviat" or "Wihåvjat," was the Gabrielino name for "San José [Rancho San José] near Azusa." The name was derived from *wihåth*, meaning "cholla" or "cactus." Santos reported that *Wihåviat* was "where [a] big canyon comes out of the mountains east of Pasadena. This canyon goes to San Gabriel" (Harrington 1986:R102 F322-323, R105 F636).

Fig. 9. Large boulder covered with pictographs (rock paintings), located in San Gabriel River Canyon in the San Gabriel Mountains. The pictographs, which have been given the archaeological designation CA-LAn-164, may have been retouched in the 1930s.

COVINA

According to Felicitas Serrano Montaño, the Gabrielino community of *Weniinga* was located where the modern city of Covina was founded. José Zalvidea reported that the name *Weniinga* means "one of the place[s] where metates, etc., or anything está tirado [is discarded] as about an Indian camp." A variant name for *Weniinga* is "Guinibit" (Harrington 1986:R102 F323-324).

PUENTE HILLS

The community of *'Ahwiinga* was located on Rancho La Puente, a location which was confirmed by both Reid (1852:7) and José Zalvidea (Harrington 1986:R102 F82). According to Manuel Santos, the name *'Ahwiinga* means "quemada [burned brush]" (Harrington 1986:R105 F636).

The community of *'Ahwiinga* may have served as a provincial "capital" for several Gabrielino communities. Bernice Johnston, citing "an early record translated by Thomas Workman Temple II" as her source, wrote that

> The old text ran, "Matheo, Capitan de la Rancheria Ajuibit, whom the other rancherias regard as their chief, was baptized June 6, 1774, at the age of thirty-five or six." Here was one more of the rare instances in which one man ruled several villages. Being a chief, Matheo was faced with a dilemma which did not trouble lesser men: namely, to make a decision as to which of his wives to retain as his bride in the Christian ceremony which was to follow his baptism. The record gives the name of his choice as Francesca (Johnston 1962:143).

The author of the present volume attempted to trace this quotation to its source. Using a compilation of Mission San Gabriel baptismal entries prepared from Temple's notes by the Daughters of the American

Revolution, it appears that this quotation is derived from entry 81 in the Mission San Gabriel baptismal register. Unfortunately, the typescript prepared by the DAR is incomplete; it reads "81-June 6, 1774 was baptized MATEO, Capitan de la Rancheria Ajuibit, #Mateo Maria, by Figuer." (Temple n.d.b). Worse still, the original entry in the baptismal register is no longer available; the page containing entries 78 through 87 were removed from the register, apparently sometime after Temple's research (San Gabriel Mission Registers n.d.). Thus, for the present time Bernice Johnston's quotation must remain the primary source for this intriguing piece of data.

The placename *'Ahwiinga* appears in the account of an expedition in 1821 by two missionary priests, Fathers Payeras and Sanchez. On September 10, 1821, the expedition set out from Mission San Diego to explore the interior regions between that mission and San Gabriel. On September 26 the party reached San Bernardino, at that time in use as a rancho of Mission San Gabriel; five days later they passed "Ajuenga" on their way to San Gabriel (Engelhardt 1913:142-145).

The western slopes of the Puente Hills hold a prominent place in Gabrielino oral literature. According to one account

> . . . there was a bear which lived on the mountain above the cienega [marsh] of axǔɳa ['*Ahwiinga*], near the cienega. The place where the bear lived was called Xǎrvo. It is derived from 'aXǎrvi . . . the place was called Xǎrvo, or 'aXǎrvoɳa ['*AXaarvonga*], meaning "where it (the bear) is or was." The bear was dangerous and an Indian told a Spaniard about it and the Indian got a bad whipping for his kindness. The Spaniard went up to the place . . . on horseback and his horse threw him and left him there dead, and the horse came back alone. . . . The Spaniards and Indians went up and brought home the body of the dead Spaniard (Harrington 1986:R102 F328).

José de los Santos Juncos referred to the place as *Xārvut*, or *Qarvut*, and he noted that "Xārvut is [the] name of a canyada where only brujos [sorcerers] entered to make their hechicerias [witchcraft]. It is situated near Mission Vieja" (Harrington 1986:R105 F564). According to Santos Juncos "a white bear is seen at that place—not a real bear but of the water. And there are viboras [vipers], many, at that place. And perritos [little dogs]—they are perritos of the water. That is what the old Gab. Indians used to say"

(Harrington 1986:R102 F329). Santos Juncos was probably referring to the *Chengiichngech* Avengers, supernatural creatures sent by *Chengiichngech* to punish those who did not follow his commandments (Boscana 1933:29).

Another story told by this consultant recounted a war that the shamans of *'AXaarvonga* waged against the Indians living near the coast. Although the coastal Indians used their magic to bring rains that flooded the countryside, the shamans of *'AXaarvonga* had the wind as their ally and it blew their enemies into the sea. Eventually peace was restored after many were killed on both sides (Harrington 1986:R105 F564; see Chapter 9 for a complete discussion of this Gabrielino story).

José de los Santos Juncos also provided detailed information on the location of *'AXaarvonga*. He described it as "a deep gulch back of Petissier's [Pellissier's] place, opening to the west (near Bartolo Station)." He went on to say that "east of qarvut there is a big canyada opening through the hills. Indians used to live there" (Harrington 1986:R102 F829-830, 843).

The United States Geological Survey Map of the El Monte Quadrangle (7.5 minute topographic series, 1966, photorevised 1981) places "Bartolo" at Whittier Junction, where Beverly Boulevard and the San Gabriel River Freeway intersect in the city of Pico Rivera. This is the area known historically as the Paso de Bartolo. The most likely candidate for identification with *'AXaarvonga*, therefore, is Sycamore Canyon, which lies due east of Bartolo, although another possibility might be Turnbull Canyon farther to the south.

In this same vicinity is the place where the shamans of *'AXaarvonga* summoned the wind that defeated their enemies. José de los Santos Juncos reported that this place "is near Punta de la Loma [the Point of the Hill] by old S. G. Mission [Misión Vieja] and Xārvut. The top of the hill there is still bare to this day" (Harrington 1986:R105 F564). José Zalvidea noted that the word *Xárvo* means "stony" (Harrington 1986:R102 F473).

WALNUT

According to Reid, *Pemookanga* was located on "Rancho de los Ybarras" (Reid 1852:8). Harrington, writing in 1918, noted that Rancho de los Ybarras was "a quarter of a mile e. [east] of walnut station. The

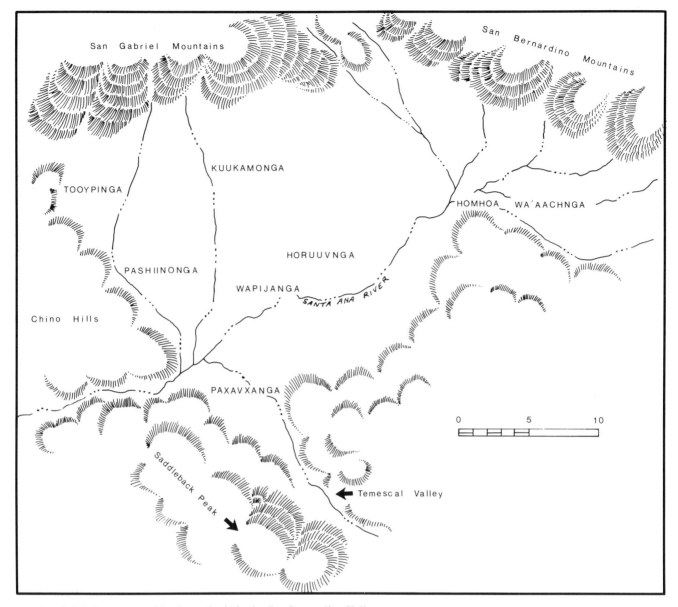

Map 7. Gabrielino communities located within the San Bernardino Valley.

old adobe house is still there and Jesus Ybarra now over 70 yrs. old but Kewen [José de los Santos Juncos] is a few yrs older, still lives there & can tell me much inf. [information.] That is certainly what Reid meant by El Rancho de los Ybarras" (Harrington 1986:R104 F81).

Variant names for *Pemookanga* include *Pimocabit* and *Pomoquin* (Engelhardt 1927a:355-356). Although José Zalvidea did not recognize either name for this community, he reported that "pɨmuka'ŋa would mean 'where he died'," while "pomŏ'okin means 'where they were sleeping according to custom, naked'." Zalvidea went on to say that "all was still dark and the earth was soft. [They] went to [the] sierra when it

was hot." The name "pomŏ'okin refers to sleeping out of doors, not sleeping in the house, sleeping naked" (Harrington 1986:R102 F225, 228-229).

SAN BERNARDINO VALLEY

The northeastern region of the Gabrielino territory is dominated by the broad prairie known as the San Bernardino Valley. The San Bernardino Valley comprises more than 400 square miles of territory surrounded on all sides by mountains and foothills. The valley is bounded in the north by the San Gabriel Mountains and in the northeast by the San Bernardino

Mountains. The Santa Ana Mountains border the valley on the east and south, and the Chino Hills are on the southwest. In the west the San Bernardino Valley is bounded by the Puente Hills and the San José Hills. A narrow pass located north of the San José Hills provides a westward route to the San Gabriel Valley, while Cajón Pass, which runs between the San Gabriel and San Bernardino Mountains, provides a northern route to the Mohave Desert. Elevations in the San Bernardino Valley range from 700 to 2,000 feet above sea level.

SAN BERNARDINO MOUNTAINS

According to Mrs. James Rosemyre, the Gabrielino knew the San Gabriel and San Bernardino valleys as "Yo-wé-hah." Mrs. Rosemyre also gave the name "Kó-kam-o-vit" for the San Bernardino Mountains (Merriam n.d.c; see also Appendix I of the present volume), which was probably derived from the name of the Gabrielino community *Kuukamonga*.

According to José Zalvidea, Mount San Antonio, popularly known as Old Baldy, was known as "joåt [*ywaat*]," meaning "snow." Another consultant, perhaps José de los Santos Juncos, offered the variant name "juit gait [*xaayy ywaat*, or snow mountain]" for the same peak. According to Zalvidea, the "Bear Mountain range [the San Bernardino Mountains]" was known as "Piwïpwi" (Harrington 1986:R102 F200, 454, R104 F34; Munro n.d.). According to Harrington, *Piwïpwi* was San Gorgonio Peak; the name may refer to a Serrano placename, *Puwipui* or *Puwipuwi*, located near San Gorgonio Mountain (Kroeber 1925:Plate 57; Harrington 1933:181).

Eight major Gabrielino communities located within the San Bernardino Valley will be discussed in the following section. Five of these appear to have been located in or near the prairie-foothill transition zone ringing the valley, including *Tooypinga*, *Wapijanga*, *Pashiinonga*, *PaXávXanga*, and *Horu-uvnga*. The remaining three, *Kuukamonga*, *Homhoa*, and *Wa'aachnga* appear to have been located near primary watercourses.

WESTERN END OF THE SAN BERNARDINO VALLEY

The community of *Tooypinga* lay near the base of the San José Hills on land that was once part of Rancho San José (Reid 1852:8; Harrington 1986:R102 F294, R103 F88). According to José Zalvidea, the name *Tooypinga* "is derived from tojtš, the devil

woman who is there at El Rincon, near San José." Harrington added that the "Inf. [informant, i.e., José Zalvidea] knows old San José at Pomona. There was lots of tunas [tuna cactus, *Opuntia* sp.] there at S. Jose. My mother [Zalvidea's mother] said that Yutas [Ute Indians] came down stealing horses & killed those women" who were gathering cactus (Harrington 1986:R102 F294, R103 F88). According to Reid (1852:75) virtually the entire population of *Tooypinga* was taken by force and relocated to Mission San Gabriel during a punitive military expedition.

Manuel Santos reported that the area around modern Pomona was known as "*ïsutkava'a*," although he volunteered no meaning for the name (Harrington 1986:R105 F636).

One of Harrington's consultants, possibly José de los Santos Juncos, offered the placename *Tsikowále*, reporting it to be near Rancho San Antonio, which lay northeast of *Tooypinga* near the base of the San Gabriel Mountains. "San Antonio is a place this side of Cucamonga—it was [the] ranch of Los Palomares. There is a canyon also this side of Cucamonga called Tsikowále—there was [an] adobe house and viña [vineyard] in there. San Antonio . . . is by the point of hill hitherward of Tsikowále. Last is an Ind. name. . . . Azusa is this side of Tsikowále" (Harrington 1986:R104 F111). The most likely identification of *Tsikowále* would be San Antonio Canyon, which lies below Mount San Antonio, popularly known as Mount Baldy.

CHINO

According to Manuel Santos, the Gabrielino community of *Wapijanga* was located on Rancho del Chino. José Zalvidea reported that *Wapijanga* received its name "because there is much guata [juniper] there," while Felicitas Serrano Montaño noted that *Wapijanga* "is now called Guapa, a place this (S. Bern.[the San Bernardino]) side of Chino" and Harrington said that it "is the old name of the place now called Guapa, a place this side of Chino (a railroad station I understand her to say)" (Harrington 1986:R102 F234, 319, 321, 460). The area later became known as Juapa Ranch (Greenwood and Foster 1989:60-70).

Also located on Rancho del Chino was the community of *Pashiinonga*. According to José Zalvidea, *Pashiinonga* was "the Indian name for Rancho del Chino" and was "derived from pǎsí, chia, for there was much chia there. There was much chia there and also at *Cucamonga*" (Harrington 1986:R102 F215). According to Reid, the inhabitants of *Pashiinonga* were forcibly relocated to Mission San Gabriel along with the population of *Tooypinga* (Reid 1852:75).

Another Gabrielino placename associated with Rancho del Chino is *Toowish Puki'*. According to Manuel Santos, *Toowish Puki'* was located below *Kuukamonga* (Harrington 1986:R102 F307). José Zalvidea translated *Toowish Puki'* as "house of the devil" and reported that "the devil there sale por noche [comes out at night], coming from Temescal to R. del Chino [Rancho del Chino]. . . . " He described *Tōwis Puki'i* as "about 2 or 3 miles from Rancho del Chino" on the "other side of [the] river—the point of the mtns. [mountains] where the mtn. range ends. . . . Or maybe only 1/2 mi [mile] from Rancho del Chino." According to Zalvidea the "Ind's [Indians] were afraid of it. [The] Americans did not believe that [the] devil was there . . . [and the] devil came with keys in its hand and the Am's [Americans] got scared [and] they carried [the] devil to the gvt. [government]. And [they] decided to turn him loose again—the men that did not believe in the devil all died" (Harrington 1986:R103 F31). Zalvidea indicated that *Toowish Puki'* was not a Gabrielino name, noting that the Gabrielino would be "Zizu 'akin [*shiishu 'akin*]" (Harrington 1986:R103 F31). In fact, *Toowish Puki'* is Luiseño and means *Toowish*'s house, referring to *Taakwesh*, the cannibal spirit who dwelled on Mount San Jacinto (Munro n.d.).

CORONA, TEMESCAL VALLEY

José Zalvidea reported that *PaXávXanga* was "below pǎmajam," a Gabrielino placename located in the Santa Ana Mountains, and that the name "means pedazo de sierra [piece of the mountain]" (Harrington 1986:R102 F217). Kroeber reported that "Pakhavkha" was "part Gabrielino" and was located on Temescal Creek (Kroeber 1907:144, 1925:Plate 57). Others have suggested that *PaXávXanga* lay further south within Juaneño territory (O'Neil and Evans 1980:229-230, 277).

Jesús Jauro reported the name *Siisovet*, or *Shiishonga*, for the region around Corona; the name is similar to *Shiisho'vet*, a placename which José Zalvidea located near Azusa (see above). According to Jauro "all the rincon donde está el pueblo de

Corona [all the corner where the town of Corona is] = SiiSuŋa" (Harrington 1986:R105 F297).

Jauro told a story in which the devil abducted a small child (variously given as a boy or girl) from its mother. The child was in the house crying and the devil took it and fled to *Shiishonga*. He placed the child's cradle in an alder tree and fed the infant chía seeds mixed with mucus. Mole warned the child of what the devil was doing, however, and the child escaped. When the devil learned what mole had done he was angry. He tried to kick mole, but mole escaped down his hole. Then the devil used a magical tray to divine the direction in which the child had fled. When the devil threw the tray in the right direction it kept rolling until it reached a settlement where a fiesta was in progress. The people attempted to hide the child in one of their homes; nonetheless, the devil discovered the child's whereabouts and kicked it to death in a fit of rage (Harrington 1986:R105 F296-297).

Two miles east of Corona was *Poruumanga*, which Jesús Jauro described as "a stone east of Corona . . . 2 miles from Corona, a rock, not on a hill, [but] on a plain, on [the] e. [east] side of [a] rd. [road] that goes from Corona to Riverside. It is a rock that stands up" and was mentioned in Indian songs (Harrington 1986:R105 F297).

RIVERSIDE

Jesús Jauro reported to Harrington that the Gabrielino community of *Horuuvnga* was located at Jurupa, referring to the Mexican land grant of that name near Riverside. José Zalvidea offered that "hurǔpa [*Jurupa*] is the sharp white hill seen to the west of Riverside," a hill that looked "as if cement . . . was being dug out of the hill. . . ." He further noted that the name *Jurupa* "is applied to all the hills we see on the other side of the San Bernardino Valley from here (Highland)" (Harrington 1986:R102 F452).

The relationship between the names *Jurupa* and *Horuuvnga* is unclear. Kroeber (1925:895) noted that *Jurupa* is a Serrano placename, the Serrano having succeeded the Gabrielino in much of the San Bernardino Valley during the early decades of the 1800s. Perhaps the Serrano name *Jurupa* is based on an earlier Gabrielino name. A number of meanings have been suggested for *Huruuvnga*. According to Jesús Jauro, *Horuuvnga* was derived from *hurúuvar*, or "romerillo [coastal sagebrush or *Artemisia californica*]" (Harrington 1986:R105 F307). José

Zalvidea, however, stated that "Jurupa means . . . se bajan [they descend it]." Zalvidea also reported that "there used to be a great rattlesnake at Jurupa in a cave. It was a rattlesnake of long ago" (Harrington 1986:R102 F452).

According to José Zalvidea, the name *Shokaava* was given to a "long range of hills at *Jurupa*—west of Riverside." Harrington added that this referred to "the long range seen from Highland as beginning near the small white hill and running far out toward the west." The range referred to is probably the Jurupa Mountains north of Rubidoux. Zalvidea went on to report that "a stone stands erect on top of this long range of hills and it is because of that stone that the hills are named *sokǎva*. That stone used to be a person" (Harrington 1986:R102 F456).

It is unclear from Harrington's notes whether *Jurupa* and *Shokaava* are separate geographical features or simply two different names for the Jurupa Mountains; both names seem to describe a range of hills west of Riverside. A sketch map prepared by Harrington offers yet another possibility. In this sketch, Harrington identifies a hill south of Mount Rubidoux and southwest of Riverside as *Shokaava*, and notes that "Victor [perhaps Victor Meza, a Luiseño consultant] says they are cutting this hill for cement or smthng [something]" (Harrington 1986:R103 F206). A comparison of Harrington's sketch map to the Riverside West USGS 7.5 minute series topographic map (1967) suggests two possible identifications for this feature: Pachappa Hill, which lies approximately one mile south of Mount Rubidoux; and Quarry Hill, which lies approximately four miles south of Mount Rubidoux.

Nearby was "juŋǎ'ᵃv," which José Zalvidea described as "the point of the hill on the side of the San Bernardino Valley opposite Highland which runs out from the Santa Ana Mountains toward the white cement hill." Zalvidea told Harrington that "there was a still bigger rattlesnake that had horns, still bigger than the one at Jurupa, at juŋǎ'ᵃv. . . . juŋǎ'ᵃv is the hill where the horned rattle snake lived." Zalvidea translated Juŋǎ'ᵃv to mean "las auras [vultures or buzzards]" (Harrington 1986:R102 F451).

CUCAMONGA

The name of the Gabrielino community of *Kuukamonga* survives in the modern city name Cucamonga. Manuel Santos reported to Harrington

that the name *Kuukamonga* meant "I shuffle my feet on the ground" (Harrington 1986:R102 F166). Although José Zalvidea offered no meaning for the name *Kuukamonga*, he recalled that "at the high sycamore trees of Cucamonga, two miles this side of Cucamonga . . . a woman once died of thirst" (Harrington 1986:R102 F164).

Manuel Santos reported that "'ǎ‿kavjat = San José (below Cucamonga) [Rancho San José]" and "San Jose is below Cucamonga. This side of Azusa. Call San Jose Indian 'ǎ‿kaviat (3 syllables). [The] name means bare white land, as river bed, means like [an] arena in sp. [Spanish]" (Harrington 1986:R102 F109, R105 F636).

COLTON

According to data collected by George Shinn, a San Bernardino Valley resident who studied the Serrano, Cahuilla, and other Indians during the late 1880s, the community of *Homhoa* was "on or near" the "farm of John Shirley Ward . . . who was the Indian agent." Shinn also noted that the community was near a mission rancho "southeast of Colton between the southerly bank of the Santa Ana river and the base of the foothills" (Shinn 1941:26, 78). The derivation of this placename is cloudy. Kroeber described "Homoa" as a "Serrano place name" (Kroeber 1925:895), although it could be based on an earlier Gabrielino name.

REDLANDS

Two other placenames reported for the Redlands region are *Kaawchama* and *Wa'aachnga*, although these may simply be variant names for the same community. The earliest San Bernardino Asistencia was built in 1820 at "Old San Bernardino," or "Old San Bernardino Mission," west of Redlands (Shinn 1941:76). The Indians who settled here gave the name *Kaawchama* to this site. The Asistencia was abandoned at the end of 1834 following the secularization of the mission properties and a series of Indian attacks that damaged the buildings and left several Indians dead (Shinn 1941:71, 91).

A second placename reported for the San Bernardino region is *Wa'aachnga*, which José Zalvidea noted was "San Bernardino," although Jesús Jauro ascribed the name to "San Bernardino Viejo," apparently referring to the site west of Redlands (Harrington 1986:R102 F390, 458, R103 F26, R105

F297, 301). José Zalvidea noted that "there used to be much wǎ'at (guata [juniper]) here in this valley, hence the name." Similarly, Jesús Jauro thought "it mentions guata, for there was lots of guata [juniper] there" (Harrington 1986:R102 F458, R105 F301). José Zalvidea also remembered that "there is an animal which comes out when the sun rises. . . . The animal lives at the cienega of wa'átšvit (San Bernardino). The Indians brought this animal with them when they first came from where the earth is soft" (Harrington 1986:R102 F457).

The information presented by both consultants supports the theory that *Kaawchama* and *Wa'aachnga* are one and the same place, and that *Kaawchama* (or *Guachama* as it is sometimes spelled) is simply the Spanish rendering of the Gabrielino name (see Shinn 1941:80).

Several other Gabrielino placenames occur in the Redlands area. According to José Zalvidea, *Tahoovanga* was "a place on the mountain back of Redlands. . . . It is so called because of a person who turned to rock there" (Harrington 1986:R102 F456). Zalvidea also reported another placename, *Shaxaanga*, "nine or ten miles from Highland, up the Santa Ana River on this (the west) side of the pass. It means willow" (Harrington 1986:R102 F455). In his annotations to *Chinigchinich*, Harrington noted that "there is a place by this name 3 miles southeast of Colton, across the Santa Ana River from Colton, and another near Rincon" (Harrington 1933:203). Jesús Jauro noted that "allá habia una ranchería grande de los indios [over there it was a large village of Indians]" at *Shaxaanga* (Harrington 1986:R103 F477).

ARROWHEAD HOT SPRINGS, BIG BEAR LAKE

Beyond the eastern border of the Gabrielino territory and high in the *Piwipwi* (San Bernardino) Mountains was Arrowhead Hot Springs, for which Jesús Jauro gave the placename *'Apuuymonga* (Harrington 1986:R103 F480). According to José Zalvidea "'apǔjmuŋa means 'bien estaban, estaban llenos [they were well, they were full]'" (Harrington 1986:R102 F445).

Zalvidea also reported that Big Bear Lake was "the lake where wijȯt [a supernatural being who was also the "first captain," or chief in Gabrielino legend] died. . . . There is no name for the lake except for an expression in Indian which means where wijȯt died. The Indians used to sing and cry there, and throw beads into the water" (Harrington 1986:R102 F447). Zalvidea also stated "'atȯ'avijat, big—said of Bear Lake. All the pines on top of the mountains here used to be people and turned into pines when wijot died. They all cried and crying turned into pines. . . . Bear Lake, cries like a person. It is the lake that cries. Wijȯt died in the water there. He was drinking water and fell in and died there" (Harrington 1986:R102 F446).

José de los Santos Juncos told Harrington that "On top of the mts. [mountains] of S. Bernardino they say there is a lake and there a bear like those of the sea (later he called it a whale) and also deers come out of the water, but if you see them they immerse again. . . . Once a man at Lake in S. Bern. mts. shot at the whale in the lake & [the] result was that a great storm rose suddenly, carrying away a sawmill & swollen creeks" (Harrington 1986:R104 F39).

Finally, Harrington was given the following information by a consultant named Antonio.

In Bear Lake [there] is charcoal, down in the water; and there are also red ants down in the water, in religion, tho now only ordinary ants are seen, outside the water, on the shore, these ants . . . are Woyoot's blood. And there are also abalorios [shell beads] in the lake. And the pines stand there—they were the tall mourners who tried to keep coy. from the pyre [coy. = Coyote, a reference to an incident in Gabrielino legend in which Coyote steals Wiyot's heart] (Harrington 1986:R103 F337).

SAN JACINTO MOUNTAINS

José Zalvidea offered that *Jamiwo* was "the mountain range of Saboba (southeast of Highland). This mountain is the younger brother of small hiḟȧkupa and piwȋpwi." He went on to state that "at jamȋwo mountain there is a great rock where tȧkwiš lives. [T]ȧkwiš makes a noise like thunder and goes out only at night" (Harrington 1986:R102 F450; See Chapter 8 for a more detailed discussion of the cannibal-spirit *Taakwesh*).

Harrington identified *Jamiwo* as Mount San Jacinto, the name perhaps being derived from *Yamiwu*, the name of a Serrano or Cahuilla clan located north of San Jacinto Peak. Harrington also associated the name *Piwȋpwi* with San Gorgonio Peak (Kroeber 1925:Plate 57; Harrington 1933:181).

SANTA ANA MOUNTAINS

South of the San Bernardino Valley lies a stretch of rugged terrain dominated by the Santa Ana Mountains. This mountainous region extends well into the territory of the Juaneño. Although the Gabrielino territory may have extended as far south as Aliso Creek, ethnographic data suggest that both the Juaneño and Gabrielino claimed usage rights in the Santa Ana Mountains (see O'Neil 1988:111-112). Following the general outline presented earlier in this chapter, primary settlements in this region are believed to have been located in lower canyons that offered protection against cold weather while providing access to several ecological zones.

The Gabrielino may have known Santiago Peak by the name *Xuungova*; Santiago Peak and Modjeska Peak together form the mountain popularly known as Saddleback. According to José Zalvidea "Xuŋŭva is the peak in the second range from here looking straight across San Bernardino Valley from the Highland Reservation. The name means cemetery. It is the snowy peak . . . in the Santa Ana Mountains" (Harrington 1986:R102 F460). Mrs. James Rosemyre, another Gabrielino consultant, gave the name of Saddleback as *Haŕ-wo-vē't* and noted that this was the name for a "peak south of San Gabriel (Santa Ana?)" (Merriam n.d.c; see also Appendix I of the present volume). The derivation of this placename is unclear. Merriam recorded the Gabrielino word for cemetery as *Koo-nas-gnă* (Merriam n.d.c) while Harrington offered *kwiλ'asvit* (Harrington 1986:R102 F460).

A number of important archaeological sites have been discovered in the Santa Ana Mountains. Orange County historian T. E. Stephenson noted that "all along the Limestone [Canyon] are evidences of early Indian occupation. Near its mouth are many acres of blackened earth where ancient campfires burned" (Stephenson 1931:94). Limestone Canyon is located on the western slopes of the Santa Ana Mountains near Santiago Reservoir, also known as Irvine Lake. Archaeological sites in this region were excavated in 1935 and 1937 under the supervision of J. W. Winterbourne. The reports of these excavations were published in 1969 by the Pacific Coast Archaeological Society (Hudson 1969).

Another important archaeological site was located northeast of the Limestone Canyon sites in the upper reaches of Black Star Canyon. Once again Stephenson provides a picturesque description of the site.

> Just at the edge of the grove of oaks we found the first unmistakable sign of early Indian habitation. It was a boulder six or eight feet long with five deep grinder holes worked into it. . . . Before us was a small hill, covered over with stunted and broken oaks. Beneath the trees were piles of boulders. . . . Worked into these boulders were dozens and scores of deep grinder holes. . . .
>
> In an open space, partly surrounded by trees and sandstone boulders ancient campfires burned. . . . The soil is here black as peat, greasy from the refuse of the camp, with bits of charcoal in it (Stephenson 1931:108-109).

The Gabrielino placename *Paamayam* refers to a place in the eastern regions of the Santa Ana Mountains, perhaps near Saddleback Mountain (O'Neil 1988:115). José Zalvidea merely noted that "PaXȧvᵃXa [*PaXávXanga*, a Gabrielino-Juaneño community located in Temescal Valley] was below påmajam" (Harrington 1986:R102 F217). According to Harrington's Juaneño consultant Anastacia de Majel, "páama'yam" means "white-headed eagle" (Harrington 1986:R127 F407).

South of Saddleback Mountain lies Bell Canyon which, according to T. E. Stephenson, received its name from Bell Rock. Bell Rock was located near the top of a mound or hillock 30 feet high, and comprised a boulder shaped "like the palm of one's hand, being some seven feet long by three and a half feet across" resting upon several other boulders; at no point did it touch the ground. "When struck by a stone, this rock sent a clear bell-like sound up and down the canyon. Old Spanish-speaking people of San Juan Capistrano who used to camp near the rock say that on a quiet day the sound of the bell could be heard for a mile" (Stephenson 1931:137-138). According to José de los Santos Juncos, the Indians knew Bell Rock as "Taráɡiŋa. . . . Gold was found there & further on. The Ind. [Indians] said because of the bell rock there must be alguna cosa [something] there & gold was discovered" (Harrington 1986:R104 F24). As if to corroborate the information provided by Santos Juncos, Stephenson, writing sometime before 1931, reported that "treasure hunters had partially destroyed the tone of the bell rock" (Stephenson 1931:137).

SUMMARY

The northern region of the Gabrielino territory can be divided into three broad inland prairies known as the San Fernando, San Gabriel, and San Bernardino valleys. Together these valleys constitute one-half of the Gabrielino territory.

The San Fernando Valley is bordered on the north and west by the San Gabriel and Santa Susana mountains, on the south by the Santa Monica Mountains and Cahuenga Peak, and on the east by the Verdugo Mountains. The valley comprises 160 square miles of prairie with elevations ranging from 500 to 1,000 feet above sea level. Major Gabrielino communities which appear to have been located in the prairie-foothill transition zone included: *'Atavsanga, Siutcanga, Pasheeknga, 'Achooykomenga, Pakooynga, Tohuunga, Muuhonga, Wiqanga, Kaweenga,* and *Haahamonga.* An important ritual site complex was located at Burro Flats in the Simi Hills west of Chatsworth.

The San Gabriel Valley is bordered on the north by the San Gabriel Mountains, on the east by the San José Hills, on the west by the San Rafael Hills and Cahuenga Peak, and on the south by the Puente Hills. The valley comprises 200 square miles of prairie with elevations ranging from 300 to 1,000 feet above sea level. Major Gabrielino communities that were located near watercourses associated with the Río Hondo river included: *Shevaanga, Sonaanga, Sheshiikwanonga, 'Akuuronga,* and *'Aluupkenga.* Significant communities that were located in the prairie-foothill transition zone included *'Ashuukshanga, Weniinga, 'Ahwiinga,* and *Pemookanga.* In addition, a ritual site known as *'AXaarvonga* was located near Sycamore Canyon in the Puente Hills.

The San Bernardino Valley comprises 400 square miles of prairie ranging from 700 to 2,000 feet above sea level. The valley is bordered on the north by the San Bernardino and San Gabriel mountains, on the east and south by the Santa Ana Mountains, on the southwest by the Chino Hills, and on the west by the Puente and San José hills. Major Gabrielino communities that appear to have been located in the prairie-foothill transition zone were *Tooypinga, Wapijanga, Pashiinonga, PaXávXanga,* and *Horuuvnga.* Important Gabrielino communities located near primary watercourses were *Kuukamonga, Wa'aachnga,* and *Homhoa.*

A number of important archaeological sites have been identified in the Santa Ana Mountains in Limestone and Black Star canyons. The twin-peaked mountain popularly called Saddleback was known the Gabrielino as *Xuungova;* somewhere nearby was the place the Gabrielino referred to as *Paamayam.*

East of the Santa Ana Mountains lay the foothills and coastal plains held by the Juaneño, while to the northeast were the mountain and desert territories occupied by the Cahuilla and Serrano. Toward the west, however, the valleys and foothills of the Santa Anas gradually merged into a broad, brush-covered prairie dotted with marshes and cut by the winding courses of rivers and streams. This rich coastal land was Gabrielino territory. Here, along the coast and on the hills and bluffs that rise above the floodplain, some of the most important Gabrielino communities flourished. Their story is taken up in the next chapter.

CHAPTER 4

THE PEOPLE OF THE COASTAL PLAIN

The Los Angeles—Santa Ana Plain is a broad, level expanse of prairie comprising more than 800 square miles that extends from Cahuenga Peak south to the coast, and from Topanga Canyon southeast to the vicinity of Aliso Creek. During Gabrielino times the plain was characterized by extensive inland prairies and a lengthy coastal strand, with elevations for the most part 500 feet above sea level or less. The plain is traversed by a number of important watercourses, including the Los Angeles, Río Hondo, San Gabriel, and Santa Ana rivers. Marshlands fed by fresh or salt water also once covered many portions of the countryside. The coastal communities developed mainly along the sheltered bays and inlets of San Pedro and Newport.

INLAND COMMUNITIES

The inland Gabrielino communities of the Los Angeles—Santa Ana Plain were distributed in a broad arc stretching from Cahuenga Peak southeast to the foothills of the Santa Ana Mountains. A short distance east of Cahuenga Peak the plain merges with the southern reaches of the San Gabriel Valley; for approximately 12 miles there are few natural barriers separating these two great plains. Further east, the Puente Hills and the Santa Ana Mountains form a northern boundary to the Los Angeles—Santa Ana Plain.

The inland Gabrielino communities discussed in the following section include: *Maawnga, Yaanga, Geveronga, 'Ochuunga, Chokiishnga, Huutnga* and *Naxaaw'nga-Sejat, Tevaaxa'anga, Hotuuknga, Pasbenga.* Each of these communities appears to have been situated near a major river system, but in some cases they also fell near the foothill-transition zone.

LOS ANGELES

According to Reid the Gabrielino community of *Maawnga* was located on "Rancho de los Felis" (Reid 1852:8). Rancho de los Feliz was one and one-half leagues in size (about ten square miles); it included within its boundaries Griffith Park (Hanna 1946:104; a Spanish league was approximately 2.63 miles, see Webb 1952:9, note 7). Harrington's consultant José Zalvidea concurred with this location and reported that the name means "despacio [slow or deliberate]" (Harrington 1986:R102 F185). José de los Santos Juncos located "Reid's 'Rancho de los Féliz' by the Jewish cemetery of Los Angeles" (Harrington 1986:R102 F185). Sétimo López reported that "máwŋa = los Corralitos [little corrals]"

> and mas abajo (de los Corralitos) estaba el "Rancho de los Féliz." . . . Los Corralitos is en frente de la Loma grande [Further down from los Corralitos was the "Rancho de los Féliz." . . . Los Corralitos is in front of the large hill] and towards the river and the Rancho de los Féliz queda mas abajo [is further down] (Harrington 1986:R106 F059).

South of *Maawnga* lay a fertile, well-watered region that was described in 1769 by Father Juan Crespí, a member of Gaspar de Portolá's expedition. In his entry for August 3, Father Juan noted that "after crossing the river we entered a large vineyard of wild grapes and an infinity of [wild] rosebushes in full bloom. All the soil is black and loamy, and is capable of producing every kind of grain and fruit which may be planted" (Bolton 1927:148). Continuing westward that same day the explorers crossed "good land well covered with grass" and discovered a "village . . . the people of which, on seeing us, came out into the road. As they drew near us they began to howl like wolves;

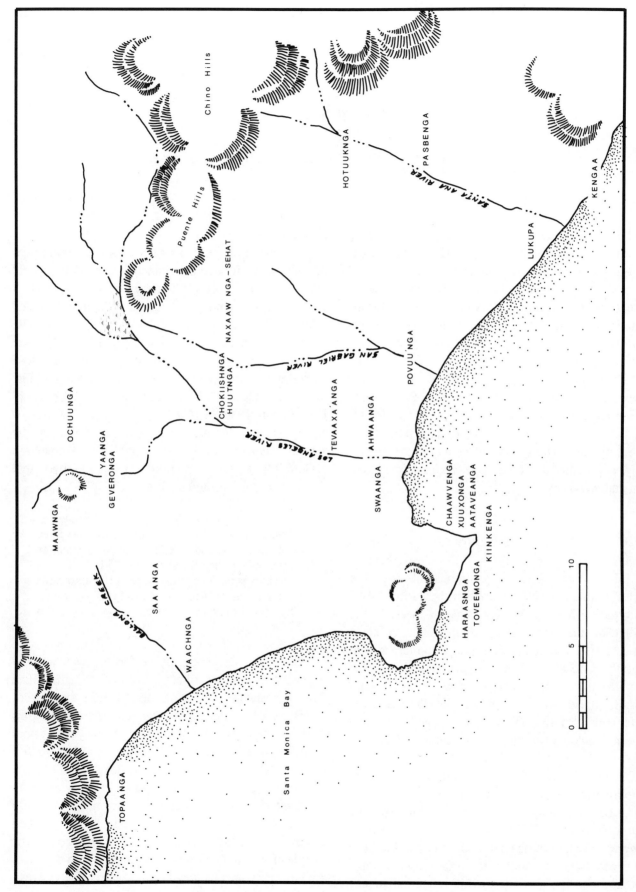

Map 8. Gabrielino communities located on the Los Angeles-Santa Ana Plain. The modern river courses are depicted; however, prior to 1867 the San Gabriel River lay farther west and emptied into San Pedro Bay.

they greeted us and wished to give us seeds, but as we had nothing at hand in which to carry them we did not accept them. Seeing this, they threw some handfuls of them on the ground and the rest in the air" (Bolton 1927:148).

The explorers then traveled across a plain until they came to the "Spring of Alders," which was "a grove of very large alders, high and thick, from which flows a stream of water. . . . The banks were grassy and covered with fragrant herbs and watercress. The water flowed afterwards in a deep channel toward the southwest" (Bolton 1927:148). Here the party camped. Throughout the day the explorers were astonished by a continuing series of earthquakes, causing them to conclude "that in the mountains that run to the west in front of us there are some volcanoes . . . for the explorers saw some large marshes of . . . pitch; they were boiling and bubbling, and the pitch came out mixed with an abundance of water. . . . The water runs to one side and the pitch to the other" (Bolton 1927:148-149). The intrepid explorers had discovered the great asphalt beds at La Brea.

The Gabrielino community of *Yaanga*, located near the present Civic Center, is popularly regarded as the Indian precursor of modern Los Angeles. According to José Zalvidea, "jǎ̱ŋa [was] the Pueblo of Los Angeles, and [an] Angeleño is called jǎ̱vit. . . . This is the old name of the site of Los Angeles plaza," and "it means . . . it is alkali, like the earth is salty" (Harrington 1986:R102 F146-147). Reid (1852:7) noted simply that "Yang-na" was "Los Angeles."

A curious variety of names is associated with *Yaanga*. Kroeber reported that "an old Luiseño informant on the San Luis Rey River," perhaps Félix Calac, gave the Indian name of Los Angeles as *Iyakha*, noting that in Luiseño *iyala* means "poison oak." Kroeber suggested that *Iyakha* might simply be the Luiseño equivalent of *Yaanga* (Kroeber 1907:70, 143-144). Kroeber also offered *Wenot* as yet another name for Los Angeles (Kroeber 1925:621, Plate 57). The word *wenoot* or *weenot* means "river" in Gabrielino, although Gatschet gives river as *otcho'o*, (Gatschet 1879:441; Munro n.d.).

The exact site of *Yaanga* is uncertain. The original community was abandoned sometime prior to 1836 (Robinson 1952:16) and was succeeded by a series of later rancherías inhabited by Gabrielino and other Indian refugees (see Chapter 10).

The community of *Geveronga* may also may been located in this region. The San Garbriel baptismal registers list the community of "Geberovit" or "Geverobit" as "en la ranchería inmediata al Pueblo Los Angeles [in the ranchería adjoining the Pueblo of Los Angeles]." Mission San Gabriel recruited 31 converts from this community between 1788 and 1809 (Merriam 1968:107).

Kroeber located the placename *Apachia* east of Los Angeles (Kroeber 1925:Plate 57). Unfortunately, at the present time there is no further data available on this placename. The spelling of this name does not seem to correspond with any of the communities listed in the San Gabriel Mission registers as compiled by Merriam (1968), and it may have been a geographical feature rather than a settlement.

According to José Zalvidea, the community of *'Ochuunga* was "on the road from San Gabriel to Los Angeles, about three miles from San Gabriel." Felicitas Serrano Montaño reported to Harrington that "Basques used to live there. There were many wild roses. There is a big matanza (slaughter house) there now at the site of 'otsuvit ['Ochuunga], about half way between Los Angeles and San Gabriel. [A] railroad and wagon road pass by ['Ochuunga]" (Harrington 1986:R102 F316). She went on to say that the name *'Ochuunga* is derived from *'ochuur*, meaning "wild rose," and the Spanish placename for this location was "Rosa de Castilla" because "there were many wild roses there" (Harrington 1986:R102 F316).

WATTS

Between Watts and Lynwood was the 4,438 acre Rancho Tajauta granted to Anastasio Avila in 1843 (Cowan 1956:101; Beck and Haase 1974:Map 37). Kroeber suggested that *Tajáuta* was probably based on a Gabrielino placename (Kroeber 1925:897). In his 1918 fieldnotes Harrington reported that he

> interviewed Mr. Lugo of [the] S. [San] Gabriel poolroom. He says that the ranch at Watts was of the Lugos and was known as El Rancho Nuevo. The old adobe house was a quarter of a block west of the spring site. [There] used to be tules at the spring. He volunteered that the old name of the place was *Tajáuta*. . . . [Lugo] and told Kewen [José de los Santos Juncos] that it was an Ind. [Indian] name (Harrington 1986:R104 F80).

The name survives in the present Tajauta Avenue in the City of Compton. The name *Tajáuta* may be a

Spanish corruption of *Huutnga*, a community that Reid placed on the "Ranchito de Lugo" (see the following section).

BELL, LOS NIETOS

Reid located the Gabrielino community of *Chokiishnga* at the Jabonería, or "soap factory" (Reid 1852:8). Harrington's consultant José de los Santos Juncos reported that "La Jaboneria [the soap factory] is on L.A. ward bank [west bank] of [the] S. Gabriel River. Sierra Madre w [west] of where train crosses river. Old adobe ruins [are] there." Harrington noted that this factory was established by an American, Lemuel Carpenter, probably in 1833, "on the west side of Rio Hondo just a little south of Telegraph Road." Writing sometime before 1933, Harrington stated that "the old adobe house that is still standing there is west from the soap factory site" (Harrington 1933:206, 1986:R104 F35). La Jabonería was reportedly located at the lower crossing of the San Gabriel River, on the road between Los Angeles and San Diego (*Los Angeles Star*, May 24, 1851, cited in Black 1975:251; Bancroft 1886:390). Another early historical account, written in 1876, noted that the factory was "not far from the present road to Los Nietos" (Warner et al. 1876:35).

The location of *Chokiishnga* is clouded somewhat by the fact that La Jabonería refers not only to the soap factory, but also to a 2,400-acre rancho owned by Vicenta Lugo, daughter of Antonio María Lugo (*Los Angeles Star*, December 12, 1859, cited in Black 1975:251). Sometime prior to 1843, Carpenter had abandoned the original soap factory site and relocated his operations to Rancho Los Nietos (Harrington 1933:206; Black 1975:250-251). Reid's mention of La Jabonería probably refers to the later rancho, which presumably included the site of the original soap factory.

The community of *Huutnga* was also located in this vicinity. Reid (1852:8) placed *Huutnga* on the "Ranchito de Lugo"; José de los Santos Juncos reported that "Ranchito de Lugo is to [the] right of . . . [La Jaboneria] by [the] tile factories" (Harrington 1986:R104 F35). Another Harrington consultant, Felicitas Serrano Montaño, reported "xáwtŋa, Ranchito de Lugo. [It] was at the Jaboneria" (Harrington 1986:R126 F251). According to José Zalvidea the name *Huutnga* means "en los sauces [in the willows]" (Harrington 1968:R102 F128).

Another early placename in this region is *Curunga*. An historical account of Los Angeles prepared in 1876 by several early residents notes that "Pico Crossing," the site of an 1847 battle between the Californian forces under General Flores and the Americans under General Kearny, was "by the Californians always named CURUNGA" (Warner et al. 1876:43). The *nga* ending suggests that *Curunga* may be based on an earlier Gabrielino placename; however, at the present time no additional information is available for this name.

Naxaaw'nga and *Sehat* were two Gabrielino communities located near the modern community of Los Nietos. Reid placed "Nacaug-na" on "Carpenter's Farm," a reference to Lemuel Carpenter, mentioned above in the discussion of *Chokiishnga* (Reid 1852:8). Harrington concluded that "the Carpenter place was the old Nieto . . . headquarters," referring to the adobe home of José Manuel Nieto—Nieto held one of the earliest California land grants, an enormous tract of land known as Los Nietos, which he received in 1784. Lemuel Carpenter apparently purchased the adobe and 24,000 acres of property from the widow of one of the Nieto heirs around 1843. The adobe home was later washed away when the San Gabriel River flooded in 1867 (Harrington 1933:203-207).

José de los Santos Juncos, whom Harrington often referred to by the nickname of "Kewen," confirmed the identification of *Naxaaw'ŋa* with the Nieto-Carpenter adobe. "Kewen knew the name of the Carpenter adobe house site as Nakaw'ŋa and volunteered the location of the site as being somewhere in the bed of New River [the San Gabriel River] a little upstream of the Downey (= the Sanford) adobe house. In this information he agreed with Reid" (Harrington 1933:207).

Naxaaw'nga, then, was lost long ago to a rampaging flood on the San Gabriel River. But what of *Sehat*? Father Gerónimo Boscana noted that "it may not be uninteresting to know the beliefs prevailing among the Indians about the origin of those who first settled in the neighborhood of San Juan Capistrano. . . . The first, or earliest people . . . emigrated from a place called Sejat . . . in the middle of a valley now known by the name of 'el Rancho de los Nietos'" (Boscana 1933:83). Kroeber also placed "Sekhat" at Los Nietos, on the basis of information obtained from a Luiseño consultant; Kroeber suggested that the name was derived from *sakhat*, the Luiseño word for willow

(Kroeber 1907:144; also Kroeber 1925:Plate 57).

Harrington, on the other hand, believed that the placename *Sejat* was derived from *shokaa*, the name for the Acute-tongued Borrowing Bee, *Andrena rugarea*. On the basis of his research, Harrington suggested that "although the site of the Carpenter adobe house was called Nakaw'ŋa, the site is the same as that of the José Manuel Nieto headquarters, and it may have been some place nearby that was called Sʋká'. . . . There was a bank there, and the Acute-tongued Burrowing Bee frequently makes its home in [earthen] banks" (Harrington 1933:208). Harrington reported a number of possible sites for *Naxaaw'nga-Sehat*, all lying between Los Nietos and the present course of the San Gabriel River. Foremost is the former site of the Nietos adobe, now lost somewhere in the San Gabriel River channel. Also worthy of note is the site once known as "La Rancheria," described by Mr. Juan Ramírez, a local landowner, as "the best known Indian village site in the whole region. It is a little knoll of rich black sandy soil on the east bank of New River [the San Gabriel River] only a little downstream of the Pico house. . . . It is on the present Holbrook ranch. . . . The ground there is said to be full of Indian relics of many kinds" (Harrington 1933:209).

LONG BEACH

Reid placed the Gabrielino town of *Tevaaxa'anga* on "Serritos," or Rancho Los Cerritos, the headquarters of which was located in the city of Long Beach near the present course of the Los Angeles River (Reid 1852:8). This agrees with the location provided by Kroeber (1925:Plate 57). One early historical account describes this region as "a forest, interspersed with tracts of marsh," and notes that

> until 1825, it was seldom . . . that the river discharged, even during the rainy season, its waters into the sea. Instead of having a river-way to the sea, the waters spread over the country . . . forming lakes, ponds, and marshes. The river water, if any, that reached the ocean, drained off from the land at so many places, and in such small volumes, that no channel existed until the flood of 1825, which, by cutting a river-way to tide water, drained the marsh land and caused the forests to disappear (Warner et al. 1876:17-18).

Although Zalvidea did not recognize the placename *Tibajabit* (a variant spelling of *Tevaaxa'anga*),

he suggested two possible etymologies for the name. According to Zalvidea, "Kivȧhaŋa" meant "in the old houses" and, "tivȧXavit [i.e. *Tibajabit*] would mean 'de ay de la casa [de alí de la casa—there from the house]'"; however, Harrington expressed reservations about the second etymology, noting that the "man [Zalvidea] does not know" the placename (Harrington 1986:R102, F375-377).

BUENA PARK

Harrington noted two Indian settlements located on a "Map of Part of Los Angeles County" prepared around 1870 by "C. B. Polhemus" and "E. F. Northam." The first settlement, "Indian Camp" was described by Harrington as having been located "3 miles due west of Coyote Ranchhouse," and the second, "Old Indian Camp," was "a little south of 'Indian Camp' . . . in sect. 33, township 3 south, range 11 west" (Harrington 1986:R106 F174; Polhemus and Northam n.d.). These locations place the settlements along the present course of Coyote Creek northwest of the modern community of Buena Park.

BREA CANYON

Brea Canyon is situated near the edge of the Los Angeles—Santa Ana Plain along the western slopes of the Chino Hills. Traveling through this region with Portolá in 1769, Father Juan Crespí reported that on July 29 the party encountered "a small pool of water, on whose bank there is a very large village of very friendly" Indians. The population of this community "numbered more than seventy souls"; they were "having a feast and dance, to which they had invited their neighbors of the river called Jesús de los Temblores [the Santa Ana River]" (Bolton 1927:142-143). Father Crespí did not record the name of this community.

ANAHEIM

In 1852, Reid reported that the community of *Hotuuknga* was located on "Santa Ana [Yorbes]," referring to the 79,000-acre Mexican land grant of Rancho Santiago de Santa Ana owned by the Yorba family (Reid 1852:8, brackets in original; Beck and Haase 1974:Map 37). This identification was confirmed by Kroeber (1907:144, 1925:Plate 57). An entry in the San Gabriel mission registers states "Jutucunga en el rio Santa Ana [on the Santa Ana River]" (Merriam 1968:112).

Writing sometime before 1933, Harrington reported *Hotuuknga* as the "site of the former Bernardo Yorba adobe house, on the north bank of Wanawna, the Santa Ana River, a little downstream of Santa Ana Caynon [sic], 1/4 mile upstream of the Yorba church, across the river from Peralta. The old adobe house was visited by me [Harrington] with Acú [a Juaneño consultant, José de la Gracia Cruz]. . . . It was torn down about 1926. . . . The Yorba church is on the south side of the main north-bank road, between [the] road and [the] Santa Fe railway. The Yorba house site is on the north side of this road" (Harrington 1933:114).

When the Portolá Expedition forded the Santa Ana River on July 28, 1769, Father Crespí described it as "a river which has a bed of running water about ten varas wide [about 27 feet wide; a Spanish vara was about 33 inches. See Webb 1952:63, note 5] and half a vara [about 16 inches] deep. . . . Its course is from northeast to southwest. The bed of the river is overgrown with sycamores, alders, willows, and other trees. . . ." On the right bank of the river there was

> a populous village of Indians, who received us with great friendliness. Fifty-two of them came to the camp, and their chief told us by signs which we understood very well that we must come to live with them; that they would make houses for us, and provide us with food, such as antelope, hares, and seeds. They urged us to do this, telling us that all the land we saw, and there was certainly a great deal of it, was theirs, and that they would divide it with us (Bolton 1927:141).

These Indians were seen by Father Crespí again the following day at the fiesta near Brea Canyon. Although Father Crespí did not report a name for this community, it appears to have been situated near the location of *Hotuuknga*.

José Zalvidea reported to Harrington that *Hotuuknga* ". . . means night, for at the beginning of the world, they went no more in the night" (Harrington 1986:R102 F129).

SANTA ANA

A number of additional Gabrielino placenames have been reported for the Santa Ana region. According to Harrington the Santa Ana River was known as *Wanaawna*, while Red Hill, "El Cerrito Colorado near Irvine," was "Katuktu" (Harrington 1933:114, 185). The name *Katuktu* may be Luiseño,

for it duplicates their name for Morro Hill located near Oceanside. According to the oral literature of the Luiseño, the ocean once rose and overflowed the countryside, and only those Indians camped atop *Katuktu* were saved from the flood (DuBois 1908:157).

A map prepared in 1864 by Alexander Taylor placed the settlement of "*Pasbengna*" along the Santa Ana River in the vicinity of the city of Santa Ana (Heizer 1941b). This is confirmed by a comment in the San Gabriel baptismal register which noted "Pajbenga cerca del Rio de Sta. Ana [*Pasbenga* near the Santa Ana River]." Thirteen baptisms from this settlement were recorded at the mission between 1776 and 1807 (Merriam 1968:114).

Manuel Santos reported that the name of Santa Ana was "hǎnpjat," meaning "that black manteca de sierra (evidently mineral oil, he does not know the Spanish word brea)." The name was derived from "hǎnat, brea [tar or pitch]" and was given to the place because there "used to be mineral oil there" (Harrington 1986:R102 F124, 239).

José Zalvidea reported the placename "'AXawkηa" as a location "near Santa Ana." According to Zalvidea the name means "en la rede," or "in the net," and was derived from *'aXáwk*, meaning "la reda [the net]" (Harrington 1986:R102 F81).

COASTAL COMMUNITIES

The coastal region of the Gabrielino territory begins midway between Malibu and Topanga canyons and stretches southwestward 75 miles, ending near Aliso Creek. The coastal region, which has been defined as a narrow strip extending five miles or so inland from the ocean (Hudson 1969:10), encompasses 375 square miles of varied terrain. West of Topanga Canyon the terrain is rugged; the steep, ocean-ward slopes of the Santa Monica Mountains reach 1,000 feet or more in elevation, except where stream-cut ravines and canyons open onto narrow beaches at the water's edge. From Topanga Canyon southward to the Palos Verdes Peninsula, a distance of 22 miles or so, the coast is flat and level; extensive marshlands once existed near the mouth of Ballona Creek in the area now known as Playa del Rey.

The terrain becomes rugged once again as the coast follows the Palos Verdes Peninsula for a distance of approximately 12 miles before reaching San Pedro

Bay, which in Gabrielino times was typified by extensive mud flats and sand bars. From Long Beach southward to Newport Bay, a distance of 24 miles, the coastline is flat and level; this region once consisted of beaches interspersed with fresh and saltwater marshes. The San Joaquin Hills reach the coast at Newport Bay, and for the remaining 12 miles of Gabrielino coastline the terrain is steep, although elevations are generally less than 1,000 feet.

The major Gabrielino coastal communities located north of San Pedro which will be discussed in the following section include: *Topaa'nga*, *Saa'anga*, *Waachnga*, *Toveemonga*, *Chaawvenga*, *Swaanga*, *'Aataveanga*, *Xuuxonga*, *Kiinkenga*, and *Haraasnga*. Those communities south of San Pedro that will be discussed are *'Ahwaanga*, *Povuu'nga*, *Lukúpa*, and *Kengaa*.

TOPANGA CANYON

The westernmost Gabrielino coastal community was *Topaa'nga*, a placename that survives in Topanga Canyon. José Zalvidea reported that *Topaa'nga* meant "the point of that mountain range which ends there in the sea." Zalvidea reported "a large cemetery" there, and went on to say that "topǎ'ŋa is the name of the place where the mountains run out into the sea. A road passes through the mountains from topǎ'ŋa to San Fernando. There was a graveyard at topǎ'ŋa close to the beach with whale ribs erected over the graves. Z [Zalvidea] has many ancestors buried there" (Harrington 1986:R102 F378). Sétimo López reported that the name *Topaa'nga* "is [in the] V. [Ventureño] language" (Harrington 1986:R106 F058).

SANTA MONICA BAY

A number of Gabrielino placenames have been reported for the Santa Monica area, although it is unclear whether they were settlements or merely geographical placenames. José de los Santos Juncos reported that the name "Kitsĕpet [*Kecheekvet*]" was "Santa Monica or rancho de San Vicente," referring to the 30,260-acre Rancho San Vicente y Santa Mónica (Beck and Haase 1974:Map 37; Harrington 1986:R102 F348, R105 F572).

Felicitas Serrano Montaño reported the placename *Koruuvanga* for "Santa Monica," although Harrington noted that she "does not seem to know clearly." José Zalvidea reported the name to mean "en calor estamos, estamos en el sol ahora dice [we are in

warmth, it says we are in the sun now]" (Harrington 1986:R102 F100, 344-345).

BALLONA CREEK

The Gabrielino community of *Saa'anga* was located in the vicinity of Ballona Creek. According to Harrington (1933:195), the "old Machado Ranch at La Ballona was Saa'an, locational of Saanat, pitch, tar." A Juaneño consultant told Kroeber that "Saan" was located at "Ballona," a reference to Rancho Ballona, a 13,920 acre rancho granted to Agustin and Ignacio Machado and Felipe and Tomás Talamantes in 1839. The rancho included present day Playa del Rey, Venice, and Culver City (Kroeber 1907:144, 1925:Plate 57; Cowan 1956:18; Beck and Haase 1974:Map 37).

According to José Zalvidea, a prominent inlet at the mouth of Ballona Creek was known as "Pwínukipar." According to Zalvidea, the name "is applied to any estero [estuary or marsh]. It means that it is full of water" (Harrington 1986:R102 F346).

José Zalvidea reported the Gabrielino placename "Waachnga" to be "only a mile and a half" from Las Salinas (Harrington 1986:R102 F334). Las Salinas, as discussed below, is "near Redondo . . . where they used to get salt" (Harrington 1986:R102 F845, R104 F11). According to Zalvidea, "wǎtšŋa is near San Pedro by the sea, but wa'ǎtšŋa is San Bernardino. . . . Z [Zalvidea] says that . . . where [it] is . . . there is a big church there and a big sycamore tree and many Indians . . . were buried under the sycamore tree" (Harrington 1986:R102 F390). Harrington went on to note that "the catholic church at Wilmington is on land extending from 6th to 7th Streets and from F to G Streets. . . . A sycamore tree, a big one, formerly stood in front of the church. The cemetery was west of the church, but the bodies have been removed" (Harrington 1986:R102 F846).

However, José de los Santos Juncos offered a different site for *Waachnga*, placing it "on the Long Beach side of the [San Pedro] Bay not far from Long Beach" (Harrington 1986:R102 F824). Harrington concluded that his attempts to locate this placename "were very unsatisfactory" (Harrington 1986:R102 F390).

Variant spellings of *Waachnga* found in the mission registers at San Gabriel include *Guasna*, *Guashna*, *Guaspet*, *Guachpet*, *Guashpet* and others (Merriam 1968:109). These variant spellings provide an important clue to the location of this community.

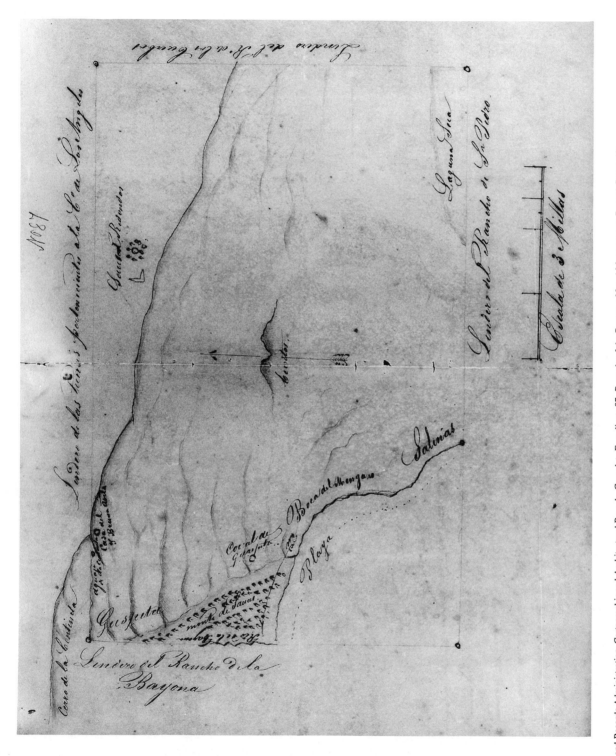

National Archives and Records Administration, Cartographic and Architectural Branch, Complete Expediente 87, Records of the Bureau of Land Management, Record Group 49
Fig. 10. A diseño (map) of Rancho Sausal Redondo showing the Mexican land grant of Guaspita located on the east bank of Ballona Creek. This grant included the site of the Gabrielino community of *Waachnga*; the name Guaspita was probably derived from the earlier Gabrielino placename.

Antonio Ignacio Avila received the grant of "Gua-spita" in 1822, 1837, and 1846; Guaspita and the grant known as Salinas eventually became part of Rancho Sausal Redondo (Cowan 1956:38). The similarity of names suggests that Guaspita was derived from the earlier Gabrielino placename, and that the grant included the site of *Waachnga* within its boundaries. A diseño (map) of Rancho Sausal Redondo clearly shows "Guaspita" as located a short distance from the coast on the hills overlooking Ballona Creek (California Private Land Claims n.d.a).

REDONDO BEACH

'Ongoovanga was a Gabrielino placename located at "Redondo Beach . . . [which was] formerly called El Redondo or Las Salinas" according to José de los Santos Juncos. He went on to note that "Californians used to get salt by the wagonload there" (Harrington 1986:R102 F339, R104 F11). José Zalvidea also placed *'Ongoovanga* at "Salinas (Redondo)" and offered the variant placename "*Ongoving*" for the site (Kroeber 1907:143, 1925:621, Plate 57). The name *'Ongoovanga* was probably derived from the Gabrielino word *ongoova*, meaning salt (Merriam n.d.c; Munro n.d.). It is unclear whether a permanent community existed at *'Ongoovanga*, or whether the location was merely a geographical placename.

A number of important archaeological sites once dotted the coast from Redondo Beach south to Palos Verdes. These sites include Palmer-Redondo, Hollywood-Riviera, and Malaga Cove; Palmer-Redondo and Malaga Cove may have been occupied during the Gabrielino period. All of these sites have been impacted or destroyed by urbanization (Wallace 1984).

PALOS VERDES

According to the data presently available, nine Gabrielino placenames were located on the Palos Verdes Peninsula. This represents a greater concentration than is found in any other region of similar extent in the Gabrielino homeland. The peninsula is unique not only because of the large number of placenames, but also because of its geographical position. Palos Verdes is located within the "sheltered coast," which runs northward from San Pedro Bay; the sheltered coast is characterized by protected bays and inlets which offered attractive sites

for the establishment of communities (Hudson 1971). By virtue of its location and topography the peninsula shelters San Pedro Bay from all but southeasterly winds. This location also provides the shortest maritime route to the Channel Islands, the straight-line distance from Point Fermin to Isthmus Cove on Santa Catalina being 21 miles. As a result, the peninsula was a likely port of call for goods brought from the islands to the mainland (Kroeber 1925:629; Davis 1961).

The Palos Verdes Peninsula encompasses approximately 40 square miles of territory. It is eight miles in length from east to west and five miles in width from north to south. The topography comprises a series of hills and terraces rising to a central ridge 1,000 feet above sea level. Steep cliffs and narrow beaches typify the western and southern coasts, and prior to modern dredging and filling operations the eastern coast was dominated by a large estuary surrounded by tidal mudflats. During Gabrielino times the southern, ocean-facing slopes of the peninsula were probably covered by open grassland, while the northern slopes consisted of grasslands alternating with wooded ravines and canyons. Land mammals in the Palos Verdes region were typical of those found throughout the Gabrielino territory and included coyote, fox, and deer as well as several species of rabbit, skunk, and squirrel. The peninsula also offered the Gabrielino a rich assortment of sea mammals, such as otter, seal, and sea lion, as well as fish and shellfish (Butler 1974).

Human occupation began on the peninsula at a very early date. Malaga Cove, located on the western coast of the peninsula, contained a rich archaeological site with four stratigraphic layers of occupational debris, the earliest of which appears to predate the Millingstone Horizon period. The discovery of historic trade beads at Malaga Cove suggests that occupation continued until the arrival of Europeans in southern California, and perhaps well into the 1800s (Walker 1952:68).

The San Pedro Harbor Site, a large shell midden once located on the eastern slope of the peninsula overlooking San Pedro Harbor, appears to have been occupied as early as 4,000 years ago and periodically thereafter until A.D. 1500. Data recovered during archaeological excavations in early 1968 indicate that the site was occupied primarily during the spring while the inhabitants were gathering shellfish. During the

San Pedro.   California

Fig. 11. A watercolor painting of the Palos Verdes Peninsula, completed in 1842 by William Meyers. The hide house, a small adobe that was the first structure built on the peninsula, is visible left of center and near the shoreline.

summer the Indians may have moved inland to hunt game and gather plant foods, remaining through the winter and returning to the harbor site again the following spring (Butler 1974).

The earliest description of the peninsula and its Indian occupants was recorded by the Cabrillo Expedition in 1542. On Sunday, October 8, the party arrived at "the mainland in a large bay, which they named 'Baia de los Fumos' on account of the many smokes they saw there. Here they engaged in intercourse with some Indians they captured in a canoe, who made signs to them that towards the north there were Spaniards like them. The bay is in 35°, it is an excellent harbor and the country is good, with many valleys, plains, and groves of trees" (Wagner 1929:85-86).

The next observations of the region were recorded by the Sebastián Vizcaíno expedition in 1602. According to Vizcaíno's diary, while the main party

explored Santa Catalina Island, one ship was sent to inspect "another island apparently belonging to the mainland" (Bolton 1908:86). A map published with Father Antonio de la Ascensión's account depicts the Palos Verdes Peninsula and San Pedro Bay, referred to as the "Ensenada de S. [San] Andres." Depicted on this map is the "Isla raza de buena gente," or "flat island of good people," probably a reference to Dead Man's Island or Rattlesnake Island, both prominent harbor landmarks prior to port development early in this century (Wagner 1929:235, 402, note 137; see also Bolton 1908:86.).

It is unfortunate that a more complete survey of the peninsula was not attempted during this expedition. Certainly the cursory observations reported by Father Antonio do not approach the level of detail recorded in his description of the *yovaar* (sacred enclosure) at Isthmus Cove on Catalina (see in Chapter 1). Wagner (1929) offers an explanation for the explorers' apparent

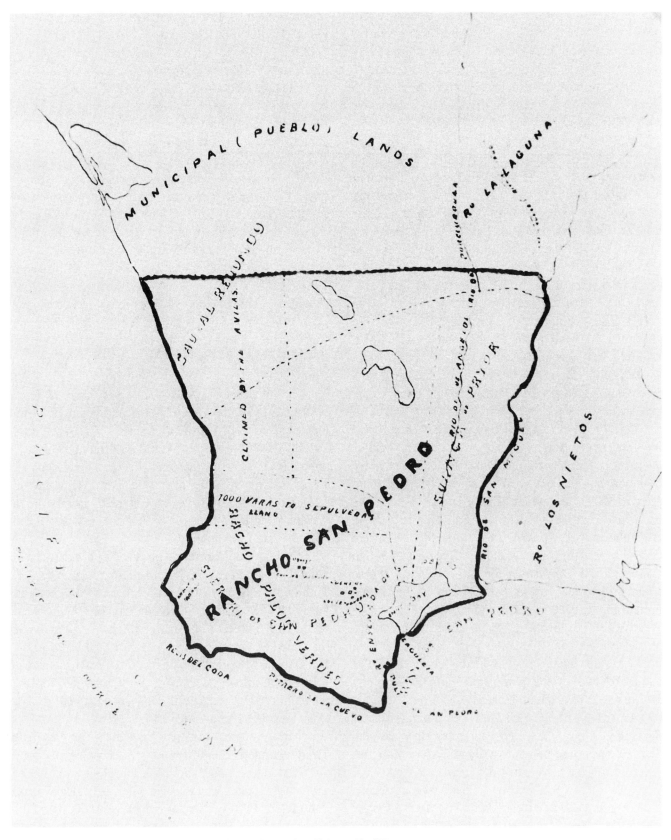

Fig. 12. A map of Rancho San Pedro reproduced in the Abstract of Title by Grove and Wilkinson, 1891. The 4000-acre Suanga tract claimed by Nathaniel Pryor in 1839 lies north of the Bay of San Pedro and adjacent to the eastern boundary of the rancho. It was bounded on the east by the San Gabriel River (Rio de San Miguel). During the flooding of 1867 the San Gabriel changed course; the river now empties into Alamitos Bay.

lack of interest in the mainland: "a set of twenty-five instructions was given him [Vizcaíno] to govern his conduct while on the voyage. . . . He was directed to be very cautious if Indians were encountered and to treat them well, and was forbidden to allow anyone to go inland to look for them, as that was not a necessary part of his business" (Wagner 1929:175).

In 1769 Palos Verdes was visited by the *San Antonio*, a supply ship supporting Gaspar de Portolá's expedition to Alta California. Father Juan Vizcaíno, who sailed aboard the *San Antonio*, mistakenly described Palos Verdes as an "Island which must be near the port and the mainland." In his entry for March 23, 1769, he sighted an Indian settlement and reported that "from afar we could see their small cabins and some trees." The following day the padre realized that the "Island above-mentioned is not an Island, but a promontory" (Vizcaíno 1959:18-19). In his entry for March 26, Father Juan observed that "smokes have been seen all day in a ravine. . . . There is only one cut through which it seems flows a river into this large bay, formed by the point which reaches as far as the Port" (Vizcaíno 1959:20-21).

Five of the nine Gabrielino placenames reported for the peninsula, *Toveemonga*, *Chaawvenga*, *Swaanga*, *'Aataveanga*, and *Xuuxonga*, appear to have been communities occupied during the late 1700s and early 1800s, as evidenced by notations in the baptismal registers of Mission San Gabriel. Two other placenames, *Kiinkenga* and *Haraasnga*, duplicate Gabrielino names for islands, *Kiinkenga* for San Clemente and *Haraasnga* for San Nicolas. These communities may have been occupied by island Indians relocated to the mainland during the late 1700s or early 1800s, perhaps to escape attacks from Indians brought down from Russian-owned Alaska to hunt sea otter near the Channel Islands during those years. The nature of two of the placenames, *Moniikanga* and *Masaawnga*, remains unclear.

A variety of locations has been suggested for *Swaanga*, which Reid (1852:9) described as the "largest and most populous village." José Zalvidea reported to Harrington that *Swaanga* was "one mile this side [?] of San Pedro. There was a cienega [marsh] there and a few cottonwood trees. . . . Swáŋa was in the plain." He also noted that the community was "near San Pedro, but inland" (Harrington 1986:R102 F371). According to José Zalvidea the name *Swaanga* "means junco [rush]. There was lots

of junco there about the village. Junco is called in G. [Gabrielino] swar" (Harrington 1986:R102 F371).

Reid (1852:8) simply noted that *Swaanga* was located at "Suang-na," suggesting that this was still a recognizable placename as late as 1852. This is borne out by an 1839 report by a special commission of the Los Angeles *Ayuntamiento* (city government). The commission was convened to investigate an ownership claim by Nathaniel Pryor to a 4000-acre portion of Rancho San Pedro commonly known as the *Suanga* tract; the claim was denied. An 1891 map reproduced in "Abstract of Title" for Rancho San Pedro clearly shows the "Suanga of Pryor" tract lying along the eastern border of the rancho, north of the Inner Bay of San Pedro (Gillingham n.d.; see also Gillingham 1961:54, 166-167). This location supports José Zalvidea's comments that *Swaanga* was located "in the plain" and "inland." Baptismal records from Mission San Gabriel confirm that the community of *Swaanga* was occupied at least as late as 1813 (Merriam 1968:117).

The placename *Masaawnga* was derived from information obtained from a Luiseño consultant, who located it at "San Pedro" (Kroeber 1907:144). José Zalvidea did "not seem to know well the placename," although he did note that *Masaawnga* "means junco. There is a lot of junco near San Pedro" (Harrington 1986:R102 F355). *Masaawnga* may simply be a variant name for *Swaanga*, or in some way associated with the latter community.

A number of Gabrielino placenames are associated with the San Pedro region, including *Chaawvenga*, *Tsauvinga*, *Sow-vingt-ha*, *Unavnga*, and *Navungna'a*. Reid (1852:8) placed the community of *Chaawvenga* on "Palos Verdes"; the name *Chaawvenga* may be translated as "place of the tip or thorn" (Munro n.d.). San Gabriel Mission baptismal records offer the names *Chaubit*, *Chauvit*, *Chautbit*, and *Chaubipet* for the community, and indicate that it was occupied until at least 1813 (Merriam 1968:106).

Variant spellings of *Chaawvenga* include *Tsauvinga* and *Sow-vingt-ha*. According to José Zalvidea, *Tsauvinga* "applies to San Pedro and not to any other place near San Pedro" (Harrington 1986:R102 F384). Taylor wrote in 1860 that "the beach or playa of San Pedro was called Sow-vingt-na" (Taylor 1860a, n.d.). Other names that may have referred to this community include *Unavngna* and *Navungna'a*. Kroeber, referencing information obtained from a Luiseño, reported the name "Unavngna" for the community (Kroeber 1907:144). Manuel Santos, in response to the name *Unavngna* offered "Nǎvŋa," derived from the Gabrielino word "nǎvut, tuna [tuna cactus, *Opuntia* sp.]." José Zalvidea added that "there used to be lots of tunas at Palos Verdes antes [formerly]" (Harrington 1986:R102 F388).

According to José Zalvidea, *Xuuxonga* was located "on the shore below San Pedro." In reporting the name, Zalvidea mentioned the phrase "mandaba el. The name means principal or ruling place" (Harrington 1986:R102 F392). Interestingly, Harrington noted that *Xuuxonga* seemed in some way to be associated in Zalvidea's memory with the San Fernando Valley community of *Muuhonga*, for the consultant "mentioned the story of how the animals were treacherously killed at muhu'ŋa in connection with this name" (Harrington 1986:R102 F392).

José Zalvidea identified *Moniikanga*, as "a place in the hill by San Pedro near the beach," and as a "hill by Pt. [Point] Fermin." According to Zalvidea *Moniikanga* means "lomita [hill] or loma poco grande [not very big hill]" (Harrington 1986:R102 F356,357). *Moniikanga* would seem to have been a small settlement, or perhaps merely a geographical placename.

Haraasnga appears on Reid's list of Gabrielino communities, although he offered no locational data (Reid 1852:8). José Zalvidea reported that *Haraasnga* was located near *'Aataveanga* and *Kiinkenga* (Harrington 1986:R102 F391), although on another occasion he offered that it was "otra sierra adendro del agua near pimú'ŋa [the other mountain in the water near pimú'ŋa]," to which Harrington added the comment "surely and clearly San Clemente Island" (Harrington 1986:R102 F462). *Pimú'ŋa* was the Gabrielino name for Santa Catalina Island, and the implication is that *Haraasnga* may have been both a mainland community located on the Palos Verdes Peninsula and an island community on San Clemente.

José de los Santos Juncos told Harrington that *Haraasnga* was "a little west of kíŋkiŋa, just [the] other side (west) of [the] first point west of kíŋkiŋa (kíŋkiŋa equals Point Fermin lighthouse)" (Harrington 1986:R102 F826). As White's Point is the first point west of Point Fermin, José de los Santos Juncos's information would place *Haraasnga* west of Royal Palms Beach Park, along the stretch of coast between

the park and Portuguese Bend (Harrington 1986:R102 F852).

The association of *Haraasnga* with both a mainland community and one of the Channel Islands is an intriguing puzzle. Although Harrington believed that the name *Haraasnga* referred to San Clemente Island, Kroeber disagreed, pointing out that *Haraasnga*, when translated into Chumash, was *Ghalas-at*, the name for San Nicolas Island (Kroeber 1925:635). It may be that groups of island Gabrielino relocated to the mainland and founded the community of *Haraasnga*, bestowing upon it the name of their traditional island home (see also Heizer 1968:110-111, note 24). Hints contained in historical and ethnographic accounts suggest that lineages did relocate from the islands to the mainland. When San Nicolas Island was abandoned in 1835, the Nicoleño were brought to San Pedro; although most of the islanders were dispersed among the missions, at least one, a man known as Black Hawk, remained in San Pedro until his death (see Hardacre 1880; Roberts 1933:77; Nidever 1937:38; Cheetham 1940:43; Phelps 1961).

According to José Zalvidea and José de los Santos Juncos, *Toveemonga* was "a place about one and one-half miles from San Pedro, up the coast from San Pedro, on the coast. . . . It refers to a great stone on the beach. . . . There was a big village there of Indians. . . . Tověmur is a rock at the very point of San Pedro hill, west of San Pedro" (Harrington 1986:R102 F382). José de los Santos Juncos reported that *Toveemonga* was "where [a] spring is, near [the] top of [a] sea cliff where a big hill runs out to form a second point west of Point Fermin lighthouse" (Harrington 1986:R102 F825). These descriptions place the community in the White's Point—Royal Palms Beach vicinity.

José de los Santos Juncos prepared a sketch map of the *Toveemonga* area, and according to Harrington "M. Palmer has dug there," a reference to early excavations conducted by the antiquarian Dr. Palmer, a local dentist who donated his collection to the Southwest Museum and also served as its director (Harrington 1986:R102 F852, R105 F589; see Chapter 1 for a discussion of Palmer's work). Mission records indicate that the community was occupied until at least 1804 (Merriam 1968:118).

José Zalvidea reminisced that "tovjěmur was one of the first people and was turned into a great rock which stands erect on the shore of the ocean near San

Pedro." He went on to report that "the name means 'lo que para'[a thing which stands up]" (Harrington 1986:R102 F382). José de los Santos Juncos's comment that *toveemor* was "mentioned in [the] mourning songs of San Gabriel" suggests that it represents an important figure in the rituals and mythology of the Gabrielino (Harrington 1986:R102 F826).

Kiinkenga is another example of a Gabrielino placename that appears on both the Channel Islands and the mainland. Reid attributed the placename "Kinkipar" to "San Clemente Island" (Reid 1852:8). Manuel Santos reported that *Kiinkenga* was an "<u>island in the sea</u>." After confiding to Harrington that José Zalvidea originally came from *Kiinkenga*, Santos went on to state that they "call the people [of *Kiinkenga*] <u>kiŋkijam</u>. . . . They are pipïmaram [Gabrielino]" (Harrington 1986:R102 F475, underlining in original).

José Zalvidea, however, told Harrington that *Kiinkenga* was "two miles south of San Pedro on the beach," while José de los Santos Juncos was even more definite, describing it as "back of Point Fermin lighthouse" (Harrington 1986:R102 F340, 824). According to José Zalvidea the name "Kíŋki pár or par Kíŋki would mean sea or water of K'íŋki" and "must be called that way because it was on the shore" (Harrington 1986:R102 F341). Zalvidea also reported that "Pipímaris, Pico and other Indians are living there now and in Los Angeles," indicating that *Kiinkenga* remained a recognizable location and placename among the Gabrielino until well into the twentieth century (Harrington 1986:R102 F340).

Two separate locations have been reported for *'Aataveanga*. According to José Zalvidea the community was located "between San Pedro and Kïŋkiŋa and is on the shore." Zalvidea noted that *'Aataveanga* was "an old, old name and there is a big cemetery there" and went on to report that the name *'Ataaveanga* means "de antes pusieron toda la rancheria, le pusieron [before they placed each ranchería, they placed it]," they settled there and put a village there and at Kïŋki" (Harrington 1986:R102 F333-334).

José de los Santos Juncos reported, however, that "akáviaŋa was where [the] Indians lived on [the] plain above where [the] Palos Verdes ranch house was" (Harrington 1986:R102 F827), and he said that the name "means where they used to stay" (Harrington 1986:R102 F332). Although Harrington noted that

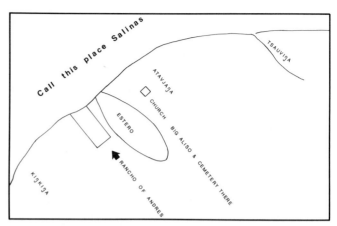

Map 9. A redrawing of a sketch map, prepared in 1914-1915 by José Zalvidea; the map shows the relative positions of three Gabrielino communities located on the east coast of the Palos Verdes peninsula. This redrawing by the author is based on a microfilm copy of the original; Harrington's phonetic spellings of the Gabrielino placemanes have been simplified. Compare this sketch map to plat map shown in Figure 13.

Santos Juncos' memory of the site seemed unclear, he did report that "Mr. A. G. Sepulveda says that the old Palos Verdes ranch house stood where the pepper trees are just east of the corner of Channel Street and Ancon Street, San Pedro. Quite a little valley there enters from the hills of the west. Kuhn [José de los Santos Juncos] says there was a spring there" (Harrington 1986:R102 F827). The reference is most likely to the adobe home of José Diego Sepúlveda, built in 1853 and razed before 1910. This ranch house, a Monterey-style, two-story adobe, once stood at the intersection of Channel and Gaffey streets. Another early Sepúlveda home stood at Gaffey and Anaheim streets, while a third lay somewhat west of Gaffey, near the present Capitol Drive (Silka 1984:15, 24-25).

While interviewing José Zalvidea in 1914-1915, Harrington obtained a sketch map from the consultant showing the relative locations of *Chaawvenga*, *'Aataveanga*, and *Kiinkenga* (Harrington 1986:R103 F26). Harrington was dissatisfied with the drawing, noting that "according to the map which Jose drew on the ground the ranch of Andres is below an estero [inlet], and [the] estero is between 'atåvjaŋá and Kïŋkiŋa . . . 'atåvjaŋá being between San Pedro and Kïŋkiŋa. But when he drew a second map he had the places arranged differently" (Harrington 1986:R102 F334).

A comparison of the Zalvidea sketch map, made in 1914-1915, with an 1859 plat map of Rancho Los Palos Verdes (Hancock 1859) suggests a possible correlation. Zalvidea's sketch of the coastline appears to be fairly accurate; however, he has placed the topographical features on the ocean side of the coastline (as if they were situated in the ocean) rather than on the mainland side. If the map is corrected for this error Zalvidea's shoreline resembles the coast before modern harbor development. The placements of *'Aataveanga* and *Kiinkenga* agree quite well with Zalvidea's data, although *Chaawvenga* seems too far east.

Two of the landmarks on the Zalvidea map, the "rancho of Andres" and the "church [and] big aliso [alder] and cemetery" remain unidentified, although the church may be the Catholic church in Wilmington with a big sycamore (not an aliso, i.e. alder, tree) and a cemetery (see the above discussion of *Waachnga*). Other churches that existed in San Pedro early in this century included the Presbyterian Church at Tenth and Mesa streets, and the second Mary Star of the Sea Catholic Church at Ninth and Centre streets (Silka 1984:40, 91). The "rancho of Andres" appears to coincide with the "Government Reserve" shown on the 1859 map, a 42-acre square designated by the Mexican and later American governments as a public landing place. At one time an adobe building that was used for storing cow hides intended for trade stood on this reserve. This building, which may have been constructed during the Mission Period, was visited by Richard Henry Dana in 1835 and described in his book *Two Years Before the Mast* (1840). Early records indicate that the hide house was abandoned around 1848, at which time squatters built corrals and began sheep ranching on the reserve until it was reclaimed by the government sometime after 1898 (Weinman and Stickel 1978:93-94).

The Palos Verdes Peninsula remains in many ways the most intriguing region of the Gabrielino homeland, due primarily to the large number of placenames recorded within its limited area. Economic factors, such as the availability of both marine and mainland food resources and a favorable location along the maritime trade route from Catalina Island, may have allowed the peninsula to support a large concentration of communities within a relatively small area. One might also speculate that some type of political confederation existed on the peninsula. At the present time there is little ethnographic or ethnohistoric data to support such speculation; however, political confederations have been reported for the Chumash, and (as noted earlier) there are some ethnohistoric data

to suggest that the inland community of *'Ahwiinga* served as a provincial "capital."

LONG BEACH

Three important Gabrielino communities located within the present boundaries of the city of Long Beach were *Tevaaxa'anga*, *'Ahwaanga*, and *Povuu'nga*. According to a Gabrielino story recalled by José de los Santos Juncos, these communities were founded by refugees from the San Gabriel area. Santos Juncos stated that "the Indians originally all lived together, but strife arose between them, and those of S. G. [San Gabriel] drove the other faction down to the orilla del mar [seashore], by Los Cerritos, Los Alamitos, etc." (Harrington 1986:R105 F564-565). One early historical account notes that the Indians fought "constant wars, making it impossible for them [the Indians living in the interior] to . . . fish, although . . . there is a very suitable beach on the bay of San Pedro, where barks can anchor in safety" (Bolton 1926:219-220).

The first of these communities, *Tevaaxa'anga*, has already been discussed as one of the inland Gabrielino communities. The second settlement was *'Ahwaanga*; Kroeber placed this community in the Long Beach vicinity and noted that *'Ahwaanga* was at "Los Alamitos, Cerritos [ranchos]" (Kroeber 1907:144, 1925:Plate 57).

The third Gabrielino community in Long Beach was *Povuu'nga*. According to Father Gerónimo Boscana, *Povuu'nga* was the birthplace of both *Wewyoot*, the first *tomyaar*, and the creator-god and spiritual being *Chengiichngech* (Boscana 1933:32-33). *Povuu'nga* was an important ceremonial site and probably served as a ritual center for the Gabrielino communities of the region.

Harrington's Juaneño consultant José de la Gracia Cruz, also known as Acú, recalled a story in which

> two químicos [sorcerers or shamans] were going from Pobuna to another rancheria on their way from one fiesta to another. They were brothers, the one was stronger (mas fuerte, i.e. a better químico than the other). They were passing over a plain between two mountains and one of them saw a bear in a barranca [ravine] at the foot of one of the mountains, which stood up and looked at them for a moment and then started across the plain toward the other mountain. The lesser químico said to the stronger "surely that is Cheng-ee-ching-itch, don't you do something to him?" Then

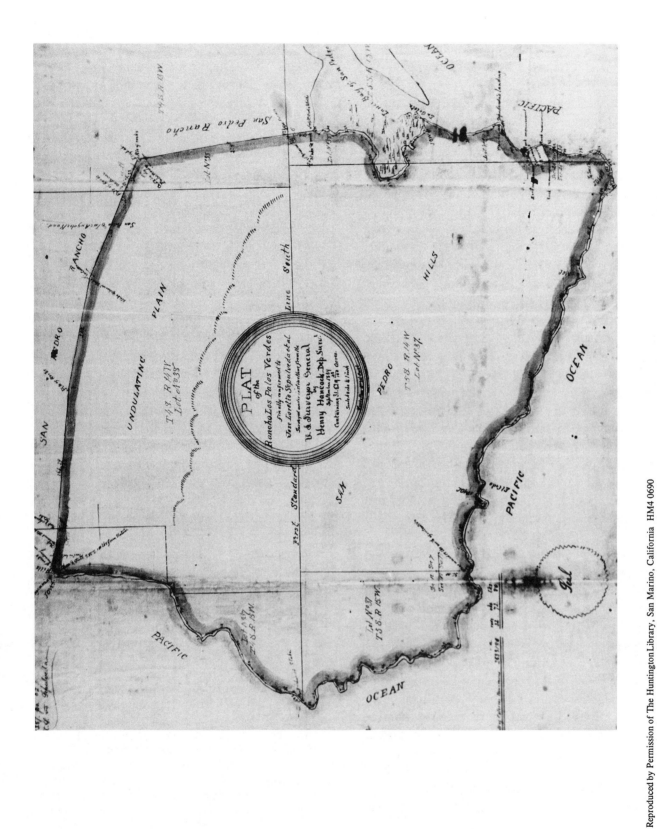

Fig. 13. A plat map of Rancho Palos Verdes prepared in 1859 by Henry Hancock. The marshy areas along the Inner Bay are clearly noted. Compare the shoreline shown on this map to the sketch of this region prepared by José Zalvidea (see Map 8).

the stronger químico gave three shouts at the bear and the bear immediately fell down as if he were shot. His hind legs dragged on the ground and he crawled along by means of his forelegs and began to scratch the earth with them to throw the dirt upon his back where he was wounded. Presently the earth cured him and he arose on all fours and went away (Harrington 1986:R121 F566).

Reid placed *Povuu'nga* on "Alamitos [Rancho]" (Reid 1852:8), and José Zalvidea confirmed this location, noting that *Povuu'nga* "is the correct form of the name of Los Alamitos" (Harrington 1986:R102 F360). A strong contender for the location of *Povuu'nga* is the hilltop site occupied by Rancho Los Alamitos. The ranch house, which incorporates the original adobe constructed in the early 1800s, is now maintained as an historical site by the City of Long Beach. Archaeological remains may still lie buried beneath the ranch buildings (Dixon 1972:88). A sketch map by Harrington locates a "rancheria" south of the adobe residence (Harrington 1986:R104 F28), and the anthropologist noted that "just east of the tennis court in the alfalfa field which constitutes the lowest reaches of the point of the hill, the ground is covered with shell debris—the remains of the rancheria of Puvú'." An important freshwater spring once flowed near the base of the hill and watered an extensive forest of cottonwood trees (Harrington 1933:149).

Povuu'nga existed as a recognizable community at least until 1805, as evidenced by baptismal records from missions San Gabriel and San Juan Capistrano (Merriam 1968:116, 135). José Zalvidea reported that the name *Povuu'nga* means "en la bola [in the ball]." Zalvidea conjectured that "there must have been a bola [ball or sphere] of stone, maybe, there, antes [previously]" although Harrington noted that the reference was unclear (Harrington 1986:R102 F360). Another possible translation of "en la bola" is "in the crowd" based on the Mexican usage of the word bola. The author of the present work has wondered if perhaps Zalvidea could have meant "en la bolsa," or "in the pouch." The numerous bays and inlets in this region were referred to as "las bolsas," a tradition that is preserved in the name of Rancho Las Bolsas.

A few miles north of Rancho Los Alamitos is the Los Altos Site (LAn-270). Excavations at the Los Altos Site during 1952 and 1953 recovered a number of Late Period artifacts (Simpson 1953; Bates 1972); a number of these are included as illustrations in the present volume. Although the limited archaeological data suggests that the Los Altos Site was occupied during the Gabrielino period, the relationship between *Povuu'nga* and LAn-270 remains unclear.

SEAL BEACH, HUNTINGTON BEACH, COSTA MESA

The coastal region between the present cities of Long Beach and Huntington Beach once largely consisted of low-lying marshlands subject to flooding by the Santa Ana River. Until the completion of the Prado Dam Flood Control Project in 1942, winter storms often flooded portions of Orange County. Perhaps for this reason many of the archaeological sites in this low-lying coastal region consist primarily of shell middens located along the peripheries of bays, lagoons, and marshes (Chace 1969). The archaeological evidence suggests that these Gabrielino settlements were primarily temporary or seasonal camps occupied while hunting or gathering shellfish and plant foods (Hudson 1971). Important Gabrielino sites in this region of Orange County were located on bluffs and knolls elevated above the Santa Ana River floodplain.

Motuuchey was reported by José de los Santos Juncos to be the Gabrielino name for "El Puerto de los Alemanes [the Port of the Germans]," or the former Anaheim Landing near Seal Beach, also once known as "El Piojo [the Louse]." According to Santos Juncos the name *Motuuchey* means "pulga [flea]" (Harrington 1986:R104 F24).

Kroeber (citing data from a Luiseño consultant) placed the Gabrielino community of "Lukup" at "Las Bolsas [Rancho]" in the Huntington Beach area (Kroeber 1907:144, 1925, Plate 57). Harrington's consultant José Zalvidea reported that "*Lukúpa*" was "a place east of Long Beach." Zalvidea noted that the name *Lukúpa* means "plateado [silvery]" (Harrington 1986:R102 F850). Constance Goddard DuBois, referring to information obtained from Luiseño consultants, identified "Lukup" as "a large rancheria south of Santa Ana on the coast" (DuBois 1908:122). One possibility for the location of *Lukúpa* is the Newland House Site (Ora-183); the site is situated on one of the few knolls in that region that rises above the Santa Ana River floodplain. The Newland House Site has been the subject of various archaeological excavations since the 1930s (see Winterbourne 1968a; Cottrell et al. 1985; O'Neil 1988:108-110).

Other important archaeological sites in this region include the Banning Estate or Fairview Site (Ora-58) and the Griset Site (Ora-135), both of which were located on promontories overlooking the Santa Ana River in the city of Costa Mesa. These sites were excavated in the 1930s under the supervision of J. W. Winterbourne; the Banning Estate Site was excavated again in the 1960s by Dixon. The Griset Site is especially noteworthy because of the discovery of ceramics dating to the Mission Period, which suggests that the site was occupied well into the historic period (Winterbourne 1968b, 1968c; Dixon 1968, 1970, 1971).

NEWPORT BAY

The community of *Kengaa* was located on Upper Newport Bay. According to records from Mission San Juan Capistrano, it may have been occupied as late as 1829 or 1830 (Merriam 1968:125-126). The placename remained in use for much of the nineteenth century—an 1853 diseño (map) of this region identifies Newport Bay as the "bolsa de gengara [Bay of Gengara]," *Gengara* being a variant spelling of *Kengaa*. Archaeological sites that may have been associated with *Kengaa* include Ora-119A and Ora-111 (O'Neil 1988:110; California Private Land Claims n.d.b).

Kroeber placed "Moyo" at "Saucal, San Joaquin [Rancho]" (Kroeber 1907:144, 1925:Plate 57). It is unclear whether *Moyoonga* was a community or simply a geographical placename, although archaeological research in the San Joaquin Hills indicates that permanent, year-round settlements existed in this region (Howard 1977).

SUMMARY

The Los Angeles—Santa Ana Plain is a broad, level expanse of prairie covering more than 800 square miles from Cahuenga Peak to the coast, and from Topanga Canyon to the vicinity of Aliso Creek. The plain is characterized by a lengthy coastal strand; four major watercourses traverse the plain including the Los Angeles, Río Hondo, San Gabriel, and Santa Ana rivers. During Gabrielino times many portions of this region were covered by fresh and saltwater marshes.

The major inland Gabrielino communities discussed in this chapter include the following: *Maawnga, Yaanga, Geveronga, 'Ochuunga, Chokiishnga, Huutnga, Naxaaw'nga-Sejat,*

Tevaaxa'anga, Hotuuknga, Pasbenga. Each of these communities appears to have been situated near a major river system, although in some cases these locations also fell near the foothill-transition zone.

The coastal strand is defined as a narrow strip extending along the ocean's edge for 75 miles and inland for five miles. It includes 375 square miles of territory and, based on geographical features, is divided into two regions: the northern (sheltered) coast; and the southern (exposed) coast.

The sheltered coast extended northward from San Pedro to Topanga and offered numerous bays which were attractive sites for settlements. The topography of this coast is varied. In the vicinity of Topanga Canyon the ocean-ward slopes of the Santa Monica Mountains reach 1,000 feet or more in elevation and beaches are limited to canyons and ravines at the water's edge. From Topanga Canyon south to the Palos Verdes Peninsula the coast is flat and level, and was once characterized by extensive marshlands in the Playa del Rey region. The terrain becomes rugged again as the coast follows the Palos Verdes Peninsula to San Pedro. The major Gabrielino communities located on the northern coast which were discussed in this chapter are: *Topaa'nga, Saa'anga, Waachnga, Toveemonga, Chaawvenga, Swaanga, 'Aataveanga, Xuuxonga, Kiinkenga,* and *Haraasnga.*

The exposed coast extended from San Pedro southward to the vicinity of Aliso Creek. During Gabrielino times the shoreline of San Pedro Bay was characterized by extensive mud flats and sand bars. From Long Beach southward to Newport Bay the coastline was flat and level and characterized by fresh- and saltwater marshes. At Newport Bay the San Joaquin Hills reach the coast and the terrain becomes steep, although elevations generally remain below 1,000 feet. Those communities located on the southern coast which were discussed are *'Ahwaanga, Povuu'nga, Lukúpa,* and *Kengaa.*

On a clear day Santa Catalina can easily be seen from the coast; the island's dark silhouette draws the viewer's gaze even as it once drew the attention of Gabrielino seafarers. Strong political, economic, and social ties united the coastal Indians with their relatives on the Channel Islands of Santa Catalina, San Clemente, and San Nicolas; a common dialect may also have strengthened these bonds. In recent years

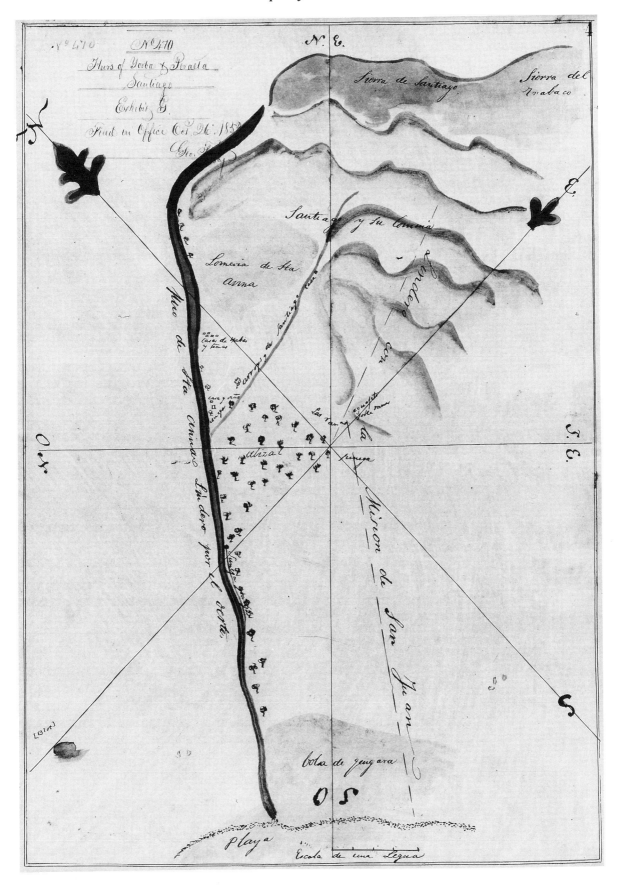

Fig. 14. A diseño (map) of Rancho Santiago de Santa Ana showing the Bolsa de Gengara (Bay of *Kengaa*).

archaeological work has begun to unravel the complex patterns of settlement and subsistence on these Gabrielino outposts. These exciting discoveries offer a different perspective on the First Angelinos and form the subject of the next chapter.

CHAPTER 5

THE PEOPLE OF THE CHANNEL ISLANDS

The southern Channel Islands of Santa Catalina, San Clemente, and San Nicolas were occupied by the Gabrielino, who also utilized tiny Santa Barbara Island for quarrying activities. Although the islands received their current names from the Spanish explorer Sebastián Vizcaíno (Wagner 1941:30-31; Jones 1969:87), according to José Zalvidea they were collectively known to the Gabrielino as "we Xaj mómte 'ašunηa wow, all the mountain ranges which are in the sea" (Harrington 1986:R102 F463). Each island had its own name as well.

The Gabrielino occupation of the southern Channel Islands may have come rather late in California prehistory. Archaeological evidence suggests that these islands may originally have been under the cultural influence of Hokan-speaking Chumash peoples. Sometime prior to European contact these Hokan-speaking peoples were replaced by Uto-Aztecans (Meighan personal communication, 1984; Raab and Yatsko 1990:19). Perhaps as the Gabrielino came into contact with the Chumash and became more sophisticated in the exploitation of marine food resources they adopted the plank canoe, gradually migrating to the Channel Islands to join or displace the resident Chumash peoples. Regardless of the process, by the time Spanish seafarers began arriving in the sixteenth century the southern Channel Islands were firmly in Gabrielino hands.

SANTA BARBARA ISLAND

Santa Barbara Island, the smallest of the southern Channel Islands, is administered by the National Park Service as part of Channel Islands National Park. Santa Barbara Island lies 38 miles from the mainland and about 24 miles west of Santa Catalina Island. The island is triangular in shape, one and one-half miles in length from north to south and one mile in width, with an area of about one square mile. A central ridge with two peaks dominates the island. Signal Peak, the highest point on the island at 635 feet above sea level, is located near the southwest coast, while North Peak near the northwest coast is 562 feet above sea level. Two islets which are detached segments of the main ridge lie off the north and southwest coasts respectively. A few narrow beaches exist in coves on the southern and northwest coasts (Gleason 1958:93; Swartz 1960; Glassow 1980:13-14).

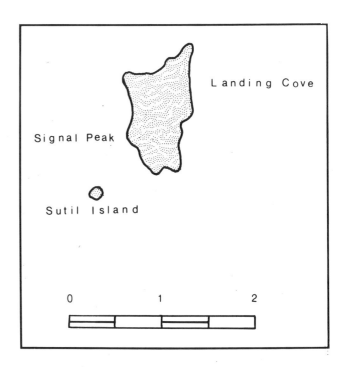

Map 10. Tiny Santa Barbara Island comprises one square mile of territory. Although visited by the Gabrielino, it was too small to support a permanent population. The Gabrielino name for Santa Barbara Island was *'Ichunash*.

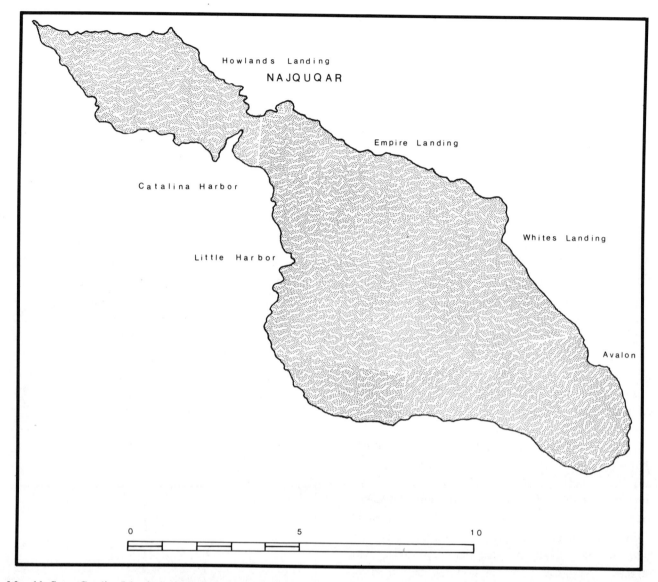

Map 11. Santa Catalina Island, the largest of the southern Channel Islands occupied by the Gabrelino. The Gabrielino name for the Island was *Pemuu'nga*, while the Isthmus was known as *Nájquqar*

The water supply on Santa Barbara Island is limited; the island receives about 12 inches of rainfall per year during the winter months. The only animals indigenous to the island are the white-footed mouse, the island night lizard, and a small bat. Sea lions are abundant during the breeding season. The island is also frequented by several species of seal, including harbor seal, northern elephant seal, and northern fur seal (Swartz 1960; Glassow 1980:16).

Santa Barbara is believed to have been used primarily for quarrying activities, with occupation limited to periodic, temporary visits. The island's central location with respect to the mainland and San Nicolas, Santa Catalina, and Anacapa islands may also have made it an important "stopping-off" point for

seafarers (Swartz 1960; Glassow 1980:36; Hudson 1981:193-194). The Spanish explorer Pedro Fages reported that the "Indians of the plain of San Gabriel communicate with the islanders of San Clemente and Santa Barbara" using "their rafts of reeds" (Fages 1937:23). Harrington (1933:145, note 66) speculated that the island may have been an important source of the black basaltic stone used in the manufacture of ritual charmstones used by shamans.

Archaeological work conducted on Santa Barbara Island up to 1980 had identified 15 archaeological sites, including a workshop area for the production of stone tools. Artifacts recovered from these sites include fishhook fragments, a bone fishing barb, a bone abalone pry, steatite bowl fragments, projectile

Fig. 15. The southern shore of Santa Catalina Island looking west. Note the steep cliffs and narrow beaches. Photograph by author.

point fragments, and mortar and pestle fragments (Swartz 1960; Glassow 1980:28). A summary of the survey and excavation project undertaken on the island is presented in Glassow (1980:19-33).

According to Fernando Librado, a Chumash consultant employed by Harrington, both the Fernandeño and the Gabrielino referred to Santa Barbara Island by the Chumash name *'Ichunash*, meaning "'a notice,' as for example the blow of a trumpet." The name is based on the Chumash word *'Ichunash*, which reportedly means "whistle" (Hudson 1981:193-194).

SANTA CATALINA ISLAND

Santa Catalina, which is the island nearest the mainland, lies approximately 21 miles from the Palos Verdes Peninsula. The island is 20 miles in length and varies in width from eight miles at its widest spot to one-half mile at its narrowest point. The total area of the island is 75 square miles. The terrain on Santa Catalina is rugged, with some peaks reaching or exceeding 2,000 feet above sea level. Beaches are for the most part limited to the mouths of canyons.

During Gabrielino times, water was available throughout the year in at least a half-dozen springs and creeks. The primary land mammals were ground squirrel, fox, and quail (Williamson 1903:14; Bean and Smith 1978:540; Rosenthal et al. 1988). Some acorn groves may have existed on the island, although they were not extensive (Finnerty et al. 1970:7). However, maritime food resources such as fish, shellfish, and sea-mammals were plentiful.

Juan Rodríguez Cabrillo visited Santa Catalina in 1542, perhaps anchoring at Avalon, where "a great number of Indians came out of the bushes and grass, shouting, dancing, and making signs to come ashore" (Wagner 1941:46). Avalon may have been visited again in 1602 by Sebastián Vizcaíno. On this occasion Indians "began to raise smokes on the beach," and when the Spaniards anchored "the women, children, and old men began to shout and make demonstrations of joy in proof of their happiness. They came running to the beach to receive the guests who were arriving" (Wagner 1929:236). On the following day a tent was set up on the island and mass was said with more than 150 "Indian men and women" present (Bolton 1908:84). Two days later the Spaniards sailed to the isthmus, which they described as the "Puerto de Santa Catalina" and where they found a "pueblo [town or village] and more than three hundred Indians, men, women and children" (Bolton 1908:85).

A map of Catalina drawn in 1602 by Father Antonio de la Ascensión places the pueblo at the isthmus; excavations by both antiquarians and modern archaeologists have confirmed the presence of an important settlement that may have served as a depot for the maritime trade with the mainland (Holder 1910:27-28; Wagner 1929:235; Finnerty et al. 1970). The Ascensión map also locates another settlement near the first anchorage at the midpoint of the northern coast; however, it has been suggested that Avalon Bay was the probable anchorage (see Wagner 1929:401, note 133).

While anchored at Isthmus Cove the Spaniards explored the island's interior, discovering "a level prairie, very well cleared, where the Indians were assembled to worship an idol which was there" (Bolton 1908:85). Father de la Ascensión described the "place of worship" as "a large flat patio" which held an altar and "a great circle all surrounded with feathers of various colors and shapes" (Wagner 1929:237). His description of the sacred enclosure was quoted at length in Chapter 2.

Santa Catalina was visited in 1769 by the *San Antonio*, a supply ship attached to the Portolá Expedition. During this voyage Father Juan Vizcaíno described "some ravines, and particularly one very green one, and a flat place where there are Indians" (Vizcaíno 1959:17). The ship was visited by Indians who "came up to us in two canoes with signals of peace," and from them the sailors obtained fresh

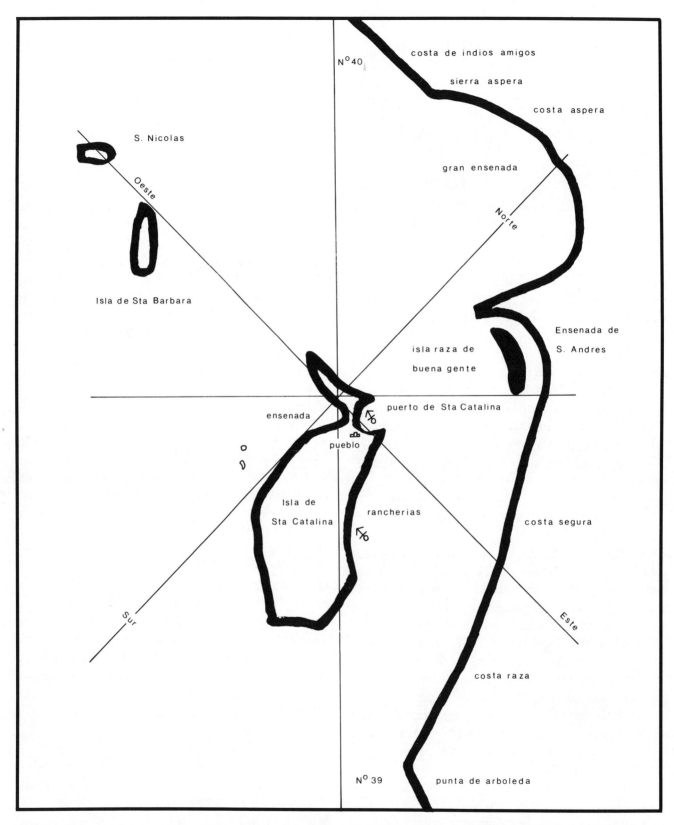

Map 12. Redrawing by the author of Father Antonio de la Ascension's 1602 map of Santa Catalina, Santa Barbara, and San Nicolas islands and the adjacent mainland. The "puerto de S. Catalina [Port of Santa Catalina]" was located at Isthmus Cove; nearby was a "pueblo" or large Indian community. A smaller Indian settlement ("rancheria") was located east of the isthmus near the north shore. Across the channel was the "isla raza de buena gente [flat island of good people]"; this is probably a reference to Dead Man's Island or Rattlesnake Island, both of which were prominent landmarks First to harbor devlopment during the early 1900s.

water in "a bottle made of reeds tarred on the inside, from which we drank, and it is good" (Vizcaíno 1959:18).

In March, 1805, Santa Catalina was visited by the brig *Lelia Byrd* captained by William Shaler; the vessel returned again in May of the same year. According to Shaler the island was occupied by "about 150 men, women, and children" (Shaler 1935:47). The historian Hubert Howe Bancroft reported that in 1807 Santa Catalina was visited by another ship, the *O'Cain*, under the command of Jonathan Winship. According to Bancroft, the crew found 40 to 50 Indians living on the island, although it is not clear whether they represented the entire population of the island. The Indians offered the visitors "grain and vegetables," which might be an indication that agriculture had reached the island (see Bancroft 1886:84).

Unfortunately, despite the historical accounts and more than a century of relic hunting by antiquarians and scientific excavations by modern archaeologists, the site distribution and settlement patterns of the Catalina Gabrielino remain poorly understood. Coastal middens suggest the presence of communities or settlements where beaches have developed at the mouths of canyons. Such places include Avalon, White's Landing, Empire Landing, Isthmus Cove, Howland's Landing, Catalina Harbor, and Little Harbor. One early writer noted that "every cañon having a beach on the north coast . . . had its ancient town-site—some large, some small" (Holder 1910:27-28; Wlodarski 1982:Figure 1).

Numerous sites in the island's interior served a variety of special economic purposes such as soapstone quarrying, seed and plant food gathering, and the processing of meat from fish, shellfish, and sea-mammals (Cottrell et al. 1980; Bickford and Martz 1980; Rosenthal 1981:60-61; Rosenthal et al. 1988). Extensive steatite quarries were located near the present-day airport, and occupation sites existed in conjunction with some of these (Meighan and Rootenberg 1957; Rosen 1980; Reinman and Eberhart 1980; Williams and Rosenthal 1993).

Although early population estimates based upon archaeological data suggest populations for the island as great as 2,000 to 3,000 (Meighan and Johnston 1957:24; Gleason 1958:16), ethnographic data are not available to substantiate such estimates. A detailed

bibliography of Santa Catalina Island archaeology appears in Wlodarski (1982).

Reid recorded the name "Pineug-na" for Santa Catalina, but this spelling is likely a printer's error for *Pimugna* (Reid 1852:8). The name "Pimu" appears to have been applied to both the island and a settlement on the island (Heizer 1968:109, note 12). José Zalvidea reported the names "Pimú" and "Pimú'ŋa" for Santa Catalina, although he did not give names for any settlements on the island (Kroeber 1907:143; Harrington 1986:R102 F467, 850). A Juaneño consultant gave Kroeber the name "Pipimar" for Catalina (Kroeber 1907:144, 1925:621). In the present volume this name will be spelled *Pemuu'nga*. According to José Zalvidea "the isthmus is called Nájquqar" (Harrington 1986:R102 F850); this was probably also the name of the Gabrielino community once located at the isthmus.

SAN CLEMENTE ISLAND

San Clemente Island lies 20 miles south of Santa Catalina and approximately 57 miles from the mainland at its nearest point. This island, which is a restricted area under the jurisdiction of the United States Navy, is 21 miles in length, and although its width varies, it nowhere exceeds four miles. The area of the island is 57 square miles (McKusick and Warren 1959; Yatsko 1989).

The topography of San Clemente Island consists of six primary zones. The predominant topographic zone is the central plateau, which covers 40% of the island's surface. The second largest zone comprises the

U.S. Navy Photograph, Courtesy of the Natural Resources Office, NAS North Island
Fig. 16. San Clemente Island looking southeast. Although San Clemente is 21 miles long, nowhere does its width exceed 4 miles. The central plateau and the steep cliffs along the eastern shore are clearly visible in this photograph.

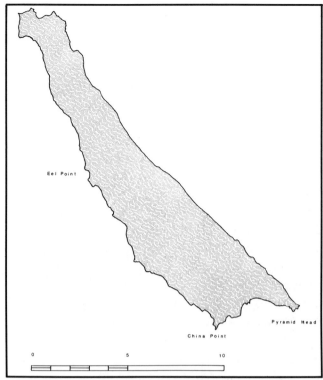

Map 13. San Clemente Island, known to the Gabrielino as *Kiinkepar*.

upland marine terraces, which are located along the western side of the island and account for another 34% of the island's area. A precipitous escarpment extends along the eastern margin of the island and accounts for another 11% of the surface area, while the northern, western, and southern coastlines are typified by a series of coastal terraces that comprise 8% of the island's surface. Canyons (located on the southwestern slopes of the island) and sand dunes account for another 7% (Yatsko 1990).

During one 15-year period (1962—1977) rainfall on San Clemente varied from 3.21 inches to 11.53 inches per year, with an average of about 5 inches or less per year. Water is generally available on the island from a number of ponds and springs and from natural tanks located in the canyons along the southwestern slope of the island (Holder 1910:156; McKusick and Warren 1959:110; Zahniser 1981:3-16; Yatsko 1990:7; Raab and Yatsko 1990:26). Native grasses on San Clemente are believed to have once reached a foot in height, and grasslands on the island were interspersed with trees and shrubs; however, the introduction of sheepherding around 1868 quickly decimated this vegetation. Today the original grasses have been replaced by introduced oats gone wild, and trees are reported to be extremely rare (McKusick and

Warren 1959:110; Hathaway and Greenwood 1981:27-28; Yatsko 1989:188-189).

The primary land animals on San Clemente are the island fox, the white-footed mouse, the island night lizard, and land snails. Middens on the island provide ample evidence that shellfish, fish, sea-mammals, birds, and foxes were important elements in the diet of the Indian inhabitants of the island (McKusick and Warren 1959:109-110).

In 1769, San Clemente was visited by the *San Antonio*, and Father Juan Vizcaíno recorded his observations, which include descriptions of the island and its Indian occupants. Approaching China Point on March 15, 1769, the padre observed "people who raised smoke," and passing Pyramid Head he saw "not a tree, only the grass was beginning to grow green" (Vizcaíno 1959:8). Two days later, on March 17, Vizcaíno wrote of San Clemente that "it is a rugged land, green, with many ravines cutting deep into the sea, and no trees, save in one huge ravine, which opens out on the beach in a small bay, where we could see small trees, and two or three Indians. They made a little smoke. Almost all the lower coast stood like a rampart, green against the hills" (Vizcaíno 1959:9-10).

During the following days the *San Antonio* remained in the vicinity of San Clemente, and the crew members traded with the Indians who paddled out to the ship in their plank canoes. Padre Vizcaíno used the opportunity to record his observations of these Indians, describing their fur robes, the cord they made from plant fiber, their plank canoes, and their fishing techniques (Vizcaíno 1959:11-16). These observations will be recounted in greater detail in Chapter 7.

In 1803, the Boston ship *Lelia Byrd* visited San Clemente and discovered 11 men, women, and children living in a cave and subsisting on baked fish. Although this small group may not have represented the island's entire population, the observation does suggest that San Clemente had experienced a severe population decline by the early years of the nineteenth century (Cleveland n.d.:194; Johnson 1988:5).

Culturally, San Clemente is believed to have been closely associated with Santa Catalina (Kroeber 1925:620). Fernando Librado, a Chumash consultant for Harrington, reported that San Clemente was occupied by a mixture of Gabrielino and Fernandeño (Hudson 1981:194). Data from the mission registers of San Gabriel, San Fernando, and the Plaza Church document marriages between people from the two islands, as well as examples of close relatives living on different islands. In addition, there exist instances where people born on one island (as reported in the baptismal registers) have relocated to the other island by the time their marriages are recorded (Johnson 1988:15).

San Clemente has been the focus of considerable archaeological research in recent years, including extensive resurveying of the island (Yatsko 1989). As a result of this work a new understanding of the settlement distribution patterns on San Clemente is emerging.

Radiocarbon dates demonstrate that the island has a history of occupation extending at least 10,000 years into the past (Salls 1990b:62). Eel Point, an important site located on the west coast of San Clemente, was occupied from as early as 7785 B.C. until the late prehistoric or early Mission Period. Data obtained from Eel Point demonstrate important adaptations in subsistence patterns which occurred during the ten-thousand-year span of the site. An early dependence upon shellfish, such as mussel and abalone, gradually gave way to an increase in fishing. The extensive exploitation of one particular species of fish, the sheephead, suggests the use of specialized techniques such as spear fishing. The remains of barracuda and other offshore species also demonstrate the use of watercraft (Salls 1990b).

Preliminary data from archaeological work on San Clemente suggest that the characteristic site type was the seasonally occupied individual household and that the family was the primary social unit on the island. Individual families engaged in a nomadic, foraging economy in which sites were occupied and abandoned on a seasonal basis (Yatsko 1989:198). Large, complex sites are also reported to extend over portions of the island's central spine. Based upon Father Juan Vizcaíno's account written in 1769, a number of settlements are believed to have been occupied between China Point and Pyramid Head at the eastern end of the island (Woodward 1959:xiv-xvi; Zahniser 1981:3-13).

Caves were utilized as shelters by the San Clemente Gabrielino, and perhaps the most interesting site is Big Dog Cave, located at the southern end of the island. Big Dog Cave is 70 feet wide at the mouth and 34 feet deep. Most important from an archaeological viewpoint, the cave contained a stratified archaeological deposit consisting of four distinct layers totalling 36 inches in depth.

Big Dog Cave was first excavated in 1939 by an expedition sponsored by the Natural History Museum of Los Angeles County (Woodward 1959:xvii, xxii, xxv). Included among the finds from this impressive site were a number of human and animal burials, two fragments of a plank canoe, arrow and harpoon fragments, fire drill fragments, stone knives hafted in wooden handles, shell artifacts, bone artifacts, and fragments of cloth that was woven at one of the mainland missions (McKusick and Warren 1959:128-136). The cave was re-excavated in 1985 by the Archaeological Field School at UCLA. A subsequent analysis of the fish remains recovered from the cave disclosed that 59% of the species taken by the islanders could be caught from the shore, while the remaining 41% required watercraft to reach the nearby kelp beds (Salls 1990a).

A number of the animal burials discovered in Big Dog Cave during the 1939 excavations were accompanied by offerings, providing evidence of ritual activities performed by the islanders. Included in these animal burials were a large dog wrapped in a robe of sea otter fur, a hen wrapped in fur and cord netting, and a fighting cock wrapped in tan and blue mission cloth. These burials were believed to have been interred by Indians living on San Clemente between 1780 and 1800 (Woodward 1941:151-152; McKusick and Warren 1959:135-136).

Important evidence of ritual activity was also discovered at Lemon Tank, an archaeological site situated on the central plateau not far from the eastern coast. Lemon Tank is located near the midpoint of

U.S. Navy Photograph, Courtesy of the Natural Resources Office, NAS North Island
Fig. 17. China Cove, located at the southeast end of San Clemente Island. Ethnohistorical accounts suggest that a number of Gabrielino settlements were located near the southeast shore of the island. This view is looking south.

Fig. 18. Big Dog Cave, located at the southern end of San Clemente Island. The cave was first excavated in 1939 during an expedition sponsored by the Natural History Museum of Los Angeles County. A number of human and animal burials were recovered in 1939, including that of a large dog wrapped in a robe of sea otter fur.

San Clemente, with ready access to most areas on the island. Basketry, fishing lines and netting, animal burials, and floral remains were recovered from the site, generally in an excellent state of preservation. More important, however, the site contained numerous cache pits, hearths, and post holes that showed evidence of important ritual activity (Eisentraut 1990).

Several of the cache pits discovered at Lemon Tank contained animal burials, including a dog, a fox, and two raptors, one of which was identified as a red-tailed hawk. The dog appears to have been buried with grave goods such as red pigment, asphaltum-impregnated basketry, and burned plant remains, suggesting it was ceremonially interred. Grave goods also accompanied the red-tailed hawk burial. Many of the artifacts found at the site, including "flower pot" mortars and pigment pots, may have been ceremonially broken. Caches of red maid seeds (*Calendrinia ciliata*) were stored inside containers made from two abalone (*Haliotis*) shells cupped together. Sometimes these seed caches included human teeth (Eisentraut 1990).

The archaeological evidence suggests that Lemon Tank may have been the site of the annual mourning ceremony held by the Gabrielino on San Clemente (the Gabrielino mourning ceremony is described in Chapter 8). Seed caches on San Clemente Island have been reported from only two other sites, the Ledge Site and the Old Airfield Site, both of which are also situated on the central plateau within view of Lemon Tank. Together these three sites may have formed an important ritual complex for the San Clemente Gabrielino (Eisentraut 1990).

There are presently too few data from San Clemente to attempt a population estimate, although the island is believed to have been occupied on a permanent, year-round basis (Zahniser 1981:3-16). Interestingly, the antiquarian Ralph Glidden suggested that San Clemente was the least populated of the Channel Islands on the basis of his failure to locate large numbers of burials (see Zahniser 1981:1-10).

The archaeology of San Clemente Island has been discussed in a number of important professional publications (Woodward 1941, 1959; McKusick and Warren 1959; Meighan 1983). Bibliographies of investigations and publications are also available (Zahniser 1981; Yatsko 1989).

Reid (1852:8) reported the name "Kinkipar" for San Clemente. This is substantiated by an entry from the mission register of San Gabriel which notes "Guinguina, ra. de la ysla [ranchería or village of the island]" (Merriam 1968:109). Manuel Santos reported to Harrington that "Kiηki . . . is [an] island in the sea. Call the people Kiηkijam. . . . They are pipĭmaram [although the term pipĭmaram properly refers to the Catalineños, it also appears to have been used during the early 1900s as a general term for the Gabrielino]" (Harrington 1986:R102 F475). In the present volume the name for San Clemente Island will be spelled *Kiinkepar*. As noted earlier in this chapter, *Kinki* or *Kinkipar* essentially duplicates the name *Kiinkenga*, the name of a community on the Palos Verdes Peninsula.

SAN NICOLAS ISLAND

San Nicolas is the most distant of the southern Channel Islands, lying 60 miles from the mainland. The island is about 9 miles in length, 3.5 miles in width, and 22 miles in area. Although the coastal regions are less than 400 feet above sea level, elevations near the center of the island can reach 900 feet (Schwartz, personal communication, 1989).

San Nicolas can be divided into three broad topographic zones. A broad, grassy plateau dominates the center of the island, while deeply eroded ravines characterize the coast along the northeast, east, and southeast shores. Sand dunes typify much of the western end of the island, especially near the coast (Schwartz, personal communication, 1989).

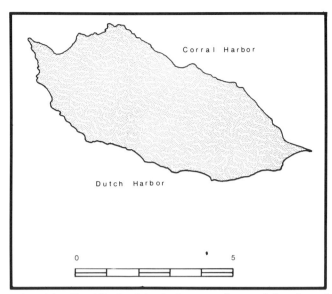

Map. 14. San Nicolas Island, the most distant of the channel islands occupied by the Gabrielino. The Gabrielino knew San Nicolas as *Xaraashnga*.

During Gabrielino times a large portion of San Nicolas was covered with grass and scrub growth, which at the west end of the island extended to within a quarter mile of the coast. The introduction of sheepherding in 1852 or 1853 quickly denuded the island, and by 1866 extensive sand dunes had begun to form (Jones 1969). Ranching on the island ended around 1941, and since that time the native vegetation has made a gradual comeback. By the time the author of the present volume made his first visit in late 1989, much of the island had regained a cover of vegetation.

Fresh water can be found at several springs in the northwest corner of San Nicolas. Land animals on San Nicolas are limited to the island fox, the white-footed mouse, the island night lizard, and the land snail (Meighan and Eberhart 1953:113-114; Schwartz, personal communication, 1989). Important marine food resources for the Nicoleño included seals, sea lions, sea otter, shellfish, fish, and marine birds (Meighan 1954).

Prime locations for Nicoleño communities appear to have been the coastal strip extending inland 200 yards from the shoreline and the island's central plateau (Meighan and Eberhart 1953:114). The occurrence of coastal settlements on sand dunes, a feature often reported on San Nicolas, may simply be the result of differential erosion which has worn down the soil surrounding the middens to a greater extent than the midden itself (Jones 1969:93).

Although early estimates of the island's Indian population based on archaeological data ranged from 1,000 to 2,000 inhabitants (Meighan and Eberhart 1953:119; Meighan 1954:23; Reinman 1962:13), these early estimates assumed that all of the sites on San Nicolas were occupied during a recent and fairly short span of time. Radiocarbon data now demonstrates that San Nicolas has been occupied for at least 8000 years (Raab and Yatsko 1990:18). Clearly, further work is needed before the population size and settlement patterns of San Nicolas can be understood.

One of the most intriguing sites on San Nicolas Island is the Cave of the Whales, a cavern located on the southwest shore, which the author was privileged to visit in 1990 and 1991. The Cave of the Whales has a special magic that is unmatched by any other Gabrielino site. The cave lies at the end of a narrow inlet situated between a rookery of elephant seals and another of sea lions. The main chamber extends 35 feet into the island and reaches a height of nine feet near its center. Petroglyphs (rock carvings) of sharks or killer whales decorate a large boulder near the cave entrance and the east wall of the cavern.

Further inside, the cave takes on a dark, eerie aspect. The crashing of waves echoes from the chamber's damp, mossy walls. In the spring, the barking of sea lions adds to the din; occasionally a lone sea lion pup wanders into the cavern. At the rear of the main chamber lies a small, crumbling stone panel decorated with pictographs executed in black paint. Once again the subject of the art is killer whales, their faint outlines still visible on the sandstone surface (see Rozaire and Kritzman 1960).

Another unusual feature on San Nicolas is the Spring Site, located on the island's northwest shore. The site is named after a freshwater spring that seeps from a sandstone exposure located at the base of a large sand dune. The freshwater that drips from this spring runs out onto a sandstone shelf that varies from 2 to 12 feet in width. A shallow groove carved into the surface of the soft sandstone channels the fresh water to the edge of the shelf. Here the lip of the shelf has been undercut so that a tarred water bottle could collect the fresh water trickling from the channel.

The artificial groove, which is more than 40 feet in length, actually consists of two primary channels, one 38 feet long, the other 5 feet long, and a number of small feeder channels. A test performed on this

U.S. Navy Photograph, Courtesy of the Natural Resources Office, NAWS Point Mugu
Fig. 19. San Nicolas Island looking northwest. The broad central plateau is clearly visible in the photograph.

Fig. 21. A petroglyph located near the entrance to the Cave of the Whales. The erect dorsal fin suggests a shark or killer whale. Photograph by author.

Fig. 20. The Cave of the Whales, located on the southern shore of San Nicolas Island. The cave lies at the end of a narrow inlet and is occasionally flooded during periods of exceptionally high tides. The entrance to the cave is located to the right of center in this photograph. Photograph by author.

Fig. 22. The Spring Site, on the northwest shore of San Nicolas, view looking east. The long, narrow groove carved into the surface of the rock (to the right of center) captures fresh water seeping from the base of the hill and channels it to the collection point where it can be captured in a container. Photograph by author.

water system in 1962 demonstrated that the flow of freshwater was sufficient to fill a 16-ounce jar in one minute, 35 seconds (Reinman 1962:12). During the author's visit in 1991 the flow filled a 16-ounce measuring cup in six minutes.

A number of archaeological reports on San Nicolas Island have been published; a general synthesis of the work done on the island is also available (Schwartz and Martz 1992). Further information can be found in the bibliography of the present volume (see Meighan and Eberhart 1953; Meighan 1954; Rozaire 1959; Reinman and Townsend 1960; Heizer and Elsasser 1961; Reinman 1962). Today San Nicolas is a restricted area under the control of the United States Navy.

San Nicolas is perhaps best known as having

once been the home of Juana María, also known as the "Lone Woman of San Nicolas," a Nicoleño who was accidentally abandoned on the island in 1835 when the Indians were removed to the mainland. She lived alone on the island until 1853, when she was taken to Santa Barbara. Unfortunately, she became ill shortly after arriving on the mainland, perhaps due to a dietary change imposed by her move. She was christened Juana María on her deathbed and buried in the cemetery at Mission Santa Barbara. Her tragic, yet heroic, story is the basis for the novel *Island of the Blue Dolphins* by Scott O'Dell. The story of Juana María will be told in greater detail in Chapter 11.

According to Harrington's Chumash consultant Fernando Librado, the Nicoleño people originally came from Santa Catalina Island and were Gabrielino

Fig. 23. Another view of the Spring Site (see Figure 22). Photograph by author.

(Hudson 1981:194). A number of Gabrielino names for San Nicolas have been reported. Librado reported that "minar is the Gabrieleño name for San Nicolas Island. [It] means 'only one who would know where good water was in island, but yet good water.' For the water shot up a foot and a half at low tide, and then only" (Harrington 1986:R102 F480).

José Zalvidea stated that "Harásvit" was "otra sierra adendro del agua near pimú'ngna," that is, "another mountain in the water near pimú'ŋa [Catalina]," leading Harrington to conclude incorrectly that *Harasvit* was "surely and clearly San Clemente Island" (Harrington 1986:R102 F462). However, Kroeber (1925:635) reported that the Chumash pronunciation of "Haras-nga" was "Ghalas-at," and *Ghalas-at* was the Chumash name for San Nicolas Island (Kroeber 1925:635). José Zalvidea also gave the names "*Xárvo*" and "*Xárásŋa*" for San Nicolas. According to José, "the other island beyond Santa

Catalina is called Xárvo," and he went on to say that the name *Xarásŋa* "means the same as 'stony.'" Harrington noted that "[It] is the etym. [etymology] which he gives for Xárvo" (Harrington 1986:R102 F473). Reid reported the name "Harasg-na" in his list of Gabrielino placenames; however, he gave no locational information (Reid 1852:8; see also Heizer 1968:110-111, note 24). Other possible names for San Nicolas include "*Jalashat*" and "*Ha-la-ca't*." In reporting the latter name, H. W. Henshaw noted that "magicians' stones [come] from this island" (Heizer 1955:198). In the present volume the Gabrielino name for San Nicolas will be spelled *Xaraashnga*.

SUMMARY

The Gabrielino occupation of the southern Channel Islands may have come rather late in California prehistory. Prior to the arrival of the Uto-Aztecan-speaking Gabrielino, the southern Channel Islands may have been held by Hokan-speaking Chumash peoples.

Santa Barbara Island's small size (about one square mile) and limited water supply restricted Gabrielino occupation to temporary visits used primarily to gather lithic materials. Archaeological work conducted on the island until 1980 had identified 15 sites, including a workshop for the production of stone tools. Fernando Librado, a Chumash consultant who worked with Harrington, reported *'Ichunash* as the Chumash name for Santa Barbara; according to Librado, the Gabrielino also referred to the island by this name.

Santa Catalina, the southern Channel Island that is nearest to the mainland, lies approximately 21 miles from the Palos Verdes Peninsula. It is also the largest of the southern islands, encompassing 75 square miles. During Gabrielino times water was available on the island in at least a half-dozen springs and creeks. Some acorn groves may have existed on Catalina; however, the primary food resources were fish, shellfish, and sea-mammals.

Santa Catalina was visited by several Spanish explorers including Juan Rodríguez Cabrillo (in 1542) and Sebastián Vizcaíno (in 1602). In his account of the latter voyage, Father Antonio de la Ascensión described a Gabrielino *yovaar*, or sacred enclosure, which the explorers observed near Isthmus Cove. In 1769, the island was visited by the *San Antonio*, a supply ship for the Portolá Expedition. Father Juan

Vizcaíno's account of this visit provides important ethnographic data on Gabrielino fishing and seafaring technologies.

Archaeological sites reportedly once existed at the mouths of most of the island's canyons opening onto the beaches. Avalon, White's Landing, Empire Landing, Isthmus Cove, Howland's Landing, Catalina Harbor, and Little Harbor are specifically reported to have had sites. Sites located in the island's interior served a variety of special economic pursuits including soapstone quarrying, seed and plant food gathering, and meat processing. The Gabrielino name for Santa Catalina was *Pemuu'nga*. José Zalvidea gave the name of the isthmus as *Nájquqar*; this was probably also the name of the community situated at that location.

San Clemente Island lies 20 miles south of Santa Catalina and approximately 57 miles from the mainland. The total area of the island is 57 square miles. Water is generally available on San Clemente in a number of ponds and springs and from natural tanks in canyons located along the island's southwestern slopes. Archaeological remains indicate that the primary food resources for the Gabrielino of San Clemente were fish, shellfish, sea-mammals, marine birds and foxes.

San Clemente was visited in 1769 by the *San Antonio*; the vessel remained near the island for several days while crew members traded with the Gabrielino, receiving lengths of cordage and robes made from woven otter fur in exchange for articles of European clothing. Important observations concerning the islanders and their culture were recorded by Father Juan Vizcaíno during this visit. San Clemente was visited again in 1803 by the *Lelia Byrd*, a vessel out of Boston. By the time of this visit the island population seems to have declined dramatically.

Archaeological evidence indicates that San Clemente has been occupied for at least 10,000 years. During the Gabrielino period the island is believed to have maintained extensive social, political, and economic ties to Santa Catalina. A number of important archaeological sites have been investigated on San Clemente including Big Dog Cave, Lemon Tank, the Ledge Site, and the Old Airfield Site. Each of these locations offered important data regarding Gabrielino ritual and mortuary activities. Big Dog Cave is also one of the few archaeological sites in the Gabrielino territory with a clearly stratified deposit, each strata relating to a phase in the cultural history of the cave.

The Gabrielino name for San Clemente Island was *Kiinkepar*; this may also be the name of a community located on the island.

San Nicolas Island is the most distant of the four southern Channel Islands, lying 60 miles from the mainland. San Nicolas is 22 square miles in area; of the four islands held by the Gabrielino only Santa Barbara Island is smaller. Fresh water is available at several springs located in the northwest portion of the island. Important Gabrielino food resources on San Nicolas resemble those of the other islands and included fish, shellfish, sea-mammals, and marine birds. Nicoleño communities appear to have been located along the shoreline and on the island's central plateau.

One of the most intriguing of the archaeological sites on San Nicolas is the Cave of the Whales. The cave receives its name from the petroglyphs and pictographs that decorate its walls. Sharks and killer whales appear to be the most prominent of the creatures depicted in the images that have survived the natural erosional processes of the cave.

Another important archaeological site on San Nicolas is the Spring Site, located on the island's northwest shore. The site takes its name from a freshwater spring at the base of a large sand dune. Water seeping from the spring enters a shallow groove that has been carved into the surface of the rock shelf at the base of the dune. This artificial groove then channels the water to a spot where it can be conveniently captured in a container.

San Nicolas is perhaps best known as the home of Juana María, a Nicoleño woman who was stranded on the island for 18 years between 1835 and 1853. During Gabrielino times San Nicolas may also have been the primary source of the ritual implements known as *tooshawt* stones. Several different names have been offered for San Nicolas including *minar* and *Xaraashnga*; the latter name may mean stony.

The islands of Santa Catalina, San Clemente, San Nicolas, and Santa Barbara were the most distant outposts of the Gabrielino homeland, yet each was an integral part of the political and economic framework that united the First Angelinos. Throughout this homeland a sophisticated social organization evolved

and functioned under the leadership of an elite group
of *tomyaars* and shamans.   Through their collective
wisdom the Gabrielino prospered to become one of the
most influential Indian societies of southern California.
The organization and structure of this complex society
are explored in depth in Chapter 6.

CHAPTER 6

THE FABRIC OF GABRIELINO SOCIETY

Gabrielino society was a complex blend of political and economic institutions that functioned to provide a stable social structure and minimize incidents of violence and warfare. Several levels of social organization existed within this system, including the family, the lineage, and the community. Ritual, social, and economic alliances cut across geographical and political divisions to integrate lineages and communities at a regional level. Gabrielino society was also organized into hierarchical social classes distinguished by ancestry, wealth, and political influence.

KINSHIP ORGANIZATION

Gabrielino society was composed of numerous kinship groups known as lineages, each of which consisted of a number of individual, related families sharing a common ancestor. Membership in a lineage was traced through the father and allowed an individual to claim use rights over hunting and gathering territories owned by the lineage. Typically such areas included oak groves, fields of seed-bearing plants, hunting grounds and shellfish beds. Trespassing upon lineage-owned territories by a foreign group was a serious offense and a potential cause of conflict (Bean 1972b:xvi; Bean and Smith 1978:547).

The Gabrielino lineage was capable of being split and reorganized, and this "segmented" lineage organization served as an important mechanism of territorial expansion. In fact, it may have been a prime factor in the eventual expansion of the Uto-Aztecans into southern California (see Bean 1972b:xvii, xviii). When a lineage population became too great for the surrounding territory to support, or food supplies became diminished as a result of environmental change, the lineage divided, one group leaving to settle in a new location (Bean 1972a:90). The departing group might enact deliberate changes in language and customs to foster an independent identity. According to Father Boscana, "as they were to change their place of residence they were necessarily obliged to alter their mode of speech as well as their customs, in order to become a distinct nation" (Boscana 1933:85).

Lineages were grouped into two separate divisions, termed "moieties" by anthropologists. Organization into moieties seems to have evolved after the Uto-Aztecans entered southern California and existed among the Cahuilla and Serrano as well as the Gabrielino, although the Gabrielino may have been the originators of the institution (Bean 1972b:xv; Strong 1929:344).

The importance of moiety organization stems from the influence it had upon ritual and economic interaction among lineages. Every lineage belonged to one of the two moieties, which were named either "wildcat" or "coyote" (Harrington 1942:32, items 1242-1243). Because each moiety possessed only a portion of the components necessary for a ritual performance, components which might include songs, ritual paraphernalia, and other items, it was necessary to bring two or more lineages together (at least one from each moiety) for a successful ceremony. In turn, these gatherings offered opportunities for the redistribution of food supplies over a wide geographic area, thereby strengthening the economic base of the entire region. These festivals were reciprocal, that is, lineages took turns hosting them, and the ritual-political-economic alliances that resulted from this system are what anthropologists call "ritual congregations" (Bean 1972a:151-153).

REGIONAL DIALECTS

There is considerable evidence that the Gabrielino spoke three or more regional dialects of the same Uto-Aztecan language. José Zalvidea reported that "all the villages and tribes had somewhat different languages and dialects" (Harrington 1986:R102 F007). Although there were distinct differences in dialect, the speakers could nonetheless readily communicate with one another. As José de los Santos Juncos observed, "the San Gabriel Indians talk heavier, the San Fernando Indians talk lighter, but they understand each other" (Harrington 1986:R102 F009).

According to the missionaries at San Fernando, the Indians at that mission spoke "three distinct languages," while the priests at San Gabriel reported that "four distinct dialects are spoken corresponding to the four directions of its location. One is called Kokomcar; another Guiquitamcar; the third, Carbonamga; and last, Simbanga" (Geiger and Meighan 1976:19). Kroeber identified *Guiquitamcar* as Kitanemuk, a non-Gabrielino language of a neighboring group of the same name, while *Simbanga* may be the language spoken in the vicinity of *Shevaanga* (Kroeber 1925:621). The origin and location of the other dialects has not been established.

On the basis of this and other ethnographic data it seems reasonable to suggest that in addition to Fernandeño, which was the Gabrielino dialect spoken in the San Fernando Valley, there was a second dialect, *Shevaanga*, that was spoken in the interior region near San Gabriel. A third dialect may have been spoken in the coastal areas near San Pedro and on some of the Channel Islands. Harrington's consultant Felicitas Serrano Montaño reported that "the San Pedro Indians talk different from those of San Gabriel" (Harrington 1986:R102 F007). A fourth dialect may have been spoken on San Nicolas Island, although there are not enough data available to draw a firm conclusion (Kroeber 1925:633; Munro 1994).

Although there is not enough information presently available to determine whether these dialects corresponded to any political divisions among the Gabrielino, it is interesting to note that an enduring pattern of warfare and feuding is reported to have existed between the Indians of the interior near Whittier Narrows and those living closer to the coast (Bolton 1926:219-220; Temple 1959:159-160). Father Francisco Palou, writing in 1773, observed that the Indians living near Misión Vieja in the Whittier Narrows region

> are very poor, on account of the small crops of wild seeds they receive from the plains and on account of the poor results of the chase [it is unclear whether this lack of food was a temporary, i.e., due to drought]. They lack also the aid from the fisheries, since the beach is about eight leagues distant [or about 12 miles; a Spanish league was about 1 1/2 miles. See Webb (1952:9, note 7)]. Though the valleys are covered with large rancherias, these wage continual wars among themselves which makes it impossible to go to the beach to fish . . . at the shore. This shore is the roadstead [harbor] of San Pedro . . . (Engelhardt 1927a:19).

A similar pattern of enmity is clearly reflected in the story told by José de los Santos Juncos of the war between the shamans of *'AXaarronga* and those of the coast, as recounted in Chapter 3.

THE *TOMYAAR*

At a local level, each Gabrielino community was composed of one or more lineages united under the leadership of a chief known as the *tomyaar*, who was typically the chief of the oldest or largest resident lineage (Taylor 1860a; Harrington 1942:32, item 1263; 1986:R102 F642; Temple 1960:166; Bean and Smith 1978:543-544). The *tomyaar* was the focus of the religious and secular life of the lineage and community, serving as chief administrator, fiscal officer, religious leader, legal arbitrator, and commander-in-chief. *Tomyaars* were usually 30 to 35 years of age when elevated to office (Bean and Smith 1978:544), and upon assuming their responsibilities they adopted as their new name the name of the community "followed by *ie*, with sometimes the alteration of one or more final letters" (Reid 1852:9). Although Gabrielino men generally went nude, *tomyaars* may have worn ankle-length capes of animal fur as a mark of office (Hudson and Blackburn 1985:43-56).

DESCENT

The position of *tomyaar* was hereditary, descending to the eldest son upon his father's death or, in the absence of a direct descendent, to the nearest male relative. In extreme situations the firstborn son of the *tomyaar*'s daughter might be proclaimed chief at birth, although during his childhood the nearest male relative would serve as regent (Boscana 1933:42; Harrington 1942:33, items 1264,1265). Female *tomyaars* have been reported for the Gabrielino as well. José de los Santos Juncos told of "old Luisa who died in Los Angeles long ago [and who] was a capitana at San Gabriel and sang and danced and could have told . . . all the Indian placenames" (Boscana 1933:83-85; Harrington 1942:33, item 1268, 1986:R102 F654).

PROVINCIAL LEADERS

Some Gabrielino *tomyaars* may have served as provincial leaders, exercising authority over several communities simultaneously. Provincial leaders are believed to have existed among the Chumash, and ethnographic information collected from the Gabrielino suggests that the *tomyaar* of *'Ahwiinga* may have held such a position (Hudson and Underhay 1978:27; see the discussion of *'Ahwiinga* in Chapter 3). According to data gathered by Harrington, during the mission period a Fernandeño chief named "Odon . . . was the chief of all the Indians of the SW end of the valley. Rogerio . . . was chief at San Fernando" (Harrington 1986:R106 F111). Although data confirming the existence of Gabrielino provincial capitals remains tenuous, it can be speculated that such political centers might have developed as lineages "budded off" from parent communities and formed new settlements that later grew in size and population (see Galdikas-Brindamour 1970:129).

DUTIES OF THE *TOMYAAR*

Among the most important of the *tomyaar*'s secular responsibilities was the management of the economic affairs of the lineage or community, especially the collection and redistribution of surplus food. It was the *tomyaar*'s duty to maintain the food stores from which the poor would be fed, and mismanagement of these reserves was a serious offense that might be punished by death (Boscana 1933:39). Hunters regularly deposited a portion of their kill with the *tomyaar*; those who collected plant and seed foods also contributed some of their gatherings to the reserves. Often a *tomyaar* had two or more wives whose labors were of great value in maintaining food stores (Boscana 1933:44; Fages 1937:21).

The *tomyaar* also managed the ritual exchanges

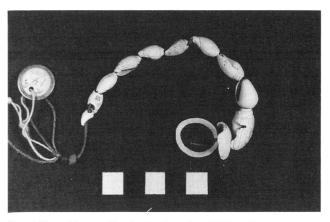

Natural History Museum of Los Angeles County No. A9464.71-395

Fig. 24. A string of whole *Olivella* shell beads; the spire at the end of each shell has been removed to create a hole for stringing the bead. These beads were collected at Malaga Cove on Santa Monica Bay. Photograph by author.

Natural History Museum of Los Angeles County No. A9464.71-394

Fig. 25. *Olivella* disc beads were manufactured by removing a portion of the shell and carefully chipping or grinding it to the proper shape and dimension; a hole was drilled in the bead for stringing. According to Harrington, the Gabrielino used both whole *Olivella* shell beads and *Olivella* disc beads as currency. These beads were collected at Malaga Cove. Photograph by author.

of shell-bead money that occurred between his community and other lineages and communities. Networks of shell-bead exchange existed between the Gabrielino, Cahuilla, Serrano, Chumash, Salinans, and others (Bean 1972a:152-153; 1974:17), and one of the oldest of these networks once linked all the Cahuilla, Serrano, Luiseño, and Gabrielino lineages from the San Gorgonio Pass to the Pacific Ocean (Strong 1929:98). In fact, archaeological evidence suggests that shell-bead exchange between the southern Channel Islands and the adjacent mainland coast of Orange County was occurring as long ago as 5,000 years (Howard and Raab 1993).

Among the Cahuilla it has been reported that strings of shell-bead money were sent out to guest communities by a lineage planning a mourning ceremony. Any lineage that did not receive such an invitation could attend by sending a string of beads to the host. In turn, when the visiting lineages held their own ceremonies they would invite their former hosts (Bean 1972a:137). Failure to abide by the rules of this reciprocal exchange could lead to serious conflict, and war often resulted "when a chief neglected to return the customary present at their festivities" (Boscana 1933:69). Other items that were used in such ritual exchanges included ceremonial staffs decorated with quail and eagle feathers, and wooden wands inlaid with shell and tipped with quartz crystals (Hudson and Blackburn 1986:252-264).

The *tomyaar* used his ability to support multiple wives to forge alliances with chiefly or wealthy families from other communities, often cementing these pacts by marrying the daughter of the allied chief (Bean 1974:25). In times of war these close ties with outside groups provided important allies, while during periods of drought or food shortage they provided ready avenues for the exchange and distribution of surplus food. The *tomyaar* also served as final arbitrator in the resolution of legal disputes and as war leader during periods of inter-community conflict (Reid 1852:15-16; Boscana 1933:43; Fages 1937:21). As religious leader the *tomyaar* managed the ritual interaction between his lineage or community and the supernatural world, it being his duty to pre-serve and maintain the ritual implements stored in the "sacred bundle," (a length of reed matting in which ceremonial objects were wrapped) and to schedule the dates for religious celebrations (Boscana 1933:43; Bean and Smith 1978:544; Harrington 1986:R105 F99; see Bean 1972a:88-89 for a discussion of the sacred bundle among the Cahuilla).

THE *TOMYAAR*'S AUTHORITY

The *tomyaar*'s prestige and authority derived in large measure from his knowledge of, and access to, supernatural power (Bean 1972a:105, 1975). Such power was potentially available to anyone who possessed the ability to use it, and this ability could be innate or acquired. An individual could acquire supernatural power in a number of ways: he could be instructed by a supernatural power-giver, that is, a supernatural being; he could be instructed by ritual specialists; he could have such power "put in" by someone who already possessed supernatural power;

or he could inherit or purchase ritual paraphernalia and so obtain the power it conferred. In addition, power could be obtained from certain sacred locations where it resided (Bean 1975).

The *tomyaar* had access to all of these avenues for acquiring power. As he was descended from a line of leaders, some ability to handle power was inborn. In addition, he had access to supernatural "power-givers" through his authority as ceremonial leader. The *tomyaar* was instructed by the ritual specialists of the community, he consorted with the most powerful shamans, he maintained the sacred bundle of ritual paraphernalia for the community, and he had the wealth to purchase additional items of ritual equipment. Furthermore, the *tomyaar*'s home was located adjacent to the *yovaar*, the most sacred and powerful location within the community, and he was one of the few individuals in the community privileged to enter the sacred enclosure.

The *tomyaar*'s authority was further enhanced by his association with a number of supernatural beings. This association is apparent in the sacred oral literature as well as in Gabrielino rituals and extended to other members of his family as well. Both the chief and his eldest son bore the title *tomyaar*, which may have been derived from *Taamet*, the name of the solar deity, while his eldest daughter bore the title *Maniisar*, derived from "Maanet," the name of the deity associated with the hallucinogenic *Datura* plant used in puberty ceremonies (Hudson and Blackburn 1978:228).

The *tomyaar* was linked through Gabrielino ritual with the legendary "First Chief" *Wewyoot* and the supernatural being Eagle (Kroeber 1925:624). A missionary from San Fernando reported that "the first Indian settlers came here from the north and were led here by a captain general who they declare lives on an island and to whom they attribute life without beginning or end" (Geiger and Meighan 1976:93, answer from Mission San Gabriel). Reid wrote of "a *remarkably clever, industrious man*, chief of a large tribe . . . who, when dying, told his people that he intended becoming an eagle, and that he bequeathed them his *feathers*, from henceforth to be employed at their feasts and ceremonies. Feasts are in consequence held *in honor of his memory*; and great reverence is shown the bird" (Reid 1852: 20).

Wewyoot was a central figure in the sacred oral literature of the Uto-Aztecans throughout southern California. The Luiseño knew him as *Wiyot*, while to the Cahuilla and the Cupeño he was the creator-god *Mukat*. In the Gabrielino creation stories he was descended from the Earth-Mother and was a dynamic, powerful leader whose reign ended when his followers assassinated him by poisoning, alleging that he had grown too old to govern, or that he had abused his authority by becoming ruthless and cruel. Although the Earth-Mother attempted to cure her son with a special remedy she prepared in a large shell, her efforts were thwarted when Coyote (always a mischievous figure in Gabrielino oral literature) overturned the shell while the medicine was fermenting in the sunlight. *Wewyoot*'s followers placed his corpse on a pyre but Coyote, who had been sent away lest he try to devour the dead body, leapt upon the pyre, tore free the heart, and ran off to consume it (Boscana 1933:27-35; Harrington 1933:116-124, note 39).

In ritual performances the *tomyaar* often served as an intermediary with the supernatural world by assuming the identity of Eagle. In such performances the *tomyaar* wore a ceremonial skirt sewn from the feathers of an eagle and performed dances which symbolized a soul's magical flight into the afterworld. The feathers for the ceremonial skirt were obtained from an eagle that was sacrificed at the Eagle Killing Ceremony, a ceremony that, according to tradition, was first held following the death of *Wewyoot* (Strong 1929:309; Boscana 1933:57; Merriam 1955; Bean and Smith 1978:544; see Chapter 8 for a further discussion of the Eagle Killing Ceremony).

THE INSTALLATION RITUAL

The *tomyaar*'s role as mediator with the supernatural world was vividly portrayed in the Gabrielino installation ritual. Preparations for the festival began weeks in advance with the collection of large amounts of food. Invitations were delivered to neighboring chiefs as well as the inhabitants of nearby communities, and on the day before the ceremony the leaders of these settlements met and pledged their support to the new leader in his office. Criers then went throughout the community to announce the upcoming ceremony (Boscana 1933:41).

The actual installation ceremony may have been held at night, as it was among the Luiseño (Kroeber 1925:688). The new chief, his body painted black with ash from a charred feather, was enrobed in the feather skirt, and a band of human hair was tied

around his head. Attached to this band was "a thin piece of wood, about half a yard in length, sometimes of a shape similar to the blade of a sword and often rounded like a wire . . . which they adorned with feathers of the hawk, the crow, and other birds" (Boscana 1933:41; Harrington 1933:157, note 109; see also Hudson and Blackburn 1985:119-123).

Once clothed in the ritual costume the *tomyaar* entered the *yovaar* and began his ceremonial dance, accompanied by singers who chanted to the music of turtle-shell rattles. The visiting leaders attending the ceremony joined the dance, and the new *tomyaar* continued until fatigue overcame him. When the ceremony concluded, the new leader was acknowledged as *tomyaar*, and a feast of three or four days duration was held (Boscana 1933:42).

A similar ceremony was held upon the "introduction" of a *tomyaar*'s son to the community. The young man was painted black and red and dressed in the feather skirt and crown. The future leader then danced until exhausted, all the time accompanying himself with a turtle-shell rattle while singers performed. When the youth was too tired to continue, one of the shamans held him on his shoulders and continued dancing until the ceremony ended (Boscana 1933:60).

THE COUNCIL OF ELDERS

The *tomyaar* was aided in his religious and secular duties by a Council of Elders, which consisted of the leaders of the lineages resident in the community, as well as other wealthy and influential individuals. The Council of Elders, which normally comprised men over 40 years of age, advised the *tomyaar* on important issues such as declarations of war. Members were often relatives of the *tomyaar*. It was not unusual, in fact, for the *tomyaar* himself to have served on the council before assuming office. Council positions were hereditary and descended from father to son (Bean 1974:26).

Important members of the Council of Elders included an "assistant cult chief," or *paxaa'*, who functioned as an announcer, treasurer, and general assistant, and who delivered moral lectures to the community. Other members included a *Maanet* official who was responsible for preparing *maanet*, the hallucinogenic *Datura* drink that was administered during puberty rituals; a firetender for ritual gatherings; a rabbit drive official; messengers; and storytellers (Harrington 1942:33, items 1295-1296, 1298, 1300, 1308, 1310; 1986:R105 F388).

Reid wrote that "boys were trained to carry messages from one chief to another. . . . It required a retentive memory." Elsewhere he noted that "a small string of buckskin was tied around the neck of those who were swift of foot" (Reid 1852:37, 40). Specially chosen boys were trained as storytellers by the *tomyaar*. It was the duty of the storyteller to memorize the oral literature of the community and be able to repeat it word for word, thus preserving the historical, traditional, and sacred knowledge of the community (Heizer 1968:118-119, note 54).

Another important official, the *Taakwa*, was responsible for managing the elaborate mourning ceremonies and for distributing food after the communal hunts (Bean and Smith 1978:544; Harrington 1942:33, items 1297-1297a; 1986:R105 F388). The *Taakwa* also played a critical role in the funeral ceremonies that followed the death of a *tomyaar*. According to Father Boscana,

> they had amongst them certain individuals who pretended to be descendants of the Coyote, eaters of human flesh [but] not as the cannibals. . . . Whenever a captain, or one of the *puplem* [the religious or shamanic officials], died, they sent for the Eno who was thus called before he officiated in his duties, and afterwards *tacue*, signifying "an eater." Having arrived at the place where they had placed the body, he immediately cut off a large piece from the neck and the back, near the shoulder, and consumed the flesh in its raw state. . . . This was always done in commemoration of the feat performed by the Coyote upon the body of the great captain, Ouiot (Boscana 1933:62-63).

Later in his account Father Boscana explains that this ritual was performed out of devotion to the dead leader and allowed his spirit to rise to "the heaven of stars," and "if it happened that he did not eat of them . . . then they did not go to the stars but to another place, to which they were destined by Chinigchinich" (Boscana 1933:77).

GABRIELINO SHAMANISM

Shamans occupied a pivotal role in Gabrielino society and were an integral part of the political, economic, legal, moral, and religious affairs of every community. Among many California Indian groups the shaman was the principal doctor, psychotherapist, philosopher, and intellectual of society, and he served as an important mediator with the supernatural world (Bean 1976). Like the *tomyaar*, the shaman owed his authority in large part to his possession of supernatural power, and it was not unusual for the chief himself to be an important shaman (Bean 1974:25, 1976). Reid told of a *tomyaar* from Santa Catalina Island named Canoa who was "accounted a great wizard," and another from the community of *Muuhonga* "who was a great wizard and enchanter" (Reid 1852:27, 55). Among the Gabrielino a woman could become a shaman, and according to Father Boscana there were "men, and also females, who are believed to possess the power of enchantment to such a degree that no one can withstand their powers" (Boscana 1933:61). A female shaman might achieve considerable power and influence, as illustrated by a shaman named Toypurina who led a revolt against Mission San Gabriel in 1785 (Temple 1958; see Chapter 10 for details on Toypurina's Revolt).

TYPES OF SHAMANS

Shamans were ranked according to the amount of power they could demonstrate through curing, transforming themselves into other life forms such as bears and wolves, divination, and control of natural and supernatural phenomena (Bean 1976). According to Harrington, there existed four primary categories of shamans, each possessing varying degrees of power and skill. The most powerful of these "has his medicine . . . within him, and he can extract this medicine through his mouth in an instant and use it for killing anything" (Harrington 1933:195, note 199). Shamans of this category were believed capable of transforming themselves into were-animals (Bean 1976); Reid wrote that they "changed themselves into the form of divers [sic] animals," and "the transmigration of the souls of wizards . . . into the bodies of animals, particularly of the Bear, is firmly believed in" (Reid 1852:21, 32).

Harrington's Gabrielino notes contain a number of accounts describing shamans who transformed themselves into bears. José de los Santos Juncos told of a shaman named Ramon Valencia who was an

Indio de S. G. [Indian of San Gabriel]. Muy hechicero [a great sorcerer]. He turned into a bear at times & went in mts. [mountains] or anywhere para matar res [to kill cattle]. . . .

One time he went up [the] other side of Sandy Sloop. . . . He was looking at res [cattle] near the cienega. . . . He went like people—in human form looking to see where he would find a res to get & then he would turn oso [bear] & catch it secretly. . . .

A big oso del monte [mountain bear] came out on him. He seized 2 stones & when [the] bear was near V. [Valencia] turned [into a] bear and sprang on him & the two grappled and . . . V. hit [the] other bear with a stone in [the] head . . . and [the] bear . . . left him grunting for his head was broken. . . . V. killed a res as soon as it grew dark & carried the meat home in his carrying net. Thus he did the whole time.

All the Mexicans got to know him & all the Ind's [Indians] feared him. . . . Wherever he went the Ind's gave him atole, pinole, wine, all, for they feared him (Harrington 1986:R105 F562).

Another Harrington consultant described a shaman's transformation into a bear with the clarity of a snapshot. The incident involved a messenger named Avila. "Rain was threatening. And they watched him as he departed & he was galloping & he was already a bear as he went out of sight" (Harrington 1986:R103 F703).

The island shamans were held in special awe. It was believed that these shamans lived 200 or 300 years and were strong enough to bend tough trees (Roberts 1933:4). According to José de los Santos Juncos the "island Ind's [Indians] were most brujos [the greatest magicians], [they] used lobos del mar to kill people [lobos del mar—literally sea wolves, the Spanish term for sea lions. See Venegas 1759:276; also Harrington 1986:R102 F601]. People here used yerbas [herbs] but [the] islanders were [the] worst hechiceros [sorcerers]" (Harrington 1986:R104 F005). These shamans were also believed to have the power to talk to the ocean and calm the waves during channel crossings (Harrington 1986:R104 F40).

The second category of shaman consisted of men who used preparations of herbs, magical paraphernalia, effigies, or painted figures to achieve their ends (Harrington 1933:195-196, note 199). For example, among the Chumash Indians, and probably the Gabrielino also, a distinction was recognized between shamans who could actually transform themselves into bears, and those who merely used a magical bear costume to achieve their ends (Blackburn 1975:40; Hudson and Blackburn 1985:154-158). The third type of shaman consisted of individuals specializing in the use of second sight, while the fourth was the mesmerizer or hypnotist (Harrington 1933:195-196, note 199).

SHAMANIC ASSOCIATIONS

California Indian shamans increased and consolidated their political influence by organizing themselves into associations that cut across lineage boundaries and provided a regional framework of religious and political authority. Through these organizations shamans controlled the recruiting, testing, and training of candidates and established rules of conduct for their profession. Shamanic associations provided an important check on the power of the shamans and prevented abuses by unscrupulous individuals. Members found guilty of abusing their authority might lose their professional standing; in severe cases punishment might include execution (Bean 1976). The importance of this "self-policing" authority is made evident by Reid's comment that "if a seer or wizard . . . was known or suspected of having made away with any one, the chief had no jurisdiction over him, because he conversed with the *Great Spirit*. But other seers could do him the damage they saw fit" (Reid 1852:16-17).

Shamanic associations are reported to have existed among the Cahuilla Indians as well as the Chumash (Bean 1972a:113-114; Hudson and Underhay 1978:29). The Gabrielino participated extensively in the Chumash organization, which was known as the *'antap*, and in their own association, which has been called the *yovaarekam*, a reference to the *yovaar*, or sacred enclosure (Hudson and Blackburn 1978:231, 238, 242-243). A Kitanemuk Indian living near the southern end of the San Joaquín Valley told Harrington that the *'antap*, "the religion of the coast—that religion in which they knew all things . . . was very strong at San Gabriel," and that "*y+var* was the same as Ventureño *'antap*. They called the *'antap* in Kitanemuk *y+varakam*" (Hudson and Blackburn 1978:231).

Few details are available on the organization of the *yovaarekam*; however, the membership of the *'antap* was divided into two groups, the *'antap* and the *shan*. The *'antap* was a regional assembly consisting of community leaders who conducted important rituals and festivals and advised provincial leaders. Members of the *shan* served as assistants to the *'antap*, travelling throughout the provinces and relaying important information back to the leaders (Hudson and Underhay 1978:29-30).

GUARDIAN SPIRITS

The majority of shamans came from shamanic families or were recruited by other shamans, and a divine call, often received through a dream, was an important factor in the choice of candidates (Bean 1972a:109, 1976). Young men and women were required to undergo an arduous apprenticeship, during which they were repeatedly tested not only by other members of the profession, but by supernatural beings as well (Bean 1976). In cultures throughout the world, the shamanic initiation typically involves a series of trances, during which the candidate undergoes ordeals of suffering, death, and rebirth at the hands of supernatural beings (Eliade 1951:33-34). This initiation serves to transform the "profane" individual of the secular world into a new person capable of possessing and managing supernatural power.

It was during the trance that the candidate received instruction from supernatural beings, especially from his special guardian, in power, knowledge, and ritual techniques (Bean 1976). Each shaman possessed a guardian spirit which resided in his body, specifically within his heart, and which had been passed to him from another shaman who served as his sponsor. A variation of this concept existed among the Cahuilla, who believed that it was not the guardian spirit itself that was carried within the shaman's body, but rather a special agent called *Teyawa* that maintained the link between the shaman and his guardian (Bean 1972a:168).

A guardian spirit could be an animal spirit, a personified natural force like thunder or ball lightning, a supernatural creature, or even a plant. Especially powerful shamans might have more than one helper. A shaman was able to produce the guardian through his mouth and present it to the apprentice he was sponsoring, whereupon the apprentice swallowed it, or touched it against his neck or chest, thereby acquiring

its powers for life (Harrington 1933:161-162, note 123; Bean 1972a:109).

MAGICAL FLIGHT

In many cultures throughout the world, shamans were distinguished from other individuals possessing supernatural power by their ability to leave their bodies during "magical flights" to ascend into the sky or descend into the underworld (Eliade 1951:5). Among many California Indian groups the shaman used this ability for a number of purposes, including gaining supernatural aid for the community; learning about the universe; leading souls of the dead to the afterworld; and receiving instructions from supernatural beings regarding proper lifestyles and medical techniques (Bean 1976).

Shamans and apprentices employed a number of techniques to bring about the trance that enabled them to contact the supernatural world. A hallucinogenic drink called *maanet* prepared from the dried root of *Datura wrightii*, more popularly known as Jimson weed, was used to bring about a trance that enabled the shaman's soul to undertake magical flight (Geiger and Meighan 1976:89; answer from Mission San Gabriel). *Datura wrightii* contains a number of powerful alkaloids that can be extremely toxic, and consequently a great deal of knowledge and experience was required to use the plant safely. Casual experimentation with this drug often proves fatal. Hallucinations involving flying, frenzied dancing, and bodily dissolution are typical of *Datura* intoxication, and the plant's ritualistic use has been documented among societies in Asia and Africa as well as Medieval Europe and North America (Harner 1973:128-140; Armstrong 1986).

The Gabrielino also achieved intoxication by eating a potent mixture of tobacco, lime, and water (or urine) called *peeshpevat* (Geiger and Meighan 1976:89, answer from Mission San Gabriel). A Chumash Indian at Mission Santa Barbara reported to a priest that eating tobacco made a person feel fine, and that "you do not think of women or anything, just sleep" (Librado et al. 1979:148). According to Harrington's consultant Jesús Jauro,

> con ese curaban el estómago [with that they used to treat the stomach] . . . para q. quedara liviano el cuerpo [in order that the body will remain light], para tornar un oso [in order to become a bear]. . . . they pounded up the tobacco fine, and added

some cold water, making it the consistency of mush, and put some with 2 fingers into [the] mouth, and then took a drink of water to wash it down. . . . They kept eating it & drinking water, until they finished the mortar full . . . & when through they drank some warm water & went outside & vomited (Harrington 1986:R103 F522).

It is possible that tobacco ingestion was also used for other ritualistic purposes that were concealed from the mission clergy.

A third possible technique of ritual intoxication used by the Gabrielino involved the ingestion of live, poisonous red ants; the exact mechanism of intoxication through ant ingestion is unclear (Reid 1852:36; see Blackburn 1976 for a more complete discussion of the ethnographic data concerning ant ingestion).

POWER OBJECTS

Shamans derived considerable power from the ceremonial costumes and ritual paraphernalia they possessed. During ritual performances the shaman wore a special costume that consisted of

a kind of wig . . . that was made secure by a braid of hair passed around the head, into which they inserted various kinds of feathers, forming a crown. . . . [and a] covering for the body . . . prepared from the feathers of different kinds of birds, which were sewed together and, like a sort of petticoat, reached down to their knees. . . . The parts exposed were generally painted red and black and, not unfrequently, white (Boscana 1933:57).

Shamans carried wooden wands inlaid with shell and tipped with flint knives or crystals (Harrington 1942:17, item 585). According to Jesús Jauro, the *maahevat* was "a flat stick with 2" or 3" of shell inlay near one end. [T]he paxá' holds this in his hand when he dances. . . ." The *maahevat* was one of the articles that the *tomyaar* kept stored in the sacred bundle (Harrington 1986:R103 F162). A flat board, painted red and bearing rattlesnake rattles, was worn on the forehead (Harrington 1942:17, 40, items 584, 1592; Hudson and Blackburn 1985:202-222).

A review of the Harrington notes and other sources of ethnological and archaeological data reveals that a wide variety of naturally-occurring items were used by the Gabrielino shamans as power objects. Small dried animal skins, curiously shaped vegetable growths, and rare, sparkling minerals were utilized as talismans (Heizer 1968:123-124, note 69). Merriam (1955:80) reported that Gabrielino shamans wore collars of beads, stones, and bear claws during the mortuary ceremony given to honor the memory of the dead. José de los Santos Juncos reported that one shaman was known to wear "a fillet of hair around his head under his hat. It was that that gave him his hechicero [sorcerer] power" (Harrington 1986:R102 F738). He also told of the "bird called pito real [green woodpecker] . . . which carries a stone of virtue. The brujos [sorcerers] at S. G. [San Gabriel] had these stones . . ." (Harrington 1986:R105 F563). José explained that

to get its stone a G. [Gabrielino] went over back of the mtns. [mountains]. Must find [a] nest. First [they] clean all around the base of the cave or the hollow tree where the nest is. Then [they] plug the cave or tree. [They] [h]ide themselves and [the] bird comes & breaks open to nest. [They] must hide themselves, for if [the] bird sees them she won't use the stone. Then after she has used it, they look on [the] ground & find it & thus make themselves brujos, sabios [sorcerers, wise men] (Harrington 1986:R105 F561).

In addition to "pito real" stones, Gabrielino shamans used the "aura [turkey vulture] egg which is of great virtud [power]." José de los Santos Juncos "once saw [a] hollow in rocks with aura eggs in it back of Cahuenga somewhere" (Harrington 1986:R105 F564; see also Hudson and Blackburn 1986:152-153).

Quartz crystals were powerful talismans associated with thunder, lightning, and rain (Hudson and Blackburn 1986:154-156). Alliott (1916:129-130), citing Harrington's research among the Luiseño, reported that quartz crystals were believed to be capable of opening a way through any obstacle of wood or rock. *Chengiichngech* was believed to use crystals as arrows, shooting them into those who offended him by breaking his commandments (Harrington 1933:134). As mentioned above, quartz crystals were sometimes used to tip the wands carried by shamans as symbols of authority.

Another mineral used by shamans was referred to as a "noot stone" and was of "gray color with sparkling pieces in it that look bright as silver" (Harrington 1986:R103 F342). Harrington described a noot stone as "consisting mainly of kaolin, and occurring in various colors, blue, green, white, red, etc. This rock is pulverized and rubbed on the legs and imparts great swiftness and fortitude in running. . . . This rock whistles . . . when one has some of it in the house and forgets about it" (Harrington 1933:134-135). He also reported that "one must never merely pick up a *noot* stone. You must walk 3 times around it in [a] clockwise direction & then soplar [blow], and then pick it up." One could easily tame a horse by chewing a bit of *noot* stone and spitting it on the horse's face (Harrington 1986:R103 F342). *Noot* is the Luiseño word for chief; the name *noot* stone indicates that only the chief and other members of the elite having access to supernatural power could possess these talismans.

Another important mineral employed by Gabrielino shamans was the *toshaawt* stone. The earliest reference to the *toshaawt* stone occurs in Boscana's *Chinigchinich*. According to Father Boscana, *toshaawt* was "a black rock . . . from a small island near the beach" that was placed in the center of the world to secure it in place. In the center of the rock was "a ball formed like a bladder and filled with gall" which, upon being emptied into the sea immediately changed the former fresh water sea to salt (Boscana 1933:31). Chumash consultant Fernando Librado suggested that *toshaawt* was the name given to black basaltic rocks obtained from Santa Barbara Island that were used as shaman's charmstones (Harrington 1933:145, note 66). Other evidence, however, suggests that *toshaawt* stones originated on San Nicolas Island. Several Chumash artifacts identified as *toshaawt* stones, and preserved in the collection of the Santa Barbara Museum of Natural History, match iron concretions that occur naturally on San Nicolas Island (Howorth 1988). Furthermore, ethnographic evidence for a source on San Nicolas can be found in the notes of Henshaw, who wrote that "magician's stones [come] from this island" (Heizer 1955:198).

Merriam described how a *toshaawt* stone was used by the Gabrielino in the Girls' Puberty Ceremony: "A curious porous stone called to-sow't came from the sea. It belongs to the chief but is borrowed by an old woman who gives the Puberty dance. . . . The stone to-sow't is put into a basket of hot water, when it at once begins to gurgle and sing. . . . Then the stone is taken out of the water . . . " (Merriam 1955:86).

Gabrielino shamans also employed a diverse assortment of manufactured ritual paraphernalia in their ceremonies. Father Boscana described a charm worn beneath the shaman's left arm, which consisted of a leather bag containing a ball of mescal, or yucca, mixed with wild honey. To use the charm a shaman simply touched it with his right hand "and such demands as are made are complied with without question" (Boscana 1933:61; see also Harrington 1933:178, note 175). Pipes made from stone or baked clay were used for ritual tobacco smoking (Hudson and Blackburn 1986:118-129). In 1769, Father Juan Crespí described several shamans from a settlement near the Los Angeles River who "were smoking pipes well made of baked clay and they puffed at us three mouthfuls of smoke" (Bolton 1927:147).

Cigar-shaped charmstones, sometimes known as plummet-stones, were also used in shamanic rituals (Heizer 1968:123-124, note 69). Generally these stones were of cylindrical shape with tapered ends and a smooth finish, and sometimes one or both ends were grooved (Hudson and Blackburn 1986:157-165). According to information provided by Mrs. James Rosemyre, the "doctor's charm stone is suspended on [the] breast and is heated and used as [a] counter irritant on patients" (J. W. Hudson n.d.).

Effigies carved in the forms of whales, fish, birds, mammals, canoes, and various abstract shapes were used by shamans for ritual purposes and were quite common in archaeological sites located in coastal regions and on the Channel Islands (Lee 1981; Hudson and Blackburn 1986:171, 219). Perhaps the largest and most diverse assemblage of steatite artifacts ever found was recovered in 1962 near the mouth of Santa Monica Canyon in Pacific Palisades, just outside the territory traditionally assigned to the Gabrielino. The collection included 29 spike-shaped objects of stone, 22 bird-like effigies commonly referred to by archaeologists as "pelican stones," three owl-shaped effigies, three canoe models, and a varied assortment of soapstone and sandstone vessels and utensils, as well as artifacts of chipped stone. Unfortunately, the collection was reportedly dispersed after the artifacts were photographed and recorded (Wallace 1987).

Ritual plaques manufactured from soapstone are believed to have a long association with shamanism; in fact, their use may predate the arrival of the Uto-Aztecans in southern California (Moriarity 1982). Such plaques have been recovered from archaeological sites along the coast from Ventura to Seal Beach, and on the Channel Islands (Pond 1968; Cameron 1990).

Catalina Island Museum No. G-121

Fig. 26. A soapstone plaque decorated with an incised design. A variety of uses has been suggested for these plaques including: as personal ornaments (worn suspended from the neck on a cord), to decorate grave stones, or to warm water. This specimen, collected by Ralph Glidden, is from Catalina Island. Photograph by author.

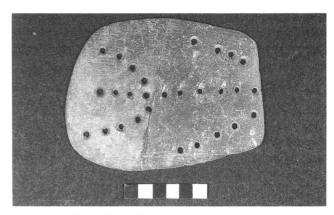

Catalina Island Museum No. G-152

Fig. 28. A drilled stone tablet from Catalina Island; this artifact was collected by Ralph Glidden. The purpose of these plaques is unclear; they may have served as effigies or ritual objects. Photograph by author.

Catalina Island Museum No. G-121

Fig. 27. A view of the incised design on the reverse of the plaque shown in Figure 26. Apparently this artifact was fragmented at the time of its discovery and later repaired. Photograph by author.

California State Univeristy, Long Beach Nos. 66-27 (large plaque) and 66-875 (small plaque)

Fig. 29. Drilled stone tablets from Los Altos Site LAn-270, located in the City of Long Beach. These plaques were recovered during archaeological excavations conducted at the site during the early 1950s. Photograph by author.

A variety of uses has been suggested for these ritual plaques, including warming stones to heat water for washing infants or wounds, and as ornaments worn suspended from a neck cord or used to decorate grave markers (Moriarity 1982; Hoover 1973). The plaques from the southern Channel Islands are unique in that they are often decorated with incised designs representing different types of creatures (Lee 1981:40-45). Other styles of stone plaques probably also served ritual or shamanic functions, as did stone tubes decorated with drilled holes (Hudson and Blackburn 1986:218-219).

Shaman's kits containing ritual artifacts of shell, soapstone, and bone have been recovered from burials within the Gabrielino territory at Goff's Island on the coast near Aliso Creek and also on San Nicolas Island. Both of these kits, which were apparently buried with their owners, were notable for the quality of the soapstone artifacts they contained (Winterbourne 1967:42, 44, Plates 25, 34, 35; Lee 1981:54-55).

SHAMANIC AUTHORITY AS AN INSTRUMENT OF SOCIAL CONTROL

Shamans deliberately cultivated a public image of superiority and power to inspire respect and obedience, and this enabled them to serve as important instruments of social control. Not only could the shaman's power be used to ward off enemies, but it could also enforce adherence to the laws and precepts of *Chengiichngech*. To this end shamans engaged in elaborate shows of magical power and extravagant displays of ritual paraphernalia.

José de los Santos Juncos told another story about the shaman Ramon Valencia in which the hechicero hosted a fiesta that was attended by many guests including Ventureño and Cahuilla Indians. This fiesta may have taken place during the mid-1800s as the Cahuilla chief Juan Antonio is mentioned as being in attendance; Juan Antonio first became a leader of the Cahuilla during the early 1840s (see Phillips 1975:48). During the fiesta Valencia was buried alive and then rose from his grave. After Valencia was buried

> an old Indian stayed outside & had a fire [at the] side of the pit. . . . The old man waved [a] fire brand in 4 directions and as he did so he gave the cry—this same kind of cry with falling scale & slapping hand over mouth. . . . At this first cry [the] earth trembled some. At [the] second waving & cry it trembled more. At [the] 3rd waving & cry it rocked & [the] people asked one another if they had ever seen anything like that. At [the] second cry V. had started to rise from [the] earth—at [the] 3rd he came out (Harrington 1986:R105 F563, see also R104 F40, 41).

Harrington visited the site of Ramon Valencia's fiesta with José de los Santos Juncos sometime between 1914 and 1918 and prepared a sketch map of the location (see Harrington 1986:R104 F41).

Shamans were believed to be capable of preparing a variety of poisons, some of which became effective merely through contact with flesh (Reid 1852:35). José de los Santos Juncos described a "kind of poison powder which a man carried, e.g., in his belt and poisoned Indians with it when [a] breeze blew from him to someone. . . . [They] also put it in the food and thus poisoned their enemies, and one would fall over dead quickly" (Harrington 1986:R102 F736). In addition, shamans were able to use their supernatural powers to control the weather and to "witch" enemies from a distance (see Harrington 1986:R105 F564, R104 F40).

To cause earthquakes or send sickness to an enemy, Gabrielino shamans of the San Fernando Valley prepared a special four-sided sandpainting that was surrounded by a rope fence. The shaman stood in the center of the painting holding twelve strings that radiated outward to an equal number of assistants. When the shaman shook the strings the earth quaked and sickness befell the person he had in mind (Kroeber 1925:626). While camped near a Gabrielino

settlement on the Santa Ana River in 1769, the members of the Portolá Expedition experienced a "horrifying earthquake" that caused one of the shamans to begin "with frightful cries and great demonstrations of fear to entreat heaven, turning to all the winds" (Bolton 1926:129).

A Chumash legend told of a Gabrielino shaman who painted a stone tablet with figures of men and women bleeding from the mouth and falling down. The shaman exposed the paintings to the sun and prayed for sickness, and soon the acorn crop failed and a five-year drought fell upon the land. The crisis was ended only when an opposing group of shamans discovered the tablet and immersed it in water, thereby neutralizing its power. Immediately clouds formed and rain began to fall, bringing the drought to an end (Blackburn 1975:276, narrative 79).

ASTRONOMY, ASTROLOGY, AND THE GABRIELINO CALENDAR

The Gabrielino shaman possessed an extensive knowledge of astronomy and cosmology that he used to predict the future and to schedule the proper dates on which to celebrate religious festivals (Reid 1852:32; Boscana 1933:43). The Gabrielino made use of both solar and lunar calendars, a solar calendar being used for long periods of time and a lunar one for days and months (Reid 1852:39; Heizer 1968:118-119, note 54). According to Father Boscana, the lunar calendar began on December 21 and was corrected twice a year at the solstices to bring it into agreement with the solar year. For this reason the Gabrielino year had only ten months, December and January, the time of the winter solstice being combined to form one month, and June and July, the time of the summer solstice, combined to form another (Boscana 1933:65-67). José de los Santos Juncos reported that the Gabrielino had names for all the months of the year (Harrington 1933:186-191, note 185, 1986:R104 F005).

Gabrielino shamans belonging to the Chumash *'antap* society may have also used the Chumash solar calendar. This calendar consisted of twelve months of 30 days each, and was calculated by observing the changing positions of the constellations near the horizon before sunrise. Star charts made of stone tablets inlaid with tiny shell beads may have aided the shamans in this task. Every three or four years this calendar was adjusted to correct for the difference between the calendar year of 360 days and the solar

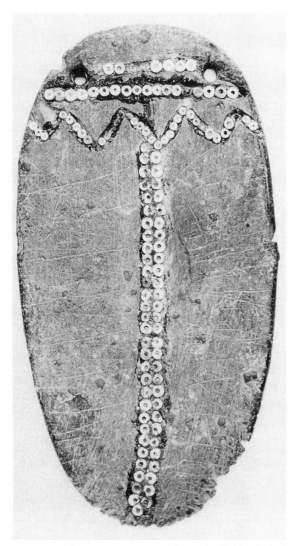

Courtesy of the National Museum of the American Indian, Smithsonian Institution, No. 20/3709

Fig. 30. A soapstone plaque that has been decorated with inlay of asphaltum and shell beads. This artifact, which measures 6 1/2" in length, was recovered from Huntington Beach in Orange County.

year of 365¼ days (Harrington 1942:29, item 1126; Hudson and Underhay 1978:126-139; Hudson and Blackburn 1986:225-226).

ORAL LITERATURE AND STORYTELLING

Shamans were responsible for preserving sacred and historical knowledge contained in the oral literature. This knowledge was passed by word of mouth and memorized by each generation. Certain males were trained from youth as bards, or storytellers, with the ability to memorize long stories and orations and repeat them word for word (Heizer 1968:118-119, note 54).

DISEASE AND MEDICAL TREATMENT

Shamans represented the highest level of expertise in a hierarchy of medical practitioners. Folk medicine techniques were available to anyone, and herbalists and midwives could be found in every community. However, only a shaman could undertake magical flight and visit the supernatural world to reverse the course of a serious illness.

Generally speaking, five causes of medical problems were recognized among California Indian groups, including natural causes, such as wounds and snakebite; sorcery by enemy shamans; supernatural punishment resulting from the breaking of taboos; soul loss; and the malevolence of spirits prior to a death ceremony (Bean 1972a:111). Ultimately, however, all misfortunes and illnesses were explainable as the result of the absence or the abuse of supernatural power. Mismanagement of power led to opposition and conflict, and frequently the outcome was disease. If the mismanagement became excessive, supernatural beings might intervene in human affairs. Methods of treatment employed a "holistic" approach that emphasized rest, the re-establishment of emotional harmony (whether in nature, human relationships, or human-supernatural relationships), and the re-integration of the patient with society (Bean 1976).

MEDICINES

At the outset of an illness help might be sought from an herbalist. Elements from each of the major resource categories (i.e., floral, faunal, and mineral resources) were utilized in Gabrielino medical treatment, and medicines prepared from a combination of ingredients were sometimes administered in conjunction with shamanic rituals. Although it is no longer possible to reconstruct a complete inventory of Gabrielino medicines, more than 20 different species of plants having medicinal uses have been reported for the Luiseño, while more than 200 separate uses of medicinal plants have been documented for the Cahuilla (Kroeber 1925:650; Bean 1972a:48-49; see also Bean and Saubel 1972). Given this information it is clear that the Gabrielino medical knowledge that has survived to the present day is but a tiny remnant of a once rich fund of information on the treatment of illnesses and injuries.

Although the efficacy and method of operation of many Gabrielino medical treatments remains unclear, it should be remembered that these techniques represented components of a holistic approach to healing. Among the more common methods of treatment was the use of prolonged periods of sweating followed by cold baths. This procedure was especially favored in the treatment of headaches and fevers. To aid the sweating, yerba de pasmo (*Baccharis viminea*) or chilicote (*Echinocistis macrocarpa*), called *Yjaihix* in Fernandeño, were boiled and taken internally. Sunbathing, bathing in thermal waters, and "baking" in an earthen pit on a bed of ashes were also frequently used in the treatment of illness. Bloodletting using sharp flints was a common method of treatment for inflammations (Reid 1852:33; Boscana 1933:71; Geiger and Meighan 1976:72-73, answers from Mission San Gabriel and Mission San Fernando).

A technique known as "counter-irritation" was used to treat pains in the side and upper torso as well as *"paralytic affections, stagnation of the blood, and loss of action in the limbs"* (Reid 1852:33). Different methods were used to create a counter-irritation. In one technique, live red ants were swallowed while more ants were applied externally to the affected part, which was also whipped with nettles (Geiger and Meighan 1976:73, answer from Mission San Fernando). Rheumatism was treated with another kind of counter-irritation in which a row of blisters was raised across the affected part by affixing small wads of dried nettle plant to the skin with saliva. The nettle was set afire and allowed to burn down to the skin, and the resulting blisters were opened immediately (Reid 1852:32). As noted above, shamans' charmstones were also heated and used to create another type of counter-irritation.

Wild tobacco (*Nicotiana* sp.) had a number of medical uses among the Gabrielino. Fevers were treated by inducing vomiting through the ingestion of wild tobacco and other herbs, followed by massage and singing (Reid 1852:33). A large ball of masticated tobacco was swallowed as part of the course of treatment for strangury, a urinary affliction. Apparently the tobacco acted as a sedative or muscle relaxant (Reid 1852:33-34). A mixture of tobacco, lime (obtained from crushed, burned sea shells), and water or urine was known as *peeshpevat* and was taken to relieve stomach pains and heal wounds (Geiger and Meighan 1976:73, answer from Mission San Fernando; Harrington 1986:R103 F522).

Chilicote (*Echinocystis macrocarpa*), which is also variously known as wild cucumber or manroot, was used to treat a wide variety of medical problems. According to a missionary stationed at San Fernando, chilicote was toasted and mixed with the powder of a crushed stone known to the missionaries as *"Bafa,"* and to the Indians as *"Paheasa."* The remedy could then be used as a wash or taken internally to treat a variety of complaints including film on the eye, inflammation, delayed menstruation, wounds, and urinary maladies (Geiger and Meighan 1976:73, answer from Mission San Fernando). To relieve stomach pains the seeds of chilicote were burned on a hot coal and the resulting smoke inhaled (Boscana 1933:71; Harrington 1933:194-195, notes 195-196).

The root of *Lomatium californicum*, known to the Spanish missionaries as "chuchupate" and to the Indians living in the vicinity of San Fernando as *cayat*, was chewed and then rubbed on body parts afflicted with pain. The plant was also used to relieve headache (Geiger and Meighan 1976:73, 158, answer from Mission San Fernando; see also Librado and Harrington 1977:116). Salt from the saltgrass plant was used to treat fevers, and tea made from elder pitch was used as a laxative (Merriam n.d.c). Anise was commonly used as a purgative, while yerba de pasmo, also known as guatamote or mule-fat (*Baccharis viminea*), was used to relieve toothache. This same plant, when boiled, was taken to induce perspiration, and when ground was used like snuff tobacco (Geiger and Meighan 1976:73, answer from Mission San Fernando).

The flower of wild rose was used as a gentle purgative for babies (Harrington 1986:R104 F94). Poultices of sage (*Salvia* sp.), coastal sagebrush (*Artemisia californica*), or nettle (*Urtica* sp.) were used for sores, swellings, tumors, and rheumatic pains. Coastal sagebrush was also used in the preparation of eye medicine (Boscana 1933:71; Harrington 1933:163, note 127, 193-194, notes 191-194; 1986:R105 F307). Oak bark was used as a general, all-purpose antiseptic wash, and water derived from the ash tree was taken as a refreshing tonic (Bean and Saubel 1972:129; Geiger and Meighan 1976:72-73, answers from Mission San Gabriel and Mission San Fernando). *Datura wrightii* was sometimes administered when psychosomatic illness was indicated by symptoms such as paralysis or loss of action in the limbs (Reid 1852:33). *Datura* could also have been used as an anaesthetic, although any application of this potent drug would have required the skills of an experienced shaman.

Animal and mineral substances were also used by the Gabrielino to treat illness. Two commonly used purgatives included small cakes of lime made from burned sea shells and water mixed with salt. Powdered alum mixed with ferrous sulphate, known to the missionaries as *copperas*, was used as a cleansing agent for the treatment of venereal disease, poisoning, or crippling (Reid 1852:33; Geiger and Meighan 1976:72-73, answers from Mission San Gabriel and Mission San Fernando). Snakebite was treated by applying herbs and ashes to the wound while a mixture of herbs, ashes, and the fine, powdery dust found at the bottom of ant nests was taken internally. "Decline," that is, the gradual loss of bodily function due to age or illness, was stemmed by feeding the patient the meat of cooked mud turtles (Reid 1852:33-34).

MAGICAL FLIGHT AND THE TREATMENT OF DISEASE

If the efforts of an herbalist failed, or if it was suspected that an illness resulted from other than natural causes, a shaman was consulted. Some shamans could only diagnose disease, while others could both diagnose and treat an illness. Gabrielino curing shamans were called *ahuuhvorot* (Reid 1852:32; Bean 1976; Harrington 1986:R103 F342). A fee or gift was paid to a shaman for performing a cure, but if the treatment was unsuccessful the payment was refunded and another shaman consulted; however, if a failure resulted from a patient's refusal to follow the prescribed course of treatment the shaman was absolved of any responsibility (Bean 1976).

Serious illnesses were diagnosed through the use of magical flight (Bean 1976). If a disease was caused by a supernatural being, the shaman would consult with that spirit to determine what propitiation was necessary. If the illness was the result of soul loss, the shaman would undertake magical flight to retrieve the lost soul and return it to the owner's body. Shamans also used magical flight to detect witchcraft, which most often involved "object intrusion," that is, the introduction of a foreign object, such as an animal hair, a stone, a splinter, or such, into the body by an enemy shaman. This object could only be located and removed by a curing shaman, who used a special technique known as "sucking." In one account by Father Boscana describing the sucking method, shamans placed feathers on the patient's head

and encircled him entirely with these and other articles such as horse hair, grass, beads, and hairs of the head, blowing at the same time with their mouths towards the four cardinal points, and muttering to themselves certain low sounds—certain mysterious words accompanied with antic gesticulations. . . . After this, one of them applied his lips to the part affected and pretended to draw from it by suction the particles which they had stated as being within, and exposed them to all present (Boscana 1933:72).

In addition to magical flight and sucking, shamans employed a number of other curing techniques, including massage, sweating, hypnosis, and surgery (Reid 1852:32-35; Boscana 1933:71-73). A number of different curing techniques were also used in combination to treat both the physical and emotional aspects of an illness. Reid described a treatment for a urinary affliction known as strangury that incorporated steaming, narcotic inebriation, sucking, smoking, massage, and ritual singing. The treatment began

by steaming the patient. . . . Immediately after a very large ball of masticated tobacco was given, which caused great depression and relaxation of the nervous system, often times producing the desired effect. If not, blood was drawn by sucking the abdomen immediately over the region of the bladder. This operation was performed with many prior rights [rites], such as smoking to the Great Spirit, pressure and rubbing of the part with the hands, and a song, every verse of which concluded with
NOM IM MANOC, IN MANOC
NOM IM MANOC, IN MANOC
        YOBARSE!
I do, what I am doing,
I do, what I am doing.
        Oh Church!
(Reid 1852:33-34; comment in brackets in original).

ABUSES OF SUPERNATURAL POWER

Despite the wealth, power, and prestige often attained by shamans, the divine call to assume the duties of the profession was not without certain risks. Society had a decidedly ambivalent attitude toward the shaman. Supernatural power could be used for evil as well as good, and the shaman capable of curing a suffering patient was probably also skillful enough to murder an unsuspecting victim. The abuse of supernatural power could result in severe punishment, and even death.

Harrington recorded a story that well illustrates the fate that might befall shamans who ran afoul of society. In this account two brothers, both powerful shamans, were summoned to a festival at San Gabriel. Their host, a *tomyaar* who had many enemies, offered them a handsome reward of shell-bead money to destroy his opponents.

When the festival concluded, the two shamans returned to their home in a remote canyon on Santa Catalina Island, accompanied by a young apprentice. They began their work by creating a sandpainting depicting the world, adding to it representations of blood, infirmities, and dangerous animals. They then hung 12 rag dolls face downward and uttered three shrill cries that caused the earth to tremble.

Soon people at San Gabriel began to die in great numbers. Unfortunately, among the casualties were many innocent victims, including the *tomyaar*'s own daughter. The chief, grieving over his loss, called together his council and explained the cause of the epidemic. The council agreed that the shamans must be stopped, and a war party was quickly sent to Santa Catalina.

Upon arriving at the island, the warriors made their way to the remote canyon where the shamans practiced their arts. A great battle ensued. Both sides used sorcery to try to gain the advantage, but eventually the two shamans and their apprentice were captured. The brothers were executed, and their hearts were cut out and burned so that they could not return to life. The apprentice was also put to death after he was forced to destroy the sandpainting and the rag dolls. Thus the malevolent shamans were punished for misusing their supernatural powers, and the epidemic at San Gabriel was brought to an end (Hudson 1979a; Harrington 1986:R105 F565-568).

SOCIAL CLASSES

Archaeological and ethnographic evidence suggests that Gabrielino society included a number of hierarchically-ordered social classes (Finnerty et al. 1970:18; Galdikas-Brindamour 1970:136; Bean and Smith 1978:543). Three primary social classes have been identified, including the elite, the middle class,

and the commoners. Two additional classes that can be distinguished were the poor, and the slaves and vagabonds (Boscana 1933:70; Bean 1974:22; Bean and Smith 1978:543). Class membership depended not only upon wealth but also ancestry, and it played a large role in determining individual lifestyles.

At the top of the social order was the elite class. The Gabrielino elite formed a privileged class of wealthy families that included the *tomyaar* and the Council of Elders. Members of the elite inherited their wealth and were typically the most politically and economically active individuals in the community. They were readily distinguished from others by their occupations and their large homes, and there is some historical evidence to suggest that certain clothing styles, such as the length of the hide capes worn by the men, were determined by the wearer's social status (Fages 1937:32; Hudson and Blackburn 1985:45). Members of the elite were supported in large measure by gifts and payments they received for professional services (such as medical care) they rendered to the community. This released them from much of the burden of daily food-gathering activities. Because they tended to choose marriage partners from their own class, elite families possessed extensive social ties with other communities, and this gave them greater freedom to travel than was enjoyed by the lower classes (Bean 1974:29).

Members of the elite spoke a refined language; Reid reported that "there is now at San Gabriel an old woman named *Bona*, who takes a pride in speaking sometimes the 'court language' to the 'young ones' to stultify their intelligence" (Reid 1852:14). Members of the elite also participated in secret religious ceremonies not open to commoners (Reid 1852:14; Bean 1974:29). The highest levels of sacred, esoteric knowledge of the *Chengiichngech* religion were restricted to devotees from the upper class, and this restriction was sanctioned by *Chengiichngech* himself, who "separated the chiefs and elders from among them, and directed that they alone should wear the kind of dress which had adorned his person, and then taught them how to dance" (Boscana 1933:33-34). Only the *tomyaar* and other members of the elite could enter the *yovaar*, and "those who entered, would be called Tobet, and the remainder of the people, Saorem" (Boscana 1933:34). A loose translation of the word *Tobet* might be "the initiated," while *Saorem* meant "persons who do not know how to dance" or "could not make use of the vestments of Chinigchinich" (Boscana 1933:34). Religious knowledge was communicated to boys when they underwent the rite-of-passage ceremony at puberty, but Father Boscana noted that "when they reveal anything to their children, it is only to such as they intend to rear for their successors, and these are enjoined to keep fast the secrets" (Boscana 1933:17).

Among most California Indian groups the middle class consisted of bureaucrats, craftsmen, and other skilled individuals who had earned the patronage of the elite. Individuals of special skill or talent were capable of considerable social mobility, and craftsmen who earned the patronage of the elite were often candidates for bureaucratic positions (Bean 1974:22-23).

In contrast, commoners did not possess the inherited wealth of the upper class, nor did they receive the patronage accorded to members of the middle class. They did not have the extensive social ties enjoyed by the elite, and this tended to restrict individual travel. They were not privy to the higher levels of religious knowledge, and they were excluded from much of the ritual activity (Bean 1974:29).

Beneath the commoners were a class of poor who were considered undesirable and were characterized as dishonest and irresponsible (Bean 1974:30). Further yet down the social ladder were slaves taken in battle. These consisted primarily of women and children, for most warriors captured on the battlefield were decapitated immediately, although some might be taken as prisoners for later torture and public execution. Slaves were sometimes returned to their families as part of a negotiated settlement (Reid 1852:15; Boscana 1933:70).

Homosexuals and transvestites represented a unique subgroup within Gabrielino society; these individuals might originate from any of the social classes (Bean 1974:23). According to Father Boscana, in pre-mission times these individuals were selected

> whilst yet in infancy . . . and instructed as they increased in years in all the duties of the women—in their mode of dress, of walking, and dancing; so that in almost every particular, they resembled females. Being more robust than the women, they were better able to perform the arduous duties of the wife, and for this reason, they were often selected by the chiefs and others, and on the day of the wedding a grand feast was given (Boscana 1933:54).

Prostitution was reported among the Gabrielino, although few details beyond its existence have been recorded (Harrington 1942:31, items 1202-1204).

SOCIAL CONTROL

The Gabrielino had extensive laws and codes of behavior that were enforced through a wide variety of social and supernatural sanctions. The *tomyaar* was the final arbitrator of disputes, and he was aided in the administration of justice by the Council of Elders (Reid 1852:15). The decisions of the *tomyaar* were announced by an elder, probably the *paxaa'*, who

> was appointed to make public the crime, which he did by crying most bitterly throughout the *rancheria*, saying that "so and so has said or done this or that to our captain;" that "Chinigchinich is very angry and wishes to chastise us by sending upon us a plague, of which we may all die. Arm yourselves, then, both old and young, to kill the offender, so that by presenting him dead to Chinigchinich he may be appeased and not kill us" (Boscana 1933:42-43).

Members of the community then armed themselves and "immediately went out . . . in search of the delinquent, and when they fell in with him they despatched him, and together with the arrows . . . he was borne to the presence of Chinigchinich" (Boscana 1933:43). The parents of the executed offender were later allowed to take possession of the body.

Many of the laws and rules regulating Gabrielino society were contained in the sacred precepts of *Chengiichngech* and reinforced through the moral lectures delivered by the *tomyaar* and the *paxaa'*, as well as through the legends, stories, and anecdotes that comprised Gabrielino oral literature. Father Boscana wrote that it was *Chengiichngech* himself who instructed the elders "how to rear the young, as well as in the rules they were to observe for the future" (Boscana 1933:34). Prior to his death, *Chengiichngech* warned that he would ascend to the stars and keep watch, and "those who obey not my teachings, nor believe them, I shall punish severely. I will send unto them bears to bite, and serpents to sting them; they shall be without food, and have diseases that they may die" (Boscana 1933:34).

Children remained under their parents' authority until the age of puberty (Reid 1852:16). Moral instruction consisted of the teachings of *Chengiichng-ech*, which were "strongly impressed upon their minds that they might become good and avoid the fate of evil. The perverse child invariably was destroyed, and the parents of such remained dishonored" (Bos-cana 1933:45). These teachings were later reinforced at puberty through instruction given at the rite-of-passage ceremony (Boscana 1933:45-46).

Reid reported that murder was a rare occurrence among the Gabrielino and robbery was unknown (Reid 1852:15-16). Crimes punishable by death included murder, incest, mismanagement of the community food reserves by the *tomyaar*, and violations of the protocol governing behavior within the *yovaar* (Reid 1852:15; Boscana 1933:39, 46). Execution was ac-complished by shooting with arrows, although burning alive as a form of execution also appears in some Gabrielino accounts (Reid 1852:54; Boscana 1933:88). Lesser offenses were punished by the assessment of fines in food, skins, or shell-bead money. Whipping was never resorted to as a punishment (Reid 1852:16).

Adultery was handled by the Gabrielino in an innovative fashion. Legally, a dishonored husband was at liberty to kill or wound his wife if he caught her in the act of adultery, and anyone who interfered or avenged the woman's death was answerable to the *tomyaar*. However, according to Reid, as a more general practice the wronged husband rejected his wife, informing her lover that he was free to take her, and the husband then took possession of the other man's spouse as his own. The exchange was legal and not subject to appeal (Reid 1852:16).

Respect for the *tomyaar* and his decisions was rigorously enforced, as were the rules and etiquette for religious ceremonies (Boscana 1933:29, 34, 42-43, 46). Reciprocity was vigorously promoted, especially with regard to food and its procurement. Hunters and fishermen were expected to share their catch, a portion of which was deposited with the *tomyaar* as part of the community food reserve. In fact, according to Boscana, a hunter could not partake of his own kill, but could eat only that taken by others (Boscana 1933:43, 62). Such reciprocity rules reduced stress within the community by mitigating the most severe effects of food shortages (Bean 1972a:174-175).

One avenue of appeal lay open to those convicted of a crime by a ruling of the Council. A criminal could appeal his case directly to *Chengiichngech* by seeking sanctuary within the *yovaar*. Regardless of

the nature or severity of the crime, should the offender safely reach the grounds of the sacred enclosure he was free to leave the settlement without being attacked. *Chengiichngech* himself would decide the issue, while the people restricted their actions to banishment of the guilty party. However, vengeance could be taken out on the relatives and descendants of the offender and could continue until the entire punishment was meted out (Boscana 1933:39).

At the inter-community level, disputes between individuals were resolved through joint action of the *tomyaars*, and in the event that they were unable to reach agreement, an impartial third *tomyaar* was brought in to decide the case (Reid 1852:15-16). If the dispute affected the welfare of the community, or if certain offenses (such as witchcraft) were involved, or if negotiations had already failed, war might be declared.

CONFLICT AND WARFARE

A declaration of war might be made for a number of reasons: failure to observe the responsibilities of the reciprocity system, abduction of women, trespassing, sorcery, robbery, and revenge for insults (Boscana 1933:69; Bean and Smith 1978:546-547). Although Reid noted that robbery was unknown, his comment probably referred to its incidence among members of the same lineage or community, and not to incidents between different communities. Trespassing on lineage-owned hunting or gathering areas by a non-member threatened vital community food resources and was considered a most serious offense. A long-enduring pattern of enmity seems to have existed between the coastal Gabrielino and those of the interior communities, and this conflict may have resulted from intense competition between these two groups for food resources (Bolton 1926:219-220; Temple 1959:159). Similar competition may have been at the heart of warfare between the Gabrielino living in the community of *'Aluupkenga* (near Arcadia or Sierra Madre) and those near San Gabriel (see Taylor 1860a, n.d.).

The decision to declare war was made by the *tomyaar* in consultation with the Council of Elders. In the event that additional troops were needed, gifts would be sent to the leaders of other communities to enlist allies (Boscana 1933: 69). Communities allied

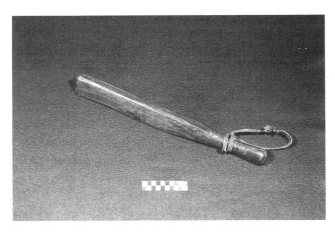

Natural History Museum of Los Angeles County No. A110.14/1102C

Fig. 31. A three-sided wooden Gabrielino war club; a leather thong is attached to the handle. This club and the one in Figure 32 are from the Coronel Collection; a number of other Gabrielino artifacts from the Coronel Collection are also illustrated in the present volume. These artifacts were first published in Hoffman (1885); Hoffman's notes concerning the Coronel Collection are summarized in Heizer (1968:104). Photograph by author.

Natural History Museum of Los Angeles County No. A110.14/1102B

Fig. 32. Another wooden Gabrielino war club from the Coronel Collection. The head of this club has four faces, each with four sharpened wooden spikes; a leather thong is attached to the handle. Photograph by author.

through marriage generally supported each other in such conflicts (Bean and Smith 1978:546).

After a decision was made to declare war a general community meeting was held at the *tomyaar*'s home. Smoke signals were used to summon allies from neighboring settlements. At this meeting the men were ordered to make ready their weapons and the women were instructed to prepare food; however, the reason for the preparations was not announced. Once a date was chosen for the attack, a second meeting was held and a formal declaration of war was announced. An attempt was made to keep the attack secret; however, such efforts were rarely successful (Boscana 1933:69-70; Temple 1959:159-160).

The *tomyaar* (or his representative) led the war party followed by the adult men, the old men, and the women and children. The fighting was hand-to-hand. Ambush was used whenever possible. Weapons included bows with arrows dipped in rattlesnake poison, clubs, slings, and stones. Homes were fired by tossing burning brands onto the roof tops (Harrington 1942:14-15; Bean 1972a:130; Bean and Smith 1978:546).

The women and children assisted their warriors by gathering up the enemy arrows for reuse by their own warriors, while shamans and medical practitioners administered care to the wounded. Warriors unfortunate enough to be captured by the enemy were decapitated on the battlefield or carried off for subsequent torture and execution. Scalps were taken as trophies and suspended from a pole near the *yovaar*, although they might be ransomed by relatives. Women and children captured during the fighting were held as slaves unless they were able to escape (Boscana 1933:70; Reid 1852:15; Bean 1976).

The verbal feud or "song duel" was a less violent form of conflict that served as a safety valve to "let off steam" and prevent physical aggression. Song duels were acted out during ceremonies lasting as long as eight days; during these duels obscene songs that ridiculed the enemy were composed and performed. During the performance the participants continually stamped their feet upon the ground to indicate the pleasure they would derive from trampling their enemies' graves. According to Reid, verbal feuds sometimes persisted over several generations. Writing in 1852, Reid noted that "there are two families at this day whose bad feelings commenced before Spaniards were even dreampt [sic] of and they still continue yearly singing and dancing against each other. The one resides at the Mission of San Gabriel, and the other at San Juan Capistrano; they both lived at San Bernardino when the quarrel commenced" (Reid 1852:38).

SUMMARY

Gabrielino society was a complex blend of political and economic institutions that functioned to stabilize the social structure and limit violence and warfare. Gabrielino society was composed of numerous kinship groups known as lineages, each of which consisted of a number of individual, related families sharing a common ancestor. Membership in each lineage was traced through the father and allowed individuals to claim use rights over hunting and gathering areas owned by the lineage.

Lineages were grouped into two separate divisions, which anthropologists call moieties. Every lineage belonged to one of the two moieties, which were named either wildcat or coyote. Because each moiety possessed only a portion of the components necessary for a ritual performance, it was necessary to bring together two lineages of opposite moieties to perform a ceremony successfully. In turn, these ritual occasions offered opportunities to redistribute food resources over a wide geographical area and thereby strengthen the economic base of the region.

There is considerable evidence that the Gabrielino spoke several regional dialects of the same Uto-Aztecan language. Four Gabrielino dialects have been suggested, including: Fernandeño, which was spoken in the San Fernando Valley; *Shevaanga*, which was spoken in the San Gabriel Valley; an unnamed dialect, which was spoken in the coastal areas and on some of the Channel Islands; and Nicoleño, which was spoken on San Nicolas Island.

Each Gabrielino community consisted of one or more lineages united under the leadership of a *tomyaar*, or chief, who was typically the chief of the oldest or largest resident lineage. The *tomyaar* served as the chief administrator, fiscal officer, religious leader, legal arbitrator, and commander-in-chief. Some *tomyaars* may also have served as provincial leaders; there is some ethnographic data to suggest that the *tomyaar* of *'Ahwiinga* served in this capacity.

The *tomyaar* was aided in his duties by a Council of Elders that consisted of the leaders of the lineages residing in the community as well as other wealthy and influential individuals. Important council members included: the *paxaa'* or assistant cult chief, who functioned as an announcer, treasurer, and general assistant, and who delivered moral lectures to the community; an official who prepared the hallucinogenic *Datura* drink; a firetender for ritual occasions; a rabbit drive official; messengers; and storytellers.

Shamans occupied a critical position in Gabrielino society, serving as the primary doctors, psycho-therapists, philosophers, and intellectuals. The shaman served as a mediator with the supernatural world, and he owed his authority in large part to his possession of supernatural power. It was not unusual for the *tomyaar* himself to be an important shaman. Shamans were ranked according to the type of powers they possessed; the most powerful shamans were believed to be capable of transforming themselves into animals, especially bears. Gabrielino shamans were organized into a professional society known as the *yovaarekam*; some Gabrielino shamans also belonged to the organization of Chumash shamans known as the *'antap*.

Archaeological and ethnographic data suggest that Gabrielino society was organized into several hierarchically-ordered social classes. The three primary social classes included the elite, the middle class, and the commoners. Beneath the commoners was a fourth class consisting of the poor and other undesirable individuals; beneath them were slaves taken in battle.

The Gabrielino had extensive laws and codes of behavior that were enforced through social and supernatural sanctions. Many of these laws were contained in the sacred precepts delivered by *Chengiichngech* that were reinforced through moral lectures given by the *tomyaar* and the *paxaa'*. At the inter-community level, disputes were resolved through joint decision by the *tomyaars*, or in the event that they were unable to reach a decision, by a third, impartial *tomyaar*. In extreme cases the failure to arbitrate a dispute could lead to war.

War might be declared for a number of reasons including: failure to observe the responsibilities of the reciprocity system; abduction of women; trespassing; sorcery; robbery; and revenge for insults. The decision to declare war was made by the *tomyaar* in consultation with the Council of Elders. The *tomyaar* (or his representative) led the war party. Fighting was hand-to-hand, and weapons included bows with arrows dipped in rattlesnake poison, clubs, slings, and stones. Homes were fired by tossing burning brands onto the roofs. Warriors captured on the battlefield were decapitated or carried off for later torture and execution; women and children captured during the fighting were held as slaves.

Despite periodic disruptions brought about by warfare and social conflict, the Gabrielino achieved a remarkable adaptation of the hunter-gatherer lifestyle to the environment of southern California. They created a stable social, political, and economic system that was organized at the local level through the lineage and community. This system was capable of expanding during favorable periods, maintaining itself during times of stress, and segmenting to form new units when the original population outgrew the environment's ability to support it. The Gabrielino economy was organized at a regional level through a complex system of reciprocal exchanges between lineages and communities. Political and military alliances helped keep breakdowns in this system to a minimum. This dynamic economic system and its interrelationship with the rich and varied environment of southern California forms the subject of the next chapter.

CHAPTER 7

ENVIRONMENT AND ECONOMY

The Gabrielino homeland offered an environment rich in natural resources, and this wealth of resources, coupled with an effective technology and a sophisticated system of trade and ritual exchange, resulted in a society that Kroeber characterized as "the wealthiest and most thoughtful of all the Shoshoneans of the State" (Kroeber 1925:621).

At the heart of the Gabrielino economy lay an extremely effective system for the utilization of food resources. Floral and faunal resources varied in availability from location to location and from season to season, and this variability placed a distinctive stamp upon the settlement patterns of the Gabrielino and other Indian cultures of southern California. Some food resources, such as rabbits, shellfish, and roots or bulbs, were available throughout much of the year. Other crops, such as acorns, matured only once a year; at collecting time large numbers of people migrated to the acorn groves to gather the wild crop before it spoiled or was devoured by predators and insects. In addition, winter was typically a time of food stress for most southern California Indian groups because of the lack of fresh plant foods in that season (Bean 1972a:155), and although the coastal Gabrielino may have fared somewhat better because of their access to marine food resources, inland communities undoubtedly faced the season with misgivings.

Variations in topography and geography also affected the availability of local food resources, and this was reflected in the lifestyles of the Gabrielino (Boscana 1933:65). For example, while the Channel Islands were rich in marine food resources, plants and land mammals were noticeably scarce. Similarly, although the mainland Gabrielino living near the coast had access to food resources that included plants, land mammals, and marine foods, those of the interior were less well endowed.

It would be misleading, however, to characterize the Gabrielino economic system as completely dependent upon the natural environment. In fact, the Gabrielino developed a viable economic system in which the careful management of resources, coupled with vigorous trade and ritual exchange, helped to distribute food resources more evenly. Thereby, population growth was promoted and the social disruption that would result from shortages was lessened. In addition, technological developments such as the plank canoe and the sinew-backed bow greatly expanded the range of available foods and enhanced the nutritional value of the Gabrielino diet.

MANAGEMENT OF FOOD RESOURCES

A deep concern for the proper management of food resources is evident throughout Gabrielino culture. A portion of the food procured from a day's hunting or gathering was deposited in the communal reserve, and a *tomyaar* who was found guilty of mismanaging the food reserve would be banished or executed (Boscana 1933:39, 43). Greediness, gluttony, and food hoarding were depicted as reprehensible traits in Gabrielino oral literature (Reid 1852:49-51, 55, 63; Harrington 1986:R106 F188-189). To discourage hoarding, hunters and fishermen were, under certain circumstances, prohibited from eating of their own kill (Reid 1852:36; Boscana 1933:62); however, family food caches might be maintained at locations away from the primary community site in case of special need (Reid 1852:57; see also Bean 1972a:53-55).

Food gathering responsibilities were generally divided on the basis of sex and age. Men were primarily responsible for hunting and fishing, while women gathered plant foods, roots, nuts, and seeds, perhaps aided by the elderly (Boscana 1933:56; Bean and Smith 1978:546). During certain times of the year a majority of the people joined in communal efforts to collect seasonal crops or cooperate in large-scale rabbit hunts (Hudson 1971:59, 70; see also Boscana 1933:65 and Bean 1972a:37, 59). In August of 1769, shortly after fording the Los Angeles River on their route north to Monterey, the members of the Portolá Expedition encountered "the entire population of an Indian village engaged in harvesting seeds on the plain" (Teggart 1911:21).

TRADE AND RITUAL EXCHANGE

The Gabrielino homeland lay at the center of an extensive network of trade associations that extended eastward to the Colorado River and westward as far as San Nicolas Island (Davis 1961). The mainland Gabrielino maintained trade relations with the Cahuilla, Serrano, Luiseño, Chumash, and Mojave, as well as the island Gabrielino of Santa Catalina, San Clemente, and San Nicolas. The Gabrielino traded soapstone, asphaltum, and shell beads with the Cahuilla in exchange for food products, furs, hides, obsidian, and salt (Bean 1972a:123). The Serrano received shell bead money, fish, sea otter skins, and soapstone vessels from the Gabrielino in exchange for deerskins and seed foods (Reid 1852:43-44; Strong 1929:95-96). Obsidian from Obsidian Butte near the Salton Sea was traded to the Luiseño, and thence to the Gabrielino (Koerper et al. 1986). José de los Santos Juncos reported that the "Tejon Indians used to come to Los Angeles with quantities of deer skins and sell them. They used to come to San Gabriel and attend fiestas there" (Harrington 1986:R102 F33).

RITUAL EXCHANGES

The Gabrielino are known to have maintained ritual exchanges involving shell bead money with the Luiseño (Strong 1929:98), and archaeological evidence demonstrates that the Chumash of the Santa Monica Mountains received ollas, bowls, and smoking pipes of Catalina soapstone from the Gabrielino (King 1971). The Chumash of the northern Channel Islands obtained soapstone vessels through direct trade with the island Gabrielino, perhaps later trading these articles with the Chumash of the Santa Barbara coast (Kroeber 1925:629). The use of soapstone by the

Ventureño Chumash is known to have continued well into the Mission Period (Wlodarski and Larson 1976).

TRADE WITH THE SOUTHWEST

Colorado River peoples, such as the Mojave, regularly visited the Gabrielino to trade, making the trip from the Colorado River to the coast on foot in 15 or 16 days (Cook 1962:161). The presence of Southwestern ceramic sherds at several archaeological sites in Los Angeles County suggests that such coastal-inland trade was already ongoing by A.D. 900 to 1000. Fragments of Hohokam pottery dated prior to A.D. 900 have been recovered from *Tohuunga* in the San Fernando Valley and from a coastal midden at Redondo (Heizer 1941; Walker 1952:112-116; Forbes 1961), and similar finds have been made at the Century Ranch Site (LAn-227) and in the Wilmington area (Ruby and Blackburn 1964).

During Gabrielino times, the main articles of this long distance trade were luxury goods. Red ochre, soft black blankets, and shirts of deer or antelope skin were provided by the Colorado peoples in exchange for shell and soapstone (Cook 1962:158-159; Ruby 1970:96, 266-267). In the year 1776, while traveling from the Colorado River to Mission San Gabriel, Father Francisco Garcés encountered a number of trading parties from the Colorado River making their way to the coast "for their commerce in shells" (Garcés 1900:254). As late as 1819, trade parties from the Colorado River continued to visit the California missions, following routes that led from the Colorado through Cajón Pass into the San Bernardino Valley, and then on to the San Fernando Valley and Newhall Pass, or through Antelope Valley, which lies north of the San Gabriel Mountains, and on to the lower San Joaquín Valley (Farmer 1935).

ISLAND TRADE

Within the Gabrielino territory a vigorous trade existed between the islands and the mainland. The island Gabrielino of Santa Catalina offered the mainlanders goods of soapstone such as bowls, ollas, and pipes, as well as roots (especially *Brodiaea* sp.), seal and otter skins, red ochre, shell beads, and lumps of lead ore, which were prized as a source of supernatural power as well as a raw material for the production of black paint (Strong 1929:95-96; Wagner 1929:237; Martínez 1938:52; Meighan and Johnson 1957:26; Vizcaíno 1959:14-16; Finnerty et al.

1970:22-23). In return, they probably received goods that were in short supply on the island, such as plant foods and perhaps certain manufactured goods (Meighan and Johnson 1957:29). The San Clemente islanders traded kaolin, a white clay found on the island, and a mineral, sulphate of iron, in return for raw stone suitable for flaking into usable tools (Zahniser 1981:3.20, 21). According to the nineteenth century explorer Duflot de Mofras, the Gabrielino continued making trips to San Clemente to gather these articles after the island was abandoned (Wilbur 1937:191).

Of the items offered for trade by the islanders, soapstone was perhaps the most important. Soapstone quarrying and manufacturing sites existed in several locations on Santa Catalina, including the Valley of the Ollas, (or Pots Valley), Empire Landing, and the vicinity of Little Springs Canyon (Wlodarski 1979a:337-338). A major center for the distribution of soapstone goods to the mainland was located at Isthmus Cove (Finnerty et al. 1970). Mainland trade depots were reportedly located at Redondo and San Pedro (Kroeber 1925:629), and it is likely that ceremonial centers such as *Povuu'nga* also played an important role as gathering places for trade and ritual exchange.

MAINLAND TRADE

Mainland trade occurred between coastal and inland lineages and communities, and this trade may have been an important factor in the establishment of permanent settlements in areas having less reliable food supplies. Marine food resources such as fish, shellfish, and marine mammals were traded by coastal communities to the interior communities, thereby helping to stabilize the winter and spring food supply in areas such as the Santa Monica Mountains (see Galdikas-Brindamour 1970). A variety of other items were traded as well. Duflot de Mofras, who visited Mission San Gabriel around 1840, observed that "the Indians often bring bits of native copper, fragments of opals, and specimens of sulphureted lead down from the mountains" (Wilbur 1937:187).

A number of mainland trade routes that led across the San Gabriel Mountains to the desert were traced out by Will Thrall, an early collector of San Gabriel Mountains history. Some or all of these routes could have been utilized by the Gabrielino. The first route followed Millard Canyon to Red Box Divide, down

the west fork of the San Gabriel River perhaps to Valley Forge Canyon, then to Barley Flats and across Big Tujunga Canyon to Chilao where the trail forked. One branch followed the high country and eventually descended into the south fork of Little Rock Creek and out into the desert; the other ran northwest to Alder Creek, then climbed the west slope of Mount Pacifico, descended Santiago Canyon to Little Rock Creek, and then ran out to the desert. A second route ran up the north fork of the San Gabriel River, climbed over the Islip saddle, then dropped down into Big Rock Creek and out onto the Mohave. A third trail is reported to have led up Little Santa Anita Canyon to Mount Wilson, then north into the west fork of the San Gabriel River, and up the fork to Valley Forge Canyon where it met the first trail (Vernon 1956:145-148; Robinson 1977:13-14).

RITUAL CONGREGATIONS AND TRADE

Ritual lineage gatherings served as an important mechanism for trade and the redistribution of surplus food resources among mainland groups. As noted in Chapter 6, Gabrielino lineages were grouped into two separate divisions, known as "moieties." Every lineage belonged to one of these two moieties, which were named either "wildcat" or "coyote." Because each moiety owned only a portion of the components necessary for a successful ritual performance, two or more lineages were required to join together to produce a ritual or fiesta. Thus, while passing through the Gabrielino territory in 1769, the members of the Portolá Expedition observed that the inhabitants of one "village were having a feast and dance, to which they had invited their neighbors of the river called Jesús de los Temblores" (the Santa Ana River) (Bolton 1927:143). Lineages joining together in such ceremonial-political-economic alliances made up everchanging "ritual congregations," arguably "the most important social units" (Bean 1972a:85, 151-153).

The reciprocal hosting of ritual activities, and the trade and food exchange activities that accompanied them, were an integral part of the Gabrielino economy, and a violation of the rule of reciprocity could result in warfare. As Father Boscana noted, war often resulted "when a chief neglected to return the customary present at their festivities" (Boscana 1933:69). A special feature of this economic system was the exchange of shell bead money that occurred between the Gabrielino and the Cahuilla, Chumash, Salinans,

and others (Bean 1972a:152-153; 1974:17). One of
the oldest systems of shell bead exchange once linked
all of the Cahuilla, Serrano, Luiseño, and Gabrielino
lineages from the San Gorgonio Pass to the Pacific
Ocean (Strong 1929:98). Archaeological data suggests
that an exchange system using *Olivella* Grooved
Rectangle beads linked the southern Channel Islands of
Santa Catalina, San Clemente, and San Nicolas to the
adjacent mainland coastal area as long as 5,000 years
ago (Howard and Raab 1993).

Information gathered from among the Cahuilla
indicates that when a lineage decided to hold a ritual,
such as a mourning ceremony, the *net*, who was the
equivalent of the Gabrielino *tomyaar*, sent a string of
shell bead money as an invitation to the other lineages.
A lineage that did not receive a string of beads yet
wished to attend the ceremony would send a string to
the host lineage. Once again, the actual ceremony
offered an important opportunity for the exchange of
surplus food and the conduct of trade. Later, when
the visiting lineage held its own mourning ceremony,
it would reciprocate by extending an invitation to its
former host (Bean 1972a:137).

ECONOMIC PRINCIPLES

Although research on the Gabrielino economy is
limited, a general outline can be presented based upon
work done with the Chumash, whose economic
organization had much in common with the Gabrielino
(see King 1971). The individual profit motive,
coupled with the law of supply and demand, was the
guiding principle of this economic activity. A number
of important features of this economy can be
delineated:

1) Food and manufactured goods were kept in
circulation through trade networks and ritual
exchanges.
2) Manufacturing was promoted by the evolution
of craft specialists who were organized into
professional associations. Craftsmen
specialized in the manufacture of wooden
plank canoes as well as other items (Boscana
1933:56; Fages 1937:34-35; King 1971:299;
Hudson et al. 1978:153-156, notes 331-335).
New association members may have been
inducted either from natural family members

or through a fictive "kinship" system in which
members "adopted" newcomers (Hudson et al.
1978:154, note 331).
3) The development of professional associations
promoted trade among the communities by establishing a network of partnerships that extended across political boundaries. Some
Gabrielino traders may have resided in
Chumash communities on a permanent basis,
cementing a network of economic relationships
across boundaries of language and topography
(Librado and Harrington 1977:25, 101, note
28; Hudson et al. 1978:142, note 308).
4) A standardized medium of exchange was
developed using *Olivella* shell beads, and
knotted cords were used to record the amount
and value of trading transactions. The value
of a string of shell bead money was related to
both the size and the quality of the individual
beads as well as the length of the string. One
unit of currency, a *pokuu' ponto*, consisted of
a string of beads that stretched from the
knuckles of the left hand to the tip of the
middle finger, back to and around the wrist,
out again to the tip of the same finger, and
back again to the wrist. Two units, *wehee'
paaka'*, was twice that amount (Reid 1852:43;
Martínez 1938:45; Heizer 1968:121-122 note
62; Harrington 1986:R104 F006).
5) The *tomyaar* was frequently the most important entrepreneur in trade activities. *Tomyaars*,
as well as other wealthy individuals, owned
the *te'aats* and were responsible for organizing
the ritual gatherings that were an integral part
of trade activity. Furthermore, the *tomyaar*
held general responsibility for the management
of economic affairs in his community. The
development of trade centers at Isthmus Cove,
San Pedro, and Redondo may have further
enhanced the social prestige and economic
control held by this special group (Kroeber
1925:629; Finnerty et al. 1970:21; Bean
1972a:104-105; Hudson et al. 1978:155, note
335).
6) The ritual destruction of food and manufactured items during ceremonial activities, such
as the Mourning Ceremony, may have served
to restrict the amount of goods available at
one time. The constant need to replace these

goods helped maintain a demand for the skills and services of the Gabrielino craftsmen.

ECONOMIC RESOURCES

The foundation of the Gabrielino economy was the wealth of natural resources available throughout the Gabrielino homeland. These can be divided into three resource categories; faunal, floral, and mineral. Faunal resources included land mammals, sea-mammals, fish, shellfish, insects, and reptiles. Floral resources included trees, plants, bulbs, and seeds, as well as sea grasses that were used to make netting and cord. Mineral resources included cherts, obsidian, and other types of stone that might be suitable for flaking into tools, as well as soapstone, sandstone, asphaltum (which was used as an adhesive and caulking compound), clays, salt, lead ore, and paint pigments. Together, this variety of natural resources satisfied virtually every material need of the Gabrielino.

Much of the diversity of floral and faunal resources available to the Gabrielino stemmed from the wide range of habitats or biotic zones in their territory. There were at least nine distinct habitats including the coastal sage-scrub, the freshwater marsh, the saltmarsh-estuary, the beach and coastal strand, the chaparral, the grassland-herbland, the southern oak woodland, the riparian or streamside woodland, and the mountains (Dixon 1974:40-43). Each of these zones or habitats offered a variety of resources to Gabrielino hunters and food-gatherers. Regions containing two or more such zones were especially rich in resources and were therefore particularly attractive as sites for permanent settlements.

COASTAL SAGE-SCRUB

The coastal sage-scrub zone covered much of the open prairie and hillslopes of the Gabrielino homeland, with cactus and low shrubs making up the primary vegetation. The coastal sage-scrub zone offered Gabrielino food-gatherers a rich variety of edible seeds as well as prickly-pear cactus, which was a special delicacy. The buds of the prickly-pear were picked with wooden tongs and then singed or peeled to remove the hundreds of tiny spines covering the fruit (Harrington 1942:8, item 134). In addition to edible seeds and prickly-pear cactus, the coastal sage-

scrub zone provided an important habitat for many of the small mammals hunted by the Gabrielino.

FRESHWATER MARSH

The freshwater marsh zone existed throughout the Gabrielino lands, being seasonally replenished by the flooding of streams and rivers. A large number of plants used in Gabrielino basketry and house building were gathered from this zone including cattails, rushes, sedges, and willows. In addition, this habitat offered important food resources such as birds, waterfowl, and small mammals.

SALTMARSH-ESTUARY

Near the seashore, saltmarsh-estuary habitats were interspersed with sand or mud flats and connected to the ocean through saltwater channels. The saltmarsh-estuary zone may have been less rich in plant resources than the freshwater marshlands; however, it offered a similar variety of waterfowl, as well as edible shellfish such as pectens, cockles, and oysters.

BEACH AND COASTAL STRAND

The beach and coastal strand offered a number of food resources that included land and sea-mammals, sea birds, fish, shellfish, and seaweed. The variety of fish species available to the Gabrielino was expanded through the use of ocean-going craft such as the plank canoe for offshore fishing activities. In addition, sea-mammals provided a variety of useful non-food resources such as furs and pelts for clothing, and bone for tools and other utilitarian items.

CHAPARRAL ZONE

In the interior, the chaparral zone consisted of a dense, evergreen shrubbery that covered much of the hillsides of the Gabrielino homeland. The two most important resources offered by this habitat were deer, which were hunted by the Gabrielino, and scrub oak, the acorns of which were consumed when more desirable varieties of oak were not bearing.

GRASSLAND-HERBLAND

The grassland-herbland zone extended from the prairie onto the lower hillslopes; it was home to antelope and deer as well as rabbits and other small rodents. The Gabrielino sometimes hunted rabbits by setting fire to the brush and driving the animals into nets. Father Juan Crespí reported seeing one burned area on July 24, 1769, when the Portolá Expedition approached Alisos Creek near the southern boundary of the Gabrielino territory, and another six days later on July 30, as the party crossed the Puente Hills (Bolton 1927:137, 143).

The Chumash Indians are believed to have practiced burning to control the spread of chaparral, maintain open grasslands and increase the availability of wild seeds from plants that sprout following a fire. Burning may also have increased the size of deer herds by improving the browse (Heizer and Elsasser 1980:73; Timbrook et al. 1982).

SOUTHERN OAK WOODLAND

The southern oak woodland was often interspersed with grassland-herbland. As the name suggests, the southern oak woodland zone offered stands of acorn-bearing oaks. The acorn was one of the staples of the Gabrielino diet, especially in inland locations where marine food resources were not available. Oak groves were probably owned by lineages who collected the acorns each autumn, then stored them for use throughout the winter.

RIPARIAN WOODLAND

The riparian or streamside woodland zone was one of the richest habitats in the Gabrielino territory and was characterized by plants that require water year-round. Vegetation typical of the riparian zone included sycamores, alders, willows, cottonwoods, grasses, and herbs; many of these plants were used by the Gabrielino in basket making and home building. In addition, the riparian zone was rich in food resources, the abundant vegetation attracting and sheltering deer, antelope, and a variety of birds.

MOUNTAINS

The mountain zone, which bordered the Gabrielino territory on the north, northwest, and east, offered numerous food resources including acorns, piñon nuts, sage, deer, and small mammals. Groups living near this zone probably hunted and gathered in the lower reaches of canyons during spring and summer, moving into the higher elevations in late summer and fall to harvest acorns. During the winter they returned to their primary settlements which were located in the lower canyons where warmer temperatures prevailed (Hudson 1971:56, 70).

FAUNAL RESOURCES

Faunal resources were a vital element in the Gabrielino economy. Pedro Fages, who accompanied Gaspar de Portolá on the first land expedition to Alta California in 1769, noted that "besides deer, antelope (which is a kind of mountain goat), coyote, wolf, fox, cony, hare, squirrel, and skunk, there is here another land animal just like a sucking pig, which they call *mantugar* [the identification of this animal is uncertain], and the flesh of which they eat, just as they do that of the other animals mentioned" (Fages 1937:22).

A missionary from San Fernando observed that "the meat they eat is obtained from the deer, coyote, antelope, jackrabbit, rabbit, squirrel, rat, dog, all birds, mole, snakes, and rattlesnakes" (Geiger and Meighan 1976:85, answer from Mission San Fernando).

Reid wrote that "the animal food in use among them was deer meat, young coyotes, squirrels, badgers, rats, gophers, snakes, raccoons, skunks, wildcats, the small crow, the blackbirds, hawks, ground owls, and snakes, with the exception of the rattle snake" (Reid 1852:22).

Harrington added dog, bear, dove, and mud hen to the list of animals eaten by the Gabrielino (Harrington 1942:7-8, items 70, 74, 86-87).

Although land mammals were fairly plentiful in most areas of southern California, some seasonal variation in availability existed. For example, late summer was probably the best season for deer hunters because of the tendency of herds to concentrate at lower elevations while searching for water (Landberg 1965:51). Extended periods of drought would also have had an impact on the availability of meat.

It was during the winter, however, that the Indians were forced to rely most heavily upon meat because of the scarcity of plant foods. Thus, at this time of year Cahuilla communities held large-scale hunts to obtain meat for distribution to the general population during ritual gatherings (Bean 1972a:156). The Gabrielino held similar communal drives during which rabbits were run into long nets stretched across the ground (Harrington 1942:6, item 5, 1986:R102 F578).

MEAT TABOOS

Despite the wide range of animal foods consumed, some meats were avoided, perhaps for religious reasons. Included among these was the meat of the animals used as messengers or "avengers" by the god *Chengiichngech*: bears, rattlesnakes, stingrays, and ravens (Boscana 1933:29; Harrington 1933:130-132). According to Reid, snakes were eaten "with the exception of the rattlesnake," and "a few eat the bear, but in general it is rejected" (Reid 1852:22). Probably the belief that shamans transformed themselves into grizzly bears contributed to the taboo on bear meat. In addition, "the owl was held in deep reverence, and supposed to predict death, by screeching near the residence of the doomed one. It was never killed" (Reid 1852:20). Other foods may have been avoided out of fear of witchcraft. Reid recounted a tale in which shamans secretly poisoned a young woman by feeding her a rabbit stuffed with toads and "pieces of lizards and other disgusting matter" (Reid 1852:56).

MEAT PREPARATION

The Gabrielino prepared meat foods in a variety of ways. Father Boscana reported that meat was sometimes consumed raw, and blood was drunk while still fresh (Boscana 1933:24). Harrington noted that the Gabrielino prepared some meat foods by jerking, while other food preparation techniques commonly used by the Indians of southern California included roasting, boiling, and baking in a covering of clay. Small rodents were often crushed, bones and all, and consumed in mush or soup (Harrington 1942:9, item 168; Bean 1972a:60). According to José de los Santos Juncos, "it was the . . . custom to give the bones of . . . liebres [hares] or deers to old women or old men—the old women or old men pounded the bones up fine in a mortar, added salt and ate them together with chia" (Harrington 1986:R105 F571).

FURS AND SKINS

In addition to providing meat, land mammals filled a number of other important needs for the Gabrielino. Skins and pelts were tanned and used for clothing and containers. Deerskins were used by the women of the interior regions for making skirts (Reid 1852:23-24), while robes and capes were sewn from the pelts of deer, rabbit, foxes, squirrels, wildcats, and coyotes (Boscana 1933:56; Harrington 1942:19, 629; Woodward 1959:xxvi; Hudson and Blackburn 1985:43-54, 104-105). Blankets were made from strips of twisted rabbit fur woven on a string weft, and Reid also reported that bedspreads were made from

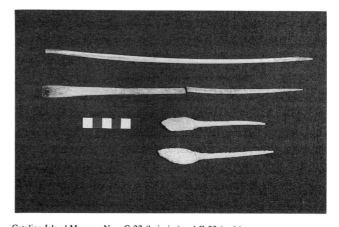

Catalina Island Museum Nos. G-23 (hairpins) and G-22 (awls)
Fig. 33. Bone artifacts from Santa Catalina Island. The two longest items may be hairpins; the shorter artifacts were probably used as awls. Photograph by author.

"rabbit skins, cut square and sewed together" (Reid 1852:24; Harrington 1942:23, items 861-862).

The Gabrielino dressed skins and furs using an oil tanning technique. Excess fat and meat were removed from the hide by pounding and scraping, using a split cobble or a fleshing tool of bone or shell. The hide was then placed against an inclined post or a wooden framework and rubbed with a preservative consisting of oil and grease or brains and wood ashes (Harrington 1942:13, items 347, 349-350, 375-377; Hudson and Blackburn 1987:139-147).

OTHER UTILITARIAN ITEMS

A number of other utilitarian items were obtained from land mammals. Tools and implements were made from bone, including needles, fishhooks, and awls. Wedges for splitting wood were made from deer bone. Deer sinew was employed by the Fernandeño in the manufacture of sinew-backed bows (Reid 1852:44; Harrington 1942:13-14, items 363, 403-408; Hudson and Blackburn 1982:92-95). Whistles and flutes were made from bone and elder wood, and deer hooves were tied in bundles for use as rattles. Another type of rattle was made from a turtle shell filled with pebbles and mounted on a wooden handle. Sometimes two shells were mounted one atop the other (Harrington 1942:28-29, items 1077-1079, 1100, 1103, 1108-1109, 1111, 1113, 1116, 1118; Wallace 1980). Hair oil was made from animal fat or bone marrow (Hudson and Blackburn 1985:352).

HUNTING EQUIPMENT AND TECHNIQUES

The Gabrielino were expert hunters, and their weapons and technology reflected a versatile set of strategies for utilizing animal resources to the best advantage. Large animals were hunted with bow and arrow, while small animals were taken with deadfalls, snares, traps, nets, slings, and throwing clubs. Burrowing animals were smoked from their nests and clubbed to death (Harrington 1942:6, items 5, 22-23, 33; Bean and Smith 1978:546).

BOWS

The Gabrielino hunter employed two types of bows, a simple or "self" bow, and a composite or "sinew-backed" bow. The more powerful sinew-backed bow was manufactured by the Fernandeño, while the self-bow was in more widespread use, especially for small game. Both the self- and sinew-backed bow averaged three to three and one-half feet in length. Buckeye and perhaps elderberry woods were used for manufacturing self-bows, while the sinew-backed bow was made from holly, elder, piñon, and juniper. Deer sinew held in place with pine pitch was used for the backing, and bowstrings were two- or three-ply vegetable fiber. Bows were held in a slanting position when shooting, and wrist guards of buckskin were worn for protection (Harrington 1942:14, items 399-414, 416, 419; Hudson and Blackburn 1982:81-87, 92-95, 132).

ARROWS

Gabrielino arrows were of two primary types: a "self" arrow with a wooden shaft, and a compound arrow consisting of a cane shaft in which a wooden foreshaft was inserted and secured with adhesive and fiber cord. Merriam reported that wild rose stems were also used for arrow shafts. Arrows were fletched with three feathers held in place with sinew and tar or glue, and sometimes designs were burned on the arrow shafts. Crooked cane joints were straightened using a tool consisting of a single piece of steatite with one or more grooves cut into its face. In use, this steatite arrowshaft straightener was heated and the crooked joint placed against it. As the heat softened the cane shaft, the crooked joint was carefully forced into the groove. Once straightened, the cane shaft was set aside and allowed to cool. The process also served to harden the shaft (Harrington 1942:14-

15; Heizer and Treganza 1944:347; Hudson and Blackburn 1982:96-100, 113-120; 1987:105-111).

Arrows were tipped according to their use. Sometimes the hardwood foreshaft was sharpened and used with no other point. At other times, points of stone or bone were inserted into a cut in the foreshaft and bound or glued in place. They were sometimes poisoned with rattlesnake venom or gall. Birds were stunned (rather than pierced) using arrows tipped with crossed sticks (Reid 1852:35; Harrington 1942:14; Hudson and Blackburn 1982:103-111).

Arrows were carried in quivers made from animal skins sewn up the middle. Quivers were also manufactured from skins stripped whole from the animal without slitting the belly. The head of the animal was left intact. The quiver was carried on the hunter's back, and arrows were inserted through the animal's open mouth and drawn out over the hunter's

Catalina Island Museum No. G-257

Fig. 34. A soapstone arrowshaft straightener used in the manufacture of cane arrows. The stone was heated and crooked cane joints were pressed into the central groove. The heat from the stone softened the cane and rendered it pliable; the groove acted as a mold to straighten the crooked joint. Photograph by author.

Natural History Museum of Los Angeles County No. A1346 (all)

Fig. 35. Stone arrow points collected during archaeological excavations at Malaga Cove on Santa Monica Bay. Photograph by author.

shoulder (Harrington 1942:15, items 466, 468, 1933:155, note 97; Hudson and Blackburn 1982:127-129). The incorporation of coyote and wildcat skin quivers as part of the *Chengiichngech* image in the sacred enclosure suggests that hunters may have carried one or the other of these quivers as a badge to designate their moiety affiliations (Boscana 1933:37-38; Harrington 1933:155, note 97).

DECOY HEADDRESSES

To aid in stalking their prey, Gabrielino deer hunters wore decoy headdresses made from the heads and necks of deer (Harrington 1942:6, item 28). Reid wrote that "the skin of a deer's head and neck was put on their own, and on seeing game they would feign to be grazing—lifting up the head occasionally to stare about. By such means they approached so near to make the first arrow 'tell'" (Reid 1852:36).

Generally the head of the deer was stuffed with grass to maintain the shape of the headdress, which was held in place with chin and arm straps. Wearing the decoy headdress and mimicking the movements of the deer, a skilled hunter was able to approach within 10 feet of his quarry (Hudson and Blackburn 1982:74-77).

HUNTING SMALL ANIMALS

The experienced hunter employed a number of other tools and techniques to aid him in his work. Fire was used to drive rabbits into large nets reaching lengths as great as 100 feet (Harrington 1942:6, item 5; Hudson and Blackburn 1982:70). According to José Zalvidea, "the Indians used to have long traps made of network. . . . They used them for catching animals for the festival" (Harrington 1986:R102 F578). Fire was also used by the Gabrielino to drive rats from their nests (Harrington 1942:6, item 33).

Birds and small game were hunted with slings, and rabbits were taken with curved, wooden throwing sticks (Harrington 1942:15, items 475-476, 483). Pedro Fages described the wooden throwing club as "a kind of war club of tough wood in the shape of a well-balanced cutlass, which they use in war and in hunting conies, hares, deer, coyotes, and antelope, throwing it so far and with such certain aim, that they rarely fail to break the bones of such of these animals as come within range" (Fages 1937:22). The Gabrielino used deadfalls to hunt such small mammals as squirrels and rodents. This kind of trap probably consisted of a large stone resting upon a stick, which in turn rested upon an acorn "trigger." The deadfall was carefully balanced so that when the acorn was removed the stick fell and the stone crushed the prey (Harrington 1942:6, items 22-23; Hudson and Blackburn 1982:59-60).

BUTCHERING TECHNIQUES

To dress their kill the Gabrielino hunters used scraping and fleshing tools made from rib bones, while a split cobble was used for cutting (Harrington 1942:13, items 344, 347; Hudson and Blackburn 1987:138-141). Reid reported that a cane knife was used for cutting up meat (Reid 1852:44). Hafted knives of flint and bone were used for butchering as well; they were sometimes wrapped in buckskin to protect the user's hand (Harrington 1942:13, items 340-343; Woodward 1959:xxii). Father Juan Vizcaíno wrote of the Catalina Gabrielino that "they carry as arms, a kind of knives with wide stone points, hafted in little wide wooden handles, which they carry on the head" (Vizcaíno 1959:14-15; see also M. R. Harrington 1934).

HUNTING RITUALS

In addition to the tools and implements already described, the Gabrielino hunters employed ritual and self-discipline to ensure success in the hunt. Reid wrote that "during a hunt they never tasted food; nor on their return did they partake of what they themselves killed, from an idea that whoever ate of his own game hurt his hunting abilities. Before going on a hunting expedition they stung themselves all over with nettles, more particularly the eyes, the lids of which were opened to introduce the leaves" (Reid 1852:36).

Men were prohibited from hunting or fishing when their wives were menstruating, and they avoided sexual intercourse before or during a hunt, perhaps to avoid the strong human body odors that result from sexual activity (Harrington 1942:37, items 1438-1439). The hallucinogenic *Datura* plant was also used in hunting rituals. One of the missionaries stationed at San Fernando reported that "for hunting deer they drink salt water and eat of a plant the leaf of which is large and dark green, has the shape of a sharply pointed heart while the flower is white like a lily. The Spaniards call the flower *Toluache* but in the Indian language it is called *Manit*" (Geiger and Meighan 1976:48, answer from Mission San Fernando).

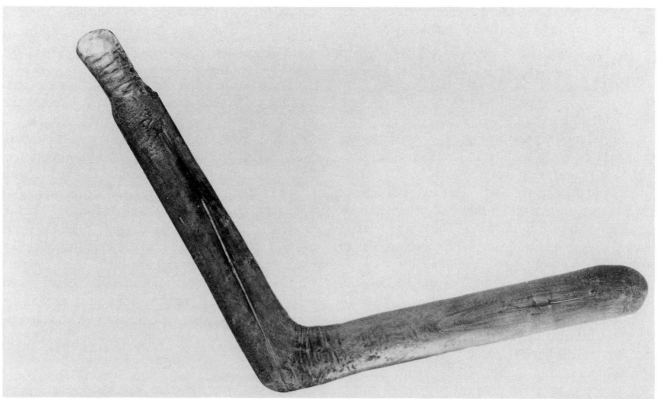

Courtesy of the Phoebe A. Hearst Museum of Anthropology, University of California, Berkeley No. 1-67252

Fig. 36. A flat Gabrielino throwing stick 24 inches long; this specimen and the one shown in Figure 37 were reportedly collected from the Indians in Santiago Canyon (located in the Santa Ana Mountains) by Samuel Shrewsbury in January, 1872.

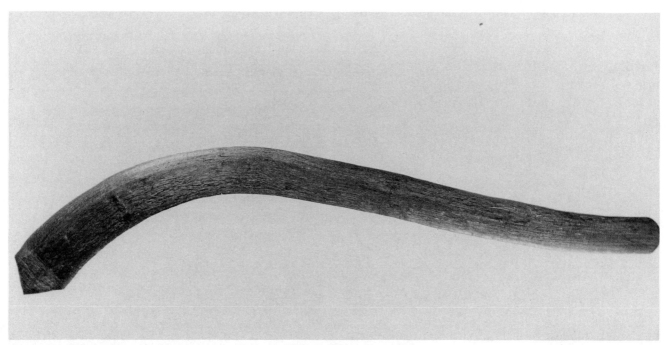

Courtesy of the Phoebe A. Hearst Museum of Anthropology, University of California, Berkeley No. 1-67253

Fig. 37. A flat Gabrielino throwing stick, 26.5 inches in length, made from oak.

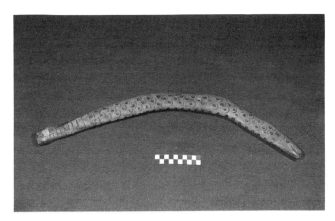

Natural History Museum of Los Angeles County No. A110.14/1274.5

Fig. 38. A decorated Gabrielino throwing stick. The design, which appears to be burned into the wood, comprises the head and body of a snake or eel; the markings on the shaft may represent scales. This artifact is from the Coronel Collection. Photograph by author.

Natural History Museum of Los Angeles County No. A110.14/1274.5

Fig. 39. Detail of the throwing stick in Figure 38; the design may represent the head of a snake or eel. Photograph by author.

Catalina Island Museum No. G-274

Fig. 40. A stone knife hafted in a wooden handle; this specimen is from Catalina Island. In 1769, Father Juan Vizcaíno reported that the island Gabrielino "carry as arms, a kind of knives with wide stone points, hafted in little wide wooden handles, which they carry on the head" (1959:14-15). Photograph by author.

Father Boscana described a ritual held prior to a communal hunt that was designed to obtain the aid and protection of *Chengiichngech*. The ceremony began when a shaman drew a spiritual being upon the ground in front of the *Chengiichngech* figure. The *tomyaar* and the shamans then passed in procession before the drawing, accompanied by the hunters, who were fully costumed and painted for the occasion. The leader then jumped "springing very high from the ground, shouting loudly, and with his bow and arrow prepared as if to shoot at something in the air. Each one in turn performed the same evolution." Next the women passed before the *Chengiichngech* figure, inclining their heads and displaying their basketry trays to *Chengiichngech* as they did so. When the ceremony was complete, the men and women departed (Boscana 1933:38).

Other general hunting practices were observed by Indian peoples throughout southern California. Thus, Cahuilla hunters ate bland foods for several days before a hunt, and they gathered in the sweathouse to sweat, bathe, and rub their bodies with herbs to reduce human odors (Bean 1972a:153-154). Chumash hunters chewed sage leaves, probably to reduce breath odors, and hunted in the early morning or late afternoon when deer were feeding. They also built small fires in which they burned green laurel leaves to attract deer (Hudson and Blackburn 1982:76). Luiseño hunters built fires of white sage (*Salvia*) and coastal sagebrush (*Artemisia*) and stood in the smoke to purify themselves before a hunt (Sparkman 1908:199).

INSECT FOODS

Insects formed an important and nutritious part of the Gabrielino diet; in fact, throughout California insects were an important dietary supplement, serving especially well as a form of "fast food" for men and women on hunting or gathering expeditions. Reid wrote that "the large locust or grasshopper was a favorite morsel, roasted on a stick at the fire," and Harrington reported that yellow-jacket larvae were also consumed by the Gabrielino (Reid 1852:22; Harrington 1942:8, item 135). The larvae of bees, wasps, ants, and beetles as well as white grubs, termites, maggots, and other insects were often eaten raw as they were found. The sticky excrement of plant lice, known as honey-dew, was eaten with gusto (Essig 1934:315-318). Honey-dew was also an important trade item, being carried to the Chumash and probably to the

Gabrielino as well by the Yokuts from the San Joaquín Valley (Woodward 1934:119).

FISHING, SEA-MAMMAL HUNTING, AND SHELLFISH GATHERING

Important faunal resources were also obtained through fishing, sea-mammal hunting, and shellfish gathering. Pedro Fages wrote that the Gabrielino were "better equipped [than those Indians to the south] for fishing; they have their rafts of reeds on which to go out to sea" (Fages 1937:23). Reid wrote that "fish, whales, seals, sea-otters, and shellfish, formed the principal subsistence of the immediate coast-range of Lodges and Islands" (Reid 1852:22), while a missionary from San Fernando noted that "those on the coast are fond of every species of fish especially the whale" (Geiger and Meighan 1976:85, answer from Mission San Fernando).

The Gabrielino utilized both shallow water and pelagic, or deep water, fishes. Along the coast and in sheltered bays and inlets such as Newport and Alamitos bays, leopard shark, gray smoothhound, shovelnose guitarfish, bat stingray, California halibut, spotted sand bass, and slim midshipmen were taken with hook and line (Follet 1966:189). The Gabrielino may have used canoes made of rushes to fish in such protected areas, as did the Luiseño to the south (Sparkman 1908:200).

The Gabrielino and the Chumash also used the plank canoe to fish the rich kelp beds that lie off the shores of the mainland and the Channel Islands. During the spring and summer seasons, large schools of tunas such as bonito, yellowtail, albacore, yellowfin, bluefin, and skipjack are present in this rich marine environment. The retreat of these fish southward during the fall and winter, as well as the increased danger of ocean travel at this time of year due to winter storms, probably restricted most deepsea fishing to the summer months (Holder 1910:54-55, 179-184; Landberg 1965:70; see also Hudson et al. 1978:122 note 258). Other fish taken by the Gabrielino included white croaker, white sea bass, skipjack, shark, guitarfish, and rockfish (Galdikas-Brindamour 1970:146; Ross 1970; Butler 1974:18, Table 4; Craib 1982:22, Table 2). Smaller fish, such as sardines, were probably taken with nets and used to supplement the Gabrielino diet.

Shellfish served as a major food source for the Gabrielino. Although in many communities shellfish were probably utilized throughout the year (see Howard 1977), it was especially during the winter when plant foods were scarce that the availability of this resource became critical (Sparkman 1908:190; Landberg 1965:72-76; Chace 1969; Hudson 1971:70). Commonly collected types of shellfish included pecten, *Chione* (cockle), *Haliotis* (abalone), oyster, limpets, clams, and octopus (Vizcaíno 1959:15; Galdikas-Brindamour 1970:144-145; Bates 1972:8). José de los Santos Juncos noted that "at Newport [there] used to be lots of white clams," which undoubtedly were collected for food by the Gabrielino (Harrington 1986:R104 F96).

Marine and shore birds also formed a regular part of the coastal Gabrielino diet. The species taken probably included those used by the Chumash, such as quail, duck, geese, cranes, gulls, and others. Sea birds were probably taken with bows and arrows, although nets, slings, and traps could also have been used (Harrington 1942:15, item 475; Landberg 1965:76-77).

In addition to food, marine fauna offered the Gabrielino a number of other important resources. Otter and seal pelts were used in the manufacture of skirts and robes (Reid 1852:23-24; Bolton 1908:84). Father Juan Vizcaíno wrote that the Gabrielino of San Clemente Island

> gave us of their possessions: two robes made of twisted skins held together with some fiber ropes of small cords, which it seems is their covering. It appears to be made of alternating black and brown strips of otter fur, three or four fingers wide, arranged vertically; and the cords have the fur twisted inside and out and these are fastened together with some small cords which look like hemp and are the color of the coconut husk (Vizcaíno 1959:12).

Other uses of marine resources included the utilization of whale vertebrae for stools, whale ribs for house frames (on the islands and on the mainland coast), and whalebone for grave markers (Holder 1910:245; Kroeber 1925:634; Harrington 1942:10; item 230; Winterbourne 1967:44; Morgan 1979).

Abalone (*Haliotis* sp.) shells were modified with asphaltum hole plugs and utilized for dishes, and when specially cut and shaped these shells were used for fishhooks and ear ornaments (Reid 1852:44;

Harrington 1942:7, items 60-61; Hudson and Blackburn 1983:278-279). Beads were manufactured from *Olivella*, *Haliotis*, and *Tivella* shells and were used both as ornamentation and as currency (Reid 1852:43; Harrington 1942:27, items 1026, 1028). Clamshells were commonly used by men as tweezers for plucking whiskers (Hudson and Blackburn 1985:353-354).

Shell beads might be manufactured from entire shells or from portions of shells that were carefully shaped by grinding. Piercing was accomplished using a stone drill followed by a bristle, perhaps using a sea lion whisker with abrasive sand. The value of a particular shell bead depended primarily upon the labor spent in its manufacture, disk-shaped beads of *Olivella* shell being typically less valuable than tubular shell beads of *Tivella* (Heizer 1968:121-122, note 62; King 1978:59-60; Hudson and Blackburn 1985:269-294).

BOATS AND FISHING EQUIPMENT

The Gabrielino utilized a variety of techniques in their pursuit of marine faunal resources. Shallow-water fish could be taken with a hook and line, as could deep-water fish, and nets were used as well. Shellfish could be easily gathered, although abalone required the use of bone pry bars (Bryan 1970a:88). Sea-mammals, as well as fish, could be taken with harpoons, tridents and spears, while herds of sea-mammals such as seals could be surprised on land and individual animals run down and clubbed to death (Wagner 1929:236; Vizcaíno 1959:16; Landberg 1965:61-62; Hudson and Blackburn 1982:193-220).

Sea otters were probably hunted while the animals were swimming. One hunting method reported for the California Indians employed an otter pup as a decoy. The pup was snatched from the ocean's surface while the parent otter was diving for food. A cord was then tied to the pup's leg; attached to the cord were several fishhooks. Once the decoy was prepared, the hunter released the pup and moved off. To bring the parent otter to the surface the hunter tugged on the cord, thereby causing the pup to cry out. Hearing this, the parent otter surfaced to rescue its pup, became entangled in the hooks and line, and was rendered an easy target for the hunter's club (Ogden 1941:14; Rudkin 1956:19, cited in Landberg 1965:60).

THE PLANK CANOE (*TE'AAT*)

Deep-sea fishing and sea otter hunting required

sea-worthy vessels, of which the Gabrielino had several types. By far the most impressive of these was the plank canoe, or *te'aat*, perhaps better known by the Chumash name of *tomol* (Hudson and Blackburn 1982:341-348; Harrington 1986:R102 F582). Archaeological and ethnographic data indicate that the plank canoe was built and used by the Chumash as far north as Point Conception, and by the Gabrielino, and perhaps the Luiseño, as far south as San Clemente Island (Sparkman 1908:200; Woodward 1959:xviii-xxi; Vizcaíno 1959:16; McKusick and Warren 1959:129; Landberg 1965:38). Plank canoes holding eight to ten Indians were observed off Catalina Island by the Cabrillo Expedition in 1542 (Wagner 1941:46), and in 1602 the Sebastián Vizcaíno Expedition, also visiting Santa Catalina, observed Gabrielino

> fishing in some small well-made canoes of boards fastened together, with their poops and bows like barks. Some of these canoes were so large that they would hold more than twenty people. In the small ones there are ordinarily three when they go fishing, two men with their paddles and two-bladed oars, seated or on their knees, one in the stern and the other in the bow, and a boy between to throw out such water as the canoe might make (Wagner 1929:236).

More than a century later, in 1769, Father Juan Vizcaíno wrote of the Gabrielino that

> their little canoes which at the most would hold seven men were made of planks of wood, about one finger thick, and in pieces sewed together and tarred on the outside. One of the Indians was ever bailing out the water that enters. Nevertheless they know how to handle them even in heavy seas, the oars are two pieces of wood and they stroke to one side, and the other, with much agility (Vizcaíno 1959:16).

The design of Gabrielino and Chumash canoes was essentially the same, the Gabrielino *te'aat* differing only in that the prow and stern had wash strakes (an extra row of hull planks) with squared edges (probably to aid in running the canoe through heavy surf) while Chumash canoes had rounded strakes (Hudson et al. 1978:96-97, note 199). The details of plank canoe construction were recorded by Harrington; there were three stages (see Hudson et al. 1978; Hudson and Blackburn 1982:341-348).

In the first stage of canoe construction the wood was carefully chosen (driftwood logs of pine being

Fig. 41. The *Helek*, a replica of a Chumash *tomol* (plank canoe) constructed using data from the ethnographic notes of Harrington. The 27 foot-long vessel proved capable of speeds of six to eight knots under favorable wind and swell conditions.

preferred) and then split into planks using bone wedges. The planks were shaped with tools of stone and shell and then smoothed with sandpaper made from sharkskin. An alternative method used by the Gabrielino for smoothing planks involved attaching a rope to the plank and dragging it across the sand at low tide. One man stood on top of the plank, and his weight combined with the abrasive action of the sand gradually smoothed the wood surface (Alliot 1917). The bottom board of the canoe was carefully shaped, wide in the center and tapering to a point at each end, and the finished bottom board was placed on forked posts to await the addition of the hull boards.

In the second stage of construction, hull boards were fitted to the bottom board. Planks were soaked in water or heated over a flame to render them pliable, and then they were bent to fit the contours of the hull. The ends of the boards were mitered to produce a stronger joint, and the edges were beveled to permit

caulking to be forced into the seams. Following this, the hull boards were glued in place with tar; the partially assembled hull was shaded by tule mats to prevent the sun's heat from softening the adhesive. Next, the planks were "sewn" together for greater strength. Along each seam, pairs of holes were drilled into adjoining boards and several stitches of vegetable fiber cord taken through each. The stitches, which were recessed in grooves previously cut into the planks, were then knotted and glued into place.

In the third and final stage of assembly a crossbeam was added amidships to strengthen the hull. Gunwale boards were added (the gunwale is the upper edge of the hull), a V-shaped gap being left open at the prow and stern to allow lines to be run out of the vessel. Reinforcing posts were installed inside the canoe at both ends. The raised wash strakes, known as the "ears" of the *te'aat,* were then added. The finished vessel was carefully caulked with plant fibers

Catalina Island Museum Nos. G-237 (container) and G-238 (applicator)

Fig. 42. A soapstone vessel for melting and applying asphaltum; asphaltum was used as an adhesive and as a waterproofing agent. Soapstone, which can be placed directly over a flame without shattering, provided an ideal raw material for many applications. The applicator is of shale. Photograph by author.

and tar, stained with red ochre and pine pitch to seal the wood, and decorated with shell inlay or spangles of crushed abalone shell.

A replica of a Chumash tomol was built for Harrington by Fernando Librado in 1913 for the Panama-California Exhibition, held in San Diego in 1915. Today this canoe is on display at the Santa Barbara Museum of Natural History. The first canoe to be constructed using data from the ethnographic notes of Harrington was built in Santa Barbara in 1976 and christened the *Helek*. An account of this project has been published in Hudson et al. (1978). Following construction the *Helek* participated in several sea trials including a circumnavigation of the northern Channel Islands by an Indian crew. During these trials the vessel—27 feet in length—proved capable of speeds of six to eight knots under favorable wind and swell conditions (Hudson et al. 1978).

DUGOUTS AND TULE CANOES

Other less sophisticated watercraft were used by the Gabrielino as well; these included dugout canoes and boats made of tule reeds. Regarding the dugout, Father Boscana wrote that "they constructed out of logs very swift and excellent canoes for fishing" (Boscana 1933:24). Due to their inherent instability, dugouts were used primarily on sheltered bodies of water and were paddled or poled from place to place. In constructing a dugout, a willow or cottonwood log was chosen and the bark removed. Next, the top of the log was flattened, although the prow and stern were left slightly higher, and the interior was

hollowed by burning with hot coals. Final shaping was accomplished using hand adzes made of stone (Hudson et al. 1978:31-36; Hudson and Blackburn 1982:338-340).

Unlike the dugout canoes, boats made from tules were stable enough to be used for ocean travel. Pedro Fages (1937:23) wrote that the Gabrielino "have their rafts of reeds . . . and by means of these the Indians of the plain of San Gabriel communicate with the islanders of San Clemente and Santa Barbara." One of Strong's consultants noted that shell bead money was brought from Santa Catalina to the mainland Fernandeño on tule boats (Strong 1929:95-96). José de los Santos Juncos reported that "The island Indians were powerful witches. They used to pass to and from the islands on balsas of tules" (Harrington 1986:R104 F40). According to Mrs. James Rosemyre, the Gabrielino word for tule canoe is *tah-rī'ng-hah* (Merriam n.d.c).

Tule canoes were of two types: a three-bundle canoe and a five-bundle canoe. The three-bundle canoe utilized one bundle for the bottom "board" and another for each side, while the five-bundle canoe utilized one bundle for the bottom and two for each side. Construction details were similar for both vessels, and three days was the required time for completion. The tules were cut green and then allowed to dry. They were tied into bundles that tapered at both ends. A willow rod was inserted into each bundle for added strength. The bundle that served as the "bottom board" was always longer than the others so that when the bundles were tied together the prow and stern would be raised. A layer of tar was applied to the craft for waterproofing, and clay was sprinkled on top of the tar to remove the stickiness.

A replica of a tule canoe was built by the Santa Barbara Center for Archaeological Preservation, Research, and Education in 1979. This vessel, which was built using authentic materials and techniques, was 18 feet long and 3 feet wide and supported a total payload of 470 pounds. It could average a speed of two miles per hour (Hudson et al. 1978; Hudson and Blackburn 1982:331-335).

SPEARS, HARPOONS, AND TRIDENTS

The Gabrielino often used spears, harpoons, and tridents when fishing from their canoes, and these implements were studied with interest by the early

Spanish explorers.   In 1602 Father Antonio de la Ascensión observed that the Gabrielino used long, slender poles

> for their fishing, as our people do harpoons. At the end of the pole they fasten a harpoon made of fishbone, and to this they tie firmly a long strong line like twine. Carrying these in their canoes, when they see in the bottom near the canoes some large fish or one of reasonable size, they strike them with these harpoons. When this is fast to the fish, they give it the line if it is a large one, and follow it, little by little nearing the beach, where they finish by killing it and drawing it on land. The small ones they at once raise into the canoe (Wagner 1929:236).

Father Juan Vizcaíno, writing in 1769, observed of the Gabrielino of San Clemente Island that "they carry shafts with harpoon points which they use in fishing. Each harpoon has three barbs" (Vizcaíno 1959:16).

The Gabrielino used a simple fish spear consisting of a straight wooden shaft with a barbed point of wood or bone permanently fixed to one end, as well as a harpoon with a detachable foreshaft equipped with a retrieval line. Harpoons with barbed points of wood or bone were used for fishing, while harpoons with stone points were used for sea-mammal hunting. Fragments of such harpoons have been found at a number of archaeological sites including Big Dog Cave on San Clemente Island and Goff's Island on the coast near Laguna Beach. The Channel Islanders may also have combined the arrow and the harpoon to create a "harpoon arrow" with the advantages of both

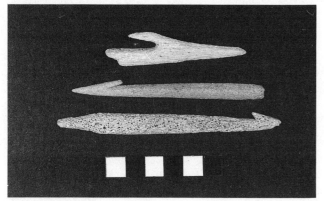

Catalina Island Museum No. G-21 (all)

Fig. 43. Bone spear or harpoon points from Catalina Island. In 1602, Father Antonio de la Ascension reported that "In the island there are many elder trees, which grow some long slender poles the Indians use for their fishing. . . . At the end of the pole they fasten a harpoon made of fishbone, and to this they tie firmly a long strong line like twine" (Wagner 1929:236). Photograph by author.

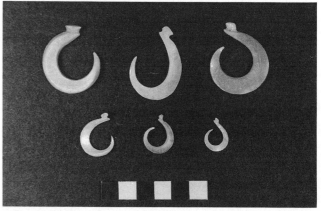

Catalina Island Museum No. G-270 (all)

Fig. 44. Circular fishhooks made from abalone shell. The glittering shell served as its own lure, although the hook could also be baited with mussel; the line was tied around the knob and secured with asphaltum. In operation, the circular hook became lodged in the mouth or stomach of a fish. Photograph by author.

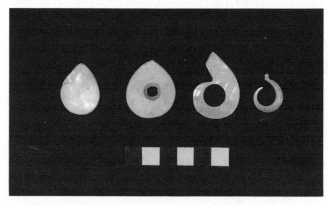

Catalina Island Museum Nos. G-264, G-266, G-267, G-270 (left to right)

Fig. 45. Four stages in the manufacture of a shell fishhook from rough blank to finished hook. Photograph by author.

weapons (McKusick and Warren 1959:129-130; Winterbourne 1967:33; Hudson and Blackburn 1982:189-219).

Harpoons were manufactured from ironwood or holly, while foreshafts were made of willow or elder. The completed harpoon measured approximately eight feet in length. Harpoon points were manufactured from wood, bone, or stone and could be unilaterally or bilaterally barbed. Retrieval lines 300 feet or more in length were manufactured from horsenettle or red milkweed (Hudson and Blackburn 1982:205-220).

FISHHOOKS

Several different types of fishhooks were used by the Gabrielino. Juan Vizcaíno noted in 1769 that the Gabrielino "use fishhooks of cactus thorns twisted like hooks" (Vizcaíno 1959:16). Reid reported that "fishhooks . . . and many other articles were made of either bone or shell" (Reid 1852:44). Circular fishhooks were made of abalone or mussel shell or of bone and were manufactured in stages from a rough blank to a finished hook. Fish lines were attached by means of grooves or a small knob on the shaft and were secured with tar. In operation the circular fishhook became lodged in the mouth or stomach of bottom-feeding fish. The glittering shell may have served as its own lure, although sometimes black mussel meat was used as bait (Schumacher 1875; Harrington 1942:7, items 60-61; Winterbourne 1967; Bryan 1970a:39-40; Ross 1970; Hudson and Blackburn 1982:172-178; Craib 1982:38; Strudwick 1985).

Other types of hooks used by the Gabrielino included a gorge consisting of a short piece of bone pointed at both ends, and composite fishhooks made from two pieces of bone bound together in a V-shape. Special decoys of abalone shell were used to troll for fish. Fish lines were generally made from surf grass, nettle, yucca fiber, or red milkweed, and rocks served as sinkers (Reid 1852:44; McKusick and Warren 1959:130-134; Hudson and Blackburn 1982:165-171, 179-183).

NETS

The Gabrielino used a variety of nets for fishing and for hunting birds and small mammals. These nets were made by craftsmen, of whom Father Boscana wrote that "the old men and the poorer class devoted a portion of the day to constructing . . . nets of various sizes, which were used for sundry purposes, such as for catching fish and wild fowl" (Boscana 1933:56). Reid wrote simply that "hemp was made from nettles, and manufactured into nets, fishing lines, thread, &c." (Reid 1852:44).

The Gabrielino very likely made use of dip nets, gill nets, drag nets, and seine nets. Dip nets were small, bag-like nets that could be mounted on a circular or semi-circular hoop two or three feet in diameter. Gill nets were used for catching sardines and small fish; they had a mesh one and one-half inches wide. These nets were suspended in the water vertically and functioned by entangling fish that tried to swim through the mesh. Sea-grass, surf grass, and yucca fiber were used in their manufacture. Drag nets had a large, four-inch mesh and were pulled behind a canoe to catch large fish such as bonita. These nets might be six or eight feet in length and were made of

milkweed or willow-fiber string. The seine net was suspended in the water vertically by means of floats and stone sinkers and was drawn by canoes to encircle schools of fish (Hudson and Blackburn 1982:153-164).

RITUALS

Despite the seaworthiness of the plank canoe and the effectiveness of Gabrielino fishing techniques, seafaring remained a risky undertaking. Ocean travel was always hazardous, as illustrated by a Chumash account from the Mission Period in which 27 canoes were lost during an expedition to San Miguel Island (Hudson et al. 1978:148-150). In addition, no amount of skill could guarantee the timely arrival of migrating schools of fish such as the tuna. It was quite natural, therefore, that Gabrielino mariners sought aid from the supernatural world to help them in their efforts.

Gabrielino fishermen observed rituals and practices similar to those followed by hunters. For example, Father Boscana reported that, just as deer hunters were prohibited from eating of their own kill, "the fishermen also possessed the same idea with regard to their fish" (Boscana 1933:62). The most notable evidence for the Gabrielino mariner's reliance upon the supernatural world, however, is the extensive assortment of handsome soapstone carvings found in archaeological sites on the Channel Islands and the mainland coast (Kroeber 1925:629-630; Cameron 1983, 1988). These soapstone effigies display a variety of naturalistic and abstract forms. They may have served as talismans that were used to channel supernatural power from a guardian spirit or dream helper to an individual. In some cases they served as physical representatives of the spiritual beings, although objects other than carvings, such as crystals or parts of animals, could be used as well. A talisman might be held or rubbed to activate its power, and *Datura* intoxication might have been an important part of the ritual (Applegate 1978:53-59; Wallace 1987:52).

Some effigies seem to relate to specific supernatural beings. Thus, carvings of canoes were most likely symbolic representations of Peregrine Falcon, who conferred skill in canoemanship. Similarly, killer whales and swordfish were believed by the Chumash to drive whales ashore where they would be stranded and could be taken for food. In Chumash mythology, swordfish appear as powerful supernatural beings dwelling at the bottom of the ocean (Heizer 1957; Landberg 1965:67; Blackburn 1975:175-190). Other

Natural History Museum of Los Angeles County Nos. A3121/2 (both)
Fig. 46. Small effigies of soapstone carved in the form of water birds. These specimens were reportedly collected from the Redondo Beach vicinity. Photograph by author.

forms chosen for representation by soapstone carvers included seals, birds, fish, and abstract compositions generally referred to by archaeologists as "pelican stones."

Regardless of their form, the use and purpose of these talismans was probably the same, that is, the acquisition of supernatural powers conferred by a guardian spirit. As such, these carvings represent sensitive works of art as well as testaments to the religious beliefs and faith of Gabrielino seafarers (Lee 1981; Hudson and Blackburn 1986:171-219; Koerper and Labbé 1987; Koerper and Cramer 1988). (It must be noted that the authenticity of a number of elaborate soapstone effigy carvings attributed to southern California sites remains questionable. For a more comprehensive discussion on this subject see Hoover 1974; Lee 1981:16, 47-50, 58, 1993.)

FLORAL RESOURCES

The second important group of resources available to the Gabrielino was floral, or plant resources. The Gabrielino gathered and utilized a large number of plant species for food and manufacturing needs. Although the total number of plants used by the Gabrielino is unknown, an indication of the extent of usage can be gained through comparison with neighboring Indian groups. For example, more than 200 plant species were used by the Cahuilla Indians for foods, crafts, and medicines (Bean and Saubel 1972; Bean 1972a:36; 1978:578). Similarly, the use of more than 100 plant species has been documented

for the Luiseño, while 150 different species have been reported for the Chumash (Sparkman 1908:228-234; Kroeber 1925:649-651; Landberg 1965:77-81; Timbrook 1990).

Plants provided a versatile and readily available resource for Gabrielino manufacturing. Trees supplied the wood used for building Gabrielino homes and manufacturing bows and arrows, spears, harpoons, bowls, platters, and dishes, while driftwood was used in building the *te'aat*. Tules, also known as bulrushes, were used in making houses and reed canoes as well as baskets and containers. Two-ply, three-ply, or four-ply cordage was made by rolling fibers of Indian hemp, milkweed, or nettle on the thigh. Heavier rope was woven from several strands of two-ply cordage (Harrington 1942:24-25, items 906-907, 910, 912-914, 916; Hudson and Blackburn 1987:154-160). Nets and fish lines were manufactured from nettle, willow-fiber, milkweed, seagrass, and yucca-fiber (Reid 1852:44; Hudson and Blackburn 1982:153-158, 163-164). José de los Santos Juncos reported that the Gabrielino "twisted string on the thigh. [They] made it long. They then made redas, carrying nets. They had a jarete (drawstring). Women carried things in them on [their] back" (Harrington 1986:R102 F745).

Other items made from plant materials included brushes of soaproot fibers and matting manufactured from tules by twining or by piercing and sewing together the stems (Harrington 1942:12, 24, items 309, 871). The sap of the milkweed plant was boiled and used for chewing gum. Pepper grass provided a condiment used in cooking and seasoning food. The insides of gourds were used as soap and as a stain remover for washing clothing (Reid 1852:23; Harrington 1942:9, item 153; Merriam n.d.c). In addition, as was discussed in Chapter 6, most Gabrielino medicines were derived in whole or part from plants such as wild tobacco, *Datura*, nettles, or marsh mallows.

PLANT FOODS

Early explorers and writers provided important information on Gabrielino plant usage. Pedro Fages wrote that the women

. . . collect their seeds, pine nuts, madroña berries, acorns, etc. . . . Cactus fruit of superior flavor, wild grapes, and brambleberries abound in the country. . . . There are many willows, from fruit of which in season the Indians know how to make a certain wine which has no unpleasant flavor. The mountaineers know how to make also a kind of sweet paste, and sugar. . . . They utilize the *tule* (cattail reed), making *atole*—gruel—from the seeds, and bread from the roots (Fages 1937:22).

Reid also discussed the plant foods eaten by the Gabrielino. According to Reid acorns were crushed and made into "a sort of mush" that "was eaten when cold."

> The next favorite food was the kernel of a species of plum which grows in the mountains and Islands, called by them *Islay*, (pronounced eeslie). Some Americans call it the *Mountain Cherry*. . . . *Chia*, which is a small, gray, oblong seed, was procured from a plant apparently of the thistle kind. . . . Pepper grass seed was also much used, the tender stalks of wild sage, several kinds of berries and a number of roots (Reid 1852:23).

ACORNS

One of the most important plant foods consumed by the Gabrielino was the acorn. In fact, the utilization of the acorn as a food resource was a development of crucial importance in the evolution of sedentary hunting-gathering cultures; it has been suggested that acorn-harvesting cultures such as the Gabrielino reached a level of complexity equal to or greater than some agricultural societies (Bean and Saubel 1972:121-122).

The acorn's importance is derived from its high nutritional value. Acorns are superior to corn and wheat in fat and fiber content, virtually equivalent to those grains in carbohydrates, and inferior only in ash and protein. In fact, because of its high nutritional value the acorn was consumed in European and Mediterranean countries such as England, France, Italy, Spain, and Algeria until well into the 1900s; in these countries acorns supplied as much as 20 percent of the food consumed by peoples of lower socio-economic levels (Merriam 1918). Acorns were harvested by California Indians from Mexico to Oregon, and although the coast live oak was considered the most desirable, even the nuts of the scrub oak would be eaten during times of crop failure (Balls 1962:10-14).

The key to the successful use of the acorn lay in the development of a technique for leaching out the tannic acid that is naturally present in the nut, thereby

making the meat more palatable. Leaching not only removes the bitter flavor, leaving a sweet, nutty-tasting meal, but it also improves the digestibility of the acorn by as much as ten percent (Merriam 1918:136; Gifford 1936:302-303). Reid described the leaching process used by the Gabrielino in some detail.

> Acorns, after being divested of their shell, were dried, and pounded in stone mortars, put into filters of willow twigs worked into a concave form, and raised on little mounds of sand, which were lined inside with a coating of two inches of sand; water added and mixed up.—Then filled up again and again with more water, at first hot, then cold, until all the tanning [tannin] and bitter principle was extracted. The residue was then collected and washed free of any sandy particles it might contain. On settling, the water was poured off. After being well boiled, it became a sort of mush, and was eaten when cold (Reid 1852:22-23; comment in brackets in original).

Acorns were normally collected in October, and expeditions to acorn-gathering sites were an important part of the seasonal migration patterns of the mainland Gabrielino. An intense, cooperative communal effort was necessary to avoid crop loss to birds, rodents, and other animals. The men climbed the trees and shook the acorns free while the women and children collected

Southwest Museum No. 585.G.6

Fig. 47. A wooden mortar from the San Fernando Valley. Wooden mortars were used in the processing of acorns. Photograph by author.

them (Hudson 1971:59; Bean 1972a:37). Some acorns might be processed on the spot, while the rest were transported to the primary settlement to be stored in large, coiled granary baskets. During the summer the granaries remained outdoors to allow air to circulate and dry the nuts; during winter they were moved inside. To discourage rodents, the granaries were placed on elevated platforms of poles (Harrington 1942:9, item 174; Bean 1978:578, figures 4 and 5; Hudson and Blackburn 1983:58-68).

Acorns could be ground in mortars of wood or granite, the latter hollowed from small boulders or bedrock outcroppings. Stone pestles were used in stone mortars, while wooden pestles were used with wooden mortars. To prevent the meal from being scattered during grinding, a bottomless basket was sometimes glued with asphalt to the working surface to create a basket-hopper mortar. Brushes of soaproot fiber or hair were used for sweeping together scattered meal (Harrington 1942:11-12, items 273-274, 290, 292, 309-311; Hudson and Blackburn 1983:100-129).

Acorn mush was prepared in watertight cooking baskets or soapstone bowls. Heated stones were dropped into the cooking baskets to bring the water to a boil, but soapstone bowls with rounded bottoms could be placed directly over the flames. The mush was stirred using a wooden paddle (Harrington 1942:9, 12, items 164, 320, 337, 339, 1986:R105 F679-680).

ISLAY

Another important plant food used by the Gabrielino was islay (*Prunus ilicifolia*). Although the pulp of this fruit was little used, the seeds were ground into meal and made into gruel (Harrington 1942:8, item 132; Balls 1962:15). Reid wrote of islay that "it has a large stone, to which numerous fibres are attached, pervading the pulp, of which there is very little. . . . This, cooked, formed a very nutritious, rich, saccharine aliment; and looked much like dry boiled frijoles" (Reid 1852:23).

CHIA

Chía (*Salvia columbariae*) was widely used by the Gabrielino and other California Indians, as well as by the Spanish and Mexican settlers. As late as 1894, chía seeds were regularly sold in Los Angeles stores (Reid 1852:23; Balls 1962:23-24). Chía seeds were collected by bending the plant stalks over a flat,

tightly-woven basket and brushing them with a fan-shaped seed beater of twined basketry construction (Harrington 1942:21, item 746; Balls 1962:24; Hudson and Blackburn 1982:235-238). When the basket was full it was dumped into a large carrying basket shaped like an upside-down truncated cone. The carrying basket was worn on the back and secured by a strap that passed across the forehead; a basketry cap was worn to protect the skin from chafing (Harrington 1942:21-22, items 737-738, 740-741, 795; Hudson and Blackburn 1982:259-265, 267-268, 1985:66-75).

Chía could be prepared in a number of ways. Young *Salvia* shoots were eaten raw. The seeds could be roasted and ground into flour which was eaten raw, mixed with water to form gruel, or used to make a drink (Balls 1962:25; Harrington 1986:R102 F532, R105 F314). José de los Santos Juncos remembered that "Indians used to eat raw tender shoots of salvia. It made their tongues black" (Harrington 1986:R102 F764). Reid reported that "*Chia* . . . roasted and ground into meal, was eaten with cold water, being of a glutinous consistency, and very cooling" (Reid 1852:23). The Chumash are known to have made chía seeds into loaves, and a refreshing beverage could be made by dropping the seeds into water and stirring (Balls 1962:25; Landberg 1965:79).

ROOTS AND BULBS

Roots and bulbs were an important part of the Gabrielino diet, a fact noted by several early Spanish explorers. In 1602, Father Antonio de la Ascensión observed that "in the island [Santa Catalina] there is a great quantity of something like potatoes . . . which the Indians carry to the mainland to sell" (Wagner 1929:237). In his diary, expedition leader Sebastián Vizcaíno reported that upon landing at Santa Catalina "many Indians were on the beach, and the women treated us to roasted sardines and a small fruit like sweet potatoes" (Bolton 1908:83). In 1769, Father Juan Vizcaíno noted that the San Clemente Indians "brought little roots, which have no flavor, resembling little onions or heads of garlic, they have two little heads joined together with skin the same as onions" (Vizcaíno 1959:16). Wild hyacinth, called "caco-mites" by the Spaniards (*Broadiaea* sp.), was one of the important roots gathered by the Gabrielino. Harrington's consultant Jesús Jauro remembered that "there are cacomites here in the hills. We used to eat them when children" (Harrington 1986:R105 F317).

Roots and tubers were harvested using a long, straight digging stick that could be weighted for greater effectiveness (Harrington 1942:9, item 146; McKusick and Warren 1959:145). The Chumash are reported to have manufactured such sticks from mountain mahogany, ironwood, holly, or whalebone (Hudson and Blackburn 1982:241-251). Roots were cooked by roasting or baking in earth ovens. When the last Indian was removed from San Nicolas Island in 1853, she prepared a meal of "roots of two different kinds, one called *corcomites* . . . and placed them in the fire which was burning within the inclosure" (Nidever 1937:83).

OTHER PLANT FOODS

Other plant foods consumed by the Gabrielino included clover, wild sunflower seeds, and cholla cactus seeds. The pulp of pounded cholla leaves was eaten as well (Harrington 1986:R105 F571, 573; Merriam n.d.c). Other plant foods used by neighboring Indian groups and likely to have been gathered by the Gabrielino included piñon, cresses and celery, buckeye nuts, wild strawberries, laurel berries, mushrooms, and seaweed (Landberg 1965:77-81; Bean 1972a:38-42). Curiously, Harrington specifically denied the use of mesquite, yucca, and agave (also known as century plant) as food resources by the Gabrielino (Harrington 1942:8, items 124-126).

Wild tobacco (*Nicotiana* sp.) was used by the Gabrielino as both a sedative and a narcotic, in addition to the medicinal uses described in the last chapter. Juan Meléndrez reported to Harrington that his grandfather and "all the other ind. [Indians] of his time in San Fernando" took *peeshpevat*, or wild tobacco, at bedtime. According to Meléndrez "they had a morterito [small mortar] full of pounded up pespibata made into 'atole' [gruel] with water. . . . They 'wet' (dipped in) the three fingers of r. [right] hand . . . & put it in mouth & swallowed, then drank a little cold water [and] then went outside & got dizzy & vomited. . . ." According to Juan Meléndrez, the Fernandeño also made cakes of wild tobacco which they formed in sardine tins. These cakes were traded for $1.00 each to the Tejón Indians attending fiestas at San Fernando (Harrington 1986:R106 F195). A Chumash Indian observed that after taking tobacco "you do not think of women or anything, just sleep" (Librado et al. 1979:148).

BURNING

The Gabrielino increased the yield of a number of wild plant foods by periodically burning off large areas of grassland. When traveling through the Gabrielino territory in July, 1769, Father Juan Crespí observed several locations that had been burned. After passing the spot that would later become the site of Mission San Juan Capistrano, the explorers "descended from the high hill" on which they had stopped "to a valley in the same direction." They "came to two good villages, whose people were all very friendly" and "traveled through this valley for about two leagues; it is of good land, but they had burned all the grass." Sixteen days later while crossing the Puente Hills the party "ascended a pass and entered a valley of very large live oaks and alders." They continued on to "a broad and spacious plain of fine black earth, with much grass, although we found it burned" (Bolton 1927:137, 143). Some of the plants that reach peak abundance in areas that were previously burned include bunch grasses, chía (*Salvia columbariae*), red maids (*Calandrinia* spp.), clover, and bulbs. Burning off the grasslands may also have improved hunting by increasing the browse for deer and smaller animals (Timbrook et al. 1982).

MANUFACTURING USES OF PLANTS

In addition to food, plants provided many of the materials used in Gabrielino crafts and manufacturing. Wood from oak, willow, sycamore, pine, and other trees was used in constructing houses, canoes, bows, harpoons, bowls, mortars, platters, and a variety of other utensils (Harrington 1942:11-12; J. W. Hudson n.d.). Tule was the primary material used in the construction of reed canoes. Tule, wild alfalfa, fern, and carrizo were used as thatching on Gabrielino homes (Harrington 1942:10-11, items 206, 262).

BASKETRY

The basketry skills of the Gabrielino elicited praise from the early explorers. Father Antonio de la Ascensión reported that when the Spaniards visited Santa Catalina in 1602 "our people asked them [the Indians] by signs for water. They at once brought a rush barrel full of water, which was good" (Wagner 1929:236). Father Juan Vizcaíno made a similar observation of the San Clemente islanders and wrote

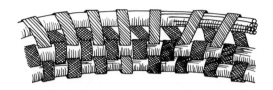

Multiple Rod Foundation

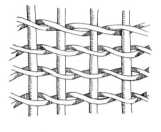

Twining

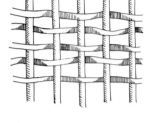

Wickerwork

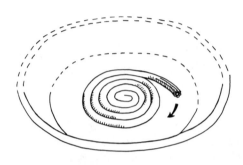
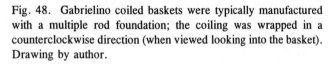

Clockwise Coiling

Fig. 48. Gabrielino coiled baskets were typically manufactured with a multiple rod foundation; the coiling was wrapped in a counterclockwise direction (when viewed looking into the basket). Drawing by author.

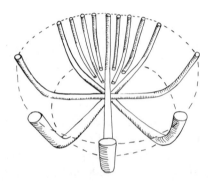

Warp Foundation

Fig. 49. The Gabrielino manufactured woven baskets using both twining and wickerwork. Drawing by author.

that "signals were made asking if they had water, then they went away and brought back a bottle made of reeds tarred on the inside" (Vizcaíno 1959:18). Father Juan Crespí reported in 1769 that the Spaniards "observed that they have houses made of willows, and large baskets of reeds so tightly woven that they hold water" (Bolton 1926:126). Pedro Fages observed that "the women know how to weave baskets of varying capacity" (Fages 1937:22); Reid wrote that "their baskets made out of split rushes are too well known so [to] require description; but though water-proof, they were used only for dry purposes. The vessels in use for liquids were roughly made of rushes and plastered outside and in with bitumen or pitch, called by them *sanot*" (Reid 1852:44-45; brackets in original).

The Gabrielino manufactured both coiled and woven baskets. Coiled baskets were manufactured with a multiple-rod foundation, the coiling wrapped in a clockwise direction when looking into the basket.

Woven baskets were manufactured using both close-work and openwork twining, work beginning at the bottom of the basket with four warps in two pairs (Harrington 1942:20-23, items 708, 714, 716, 732, 735, 821). Gabrielino baskets were manufactured from the stems of rushes (*Juncus* sp.) and squawbush (*Rhus trilobata*), as well as grass (*Epicampes rigens*) and willow shoots. Decorative motifs included both geometric and realistic designs executed in three colors. Red and green were obtained by using rushes of the proper shade, while black was obtained by dyeing (Harrington 1942:22-23, items 819-821, 835, 843-844, 849; Hudson and Blackburn 1987:212-240). Harrington noted that rushes could be dyed black by soaking them in water

in which a small blue-flowered plant had been soaked. That plant grows hereabouts in the rainy season. It is about a foot or a foot and a half tall, has leaves like those of freesias (a bulbous plant which grows in our gardens), and a blue flower shaped like a daisy flower. . . . no decoction was

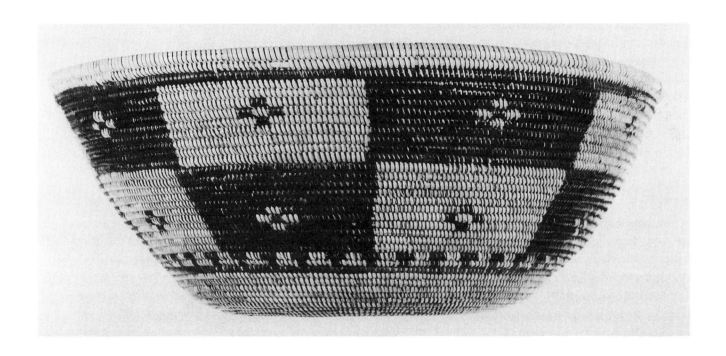

Courtesy of the Phoebe A. Hearst Museum of Anthropology, University of California, Berkeley No. 1-20916

Fig. 50. A coiled Gabrielino basket, 13.75 inches in diameter and 4.75 inches deep. The Gabrielino created basketry designs by utilizing natural color variations in the rushes (*Juncus* sp.) or by dyeing.

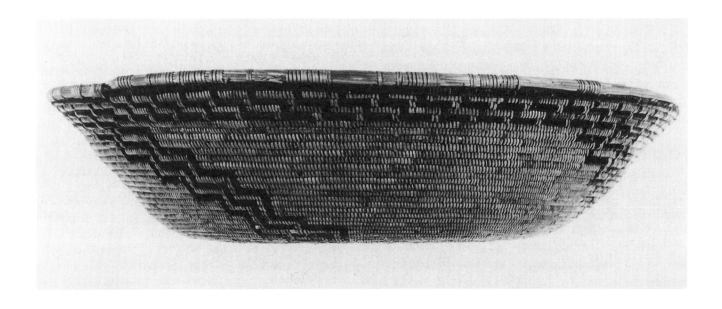

Courtesy of the Phoebe A. Hearst Museum of Anthropology, University of California, Berkeley No. 1-157455

Fig. 51. A coiled basket attributed to the Gabrielino; this specimen is 17 inches in diameter.

made for dyeing the junco but . . . the plant was merely pounded up perhaps and . . . the junco was soaked in the water in which the pounded up plant was (Harrington 1986:R105 F684).

The Gabrielino manufactured baskets in a variety of shapes and styles. Winnowing and sifting baskets were made in small and large sizes and were manufactured by coiling. Tightly coiled, watertight baskets were used for cooking, and typically these baskets were made in the shape of a truncated cone with a flat bottom. In use, these baskets were filled with water, and hot stones were added to bring the liquid to a boil (Harrington 1942:21-22, items 752, 757-758, 764; Hudson and Blackburn 1983:132-148, 175-182).

Basket-hopper mortars were used to prevent seeds and meal from blowing away during grinding. The basket-hopper consisted of a bottomless basket, either coiled or twined of *Epicampes* grass; it was glued to the top of a shallow mortar using asphaltum (Harrington 1942:22, items 778-779, 813-814; Hudson and Blackburn 1983:112-117). Large and small basketry bowls were used for serving food; typically these bowls were manufactured by coiling and were made in the shape of a truncated cone or a shallow basin (Hudson and Blackburn 1983:221-243).

Small items such as needles, awls, and strings of shell bead money were stored in globular or bottle-necked trinket baskets manufactured from coiled grass (*Epicampes* sp.). Trinket baskets were decorated with both abstract and realistic designs (Harrington 1942:22-23, items 813, 818-820; Hudson and Blackburn 1983:396-421). A basketry cap was worn to protect the forehead from chafing when wearing a carrying basket with a head strap (Hudson and Blackburn 1985:66-75).

WATER BOTTLES

Perhaps the most intriguing of the baskets made by the Gabrielino were the tarred water bottles, which came in both large and small sizes. The larger bottles stood as tall as three feet and were used for storing water inside the home. These were made of rushes or tules. Each bottle had a neck and a rounded bottom. Stoppers were made of tules (Harrington 1986:R102 F502; Hudson and Blackburn 1983:39-54).

George Nidever, the captain of the vessel that removed the last Nicoleño (a woman who was later christened Juana Maria; see Chapter 11) to the

Courtesy of The Bancroft Library, University of California, Berkeley

Fig. 52. A basketry water bottle waterproofed using asphaltum. This artifact, which may have been maufactured by Juana María, the last Indian inhabitant of San Nicolas Island, was reportedly lost in the earthquake and fire which destroyed the California Academy of Sciences in San Francisco in 1906.

mainland in 1853, once observed this Indian woman preparing a basketry water bottle. According to Nidever,

she had built a fire and had several small stones about the size of a walnut heating in it. Taking one of the vessels, which was in shape and size very like a demijohn, excepting that the neck and mouth were much longer, she dropped a few pieces of asphaltum within it, and as soon as the stones were well heated they were dropped in on top of the asphaltum. They soon melted it, when, resting the bottom of the vessel on the ground, she gave it a rotary motion with both hands until its interior was completely covered with the asphaltum. These vessels hold water well, and if kept full may be placed with safety in a hot sun (Nidever 1937:87).

Catalina Island Museum No. G-121

Fig. 53. A small decorated soapstone slab. In form, this artifact resembles the soapstone comals (frying pans) used during the early historic period for preparing tortillas. A stick was inserted through the hole and used as a handle. Photograph by author.

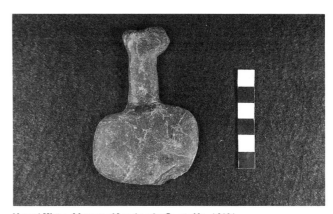

Natural History Museum of Los Angeles County No. A3121

Fig. 55. A paddle-shaped artifact of soapstone, perhaps used as an effigy or ritual item. Collected near Redondo Beach. Photograph by author.

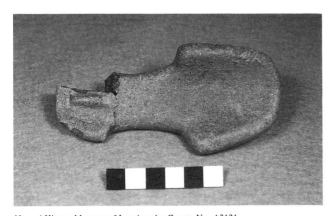

Natural History Museum of Los Angeles County No. A3121

Fig. 54. A small artifact of soapstone, perhaps once used as an effigy. This specimen was collected from the Redondo Beach vicinity. Photograph by author.

Natural History Museum of Los Angeles County No. A-1664 344

Fig. 56. A small, pick-shaped artifact of soapstone, perhaps a ritual implement. Photograph by author.

MINERAL RESOURCES

A variety of useful mineral resources were located within the Gabrielino territory, and these played a large role in the development of trade and manufacturing. Soapstone is a soft, easily worked rock that contains varying amounts of the mineral talc; soapstone is also commonly known as talc, steatite, or serpentine. It was mined extensively on Santa Catalina Island and was used in the manufacture of cooking vessels and for the carving of small sculptures and effigy figures. Flints and other types of stone suitable for flaking were used for arrowpoints, small drills, and the hafted knives used for butchering (Harrington 1942:13, items 343, 357; Wlodarski and Larson 1976:40; Wlodarski 1979a; Hudson and

Blackburn 1982:103-107). Natural cobbles were used for mauls and split cobbles for scraping, fleshing, and cutting tools (Harrington 1942:13, items 344-345, 349, 368, 370-371).

On Santa Catalina Island, slate was shaped into picks, saws, and choppers used in soapstone quarrying, while quartz was used for hammerstones, drills, and scrapers (Meighan and Johnson 1957:25; Wlodarski 1979a:346-347). Granite and sandstone were utilized in the manufacture of mortars and bowls, and crystals and curiously-shaped stones were used for ritual implements. Boulders and outcroppings of stone were selected as sites for rock art in the form of paintings, known as pictographs, and carvings, known as petroglyphs (Reid 1852:44; Harrington 1942:14, items 397-398; Heizer 1968:123, note 69).

Asphaltum was used extensively by the Gabrielino as an adhesive for applying shell inlay to stone, bone, or wood utensils and ornaments. In addition, asphaltum was used to waterproof basketry bottles and tule canoes and to caulk the seams of plank canoes (Harrington 1942:11, 13, 22, items 260, 381, 768). Much of the asphaltum used by the Gabrielino was collected as it floated ashore from marine seepages, although an alternative source was the tar pools at La Brea (Alliot 1917; Bolton 1927:148-149; Walker 1952:44). The French explorer Duflot de Mofras, who visited Mission San Gabriel in the early 1840s, offered a colorful description of the asphalt beds at La Brea. The beds consisted of

> four large deposits of asphalt . . . that spread over the surface of the ground. Among these areas are interspersed pools of cold water that lower the temperature of the bitumen. Although this water has a distinct mineral flavor, yet this does not prevent its use by animals. At sunrise these springs are coated with heavy deposits of asphalt, often a meter high, resembling great soap bubbles. As the air grows warm, the gas in these balls expands and the bubbles finally burst with a loud report (Wilbur 1937:187).

Clays of different grades and composition were another important resource and were utilized in the manufacture of ceramics, body paint, and even soap (Reid 1852:34-35; Harrington 1933:125, note 42, 1942:16, 25, items 508, 923-924, 927). Mineral stones containing lead ore were burned and used in black paint, and red ochre from Santa Catalina Island may also have been used extensively for pigment (Meighan and Johnson 1957:26; Vizcaíno 1959:14).

SOAPSTONE

The Gabrielino were skillful stoneworkers, and their mastery of the craft was most evident in their use of soapstone. The quarries of Santa Catalina Island provided the best and most extensively used source of this material in southern California, and through trade this soapstone reached the Chumash and other Indian groups. Although mainland deposits of soapstone may have been worked locally, Catalina was the preferred source. Soapstone mining on Catalina began before the Gabrielino reached the island, perhaps as much as 4,000 years ago, and continued well into the nineteenth century. During the Gabrielino period, trade in soapstone was an integral part of the vigorous economic activity linking Catalina with the mainland coastal communities north of San Pedro Bay (Kroeber

1925:629; Winterbourne 1967:23; Wlodarski and Larson 1976:54; Wlodarski 1979a:331; Williams and Rosenthal 1993).

Soapstone's value lies in its unique physical qualities. Soapstone can be easily carved and worked with stone tools. It also resists shattering when placed over an open flame and therefore makes an ideal material for cooking vessels. This unique physical property results from soapstone's low index of thermal expansion, which renders it relatively immune to temperature-induced stress (Heizer and Treganza 1944:347).

Early soapstone mining activities on Santa Catalina were probably limited to the collection of cobbles and loose surface fragments. This mining activity apparently increased around A.D. 700-900; however, the most dramatic upsurge in activity seems to have occurred fairly late, around A.D. 1650 (Meighan and Rootenberg 1957:182; Wlodarski and Larson 1976:54; Wlodarski et al. 1984:38). Important soapstone quarries were operated near the present-day airport, in the "Valley of the Ollas" near Empire Landing, and in the vicinity of Little Springs Canyon; smaller quarry sites were scattered across the island (Wlodarski 1979a:337-338). Paul Schumacher, who surveyed Santa Catalina in the late nineteenth century, reported more than 300 quarry sites at the southeastern end of the island alone (Schumacher 1878a; 1878b).

The extent to which a particular quarry site was utilized depended upon two factors. The first was the quality of the soapstone available at the quarry, while the second was the distance the raw material had to be transported to reach a processing and manufacturing site (Wlodarski 1979a:336-337). Two primary grades of soapstone were quarried and utilized. Fine-grained soapstone, which occurs in thin slabs, was used for manufacturing pipes, carvings, beads, dishes, and similar finely carved items. Coarse-grained soapstone, which occurs in large surface outcroppings or underground deposits, was used for manufacturing large items such as ollas and bowls (Wlodarski 1979a:333).

A number of effective mining techniques were employed by the Gabrielino. To separate a lump of soapstone from a surface deposit a spherical "bulb" was created by chiselling a groove around a section of the outcropping. This groove was expanded until the bulb was sufficiently raised from the outcropping to be broken free. Access to subsurface deposits was gained by digging open-pit mines that might reach 40 feet in

Fig. 57. The Gabrielino quarried soapstone from numerous locations on Santa Catalina Island. Large pieces of soapstone were obtained by cutting a bulb from an outcropping; the bulb was subsequently broken loose and shaped into a bowl or vessel. Photographed by author at the Catalina Island Museum.

Fig. 58. A large fragment of soapstone from a Gabrielino quarry; the circular scars visible on this fragment were created when soapstone "bulbs" were removed during the quarrying process. Photographed by author at the Catalina Island Museum.

diameter, with depths exceeding four feet. The actual quarrying techniques used in these pit mines were essentially the same as those used for surface outcroppings. Blade-like picks of slate hafted to wooden handles were used to work soapstone deposits, although following contact with Europeans iron implements were introduced (Holder 1910:28; Meighan and Johnson 1957:27).

Archaeological excavations conducted at a small miner's camp on Santa Catalina have provided an intriguing "snapshot" of the soapstone miners and their methods of operation. The site, which was located in the vicinity of the Catalina Airport near a small spring, consisted of a soapstone quarry, a house floor, and an associated midden. The size of the camp suggests that the quarry was operated by single-family groups. Mining activities at the site began sometime between A.D. 500 and 1000. The presence of blue and green Venetian glass trade beads suggests that the quarry may have continued in operation until the Mission Period. The initial stages of soapstone processing and manufacturing were also carried out at the camp, as evidenced by fragments of numerous soapstone vessels (Meighan and Rootenberg 1957:177-181; Rosen 1980; Wlodarski et al. 1984:37; see also Williams and Rosenthal 1993).

TOOL MANUFACTURING

The Gabrielino employed a number of specialized craft techniques to manufacture tools and utilitarian items from soapstone and other types of lithic material. Stone "edge" tools such as knives or

arrowpoints were manufactured by percussion and pressure flaking. Percussion flaking, probably the older technique, is performed by striking a stone blank, known as a "core," with a hammerstone or a baton of antler or bone to remove a flake of material. More delicate chipping was accomplished by pressure flaking. In pressure flaking the semi-finished tool is held in the palm of the hand (which is protected by a piece of buckskin) while the tip of a small baton is gently pressed against the unworked tool edge. Many small flakes are quickly removed in succession until the final edge is sharpened and shaped (Harrington 1942:13, items 370-371; Spier 1970:53-56).

STONE VESSELS

Large pots, bowls, and mortars could be manufactured from soapstone, sandstone, or granite. Vessels such as these were manufactured in stages to minimize production time and reduce the chance of breakage. In the first stage, a working surface was created by chipping a circular groove around one end of a spherical stone blank, thus creating a large knob. Removing this knob with a single blow would almost certainly fracture the blank; instead, two perpendicular grooves were cut across the knob, dividing it into four sections which could be removed without danger. This process was then repeated to hollow out the vessel; the final shaping was accomplished by chipping (Bryan 1970b).

Soapstone bowls from the Gabrielino islands were decorated with distinctive designs consisting of carved bands containing incised diagonal lines. In contrast, bowls from the Chumash islands to the north typically

Catalina Island Museum Nos. G-250 (bowl) and G-147 (pestle)
Fig. 59. A small soapstone bowl and pestle. Photograph by author.

California State University, Long Beach No. 66-7
Fig. 60. A small soapstone bowl fragment with incised decoration; this artifact was collected during archaeological excavations at the Los Altos Site (LAn-270) during the early 1950s. Photograph by author.

display patterns of zigzag, crosshatch, or dentate incising below the rim (Lee 1981:36-37).

CERAMICS

Reid (1852:44) reported of the Gabrielino that "their present clay pots were at that time unknown; the Spaniards taught them their manufacture." Although soapstone long remained the preferred material in the manufacture of cookware, ceramic vessels were also manufactured and used by the

California State University, Long Beach No. 66-582
Fig. 61. A small incised soapstone bowl from the Los Altos Site (LAn-270); although a portion of this bowl is missing, the decoration appears to have comprised a continuous band around the outside of the vessel. Photograph by author.

Catalina Island Museum Nos. G-254 (bowl) and G-255 (grinding stone)
Fig. 62. A small soapstone paint mortar and grinding stone; the mortar is filled with red ochre. A pigment like red ochre was mixed with a binder (such as animal fat) to create a paint with permanent adhesive qualities. Photograph by author.

Gabrielino. Archaeological evidence suggests that pottery making may have been adopted from the neighboring Cahuilla, Serrano, or Luiseño not long before European contact. Fragments of ceramic vessels have been recovered from many late sites in Orange County, and these appear to be locally manufactured versions of a type of pottery known as Tizon Brown Ware (Hudson 1969:47; Lauter 1977; Koerper and Flint 1978; Koerper et al. 1978; Craib 1982:54, 66; Taylor and Douglas 1982).

According to Harrington, the Gabrielino manufactured spheroid-shaped clay vessels as large as eight inches in diameter at the belly. These vessels were made from coiled clay that was smoothed and shaped using a paddle on the outer surface, and a cobble as an anvil on the inner surface. The

Courtesy of the Charles W. Bowers Memorial Museum Collection. Historical Photo No. 6538

Fig. 63. Maze Rock, one of the better-known examples of rock art executed in the Riverside Maze Style; this style of petroglyphic rock art may have been associated with hunting rituals. Maze Rock was originally located in the Santa Ana Mountains on a ridge overlooking Bell and Trabuco canyons. The petroglyphic design was enhanced (perhaps by chalking) for this photograph.

completed vessel was then dried and fired in an open bark fire (Harrington 1942:25, items 923-924, 926-927).

The Gabrielino also made smoking pipes of clay. As the Portolá Expedition approached the Los Angeles River in 1769 it was visited by eight Indians. According to Father Juan Crespí "some of the old men were smoking pipes well made of baked clay and they puffed at us three mouthfuls of smoke" (Bolton 1927:147).

PAINTS AND PIGMENTS

The Gabrielino made extensive use of clays and minerals for paint. Red ochre, kaolin (a white mineral), and charcoal were used for pigments. Other pigments included manganese (obtained through trade with the Cahuilla), and mineral stones containing lead that were collected on Santa Catalina Island (Wagner

1929:237; Martínez 1938:52; Harrington 1942:18, items 611, 613, 615-616; Meighan and Johnson 1957:26; Vizcaíno 1959:14; Butler 1974:70-72). The Fernandeño of the Santa Monica Mountains used locally available deposits of hematite and limonite. Hematite provides a red pigment while limonite varies from yellow to dark brown. Hematite was also recovered from Big Dog Cave on San Clemente Island (McKusick and Warren 1959:132; Lee 1981:25). Fuchsite, which produces a pigment of blue-green color, was obtained through trade (Galdikas-Brindamour 1970:150; Lee 1979:302).

Non-mineral sources of pigment included the scum produced by iron-depositing bacteria on the surfaces of pools and springs in late summer. This scum was collected, dried, and burned for use in the preparation of red paint (Harrington 1933:167, note 138). Generally, pigments were crushed and ground into powder in small mortars, then mixed with a binder such as animal fat to produce a paint with permanent adhesive qualities (Rogers 1929:407; Grant 1965:86; Lee 1981:25-26; Hudson and Blackburn 1985:313-323, 1987:179-192; also Webb 1952:231-233).

GABRIELINO ROCK ART

Boulders and rock outcroppings provided ready sites for the execution of rock art, some of which consisted of rock carvings known as petroglyphs, while others were rock paintings, known as pictographs. Three distinct styles of rock art have been identified within the boundaries of the Gabrielino homeland. One of these, the Riverside Maze Style, consists of petroglyphs, while the other two, the southern California Rectilinear Abstract Style and the Abstract Polychrome Style, are pictographs (Grant 1967).

Rock art of the Riverside Maze Style consists primarily of petroglyph "mazes" carved on isolated boulders or outcroppings near trails or mountain ridges. Riverside Maze art is generally believed to have been executed as part of hunting rituals and is particularly abundant near the eastern Gabrielino border, extending well into the territory of the Cahuilla (Hedges 1973:14; Minor 1973:32; Bean, personal communication, 1984). One of the best examples of Riverside Maze art from the Gabrielino homeland is Maze Rock, a petroglyph-covered boulder once located on a ridge overlooking Bell and Trabuco canyons near El Toro in Orange County. Maze Rock is now on display in the courtyard of the Bowers Museum in Santa Ana (Knight 1979). Yet another fine example of this type of petroglyphic art is on display in Maze Rock Park near the city of Hemet.

Rock art of the Rectilinear Abstract Style consists of pictographs executed on exposed boulders near Gabrielino communities. Generally these paintings were done in red, white, or black, and common motifs include zig-zags, straight lines, diamond chains, crosshatching, parallel lines, and hand prints (Grant 1967:241-242). Ethnographic information from various Indian groups suggests that many of these paintings were created during the elaborate rituals associated with puberty ceremonies. For example, at the end of the girl's puberty ritual, diamond-shaped designs representing the rattlesnake were painted in red on an exposed boulder (DuBois 1908:92; Strong

1929:298-299; Sanburg 1972; Minor 1973:32). Because of the exposed nature of these sites few examples of pictographic rock art have survived within Gabrielino territory (see Sanburg 1972).

The Abstract Polychrome Style was by far the most spectacular of the three styles of rock art. Abstract Polychrome rock art consists of pictographs painted in red, white, or black, although some elaborate Chumash paintings display as many as six colors. Design motifs include circles, spokes, rays, and cogs (Grant 1967:239). Rock art of the Abstract Polychrome Style reached its greatest expression among the Chumash, and it is noteworthy that Gabrielino examples seem especially numerous in areas where Chumash influence may have been felt most strongly, such as Santa Catalina Island and the San Fernando Valley (Quist 1978; Sanburg et al. 1978; Edberg 1985). The paintings were probably linked to shamanistic practices, which included the use of the hallucinogenic *Datura* plant (Grant 1967:239-241; see also Grant 1965).

Other less well-defined styles of pictographic and petroglyphic rock art have been discovered within the Gabrielino territory. Abstract or stylized representational designs were often carved on fixed or portable stone surfaces. The most unique and outstanding example of Gabrielino petroglyphic art is a panel of carvings representing fish and killer whales that once decorated the Cave of the Whales on San Nicolas Island. This panel has deteriorated through natural erosion; it is now preserved at the Southwest Museum (Rozaire and Kritzman 1960; Bryan 1970a:150, note 1). The Cave of the Whales, which is also decorated with pictographs of fish or whales executed in black paint, was described in greater detail in Chapter 5.

Catalina Island Museum No. G-123

Fig. 64. A small painted boulder from Catalina Island decorated with a spiral design in red and white. Photograph by author.

SUMMARY

The Gabrielino homeland offered an environment rich in natural resources. This wealth of resources, coupled with an effective technology and a sophisticated system of trade and ritual exchange, resulted in a society that was among the most materially wealthy and culturally sophisticated of the California Indian groups.

At the heart of the Gabrielino economy was an effective system for the management of food resources. A portion of the food procured from each day's hunting or fishing activities was deposited with the *tomyaar*, who was responsible for managing the community's food reserves. In addition, each family maintained individual food caches for use in times of special need. Food gathering responsibilities were divided on the basis of sex and age; men hunted and fished while women gathered plant foods, roots, nuts, and seeds. Seasonal activities, such as acorn gathering or the large-scale rabbit hunts held during fiestas, were communal efforts.

The Gabrielino homeland lay at the center of a trade network that extended east as far as the Colorado River and west as far as San Nicolas Island. The mainland Gabrielino maintained trade relations with the Cahuilla, Serrano, Luiseño, Chumash, and Mojave, as well as with the Gabrielino living on the southern Channel Islands and the Chumash living on the northern Channel Islands. Ritual lineage gatherings served as important opportunities for trade and the redistribution of surplus food resources. Two or more lineages (at least one from each moiety) were required for a successful ritual performance; lineages took turns hosting these rituals on a reciprocal basis (see Chapter 6 for a discussion of the moiety among the Gabrielino).

The individual profit motive, coupled with the law of supply and demand, was the guiding principle in Gabrielino economic activity. The *tomyaar* was frequently the most important entrepreneur in trade activities. Other wealthy and elite members of Gabrielino society also participated in the system of economic exchange, and professional associations extended across political and linguistic boundaries.

The natural resources available within the Gabrielino category can be divided into three categories, including faunal resources, plant resources, and mineral resources. The wide variety of natural resources available locally satisfied most Gabrielino needs, although luxury items could be obtained through trade.

The Gabrielino were expert hunters, and their weapons and technology reflected a versatile set of strategies for utilizing faunal resources. Both composite (or sinew-backed) and self-bows were used by the Gabrielino. Arrows included self-arrows having a wooden shaft and composite arrows having a cane shaft into which a wooden foreshaft was inserted and secured with adhesive and cord. Arrows were fletched with three feathers and tipped with a variety of points depending upon the intended use. Gabrielino deer hunters frequently wore disguises made from the heads and necks of deer. Wearing such a disguise and mimicking deer as they grazed allowed the Gabrielino hunter to more closely approach his prey. Other hunting implements included long nets used during rabbit hunts, slings, throwing clubs, and deadfall traps.

Important marine food resources used by the Gabrielino included both shallow water and pelagic (deep-water) fishes as well as shellfish and sea-mammals. Plank canoes were used to fish the rich kelp beds that lie off the coasts of the mainland and islands. These canoes were made from wooden planks that were carefully shaped, then glued and stitched together with cord made from vegetable fiber. Other watercraft used by the Gabrielino included canoes made from bundles of tule reeds and wooden dugouts. Fishing and sea-mammal hunting equipment comprised spears, harpoons, tridents, and several varieties of fishhooks as well as dip nets, gill nets, drag nets, and seine nets.

Among the most important of the floral resources used by the Gabrielino were acorns, islay, chía, and wild hyacinth; other important floral resources were roots, nuts, and seeds. Seeds and nut foods were typically prepared by pounding in mortars or grinding on stone metates; acorn also had to be leached to remove the bitter-tasting tannic acid. The resulting meal could then be cooked in gruel or made into cakes. Wild tobacco was utilized as a purgative and sedative, and may also have had ritual uses. The Gabrielino improved the yield of their seed-bearing fields by periodically burning off large areas of grassland.

Plants also provided important manufacturing materials for use in building homes, tule canoes, and a wide assortment of baskets. The Gabrielino manufactured both coiled and woven baskets; decorative designs included realistic and geometric motifs executed in red, green, and black. Water bottles were manufactured from baskets that were waterproofed with a coating of asphaltum.

A variety of useful mineral resources were available in the Gabrielino homeland. Soapstone was used in the manufacture of cooking vessels as well as small sculptures and effigy figures. The highest quality of soapstone was found on Santa Catalina Island, and more than 300 soapstone quarries have been identified on the island. Large bowls, pots, and mortars were also manufactured from sandstone and granite using stone tools.

Locally available clays were used in the manufacture of spheroid-shaped ceramic vessels as large as eight inches in diameter at the belly. A coiling technique was used in their manufacture, and the vessels were smoothed and shaped using a paddle on the outer surface and a cobble as an anvil on the inner surface. The completed vessels were fired in open bark fires.

The Gabrielino also used clays and minerals (as well as a variety of other naturally-occurring items) in the preparation of pigments. Boulders and rock outcroppings provided ready sites for the execution of rock art. Gabrielino rock art can be divided into three primary categories including: the Riverside Maze Style of petroglyphs (rock carvings); the Rectilinear Abstract Style of pictographs (rock paintings) that were typically geometric paintings executed during puberty ceremonies; and the Abstract Polychrome Style that included a variety of abstract pictographs executed in red, black, or white. The most spectacular Gabrielino rock art sites are found at Burro Flats in the Simi Hills at the western end of the San Fernando Valley, and in the Cave of the Whales on San Nicolas Island (see Chapters 3 and 5 for more complete discussions of these sites).

In addition to the trade in material goods that was a regular feature of the interaction between the Gabrielino and their Indian neighbors there also existed an intellectual exchange of religious and philosophical ideas. The first Angelinos were religious innovators, and the *Chengiichngech* religion, which developed among the Gabrielino and later spread to the Luiseño and other Indian groups, was their greatest achievement. The rituals and practices associated with the *Chengiichngech* religion and other ritual beliefs of the Gabrielino are examined in greater detail in Chapter 8.

CHAPTER 8

RELIGION, RITUAL, AND THE CYCLE OF LIFE

The Gabrielino were a deeply spiritual people whose lives were profoundly touched by ritual and ceremonialism. Virtually every aspect of Gabrielino life was influenced by religious beliefs and practices. The political leadership of the community was made up in large part by an elite group of religious officials who sought divine sanction for political and legal decisions through the performance of special rituals and ceremonies. An important feature of the Gabrielino economy was the redistribution of food and luxury goods that accompanied festivals and other ritual occasions. Morality and codes of behavior were defined through religious precepts, and sacred knowledge was preserved through the recital of Gabrielino oral literature. Marriage, childbirth, and other personal events were celebrated by rituals marking the individual's transition to a new role in life.

THE *CHENGIICHNGECH* RELIGION

Gabrielino religion and ritual evolved over many generations through the fusion of a number of distinct currents of religious thought. Some of the elements that contributed to this religion were the beliefs and practices of the pre-Uto-Aztecan population of the Los Angeles area, the beliefs and rituals of the Uto-Aztecans themselves, the highly developed *'antap-yovaar* religion of the coastal Gabrielino and Chumash, the *Chengiichngech* religion that may have originated in the Gabrielino community of *Povuu'nga*, and, during the historic period, Christianity as it was taught by the Franciscan missionaries. Other potential sources of influence on Gabrielino religion include the elaborate religious systems of the agricultural societies of Arizona and New Mexico.

Each of these elements was redefined and incorporated into a complex and sophisticated religious system known as the *Chengiichngech* religion (Kroeber 1925:622-624, 645; Strong 1929:346-349; Hudson and Blackburn 1978).

Many of the details surrounding the development and practice of Gabrielino religion remain unclear, due in large measure to the unwillingness of the Gabrielino themselves to divulge sacred knowledge to outsiders. Father Boscana noted that "a veil is cast over all their religious observances and the mystery with which they are performed seems to perpetuate respect for them" (Boscana 1933:17). Especially unclear is the emergence of the *Chengiichngech* beliefs as the dominant element of Gabrielino religion. A thoughtful reading of the creation story related by Father Boscana suggests that these beliefs may have developed in part as a reaction to the disruption of Gabrielino society.

> To his [*Chengiichngech's*] enquiry as to why they [the Indians] were thus congregated, they answered that their grand captain [*Wewyoot*] was dead, and that they had met together to assist at the funeral ceremonies, and now, previous to their retirement, the elders were consulting as to the manner they should subsist in the future (Boscana 1933:33).

Some theories on the origin of the *Chengiichngech* religion suggest that it was a relatively recent phenomenon resulting from contact with the Hispanic Catholic culture. Kroeber suggested that the prophet-spiritual being *Chengiichngech* was "a reaction formation . . . an imitation of the Christian God of the missionaries, whom they took over and furnished with a native name and added to their own beliefs." Kroeber asked rhetorically if "the prophet or his followers were born so late as to live in mission times, and therefore to have heard of a far away Messiah who was the Son of God, and [if] . . . they were emulating Him?" (Kroeber 1959:291, 293).

Yet another theory attributes the rise of the *Chengiichngech* religion to the direct influence of Europeans who were perhaps stranded or shipwrecked along the California coast in the sixteenth century. According to this theory, the prophet *Chengiichngech* may have been a traveler with a background in one of the world's major religions, such as Buddhism, Judaism, or Christianity (White 1963:94-95).

An alternative to these "foreign influence" theories suggests that the *Chengiichngech* religion arose as an indigenous reaction to the social stresses brought about in Gabrielino society by European diseases introduced by the Spaniards in the sixteenth century. A similar explanation has been suggested for the emergence of the *'antap* religion among the Chumash (Hudson and Underhay 1978:72). According to this theory, the traumatic impact of these diseases inspired a religious reaction that included a heavy emphasis upon shamanism.

It would be misleading, however, to view the *Chengiichngech* religion solely as a product of foreign influence. Indeed, some of the most visible elements of the religion, such as the *yovaar* and the sacred *Chengiichngech* image, seem to have been present on Santa Catalina Island at an early date, certainly prior to the arrival of the Sebastián Vizcaíno Expedition in 1602, and long before the Mission Period (Wagner 1929:237). Furthermore, the possibility that seemingly Christian elements represent late additions to an already existing religious system must be considered.

Regardless of its origin, the *Chengiichngech* religion struck a responsive chord in the Gabrielino as well as many other southern California Indian groups. As it was articulated in its most developed form, the primary features of this religion included a pantheon of deities arranged beneath the supreme creator-god *Chengiichngech*; an elaborate cosmology; a religious elite that possessed knowledge and supernatural power not available to the general population; the maintenance of a sacred location, the *yovaar*, within the community; a strict code of morality; a sacred oral literature; and an extensive array of rituals and ceremonies.

CHENGIICHNGECH

The Gabrielino recognized a diverse pantheon of supernatural beings, and it was the shaman's duty to define the relationships between these deities and prescribe the correct worship to be accorded each. These supernatural beings were arranged in a hierarchy of importance and function beneath the supreme creator-god, *Chengiichngech*, who was known by a number of names, and who was "the maker and creator of all things, whose name was (and is) held so sacred among them, as hardly ever to be used; and when used only in a low voice. That name is *Qua-o-ar*. When they have to use the name of the Supreme Being on any ordinary occasion, they substitute in its stead, the word *Y-yo-ha-rivg-nain*, or 'The Giver of Life'" (Reid 1852:19). Father Boscana reported that

> Chinigchinich was known under three distinct names: Saor, Quaguar, and Tobet. . . . Saor means that period in which Chinigchinich could not dance; Quaguar, when enabled to dance; and Tobet, when he danced enrobed in a dress composed of feathers with a crown of the same upon his head and his face painted black and red. They say that once, while dancing in this costume, he was taken up into heaven where are located the stars (Boscana 1933:30).

Other names ascribed to *Chengiichngech* include "Ouiamot" and "Attajen," the latter meaning "rational being," while the former was reported as the "son of Tacu and Auzar" (Boscana 1933:33). *Chengiichngech* is reported to have come from the community of *Povuu'nga* on Alamitos Bay, and he is credited with "establishing the rites and ceremonies necessary to the preservation of life" (Boscana 1933:33).

THE "NORTHERN COMPLEX"

The Gabrielino recognized other deities of lesser importance as well. A missionary from San Fernando reported that the Indians had "five gods and one goddess. They are called *Veat*, *Jaimar*, *Chuhuit*, *Pichurut* and *Quichepet*. The last mentioned is the husband of the goddess *Manisar* who gives the Indians corn or seeds" (Geiger and Meighan 1976:58, answer from Mission San Fernando). These six deities, here spelled *Wewyoot*, *Taamet*, *Chuuxoyt*, *Piichorot*, *Kwiichepet*, and *Maniishar*, make up a grouping that Kroeber referred to as the "northern complex," and that was recognized not only by the Gabrielino but also by a number of their northern neighbors. The northern complex appears to have been unknown south of the Gabrielino (Kroeber 1925:623).

One of Harrington's consultants, probably Juan Meléndrez, recalled a shrine near El Escorpión which may have been associated with these deities. According to Meléndrez,

> in the Escurpión there were 7 stones in the form of men—these were the Siete Viejos [Seven Old Ones]. People always threw chia, etc., there so that there would be good crops the next year and when they finished pounding chia or bellota [acorns] or anything they always threw the last bit in the fire—whatever went in the fire was for the 7 Viejos. One time inf's suegra [informant's mother-in-law] & inf. & Estevan were sitting at the table in this same room. . . . They were talking about the 7 Viejos. . . . Estevan said that when he was hunting . . . either on the island of Anacapa or Santa Rosa . . . he & his companions looked down a deep poso [pozo, a well or pit] (no water in it) & saw the 7 Viejos seated in a circle at the bottom—shoulders hunched & heads bent. Estevan & his companions threw clothes & food down as offerings to them (Harrington 1986:R106 F215).

The deities comprising the northern complex may also have been associated with specific celestial objects such as the sun and moon and certain stars (Hudson and Blackburn 1978:235-236). Supporting evidence for the association of astronomical objects with Gabrielino deities can be found in a description of the *yovaar* penned in 1602. According to Father Antonio de la Ascensión, within the *yovaar* "there was a figure like a devil painted in various colors. . . . At the sides of this were the sun and the moon" (Wagner 1929:237).

The northern complex may represent a religious system of considerable antiquity, one that predates the development of the *Chengiichngech* religion. In fact, many of the concepts embodied in the *Chengiichngech* religion may have been based upon this earlier system and its pantheon of supernatural beings. Attempts to reconstruct this pantheon, although preliminary, are worth reviewing.

The supernatural being named *Veat* mentioned in the report from San Fernando is almost certainly the "grand captain" *Wewyoot* whose death preceded the appearance of *Chengiichngech* (Boscana 1933:28-29, 32-33; Hudson and Blackburn 1978:228-229). As discussed in Chapter 6, *Wewyoot* is closely associated in Gabrielino oral literature with the *tomyaar* and with

the supernatural being Eagle. To quote Reid once again, the Gabrielino spoke of "a *remarkably clever, industrious man*, chief of a large tribe . . . who, when dying, told his people that he intended becoming an eagle, and that he bequeathed them his *feathers*, from henceforth to be employed at their feasts and ceremonies" (Reid 1852:20). Among the Luiseño the new moon was believed to be *Wewyoot* risen from the dead, and foot races were held in his honor (DuBois 1908:135, 148; Boscana 1933:62; White 1963:141). The Gabrielino may have shared this belief, as Harrington reported that they regarded the moon to be a male deity (Harrington 1942:42, item 1660).

The deity "*Jaimar*," a name that Kroeber translated as "Tamur" or "Tomar," probably refers to *Taamet*, the supernatural being represented by the sun (Kroeber 1925:623; Hudson and Blackburn 1978:228). The importance of the sun in Gabrielino religion is suggested by the description of the *yovaar* quoted above, and by the fact that the summer and winter solstices were times of important ritual activity for the Gabrielino (Boscana 1933:65-66). The Chumash conceived of the sun as a powerful anthropomorphic being named *Kakunupmawa* who lived in a crystal house with his two widowed daughters. Each day *Kakunupmawa* circled the world carrying a torch in his hand and collecting human beings to devour; each night he played a game of peon with Sky Coyote. At the winter solstice the scores of *Kakunupmawa* and Sky Coyote were tallied; if *Kakunupmawa* was the victor his prize was taken in human lives the following year (Blackburn 1975:36-37; Hudson and Underhay 1978:51-53).

As noted in Chapter 6, a strong ritual connection may have existed between the *tomyaar* and the supernatural being represented by the sun. The name "Tamur," which is derived from the Fernandeño *tamiat* and the Gabrielino *taamet*, may also be related to the title *tomyaar* held by the Gabrielino chief (Hudson and Blackburn 1978:228, but also see note 2; Harrington 1986:R102 F491, 568).

"*Chuhuit*" or *Chuuxoyt*, which was translated by Kroeber as "Chukit," meaning "deer," is equivalent to the Kitanemuk Indian deity *Tsuqqit*, the mother of mankind, who represents the earth (Kroeber 1925:623; Hudson and Blackburn 1978:233, Table 2). In Gabrielino creation stories the earth was portrayed as the "first woman," and according to one version related by Father Boscana, everything that exists in the world was produced through the sexual union of the sky "brother" and the earth "sister" (Boscana 1933:27). The neighboring Chumash knew the earth as the female supernatural being *Chup* or *Hutash*, who provided all living things with food. *Hutash* was honored each year during August in a fiesta that gave thanks for the harvest of wild plant foods; the harvest festival was often held in conjunction with a ceremony of mourning for the dead (Hudson and Underhay 1978:45-48).

The identities of the supernatural beings *Piichorot* and *Kwiichepet* remain unclear. *Piichorot* may have been equivalent to the male deity Morning Star, although Kroeber translated the name to mean the "breath of life" (Kroeber 1925:623; Hudson and Blackburn 1978:233, Table 2, 246).

The name *Maniishar* may have been derived from the word *maanet*, meaning *Datura*, and this suggests that the female supernatural being *Maniishar* was associated with that hallucinogenic plant. It is interesting to note that the eldest daughter of the *tomyaar* held the title *Maniishar*, which suggests an important ritual connection between that deity and the chief's female descendent (Reid 1852:9; Kroeber 1925:623; Hudson and Blackburn 1978:228, 233, Table 2).

LESSER DEITIES

A number of other important supernatural beings can be identified from Gabrielino oral literature. Many appear as the "first people," animal beings who once occupied the earth and assumed their present form prior to the appearance of mankind. Others appear primarily as character figures in stories and fables.

A special class of animals was designated "*Chengiichngech* Avengers," that is, creatures that *Chengiichngech* sent to watch over mankind and punish those guilty of breaking his commandments. According to Father Boscana, upon his deathbed *Chengiichngech* warned that "those who obey not my teachings, nor believe them, I shall punish severely. I will send unto them bears to bite, and serpents to sting them" (Boscana 1933:34). José de los Santos Juncos referred to these beings as the "tsåtSηitSam" and reported that they were the "sabes del mundo [wise ones of the world] for that is what the name means. [They are] below God, whom the Indians knew as dwelling in the sky" and it is they "who rule the world." Santos Juncos told a story about "the

cave of the tsåtSηitSam near S.J.C. [San Juan Capistrano]."

> A Sonoreño . . . went to a place spoken of as the aguaje de la loma blanca [water hole of the white hill], by the seacoast. He entered . . . and there were the tsåtSηitSam. They talked . . . [a] strange language of course, but they gave him power to understand them. There were viboras [vipers] and cuervones [crows or ravens] (thus they called the big cuervas who talk) and the tsåtSηitSam started to dance that dance which . . . uses feather headdresses. . . . And as he left they gave him something to take so that he was wise, and they told him never to mention what he had seen, for if he did he would die at once (Harrington 1986:R105 F559).

Upon his visit to Santa Catalina Island in 1602, Father Antonio de la Ascensión observed a scene that corroborates the special reverence with which the Gabrielino regarded the raven. When the landing party led by Sebastián Vizcaíno reached the sacred enclosure they saw that

> inside the circle there were two large crows larger than ordinary ones, which flew away when they saw strangers, and alighted on some near-by rocks. One of the soldiers, seeing their size, aimed at them with his harquebus [matchlock rifle], and discharging it, killed them both. When the Indians saw this they began to weep and display great emotion (Wagner 1929:237).

Father Antonio offered his opinion that "the Devil talked to them through these crows, because all the men and women hold them in great respect and fear." Other animals that may have served as *Chengiichngech* avengers besides ravens, bears, and snakes were mountain lions, spiders, centipedes, and stingrays (Harrington 1933:129-135, note 54).

Some animals were regarded as helpers or protectors of mankind. Porpoises were believed to guard the world, their duty consisting "of going round and round the earth to see that all is safe" (Reid 1852:20). Although the swordfish were believed to be malevolent by nature, they benefitted mankind by driving whales ashore for people to eat. The Chumash knew swordfish as old men with long beards and wooden swords projecting from their heads. They were believed to live in a crystal house on the ocean floor (Blackburn 1975:37). The Gabrielino and Chumash sang special songs dedicated to the swordfish at the

Winter Solstice Ceremony. These songs were called *papu marata*, which was probably the Gabrielino word for swordfish (Librado and Harrington 1977:61, 105, note 65).

Other animal beings might serve as personal protectors or guardian spirits. Thus, peregrine falcon was commonly believed to be a guardian spirit for fishermen and canoe owners (Applegate 1978:55). Young men commonly received a protector or guardian spirit at the time of their initiation in the Puberty Ritual, a ceremony that will be more fully discussed later in this chapter.

Unlike the porpoise and the swordfish, other spirits were believed to be distinctly malevolent. Perhaps the most notable of these was *Taakwesh*, a cannibal spirit believed to dwell at Lily Rock near Idyllwild. Harrington suggested that *Taakwesh* was associated with ball lightning, a terrifying and dangerous meteorological phenomenon (Harrington 1933:180-185). José Zalvidea reported that "at jamɨwo mountain [San Jacinto] there is a great rock where tằkwiš lives. Tằkwiš makes a noise like thunder and goes only at night" (Harrington 1986:R102 F450). Another consultant reported that "taakwic used to be frequently seen. . . . The light used to be seen at taakwic peak & at the same time it reach[ed] over to Bernasconi Peak and simultaneous rumbling was heard there" (Harrington 1986:R105 F376; underlining in original).

GABRIELINO COSMOLOGY

In conjunction with this pantheon of supernatural beings, Gabrielino religion evolved an elaborate cosmology to explain the mysteries of the universe. It was the shaman's responsibility to investigate and explain these mysteries. Shamans used magical flight, a trance state brought about by the ingestion of *Datura*, to consult with supernatural beings and then share this information with other initiates or convey it in abbreviated form to the general population.

Just as the Gabrielino and Chumash held many religious beliefs in common, so also did they share many cosmological concepts. The universe was believed to consist of a number of parallel worlds placed one above the other. Although some accounts mention as many as five such worlds, the usual number given is three (Blackburn 1975:30).

The world of the humans was the middle world, which the Gabrielino knew as *Tovaangar* meaning "the whole world," and which they believed was fixed on the shoulders of seven giants, perhaps associated with the "seven old ones" of the northern complex. When the giants moved, earthquakes occurred (Reid 1852:19; Blackburn 1975:30; Harrington 1986:R102 F566). The world above was the home of supernatural beings such as *Taamet*, the sun. The Gabrielino knew this upper world as *Tokuupar*, the sky or heaven, and in creation stories it was personified as the "husband-brother" of the earth (Reid 1852:67; Boscana 1933:27; Harrington 1933:115-116, note 35, 1986:R102 F570; Blackburn 1975:30). When a shaman or *tomyaar* died his heart, which was the manifestation of his soul, rose toward *Tokuupar* to become a star, a planet, or a comet (Boscana 1933:77). Finally, the lower world was generally regarded as the abode of malevolent spirits, who the Chumash called *nunašɨš*, and who were believed to wander the earth after darkness fell (Blackburn 1975:30).

The *yovaar* represented a supernatural "transition zone" which allowed access to both the upper and lower worlds; most likely a passage through the firmament to the upper world was believed to exist in the region of the pole star (Reid 1852:65-66; Sparkman 1908:225; also see Eliade 1951:260-261, 1957:36 for a general discussion of cosmological concepts as they appear in shamanistic societies throughout the world). Eclipses were believed to be caused by a monster devouring the sun or moon, although the Chumash believed that the moon was eclipsed by the wings of a great eagle (Boscana 1933:62; Hudson and Underhay 1978:52-53).

The Gabrielino names for some celestial objects were recorded by Harrington. The north star was *Roomish*, and according to José de los Santos Juncos "there were robber stars around the north star, who wanted to steal it, but other constellations or stars were guarding it" (Harrington 1986:R102 F732). The morning star was *Pahiiyot*, while the three stars that form the belt of the constellation Orion were known as *Paahe' Sheshiiyot*. The constellation of the Pleiades was called *Chechiinoy sheshiiyot* (Harrington 1986:R102 F588-590).

RELIGIOUS OFFICIALS

A central feature of Gabrielino religion was a hierarchy of religious officials chosen from the elite class of society. Members of this hierarchy were distinguished by their wealth and prestige, their possession of sacred knowledge and supernatural power, and their access to the interior of the *yovaar* (Boscana 1933:34, 38; Bean 1974:29). According to the Gabrielino creation story, the religious elite were separated by *Chengiichngech* from the general population and given the name *Toovet*, which corresponds to the name *Chengiichngech* took for himself when he donned the ritual feather-cloak and danced the sacred dances (Boscana 1933:33-34). A loose translation of the word *Toovet* might be "the initiated," although among the Gabrielino living near Tejón at the beginning of the present century the title "To-vē't" meant "son of a chief" and was reserved for the young man who performed the Eagle Dance at the close of the Mourning Ceremony (Merriam 1955:83). *Chengiichngech* named the remainder of the population "Saorem," or "persons who do not know how to dance" or "could not make use of the vestments of *Chengiichngech*," or in other words, the uninitiated. The name *Saorem* corresponds to the name used by *Chengiichngech* before he acquired sacred knowledge (Boscana 1933:34). The title *Yovaarekam* has also been reported for the Fernandeño-Gabrielino ceremonial officers and is probably derived from *yovaar*, the name of the sacred enclosure (Hudson and Blackburn 1978:231, 238; see Chapter 6 for a more complete discussion of Gabrielino shamanic societies).

THE SACRED ENCLOSURE—THE *YOVAAR*

The construction of the sacred enclosure, the *yovaar*, was an integral aspect of Gabrielino religion. The earliest description of a *yovaar* was reported in 1602, and in design the structure seems to have changed but little over the following 200 years (see Chapter 2 for a complete description of the *yovaar*). Feather poles designated the four cardinal directions, and figures of the sun and moon were contained within the enclosure walls (Reid 1852:41; Wagner 1929:237; Boscana 1933:37-39).

The *yovaar* was ordered by *Chengiichngech* to be a place "where they might pay to him adoration, offer up sacrifices, and have religious worship. The plan of this building was regulated by himself" (Boscana 1933:29). To enter the *yovaar* was to experience the sacred and be in contact with *Chengiichngech*, and thus admittance was strictly regulated (Boscana 1933:34). No act of irreverence was permitted to occur within the *yovaar*, and silence was observed

during important ceremonies (Boscana 1933:38). Mircea Eliade, a historian of religion who has studied the symbolism of religious architecture in shamanistic societies throughout the world, reports that such structures represent a sacred place where communication between the secular and supernatural worlds was possible. In plan these religious structures were often believed to represent the universe (Eliade 1957:36, 37, 42-47).

MORAL CODE

Rules and regulations were an important part of Gabrielino life and served to maintain stable social and family relationships as well as the political and economic viability of the community. A healthy respect for the authority of the *tomyaar* and shamans was an important part of these regulations. According to the creation story it was *Chengiichngech* himself who "taught them the laws they were to observe for the future as well as their rites and ceremonies" (Boscana 1933:29). These commandments were enforced by *Chengiichngech* through the agency of his "avengers" (Boscana 1933:34). The regulations promulgated by *Chengiichngech* covered numerous situations, including ritual observances, obedience to authority, economic reciprocity, family and social obligations, child rearing, and hygiene.

It was incumbent upon the Gabrielino to observe the rituals and ceremonies "necessary to the preservation of life" (Boscana 1933:33). Respect for authority was both expected and demanded, and reverence for *Chengiichngech* was so great that the deity's name could never be used in swearing or oaths (Reid 1852:37). Punishment for disrespect or disobedience could be severe and might include execution (Boscana 1933:42-43). Reciprocity and food-sharing were also required by the laws of *Chengiichngech*. One of the strictest examples of this regulation was the prohibition against hunters eating their own kill and fishermen consuming their own catch. This rule was intended to prevent hunters and fishermen from secretly hoarding food and refusing to share it with other members of the community (Reid 1852:36; Boscana 1933:61-62).

Many family and social interactions were closely governed by the commandments of *Chengiichngech*. Incest was punished by death, and a wife's adultery gave her husband the right to kill her, although divorce was a more common solution (Reid 1852:15-16).

Respect among siblings was essential, and "no male from childhood upward was allowed to call his sister *liar* even in jest" (Reid 1852:37).

Regulations surrounding child-rearing served to socialize children into the community, and Father Boscana reported that "the moral instruction given by parents to their children was contained in the precepts of *Chinigchinich*. . . . The perverse child invariably was destroyed" (Boscana 1933:45). Although the climax of this socialization process was the puberty rituals held for boys and girls, the process began at a much earlier age. To teach children to endure patiently the rigors of the hunter-gatherer lifestyle, they were not allowed to approach a fire for warmth nor were they allowed to eat certain foods until they reached adulthood or became parents (Boscana 1933:47). To teach respect for authority, children were not allowed to drink from a cup of water until an adult had first satisfied his thirst, and if two adults were in conversation a child could not pass between them (Reid 1852:37).

The importance the Gabrielino placed upon cleanliness and hygiene is emphasized by the commandment that everyone bathe once a day, and it appears to have been the custom to bathe early each morning before sunrise (Harrington 1933:168, note 141, 1986:R105 F685). Other regulations very likely dealt with cleanliness of the home, cooking and eating habits, and general sanitation (see Bean 1972a:81 for a discussion of such rules among the Cahuilla).

ORAL LITERATURE

Gabrielino oral literature preserved both sacred and secular knowledge, passing it from generation to generation through memorization. Specially chosen males were trained from youth as bards or storytellers, with the ability to memorize long stories and orations and repeat them word for word (Heizer 1968:119, note 54). Unfortunately, much of the oral literature of the Gabrielino was far too sacred to be revealed to the uninitiated, and what has survived gives only a tantalizing glimpse of the depth and richness of this art form. Sacred literature was used by the *tomyaar* and the shaman to enforce the moral codes; among the surviving accounts important themes include marital, religious and parental obligations, and economic reciprocity. Other oral accounts include creation stories, descriptions of shamanic flight, Coyote stories, and tales describing the origin of the Pleiades constellation (Reid 1852:49-68; Boscana 1933:27-35).

RITUALS AND CEREMONIES

Ritual was a fundamental part of Gabrielino culture, touching virtually every aspect of public and private life. Through the performance of ritual the Gabrielino satisfied a wide range of political, economic, and social needs. The performance of ritual also promoted a sense of well-being among the members of the community, and encouraged an optimistic outlook for the future.

Significant personal events, such as the birth of a child, the onset of puberty, and marriage were occasions for important "rite of passage" observances. Rite of passage ceremonies sought supernatural favor and support for the individual while confirming his or her new role in the community and imparting new social duties and privileges (Strong 1929:347; Bean 1972a:141-143). Perhaps no less important were the occasions these ceremonies provided for the community to celebrate the growth and maturation of its younger members.

Legal, political, and social institutions were defined and legitimized through ritual observances. Thus, the elevation of a new *tomyaar* or the first appearance of a new shaman were important ceremonial occasions (Boscana 1933:41, 60). Ritual observances also provided an important means of obtaining divine sanction for specific legal or political decisions, such as a declaration of war or the punishment of law breakers (Reid 1852:15; Boscana 1933:43).

Political alliances between lineages and communities were also reaffirmed through rituals. The association of several lineages jointly participating in rituals created a ritual congregation. The Gabrielino formed ritual congregations with the Cahuilla and Kumeyaay (otherwise known as the Diegueño), as well as the Chumash, Salinans, Luiseño, and Serrano. Indians from the Tejón region attended fiestas at San Gabriel and San Fernando, and as late as 1869 Rogerio Rocha, a Gabrielino *tomyaar* who resided at Mission San Fernando, played an active role in Chumash rituals held at Saticoy near Ventura (Strong 1929:98; Bean 1972a:151-152; 1974:17; Librado and Harrington 1977:91; Harrington 1986:R105 F562).

Ritual played a crucial role in maintaining the economic stability of lineages and communities among Uto-Aztecan-speaking peoples by providing a mechanism for distributing food to alleviate local shortages and promote food sharing within the general population. The exchange of surplus food that accompanied many intercommunity rituals helped to maintain an economic balance among lineages and thereby lessen the possibility of violent conflict. Among the Cahuilla such rituals were induced perhaps a dozen times a year and provided for the redistribution of meat to large numbers of people during the winter months when plant resources were scarce and food shortages were most acute. Meat supplies were augmented by large scale hunts for rabbit, deer, sheep, and antelope conducted by the Cahuilla and Gabrielino in conjunction with such intercommunity festivals (Harrington 1942:6, item 5; Bean 1972a:154-156).

The Gabrielino conducted certain ceremonies to promote the welfare of the community and strengthen its relationship with the supernatural world. Some of these rituals, such as the harvest or solstice celebrations that will be discussed later in this chapter, formed a regular seasonal pattern of ceremonies; other ceremonies, such as the rituals undertaken during solar or lunar eclipses, were performed as needed (Boscana 1933:62). Certain naturally-occurring events were also commemorated out of respect for supernatural beings. Especially noteworthy in this regard were the races conducted at the appearance of the new moon to commemorate the rebirth of *Wewyoot* after his assassination (Boscana 1933:62; Harrington 1933:179-180, note 180).

RITES OF PASSAGE AT BIRTH

Religion was clearly a central element in the lives of the First Angelinos. From birth to death every Gabrielino man, woman, and child was surrounded by an intricate web of ritual and ceremonialism. Immediately following delivery, newborn babies were given a ritual drink of urine and were displayed to the community (Reid 1852:53; Boscana 1933:53). If the child was born to a *tomyaar* it was bathed by several elderly midwives, who then drank the rinse water. These women then performed "a dance around the happy father, chanting all the while the future renown of the little one" (Reid 1852:30). Mother and child underwent purification rituals for three consecutive days, during which time the mother took no food and

drank only warmed water or thin acorn mush (Reid 1852:29; Harrington 1942:34, item 1335). A special hut was prepared and

> in the centre . . . a large hole was dug; an immense fire was kindled therein, and large stones heated until red-hot; when nothing but hot embers and . . . stones remain, bundles of wild tanzy are heaped on, and then the whole is covered with earth, with the exception of a small aperture in the middle. The mother had to stand over this hole, with her child wrapt up in a mat, funnel fashion, while cold water was gradually introduced into the opening. This generated great quantities of steam. . . . When no more steam was produced, the mother and child laid down on a heap of earth, and were well covered up until the steaming process was renewed (Reid 1852:29).

Great care was taken in the disposal of the umbilical cord. The cord was cut and removed by several women who secretly buried it, sometimes within the child's home. This may have been done to prevent the cord from falling into the hands of an enemy who could use it to "witch" the baby. The afterbirth was also buried, probably for the same reason (Boscana 1933:53-54; Harrington 1942:35, items 1336, 1348). A salve of burned and crushed chilicote plant (*Echinocystis macrocarpa*) was applied to the newborn's belly-button to help it heal (Harrington 1933:194, note 195).

If the newborn was a boy the privilege of choosing a name fell to the grandfather, and if a girl, to the grandmother. If an unusual or special event was associated with the birth, the child's name might commemorate the occurrence. It is also possible that the Gabrielino followed the Chumash practice of having the child's name chosen soon after birth by a special shaman, the *'alchuklash*, who used astrology to guide him in his choice (Boscana 1933:53; Hudson and Underhay 1978:37).

RITES OF PASSAGE AT PUBERTY

Both boys and girls underwent special rite of passage ceremonies at puberty, and these rituals were among the most dramatic of Gabrielino religious practices. Puberty ceremonies served to quickly and effectively resocialize the participants, preparing them to accept the responsibilities of adulthood and membership in the community. Puberty ceremonies also created a suitable context for passing on important lineage and community traditions to new generations.

BOYS' PUBERTY CEREMONY

The Boys' Puberty Ceremony belongs to a special class of religious ritual in which the initiate undergoes a ritual death and is reborn as a new man possessing sacred knowledge. Among the Gabrielino, as well as many other peoples throughout the world, these initiation rituals included the establishment of a special relationship with a spiritual protector or "guardian spirit" who strengthened the initiate and protected him from harm (Kroeber 1925:640; Harrington 1933:161-162, note 123; see also Eliade 1957:188-192 for a general discussion of initiation rituals).

The most complete accounts of the Boys' Puberty Ceremony were compiled by Father Gerónimo Boscana (1933) and Constance Goddard DuBois (1908). Father Boscana's account was based upon observations made of the Indians at Mission San Juan Capistrano around 1813, many of whom were undoubtedly Gabrielino. DuBois' work was based upon research among the Luiseño early in the present century. Information on this ceremony from other Uto-Aztecan groups was compiled by Strong (1929). The Gabrielino may have been the originators of much of the elaborate ritual associated with this ceremony, which was subsequently adopted by the Luiseño and others (Kroeber 1925:645). The last reported celebration of the Boys' Puberty Ceremony took place among the Luiseño around 1858 or 1868 (DuBois 1908:77; Sparkman 1908:225).

The Boys' Puberty Ceremony appears to have been held every two or three years (DuBois 1908:84). According to Father Boscana, "at the age of six or seven years, the children were given a god as protector. This was an animal in which they were told to place entire confidence, and which . . . would defend them from all dangers, particularly in war against their enemies" (Boscana 1933:45). This protector was not *Chengiichngech*, "but another [spiritual being] called Touch" who "was invisible, and inhabited the mountains and bowels of the earth" and who appeared "in the shape of an animal of the most terrific description" (Boscana 1933:45). The central ritual of the ceremony involved the ingestion of a drink called *maanet*, prepared from the dried root of *Datura wrightii*, a plant that contains a powerful alkaloid and has strong hallucinogenic properties

(Harner 1973:128-140; Geiger and Meighan 1976:89, answer from Mission San Gabriel; Armstrong 1986).

The *maanet* ceremony was held after dark in a secluded location away from the ceremonial grounds. The ritual was supervised by the *tomyaar*, who was aided by a number of *paxaa's*. The dried *Datura* root was prepared by the *tomyaar* in a special stone mortar that was freshly painted red, white, and black for the occasion. When not in use this mortar was kept buried. Under the *tomyaar's* supervision the initiates drank the *Datura* beverage from the mortar. As each boy drank, the *tomyaar* pressed his palm against the child's forehead. He monitored the amount of drink consumed, raising the boy's head when the proper amount had been swallowed (DuBois 1908:78-79).

After drinking the *Datura* the initiates returned to the ceremonial ground, imitating the motions and sounds of animals as they crawled on all fours. When the initiates reached the main gathering area they continued singing and dancing around the fire until they were too intoxicated to remain standing. They were then returned to the secluded area until the intoxication wore off. During this hallucinogenic trance the boys were watched over by a number of older initiates who admonished them to stay awake and observe their visions carefully, and to remember the instructions given to them by their guardian spirits (DuBois 1908:79-80; Boscana 1933:45-46).

During the remainder of the three-day ceremony the initiates received instruction on ritual practices, and listened to lectures describing the standards of behavior imposed by *Chengiichngech*. Often, visiting lineages took part in the instruction, sharing their rituals and practices with the boys. The initiates did not partake of any food for the three-day duration of the ceremony, and they were required to continue abstaining from meat and salt for two to three weeks afterward; other dietary restrictions may have lasted for as much as one year (DuBois 1908:80-82; Sparkman 1908:222; Boscana 1933:45-46).

Three days after the *Datura* ceremony the young initiates participated in another ritual symbolizing their spiritual death and rebirth. The boys were taken to a spot where a trench had been prepared. This trench was five feet long, two feet deep, and a little more than a foot wide. In the bottom a number of round, flat stones were arranged in a straight line, and surrounding these stones was a mesh of milkweed twine woven around wooden stakes. Each initiate was required to leap from stone to stone while steadying himself against the sides of the trench, although smaller boys might be helped by a "sponsor," for it was believed that if a boy slipped and fell he would die young (DuBois 1908:85-87).

In yet another ritual the initiates were branded on the right arm. A wad of dried herb, California Mugwort (*Artemisia vulgaris*), was pressed against the skin, set afire, and allowed to burn down to the flesh. This raised a large blister which, when left to heal by itself, resulted in a distinctive scar. Father Boscana said it was believed that this branding "added greater strength to the nerves, and gave a better pulse for the management of the bow" (Boscana 1933:46).

A still greater test of endurance came during the Ant Ceremony, in which the initiates were whipped with nettle branches and stung by ants to strengthen their courage and fortitude. According to Father Boscana, this ritual was held in July or August "when the nettle was in its most fiery state" (Boscana 1933:47). After being whipped with nettles "until he was unable to walk" each initiate was "carried to the nest of the . . . most furious species of ants and laid down among them" while the onlookers "kept annoying the insects to make them still more violent" (Boscana 1933:47).

Following the Ant Ceremony, a sandpainting was created. Among the Luiseño, this painting typically had a pit in the center representing "hell," surrounded by three concentric circles; the outer circle represented the Milky Way, the middle circle night, and the inner circle blood. Figures of animals decorated the painting in the space between the central pit and the inner circle, and an opening facing north cut across all three circles (Sparkman 1908:221). A lump of sage seed flour and salt was placed in each boy's mouth, and he then spat the lump into the pit in the center of the painting. If the lump was moist after being spat, it was taken as a sign that the youth had not heeded the counsel offered him during the ceremony (Sparkman 1908:222).

Father Boscana described yet another ceremony, which Kroeber interpreted as a higher level of initiation for boys who had already completed the *Datura* ritual (Kroeber 1925:640). According to Boscana, the youths were painted black and red and adorned with feathers and were then led in procession into the *yovaar*, where they sat near the *Chengiichngech* figure. A sandpainting depicting a

"figure of an animal" was created, and the initiates fasted for the entire three-day period of instruction (Boscana 1933:46).

GIRLS' PUBERTY CEREMONIES

The Girls' Puberty Ceremony not only prepared the participants for their future roles as wives and mothers, but also announced their approaching eligibility for marriage (Bean 1972a:143). The ceremony was conducted for several girls at one time and was held when their fathers notified the *tomyaar* that the girls had begun menstruating. The *tomyaar* then contacted the members of a lineage linked by ceremonial reciprocity with the host lineage and asked them to provide an official to preside over the ceremony. The last known performance of the Girls' Puberty Ceremony occurred in the Upper San Luis Rey Valley in 1890 (DuBois 1908:93-94; Sparkman 1908:225; Strong 1929: 297-299).

A central feature of the Girls' Puberty Ceremony was a period of ritual seclusion and purification. The ritual seclusion and purification of girls at puberty and of women during menstruation has been practiced by the people of many cultures throughout the world (see Frazer 1922:690-705). According to Father Boscana, the Luiseño "made a large hole in the ground, in shape resembling a grave, and about two feet deep. This they filled with stones and burning coals, and when sufficiently heated the latter were taken out, and upon the former they laid the branches of the *estafiarte* (a kind of perennial plant), so as to form a bed" (Boscana 1933:48). In addition to *estafiarte*, which has been identified as California Mugwort (*Artemisia vulgaris)*, some of the other plants used in this ceremonial "bed" included sumac, Panicled Bulrush (*Scirpus microcarpus*), sedge (*Carex schottii*), and red and green algae. Algae were collected from springs in late summer and were called "menses of . . . the earth" (DuBois 1908:94; Harrington 1933:167, note 138).

Once the pit was prepared, the girls were gathered together and seated on the ground before the *tomyaar*. The *tomyaar* gave each girl a ball of tobacco, which she swallowed with a mouthful of warm water. The tobacco was a test of the girl's character, for if she vomited it was taken as a sign that she was not virtuous (DuBois 1908:94). Drowsy from the side-effects of the tobacco, the girls were then placed on the heated bed of fragrant brush, and "for two or three days . . . permitted to eat but very little. This constituted the term for purification" (Boscana 1933:48; Harrington 1942:36, item 1423). A loosely woven mat or basket was placed over each girl's face to protect her from flies and insects, and she was given a piece of shell or wood with which to scratch herself, for it was believed that using her fingernails would cause pimples to appear (DuBois 1908:94; Strong 1929:298).

Each day of the ceremony brought a different lineage to visit and participate in the celebration (DuBois 1908:94-95; Strong 1929:298). Father Boscana reported that "the outside of the hole was adorned with feathers of different birds, beads," and other items. A number of older women "were employed in singing songs . . . and the young women danced around her [the initiate] at intervals every day" (Boscana 1933:48-49; also Harrington 1942:36, item 1420).

Following the purification ritual, each girl's face was painted and she was adorned with necklaces of mica and bracelets and anklets of hair. An abstention from meat, salt, and grease was observed, and water was taken only when warmed (DuBois 1908:96; Harrington 1942:36, items 1397, 1401, 1403). At the end of one month, the *tomyaar* created a sandpainting and lectured the girls on proper behavior and lifestyle. A lump of ground sage seed and salt was placed in each girl's mouth, which she then spat into a hole in the center of the sandpainting, where it was buried. The ceremony closed with a foot race to a large rock, where relatives painted a design representing the rattlesnake on each girl's face. A corresponding design was then painted on the boulder (DuBois 1908:96; Strong 1929:298-299).

Mrs. James Rosemyre, a Gabrielino consultant interviewed by C. Hart Merriam, described another puberty ritual performed for girls 12 to 15 years of age. In this ritual the mothers of the initiates danced around the girls while singing about "to-sow't," a magical stone owned by the *tomyaar*. The sacred stone, which was probably a shaman's charm-stone, may represent *Toshaawt*, the black stone which *Nocuma*, the supernatural being representing "Sky," used to secure the world in one of the creation stories recorded by Father Boscana (see Chapter 9).

The dance was supervised by an older woman who was also responsible for handling the *toshaawt* stone. She placed the stone in a basket of boiling water, where it began to "gurgle and sing." The

stone was then removed from the water and placed under a bowl-shaped basket containing a bitter tea brewed from the chilicote plant, also known as manroot (*Echinocystis macrocarpa*). As each girl took a cup of the tea her mother gave the official a payment of shell beads or money. At the end of the ritual the *tomyaar* announced that the girls had become women (Merriam 1955:86).

A number of the restrictions observed by young girls at puberty were also followed by mature women during menstruation. Thus, menstruating women avoided meat, grease, and salt, drank only warmed water, and may have secluded themselves in separate dwellings. Husbands, too, were required to observe certain restrictions during their wives' menstruations, presumably to avoid the dangerous supernatural consequences of contact with menstrual blood. Accordingly, a man could neither hunt nor fish while his wife was in her period (Harrington 1942:11, 36-37, items 248, 1429, 1431, 1433-1434, 1438, 1439).

COURTSHIP, MARRIAGE, AND BIRTH RITUALS

Marriage was an important ritual occasion; through matrimony, alliances were created that united families, lineages, and communities. Marital alliances could extend across a wide geographical area and frequently crossed language boundaries; the Gabrielino chose marriage partners from among the Cahuilla and the Chumash and probably from other language groups as well. Indians living at *Tohuungna* in the San Fernando Valley took spouses from at least 11 other Gabrielino communities in the Valley region (Forbes 1966:138, 147; Bean 1972a:93).

Among the California Indians, marriage partners were generally chosen from the same socioeconomic class (Bean 1974:19-20). Thus, the children of a *tomyaar* would usually marry within the elite class. Although the ordinary Gabrielino man took only one wife, a *tomyaar* might have one, two, or three, a privilege which not only promoted the formation of alliances with other lineages and communities but also provided the chief with help in managing the community food reserves (Reid 1852:25, 27; Harrington 1942:30, item 1162). Gabrielino shamans and other members of the wealthy elite may also have taken more than one wife, as was the practice among the Cahuilla (Bean 1974:19-20).

An important concern of Gabrielino courtship and betrothal was the avoidance of incest. During historic times, individuals from the same community were allowed to marry as long as no kinship tie existed; however, previously it was a common practice among some Uto-Aztecan-speaking groups to choose a marriage partner from the opposite moiety (Harrington 1942:30, item 1177; Bean 1974:19-20; see Chapter 6 for a discussion of the moiety in Gabrielino society). The strictness of this moiety rule is illustrated by a Cahuilla prohibition forbidding marriage between partners of opposite moieties if a genealogical relationship existed during the previous five generations (Bean 1972a:91).

Betrothals could be accomplished in a number of ways depending upon local custom or the socio-economic class of the partners. In the simplest situation, the suitor approached the intended and expressed his feelings, declaring "I wish to wed you," or "We are to be married." If interested, the girl replied "It is well," or "I will inform my parents, and you shall know." Sometimes a suitor used a third party to ask the girl for her consent before her parents were approached (Boscana 1933:51).

In other betrothals, the girl's parents were approached first, either by the suitor or by a profes-sional matchmaker, or the betrothals were arranged by the parents while the partners were still infants. In the latter situation, during childhood the future bride and groom "were always together and the house of either was a home to both," and "when the individuals . . . reached the proper age they were united with the customary ceremonies" (Boscana 1933:51-52; also Harrington 1942:30, item 1175). By far the most drastic procedure, and one that was probably used but rarely, was marriage by capture, or kidnapping. Such an action was regarded as a most serious offense and was generally "the cause of war, and severe conflicts between the neighboring villages" (Boscana 1933:53).

A ritual exchange of gifts was an important part of the courtship, although the method and substance of the exchange varied. According to Father Boscana, when the suitor first visited his future bride's home he presented her family with a present of fur, beads, seeds, or some other suitably valuable item. He then began a period of work service with the bride's family, supplying them with fuel and game while the girl attended to the house. This allowed the parents to observe the suitability of the match (Boscana 1933:51-

52; Harrington 1942:30, items 1157-1158). Among the Gabrielino of the San Fernando Valley it was customary for the suitor or his representatives to present the father of the bride with a gift of "two or three pesos in beads," while the bride received "a shawl similar to a cape made of skins of a rabbit or otter, a chamois skin and a small basket" (Geiger and Meighan 1976:66, answer from Mission San Fernando).

Reid observed that when a marriage was arranged the groom announced the betrothal "to all his relations, even to the *nineteenth cousin*" (Reid 1852:25). Prior to the marriage ceremony, the groom's male relatives carried a present of money beads to the bride's family. These beads were divided equally among the bride's female relatives; however, the bride herself received nothing. A few days later the bride's relatives returned the gesture, bringing gift baskets of chía meal to the bridegroom's home (Reid 1852:25).

The actual marriage ceremony lasted three or four days and included members of both families. As the ceremony commenced, the bride, adorned in beads, furs, feathers, and paint, travelled to her spouse's home accompanied by several shamans and older women sent by the groom (Boscana 1933:52). Sometimes the bride was carried by one of her male relatives and was accompanied by her friends and family, everyone joining in a joyous dance. Halfway to their destination the bride's party was met by the groom's family and friends, who led them the rest of the distance (Reid 1852:25-26).

When the bride arrived at the groom's home she was undressed by several women who were allowed to keep her clothes and jewelry. She remained naked throughout the ceremony, unless she was the bride of a *tomyaar*, in which case she was enrobed in a feather cloak (Boscana 1933:52). In the final phase of the ceremony, baskets of seeds were emptied over the heads of the bride and groom "to denote blessing and plenty," while the guests scrambled to gather the scattered seeds (Reid 1852:26).

Following the marriage ceremony, a dance was held "where might be seen warriors and hunters in full costume. . . . old women took a part in the dance either as if carrying of game, or of dispatching their wounded enemies. . . . The younger portion of the women and old men sat around as singers" (Reid 1852:26).

Before departing, the bride's parents gave her a

final lecture, encouraging her to perform her duties faithfully and so avoid dishonoring them. They also advised her that she could return home if her husband mistreated her (Boscana 1933:52). Reid reported that it was unacceptable for a married woman to visit her parents' home, although they could visit her as they wished (Reid 1852:26-27).

A feast was given at the onset of a couple's first pregnancy, and one entire night was devoted to singing and dancing. The songs asked *Chengiichngech* to look with favor on the unborn child, as the mother was a good woman who had fulfilled the community's hopes by becoming pregnant. Prior to the child's birth, the husband observed a 15 to 20-day period of seclusion corresponding to his wife's confinement. During this time men "could not leave the house, unless to procure fuel and water, [and] were prohibited the use of all kinds of fish and meat, smoking and diversions" (Boscana 1933:53-54).

Women normally delivered their babies in a sitting position, assisted by a midwife (Harrington 1942:34, items 1326, 1328). Following childbirth, a woman was restricted from eating meat for one or two months. At the end of this time she was given three pills "the size of a musket ball compounded of one part meat and one part wild tobacco" and was again free to follow a normal diet (Reid 1852:30; Harrington 1942:35, items 1371-1372). Children were normally weaned at two years of age, although one of Harrington's consultants reported that "some Ind. [Indian] women used to suckle their children after they were big enough to run around" (Harrington 1942:35, item 1363; 1986:R105 F685).

The Gabrielino used a number of techniques to manage population growth and family size. Sexual abstinence was probably the most common and was practiced by new parents "until the child could run about" (Reid 1852:30). Infanticide may have been practiced on deformed children, and abortion was accomplished by "eating medicine" (Harrington 1942:35, items 1360, 1362). Reid reported that during historical times abortion was induced when a pregnancy resulted from rape or a casual liaison between a Gabrielino woman and a Spanish man (Reid 1852:87).

Among the Gabrielino, marriages could be dissolved for a number of reasons including infidelity, barrenness, and incompatibility (Harrington 1942:31, items 1191-1193). Although a Gabrielino man had the legal right to kill or wound his wife if he caught her committing adultery, a more common recourse allowed the wronged husband to inform his wife's lover that "*he was at liberty to keep her*," and then take possession of the lover's spouse for himself. The exchange was regarded as both legal and final (Reid 1852:16).

A Gabrielino woman could divorce her husband if he beat or abused her, in which case all of the gifts given to the girl's family would be returned (Reid 1852:27). Yet another cause of divorce was a husband's failure to support his wife and family properly. In one story recounted by Reid, seven sisters, represented by the stars in the constellation of the Pleiades, abandoned their husbands because the men were greedy and refused to share their catch from the day's hunt. According to Harrington, Gabrielino divorcees generally remarried (Reid 1852:49-51; Harrington 1942:31, item 1196).

DEATH AND MOURNING CEREMONIES

Perhaps no aspect of Gabrielino culture received greater ritual attention than death. The Gabrielino personified death as a force that entered the world with the passing of *Wewyoot* and which "when in anger with any-one, by degrees took away his breath until all was removed and then the person died" (Boscana 1933:75; Harrington 1933:198-199, note 211). Juan Meléndrez recounted a Gabrielino story in which

> the grillo [cricket] & the matavenado [Jerusalem cricket] & another insect (pinacate [black beetle], inf. thinks) were the reyes [kings]. The grillo & the other did not want death but the matavenado said there had to be death, also wars & catastrophes, etc., or there would not be room for the people. So they let people die. The matavenado wanted to kill all the females so that there would be only males in the world, but the others saw that they could not survive without the females & would not do it (Harrington 1986:R106 F221).

Death initiated a series of rituals intended to free the spirit of the deceased from this world and aid it in its journey to the land of the dead. These rituals began with the funeral observances and ended with the performance of a Mourning Ceremony one to four years later (Merriam 1955:77).

Reid reported that the Gabrielino had "only one word to designate *life* and *soul*" (Reid 1852:19).

However, Father Boscana noted that every individual possessed a "soul belonging to the body," which they called "*pusuni*, which . . . signifies 'a substance within,'" and which referred more specifically "to the heart on account of its location and particular importance to the body." This soul was distinct from "the *espíritu vital*, received from the air which they breathed, and which they called *piuts*" meaning "to live" or "breath" (Boscana 1933:75; also Harrington 1933:197-198, note 210). The soul of a deceased person was believed to linger about its former home until released by the performance of the proper funeral and mourning ceremonies. To help free the soul from earthly ties the name of the deceased was never mentioned. In addition, the dwelling of the deceased was sometimes burned, although Reid indicated that this was practiced only if "the deceased were a head of the family, or a favorite son" (Reid 1852:31; also Boscana 1933:78; Geiger and Meighan 1976:97, answer from Mission San Fernando).

The Gabrielino possessed a dual concept of the land of the dead, reflecting perhaps the social division between the elite and the commoners. Father Boscana wrote "the chiefs and *puplem* alone went to the heaven of stars. . . . Others, who were not of noble rank, were doomed to the borders of the sea, or to the hills, mountains, valleys, or forests. There they remained an indefinite time while Chinigchinich made them do penance for the faults they had committed in not obeying his precepts." Father Boscana noted that it was not clear what happened to the deceased when their penance was completed (Boscana 1933:77).

The name *Shiishonga* referred to the land of the dead which, according to different accounts, lay either below the earth or on an island in the west (Boscana 1933:76; Harrington 1933:199, note 214, 1986:R105 F434). José Zalvidea reported that

in the west beyond pimǔ'ŋa [Santa Catalina Island] there is a land which rises as a sierra from the sea with pines, fruits and flowers. That country is called 'erĕspat, and the Captain of that country is šEh₂ᴇ̆vajt. He cares for all and tolerates no evil. His name means "no quiere malo, quiere bueno, que este todo bien [he does not wish evil, he wishes good, he wishes everything well]." . . . Those who do not believe in šEh₂ᴇ̆vajt, he punishes. God made both worlds. They are connected. The one there is connected and balanced with the one here (Harrington 1986:R102 F41).

The missionaries at San Gabriel offered a similar piece of information, reporting that "one or the other declared he learned that the first Indian settlers came here from the north and were led here by a captain general who they declare lives on an island and to whom they attribute life without beginning or end" (Geiger and Meighan 1976:93, answer from Mission San Gabriel). Harrington suggested that the "captain general" was none other than *Wewyoot* (Harrington 1933:199, note 214).

To reach the land of the dead a soul underwent a series of trials that tested its courage and moral strength. One Gabrielino story told of a young man who entered the land of the dead to be reunited with his deceased wife. In his first trial, the young man retrieved a white feather from the top of a pole so tall its end could not be seen. In the second trial, he split a long hair from end to end. In the third, he drew a star map accurately depicting the location of the North Star, which was probably believed to mark a passage through the sky to the upper world of supernatural beings. Finally, he single-handedly slew a herd of deer that had been magically disguised as beetles (Reid 1852:65-66; see Blackburn 1975:33-34 for a discussion of a similar theme in Chumash oral literature).

A second land of the dead, known as *Tokuupar*, was reserved for *tomyaars* and shamans. It has already been noted that *Tokuupar* means "heaven" or "sky" and corresponds to the upper world, which was the abode of supernatural beings (Reid 1852:67). The soul of a deceased *tomyaar* or shaman "went to dwell among the stars, and like them threw its light upon the earth. For this reason they said that the planets and most luminous bodies were their hearts" (Boscana 1933:77).

According to Father Boscana, the soul of a *tomyaar* or shaman could reach *Tokuupar* only if a special funeral ceremony was performed involving the ritual ingestion of a portion of muscle taken from the neck of the deceased. To enable a soul to reach *Tokuupar* it was necessary that a special ritual official, the *taakwa*, "the eater of human flesh, had eaten of them previous to their being burnt." If this ceremony was not performed "they did not go to the stars but to another place, to which they were destined by Chinigchinich" (Boscana 1933:77). The *taakwa* "arrived at the place where they had placed the body . . . [and] immediately cut off a large piece from the neck and the back, near the shoulder, and consumed the flesh in its raw state, in the presence of the multitude. . . . This was always done in commemoration of the feat performed by the Coyote upon the body of the great captain, Ouiot" (Boscana 1933:62-63). It should be noted that ritualized consumption of human flesh, which has been reported from cultures throughout the world, is often practiced in the belief that it preserves a special quality or virtue of the deceased by transmitting it to someone still living (see Frazer 1922:576).

The Gabrielino practiced both cremation and interment. Interment may have been the more standard practice on the Channel Islands and the mainland coast directly opposite, perhaps reflecting either the influence of Chumash mortuary practices or else a scarcity of fuel suitable for funeral pyres. Harrington noted that the "coast Gabrielino both buried and burned the dead as far south as [the] mouth of [the] Santa Ana River" (Kroeber 1925:556-557, 633; Harrington 1942:37, 45, items 1456, 1465; McKusick and Warren 1959:135, 173; Reinman and Townsend 1960:28; Hudson 1969; Koerper and Fouste 1977). During the historic period, the Spanish missionaries succeeded in eliminating cremation.

Gabrielino funerary ceremonies generally lasted three days, and if the deceased was a *tomyaar* or an important personage they might include participants from neighboring communities (Boscana 1933:73; Geiger and Meighan 1976:97, answer from Mission San Gabriel).

The Gabrielino were deeply concerned with the possibility of accidentally burying someone in a coma. According to a story told to Harrington by Juan and Juana Meléndrez, the path to the land of the dead was forked; the souls of those who were buried alive took the path to the left, while those who were truly dead followed the path to the right (Harrington 1986:R106 F237). To prevent such accidental burials a wake was held. Following death, the corpse was kept in the house overnight (Harrington 1942:37, item 1447). The mourners "suffered several hours to elapse, that they might be assured of his death" (Boscana 1933:73). Reid (1852:30) noted that the wake continued "until the body showed signs of decay," and the mourners sang a dirge "accompanied by a shrill whistle, produced by blowing into the tube of a deer's leg bone."

The corpse was borne to the cemetery or place of cremation on a special litter as the mourners followed in procession (Harrington 1942:20, item 707). A

musical instrument consisting of a cylinder covered with red and white feathers and strung on a cord was carried by two men, each holding one end of the cord. The cylinder made a mournful sound as it was swung from one end of the cord to the other. At the cemetery a special song called We-vó-e-naht, named after the mystic we'-vor (probably *Wewyoot*), was sung in the presence of the body (Merriam 1955:85).

If the corpse was to be cremated, the relative's family usually hired someone from another lineage to officiate at the burning. The office of burner was hereditary and confined to certain families. All the articles owned or used by the deceased were burned with the corpse (Boscana 1933:73; Harrington 1933:197, note 205). Cremation ashes might be placed in a stone bowl or a shell dish and then buried or they might be scattered to the east (Ashby and Winterbourne 1966:27; Hudson 1969:17-18; Merriam n.d.c).

If the corpse was to be buried, the hands were crooked upon the breast and the body bound from head to foot (Reid 1852:31). Archaeological data suggest that the corpse was usually buried in a flexed position; sometimes it was wrapped in a net, a hide blanket or cape, or a mat of tule or sea grass (McKusick and Warren 1959:134; Reinman and Townsend 1960:6; Hudson and Blackburn 1986:250-251).

Archaeological and ethnohistoric data indicate that a wide variety of grave offerings might be buried with the corpse; such offerings might include seeds, pots, otter skins, baskets, wood, bone and shell implements, and shell beads. If the deceased were an official, the instrument denoting his office was included as well. The amount and value of grave goods included with a burial depended upon the social status of the deceased. *Tomyaars*, shamans, and other members of the elite were buried with the most elaborate and extensive grave goods (Reid 1852:31; Winterbourne 1967:43; Finnerty et al. 1970:15-21; Geiger and Meighan 1976:97, answers from Missions San Gabriel and San Fernando). Funeral fires were sometimes kindled on or near the grave, and on San Nicolas Island stone slabs decorated with asphaltum inlay might be buried with the corpse (Alliot 1916; Ashby and Winterbourne 1966:27; Bryan 1970a:82-84).

Graves were marked in a number of ways. The coastal Gabrielino near San Pedro erected grave markers etched with characters commemorating the deceased. One such marker, apparently commemo-

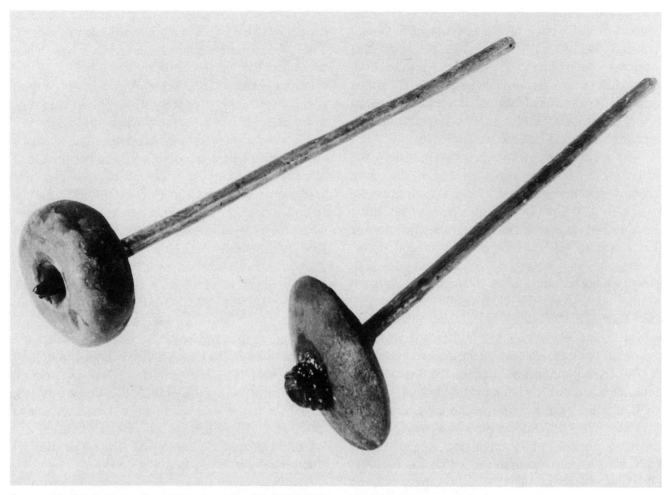

Courtesy of the Peabody Museum, Harvard University. Artifact Nos. 86-23-10/39261and 86-23-10/39264, Photo No. N29398

Fig. 65. The sunstick was a ritual implement used by shamans during the seasonal ceremonies performed at the time of the winter and summer solstices. These sunsticks were collected from Bowers Cave in the San Martín Mountains in Los Angeles County.

rating a fisherman, was etched with figures resembling killer whales (Heizer 1968:104, 123, note 66). Beautiful urn-shaped baskets and choke-mouth baskets might also be left on graves as markers, sometimes filled with food (Merriam 1955:85).

When the interment or cremation was completed the mourners retired outside the settlement to continue the ceremony. Shamans sang songs recounting the course and outcome of the disease, and mourners singed their hair and covered their face and hands with ashes as a sign of their grief. For the loss of a parent, wife, or child, the hair was completely shorn; for a distant relative, one-half the length was cut; and for a friend only the tip was removed. Merriam reported that a mourning period of one year was observed, during which time the bereaved abstained from meat. Female mourners cut their hair just below the ears and put black tar on their foreheads, cheeks, and chin.

The face paint was worn for the entire year. Although the personal effects and sometimes the home of the deceased might be burned, one item always was reserved to be burned in commemoration at the Mourning Ceremony (Reid 1852:31; Boscana 1933:73; Harrington 1986:R106 F193; Merriam n.d.c).

SEASONAL RITUALS

Large, public rituals were times of great activity and excitement for the Gabrielino. A number of these rituals were held on an annual basis, including the Summer Solstice Ritual, the Harvest Celebration held at the end of summer, and the Winter Solstice Fiesta. Others may have occurred at intervals of several years, such as the Mourning Ceremony and the Eagle Killing Rite held in conjunction with the Harvest Celebration.

Fig. 66. The Summer Solstice Site at Burro Flats. A line of "cupules" (small, artificial depressions) on top of a boulder (center, foreground) aligns with a naturally formed notch in the distant cliff; at the time of the summer solstice the rising sun is framed by this notch. Photograph by author.

Fig. 67. Another view of the Summer Solstice Site at Burro Flats showing the "cupule boulder" (right) and "face rock" (left); the outcropping between these two boulders has been drilled with five mortar holes arranged in the shape of a bear's paw. At the time of the summer solstice, a shadow cast by the cupule boulder bisects the mortar hole forming the "heel" of the paw. Photograph by author.

THE SUMMER SOLSTICE RITUAL

Information on the Gabrielino Summer Solstice Ritual is sketchy, and Father Boscana reported that the event was of less significance than the winter solstice for the reason that the latter "ripened their fruits and seeds, gave warmth to the atmosphere, and enlivened again the fields with beauty and productivity" (Boscana 1933:65-66). Details on the Chumash rite are also limited; however, it is known that at midsummer the shamans "prepared [a] soft place in the earth and inserted [the sun-] stick surmounted by this stone. . . . [The] stone was the sun. [These men] made a prayer. . . . Also in [the] midsummer [ceremony they] had a big "basket" and all put valuables in it as offerings to Sun for crop increase" (Harrington n.d. cited in Hudson and Underhay 1978:66; comments in brackets in Hudson and Underhay).

The sunstick was an item of ritual paraphernalia rich in sacred symbolism. It consisted of a wooden shaft approximately 15 inches in length, topped with a sandstone disc held in place with cord wrappings and asphaltum. The stone disc, six inches in diameter and painted green or blue, was set on the shaft at an angle. A pattern of lines radiating outward from the wooden shaft was painted on top of the disc; a red or black crescent representing the moon was painted on the side. According to Harrington's Chumash consultant Fernando Librado, the shaft of the sunstick was a physical representation of the earth's axis and the sandstone disc represented the sun. When not in use the sunstick was stored in a feather down-lined box of cottonwood or red cedar decorated with shells (Librado and Harrington 1977:56-57; Hudson and Underhay 1978:63-66; Hudson and Blackburn 1986:235-241). A number of artifacts identified as sunsticks have been recovered from Bowers Cave, a dry cave located in the San Martín Mountains near Castaic Junction, and also from Santa Catalina Island and the Santa Barbara coast (Van Valkenburgh 1952; Elsasser and Heizer 1963).

An important complex of Gabrielino-Chumash sites associated with winter and summer solstice rituals is located in the Simi Hills. Burro Flats, at the western end of the San Fernando Valley near Chatsworth, consists of several associated midden and rock art sites. The summer solstice site comprises several natural and artificial rock features that align with the position of sunrise several days before and after the solstice. The first of these is a naturally-formed notch in the skyline defined by the cliff bordering the eastern edge of the site. West of the cliff is a brush-covered flat with scattered rock outcroppings. The top surface of one of these outcroppings, a boulder that stands shoulder-high, has been drilled with a line of small depressions, or "cupules"; this line of cupules points toward the notch in the cliff. A few feet west of the cupule boulder is a second outcropping, the surface of which lies at ground level and bears five deeply-drilled mortar holes arranged in the pattern of a "bear paw."

The author visited Burro Flats in the summer of 1990, approximately one month after the summer solstice. The sun rose to the south of the cliff notch that day, although for a few days at the time of the solstice it is framed by this natural indentation. As the small crowd of visitors watched in silence the sun rose above the cliff, causing the cupule boulder to cast a long, pointed shadow across the "bear paw" stone. At the time of the solstice this shadow bisects the mortar forming the "heel" of the bear paw. Some researchers have suggested that this mortar could have been used as a receptacle for offerings to the sun, much the same as the "big basket" described by Harrington (Romani et al. 1988:127). As the sun rose higher in the sky the shadows gradually faded, bringing the phenomenon to an end.

HARVEST CELEBRATION

Details on the Gabrielino Harvest Celebration must be reconstructed in large measure from information gathered by Harrington from Chumash consultants. The Harvest Celebration was held to honor the female earth deity and give her thanks for the harvest of wild fruits and seeds. The Gabrielino name for the earth was *Tovaar*, although an important association also existed between the earth deity and the supernatural being *Chuuxoyt*, who was represented by "Deer" (see the discussion on the Gabrielino pantheon earlier in this chapter).

The Gabrielino probably held the Harvest Celebration at the same time of year as the Chumash festival; it is believed that in pre-mission times the Chumash ritual was held in August, although it was later moved to the end of September (Librado and Harrington 1977:43-50, 104, note 51; Hudson and Underhay 1978:45-46). The members of the Portolá Expedition may have witnessed a Gabrielino Harvest Celebration in July of 1769. While travelling through Brea Canyon the explorers came upon a community of "more than seventy souls" who were "having a feast and dance, to which they had invited their neighbors of the river called Jesús de los Temblores [the Santa Ana River]" (Bolton 1927:142-143).

The Harvest Celebration generally lasted four or five days, during which time different "delegations" of visiting lineages participated in the rituals. Sometimes these delegations came from considerable distances, as when Yokuts Indians from the southern San Joaquin Valley travelled to Ventura to join a Chumash Harvest Celebration (Librado and Harrington 1977:43, 46).

The *paxaa'* officiated at the Harvest Celebration. The celebration began at midmorning on the first day with a number of processions to the sacred enclosure. Visiting delegations might participate in these processions, singing songs, performing dances, and showering the spectators with corn, beans, chía, and islay seeds. Two shamans standing at the *yovaar* played deer bone whistles to accompany the dancers. When the procession reached the sacred enclosure, the participants, accompanied by the shaman's music, sang a song honoring the spirit of Deer (Librado and Harrington 1977:43-45).

More ritual processions took place in the following days. In one midafternoon performance, women of all ages carried offerings of food and beads to the sacred enclosure in a carefully orchestrated procession. The women first circled the interior of the enclosure once in a clockwise direction, then circled the exterior three times more, also in a clockwise direction. Following this, they presented their gifts to the paxaa', circled the enclosure three times more in a clockwise direction, and returned to their seats (Librado and Harrington 1977:46-47).

ANNUAL MOURNING CEREMONY

A Mourning Ceremony was sometimes held in

conjunction with the Harvest Celebration. The Mourning Ceremony honored the souls of those who had died in the interval since its last performance. It was the culmination of a series of death rituals, and through its performance the souls of the deceased achieved release from the earth and entrance into the land of the dead (Bean 1972a:136). Following the performance of the Mourning Ceremony, widows and widowers were free to marry again (Hudson and Underhay 1978:47). The ceremony was characterized by elaborate rituals; Kroeber suggested that the Gabrielino may have developed many of the rituals in the ceremony as it was performed by the southern California Indians (Kroeber 1925:860).

The Mourning Ceremony was called *Kotuumot Kehaay* in Gabrielino and was held at intervals varying from one to four years depending upon the time required to collect the food, money-beads, and other goods necessary for the fiesta (Harrington 1942:38, item 1486; Merriam 1955:77). Harrington reported that the ceremony was generally held in late summer (1942:38, note 1490); however, Father Boscana suggested that the date might vary, noting that "at the time of the death of a captain, or one of the *puplem* [shamans] . . . a *pul* [shaman] observed the moon's aspect, also the month in which the death occurred. In the following year, in the same month, when the moon's aspect was the same, they celebrated the anniversary" (Boscana 1933:67).

The Mourning Ceremony generally lasted eight days (Reid 1852:41-42; Merriam 1955:77) and consisted of four primary rites. The first of these was known as the "clothes washing." In this rite the clothes of the deceased were viewed and then ritually rinsed with cold water by the *taakwa*, who then drank the ceremonial rinse water (Harrington 1933:185, 191, notes 182, 187, 1942:38, item 1499). The second ritual was known as the "clothes burning" and was properly conducted several days or weeks after the clothes washing, although it was more common for the two to be held in conjunction with one another. During the clothes burning the *taakwa* consigned the clothes of the deceased to the flames and later gave a recital that described the death of *Wewyoot*. A number of other singing and chanting ceremonies were held as well (Harrington 1933:191-192, note 187, 1942:38, item 1500).

The third primary rite was the image-burning ceremony in which representations of the deceased

were consumed in a great fire. The fourth and final ceremony involved the distribution of the property of the dead (Harrington 1933:192, note 187, 1942:38, items 1512, 1514). A special memorial might also be held to honor those individuals who had been initiated into the most sacred mysteries of the *Chengiichngech* religion, and this memorial closed with the burying of the initiate's ceremonial regalia in the center of a sandpainting (Harrington 1942:38, item 1516).

According to information gathered by Merriam, the Mourning Ceremony was sponsored by a wealthy member of the community who was called the "mah-ne-sas" or *maniishar* and who presided over the ceremony. The *maniishar* provided the food for the fiesta as well as the baskets to be burned during the rituals. The *maniishar* invited members of other lineages to the fiesta as well (Merriam 1955:7, n.d.b). José de los Santos Juncos reported that "when S. Gab. [San Gabriel] captain went to have fiesta for los muertos [the dead], the pobres [the poor] paid capt. to make fiesta for their dead, just like people pay priest now. Gab. capt. sent his courier to Azusa, etc., to announce fiesta to the other captains" (Harrington 1986:R102 F732). Ceremonial reciprocity also played an important part in these ceremonies. Juan Meléndrez reported to Harrington that "the F. [Fernandeño] gave the burning fiesta for the dead among the G. [Gabrielino] & the G. gave it for the F. dead" (Harrington 1986:R106 F241).

From each group invited to the ceremony, the *maniishar* chose one person to be "to-me-arr'[*tomyaar*]." These individuals were generally not true *tomyaars*; however, it was necessary that they be mourners. In turn, each *tomyaar* chose two or three of his relatives, usually men, to be workers. The *maniishar* also invited a number of female mourners who brought offerings of food, beads, baskets, and money (Merriam 1955:77-78, n.d.b).

The performers in the Mourning Ceremony rehearsed for eight days in an "unconsecrated" *yovaar* prior to the beginning of the celebration, and one entire day was taken to consecrate the primary *yovaar* in which the ritual would be held. The sacred enclosure was decorated with feathers and, according to Reid, four poles carrying feather banners were erected in the cardinal directions (Reid 1852:41). Other accounts mention only one large pole, which was erected in the cemetery (Merriam 1955:78-80, n.d.b). A missionary at San Fernando described this pole as "covered with bundles of feathers from the crow and . . . adorned with beads" (Geiger and Meighan 1976:58, answer from Mission San Fernando). According to José de los Santos Juncos, the pole was called *kotuumot* and was painted, with "one vertical bunch of feathers at [the] top . . . with feathers of various colors." The pole was "painted in rings 4" broad of alternating red & white" (Harrington 1986:R104 F006-007; see also Hudson and Blackburn 1986:61-66, 76-83).

On the first day of the ceremony, the workers chosen by the *tomyaars* to prepare the *kotuumot* pole assembled at the *maniishar*'s home. They were provided with food and were sent to the mountains to cut a tall, straight pine 40 to 50 feet in height. When such a tree was located it was felled, trimmed, and transported back to the festival grounds. The bark was peeled and the trunk polished with pumice and painted in four colors: white, red, black, and gray. Paint was applied in six-inch wide bands, each of which may have represented a part of the human body (Merriam 1955:78-79, n.d.b).

Before the *kotuumot* pole was erected, "choke-mouth" and "funerary urn" baskets were attached; the bottoms of the baskets were removed so that they could be fitted over the pole. The last basket was always turned upside down and placed on top of the pole. A small vertical stick rose from the center of this basket; attached to the end of the stick were three white quills cut from eagle plumes. Two smaller sticks extended outward from the base of the first stick at oblique angles; both of these sticks were painted red and tipped with a small shell. The bases of the three sticks were bound together with an eagle feather dyed with red earth (Merriam 1955:79, n.d.b; see also DuBois 1908:103-104 for a similar description of the Luiseño pole).

The Mourning Ceremony performers were elaborately costumed. Reid reported that they were "adorned with eagle and hawk's feathers, and a plentiful supply of paint laid on the face, neck, arms, and upper part of the body" (Reid 1852:41). Merriam provided a more detailed description of the performers. The women wore ceremonial skirts that extended halfway from their knees to their ankles, and their necklaces and belts were richly decorated with beadwork. Their faces were painted with designs in red, and on their heads they wore a broad band of eagle down or rabbit fur dyed pink. More eagle down

was worn on their breasts, and they carried rattles of bear teeth and claws. The men painted their arms and bodies and placed a special mark on their breasts, while shamans wore knee length skirts, high caps decorated with eagle plumes, collars decorated with beads, stones, and bear claws, and anklets that jingled (Merriam 1955:80, n.d.b; see also Hudson and Blackburn 1985).

As the Mourning Ceremony opened, the female mourners seated themselves in a circle around the *yovaar*, leaving only the doorway open (Reid 1852:41). As the *kotuumot* pole was being decorated with baskets, the mourners tossed offerings of food, clothing, beads, and baskets against it while singing mournful chants to the dead. José de los Santos Juncos reported that *toveemor*, the rock located on the Palos Verdes coast near the community of *Toveemonga*, "was mentioned in mourning songs at San Gabriel. When the dolientes [mourners] from a certain place heard that place mentioned in the mourning song they rose and paid the singer" (Harrington 1986:R102 F826). As the workers raised the pole, the mourners shook shallow baskets filled with seeds and pine nuts and showered the contents against the pole while singing (Merriam 1955:80-81, n.d.b).

When the *kotuumot* pole was in place the workers gave three whoops by vibrating their fingers against their mouths. The singers then formed a circle around the pole and sang to it while moving forwards and backwards, all the while keeping in step. This dance, with the accompanying song, was repeated during the morning, afternoon, and night each day of the festival (Merriam 1955:81, n.d.b). Reid observed that one Mourning Ceremony dance was directed "by numerous gestures, both of hands and feet, made by the seers. Each dancer represented some animal in his movements; but the growl given simultaneously at the end of each verse, was for the Bear" (Reid 1852:41).

The last day of the celebration was reserved for the burning of offerings to the dead. Reid reported that "the old women were employed to make more food than usual, and when the sun was in its zenith it was distributed, not only among the actors, but to the spectators likewise" (Reid 1852:42). At Tejón, the *kotuumot* pole was moved to the burial ground and re-erected, and for the last time the performers gathered around the pole and sang.

Everyone then returned to the festival grounds while the *tomyaars* entered the house where the offerings were kept and withdrew enough money to pay the workers (originally this was probably shell bead money, although during historic times silver money was used; see Merriam 1955:82). The rest of the valuables were stuffed into a large sealskin bag sewn in the shape of a huge animal. This effigy, called "Chi'-e-vōr," was decorated with beads, shells, and feathers. The *Chi'-e-vōr* was carried to the center of the festival grounds by several shamans, led by one of their number who walked backwards while uttering "Huh, huh, huh." Following him was another shaman who also walked backwards, chanting and waving his hands with his palms extended downward. Next in the procession came the relatives (Merriam 1955:82-83, n.d.b).

At the festival grounds, the effigy was burned along with a portion of the deceased's hair that had been saved for the occasion (Merriam 1955:83, n.d.b). Reid reported that

> after eating, a deep hole was dug, and a fire kindled in it, when the articles reserved at the death of relatives were committed to the flames; at the same time, baskets, money, and seeds were thrown to the spectators. . . . During the burning process, one of the seers, reciting mystical words, kept stirring up the fire to ensure the total destruction of the things.—The hole was then filled up with earth and well trodden down (Reid 1852:42).

Harrington's consultants offered other significant pieces of information about this important ritual. According to José de los Santos Juncos,

> the clothes and also monitos [funeral effigies], made of rags or anything like that, with eyes, etc., represented on them, were burnt. There were old men who sang. . . . At the close the old man who was the leader (tòvit) hit his two sticks which he held in his hands together again. The tòvit was painted & with feathers on him. . . . The monito was merely the image of the dead person, and had no special name (Harrington 1986:R104 F010).

Juan Meléndrez reported that in assembling the funeral effigy

> there was no attempt made to make a face or mask. They first put 2 sticks in [the] form of a cross, then built the mono on this by hanging difunto's [deceased's] clothes on it. The head was made simply by draping a cloth over the headpiece

of the cross. . . . They kept the mono a week, then burnt it. You did not go near where it was—muy respetos (Harrington 1986:R106 F240-241).

Juana Meléndrez, the wife of Juan, offered that

> when the dolientes [mourners] decided to have a burning fiesta they sent word to all the people to ask if they had ropa [clothing] of their difuntos to burn & all would send something. If the particular dolientes who were giving the fiesta were mourning for a woman, the mono was a woman, made to look like the difunta, & the clothes of the dead men, if there were any, were put inside. They made a mask . . . for the face, & put earrings, cuentitas [beads] & everything. If the ones who were giving the fiesta were mourning a man the mono was a man & the women's clothes went inside. There was never but one mono (Harrington 1986:R106 F219-220).

Harrington noted that there was some confusion regarding the sex of the mono, or funeral effigy, and that he had previously understood that "if all the dead people were women, the mono was a woman, if all were men or if there was even one man among several women the mono was a man" (Harrington 1986:R106 F220; see also Hudson and Blackburn 1986:265-268).

The offering of gifts was a demonstration of the mourners' devotion to the memory of the dead. According to Merriam's calculations, hundreds of dollars in food, shell bead money, and gifts were consigned to the flames, many of the offerings having been made by very poor individuals (Merriam 1955:82-83, n.d.b). Archaeological excavations conducted in 1945 at Big Tujunga Wash revealed the site of a Mourning Ceremony complete with offerings. Included among the wealth of objects recovered were burnt whale bones, probably from grave markers, ceremonial stone knives, soapstone tobacco pipes, awls and gaming pieces of deer bone, arrowpoints, large projectile points, shell and soapstone beads, abalone shell, samples of red, white, and yellow paint, stone gorgets, hammerstones, stone harpoon barbs, stone bowls, mortars, pestles, and manos (handstones). Similar sites have been discovered at other locations, including San Clemente Island and Malaga Cove on the Palos Verdes Peninsula (Walker 1952:102-116; Meighan 1983; Eisentraut 1990).

Following the burning of the offerings a young, unmarried man was carried by the workers to the festival grounds. He was called *toovet*, meaning "son of a chief," (Merriam 1955:83), and may have represented *Chengiichngech* himself. Father Boscana wrote that "Chinigchinich was known under three distinct names: Saor, Quaguar, and Tobet. . . . Tobet, when he danced enrobed in a dress composed of feathers with a crown of the same upon his head and his face painted black and red" (Boscana 1933:30).

Like *Chengiichngech*, the *toovet* wore an elaborate ritual costume. A large, richly decorated headdress of eagle plumes and shell beads reached to his shoulders, while his skirt consisted of white and black feathers, the former decorating the upper half of the garment and the latter the lower half. His body was painted red, white, blue, and gray, and he wore a sacred funeral rope wound around him in a spiral fashion. On each shoulder the *toovet* wore a rattle decorated with feathers, and he carried two sticks which he struck together to keep time (Merriam 1955:83, n.d.b; see also Hudson and Blackburn 1985).

It was the duty of the *toovet* dancer to undertake a magical flight and lead the souls of the dead into the afterworld. His whirling dance was a symbolic representation of the arduous journey made by his soul as it conducted the souls of the deceased to the land of the dead; the wooden sticks he rapped together while dancing were believed to assist him magically in traveling great distances quickly (Bean 1972a:139; Hudson and Underhay 1978:90; see also Eliade 1951:477-482 for a general discussion regarding the role of magical flight in shamanistic societies). The *toovet* performed while the men surrounding him sang; the pace of his dance gradually increased until he was rapidly whirling on the spot where the fire had recently burned. When his performance ended, the Mourning Ceremony was closed (Merriam 1955:84, n.d.b).

Subsequent rituals may have included a reburial of the offerings that survived the fire, sometimes with the bones or ashes of the deceased. Among the Chumash, on the morning following the celebration the mourners were ritually bathed by an older man and woman in a specially built tule house (Hudson and Underhay 1978:47). According to Merriam, following the Mourning Ceremony the mourners washed their faces to remove the tar that they had worn as a sign of their bereavement during the previous year. The men then painted their faces and bodies down to their hips and were carried around the house three times in a big, deep bowl basket. Women painted their foreheads,

cheeks, and chins with brilliant red paint and danced. When the ceremony ended, both sexes were free to eat meat again and remarry (Merriam n.d.b).

THE EAGLE RITE

Another ritual held in conjunction with the Harvest Celebration and the Mourning Ceremony was known as the Eagle Rite. According to Father Boscana, among the Indians at Mission San Juan Capistrano "the most celebrated of all their feasts, which was observed yearly, was the one they called *panes*, signifying a bird feast" (Boscana 1933:58). The Eagle Rite was practiced by both Uto-Aztecan and non-Uto-Aztecan groups. During this elaborate and extended sequence of rituals, a bird, usually a White-headed or Golden Eagle or a California Condor, was ritually slain and its feathers used to manufacture the ceremonial skirt worn by the *tomyaar* or shamans (Harrington 1933:176, note 164). Due to an absence of eagle and condor species on the Channel Islands, the Gabrielino of Santa Catalina, San Clemente, and San Nicolas may have substituted ravens in their stead (see Geiger and Meighan 1976:160-161; and Hudson and Underhay 1978:85-88 for a more complete discussion of this topic).

As was noted earlier in this chapter, the Gabrielino and other Uto-Aztecan Indians recognized a close ritual association between the sacred figure of the eagle and the office of the *tomyaar*. Among these groups the eagle was "owned" by the lineage chief. The Cahuilla and Luiseño conducted the Eagle Rite one year after the death of a *tomyaar* or one of his close relatives (Kroeber 1925:642; Strong 1929:307; Harrington 1942:33, items 1289-1290). The eagle symbolized the continued life of the lineage; the eagle "allowed" himself to be killed so that the lineage would be preserved (Bean 1972a:138-139). Father Boscana alluded to this belief, noting that "as often as the bird was killed it multiplied, because every year all the different *capitanes* celebrated the same feast . . . and were firm in the opinion that the birds sacrificed were but one and the same" (Boscana 1933:58-59). The death of the eagle also symbolized the magical flight undertaken by the shaman to lead souls to the afterworld or make contact with the supernatural world; the eagle's feathers were used in the ritual clothing worn by the shaman or *tomyaar* as he performed the dances that represented this flight (Bean 1972a:139).

Broad similarities existed between the Eagle Rite as performed by the Gabrielino and the rituals conducted by the Cahuilla and Luiseño, and taken together these sources offer a rather complete picture of the celebration. Preparations for the Eagle Rite began with the discovery of an eagle's nest. A special individual was assigned by the chief to monitor the chick's progress, and each stage in the bird's development was celebrated with a special ritual (Bean 1972a:139-140). When the parent was observed bringing large game to the nest, a specially chosen handler captured the young eagle and cared for it. The eaglet might be raised in captivity for as little as a week or perhaps as long as a year. While the bird was in captivity the people brought it food and left it messages to carry back to the spirit world (Strong 1929:308; Geiger and Meighan 1976:160).

The culmination of the Eagle Rite, which occurred when the bird reached maturity, was a ceremony that lasted from three days to a week. Different lineages were invited to participate in each day's ceremonies—the fiesta was an important reaffirmation of the economic ties uniting lineages and communities (Boscana 1933:58; Bean 1972a:140). On the eve of the main celebration, a formal announcement was made of the upcoming ritual and a temporary *yovaar* was prepared. The next day, the celebration opened with a procession in which the eagle was carried into the temporary *yovaar* and placed on a special altar. The shamans performed a ceremonial dance while young girls ran races "to and fro with great rapidity, some in one direction, and some in another" (Boscana 1933:58).

The eagle was then carried to the main *yovaar* in a second procession led by the shamans. "Arriving at the temple, they killed the bird without losing a particle of its blood. The skin was removed entire . . . for the purpose of making their festival garment. . . . The carcass they interred within the temple in a hole previously prepared" (Boscana 1933:58). Juan Meléndrez offered a somewhat different description of the ceremony, reporting that

> it was anciently the custom in the fiesta when they caught an eagle to spread out a skin on the ground and tie the eagle sentado [sitting] on it, then all threw chía, corn, bellota [acorns], everything, till the eagle was buried up to its neck and thus paid it . . . then a good shot shot an arrow at its head and killed it (Harrington 1986:R106 F194).

Felicitas Serrano Montaño reported that "the eagle (the kind called in Spanish aguila real, she thinks) was the God and captain of the Indians. They used to catch it and bring it up and then at a big festival they would kill it, using a blanket in connection with killing it" (Harrington 1986:R102 F607). The remains of red-tailed hawks have been recovered from a number of archaeological sites within the Gabrielino territory, including the Newland House site in Huntington Beach (Ora-183), the Encino site in the San Fernando Valley (LAn-43), and Lemon Tank on San Clemente Island (SCII-1524) (Cottrel et al. 1985; Langenwalter 1986; Eisentraut 1990).

After the eagle was slain, several older women gathered about the bird's grave and mourned its death while bestowing gifts of seeds and food in thanksgiving. The fiesta continued for three days and nights after the eagle's death (Boscana 1933:58).

WINTER SOLSTICE CEREMONY

During the month of the Harvest Celebration preparations were begun for the Winter Solstice Ceremony. Among the Chumash, the *'antap* officials gathered for a brief ritual that anticipated the upcoming ceremony. Their meeting was held in the home of one of the officials and members of the community were invited as well. The meeting opened around mid-morning with a ritual display of ceremonial objects, including a large whale vertebra decorated with a painting of a solar disc done in purple with 12 rose-colored rays emanating from it.

Following this, offerings of seeds were deposited in baskets lining one side of the room. The participants performed songs thanking Sun for the gifts he had bestowed on his people, and the ceremonial objects were displayed a second time. The ceremony closed with an elaborate speech by one of the *'antap* officials warning the people of the approaching solstice and the need to make preparations for the winter, and instructing them in the proper upbringing of their children (Librado and Harrington 1977:50-53).

As winter approached, the pace of ritual activity accelerated. There is little ethnographic information presently available on the Gabrielino celebrations during the winter solstice; however, a rather complete reconstruction of the Chumash ceremony is possible, and the Gabrielino rituals may have been similar. Preparations for the Winter Solstice Fiesta probably began as early as November, when the Chumash *slo'w*, or fiesta "manager," who had been previously chosen by the *'antap* hierarchy, assembled in secret with 13 "captains" to discuss the upcoming ceremony and collect the offerings used to defray the expenses of the celebration.

At a later meeting in November or early December, workers were assigned to inspect the feather poles erected at the solar shrines during the previous year's ceremony and determine how many needed replacing. These workers would also manufacture any new poles that were needed. Each pole represented a community (Librado and Harrington 1977:55-56). Juana Meléndrez may have been referring to Gabrielino or Chumash shrines when she recalled that

> each ra. [ranchería, village] had its Dios (evidently referring to shrines). This "Dios" was buried en las lomitas [in the hills] & the people went there & threw abalorios, cuentitas [shell-beads, little beads], chia, [and] seeds. Inf. [informant] once asked her suegra [mother-in-law] what was buried there & she said she did not know—only the capts. knew—they went with it wrapped in a bundle & buried it there (Harrington 1986:R106 F219).

Sometime between December 20 and 23 the Winter Solstice Fiesta opened with a conference of the community chiefs. The *'antap* then presided over a special meeting in which each individual was required to settle any debts he had accumulated during the year. The *paxaa'*, who acted as the announcer during this meeting, was paid a percentage of each settlement (Librado and Harrington 1977:56).

The main ceremony of the fiesta took place on the afternoon of December 24. On this day the *paxaa'* erected the sunstick to ritually "pull" the sun back from its declining winter course and thereby return the earth to fruitfulness (Librado and Harrington 1977:57-58; Hudson and Underhay 1978:66). In the afternoon the *paxaa'* removed the sunstick from its wooden storage box and set it in the ground, placing it upright in a hole prepared previously. The *paxaa'* carried the ritual title of "shadow, image of *Kakunupmawa* [the sun]." Surrounded by his 12 assistants, the *paxaa'* tapped the stone disc twice. As he tapped the disc the others tossed feathers down into the air and cried "It is raining! You must go in the house!" This was done in imitation of the rainfall which, it was hoped, would water the wild crops during the upcoming spring. The *paxaa'* then addressed the spectators, exhorting them

to heed the wonder of the sun's power and making predictions regarding crops and weather for the upcoming year. The daytime ceremonies concluded with a dance performed by the assistants (Librado and Harrington 1977:57-58; Hudson and Underhay 1978:66).

Around 8:00 p.m. the people gathered outside a special ceremonial brush enclosure. Inside the enclosure the *slo'w* sat before a large fire, resting on a stool made from a whale vertebra and surrounded by his 12 assistants. One by one, members of the congregation came forward to present offerings of seeds, wheat, islay, or shell-bead money, each participant following a ritually-prescribed sequence of steps when approaching and leaving the enclosure. The completed feather poles were then brought out and carried in a solemn dance that lasted until dawn. Other dances were performed during the night while the participants feasted and tossed offerings into the flames.

On this night the sun was born anew, and in the remaining hours of darkness moral conventions were set aside and men and women were free to engage in sexual liaisons. Such ritually sanctioned promiscuity was practiced by many peoples in ancient Europe, Central America, Australia, and Africa, and was generally associated with ceremonies to promote fertility in nature (Frazer 1922:156-161; Librado and Harrington 1977:58-60).

There was little activity the following day, although some dances were performed. In one such performance three men sang "Come out, Sun! Come out so that you may see your grandfather." Six women then took up the song while motioning toward the sun with extended arms. That evening the "Dance-of-the-Widows" was performed. Recently-widowed women or orphaned girls formed a ring around the fire, surrounded by a second ring of men; the dance consisted of hand movements made to the accompaniment of singing and the music of deer hoof rattles. Gabrielino participants from San Fernando are reported to have sung *papu marata* songs which honored the swordfish at this ceremony. Other songs and dances were held that night as well (Librado and Harrington 1977:60-61).

On the morning of December 26, the newly manufactured feather poles were carried in procession to the hilltop shrines. The completed poles were made of toyon or willow, three to five feet in length, and painted red or black. The top of each pole was decorated with the wing feathers of vultures or condors, while the shafts were wrapped with strings of beads and the feathers of crows and sea gulls (Librado and Harrington 1977:61-63, 106, note 70; Hudson and Underhay 1978:67; Hudson and Blackburn 1986:93-98).

Archaeological evidence for the Gabrielino Winter Solstice Ceremony exists in the form of a solstice observatory at Burro Flats located at the western end of the San Fernando Valley (Burro Flats was mentioned earlier in this chapter in the section describing summer solstice rituals). A number of Indian solstice observatories have been identified in California; however, the Burro Flats sites are the only documented solstice sites within the Gabrielino territory.

At the heart of the Burro Flats complex is a small, shallow rock shelter decorated with pictographs painted in red and white on a black background. These pictographs include elements of ritual significance including concentric circles, bird-like creatures wearing tall headdresses, long ladder-like poles rising into the sky, and star-like objects with tails that may be comets. According to one line of interpretation, these paintings may represent characters and themes from Gabrielino-Chumash mythology; the concentric circles represent Sun and the birds symbolize Eagle. The tall ladder-like objects portray the poles erected over chiefs' graves, and comets are omens of future events. The bird-like creatures may also represent shamans dressed in ritual garb (Romani et al. 1985, 1988; Edberg 1985).

The paintings are clear and vibrant—a generous rock overhang protects the pictograph panel from sun and rain. Only once a year, for a few days around the winter solstice, does sunlight penetrate the shelter. At that time a triangle of sunlight formed by a notch in the upper rim of the overhang shines into the shelter, falling upon a series of white concentric circles located at the west end of the panel. This phenomenon was most certainly a central feature of the Winter Solstice rituals held at the site.

SUMMARY

Virtually every aspect of Gabrielino life was touched by religious beliefs and practices. The political leadership of the community comprised an elite group of religious officials who sought divine sanction for political and legal decisions through ritual performances. Important personal events were marked by rite of passage ceremonies. Large public ceremonies strengthened the community's relationship with the supernatural world. These public ceremonies were held on a seasonal basis, and the redistribution of food and luxury goods that accompanied these fiestas was a crucial feature of the Gabrielino economy.

The Gabrielino religion evolved over many generations through the fusion of several different currents of religious thought. In its most highly developed form this system of beliefs and practices is known as the *Chengiichngech* religion. Important features of the *Chengiichngech* religion included: a pantheon of deities arranged beneath a supreme creator-god; an elaborate cosmology; a religious elite; the maintenance of the sacred enclosure within the community; a strict code of morality; a sacred oral literature; and an extensive array of rituals and ceremonies.

A number of theories have suggested that the *Chengiichngech* religion developed under the influence of Christianity or one of the world's other major religions. However, historical accounts indicate that many important features of the *Chengiichngech* religion had already developed by 1602, more than 150 years before the establishment of the California missions. When the members of the Vizcaíno Expedition visited Santa Catalina Island in 1602, they observed important evidence of the *Chengiichngech* religion including the *yovaar*, or sacred enclosure, and the *Chengiichngech* figure. The descriptions of these features written by Father Antonio de la Ascension in 1602 match closely those penned by Father Gerónimo Boscana in the early 1800s and those recorded by Harrington in the early 1900s.

The Gabrielino recognized a diverse pantheon of gods arranged in a hierarchy of importance and function beneath the supreme creator-god *Chengiichngech*. Among the more important of these deities were six gods that together make up a grouping known as the northern complex. The six deities included in the northern complex were: *Wewyoot*, *Taamet*, *Chuuxoyt*, *Piichorot*, *Kwiichepet*, and *Maniishar*. Lesser deities recognized by the Gabrielino were the *Chengiichngech* avengers. *Chengiichngech* avengers were creatures sent by *Chengiichngech* to punish those guilty of breaking his commandments;

they included ravens, bears, snakes, mountain lions, spiders, centipedes, and stingrays. Other spiritual beings were regarded as helpers of mankind; for example, porpoises were believed to guard the world. There were malevolent Gabrielino spirits as well. Among the most notorious of these malevolent spirits was *Taakwesh*, a cannibal spirit believed to dwell at Lily Rock near Idyllwild.

Gabrielino ritual satisfied a wide variety of social, political, and economic needs. Significant personal events such as birth, the onset of puberty, marriage, and death were important occasions for rite of passage ceremonies. The elevation of a new *tomyaar* or the first appearance of a new shaman were also important occasions for religious rituals. Seasonal ceremonies promoted the general welfare of the community and strengthened its relationship with the supernatural world. Some of the most significant seasonal rituals

were the Summer Solstice Ritual, the Harvest Celebration, the annual Mourning Ceremony, the Eagle Rite, and the Winter Solstice Ceremony.

The Winter Solstice Ceremony concluded the year's ritual cycle; it was the culmination of an annual sequence of events designed to preserve and protect the community. Yet even as the old ritual cycle ended a new one began. In addition to the ritual elements described in this chapter these celebrations included many activities that were largely recreational. Music, singing, storytelling, and gaming were prominent activities at any Gabrielino gathering; these activities also represented important aesthetic elements of Gabrielino culture. A more complete discussion of these artistic and recreation activities is presented in Chapter 9.

STORIES, SONGS, DANCE, AND GAMES

The Gabrielino expressed their artistic and creative energy in many ways. The vivid, colorful pictographs at Burro Flats at the west end of the San Fernando Valley and the naturalistic pictographs and petroglyphs in the Cave of the Whales on San Nicolas Island are excellent examples of Gabrielino creativity in the visual arts. The elaborate traditions and rituals of the *Chengiichngech* religion testify to the First Angelinos' expressiveness in spiritual and ceremonial affairs.

The Gabrielino also expressed their creative talents and artistic genius through their stories, songs, and dance. Because the Gabrielino did not possess a written language, their narratives and songs were memorized and passed down by word of mouth from generation to generation. Through this oral literature the Gabrielino preserved important cultural knowledge such as genealogies, lineage histories, religious and medical practices, and laws. Much of this knowledge was lost during the 1800s; however, a sample has survived thanks to the efforts of several Gabrielino consultants and the anthropologists who worked with them.

ORAL LITERATURE

Oral literature served a number of functions for the Gabrielino. Important concepts about the afterlife were conveyed in Gabrielino tales, as were cultural values such as disapproval of greediness and food hoarding (Reid 1852:49-51, 55-59; Harrington 1986:R106 F188-191), the virtues of marital devotion (Reid 1852:49-51), and the dangers of egotistical pride (Reid 1852:54; Harrington 1986:R105 F572-573). The moral teachings of *Chengiichngech* were preserved in the creation stories (Boscana 1933:29-30,

33-34), and Gabrielino literature also wrestled with ethical and philosophical concepts such as the origins of life and death, inequality among men, and the proper use of supernatural or shamanic powers (Boscana 1933:27-34; Harrington 1986:R106 F221). Historical information such as migration accounts were preserved through oral literature (Harrington 1986:R105 F564-565; see also Boscana 1933:83-85 for an excellent example of a Juaneño migration legend).

Gabrielino stories were usually narrated by older individuals, and professional bards were employed as well (Heizer 1968:118-119, note 54; Blackburn 1975:26). A talented storyteller was a great asset to the community during long winter evenings. The subjects of Gabrielino oral narratives were numerous and included star lore, creation stories, Coyote stories, and curious rambling tales that explored a variety of cultural norms held by the Gabrielino. Other stories were clearly allegories of shamanic experiences such as ritual death and rebirth and magical flight to the after-world (Reid 1852:63-68; Kroeber 1925:624-626).

Gabrielino oral literature borrowed elements from the literature of other Indian groups, often blending them to make the tale more interesting. Gabrielino literature especially shares many features in common with the oral literature of the Chumash, and a comparison of the two collections provides valuable insight into the meaning and purpose of Gabrielino stories.

These oral narratives serve as a psychological "window," illuminating many aspects of Indian culture and society. Important insights into Gabrielino concepts of personality and motivation can be gained from a study of this literature. Little time was spent exploring the personalities of the main characters. Rather, as in Chumash literature, an individual's actions were viewed as the inevitable result of his or her basic nature, whatever it might be. Both Gabrielino and Chumash storytelling used the techniques of distortion and "inversion" (the reversal of normal behavior standards) to emphasize sacred or supernatural elements of a story (Blackburn 1975:24, 80-82).

Typically, Gabrielino narratives open with a brief statement of setting or theme, or both. For example, one narrative begins "In the Lodge of *Muhuvit*, which lay behind the hills of San Fernando, once lived a chief . . . who was a great wizard and enchanter" (Reid 1852:55). Another tale opens with the statement "A coyote, which, like all the rest of his kin, considered himself as the most austire [sic] animal on the face of the earth . . . came one day to the margin of a small river" (Reid 1852:54). One version of the creation story commences with the phrase "An invisible and all-powerful being called Nocuma made the world" (Boscana 1933:31).

CREATION STORIES OF THE INTERIOR INDIANS

The creation stories are, in fact, a good place to begin studying the oral literature of the Gabrielino. The most complete accounts of the creation stories were recorded by Father Boscana from the Indians living at Mission San Juan Capistrano. Although the population at this mission included both Gabrielino and Juaneño Indians, it appears likely that much of the information was collected from Gabrielino residents. In discussing this issue Kroeber concluded that "a large part, possibly the bulk, of the information . . . is certainly of Gabrielino origin" (Kroeber 1925:636; for a more complete discussion of this issue, see Chapter 1).

According to Father Boscana, the Indians at San Juan Capistrano reported two versions of the creation myth—one was told by the Indians from the inland areas, the other by those from the coastal regions. The creation story of the interior peoples begins with the sexual union of the celestial brother and sister, representing the sky and earth. This union produced all things, that is, earth, sand, rocks, trees, animals, and finally *Wewyoot*, the "first captain" or *tomyaar*. *Wewyoot* was the father of all the first people, animal beings who could think and speak as humans.

As time went on and *Wewyoot*'s children multiplied, they became disenchanted with his rule and determined to assassinate him, alleging that he had grown too old to govern. Accordingly, they poisoned

him, and although his mother, the Earth, brewed a special medicine to cure him, her efforts failed when Coyote upset the shell containing the medicine. After *Wewyoot* died, his subjects burned his body on a pyre. Before the corpse was consumed by the flames, however, Coyote leapt upon it and tore a large piece of flesh from the stomach and devoured it (Boscana 1933:27-28).

Following *Wewyoot's* death the people held a general council to devise a means of gathering the foods they needed to survive. It was at this time that *Chengiichngech* first appeared, manifesting himself as a spiritual being. *Chengiichngech* conferred shamanic powers upon specially chosen individuals, endowing them "with the power to cause it to rain . . . to influence the dews . . . to produce the acorn" and to create rabbits, ducks, geese, and deer (Boscana 1933:29). *Chengiichngech* then created humans from clay he found on the shore of a lake. He taught his new subjects the rules they were to obey, and he instructed them to build the *yovaar* and to perform the sacred dances while robed in the ritual feather skirt. One day, while dancing in the feather skirt, *Chengiichngech* rose into the heavens, but before he left he transformed the children of *Wewyoot*, the first people, into mortals like those he had created from the clays found on the shore of the lake (Boscana 1933:29-30).

CREATION STORIES OF THE COASTAL INDIANS

In contrast, the creation story of the coastal dwellers opens with a maritime theme. In the beginning an invisible and all-powerful spiritual being named *Nocuma* created the world and all it contains. The world was spherical and rested upon his hands; to secure it he placed *Toshaawt*, a large rock, at its center. A small stream encircled the world, and it was crowded with fish.

One day the fish were discussing ways to create more room for themselves as their number had become so great. Along came a large fish carrying the rock *Toshaawt*, which he broke open. In the center was a ball filled with gall, which emptied into the water. Soon the stream became salty and bitter and it overflowed the earth to become the present oceans. *Nocuma* then created the first man and woman, and from their descendants was born *Wewyoot* (Boscana 1933:31-32).

Wewyoot was an ambitious and ruthless leader who embarked on a campaign of conquest from his home base at the community of *Povuu'nga*. Eventually his followers grew unhappy under his rule and decided to assassinate him, charging that he had abused his power and authority. They poisoned him by pulverizing a small piece of the rock *Toshaawt* and creating a mixture that was applied to his breast. *Wewyoot* died soon after, and his followers assembled at *Povuu'nga* to burn his body on a pyre (Boscana 1933:32-33).

Following *Wewyoot's* funeral, a council was held to decide how the people would feed themselves. During this council there appeared a spiritual being named *Attajen*, meaning "man" or "rational being." *Attajen* granted shamanic powers to those persons charged with the responsibility of controlling the food supply (Boscana 1933:33).

Years later, *Chengiichngech* manifested himself to the Gabrielino and began his teaching at *Povuu'nga*, *Wewyoot's* home community. The true name of *Chengiichngech* was said to be *Ouiamot*, the son of *Tacu* and his wife *Auzar*. *Chengiichngech*, or *Ouiamot*, taught the people the laws, rites, and ceremonies necessary for the preservation of life, and he designated the shamans and taught them how to dance in the sacred feather garments. *Chengiichngech* also taught the people how to build the *yovaar*, and he divided the population into classes according to religious knowledge. Those who were allowed to enter the sacred enclosure were called *Toovet*, which was the name *Chengiichngech* took for himself when he danced in the ritual feather garments. Those who remained outside the walls of the enclosure were called "Saorem," meaning "persons who do not know how to dance." *Chengiichngech* took the name "Quaguar" when he ascended into the heavens, and there he remains to watch over his people (Boscana 1933:33-35).

These creation stories raise a number of interesting questions (see Kroeber 1959). For example, why is *Wewyoot* depicted as a ruthless conqueror, a characterization that contradicts the usual portrayal of this important figure by the Indians of southern California, and is this a Gabrielino innovation? Who is the mysterious *Attajen*, and is he, as Kroeber suggests, one and the same as either *Wewyoot* or *Chengiichngech*? Was *Chengiichngech* a mortal prophet, the son of *Tacu* and *Auzar*, or a god, or both? Perhaps future research will provide some answers to these intriguing questions (Kroeber 1925:638, 1959:291-293; White 1963:96; see DuBois

1908:128-148 for the Luiseño version of *Wewyoot's* death).

ASTRONOMICAL THEMES

Stories with an astronomical theme were quite common in Gabrielino literature. Several surviving stories deal with the Pleiades, an autumn constellation of six stars arranged in the form of a small "dipper" similar in shape to the better known Big Dipper. Typically, these stories center around the affairs of six or seven sisters. Pleiades stories are found in cultures throughout the world; these stories often mention a seventh star, leading some students of folklore to speculate that there was once another star which has since faded from view.

Reid recounted a Pleiades story in which "there were *seven brothers* married to *seven sisters*." Each day the wives set out to gather roots while their husbands departed to hunt rabbits. When the wives returned home they always found their husbands waiting empty-handed, complaining loudly of "bad luck" during the hunt. Only the youngest had anything to show, and each day he presented his wife with a single rabbit.

Eventually the women became suspicious and decided to learn the truth. They devised a plan whereby the youngest sister would remain at home, pretending to have a pain in her jaw. The next day the girl hid herself in the bushes behind her house and waited for the hunters to return. Several hours before sunset the brothers arrived, laden with rabbits! The young woman watched in dismay as the men built a fire and roasted and devoured the rabbits, then hid the bones. Only the youngest brother set aside a rabbit for his wife, for which he was much ridiculed by the others.

When the other wives returned home they crowded around to hear their sister's story. The young girl described how the hunters had come home laden with rabbits, and how they roasted and ate all of their catch. She then led them to the hidden pile of bones. Angered and hurt, the sisters decided to abandon their husbands. After a brief discussion, they proceeded to a nearby lagoon where they built a magical machine of reeds; they used this machine to ascend into the sky and become the stars of the Pleiades.

Although the older brothers were glad to be rid of their spouses, the youngest loved his wife dearly and missed her. One day as he sat by the edge of the lagoon crying from loneliness, the sisters took pity on him. They told him the secret of their magical machine and taught him how to use it. The younger brother then joined them in the heavens, where he became part of the constellation we know as Taurus (Reid 1852:49-51).

Jesús Jauro recounted a tale about the Pleiades and Coyote, which is similar to a Juaneño story recorded by Charles Saunders in his entertaining book *Capistrano Nights* (Saunders and O'Sullivan 1930:123-125). According to Jauro, six sisters were married to Mountain Lion. Lion was a good hunter, but Coyote coveted his wives and wanted to steal them. He decided to kill Lion, and so he told him that there was a deer grazing near the edge of a steep ravine. When Lion went to hunt the deer Coyote followed him and, sneaking up behind him, he pushed Lion to his death.

Coyote then went to visit the six sisters. "Why are you girls sad?" he asked, feigning innocence. The girls explained that they were upset because Lion had not returned from his hunt. Coyote offered to stay with the girls and hunt for them, and so he became their husband.

After Coyote had lived with the girls for a while he became ill. Feeling death approaching, he instructed the girls to burn his body on a pyre after he was gone. The girls obeyed his wishes, but Coyote was a mischievous character, and as soon as his body was placed on the pyre he revived.

The sisters were unhappy living with Coyote, and when he came back to life they tried desperately to escape. "If we turn palo [into a stick] he will be breaking us, water [and he] will be heating us. Better go [in]to [the] sky, one proposed." They agreed that going into the sky was their only chance of getting away, so one day while Coyote was hunting rabbits they made their escape.

Coyote was surprised to discover the girls missing, and he looked everywhere for them with no success. Then one day, thirsty from his long search, Coyote lowered his head to drink from a pool of water. Reflected in the calm waters of the pond were the sister's faces "flanqueando [showing] their teeth as they smiled [down] at him." Coyote tried to catch the girls but he could not. Today "Coy. [Coyote] is a red star [the star Aldebaran] behind the Pleiades. The stones are here where they ascended" (Harrington 1986:R103 F719-720).

Juana Meléndrez recalled another Pleiades legend

that involved three sisters instead of the usual six or seven. "The girls had two lovers, the *cinzonte* [mockingbird] and the *huitacoche* [huitlacoche, variously given as corn smut, a fungus that grows on ears of corn, or black mushroom; the use of this story element suggests that the tale may date to the Mission Period when agriculture was introduced to the Gabrielino]. They took the *cinzonte* because he sang so beautifully." When the *huitacoche* realized that he had been rejected he learned to sing like the *cinzonte*, and in this manner he succeeded in fooling the girls.

But the *huitacoche* was an "exceedingly hideous, repulsive man with sore eyes" and the girls were so disgusted by his appearance that they determined to flee him by going into the sky. In their haste to escape, however, the girls slipped down a high, steep bank. "Three barba de chibo [literally, goat's beard] plants growing down this reliz [slope] are the hair of the three girls." The *cinzonte* looked for the girls but could not find them, until finally he saw their reflections in a pool of water. At first he thought they were in the water, but when he looked up he realized they were in the sky (Harrington 1986:R106 F153).

COYOTE STORIES

Coyote was a favorite character in Gabrielino oral literature. He was often portrayed as a vain, foolish, and gullible fellow. For example, Reid told a Coyote story that resembles Aesop's fable of the race between the tortoise and the hare. According to the story, Coyote once challenged a small stream to a race. Although Coyote was much swifter, he soon grew tired and lost the contest to the steadily flowing river. "He walked off with his tail between his legs and had something to reflect upon for many a day afterwards," moralized Reid (1852:54).

Juana Meléndrez told the following Coyote story. "Once the Coyote came upon a pinacate [a black beetle] in this position [with his head to the ground] & cried 'Ahora te voy comer, amigo pinacate [now I am going to eat you, friend pinacate].'" Thinking quickly, the pinacate replied that he was listening "to what they say in the other world. They are getting ready the bows and arrows to kill the cagones [cowards] who defecate in el camino [the road] & dirty up the road. 'Yo soy [It is I!]' cried Coyote in alarm . . . [and] ran off" (Harrington 1986:R106 F223).

A much longer Meléndrez story concerning Coyote and Rabbit incorporated European elements, which suggests that it was composed during or after the Mission Period. One moonlit night Coyote came upon Rabbit sitting by the shore of a lake. "Aha, amigo conejo [friend rabbit]" said Coyote, "ahora te voy á comer [now I am going to eat you]." But instead of running away Rabbit simply pointed to the reflection of the moon glowing in the still waters of the lake. "Do you see that big piece of cheese" Rabbit asked, "[t]hey sent me to bring it & when I stopped to get a drink it rolled into the lake. How can we get it out?"

Now Coyote liked cheese, and so he momentarily forgot his plan to kill and eat Rabbit. Realizing that he had distracted his enemy, Rabbit suggested that they hold a contest to get the cheese out of the water. They would place stakes along opposite shores of the lake and each of them take a side. Starting at one end of the lake, they would each run along the shore until the first stake was reached, then leap across the water and continue running along the opposite shore to the next stake. In this way they would work their way down the racecourse, jumping across the water each time a stake was reached, until one of them got to the cheese. To make the contest even more difficult, they would drink water from the lake as they ran.

When the race began, Coyote followed Rabbit's rules, drinking from the lake as he ran along the shore and leaping across each time he reached a stake. But Rabbit cheated and did not drink. Eventually, Coyote became so heavy and bloated with water that when he tried to jump across the lake he fell in, and Rabbit ran away laughing.

Later Coyote came upon Rabbit again. Rabbit was crouched under a tremendous boulder, pressing his hands and side against the rock. "Aha, amigo conejo!" cried the angry Coyote. "You thought you played a trick on me . . . didn't you? Now I am going to eat you!" Rabbit remained perfectly still, as if holding the rock in place. He replied that he was holding up the world, but that he had grown very thirsty from his efforts. "Won't you hold it while I go and get a drink?" he pleaded. So Coyote took Rabbit's place under the rock while his prey ran away.

After a long while Coyote grew tired and started to let go of the rock. But he was terrified that the world would fall, and so with all his strength he pressed against the boulder. Eventually he could bear it no longer, however, and fearing that he would be crushed, he jumped far away. When the boulder did not move Coyote knew that he had been tricked again.

The next time Coyote came upon Rabbit his clever quarry was hiding in a patch of reeds. "Aha" cried Coyote, "now at last I have you." But Rabbit hushed Coyote. "There is going to be a fiesta there on the other side of the arroyo" he whispered, "you like fiestas, don't you?" "Sí, sí" exclaimed Coyote. "And they are going to have plenty of chickens for you to eat—you like chickens, don't you?" "Sí, sí!" assented Coyote eagerly. "They want me over with [the] people" Rabbit continued. "You stay here & wait till I see if it will be all right for you to come—then I will come back & tell you & when you hear the sound of something popping, that will be the fireworks . . . of the fiesta & you must begin to come." "All right" said Coyote.

Coyote waited while Rabbit ran off. But before he departed, the crafty Rabbit set fire to the reed patch. Coyote heard the reeds popping as they burned, but he thought it was the fireworks and so he began to dance for joy. He danced until the fire came so close that he was forced to jump through the flames to make his escape.

When Coyote again found Rabbit he was very angry. "Don't think you are going to escape again" he warned, "Now I have you & I am going to eat you!" "Coyote" said Rabbit, "You like chickens, don't you?" "Sí, sí, of course I do" answered Coyote, annoyed. "Well" said Rabbit, "there is a man right over there who has fine chickens & no dogs. He told me to look & see if anyone was coming to get them but I will let you eat them all if you want to." "Is that so?" asked Coyote suspiciously, "is it really true that there are no dogs?" "Yes, it is true, go on & help yourself, right over there" said Rabbit, pointing.

Of course, once again Rabbit made a fool of Coyote. When his enemy departed, Rabbit took a short cut and warned the man who owned the chickens. The man turned his greyhounds loose and they ran Coyote off (Harrington 1986:R106 F242-245).

TALES OF THE SUPERNATURAL

The Gabrielino often told stories about the supernatural world. Malevolent characters similar to the *nunašɨš* of Chumash oral literature appear in some of these stories. The *nunašɨš* were dangerous animals or demons who lived during the time of the First People. Many of the *nunašɨš* were believed to live in the world below, coming out after dark to travel in this world (Blackburn 1975:38).

Some Gabrielino *nunaš+š* lived in caves, such as the giant scorpion-like animal at Rancho El Escorpión, while others dwelled in streams, lakes, or ponds, like the "perritos del agua [literally little water dogs]" or the "madre del agua [mother of the water]" at La Presa, the artificial reservoir built during the Mission Period at San Gabriel (Harrington 1986:R106 F53, R104 F38, 42). Other supernatural creatures included Devil Women living at various places such as Rancho San José, Rancho San Antonio, and Corona, and the white bear living in the ciénega at *'AXaarvonga* near *'Ahwiinga* (Harrington 1986:R102 F265, 294, 328-329, 829-830, R104 F38, R105 F296).

Perhaps the most terrifying of all the Gabrielino *nunaš+š* was the cannibal spirit *Taakwesh*, who dwelled in his lair at Lily Rock near Mount San Jacinto. *Taakwesh* was described as "a low-flying meteor or ball of lightning, but also in bird-like form or as a man in feathers" (Kroeber 1925:680; Harrington 1933:180-185, note 181).

Jesús Jauro reported that once "when coming back from a dance, taakwic passed above them in the buggy, echando chispas [throwing sparks] & making a noise. He was heading from S. Jacinto mt. toward the mt. near Bernasconi." He went on to say that the "taakwic hill near Bernasconi spg. [spring] . . . is where taakwic se asienta [sits down] and there is green toluache [*Datura*] growing there the year around" (Harrington 1986:R103 F299-301). Jauro also recalled that he once

> saw taakwic in Lake View. He se [a]sienta a la pura cumbre de la loma [seats himself at the very summit of the hill] (the hill near Bernasconi Spgs). . . . Cuando sale el sol en la mañana se mira como una ventana de vidrio, y dicen que ese es el mi[r]ado de taakwic [when the sun rises in the morning, it shines like a window of glass, and they say this is how taakwic appears] (Harrington 1986:R105 F299).

One of Harrington's non-Indian consultants reported that "taakwic used to be frequently seen. . . . The light used to be seen at taakwic peak & <u>at the same time</u> it reached over to Bernasconi Peak and simultaneous rumbling was heard there" (Harrington 1986:R105 F376; underlining in original).

SHAMAN TALES

Perhaps the most elaborate Gabrielino stories are those describing various shamanic experiences. Some of these stories tell of the supernatural exploits of Gabrielino shamans, such as the story of the shamans' war on Santa Catalina recounted in Chapter 6. José de los Santos Juncos told a similar story in which

> the Indians originally all lived together, but strife arose between them and those of S. G. [San Gabriel] drove the other faction down to the orilla del mar [sea shore], by Los Cerritos, Los Alamitos, etc. Then began the witchery contest.
>
> There was a sort of war between the Inds [Indians] at Xārvut and those at Los Cerritos, etc., and the latter made it rain by their wishing. The Indians were starving—[they] could not hunt rabbits or anything—[there were] great aguaceros [downpours]. . . . So the magicians of Xārvut made wind (viento) and turned it and at [the] very first even it was so strong that it rose up & opened the sky and blew the rain clouds asunder. It blew the jacales [brush houses] of the Indios there of the orilla del mar into the sea. And then it blew a lot of the Indians themselves into the sea. . . . When the two groups of Indians made peace, many of both parties had been killed.
>
> The place where the wind was made is near Punta de la Loma [Point of the Hill] by old S. G. [San Gabriel] Mission [the first mission site near Whittier Narrows] and Xārvut. The top of the hill there is still bare to this day (Harrington 1986: R105 F564-565).

There are data to suggest that the events that inspired the above story took place during the Mission Period. In discussing this story, José de los Santos Juncos added the comment that "one time the Island Indians by their witcheries down by the coast made it rain up here [at *Xārvut*]" (Harrington 1986:R104 F40). Two of the southern Channel Islands, Santa Catalina and San Clemente, were largely depopulated by 1820; San Nicolas was depopulated much later, around 1835 (see the discussion of this topic in Chapter 10). Therefore, the participation of the island shamans makes it likely that this event occurred sometime prior to 1820. Santos Juncos also reported that "Ramon Valencia was one of brujos [shamans] who was present at the wind-making ceremony" (Harrington 1986:R104 F40). According to Santos Juncos, when Ramon Valencia (also spelled Valencio in the Harrington notes) was near the end of his life he hosted a fiesta that was attended by the Cahuilla leader Juan Antonio; this fiesta probably took place sometime after 1840 (see Chapter 6 for a more complete discussion of the bear-shaman Ramon Valencia and the date of this fiesta; it should be noted that although this shaman's name is variously spelled Valencio or Valencia, the context of the stories indicates that it is the same individual). On the basis of these data it appears likely that the events which inspired the story of the shamans' war occurred during Ramon Valencia's lifetime and prior to the year 1820. This would place these events during the Mission Period.

A number of long, rambling Gabrielino tales incorporate elements that may be allegories of shamanic experiences such as ritual death and rebirth, and magical flight. One such tale told by Juan Meléndrez begins with a Coyote story. Sparrow Hawk, who was an important *tomyaar*, wanted to marry but could not find a girl that pleased him. Coyote offered to find Sparrow Hawk a wife, and in return Sparrow Hawk provided him with beads and other gifts to take along as a dowry. Coyote then set out across the sea to a land where an old woman lived with her young and beautiful daughter.

When Coyote arrived at his destination, he convinced the two women to return with him so that Sparrow Hawk could marry the girl. Although he had vowed to bring Sparrow Hawk a wife, Coyote was attracted to the young girl and desired her for himself. Instead of returning to Sparrow Hawk's community he brought the women to his own home. When Sparrow Hawk saw Coyote's treachery he ordered his people to gather all the food from the countryside. Later, when Coyote went to hunt food for dinner he could find nothing. In desperation he tried to fool the women by disguising his excrement as raw meat, but the mother saw through the ruse and the two fled in disgust.

Sparrow Hawk, having outwitted Coyote, had the two women brought to his home. He married the girl and they lived together happily as husband and wife; before long the girl was with child. Little did poor Sparrow Hawk know that the deceitful Coyote had impregnated the girl on their return trip from the land across the sea!

Now at this time Sparrow Hawk's community was at war and one day he left for battle, entrusting his young wife to the care of several midwives. Before Sparrow Hawk could return home the girl gave birth. The midwives were shocked to find that the newborns were baby coyotes! They immediately destroyed the babies and the young mother died of grief shortly thereafter.

They burned the girl's body on a pyre, and as the corpse was consumed by the flames Sparrow Hawk noticed a small whirlwind of ashes swirl and move away. Sparrow Hawk knew that this was the spirit of his departed wife, and so he followed it to the edge of the sea. As the whirlwind floated across the water Sparrow Hawk cried out in sorrow. The girl took pity on her grieving husband and, pulling a hair from her head, she stretched it across the water so that he could cross it as if walking on a bridge. In this manner they traveled across the sea together.

Eventually, Sparrow Hawk and his wife reached a distant land and came to a place where two huge boulders opened and closed with a tremendous crash. Although his wife passed through safely, Sparrow Hawk was fearful and hesitated. Finally, urged on by his wife, he passed between the stones. Further on they saw two enormous ravens standing like black sentinels, one on each side of the road. As the woman walked between them the birds pecked her eyes out. Sparrow Hawk was terrified and refused to go on until his wife called out "Don't be afraid, shut your eyes tight!" Sparrow Hawk trusted his wife, and following her instructions, he passed safely between the fearsome birds.

They continued on their journey until they reached a fork in the trail. "You take the left hand road & I will go to the right" said the woman. "The people over there (to [the] left) eat food & those where I am going do not. Because the ones to the left are those who are not really dead, who have been buried alive & the ones to the right are really dead."

When Sparrow Hawk reached his destination he recognized many of his former acquaintances. They asked why he had come and he explained that he had followed his dead wife. "What do you want with your wife?" asked one of his friends. "I would like to take her away with me" answered Sparrow Hawk. His friends warned that such a thing would be difficult and might only be possible if he had great courage. They explained that "every night they dance over there. Go at night & watch them as they go around—don't take your eyes off her an instant. As she passes you, grab her by the heel, not by any other part, & hold on no matter what happens. She will cry out & it will grow dark & all the others will disappear but hold on till she tells you what you must do to enable you to take her with you."

Following these instructions, Sparrow Hawk watched the spirits dance for three nights, and finally on the next night he grabbed his wife by her heel. "Qué quieres [what do you wish]?" she asked, "let me go!" "I want to take you with me" replied Sparrow Hawk. "I can do nothing" she answered, "I have to get permission from my Dios [God]."

The following night Sparrow Hawk seized her again in the same manner, and this time she agreed to accompany him if he promised to hold a fiesta when they arrived home. She explained that the fiesta must last for nine days, and while it was being celebrated he must not touch her or she would leave him forever. Sparrow Hawk promised to follow her instructions, and the next night they departed for home.

The return trip was uneventful. No boulders blocked their trail; no black ravens loomed by the side of the road. When they reached their home, Sparrow Hawk kept his promise and held a great fiesta. As part of his bargain, Sparrow Hawk had agreed to sleep with his wife for nine consecutive nights without touching her. For eight nights he kept his word, but finally on the last night he could restrain himself no longer. He took hold of her to make love, but his wife rose from their bed and departed without saying a word.

Sparrow Hawk followed his wife, and although she warned him to turn back, he would not listen. At last the woman turned and barked at him in anger. "What do you want with me?" she demanded, "is it this you want?" She then pulled out her vulva and flung it at him. The organ struck a rock and imprinted itself on the stone. The woman then disappeared forever, but her genital remained imprinted in stone in the hills above Chatsworth. Sparrow Hawk was so grieved that he climbed into the mountains, where he sat down and turned to stone (Harrington 1986:R106 F233-240; for a similar tale see Reid 1852:55-67; for a Chumash version see Blackburn 1975:249-251).

STORIES WITH CHRISTIAN ELEMENTS

Following the arrival of the Spanish during the late 1700s, the Gabrielino began to incorporate Christian and other European elements into their oral literature (as noted in some of the stories recounted earlier in this chapter). Some of these later stories reflect a clear identification of the Indian with a wrongfully abused and suffering hero or heroine. For example, Juana Meléndrez told a story of an old man who was returning home late at night. As he passed

some old adobe walls the sky thundered, and looking up he saw a great light descending. Saint Peter came down from the sky dressed in a long, white robe, keys hanging from his waist, accompanied by many boys and girls who were also wearing white robes. After a short time they ascended into the sky once more. Once again there was a peal of thunder and then the light disappeared.

A young Indian girl who had boils and sores all over her body lived nearby. Her masters thought she was infected with venereal disease, although in truth she was a good and innocent girl. They put her out by the old ruined walls and only sent her food or water if they happened to remember. The day after the old man saw the apparitions they went out to the walls and the girl was gone. Saint Peter had carried her to heaven, body and soul (Harrington 1986:R106 F249).

Another Meléndrez story told of an old man who had a little dog that he loved dearly. One night when the man was returning home with his pet he was amazed to see all the dogs of the town sitting in a circle and howling at the moon. The old man hid in some bushes as his little dog ran to join the others. Only Julano, a big dog that belonged to the Corporal, was missing from the group. The Corporal was an evil man who did not feed his dog; the poor animal was forced to steal food, for which he was regularly beaten by his cruel master.

As the old man watched and listened, a bright object descended from the sky and came to rest in the center of the circle of animals. It was Saint Lazarus, the protector of dogs. One by one each of the dogs reported to Saint Lazarus on the treatment he had received from his master. After the saint heard from all of the animals he inquired as to the whereabouts of Julano, but none of the other dogs had seen their companion. Lazarus sent the little dog to find Julano while the others waited.

When they returned everyone noticed that Julano was limping badly. Saint Lazarus asked how he had received his injury, and the big dog replied that his master had beaten him. ". . . what do you ask for your amo [master]?" inquired the saint. "Only this" replied Julano, "I want him to die." "All right," promised Saint Lazarus, "tomorrow morning at 11 o'clock he will die. . . . He will suffer much and then die." Saint Lazarus then rose into the heavens once more, and when he was high in the sky there was a loud clap of thunder and he was gone.

Amazed by what he had seen, the old man went home and shared his experience with his wife. She promised to watch the Corporal closely the next day. The following morning at 11 o'clock, the Corporal came to their home and asked for a drink. "While you get the water I will lie down here" he said to the woman, "I do not feel well." When she returned with the water he was dead, just as Saint Lazarus had promised.

Following his cruel master's death, Julano disappeared and was never seen again. But the Indians know that Saint Lazarus continues to watch over the dogs. Masters who treat their pets well share in the saint's blessings, for all dogs pray to Saint Lazarus (Harrington 1986:R106 F245-247).

SONG

Oral narratives were often recited to the accompaniment of songs to create a more pleasing and emotionally satisfying performance. Song was an integral element of Gabrielino rituals, and although songs could be performed independently of dance or ceremony, the latter activities could not be performed without song. Some songs were associated with specific ceremonies, while others could be adapted to virtually any performance. In addition, songs were commonly linked together to create a "song series" (Kroeber 1925:626; Heidsiek 1966:175-176, 246).

Songs were inherited along family lines and were rarely disclosed to outsiders. Lineages owned songs, as did individuals, and these could not be sung by others without permission. The *tomyaar* was responsible for the songs owned by the lineage, just as the head of each family was responsible for family-owned songs (Heidsiek 1966:151, 153, 246; Bean 1972a:127).

Song was a crucial element in recording and commemorating historical events. Not only was genealogical information preserved in song, but a lineage's claim to possession of its territory was validated through the performance of "songs of travel" that commemorated its arrival at the home site (Roberts 1933:10). One Gabrielino song, commemorating the migration of a lineage from the island of Santa Catalina to the mainland near San Luis Rey, describes the conflicts that arose when the newcomers displaced another lineage already residing at that

location. Another song described how the lineage settled into its new home and began raising crops (Roberts 1933:3-4, 77-94).

Songs were used by the Indians of southern California to define and preserve legal precepts. Song duels were sometimes used to vent hostility against enemy lineages; these duels often continued for days. Singing was also an important part of gaming and was believed to bring good luck. For example, prior to a game of peón the players spent as much as ten days in seclusion learning a song. This song was then taught to a singer hired to perform it during the game (Reid 1852:37-38, 46; Boscana 1933:63; Heidsiek 1966:230-235; Bean 1972a:121).

Some Gabrielino songs were based upon mythology, while others described ceremonial activities. The singing of special, personally-owned power songs formed an important part of the techniques used by Gabrielino shamans. Song was used by shamans to diagnose and treat illness, bewitch and kill enemies, make food plants and animals plentiful, control the weather, and aid in hunting (Heidsiek 1966). Reid told of a shaman's curing song used to treat the urinary affliction known as strangury (see Chapter 6). A Gabrielino magic song from Catalina Island told of a special stick used by shamans in food preparation rituals. The stick normally appeared dead and dry, yet when the shaman blew upon it, it sprouted and grew into anything desired (Reid 1852:34; Roberts 1933:90-94).

According to Father Boscana (1933:29, 63), it was *Chengiichngech* who gave shamans the power to control nature through song. Shamans regularly received songs from their "guardian spirits," or dream-

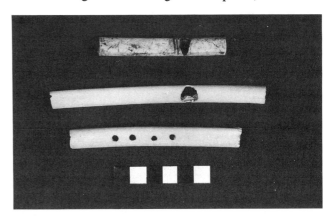

Catalina Island Museum Nos. G-6 (both whistles) and G-7 (flute)

Fig. 68. Two whistles (top and center) and a four-hole flute made from bird bone. Whistles and flutes were also made from deer tibia. Photograph by author.

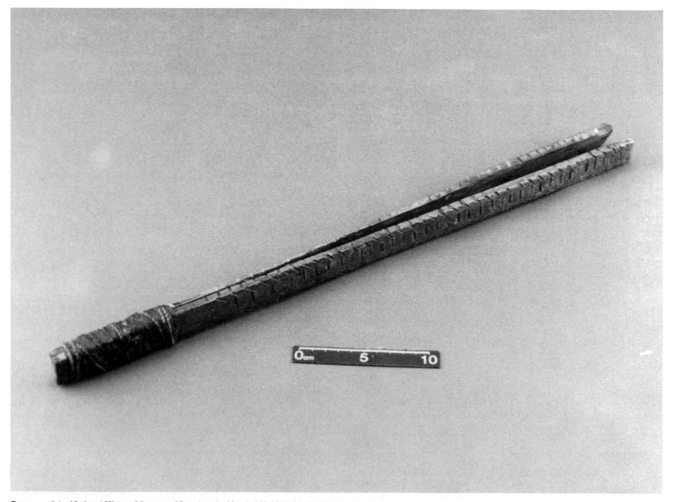

Courtesy of the National History Museum of Los Angeles No. A.110-1087NA-CA-GA
Fig. 69. A split-stick clapper; the handle is wrapped with cordage and glued with asphaltum. This artifact is part of the Coronel Collection.

helpers, as part of the dream experience. These songs were the most powerful of songs and told of the guardian spirit and the vision it provided, as well as of techniques to acquire supernatural power. They tended to be short and simple, and much less formal than ceremonial songs. And because they were performed in public rituals these songs were less secret than the songs owned by others (Applegate 1978:61-66).

MUSICAL INSTRUMENTS

Musically, Gabrielino songs (like those of the Luiseño) were constructed of repeating rhythmic patterns and were often performed to the accompaniment of musical instruments such as whistles, flutes, rattles, and bull-roarers. Whistles were made from bird bone, cane, or elder wood, and consisted of a tube with one end closed with gum or pitch. Four-hole flutes were made from elder wood or the leg bones of deer (Reid 1852:30; Harrington 1942:29, items 1100-1107, 1109). José de los Santos Juncos recalled that "small bone whistles, 4" long or so are the kind they used at S. Gab. [San Gabriel]. One man sang & a lot of women (all the women who wanted to dance) held bone whistles in the mouth and swayed body whistling to [the] song. [They] danced back and forth" (Harrington 1986:R102 F714).

Rattles might consist of a split stick or two sticks bound together with a cord and adhesive. Rattles were also constructed from cocoons attached to stick handles, deer hooves attached to a short, buckskin-covered stick, turtle shells filled with small stones, and the bladders of mountain goats filled with stones. In historic times rattles sometimes consisted of a rawhide casing attached to a wooden handle (Boscana 1933:42; Harrington 1942:28, items 1066-1079; Heizer 1968:104, 117-118, note 47; Hudson and Blackburn 1986:323-336, 339-340; Merriam n.d.c).

Courtesy of the National Museum of the American Indian, Smithsonian Institution No. 7/6779
Fig. 70. The Gabrielino made rattles from the shells of pond turtles; the two halves of the shell were filled with pebbles and cemented together with asphaltum. A bird bone handle was inserted through a hole drilled in the center of the shell. This example, collected from San Clemente Island, still retains some of the shell-inlay decoration. Photograph by David Heald.

The musical bow consisted of a flexible stave of wood with a cord stretched between the two ends; the bow was played by finger. Bull-roarers were used both for amusement and to call an assembly. The bull-roarer, which consisted of a piece of wood attached to a long string, was swung over the head to produce an eerie, fluttering sound (Harrington 1942:28-29, items 1085-1087, 1092-1093; Heidsiek 1966:288; Hudson and Blackburn 1986:317-321, 342-344).

COLLECTIONS

The music and lyrics of a number of Gabrielino ceremonial songs have been recorded, including those performed during mourning rituals (Roberts 1933:59-67, 94-100; Merriam 1955:80-84), cremations (Roberts 1933:67-69), burials (Merriam 1955:85), puberty rituals (Merriam 1955:86), marriages

(Boscana 1933:53; Harrington 1933:169, note 148), the Eagle Dance, and ceremonies involving the sacred bundle of ritual paraphernalia. Other recordings include songs performed during the Savóovet Dance, the Tatahuila Dance, and during games of peón (Harrington 1986:R105 F451-490). Three Nicoleño songs were also recorded by Harrington (Hudson 1981).

Recordings of Gabrielino songs were made at the Pala Indian Reservation in 1926 by Helen Roberts, a pioneer in the field of ethnomusicology. The original phonocylinders of the Roberts Collection are housed in the Archive of Folk Song at the Library of Congress. Additional recordings of Gabrielino songs may be contained in a collection of eight wax cylinder recordings made by Harrington and José de los Santos Juncos. These recordings are housed in the National Anthropological Archives (Heidsiek 1966:13-14, 24-25; Walsh 1976:38-39).

Natural History Museum of Los Angeles County No. A110.14
Fig. 71. An historic period rattle made from cow hide. The rattle
is formed by stretching cow hide over two small boards to create
a hollow chamber; the chamber is filled with pebbles or seeds.
The rattle was originally decorated with feathers, which were
attached at the top of the handle. Photograph by author.

DANCE

Like song and music, dance was an integral part of
most Gabrielino rituals and fiestas. Observing the
Indians residing at Mission San Juan Capistrano in the
early years of the nineteenth century, most of whom
were Gabrielino and Juaneño, Father Gerónimo Boscana wrote that "such was the delight with which they
took part in their festivities, that they often continued
dancing day and night and sometimes entire weeks. .
. . hardly a day passed without some portion of it
being devoted to this . . . ceremony" (Boscana
1933:57).

Father Boscana also noted that for the Indians
dance served much the same purpose as prayer (Boscana 1933:89).   Pablo Tac, a Luiseño Indian,
reported that "the Indians of California dance not only
for a feast, but also before starting a war, for grief,
because they have lost the victory, and in memory of
grandparents, aunts and uncles, parents already dead"
(Tac 1952:15).

Dancing was a standard component of Gabrielino
funeral ceremonies and consisted of a "monotonous
action of the foot on the ground," while war dances
were "grand, solemn and maddening" (Reid 1852:15,
30).   When a *tomyaar* was elevated to office he
danced in the *yovaar* until fatigued, when he was
joined by the visiting *tomyaars* who helped him
continue his performance (Boscana 1933:42).   The
Gabrielino also participated in Chumash dances, many
of which were named after mythical animal characters.

Examples include the Fox Dance, the Swordfish
Dance, the Bear Dance, and the Coyote Dance, as well
as the Seaweed Dance.   Indeed, a number of special
Fernandeño songs about the Swordfish were performed
at these Chumash ceremonies (Librado and Harrington
1977:61, 105, note 65).

CEREMONIAL MOVEMENT AND RITUALISTIC DANCE

On the basis of research into Luiseño dance, the
dances of the Gabrielino can be segregated into two
types; ceremonial movement and ritualistic dance
(Heidsiek 1966:256). Ceremonial movement refers to
a performance in which several members participate,
but in which no set pattern of movement has been
established. Some examples of ceremonial movement
include the boys' procession during the Puberty
Ceremony, in which the initiates imitated the noises
and movements of various animals; the fire-
extinguishing dance that was often held at the
conclusion of fiestas; and certain shamanic dances
(DuBois 1908:79-80; Boscana 1933:59; Heidsiek
1966:257-259).   Other examples of ceremonial
movement are the wedding dances and the foot-
stamping dances performed during song feuds to
ridicule enemies and to "express the pleasure they
would derive from tramping on the grave of their
foes"(Reid 1852:37,38).

Ritualistic dance, on the other hand, comprises
performances in which body movements are organized
and set, and form a part of a tradition developed and
passed down through several generations.   Such
performances sometimes lasted for several days and
required careful rehearsal (Heidsiek 1966:256, 259-
274).   Reid described one dance held during the
mourning festival in which shamans "rehearsed with
the tiros [novices] for eight days previous. . . . The
men and children . . . proceeded to dance, being
governed in the operation by numerous gestures, both
of hands and feet, made by the seers. Each dancer
represented some animal in his movements" (Reid
1852:41).

Another important ritualized dance performed by
the Gabrielino was the Eagle Dance, in which a young
shaman adorned in the eagle feather skirt whirled and
spun in a dance representing his soul's magical flight
to lead the spirits of the deceased to the land of the
dead (Merriam 1955:83-84). A ritualized dance was
held to propitiate *Chengiichngech* when it was feared
that his anger had been aroused. If there was a serious

breach of ceremonial protocol, or a sudden appearance of one of the *Chengiichngech* "avengers" such as the raven, or if a shaman diagnosed an illness as being the result of the god's anger, then such a dance might be held (Heidsiek 1966:269).

Father Boscana described a ritualized procession performed to implore *Chengiichngech's* protection from danger and sickness during a hunt. In this dance the *tomyaar* led a procession past the *yovaar*, followed by the men and women. The men carried their bows and arrows, and as they passed the *yovaar* they leapt into the air, holding their weapons as if prepared to shoot. The women made a more stately procession before the sacred enclosure, inclining their heads and presenting their winnowing trays as they passed (Boscana 1933:38).

CONTESTS AND GAMES

Contests and games of skill or chance were popular activities at most Gabrielino gatherings. The Indians held races in honor of *Wewyoot* at the appearance of the new moon, and archery contests held for distance were a favorite sport. A small bundle of tule tossed into the air was used for a mark. Cat's cradle was a popular game, and during the Mission Period a game of kickball called *gome* was played using a small wooden ball about four inches in diameter (Boscana 1933:62; Harrington 1942:27, items 1013, 1023-1024, 1986:R102 F722; Hudson and Blackburn 1986: 393-396).

RING AND POLE

Haraarekwar, or ring and pole, was played with a small ring four to eight inches in diameter made of tule or of willow wrapped in buckskin. The object of the game was to hurl a reed lance through the ring as it rolled across the ground; however, should the ring fall on one of the lances that, too, counted for a point. Usually two players competed in the sport, and the first to gain three points was the winner (Reid 1852:47; Heizer 1968:127, note 95; Hudson and Blackburn 1986:378-385; J. W. Hudson n.d.).

DICE AND PAINTED REEDS

When they gambled, the Gabrielino used dice made from reeds or walnut shells, or in historic times from the foot bones of calves (Harrington 1942:27,

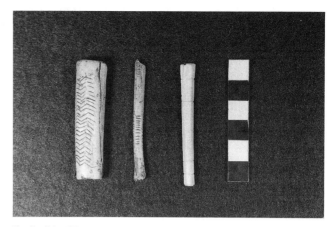

Catalina Island Museum Nos. G-8 (center and farthest from the centimeter scale) and G-18 (closest to scale)

Fig. 72. Small pieces of incised bone, perhaps used as dice or gaming pieces. These artifacts were collected by Ralph Glidden. Photograph by author.

item 1013). *Chaawchawkel* was a dice game played by two contestants using split reeds painted black on one side and white on the other. Eight reeds were tossed and scored according to the number that fell white side up, although if all eight fell black side up it also counted. Should the thrower toss all eight reeds same side up he was entitled to another throw. Score was kept with an elaborate scoreboard consisting of 50 small sticks set into the ground (Reid 1852:47; Hudson and Blackburn 1986:397-408, 416-417).

Waawre', another Gabrielino guessing game, was played by two contestants. The game used eight reed tokens that were painted on one side. One of the players hid the tokens under a basket while his opponent guessed how many lay with the painted side up (Reid 1852:47-48).

PEÓN

Peón, called *chuurchorke* by the Gabrielino, was a guessing game played by two teams of four players each. The peón was a small pawn or token only an inch or two in length and easily concealed. In play, the members of one team each took a black peón in one hand and a white one in the other while the members of the second team tried to guess which of their opponent's hands held the white tokens. Those who guessed correctly took the peón, while those who did not took a counter. The teams switched roles when all of the counters had been taken.

Peón contestants sometimes learned special power songs to bring themselves luck and hired professional singers to perform during the contest. Players and bystanders frequently wagered large sums on the

Southwest Museum No. 491-P-3449 S. Calif.

Fig. 73. A soapstone smoking pipe decorated with three bands of shell and asphaltum inlay. When in use, the pipe was held in an upright position. Photograph by author.

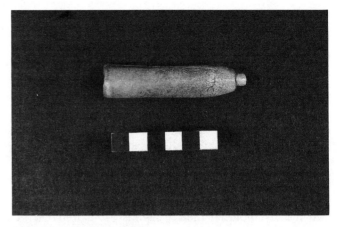

Catalina Island Museum No. G-160

Fig. 74. A small pipe made of clay; the mouthpiece is of bird bone. This specimen was collected by Ralph Glidden. Photograph by author.

outcome of the game. An umpire was usually hired to keep score during the game and settle disputes, as well as provide the firewood (Reid 1852:46-47; also Harrington 1986:R102 F713; Hudson and Blackburn 1986:410-415).

OTHER FORMS OF RECREATION

For relaxation, the Gabrielino enjoyed both sunbathing and sweating in the dry sauna of the sweathouse. At bedtime the Indians used tobacco to induce drowsiness, smoking it in clay or stone pipes made with mouthpieces of bird bone, or in "cigarettes" cut from a piece of cane. Tobacco was also mixed with lime from crushed and burned sea shells and then eaten to produce a mild sedative effect (Boscana 1933:47; Harrington 1942:27-28, items 1043-1056; 1986:R102 F718, R106 F195; Geiger and Meighan 1976:72-73, answer from Mission San Gabriel; Heizer and Elsasser 1980:122; Hudson and Blackburn 1986:115-129).

SUMMARY

The Gabrielino expressed their creative and artistic energies in many ways. Visual arts included the creation of elaborate pictographs (rock paintings) and petroglyphs (rock carvings) such as those found at Burro Flats on the mainland and in the Cave of the Whales on San Nicolas Island. Religious concepts and beliefs were expressed through the elaborate rituals

and ceremonies of the *Chengiichngech* religion. Stories, legends and oral narratives provided a literary outlet for creative impulses, while song and dance gave expression to musical creativity and innovation.

Gabrielino oral literature served a variety of functions including: conveying religious beliefs as well as moral values and other cultural norms; preserving historical accounts; examining philosophical concepts such as life and death and inequality among men; and entertainment. The subjects of Gabrielino oral literature included creation stories, star lore, Coyote tales, and allegories of shamanic experiences such as ritual death and rebirth. Often Gabrielino stories are a blend of elements borrowed from the oral literature of other groups such as the Chumash or the Juaneño. Gabrielino stories were usually narrated by older individuals, although professional bards were also employed. Typically, a Gabrielino narrative opened with a brief statement of setting or theme. Little time was spent exploring the personalities and motivations of the main characters; instead, an individual's actions were viewed as the inevitable result of his or her basic nature. Sacred or supernatural elements of Gabrielino stories were emphasized through the literary technique of inversion, that is, the reversal of normal standards of behavior.

Oral narratives were often recited to the accompaniment of songs to create a more pleasing and emotionally satisfying performance. Songs were also an integral part of Gabrielino ritual. Songs were inherited along family lines and rarely disclosed to outsiders. Lineages owned songs, as did individuals, and these could not be performed by outsiders without the permission of the owners. Songs were used by the Gabrielino for a variety of purposes including: recording genealogies and commemorating historical events; validating territorial claims; preserving legal precepts; venting hostility against enemy lineages; and bringing luck during gaming events. Shamans used song to diagnose and treat illness, bewitch and kill enemies, make food plants and animals plentiful, control the weather, and aid in hunting. Recordings of Gabrielino songs may be found in the Roberts Collection in the Archive of Folk Song at the Library of Congress. Additional recordings of Gabrielino songs made by José de los Santos Juncos and Harrington may be housed in the National Anthropological Archives.

Songs were composed of repeating rhythmic patterns and were often performed to the accompaniment of musical instruments such as whistles, flutes, rattles, musical bows, and bull-roarers. Whistles were made from bird bone, cane, and elder wood; four-hole flutes were constructed from elder wood or the leg bones of deer. Rattles might consist of sticks bound together with cord and adhesive, cocoons attached to stick handles, deer hooves attached to short, buckskin-covered sticks, turtle shells filled with pebbles, and the bladders of mountain goats filled with stones. The musical bow was played by finger and consisted of a flexible wooden stave with a cord stretched between the two ends. Bull-roarers comprised a piece of wood attached to a long string that was swung over the head to produce an eerie, fluttering sound.

Dance was also an integral part of Gabrielino rituals and celebrations. In fact, Father Boscana reported that dance served much the same purpose for the Indians as prayer served for the missionaries. On the basis of research with Luiseño dance, it is suggested that the dances of the Gabrielino can be separated into two basic categories. The first category, ceremonial movement, included performances in which several individuals might participate but in which there was no set pattern of movement. Examples of ceremonial movement were the boys' procession during the Puberty Ceremony and the fire-extinguishing dances, which were often held at the end of fiestas. The second category, ritualistic dance, included performances that followed a set pattern of body movements as part of a tradition passed down from generation to generation. Important examples of ritualized dance included the performances held during the annual Mourning Ceremony and the Eagle Dance.

The Gabrielino enjoyed games and contests. Races and archery contests were popular sports, and during the Mission Period a game of kickball called gome was a regular event. Traditional Gabrielino games included: *haraarekwar*, or ring and pole; *chaawchawkel*, a dice game played by two contestants; *waawre'*, a guessing game played by two contestants using eight reed tokens; and *chuurchorke* (peón), a guessing game played by two teams of four players each.

For relaxation, the Gabrielino preferred sunbathing and sweating in the dry sauna of the sweat hut. At bedtime they used tobacco, which was smoked in clay or stone pipes or in cigarettes cut from a piece of cane. Tobacco could also be mixed with lime and eaten for a mild sedative effect.

In 1769, the first Spanish land expedition crossed the Gabrielino territory; two years later the founding of Mission San Gabriel signalled the beginning of the Spanish colonization of the Gabrielino homeland. In the decades that followed the First Angelinos were confronted with foreign (primarily Hispanic) languages and lifestyles, religious beliefs and practices, and political, legal and economic systems. Most tragically, the Indians were infected and subsequently decimated by European diseases for which, at that time, no satisfactory treatment was available.

For the Gabrielino, the ultimate consequences of European colonization were depopulation and the fragmentation of their economic and political systems. The environment of their homeland was permanently transformed as a result of ranching, agriculture, and industrial and urban development. How did the Gabrielino survive and adapt to these overwhelming changes? Which aspects of their traditional Indian culture endured the transition and which elements were lost? The story of the Gabrielino's struggle to survive and adapt to this new and often hostile world is the subject of Chapter 10.

CHAPTER 10

THE GABRIELINO WORLD IN TRANSITION

Legends of lost ships and shipwrecked sailors have long been a romantic part of southern California history. Luiseño shamans are said to have predicted the "coming of men from big ships with white sails" long before the missions were founded (White 1963:92). According to William Shaler, a Yankee sea captain who visited California in 1804, the coastal Gabrielino and Chumash had a tradition that at some "remote" period a race of "white men" was shipwrecked on the coast, and from them came many of the advanced technological skills displayed by these Indians (Shaler 1935:57). Popular writers of more recent times have attributed the cultural advances of the Channel Island Indians to transoceanic connections with the Chinese or Japanese (Holder 1910:8), while researchers and scholarly writers have speculated upon the possible role of European or Oriental religions in the evolution and development of the *Chengiichngech* religion (White 1963:94-95).

EARLY CONTACTS

The first recorded contact between the Gabrielino and Europeans occurred in 1542 with Cabrillo's arrival at Santa Catalina Island; even at this early date the Gabrielino already knew of Spanish explorations along the Colorado River (Wagner 1941:16-17, 46). The next recorded contact came in 1602 with the arrival of Sebastián Vizcaíno at Catalina Island (Wagner 1929).

Other early European voyagers are believed to have visited the California coast, including Sir Francis Drake in 1578, Cavendish in 1586-1587, Hawkins in 1593, Dampier in 1680 and 1704, Shelvocke and Clipperton in 1719, Anson in 1740, and Wallis and Carteret in 1769. In addition, for two and one-half centuries the transoceanic route followed by Spain's

Manila Galleons passed through the Santa Barbara Channel (White 1963:92-93). There are no documented contacts between these Europeans and the Gabrielino; however, if any of these voyagers reached the southern Channel Islands, the harbors at Avalon and Isthmus Cove on Santa Catalina Island may have offered convenient and tempting landfalls.

Despite the possibility of contact between the Gabrielino and seafarers from other cultures, it would be a mistake to dismiss the technological and social sophistication of these Indians as the product of foreign influence. The complex social organization and sophisticated technological developments of the Gabrielino resulted from the interplay of many factors over a long period of cultural evolution. The maritime Indian culture of southern California, which was a contributing factor in the cultural development of the Gabrielino, was itself the product of more than 3,000 years of evolution (Meighan 1959:401-402; see also Landberg 1965:5; Hudson et al. 1978:22-23 note 6).

Ironically, the greatest impact that the arrival of European vessels had upon the Gabrielino was the decimation of the native population through the spread of contagious disease. As events of the late 1700s and early 1800s were to prove, contact with foreigners exposed the Gabrielino to bacterial and viral infections for which they had no immunities.

SPANISH COLONIZATION

Encounters between the Gabrielino and Europeans were sporadic until the second half of the 1700s. At that time the Spanish conquest of Alta California gained momentum, driven by a desire to secure the northern border against possible Russian and English settlements. The colonization was initiated by an ambitious Spanish administrator, Visitor-General José de Gálvez; under his direction an expedition to Alta California was organized in 1769. The goals of this expedition were twofold: first, to establish a base station at San Diego for use in future operations; second, to relocate Monterey Bay, discovered by Vizcaíno in 1602, and establish a settlement there.

THE PORTOLA EXPEDITION

The expedition was organized into three groups. The first was a sea-going party comprising three ships: the *San Carlos*, the *San Antonio*, and the *San José*. The *San Carlos* sailed from La Paz (near the tip of Baja California) in January of 1769, while the *San Antonio* sailed from Cape San Lucas the following month. The *San José* was lost at sea. Ironically, due to poor charts and faulty navigational data the *San Carlos* reached San Diego three weeks after the *San Antonio*, which had arrived on April 11th. Both crews suffered terribly from disease, probably typhus.

The second party was a land expedition under the command of Captain Fernando Rivera y Moncada. This party consisted of a light cavalry of *soldados de cuero*, or leather-jacket soldiers, so-called because they wore armor of quilted buckskin. This land party set out from Baja California on March 24th, driving ahead of it a large herd of cattle, horses, and mules, and arrived at San Diego on May 14th.

The third party was under the command of Gaspar de Portolá, who was also Commander-in-Chief of the expedition. Accompanying Portolá's land party was the Father President of the Franciscan missions of California, Junípero Serra. This third party departed Baja California on May 15, 1769, arriving at San Diego at the end of June. By then Portolá had lost almost half his forces to illness, yet despite his losses he immediately organized an expedition to Monterey. Father Serra, who was ill, remained behind (W. Bean 1968:36-38). The route followed by this first land expedition can be retraced through the journals left by its members. The picture that unfolds is an engrossing portrait of Indian California prior to Spanish colonization.

The Gabrielino territory was crossed twice during the 1769 expedition, with numerous contacts occurring between the explorers and the Indians. Portolá's party first approached the Gabrielino territory at the end of July, 1769. Traveling northward from present San Juan Capistrano, the Spaniards reached the Santa Ana River and followed it until they arrived at a Gabrielino community, perhaps *Hotuuknga*. They were warmly received, the Gabrielino offering them gifts of antelope and rabbit meat. The next night, after another full day of traveling, the explorers camped in the lower reaches of Brea Canyon near another Gabrielino settlement where a religious festival was underway (Bolton 1927:143).

The explorers continued westward, crossing the Puente Hills and fording the San Gabriel and Río Hondo rivers. They forded the Los Angeles River, naming it in honor of Our Lady, Queen of the Angels of Porciúncula, and passed near the community of Yaanga. Farther west they followed a route marked today by Wilshire Boulevard. Along the way they observed with wonder the marshes and tar seeps of La Brea. Portolá's visit coincided with a period of intense earthquake activity, and the explorers concluded that the tremors were caused by volcanoes lying somewhere to the north (Bolton 1927:148).

On August 4th, the Spaniards passed an empty Gabrielino settlement whose inhabitants were out gathering seeds, and that night they camped near another settlement in the upper reaches of Santa Monica Canyon. The next day they followed a route through the hills and into the San Fernando Valley, probably the course marked today by Sepulveda Boulevard.

Once in the San Fernando Valley the Spaniards took a well-deserved rest, camping for two nights near a populous Gabrielino community situated near a large pool of water (perhaps *Siutcanga*; see the discussion of this community in Chapter 3). The Spaniards departed the San Fernando Valley on August 8th, following the Santa Clara River through Newhall Valley. The expedition continued north as far as the Bay of San Francisco, but failed to recognize Monterey Bay, due in part to the exaggerated description of the bay written in 1602 by Sebastián Vizcaíno. The San Fernando Valley was traversed once again on the return trip to San Diego, the explorers crossing Cahuenga Pass and retracing their route southward, arriving in San Diego on January 24, 1770 (Johnston 1962:128; W. Bean 1968:39).

During Portolá's absence the situation in San Diego had grown desperate. The *San Antonio* had returned to San Blas in Baja California for supplies, and Captain Rivera had also returned to Baja California for the same purpose; however, by March of 1770 there was no sign of relief. Portolá decided to abandon the enterprise and return to Mexico unless one of the relief parties returned by March 19th; however, the *San Antonio* reappeared before his deadline passed (W. Bean 1968:40).

Portolá now moved quickly. Realizing that he had passed Monterey in error, he prepared a second expedition. The *San Antonio*, with Father Serra aboard, was sent on to Monterey while Portolá himself headed north accompanied by 12 soldiers. This second venture was successful, and on June 3, 1770, a mission and presidio were founded at Monterey (W. Bean 1968:40).

EARLY CONFLICTS

Although the Gabrielino accorded the Portolá Expedition a warm welcome, offering the explorers generous gifts of food, in time this initial cordiality gave way to wariness and hostility. According to Reid, the Indians

> were sadly afraid when they saw the Spaniards coming on horseback.—Thinking them gods, the women ran to the brush, and hid themselves, while the men put out the fires in their huts. They remained still more impressed with this idea, when they saw one of their guests take a flint, strike a fire and commence smoking, having never seen it [fire] produced in this simple manner before (Reid 1852:69).

Although the Gabrielino were generous in sharing their food with the newcomers, they "rejected and held in abhorrence . . . food given them by the Europeans," and "all kinds and classes of food . . . were buried secretly in the woods" (Reid 1852:70). Most likely the Gabrielino feared poisoning or witchcraft, for other materials and goods were gladly accepted.

FOUNDING OF MISSION SAN GABRIEL

By the founding of Mission San Gabriel, the Gabrielino had become openly hostile to the Spanish presence in their land. The original site chosen for the mission lay on the Santa Ana River; however, this choice was set aside in favor of an alternate location on the banks of the Río Hondo River near present day Whittier Narrows (Temple 1960:154). Two Franciscan priests, Fathers Pedro Benito Cambón and Josef

Angel Fernández de la Somera, were dispatched to found the mission, escorted by a party of ten leather-jacket soldiers who were to become the first mission guard, as well as a number of muleteers and others (Engelhardt 1927a:3; Temple 1960:153). Father Cambón's account, as translated by Thomas Workman Temple, provides a colorful eyewitness description of the resistance the party encountered from the Gabrielino,

> who, in full war-paint and brandishing their bows and arrows, with hostile gestures and blood-curdling yells, tried to prevent them from crossing the river. Our people finally fought their way to the chosen spot, dangerously pressed. . . . And having dug themselves into fox-holes behind some bales and packing boxes as best they could . . . the padres took out from one of the cases a canvas picture of Our Lady of Sorrows. . . .
> At the sight of it they became as if transfixed in wonderment, and all of them threw their bows and arrows on the ground, as two "Tomeares" or Chiefs took from around their necks the necklaces they value so highly and are accustomed to wear in those distant lands, and placed them at the feet of the Sovereign Queen of the Angels (Temple 1960:154).

Following the establishment of the mission, the priests and soldiers raised a cross and built an altar of willows and rushes, aided by Gabrielino volunteers. Mass was first celebrated at Mission San Gabriel on September 8, 1771, and in the days that followed "there came increasing numbers of men, women and children to view the painting of 'La Dolorosa,' bearing little baskets of seeds which they proffered and laid at the feet of the Sovereign Lady" (Temple 1960:154).

Unfortunately, the situation did not remain peaceful. Worried by the growing numbers of Gabrielino visitors, the priests asked Captain Pedro Fages to increase the strength of the guard. Instead of granting their request, however, Fages reduced the guard from 12 men to ten. He also ordered that only four or five Indians be allowed to enter the mission stockade at one time, although he neglected to inform the priests of this command (Temple 1960:156). The Gabrielino who had willingly provided the newcomers with land, food, and free labor now found themselves rudely restricted from access to the Christian settlement, and they were deeply offended by the slight.

The events that followed only increased the tension. In one incident, an angry crowd of Indians armed with war clubs trampled a mission guard, plundered the mission stores, and threatened the priests and soldiers. Only a show of force by the guard, who were armed with muskets, succeeded in quelling the disturbance. A plea for reinforcements was hurriedly sent to Captain Fages in San Diego, and two additional guards were allotted to the mission (Temple 1960:157).

A fragile peace lasted through the end of September and the first week of October. On October 9th, however, the Gabrielino once again crowded the stockade and threatened violence. They were infuriated by the rape of a local *tomyaar*'s wife by one of the Spanish soldiers. Reid may have been referring to this outrage when he wrote that "another event soon convinced them of their visitors' mortality, for shortly afterward they received another visit from a larger party, who commenced tying the hands of the adult males behind their backs; and making signs of their wish to procure women. . . . Harsh measures obtained for them what they sought" (Reid 1852:70).

A number of Gabrielino children living at the mission and receiving religious instruction were taken away by the Indians; only five children who concealed themselves in the priests' quarters remained behind. Among these was the son of a *tomyaar*, a circumstance which may have further agitated the Indians, for on October 10th they attacked in force (Engelhardt 1927a:6; Temple 1960:157-158, 161).

The Gabrielino plan may have been to stampede the horses while launching a coordinated attack on the settlement. At daybreak, one group of Gabrielino warriors, led by the *tomyaar* whose wife had been raped, surrounded the stockade and threatened the soldiers. Although the Spaniards somehow succeeded in dispersing most of the warriors, a number of Indians continued to block the gate. This was only a feint, however, for another group of warriors was concealed in a nearby gully waiting for the signal to attack. The Spanish position worsened when five additional bands of warriors swelled the Gabrielino ranks, two joining those in the gully while the other three positioned themselves within "a musket shot" of the mission (Temple 1960:158).

According the Father Cambón, the Spaniards were warned of their predicament by one of the Gabrielino children at the mission. The fighting began as one Spanish soldier rushed from the stockade to warn two of his comrades, who had remained outside the mission guarding a herd of horses, of the impending attack. The soldier was pursued by several Indians, and by the time he reached his companions the battle was underway.

The heaviest fighting occurred at the stockade, the Gabrielino unleashing volleys of arrows while the Spaniards responded with musket fire. Three Gabrielino were killed, including the *tomyaar* whose wife had been raped. At the height of the battle the soldiers rushed from the stockade and charged the Indians. Demoralized by the death of their leader, and fearing the arrival of Spanish reinforcements, the Gabrielino retreated (Temple 1960:158-159).

After the battle the victorious Spaniards decapitated the fallen *tomyaar* and impaled his head on a tall pole within the stockade. That afternoon, after the horses were retrieved, several Spanish soldiers visited one of the nearby Gabrielino settlements to make a show of force. The few Indians who remained in the settlement surrendered their weapons to the soldiers (Engelhardt 1927a:7; Temple 1960:159).

The following morning, October 11th, the Spaniards awoke to see the horizon ringed with the smoke of signal fires. Father Cambón believed that the Gabrielino were trying to forge an alliance between the coastal and inland communities. Their efforts apparently failed, however, for two *tomyaars* sealed pacts of peace with the Spaniards soon thereafter (Temple 1960:159).

Yet the potential for violent conflict remained high. On October 16th, a contingent of Gabrielino warriors concealed themselves in a willow thicket near the mission, and prepared for an attack. The Spanish forces were alerted to the danger, however, and the Indians retreated when four Indian boys living at the mission warned them of the Spanish preparations. The situation remained tense that night as signal fires were seen in the distance, but the following morning Captain Fages arrived at the mission accompanied by two Franciscans and a fresh contingent of soldiers. The Gabrielino withdrew, and to ensure a permanent peace Fages increased the guard to 18 soldiers (Temple 1960:159-160).

Although Mission San Gabriel was saved, the priests' efforts to recruit Indian converts had suffered a severe setback. The Gabrielino who had aided the Spaniards now shunned them, and in fact abandoned their settlements in the neighborhood of the mission and relocated some distance away. It was several months before any returned to visit the mission. It would be exactly 26 years before another mission was established in Gabrielino territory. On September 8, 1797, Mission San Fernando was founded near the communities of *Pasheeknga* and *'Achooykomenga* (Engelhardt 1927a:7-8, 1927b:12; Temple 1960:160).

THE MISSION SYSTEM

Eventually the early setbacks at Mission San Gabriel were overcome and Indians began returning to Mission San Gabriel; by October 1773, 73 adults and children had been baptized. The mission remained a rude affair, consisting of a "church, made of logs [i.e., willow poles] with tule roof; the dwelling of the missionary fathers, offices and granaries, made of the same materials; the guard-house for the soldiers of the escort; and ten little houses for the Indians of [Lower] California" (Bolton 1926:219). Corn, beans, and wheat were cultivated at the mission, and livestock comprised cattle, sheep, goats, pigs, horses, and mules. After several years the Whittier Narrows site was abandoned, perhaps in November of 1774, and a new site was chosen where the potential for agriculture was much greater. This is the site where the present San Gabriel Mission buildings now stand (Engelhardt 1927a:19; Johnston 1962:129).

The Spanish brought to California a colonial system which had evolved in medieval Spain as a means of administrating territory taken back from the Moors. This system relied upon a combination of military and religious personnel to achieve its goals. The type of mission established in Alta California was known as a *reducción*, its purpose being to "reduce," or consolidate, the Indians from the countryside into one central community.

As a general practice, two Franciscan priests were stationed at each mission, one having responsibility for temporal affairs, the other for spiritual affairs. Garrisons were stationed at the presidios established at San Diego, Santa Barbara, Monterey, and San Francisco. A smaller contingent of leather-jacket soldiers formed a guard at each mission (W. Bean 1968:28; Castillo 1978:101-102).

The mission itself was a sprawling community in which hundreds and sometimes thousands of Indians lived and worked. Indians from numerous communities, and often from different language groups as well, were brought together to live at these missions. Thus, Mission San Gabriel was home to Gabrielino, Kitanemuk, Serrano, and Cahuilla Indians. Mission San Fernando contained the Fernandeño branch of the Gabrielino, as well as Kitanemuk, Tataviam, Cahuilla, and Chumash Indians (Forbes 1966:137; Bean 1978:583; Bean and Smith 1978:573; Blackburn and Bean 1978:564; King and Blackburn 1978:536). Gabrielino were also included in the Indian population residing at Mission San Juan Capistrano.

MISSION RANCHOS

In addition to the main site where the church and residences were built, each mission also had a set of outlying ranchos where agriculture was practiced and livestock, primarily sheep or cattle, was raised. The principal San Gabriel ranchos included Rancho de la Puente, Rancho San Bernardino, Rancho Santa Anita, and Rancho Santa Ana (Engelhardt 1927a:143, 157, 201-202; Webb 1952:92-93). Reid reported that the San Gabriel ranchos included "San Pasqual, Santa Anita, Asuza [Azusa], San Francisquito, Cucumonga, San Antonio, San Bernardino, San Gorgonio, Yucaipa, Jurupa, Guapa, Rincon, Chino, San José, Ybarras, Puente, Mission Viga [Vieja], Serranos, Rosa Castillo, Coyotes, Saboneria [Jabonería], Las Bolsas, Alamites [Alamitos], and Serritos [Cerritos]" (Reid 1852:84; first comment in brackets in original). Four of these ranchos, Los Coyotes, Las Bolsas, Los Alamitos, and Los Cerritos were private holdings, being part of a massive grant made to Manuel Nieto by Governor Pedro Fages in 1795 (Engelhardt 1927a:65). They were used by Mission San Gabriel for a short period from 1815-1822, after which they reverted to Nieto's heirs (Mason, personal communication 1991). The ranchos of Mission San Fernando included El Escorpión, Las Vírgenes, Camulos, La Amarga, La Huenga, and San Francisquito. San Francisquito was apparently taken over from San Gabriel after the founding of San Fernando in 1797 (Engelhardt 1927b:63; Webb 1952:92, 107).

MISSION ARCHITECTURE

In the final stages of completion, most of the California missions conformed to the same general plan. The buildings were laid out in a large quadrangle consisting of four connecting wings surrounding an enormous enclosed courtyard. The church occupied one wing, while the priest's quarters, the *monjerio* (the single women's dormitory), the weavery, the kitchen, workshops, and storerooms filled the others. A member of the Jedediah Smith Expedition who visited San Gabriel in November, 1826, described the mission as a square in which the church faced the east, the guardhouse the west, and workshops the north and south (Rogers 1918:198-226; see also Engelhardt 1927a:149).

The structures were built with thick walls of adobe brick and roofed with tiles, although of course in the early years the buildings were far less substantial (see Engelhardt 1927a:253, 1927b:78 for the plans of Missions San Gabriel and San Fernando). The tile roofs were supported on timbers of pine cut from trees in San Gabriel and San Antonio canyons (Robinson 1977:15). José de los Santos Juncos remembered

that at the various canyons along the mountains, pines were obtained for the mission. Pines formerly grew further down the mountains than at present but have been cut. The pines were carried in the carretas, but the Indians being so numerous some Indians were employed to bring them on foot, such a bringer being required to make two trips from San Gabriel to the mountains and back in one day, each trip returning with a pine timber (of small size such as he could carry) on his shoulder. They gave azotes [lashes] to the bringers who did not complete their two trips in one day (Harrington 1986:R104 F44).

Martín Féliz (a 70 year-old Harrington consultant of mixed Indian and Spanish heritage) reported that "the Indians cut the vigas [beams] for building San Gabriel Mission up back of Mt. Wilson" (Harrington 1986:R106 F166, 185). Water to supply the mission's needs was obtained by means of irrigation ditches. José de los Santos Juncos noted that the "padres got water not only . . . at Mission Canyon and at La Presa but also in the early days there was a ditch coming all the way from Azusa, irrigating vineyards, olives, and pomegranate patches all the way down to the mission" (Harrington 1986:R104 F44).

Unmarried Indian men and women were housed in separate dormitories. To prevent sexual liaisons, girls eight years of age and older lived in the *monjerio*, which was locked at night. The keys were held by the priests. At Mission San Gabriel, an Indian matron

was in charge of the *monjerio*, and a blind Indian named Andresillo called out each girl's name as she entered the building at night. Girls who were late were punished by being locked indoors the following day (Sánchez 1929; see also Webb 1952:27-28).

In the later years of the mission period, the *monjerios* grew to become elaborate, self-contained complexes of patios, sleeping rooms, cooking areas, and workshops. They were often built adjoining the weavery, where many of the girls worked. *Monjerios* were built at San Gabriel in 1771, 1775, and 1783, and included patios with bathing pools (Webb 1952:116; Geiger 1968:33-36). The sleeping quarters were very primitive, however. The *monjerio* at Santa Barbara, for example, was a room 17 by 7 *varas* in size, a *vara* being equal to 33 inches. Thus, the sleeping area was approximately 46 by 20 feet in size, yet it accommodated 50 to 100 women! Sleeping platforms six feet wide ran the length of the two longest walls, while some women slept on the floor. Tule mats were used as mattresses, but no partitions were available for privacy. Basic toilet facilities were provided, and light and ventilation were obtained from a single wide window placed high on one wall. A fire provided heat, and a tallow candle light (Cook 1943:89-90; Webb 1952:63, note 5; Librado et al. 1979:53).

Although in the early days of the mission the married "neophytes" (a term meaning "beginners in Christianity") dwelled in traditional dome-shaped homes of willow and reeds, eventually a permanent village of adobe apartments was constructed outside the quadrangle to house them. Water was provided through an elaborate system of aqueducts, ditches, underground channels, and fountains (Bolton 1930:177-178; Webb 1952:64-65).

The apartments built at San Fernando were single, separate structures, while Reid described those at San Gabriel as "four rows of new double houses, forming three streets for the married portion of the community" (Reid 1852:78; Engelhardt 1927b:16). The interiors of these houses at San Gabriel were described in an 1807 mission report as measuring five by six *varas*, or approximately 13.5 by 16.5 feet, with doors and windows of pine (Engelhardt 1927a:75). Cooking was accomplished over an open fire built between three stones (Webb 1952:41). The ventilation in these houses was poor, as Pablo Tac, a neophyte of Mission San Luis Rey, noted in a humorous description of one family's meal: "At twelve o'clock they eat together. . . . Too bad for them if at that time they close the door. Then the smoke rising, being much, and the opening which serves as a window being small, it turns below, trying to go out by the door, remains in the middle of the house, and they eat, then speaking, laughing and weeping without wishing to" (Tac 1952:15).

POLITICAL AUTHORITY WITHIN THE MISSION

Politically, several levels of authority existed within the missions. The first and most visible was the formal, Hispanic political structure. This consisted of a hierarchy with the priests at the top. Beneath the priests was the head mayordomo, who attended to the daily business of running the mission. Often the head mayordomo was a member of the mission guard (Webb 1952:54). Beneath the head mayordomo were "other mayordomos . . . for all kinds of work, from tending of horses down to those superintending crops, and in charge of vineyards and gardens." The lesser mayordomos, or foremen, seem generally to have been Indians (Reid 1852:84; Sánchez 1929).

The neophytes elected from their own ranks officials to serve as *alcaldes* and *regidores*. The *alcaldes*, aided by the *regidores*, acted as constables, bringing wrongdoers to the attention of the priests, and they also administered punishments (Webb 1952:50). Reid reported that "they carried a wand to denote their authority, and what was more terrible, an immense scourge of raw hide, about ten feet in length, plaited to the thickness of an ordinary man's wrist!—They did a great deal of chastisement, both by and without orders. One of them always acted as overseer on work done in gangs. . . ." (Reid 1852:85). Two *alcaldes* and two *regidores* were elected annually, although the candidates seem generally to have been designated by the priests (Geiger and Meighan 1976:125-126, answers from Missions San Buenaventura and Santa Barbara).

Beneath the political structure imposed by the Spanish, there existed another political system based upon the traditional leadership of the Indian groups. The existence of such a political structure can be inferred from a statement by the priests at San Fernando that the neophytes "respect only those who were the chiefs of their rancherias in paganism" (Geiger and Meighan 1976:125, answer from Mission

San Fernando). The Franciscan priests allowed and even encouraged neophytes to hold traditional fiestas in the hope of drawing new converts into the missions. These fiestas were organized by the *tomyaar*s and required the cooperation of an Indian leadership that retained a measure of traditional authority (see Librado and Harrington 1977:104, note 50; Librado et al. 1979:26, note 3). José de los Santos Juncos noted that the "coast Indians came up to San Gabriel when invited to fiestas"; in recounting a Gabrielino story Santos Juncos noted "there was a fiesta at S.G. [San Gabriel]. The island Indians came. . . ." (Harrington 1986:R104 F11, R105 F565). Juan Meléndrez reported that the Indians of Tejón attended fiestas at San Fernando (Harrington 1986:R106 F195).

Although the office of *tomyaar* survived, it did not remain unchanged. The authority held by the *tomyaar*s declined as populations dwindled as a result of the spread of contagious diseases and as traditional social and economic patterns of interaction evolved under the impact of missionization. In addition, the priests probably modified the *tomyaar*'s traditional role in order to integrate that office into the political fabric of the mission and take full advantage of its political influence (see White 1963:158, 161).

Shamans who entered the mission community had to practice their rituals and teachings in secrecy, for the Franciscans regarded these religious officials as threats to their own authority and were intolerant of the influence they held over their followers. Thus, the missionaries of San Gabriel complained that "idolatry is still practiced by some Indians. . . . It would disappear . . . if the old people and young ones did not live together for the former are the ones who mislead the young" (Geiger and Meighan 1976:57, answer from Mission San Gabriel). Reid commented that one missionary at San Gabriel kept shamans "chained together in couples and well flogged. There were, at that period, no small number of old men rejoicing in the fame of witchcraft, so he made sawyers of them all, keeping them like hounds in couples, and so they worked, two above and two below in the pit" (Reid 1852:87).

At the lowest level of the political ladder was the individual Indian. As a neophyte, each Indian was categorized according to the work he or she performed, whether it be skilled or unskilled labor. A listing by Reid of the many jobs and positions within the community included everything from *vaqueros* and carpenters to weavers and deer hunters (Reid 1852:82-83). Another account noted that "such Indians as showed any aptitude for the various trades were given instruction in them, while the others worked in the fields, or in the care of horses, cattle, etc." (Sánchez 1929). Small children were employed in light tasks such as keeping animals out of the brickyard where adobes were drying, or chasing birds from the orchards and vegetable gardens (Cook 1943:92-94).

MISSION LIFE

The neophytes' existence at the missions contrasted dramatically with their previous lifestyle. Neophytes were required to adopt European dress patterns, and the monotonous mission diet was greatly restricted compared to the varied hunting-gathering diet of the Gabrielino. In addition, mission work patterns were directed toward vaguely-defined goals that had little in common with traditional Gabrielino community life. Traditional work patterns involved periods of strenuous labor oriented toward well-defined goals, such as hunting or gathering seasonal crops. In contrast, life in the missions demanded strict adherence to daily work routines aimed at long-term goals that were not always understood by the Indians (Cook 1943:98-99).

The average mission work week consisted of 30-40 hours of labor spread over five or six days. The ringing of bells served to regulate the daily schedule (Cook 1943:94; Webb 1952:35). A typical day began with prayers in the church at sunrise, after which came Mass. Breakfast was next, parents and small children eating in their apartments while boys and young men ate in a common kitchen known as the *pozolera*, and the single girls ate in the *monjerio* (Engelhardt 1927b:88). The meals generally consisted of *atole* (wheat, barley, or corn mush) or *pozole* (barley and beans boiled together) with meat. Sometimes *champurrado* (chocolate mixed with corn-meal gruel) was served, and on festival days the neophytes had bread and sweets (Sánchez 1929; Geiger and Meighan 1976:785-88).

Work began around eight o'clock and lasted until eleven. At noon dinner was served, which generally consisted of *pozole* made with meat and vegetables. Following an afternoon rest period, work began once again at one or two o'clock and lasted until five (Engelhardt 1927b:88; Sánchez 1929). At five o'clock prayers were said, and at six supper was taken, which

was generally the same as breakfast. After supper the neophyte's time was his or her own until approximately eight o'clock, when all would retire. Saturday afternoons were given to clothes washing, while Saturday nights were devoted to lengthy games of peón. Hotly contested races and athletic events were held after Mass on Sundays (Reid 1852:94-95; Engelhardt 1927b:88-89; Tac 1952:18-20).

Although some research suggests that the mission diet was inadequate to meet the nutritional needs of the neophyte population, it is difficult to generalize because conditions varied from one mission to another and from one period to the next. Certainly the neophytes continued consuming many of their traditional foods, gathering them while on excursions from the mission (Cook 1943:34-55; Webb 1952:41). One missionary from San Fernando wrote that "the food they partake of is the same as that of the Spaniards but at the same time they do not despise the *pinole* and seeds which they are accustomed to use in their pagan state and many even prefer them" (Geiger and Meighan 1976:85, answer from Mission San Fernando). Many of the animal foods eaten by the non-Christian Gabrielino were also consumed by the neophytes when available.

The dress worn by the neophytes represented European dress customs, rather than traditional Indian clothing. At Mission San Gabriel the men's clothing consisted of "a blanket, a short tunic which we call *cotón*, and a narrow cloth which serves as a covering for the men," while women were "supplied with a *cotón*, blanket and a skirt" (Geiger and Meighan 1976:148, answer from Mission San Gabriel).

The type of clothing provided to the neophytes seems to have depended upon the attitude of the Franciscan administrator. During the administration of Father José María de Zalvidea, who was resident at San Gabriel from 1806 to 1827 (Engelhardt 1927a:305), the neophytes were never given "any other clothing (including shirts and petticoats) than coarse frieze (Xerga) . . . which kept the poor wretches all the time diseased with the itch [xerga was a coarse blend of cotton and wooden cloth]." The reason for this severity was that "the Padre had an idea that finery led Indians to run away" (Reid 1852:86). Yet during the succeeding administration of Father José Bernardo Sánchez, resident at the mission from 1821 to 1833 (Engelhardt 1927a:306), women "dressed in petticoats of all patterns and colors, with their clean chemise protruding from the bosom, with a 'kerchief round the neck and rebosa [shawl] round the shoulders." Men wore "pants, jacket, trousers, hat and fancy silk sash," and children "sported in a white or fancy shirt, with a handkerchief tied around the head" (Reid 1852:93). The fancy men's clothing was worn primarily by the *vaqueros*, or saddle riders, while other males continued wearing the breech clout and tunic (Sánchez 1929).

RELIGIOUS CONVERSIONS

During the first 20 years of the Mission Period, recruitment appears to have been accomplished using purely voluntary methods (Cook 1943:73). Gifts of food, beads, trinkets, and clothing were used to attract the Indians. As one missionary noted with candor, "these Indians are usually caught by the mouth" (Bolton 1930:181). They were then convinced to move to the vicinity of the mission and begin receiving regular instruction (Webb 1952:25-26).

The actual period of religious instruction seems to have averaged two or three months, although in some cases it may have continued for as long as a year (Engelhardt 1927a:261; Bolton 1930:179). The kindness and special attention that the Franciscan missionaries showed the candidates during the recruitment and instruction phase was undoubtedly an important factor in maintaining the Indian's interest and cooperation (Guest 1979:63-64).

The conversion methods used by the Franciscan missionaries during the later years of the Mission Period have been debated for many years, and will not be discussed here (See Cook 1943; Castillo 1978; Guest 1978, 1979, 1985; Heizer 1978a). Rather, it is more important to understand how the Gabrielino may have viewed missionization and conversion. Reid, who probably obtained much of his information from his Gabrielino wife Victoria and her family, noted that baptism "was called by them *soyna*, 'being bathed', and strange to say, was looked upon . . . as being ignominious and degrading." According to Reid, those who were baptized "lost 'caste'" among their people (Reid 1852:74-75). One Franciscan missionary was told by an old woman at Santa Ana that the gentiles, or non-Christian Indians, would rather "be eaten by coyotes" than become neophytes (Mason 1984:130).

These comments offer an important insight into the Gabrielino's perception of life at the missions.

The Spanish mission was insensitive and antagonistic to the cultural traditions of the California Indians. Although some priests may have cared deeply about the welfare of the Indians, cultural conflict was implicit in the goals of missionization. The Indians were regarded as subjects of the crown with souls to be saved. As Spanish subjects they were extended the right to the protection of the monarchy, were taught to speak Spanish, were converted to Christianity, and were integrated into the lower strata of Hispanic society (W. Bean 1968:26-27). However, acculturation was seen as flowing in one direction only, that is, from the missionaries to the Indians. The Franciscans regarded the Indians as "adult children," and in general had little appreciation for traditional Indian culture (Guest 1985:228). Some of the important areas in which mission values conflicted with traditional Indian values included corporal punishment, overcrowding, sexual mores, work ethics, political organization, and religious beliefs and practices.

CULTURAL CONFLICT WITHIN THE MISSIONS

Indians received corporal punishment for three types of transgressions: criminal violations, such as murder, assault, rape, arson, or theft; political violations, such as fugitivism, theft of mission property, apostasy, refusal to complete assigned work, or armed opposition to soldiers; and finally, sexual offenses (Cook 1943:113-115). Several different punishments were used to discipline offenders. Men were tied to a cannon or post and lashed, or they were locked in the stocks. In another very painful form of punishment a musket was passed under the knees and tied in place, and the hands of the offender were then tied to it (Sánchez 1929). Women were flogged by another woman within the confines of the *monjerio* (Cook 1943:126).

There is no question but that the Indians found such punishment degrading and humiliating (Cook 1943:122). Reid noted that among the Gabrielino "whipping was never resorted to as a punishment; therefore all fines and sentences consisted in delivering money, food and skins" (Reid 1852:16). The effectiveness of corporal punishment is also questionable. Traditionally, punishments for transgressions such as theft or adultery were handled directly between the transgressor and the injured party. The administration of corporal punishment by a third party was probably bewildering to the Indians (Cook 1943:139).

Overcrowding was another unfortunate fact of life in the mission environment. The neophyte population of Mission San Gabriel exceeded 1,000 by 1789 and reached a peak of 1,701 in 1817 (Engelhardt 1927a:267-268). In contrast, traditional Gabrielino communities held populations ranging from 50 to perhaps 300 people. Clearly, the sheer number of people residing at the mission required a major adjustment in Gabrielino lifestyle. The effects of overcrowding were most obvious in the cramped sleeping quarters of the men and women. In the *monjerio* 50 to 100 women ages eight years and older were required to sleep on two wooden platforms, which provided approximately 700 square feet of sleeping space. Under the very best circumstances one woman might have 14 square feet of space, or an area seven feet by two feet, in which to sleep with no provision for personal privacy (Cook 1943:84-90).

Additional stress was created by the sexual deprivation that accompanied the separate confinement of single men and women. Although information on Gabrielino sexual mores is sparse, no specific prohibitions against premarital sex have been reported (see Harrington 1942:31, items 1189-1190; also Cook 1943:101-113). In this respect Gabrielino sexual mores may have more closely resembled those of contemporary American society than those of Hispanic society during the 1700s and 1800s.

The work ethic imposed by the Franciscan missionaries differed greatly from that of traditional Indian society, and this had an important effect upon the daily lives of the missionized Indians. The traditional hunter-gatherer lifestyle of the California Indians required fairly constant activity involving the gathering and redistribution of food. This system was admirably suited to the environment in which the Gabrielino lived. By contrast, under missionization Indians were required to adopt a European lifestyle in which work and recreation were segregated. Daily labor involved tedious, repetitive tasks to fulfill vaguely-defined mission goals that did little to enhance the Indian's self-esteem.

The role of traditional political leadership also underwent a change. Gabrielino *tomyaars* living within the missions were relegated to positions of authority inferior to the *alcaldes*. Shamans who practiced their skills were persecuted (Reid 1852:87; Geiger and Meighan 1976:125, answers from Missions San Fernando and San Gabriel).

Many of the religious practices of the Gabrielino were decried as superstitions, idolatry, or "vain practices" and were forbidden by the missionaries. No doubt one missionary at San Gabriel was overly optimistic in reporting that "we are successful in having them give up these practices gradually"; nonetheless, the ceremonies most offensive to the missionaries were probably modified or performed in secret (Boscana 1933:17; Geiger and Meighan 1976:47-48, 57-58, answers from Missions San Gabriel and San Fernando).

FUGITIVISM

Once an Indian was baptized he (or she) was no longer free to renounce his conversion or return home. Instead, he was required to live the remainder of his life at the mission, and if he tried to escape he was forcibly returned. Indians born of Christian parents within the mission were never given a choice as to where they might live (Guest 1979:5, 11-13, 1985:230).

The drastic changes that missionization forced upon the Indians reduced many of them to a state of profound depression. Reid reported that "at first, surprise and astonishment filled their minds; a strange lethargy and inaction predominated afterwards. All they did was to hide themselves as best they could from the oppressor" (Reid 1852:76). Ultimately, many neophytes chose freedom in spite of the risks that escape involved. If they fled to another mission they were captured, flogged, and returned in irons. Spanish soldiers regularly visited the Indian settlements in search of runaways, and inflicted severe punishments on those who aided fugitives. Thus, most of the deserters fled to the mountains, and sometimes as far as the San Joaquin Valley (Reid 1852:80).

It is clear that fugitivism represented a severe problem for the missions. It has been estimated that up to 1831 one out of every 24 neophytes successfully escaped the mission system. At Mission San Gabriel, up until 1817, 473 neophytes had escaped, which represented more than eight percent of the total baptisms performed at that mission (Cook 1943:61, Table 4). The missionaries tried to reduce the incidence of fugitivism by allowing neophytes to visit their homes for several weeks each year; however, these leaves of absence seemed to help but little (Guest 1979:11, 1985:231-232).

THE COLLAPSE OF GABRIELINO SOCIETY

At a cultural level, missionization set in motion a process that resulted in the collapse of Gabrielino society. Many factors played a part in the decline of the Gabrielino during the late 1700s and early 1800s. The incorporation of young, productive Indians into the mission system weakened the economies of the Gabrielino communities and eroded the influence of the Indian leadership. More important, however, were the numerous outbreaks of introduced epidemic diseases as well as the high incidence of new endemic diseases, especially syphilis, which resulted in a steady population decline and encouraged the flight of healthy Gabrielinos from their homeland (Reid 1852:100; Jackson 1991).

DISEASE AND POPULATION DECLINE

While statistical figures are not available for the Gabrielino as a whole, population data are available for the Indians living at Mission San Gabriel during the years 1781 to 1831. The Gabrielino population at Mission San Gabriel experienced a mean death rate of 95 per 1000 during these years, compared to a mean birth rate of 44 per 1000. This translates to a mean population decline of 51 people per 1000. Mean life expectancy at birth was only 6.4 years, with the highest mortality being among women and children (Jackson 1991). The population at Mission San Gabriel was, in fact, unable to sustain itself; it could not maintain or expand its size through natural reproduction. As a result, the missionaries were forced to maintain an active program of recruitment to ensure the survival of the mission.

Measles, influenza, tuberculosis, and dysentery were major players in the medical tragedy that tormented the Gabrielino until well into the 1800s. In addition, syphilis took its toll upon the population in several ways. First, the disease weakened the constitutions of those afflicted, making them more susceptible to other ailments. Second, children born to parents having syphilis contracted the disease at birth. One missionary at San Gabriel reported that as a result of this disease three of every four children died before reaching two years of age. Third, there is evidence which suggests that syphilis may actually have had a direct impact upon fertility and population size (Cook 1943:28-29; Geiger and Meighan 1976:72-

73, 105, answers from Mission San Gabriel; Meighan 1976b:7).

The first recorded outbreak of syphilis among the Gabrielino occurred shortly after the arrival of the Anza Expedition at San Gabriel in 1777; however, because more than two centuries had elapsed since the first contact with Europeans in 1542, it seems quite possible that earlier outbreaks went unrecorded. Members of the Portolá Expedition of 1769 were probably infected with the disease, and they could have exposed the Gabrielino to it at that time (Engelhardt 1927a:82; Cook 1943:23).

The spread of syphilis was increased by the tendency of Spanish soldiers to have sexual relations with Indian women. In 1777, soldiers at Missions San Gabriel and San Juan Capistrano were accused of visiting Indian communities at night and raping women. In 1780, one of the first *alcaldes* at Mission San Gabriel, an Indian named Nicolás, was punished for providing women to the soldiers; it was also common for soldiers to purchase women from non-missionized Indians (Engelhardt 1927a:44; Mason personal communication 1991). As a result of these incidents, in 1785, Governor Pedro Fages issued strict orders that forbade all consorting between soldiers and Indian women (Cook 1943:24-25, 105-106; Mason 1975).

The impact of venereal disease upon the California Indians is documented by mission reports. According to eyewitness accounts, many Indians were dying from syphilis; by 1810 a hospital established at Mission San Gabriel was crowded with 300-400 patients afflicted with venereal disease. Eventually a chapel and mortuary were added to the hospital so that religious services could be provided to those too ill to be moved. Women seem to have been especially hard hit by the disease, for which there was no adequate treatment (Engelhardt 1927a:86, 90-91, 94; Cook 1943:28-29, 34).

Other diseases attacked the Gabrielino as well, although the records prior to 1808 are scanty. In 1801, an outbreak of "contagious fevers" was reported at San Gabriel and San Juan Capistrano (Cook 1943:21). A missionary from San Gabriel reported that in 1804 the prevalent diseases were "venereal disease, consumption and dysentery of blood. This last mentioned ailment is seasonal, for this enemy of Indian nature recurs at the approach of winter and lasts until the beginning of summer. The number of deaths is double the number of births" (Geiger and Meighan 1976:73, answer from Mission San Gabriel). A measles epidemic struck all of the missions in 1806, and a report by the Father Comisario Prefecto of the missions for the years 1817-1819 noted that the Indians at San Gabriel, San Juan Capistrano, and San Luis Rey were still dying in large numbers from dysentery and venereal disease (Engelhardt 1927a:109; Cook 1943:19).

The Indians reacted to these waves of epidemics with fear and confusion. José Zalvidea recounted a curious tale about one epidemic. According to Zalvidea

> there was a big bodega [wine cellar] at San Gabriel. There was much odor from the wine there. There was a bad priest. He made the odor so it was bad for the Indians; many, many died from it. He took the Indians to the coast and gave them beans and so forth and to each Indian he gave a knife and a spoon and then he took them off to an island or somewhere. Z's [Zalvidea's] father told Z. this and the story is hazy in Z's mind and he is unable to make it clear or give further details. The mission church was full of Indians, just like sheep. They buried the dead Indians one on top of another in a trench. That is why the mission ended and where the Indians ended.
>
> The Indians would say: Father, the Indians are dying. The priest merely rejected them. When the Indians had died the villages ended. . . . all the people ended, became extinct (Harrington 1986:R102 F248).

José de los Santos Juncos remembered "a disease that makes [the] victim tremble and shake and makes espuma sale por la boca [foam come out of the mouth]. Had it at S. Juan C. [Capistrano] some. They say it is an animal that produces it, that it is of the water" (Harrington 1986:R102 F732). The symptoms described by José suggest hydrophobia.

The overcrowding at the missions and the generally low standard of sanitation prevalent at that time contributed to the spread of diseases (Jackson 1991). In contrast, traditional Gabrielino society placed a high value upon hygiene, as emphasized by the custom of bathing each morning before sunrise. The nutritional value of the mission diet may also have been inadequate, causing a lowering of resistance to infection (Cook 1943:34-55). In the early years of the missions, periodic crop failures sometimes brought this situation to a critical level. In 1795, one-half of the neophytes at Mission San Gabriel were sent to the mountains for several months to live on wild foods. Those that remained at the mission went on half-rations until the wheat crop was harvested (see Engelhardt 1927a:69).

CONFLICT AND REBELLION

The presence of widespread disease and other problems at the mission placed the neophyte population under a great deal of stress. The non-Christian Indians living outside the mission also suffered from disease and the gradual depopulation of the Indian communities. As a result, armed rebellions against the missions constituted a significant threat to the survival of the system. This potential danger was well illustrated in 1775 when the Kumeyaay Indians of San Diego destroyed that mission, killing three Spaniards (Castillo 1978:103). When asked the reason for the rebellion, one Indian replied that they revolted "in order to live as they did before" (Cook 1943:66).

EARLY REBELLIONS

The Gabrielino attempted a number of rebellions against Mission San Gabriel. In 1773, a revolt was provoked by the numerous rapes of Indian women by Spanish soldiers (Mason 1984:126). In November of 1779, a neophyte at San Gabriel named Nicolás José plotted the death of the priests and soldiers of the guard. The revolt, which was discovered before it began, was in retaliation for advances made upon Nicolás's wife by one of the Indians brought from Baja California by the Spaniards. Nicolás José was imprisoned with his co-conspirators (Temple 1958).

TOYPURINA'S REVOLT

The most fully documented Gabrielino revolt occurred in October of 1785 and is known as Toypurina's Revolt. Toypurina was a Gabrielino shaman from the community of *Jachivit*, the location of which is presently undetermined. Both Toypurina's father and her brother were *tomyaar*s, and although she was only 24 years of age, Toypurina herself was a person of great strength and conviction. Her resentment probably stemmed from the depopulation and social disruption of Gabrielino society caused by the founding of Mission San Gabriel (Temple 1958:148; Mason 1975:92-94).

Toypurina was encouraged by the disgruntled neophyte Nicolás José, who still resided at Mission San Gabriel and who was now angry with the Franciscans for prohibiting traditional Indian dances and ceremonies. Toypurina recruited warriors from at least four and perhaps as many as eight communities, including *Jachivit*, *Juvit*, *'Ashuukshanga*, and *Haahamonga*. The rebels were drawn from an area that extended at least 15 miles along the foothills of the San Gabriels—the region most extensively affected by missionization during the 1780s (Mason 1975:92).

The attack might have proven successful had not the corporal of the guard been forewarned of the plot (Mason 1975:92; Castillo 1991:18). Toypurina was captured within the mission grounds, as were Nicolás José, two other *tomyaars*, and 17 warriors. The others escaped over the mission wall (Temple 1958:138-139; Mason 1975:92). A trial was held and each of the 17 captured warriors was released after receiving 25 lashes. Nicolás José was sentenced to six years of presidio labor at San Diego with rationed food, no salary, and shackles on his feet. The other two *tomyaars* captured during the revolt were allowed to return to their communities after their two-year sentences were completed (Mason 1975:94; Castillo 1991:18).

Toypurina's fate was quite different. Following her capture she may have feared reprisals by the Spanish as well as retribution from the other warriors who participated in the revolt. She converted to Christianity in March, 1787, taking the name Regina Josefa, and had her Indian marriage set aside at the same time. She was exiled to Mission San Carlos in Monterey, where she married a soldier of the presidio and raised a family of four children. She died at Mission San Juan Bautista in 1799 (Temple 1958:151-152; Castillo 1991:19).

THE REBELLION OF 1810

Relations between the Indians and the Spaniards in California improved during the period from 1780 until 1810 (Mason 1986:7). However, in October and November of 1810 a massive revolt was staged against Mission San Gabriel. The rebellion included both neophytes and non-Christian Indians, the total number of participants being estimated at 800. Although the rebels did not reach San Gabriel, they came within five miles of the mission and made off with 3,000 sheep, which were later recaptured.

Indians participated in this revolt from as far as the Cajón and San Gorgonio passes, a distance of at least 80 miles from San Gabriel. The revolt was brought to an end when Gabriel Moraga arrived from northern California with seven additional soldiers in January, 1811. Forays were made against the *rancherías* involved in the raids, and many Indians were taken prisoner.

Reid may have been referring to this revolt when he wrote that some soldiers took an Indian as a guide and

> went as far as the present Rancho del Chino, where they tied and whipped every man, woman and child in the Lodge [settlement], and drove part of them back with them. On the road they did the same with those of the Lodge at San Jose. On arriving home [at the mission] the men were instructed to throw their bows and arrows at the feet of the Priest, and make due submission.—The infants were then baptized, as were also all children under eight years of age; the former were left with their mothers, but the latter kept apart from all communication with their parents.

As a result of the separation from their children, the women consented to baptism "for the love they bore their offspring," and the men followed suit soon after (Reid 1852:75-76).

By June of 1811 the revolt was over. Twenty-one neophytes and 12 non-Christian Indians were imprisoned as a result of the affair. They were later sent to the presidio at Santa Barbara, lashed for nine consecutive days, and forced to labor on the public works (Engelhardt 1927a:92; Mason 1984:136-137).

LATER REBELLIONS

In February of 1824 the neophytes of Missions Santa Barbara, La Purísima, and Santa Ynez staged the largest Indian rebellion in California history, a revolt that was ignited by the flogging of a neophyte at Santa Ynez. Major battles occurred at all three missions, and ultimately the rebels fled to the San Joaquin Valley, where further skirmishes followed. In March and April, neophytes from Mission San Fernando were reportedly running away to join the rebels, while the neophytes at San Gabriel were showing alarming signs of revolt. These stirrings quieted when a truce was arranged with the rebels in May of the same year (Castillo 1978:103-104).

In October of 1834 the mission rancho at San Bernardino was attacked by Indians; the neophytes living at the rancho were forced to retreat to Mission San Gabriel. In December of the same year a second uprising was led by two ex-neophytes of San Gabriel. The neophytes living at San Bernardino were killed and the rancho buildings burned. A short time later the rancho and other properties of Mission San Gabriel were secularized by the government of California; San Bernardino was eventually granted as a private rancho (Engelhardt 1927a:352-353; Mason, personal communication 1991).

GABRIELINO LIFE OUTSIDE THE MISSIONS

Despite the important role that the mission played in Gabrielino history, not all of the Gabrielino converted to Christianity and joined the missions. In fact, many did not. Nevertheless, even the unconverted Indians, whom the missionaries referred to as "gentiles," inevitably felt the effects of Spanish colonization.

EL PUEBLO DE LA REINA DE LOS ANGELES DE PORCIÚNCULA

In August, 1781, 11 families from Sonora arrived at Mission San Gabriel; the party was a mixed group of Spaniards, Negroes, mulattoes, Mexican Indians, and mestizos. Their goal was to found a pueblo on the Los Angeles River, and late in 1781 El Pueblo de la Reina de los Angeles de Porciúncula was founded (Engelhardt 1927a:48-52). According to the original plan the pueblo was to supply cattle, grain, and broken horses to the presidios of San Diego and Santa Barbara. In addition, the pueblo was intended to serve as a place of retirement for old soldiers whose sons would enlist in the presidio companies (Mason 1975:91).

In fact, from the very beginning the Pueblo of Los Angeles was dependent upon the local Gabrielino population for its survival. Indians provided the labor for plowing, hoeing, and weeding, as well as planting, harvesting, and grinding. They were paid in goods, such as old clothing, grain, cotton yardage, beads, and tools, especially knives and hatchets. In addition, many of the items used in daily life by the settlers were obtained from the Gabrielino. The Indians provided the colonists with baskets, trays, mats, clay and soapstone bowls and pots, tanned deerskins, sealskins, sea otter pelts, and rabbit skin blankets (Mason 1975:94).

The close ties between the Gabrielino and the settlers of the pueblo were strengthened in 1784 and 1785 when some of the settlers took Gabrielino wives. (Wilbur 1937:1861; Mason 1975:94-95). On July 4, 1784, José Carlos Rosas, son of the settler Basilio Rosas, married María Dolores, a Gabrielino woman from *Yaanga*. Two other sons of Basilio Rosas later married Gabrielino women (Wilbur 1937:186; Robinson 1952:13; Mason 1975:95, 1984:133-135).

EARLY RANCHOS

In addition to the missions and the pueblo, the Spanish also established private ranchos within the Gabrielino homeland. These ranchos were independent of the missions and were based upon grants made by the governor of Alta California. The first of these was Rancho San Pedro, also known as the Domínguez Rancho. The date of the original grant is uncertain, although it was made prior to October of 1784. Other early ranchos included San Rafael, granted in October 1784 and located near modern Glendale, and Los Nietos, granted to Manuel Nieto during the same month. Los Nietos, the largest of all, was later divided into five smaller tracts which included Los Cerritos, Los Coyotes, Las Bolsas, Los Alamitos, and Santa Gertrudis. A fourth early rancho was located at Portezuelo, about four Spanish leagues or ten miles from the Los Angeles pueblo, and a fifth, Encino Rancho, was later chosen as the site of Mission San Fernando (Engelhardt 1927a:65-66; Gillingham 1961:44, 89-91).

The Spanish *rancheros* commonly resided at the pueblo of Los Angeles and engaged non-Christian Indians to manage their ranchos. This served to acculturate the Gabrielino and teach them the skills of agriculture and animal husbandry, just as the neophytes learned these skills within the mission. As a result, the labor and subsistence patterns of the Gabrielino changed, and simple agricultural techniques were often combined with traditional hunting and gathering activities.

CHANGING LIFESTYLES

Changes in Gabrielino settlement patterns occurred as well. For example, when Father Vicente de Santa María inspected Rancho Encino in 1795 while seeking a site for Mission San Fernando, he found Indians from at least five different communities residing together and working fields of corn, beans, and melons. Several days later, while passing the "rancho of Verdugo [San Rafael]," the priest found the "gentiles . . . who live contiguous to the ranch" cultivating water melons, sugar melons, beans, and corn (Engelhardt 1927b:5-6). The Franciscan disapproved of the impact the ranchos and the pueblo had on the Gabrielino, and observed that

> the whole pagandom, between this Mission [San Buenaventura] and that of San Gabriel, along the beach, along the camino reál, and along the border of the north, is fond of the Pueblo of Los Angeles, of the rancho of Mariano Verdugo, of the rancho of Reyes, and of the [Rancho La] Zanja. Here we see nothing but pagans passing, clad in shoes, with sombreros and blankets, and serving as muleteers to the settlers and rancheros, so that if it were not for the gentiles there would be neither pueblo nor rancho. . . . Finally these pagan Indians care neither for the Mission nor for the missionaries (Engelhardt 1927b:9).

One of the priests stationed at Mission San Gabriel wrote that in the pueblo and on the ranchos "both men and women who are pagans assist in the work of the fields. Also they are employed as cooks, water carriers and in other domestic occupations." The missionary went on to note that the Indians were paid "by a half or a third of the crops" and as a result "they remain constant in the service of their masters during the season of planting and harvesting" (Geiger and Meighan 1976:129, answer from Mission San Gabriel).

Although problems arose between the Indians and the *rancheros*, informality seems to have marked relations between the Indians and their employers. Problems between the Indians and their employers centered primarily around the treatment and compensation of Indian laborers, and stock stealing. The French explorer Duflot de Mofras, who visited California during the early 1840s, reported that "all labor in El Pueblo is done by Indians recruited from a small ranchería on the banks of the river on the outskirts of the village. These poor wretches are often mistreated, and do not always receive in full their daily pay, which is fixed at one real in money and one real in merchandise" (Wilbur 1937:186).

As a precautionary measure a "Code of Conduct" to regulate interactions between the two groups was published in 1787 by Governor Pedro Fages. One of the primary duties of the Comisionado of the pueblo was to make certain that the laws governing the hiring

of local Indians were observed (Robinson 1952:13-15; Mason 1975, 1984).

CHANGING SETTLEMENT PATTERNS ON THE MAINLAND

The most obvious effect of the founding and growth of the missions, the pueblo, and the private ranchos was the decline of the Gabrielino communities. Three factors contributed to this decline. The first of these was the depopulation of the Indian communities as young, economically productive Indians joined the missions. The second factor was the low birth rate and high death rate that plagued the Gabrielino as syphilis and various other epidemic diseases spread through the population. A third cause of decline was the flight of healthy Indians away from the Los Angeles area to avoid disease or maintain their traditional lifestyle.

By using data from mission records and other sources, an overview of the population changes within the Gabrielino territory can be presented. The first communities to experience depopulation were those located near Mission San Gabriel. For example, between November 1771 and March 1774, the community of *Pemookanga* contributed more than 70 converts to the mission, a loss which probably depopulated the community (Engelhardt 1927a:264-265). *Tohuunga*, *Muuhonga*, and *Pakooynga* were most likely depopulated within a few years of the founding of San Fernando in 1797 (Forbes 1966:144-147). The important ritual center of *Povuu'nga*, located near Alamitos Bay, seems to have been abandoned somewhat later, perhaps by 1805, some of its inhabitants having entered Mission San Gabriel, while others moved to Mission San Juan Capistrano (Merriam 1968:116, 134-135; Dixon 1972:87). The coastal areas of Orange County were probably depopulated prior to 1800, although the interior mountain regions may have remained under Indian control until as late as 1850 (Chace 1966:13; Hudson 1969:61).

Other communities fared better. As late as 1821 *Kaawchama*, the Gabrielino settlement at Rancho San Bernardino, supported 200 Christianized Indians (Shinn 1941:82). *Swaanga* may also have been occupied until fairly late; Reid indicated that *Swaanga* was still a recognizable placename in 1852. The community's longevity may be attributed, in part, to its association with Rancho San Pedro, for *Swaanga* Indians reportedly worked as *vaqueros* at the rancho for many years (Reid 1852:8; Gillingham 1961:80). Another late survivor was an Indian community located near modern Pomona, which reportedly had an Indian population of 200 as late as 1870 and was finally abandoned in 1883 (Johnston 1962:144). An Indian settlement known as the *ranchería*, which was located near the traditional site of *'Akuuronga*, existed until at least the 1870s. The occupants of the *ranchería* worked as laborers at the Sunny Slope vineyards (Rose 1959:54-56).

The community of *Yaanga* survived until 1830 or 1836, although in later years it may have resembled a refugee camp more than a community. *Yaanga* was "adjacent to" the pueblo of Los Angeles. Indians from *Yaanga* supplied the pueblo with cheap labor as well as many of the material goods used by the settlers. This interdependency undoubtedly helped *Yaanga* to survive longer than most other Gabrielino communities (Robinson 1952:11-17).

Yaanga's population in 1803 was reported to be 200, and in the census of the pueblo taken December 31, 1830, Indians were heavily outnumbered by non-Indians, 198 to 764. It should be noted, however, that these figures probably represent the lower limit of the settlement's population. During the spring, *Yaanga*'s population would have swelled with an influx of seasonal laborers seeking work in the ranchos. The Indians were a mixture of Gabrielino, including some islanders, and others from Missions San Diego and San Luis Rey (Robinson 1952:15-17; Mason 1984:128, personal communication 1991).

In 1836, public pressure forced the relocation of *Yaanga* to a new district near the southeast corner of present Commercial and Alameda streets. The new community was called the "Ranchería of Poblanos [settlement of the people]" (Robinson 1952:15-17). The "Ranchería of Poblanos" lasted only ten years. Citizens of the pueblo complained that the Indians were bathing in the *zanja*, the main canal that supplied the pueblo with drinking water, and in June, 1845, the settlement was relocated across the river. Indians were not the only ones guilty of this offense, however, and the relocation may have been politically motivated. A local landowner, Juan Domingo, desired the property occupied by the ranchería; once the Indians were removed Governor Pío Pico sold the property to Juan Domingo for $200.00. The proceeds paid the governor's expenses for a trip north (Robinson 1952:17-19).

The new settlement, known as *Pueblito*, had an even shorter life. For a time it was a favorite gathering spot for American soldiers garrisoned in Los Angeles following the takeover of California; the resentment that this aroused among the Mexican population soon brought such activities to an end. In November, 1847, *Pueblito* was razed to end "disorderly gatherings." A sum total of $24.00 was paid to compensate the Indians for their homes. Thereafter, all employers were required to provide shelter and care for their Indian laborers. Self-employed Indians were required to stay outside the city limits, while unemployed Indians were assigned to the public works or jailed (Robinson 1952:20-21).

CHANGING SETTLEMENT PATTERNS ON THE CHANNEL ISLANDS

The Gabrielino living on the southern Channel Islands also suffered from population decline and displacement. Between 1803 and 1806 a measles epidemic struck Santa Catalina and Santa Cruz islands, killing over 200 Indians (Bancroft 1886:34). As a result, in 1805 the total population of Catalina was estimated to have been only 150, and by 1807 it had dropped still lower to 40 or 50 (Bancroft 1886:84; Shaler 1935:47). Some of the Catalina Gabrielino were relocated to Missions San Gabriel and San Fernando, while others settled near the present town of Carlsbad in the vicinity of Mission San Luis Rey (Roberts 1933:4; Merriam 1968:99, 116).

Although Santa Catalina had, for the most part, been abandoned by 1818, the last inhabitant was not removed until 1832 (Rosen 1980:54; Meighan and Johnson 1957:24). Harrington, writing around 1916, reported that "the last island Indian woman, named Maria . . . died at Las Calabazas 10 or 15 years ago. It is too bad that no one interviewed her. . . . She was living with but not married to Soldaño, a Mexican" (Harrington 1986:R106 F112). Sétimo López told Harrington that "they got José Chári and Maria Chári (a brother and sister) from Catalina. Chári means canasta [basket]. José and Maria lived together at Calabazas. José died first and Maria later" (Harrington 1986:R106 F11). Sétimo had a half-brother, Martin Violin, who was born of a different father; Martin's father was Nicanor Guandía. According to Sétimo, Nicanor "was the one that saco la gente de las islas en a cayuca [removed the people of the islands in a canoe]" (Harrington 1986:R106

F70). Some of the Catalina Gabrielino were allowed to live in the pueblo for a short while, but eventually they were forced to join the other Indians across the river at *Pueblito* (Robinson 1952:22).

The date and circumstances surrounding the abandonment of San Clemente Island are unclear. The first sustained contact between the Spanish and the islanders probably occurred around 1786 as a result of Spanish efforts to develop the sea otter trade. By 1803, the island's population may have dwindled to as few as 11 Indians who were observed living in a rock shelter; it is not clear, however, that these 11 individuals represented the total population of the island (Cleveland n.d.:194; Hatheway and Greenwood 1981:9).

A local tradition says that the San Clemente islanders fled to Santa Catalina to escape the attacks of Russian seal hunters. The last inhabitants may have been removed around 1814 or 1815 and assigned to Mission San Luis Rey (Kroeber 1925:622; Cheetham 1940:43; Hatheway and Greenwood 1981:11). Duflot de Mofras reported that the islanders abandoned their home "to avoid abuse at the hands of American sailors and other foreigners who came over to hunt sea otter and fur seals," although he went on to note that small expeditions were still made to San Clemente to "bring back bits of kaolin or sulphate of iron" (Wilbur 1937:191). Harrington (1933:134-135) reported that pieces of kaolin were used by shamans as power objects and were known as "noot stones" (see Chapter 6 for a discussion of shamanism and power objects); this explains the Indians' willingness to undertake a sea voyage to collect this soft stone. There is also some evidence to suggest that San Clemente may, for a time, have served as a refuge for mission runaways (Zahniser 1981:1-6; Eisentraut 1990).

Many islanders avoided missionization by migrating to the Indian community near the pueblo, where they worked as servants and laborers. An 1830 census shows that Indians from the islands were living in Los Angeles, and some of these may have come from San Clemente (Robinson 1952:22). The establishment of the Plaza Church at Los Angeles in 1826 allowed these Indians to become Christians without joining the mission; in fact, the majority of baptisms of adult islanders did not occur until the 1820s (Johnson 1988:20-21). The strong similarity between the Gabrielino name for San Clemente, *Kiinkepar*, and the community on the Palos Verdes Peninsula known variously as *Kiinkenga* or *Kiinkepar*, suggests that some of the San Clemente Islanders may also have relocated to the Palos Verdes area.

The Gabrielino of San Nicolas Island also suffered from the hardships and upheavals of this period. Groups of Indians from Alaska (which was at the time claimed by Russia) landed on the island during the early decades of the 1800s to hunt sea otter; the reported dates of arrival vary from 1811 to 1825. Quarrels over the Nicoleño women apparently led to fighting and the slaughter of all the Nicoleño men save a few. According to one account, the island had already been severely depopulated by 1825. In 1835, approximately 20 of the surviving Nicoleño were removed to the mainland (Taylor 1860b; Hardacre 1880; Phelps 1961).

Some of the displaced Nicoleño were sent to the pueblo of Los Angeles, where two of the women reportedly married citizens of the town; others went to Mission San Gabriel (Hardacre 1880). One Nicoleño, an Indian man nicknamed Black Hawk who had suffered severe head injuries in fighting the Alaskan Indians, lived for a time on the beach at San Pedro (Nidever 1937:38; Phelps 1961). The last Nicoleño to leave the island, a woman who had accidentally been left behind in 1835, was finally brought to the mainland in 1853 after having lived in isolation for 18 years. She was christened Juana María on her deathbed (more detailed information on Juana María's life is presented in Chapter 11).

THE POST-MISSION PERIOD

Just as the founding and growth of the mission system had a profound impact on the Gabrielino, so the gradual decline of that institution affected them as well. In theory, the missions were never intended to remain in the hands of the missionaries. Rather, ten years after its founding each mission was to have been turned over to Indian leaders and a secular (non-missionary) clergy. The missionaries would then move on to found new missions in a slow, steady wave of expansion across the frontier (W. Bean 1968:29).

In fact, the Franciscans had avoided secularization for many years, claiming that the Indians were not prepared to manage their own affairs (W. Bean 1968:62). Many observers of the missions, however, placed the blame for the Indian's lack of preparedness on the missionaries themselves. Support for secularization increased following Mexico's successful rebellion against Spain and culminated in the Secularization Acts, which were implemented between 1832 and 1834. As a result of these acts, the missions were despoiled by civilians, while the Indians themselves benefitted little from the wealth their labor had created (Castillo 1978:105).

Secularization came as a heavy blow to the Gabrielino, many of whom had remained closely tied to the mission. Reid reported that Indians "were continually running off" due to a lack of food and clothing. "Nearly all of the Gabrielino went north," perhaps to the San Luis Obispo region, although many travelled as far as Monterey. Indians from San Diego, San Luis Rey, and San Juan Capistrano took their places on the ranchos (Reid 1852:98-100).

DISTRIBUTION OF MISSION LANDS

A few Gabrielinos did receive shares of mission land. Victoria Reid, the wife of Reid, was one of these Indian landowners. Through his marriage Reid acquired Rancho Santa Anita, formerly a mission property, while Victoria retained possession of Rancho Huerta de Cuati (also known as Huerta de Peras, the Pear Orchard) in her own name (King 1899:111; Robinson 1952:33).

Other neophytes at Missions San Gabriel and San Fernando received property as well. Governor Pío Pico granted a small rancho near San Gabriel to an Indian named Simeon, while three other Indians, Ramón, Francisco, and Roque, owned the 4,000-acre Rancho El Encino in the San Fernando Valley. Another trio of Indians, Urbano, Odón, and Manuel, petitioned and received the valley rancho of El Escorpión. This rancho later passed to Odón's daughter, María Encarnación Chohuya and her husband (Robinson 1952:33-34, 1966; Harrington 1986:R106 F111; Cohen 1989:16-20).

A neophyte from Mission San Fernando named Samuel received a large tract of land northwest of the mission, which he planted in oranges, pears, and pomegranates; another Indian, José Miguel Triunfo, received a 388-acre grant of Rancho Cahuenga, which he later traded for Rancho Tujunga. José Miguel sold his holdings in 1850. The original site of Mission San Gabriel, known as Misíon Vieja, was until 1840 held by a neophyte on a government grant; however, in that year it was confiscated by the new Mexican government and given to Don Santiago Arguello (Engelhardt 1927a:194; Robinson 1952:33-34; 1966).

The fortunes of Mission San Gabriel reached a low point with the sale of the mission buildings and property by Governor Pío Pico to Reid and William Workman on June 8, 1846. The change in ownership was short-lived, however, for on January 13, 1847, the Californians surrendered to the Americans at Cahuenga. Shortly afterward, the mission buildings and the land on which they stood were returned to the Church (Engelhardt 1927a:221, 224-226).

THE AMERICAN PERIOD

The arrival of the Americans and the subsequent change in government brought new hardships for the Gabrielino. Perhaps the best example of this hardship was the insensitivity Americans displayed toward Indian alcoholism. During the Spanish and Mexican periods, Indians arrested for drunkenness were required to labor on the *zanja* (canal) or at the mission. The Americans added a devious twist to this custom, however. On August 16, 1850, an ordinance was passed that allowed Indians arrested for drunkenness to be auctioned to private parties for one week of labor (Robinson 1952:2-3). The officially stated purpose of the ordinance was to defray the skyrocketing costs associated with feeding and housing inebriated Indians; in fact, the plan was nothing less than a cynical form of self-perpetuating, indentured servitude that ruthlessly destroyed the lives of countless Indians.

To enforce the ordinance, special Indian deputies were locked in jail all day on Sunday to keep them sober. At sundown, these deputies were sent to patrol Los Angeles and Commercial streets as well as Nigger Alley and arrest any drunks they could find. Those arrested were taken to a corral located on the site of the present-day City Hall. The following morning they were put up for auction to the highest bidder (Robinson 1952:2-3).

Unfortunately, the vineyardists were one of the groups that made the most use of the auctioned labor. The average price paid per man was one to three dollars, two-thirds of which was paid at the end of the week to the city to cover the fine, while the rest was paid to the Indian in alcohol. Of course, this virtually ensured that on Monday morning these Indians would again be on the auction block. Individuals enmeshed in this vicious, self-perpetuating cycle usually died within one to three years (Robinson 1952:3).

Disease and starvation continued to stalk the Gabrielino throughout the American Period. The expanding ranchos and vineyards reduced the natural resources available to the Indians, and as a result, droughts and food shortages were felt more keenly than ever. The breakdown of the traditional system of economic exchange further reduced the ability of the Gabrielino to cope with local famines. A particularly severe drought with a corresponding failure of the acorn crop occurred in 1856. In 1863 a smallpox epidemic raged in Los Angeles and took a heavy toll in the Indian and Mexican districts (Newmark 1930:202-203; Cleland 1941:80).

THE GABRIELINO CULTURE IN 1852

Reid provided an important eyewitness account of the Gabrielino culture as it existed in 1852. It was, in fact, the last comprehensive survey of the Gabrielino in the nineteenth century. According to Reid, most of the traditional Gabrielino communities had disappeared by 1852, and many of the Gabrielino had migrated away from their homeland. Small Gabrielino populations could still be found at San Fernando, San Gabriel, and Los Angeles, while "those in service on ranchos are a mere handful." According to Reid, there were more Gabrielino living in Monterey County at that time than in Los Angeles, while "Death has been busy among them for years past, and very few more are wanting to extinguish the lamp that God lighted!" (Reid 1852:100).

The Gabrielino language had also declined, and Reid attributed this to the lack of "Councils" in which "wise men spoke with eloquence suited to the occasion" and "naturally elevated the minds of all" (Reid 1852:101). According to Reid, the Gabrielino practiced two religions, Christianity and their traditional Indian religion. Harrington once listened to a conversation between his consultant Juana Meléndrez and her mother-in-law concerning Indian religion. Juana "laughed . . . & said she didn't see how it was possible to have 2 creencias [beliefs] (e.g. Catholic & Ind.) at [the] same time." But her mother-in-law disagreed because "where one failed the other ayuda [helps]—they go like this (gesture of moving fingers along neck & neck)" (Harrington 1986:R106 F215).

Many Gabrielinos, however, lost faith in their traditional religion. The old Gabrielino gods, the seven "viejos," were thought to have "gone since the

Americans had come with a new religion," and *Taakwesh*, the fearsome cannibal spirit who dwelled in Lily Rock on San Jacinto Peak, had lost much of his terror. "Now taakwic only gets spirits of people who are about to die . . . taakwic no longer kills live or strong people" (Harrington 1986:R106 F215, R105 F299).

The Gabrielino still recognized the office of *tomyaar*, but in San Gabriel in 1852 there were only four and all were young. Their duties included appointing the dates for ceremonial observances and "regulating affairs connected with the church." Shell-bead money had become extremely scarce and was hoarded for use in religious ceremonies (Reid 1852:102-103).

The Gabrielino diet included traditional Indian foods as well as those introduced by the Spanish and Mexicans. Reid observed that "their clothing is of course distinct, and a cloak made of rabbit skins, has within this year or two become a novelty among themselves" (Reid 1852:102). For the most part the Gabrielinos had abandoned traditional Indian marriage rituals, preferring the Catholic ceremony instead. The purification following childbirth was still performed, although those Gabrielinos living or working with non-Indians seem to have abandoned the custom. Shamans had declined much in prestige, although they were still believed able to both cause and cure disease (Reid 1852:102-103).

Reid's Letters to the *Los Angeles Star*, published in 1852, are a twilight account of a people and a culture locked in a desperate struggle for survival. The story of the Gabrielino in the years following 1852 is far more difficult to trace.

THE GABRIELINO AFTER 1852

In June, 1875, Dr. Oscar Loew visited San Gabriel Mission and found only two Indians still speaking Gabrielino, the rest having adopted Spanish. One of these Gabrielino speakers was Fernando Quinto, a 90 year-old *tomyaar* who provided the vocabulary reproduced in Appendix III (from Gatschet 1879:475; see Chapter 1 for more biographical information about Quinto). According to Mrs. James Rosemyre, Gabrielinos in the Tejón region celebrated the Fiesta for the Dead, and perhaps the Girls' Puberty Ceremony, until late in the 1800s (Merriam 1955:84-85).

One local writer noted that Indians and Mexicans were still living in the Eagle Rock and Highland Park

Courtesy of Mr. Roy Rose and the Sunny Slope Water Company

Fig. 75. The *ranchería* at Sunny Slope Vineyards in Pasadena photographed during the late 1800s. Although the homes were constructed using traditional materials such as willow and rushes, rectangular floor plans and gabled roofs replaced the traditional dome-shaped design used prior to the Mission Period.

districts of Los Angeles in 1889. Mexican settlements could be found in the bottom lands of the San Gabriel River in the El Monte-Whittier region. Farther south, Indian settlements existed at Pala, Pauma, Temécula, Pachanga, and San Jacínto. Gabrielinos may have been living in some or all of these tiny communities (Holder 1889:67-68; Forbes 1959).

Gabrielinos resided on the Palos Verdes Peninsula throughout the 1800s. According to information gathered by Harrington, a site known as Fisherman's Camp was occupied by Indians into the 1890s. José Zalvidea reported that Gabrielinos were still living at *Kiinke*, or *Kiinkenga*, in the early 1900s, and his report was confirmed by José de los Santos Juncos (Harrington 1986:R105 F699, R102 F340, 358).

As mentioned earlier in this chapter, a settlement known as the *ranchería*, located near the traditional

site of *'Akuuronga*, survived at least into the 1870s. The Indians at the *ranchería*, some of whom could have been Gabrielino, worked as laborers at the Sunny Slope Vineyards owned by L. J. Rose. The owner's son, L. J. Rose Jr., spent much of his childhood visiting the *ranchería* and has left a brief but valuable description of Indian life in Los Angeles in the late 1800s.

According to Rose, the *ranchería* was five acres in extent and was occupied by Indians and Mexicans who frequently intermarried. Houses were constructed of tules gathered from a nearby marsh. The walls were six inches thick and held in place by willow rods lashed with cowhide; the roofs were similarly constructed. Although the floor was earthen, the buildings were "proof against rain and were quite warm and comfortable" (Rose 1959:54-55).

A simple lean-to, open on one side, served as a kitchen. Stoves were rarely used; instead, a stone fire ring supported the cooking utensils. Food consisted primarily of boiled beans refried with a small quantity of lard, sun-dried meat roasted over the embers of the fire, and coffee. Tortillas, made from corn, water, and salt, were toasted on a piece of sheet iron placed over the fire (Rose 1959:55).

Estimates of the present Gabrielino population are difficult to verify, and decades of population movement, intermarriage, and absorption into the general "Mexican" population of southern California render the task even more formidable. As late as 1952, ninth-generation descendants of María Dolores, a Gabrielino from *Yaanga*, and her husband José Carlos Rosas, a settler from the Pueblo of Los Angeles, were reported living in San Gabriel (Robinson 1952:13).

SUMMARY

The first recorded contact between Europeans and the Gabrielino occurred in 1542 with the arrival of Cabrillo's small fleet at Santa Catalina Island. The second recorded European visit came in 1602 when the Sebastián Vizcaíno Expedition visited San Clemente and Santa Catalina islands and the mainland near San Pedro. Although other voyagers may have passed near the Gabrielino coast, no other contacts between Europeans and the Gabrielino were recorded until the colonization of California by the Spanish commenced in 1769. In that year, an expedition led by Gaspar de Portolá established settlements at San Diego and at Monterey. The Portolá party crossed the Gabrielino homeland twice in 1769, and several accounts of this expedition have been published.

Mission San Gabriel was founded on September 8, 1771, at a location near Whittier Narrows. Conflict immediately erupted between the Indians and the guards at the mission; the worst violence was brought about by the rape of a local *tomyaar*'s wife by one of the Spanish soldiers. The arrival of additional guards restored the peace, but the Gabrielino permanently abandoned several nearby communities. As a consequence, the recruitment and conversion of the Indians remained slow for the first few years of the mission's existence. Mission San Gabriel was moved from its original location (near Whittier Narrows) to its present site around 1774; the reason for the move was to obtain land more suitable for agriculture. A second mission was founded within the Gabrielino territory in 1797 and named San Fernando.

The type of mission established in Alta California was known as a *reducción*; the purpose of a *reducción* was to "reduce" or consolidate the Indians from the countryside into one central community. Each mission was a sprawling community in which hundreds and sometimes thousands of Indians lived and worked. Each mission also had a set of outlying ranchos where stock raising and agriculture were pursued. Political authority within the missions was a hierarchy with the priests at the top. The missionaries delegated most of the work to a head mayordomo (who was often a soldier of the guard) and he, in turn, delegated work to lesser mayordomos who might be Indians. The Indians elected from their own ranks officials to serve as *alcaldes* and *regidores*; these officials acted as constables and were responsible for administering punishments.

Mission life was highly regimented and contrasted dramatically with the traditional Gabrielino lifestyle. Areas in which the conflict between mission life and the traditional Gabrielino customs were most apparent include the following: the use of corporal punishment rather than traditional Gabrielino punishments; overcrowding in the Indians' living quarters at the missions; the enforcement of Hispanic sexual customs and morals, which may have been more rigid than traditional Gabrielino sexual mores; the imposition of a European-style work ethic; and the imposition of Catholic religious beliefs and rituals, and intolerance for traditional Indian ceremonies and customs. Indians who converted to Christianity were not free to renounce their conversions; those wishing to leave the missions were forced to become fugitives. These runaways sometimes fled as far as the San Joaquin Valley.

Spanish colonization had a dramatic and negative impact on Gabrielino society. The traditional Indian communities were depopulated as the younger members were drawn into the labor forces of the missions or the ranchos. Epidemics caused by the introduction of European diseases (for which the Gabrielino had no immunities) further reduced the Indian population. A number of violent attacks on the mission occurred as a direct response to the social disruption brought about by missionization. Major rebellions at Mission San Gabriel have been recorded for the years 1779, 1785 and 1810.

Mexico achieved its independence from Spain in 1822. Ten years later, between 1832 and 1834, the Mexican government implemented a series of Secularization Acts that were theoretically designed to turn control of the missions over to the Indians. Although a few Indians received shares of the mission lands, most of the property was despoiled by greedy civilians. The primary result of the Secularization Acts was increased fugitivism among the Gabrielino.

The American takeover of California brought further hardships to the Gabrielino. An ordinance passed in 1850 allowed Indians arrested for drunkenness to be auctioned off to private parties for a week of labor. The result of this system was a form of self-perpetuating, indentured servitude that destroyed many lives.

During the late 1800s, Gabrielino may have been living in some of the small Indian and Mexican settlements located in Eagle Rock and the Highland Park districts of Los Angeles. Others may have resided in the El Monte-Whittier region, or further south at Pala, Pauma, Temécula, Pachanga, and San Jacínto. A site known as Fishermen's Camp on the Palos Verdes Peninsula was occupied by Indians into the 1890s, and the traditional site of *Kiinkenga*, which was also located on Palos Verdes, had Gabrielino occupants in the early 1900s.

The Gabrielino survived missionization, epidemic diseases, and the political upheavals of the 1800s. Although their population was reduced and dispersed and their culture was fragmented, the people endured. In the early 1900s, small groups of Gabrielino still gathered at scattered locations to talk and reminisce about their people and their culture. A number of these individuals also shared their memories with early researchers such as Merriam and Harrington, thereby preserving this information for future generations.

Chapter 11 recounts the stories of two Indians whose lives mirrored the tumultuous events of the 1800s. The first of these individuals is Juana María, the famed Lone Woman of San Nicolas Island; the second is Rogerio Rocha, an Indian who was born and raised at Mission San Fernando. Their brief biographies stand as testimonials to thousands of other Gabrielinos whose stories will never be told.

CHAPTER 11

VOICES FROM THE PAST

The study of the Gabrielino and their culture has enriched our understanding of the vital role these Indians played in the history of Los Angeles. This knowledge has also challenged some of the basic assumptions underlying traditional theories of cultural evolution. Many of these theories have been based on studies of early food-producing societies; in fact, agriculture has generally been regarded as the primary stimulus for advanced cultural developments such as calendars, astronomy, and complex systems of ritual and ceremony (Hudson 1988).

The Gabrielino did not practice agriculture; instead, their economy was based solely upon hunting and gathering. Nonetheless, these Indians possessed solar and lunar calendars, a well-developed astronomy, and an elaborate cycle of seasonal rituals. They also created a sophisticated theology centered on the supernatural being *Chengiichngech* and a viable system of economic exchange based upon a standardized shell-bead currency. These impressive achievements not only underscore the sophistication of Gabrielino society, but also suggest that both historically and functionally such cultural advances were not dependent on the prior appearance of agriculture and may, in fact, have been present in some early hunting-gathering societies elsewhere in the world.

Each year new research increases our knowledge of this fascinating people. Archaeological investigations, especially those on the Channel Islands where the impact of southern California's tremendous population growth has been less severe, continue to improve our understanding of Gabrielino settlement and subsistence patterns. These studies may one day also provide a more complete picture of the early maritime cultures that preceded the First Angelinos on these islands. Future ethnographic research will rely heavily upon the mission registers and other sources of archival data to expand our understanding of Gabrielino political and economic organization during the historic period.

Historical and archival research will also provide a clearer picture of the decline of Gabrielino society in the years following 1852. The history of the Gabrielino in those years is one of a creative, resolute people struggling to survive in the face of overwhelming acculturation. The lives of two individuals caught in this cultural cross fire are vivid examples of the struggle many of these Indians faced in the middle to late 1800s.

JUANA MARÍA: THE LONE WOMAN OF SAN NICOLAS ISLAND

The central character of the first biography is Juana María, the fabled "Lone Woman of San Nicolas Island." The tale of her 18 years of solitude on San Nicolas and her rescue in 1853 has been reported by a number of early writers (see O'Dell 1960; Heizer and Elsasser 1961). Many details of this story remain cloudy; nothing, however, can diminish the drama of the Robinson Crusoe-like ordeal of Juana María.

Her story begins in the early years of the 1800s, when European and American fur companies began sending hunting parties to the Channel Islands to gather sea otter pelts. These hunters, variously described as "Kodiaks" or "Russian Indians," were brought from Alaska and landed on the islands for extended periods of time. As many as three hunting ships were in the vicinity of San Nicolas during the years 1810-1811, and according to one account 30 hunters may have been camped on the island (Warner 1856; Taylor 1860b; Woodward 1957:253-255; Phelps 1961).

Conflicts between the Nicoleño and the "Russian Indians" arose when the latter tried to procure Nicoleño women. One account states that the hunters killed all but seven of the Nicoleño men, while another reports that the Nicoleño women avenged the deaths of their husbands by murdering all of the Russian Indians in their sleep. Ultimately, however, the Nicoleño were unable to defend themselves from further attacks and they agreed to relocate to the mainland. The priests at Mission Santa Barbara are credited with dispatching a schooner called the *Peor es Nada* to San Nicolas in 1835 to remove the islanders. The ship arrived at the island on August 3rd or 4th; the surviving Indians were gathered on the shore. Estimates of the number of Nicoleño removed from the island vary widely, from as few as four to as many as 20 (Taylor 1860b; Hardacre 1880; Nidever 1937:37-38; Woodward 1957:254-255; Phelps 1961).

While the Indians were waiting to board the ship a sudden storm arose, and in the urgency of the evacuation a young woman in her mid-20s was left on the island. The circumstances of her abandonment are unclear. One account states that she was gathering plant foods in the island's interior when the ship departed. Another says that she left the boarding party at the shore and returned home to find her child, who had accidentally been left behind. A third account reports that the woman was already on board one of the boats when she discovered that her child was missing and that she jumped overboard and swam ashore; due to the rising storm, the *Peor es Nada* was forced to sail without her (Hardacre 1880; Nidever 1937:37-38; Woodward 1957:255-256; Phelps 1961).

The Nicoleño refugees were taken to San Pedro and from there to Los Angeles and San Gabriel. One Nicoleño, a man nicknamed Black Hawk, had suffered head injuries in skirmishes with the Russian Indians; he remained in San Pedro, living on the beach with a group of hunters. Two of the women reportedly married wealthy men in Los Angeles. According to the existing accounts, all but two of the Nicoleño died soon after reaching the mainland. Black Hawk was blinded by disease while living in San Pedro; he later fell from a steep bank and drowned in the ocean. He may have been buried on Deadman's Island, which was a prominent landmark at the entrance to San Pedro Harbor until it was removed during harbor expansion in the years 1927 to 1929 (Warner 1856; Hardacre 1880; Nidever 1937:38; Woodward

1957:254; Gleason 1958:115-116; Phelps 1961; Queenan 1986:91).

The *Peor es Nada* was scheduled to return to San Nicolas and rescue the Indian woman; however, several prior commitments intervened. During one of these voyages, while hauling a load of lumber to San Francisco the vessel capsized at the entrance to the Golden Gate. The crew reached the shore safely, but the vessel was lost at sea. As there was no other ship on the west coast capable of making the trip to San Nicolas, all plans of rescuing the Nicoleño girl were abandoned.

Fifteen years passed before another attempt was made to locate the Indian woman. In 1850, a Californian named Thomas Jeffries came into possession of a small sailing vessel. Jeffries was reportedly paid $200 by Father Gonzales of Mission Santa Barbara to sail to San Nicolas and find the Indian girl or her child. The search was unsuccessful; however, Jeffries apparently restricted his efforts to a cursory search of the island's beaches and made no attempt to investigate the interior (Hardacre 1880; Hudson 1981:189-190).

Despite his failure, Jeffries returned to Santa Barbara with glowing tales of the herds of seal and sea otter that he had observed near San Nicolas. His stories caught the attention of George Nidever, a fur trapper and adventurer who had come to California in 1833 with the Joseph Reddeford Walker Party, and together they planned a trip to the island in Nidever's schooner (Hardacre 1880; Nidever 1937:77; Woodward 1957:257).

In April of 1852, Nidever and Jeffries sailed to San Nicolas to hunt and gather seagull eggs, which at that time were in great demand. While on the island, the two men discovered footprints in soft soil near a cluster of small brush enclosures a short distance from the beach. Nearby, strips of seal blubber dried in the open air, suspended from poles driven into the ground. These discoveries convinced Nidever that the Nicoleño girl was alive; however, the onset of a fierce gale prevented any further search. The schooner was forced to lie off San Nicolas for eight days. It finally made a run to Santa Barbara Island and thence to the mainland. An Indian crewman aboard the schooner claimed to have seen a woman running along the shore during the storm, beckoning and shouting to the sailors (Hardacre 1880; Nidever 1937:77-78).

Nidever made his second trip to San Nicolas in the winter of 1852. He was accompanied on this trip by Carl Dittman, who was also known by the nickname "Charlie Brown." Several new discoveries were made during this voyage. Dittman found a set of footprints on the beach, but unfortunately the trail disappeared where it crossed a moss-covered bank. He also found a piece of driftwood that had been accidentally dropped beside a trail.

Together, Nidever and Dittman discovered a basket lodged in the crotch of a high bush. The basket was covered with a piece of sealskin and inside was an assortment of bone needles, sinew rope, and skins of the shag, a small cormorant. The men scattered these articles upon the ground in the hope that the owner would replace them and thereby give proof of her presence. They then began hunting otter, but three or four days later were again driven from the island by foul weather, running to San Miguel Island and thence to the mainland (Nidever 1937:79-80; Dittman 1961).

The following summer, Nidever, Dittman, and an Irishman nicknamed "Colorado" travelled to San Nicolas, accompanied by four Mission Indians from Santa Barbara. One of these Indians has been identified as a Ventureño Chumash hunter named Melquiares *Shustu*. When the party arrived at San Nicolas, fresh footprints were discovered in wet soil surrounding Old Garden Spring, located near the beach on the north shore of the island. It was already late in the day when the discovery was made, so a thorough search was postponed until the following morning (Nidever 1937:80-81; Woodward 1957:260; Hudson 1981:190).

The next day the search began in earnest. The men formed two groups, Nidever and Dittman in one, Colorado and three of the Indians in the other. Colorado and the Indians rediscovered the basket that Nidever and Dittman had found on the previous trip, the contents of which had been carefully replaced. Meanwhile, Nidever and Dittman worked their way toward the northwest end of the island. While Nidever stopped for a short rest, Dittman continued on toward the island's tip, where he began climbing a long slope (Nidever 1937:81; Woodward 1957:260-261).

When Dittman reached the ridge he paused to catch his breath, allowing his gaze to wander across the landscape. In the distance he spotted a small, black dot which seemed to be moving; he imagined it was a crow sitting on a bush. His curiosity piqued, he advanced cautiously. As he drew closer he realized that he was seeing the head and shoulders of an Indian woman above the low walls of a whale bone hut. He had found the Lone Woman of San Nicolas!

When Dittman came upon the woman she was skinning a seal with a knife made from a piece of iron hoop hafted in a wooden handle. She talked to herself continuously as she worked, occasionally pausing to follow the progress of the search party, which she could clearly see from her position. Near the house were several dogs. They growled at Dittman as he approached, but the woman sent them away with a yell, unaware of the man's presence. Dittman signaled to the men in the search party by removing the ramrod from his rifle and using it to raise his hat, and they quickly surrounded the house (Nidever 1937:81-82; Woodward 1957:261; Dittman 1961).

When Nidever reached the ridge he found the other men seated around the woman. He described her as about 50 years of age, of medium height, and rather thick in build. Her hair, once black, was now thickly matted and bleached to a dull brown color. Her features were pleasant, but her teeth were worn to the gums, probably from chewing grit mixed with food prepared in stone mortars. Such tooth wear was common in Indian populations prior to the adoption of a European diet. She wore a single, sleeveless garment sewn from shag (cormorant) skins, which fitted close at the neck and reached almost to her feet. The garment was girded at the waist with a sinew cord. A second, similar dress was stored in a basket nearby (Nidever 1937:83-84; Woodward 1957:264).

The woman's home, a roofless house located near the best spring of water and the best spot for taking fish and seal, commanded a good view of most of the island. Outside the house were several baskets, some unfinished, and two tarred water bottles, as well as an assortment of bone needles, fishhooks, and sinew cords. Blubber hung from stakes and from a sinew rope stretched between two poles. During the rainy season, a nearby cave provided a dry shelter (Nidever 1937:84).

The woman served her guests a meal of roots, which she roasted in the fire burning within the hut, and then accompanied them back to the schooner. The men helped carry her personal possessions, which had been loaded into baskets. They stopped at a spring near the beach so the woman could wash herself, then proceeded to the ship. In place of her feather garment Dittman sewed her a petticoat of cotton ticking, which she wore with a man's cotton shirt and a black necktie (Nidever 1937:84-85).

The Indian woman lived at the camp on the beach for the next month while the men hunted. During this time she supplied the men with water and firewood and worked on her baskets. The hunters made a toy for her by stuffing a dead sea otter pup and hanging it by a string from the ceiling of her shelter. She amused herself by lying on her back and swinging it overhead (Nidever 1937:86).

When the hunt was complete the party set sail for the mainland, but en route they encountered yet another of the storms so frequent near San Nicolas. The woman dropped to her knees while facing the wind, apparently praying to bring the storm to an end. She repeated this behavior several times that day, and seemed quite satisfied when the storm subsided (Nidever 1937:87).

When the schooner reached Santa Barbara a variety of new experiences awaited the Nicoleño woman. She was especially delighted by the sight of an oxcart and a man on horseback. She lived with the Nidever family and received a steady stream of guests. Indians from Ventura, Santa Barbara, and Santa Ynez tried conversing with her; however, it was reported that none could understand her language. Unsuccessful attempts were also made to speak to her in Fernandeño and Catalineño (Hardacre 1880; Kroeber 1925:634; Nidever 1937:87-88; Woodward 1957:266-267; Hudson 1981:194). Four of her words were recorded: "*to-co* (reportedly pronounced to-kay')" for hide; "*nache* (nah'-chey)" for man; "*te-gua* (taý-gwah)" for sky; and "*pínche* (pin-oo-chey)" for body (Hardacre 1880). On the basis of these words Kroeber suggested that the woman's language was Shoshonean, or Uto-Aztecan, although the dialect could not be established (Kroeber 1925:633; see also Munro 1994).

The woman frequently sang and danced for her hosts, and four of her songs, or perhaps two different versions of the same two songs, were memorized by Melquiares Shustu. Later, these songs were passed on to Fernando Librado, a Ventureño Chumash, and were recorded on wax cylinders by Harrington in 1913 (Hudson 1981:191, 194; see also Munro 1994).

The woman's time following her arrival in Santa Barbara was all too brief. Her fondness for unfamiliar foods, such as green corn, vegetables, and fresh fruits, provoked attacks of dysentery, and a fall from the Nidever's porch left her with an injured spine. In addition, she became depressed when none of her kinsmen could be found. On Tuesday, October 18, 1853, seven weeks after arriving in Santa Barbara, the Lone Woman of San Nicolas died. She was christened Juana María on her deathbed, and her body was buried in the Nidever family plot in the cemetery at Santa Barbara Mission (Hardacre 1880; Woodward 1957:267-268).

Juana María's death did not dispel the aura of mystery surrounding her story, however. All of the objects brought to the mainland at the time of her rescue have since disappeared. The lost items include a feather dress, a feather cape, sandals, necklaces, fishhooks, a stone mortar, and tarred water bottles. She gave many of the smaller objects as gifts to people in Santa Barbara; the feather dress was reportedly sent to Rome by the priests at the mission, but it has never been located. Many, perhaps most, of her possessions were housed in the California Academy of Sciences in San Francisco and were burned in the great fire that followed the 1906 earthquake (Woodward 1957:268-269; Heizer 1960; Hudson 1981:195-197; Geiger n.d.:13). A photograph of a tarred water bottle reportedly made by Juana María appears in Chapter 7.

Two final notes bring to a close the strange, sad story of Juana María. Her exact place of burial in the Santa Barbara Mission cemetery is unmarked, but in 1928 a bronze plaque commemorating her life was placed on the back wall of the mission tower near the cemetery (Geiger n.d.:13-14). Eleven years later, in 1939, an archaeological expedition sponsored by the Natural History Museum of Los Angeles County visited San Nicolas Island. Using Nidever's account as a guide, the members retraced the route followed by Dittman and Nidever and rediscovered what they believed to be the remains of Juana María's whale bone hut. On a second trip, in 1940, the fragments of the house were re-erected. Years later, one member of the party returned to find the walls of the house fallen, the whale bone slowly weathering into the soil (Woodward 1957:262-264; Morgan 1979).

ROGERIO ROCHA

The second biography is the story of Rogerio Rocha, an Indian born at Mission San Fernando in 1801. Rogerio was baptized in 1810 and trained at the mission as a blacksmith; he also served as a lay reader in the church. In addition to his prominent position at the mission, Rogerio had political ties to the Chumash community at Malibu and participated in Chumash fiestas (Rust 1904:63-64; Librado and Harrington 1977:31, 91).

When Rogerio left the mission he moved to a ten-acre plot of land near San Fernando, which he may have obtained following the secularization of the mission. For 60 years this was his home. He constructed an adobe house, two wood-frame buildings, and two or three tule houses on his property, which contained a good spring of fresh water. Rogerio also planted many fruit trees on his land (Rust 1904:64). Harrington visited this site, probably around 1916, and described it as "roughly speaking one-half mile west of the center of San Fernando town and two blocks north of the S. P. [Southern Pacific] track" (Harrington 1986:R106 F155).

Despite his lengthy residence on this property, Rogerio was cheated out of his ownership through a series of deceptive legal maneuvers. Rogerio's land was part of the holdings of the De Celis family, and the original land grant specified that the owners were not to disturb any of the Indians living within the boundaries of the grant. However, in or about 1875, the property was sold to two Americans; the clause specifying the Indians' property rights was left out of the terms of sale. Although the De Celis family protested the omission, they were assured by the attorneys handling the transaction that the Indians would not be disturbed (Rust 1904:64-66).

The new owners intended to subdivide the property and use the spring on Rogerio's land to provide water to the town lots. In 1878 they brought suit to evict Rogerio, and eventually they obtained a judgement by default. Eight years later, during the winter of 1886, Rogerio and his wife were evicted; both were 80 or more years of age. Three elderly women living with them were also forced to move. On the advice of his attorney, Rogerio passively resisted the eviction; he was forcibly placed in a cart

Courtesy of the Southest Museum, Los Angeles, Photo. No. 22126
Fig. 76. Rogerio Rocha, an Indian born at Mission San Fernando in 1801. Rogerio's story reflects the tragedy that befell many of the Indians of southern California during the late 1800s.

and transported two miles to the public road, where the women and their possessions were waiting.

The eviction coincided with the onset of a four-day winter rainstorm, and Rogerio immediately set out to seek help from friends. The rain destroyed their food supplies and other perishable goods, but more tragically, Rogerio's wife contracted pneumonia in the cold, wet weather. Although the Indians eventually found shelter in an old building at Mission San Fernando, Rogerio's wife did not recover. Rogerio conducted her funeral ceremony himself.

Despite his misfortunes, Rogerio lived another 18 years. A Mexican friend loaned him a small patch of land in López Canyon west of Little Tujunga Canyon, and here he lived in peace; he died in 1904 at more than 100 years of age (Rust 1904:68; Harrington 1986:R106 F136, 166).

THE GABRIELINO HERITAGE

Today there is a growing awareness of the enormous debt that Los Angeles owes the Gabrielino. Although the city traditionally traces its cultural heritage to Spanish and American roots, it was the Gabrielino who built and supported the missions, the Pueblo, and the ranchos. It was the Gabrielino who provided the goods and labor that enabled the first settlements to survive and prosper; without them the history of Los Angeles would be very different indeed.

Reminders of the Gabrielino and their culture are scattered across the United States. Artifact collections can be found in museums in Los Angeles and Orange counties, including the Catalina Island Museum in Avalon, the Southwest Museum, and the Natural History Museum of Los Angeles County. The Peabody Museum of American Archaeology and Ethnology, Harvard University, retains a large collection of Gabrielino material gathered in the late 1800s and early 1900s. More modest artifact collections can be found in several university repositories.

Ethnographic notes on the Gabrielino are on file at The Bancroft Library, University of California at Berkeley, in the Field Museum in Chicago, in the National Anthropological Archives in the Smithsonian Institution, and in the Library of Congress in Washington D.C. The mission registers of San Gabriel and San Fernando preserve important biographical and demographic data. Reference copies of these registers are located at the Chancery Archives of the Archdiocese of Los Angeles at Mission San Fernando and at the Santa Barbara Mission Archive Library. Other early historical records are archived in Spain and Mexico. Most importantly, however, the people themselves, the descendants of the Indians described in this volume, are living testimony to the endurance of the Gabrielino spirit.

A more subtle reminder of the Gabrielino can be found in the land that was once their home. The Gabrielino understood the natural world in a special way. To the Gabrielino, Earth was a sacred being who provided food, shelter, and all the necessities of life. The Gabrielino held their homeland in reverence, and it is fitting that the protection and preservation of surviving natural areas within Los Angeles remains an important concern of their descendants. A number of local placenames such as Cahuenga, Cucamonga, Pacoima, Topanga, and Azusa are derived from Gabrielino names and serve as reminders of the Indian people who once inhabited this region.

Indeed, despite smog, congested freeways, and urban sprawl, the Gabrielino homeland still inspires feelings of awe and wonder in those sensitive enough to appreciate its natural splendor. Sometimes these feelings emerge in moments of delicate beauty: the sight of a hawk soaring gracefully over an open field; the sound of a meadowlark singing on a warm spring morning; the cool dampness of fog creeping across the land on a winter afternoon. Moments such as these link the modern Angelino to the Gabrielino of yesterday.

Perhaps the best time to appreciate the beauty of the Gabrielino homeland is during the winter, for it is then that rainstorms cleanse the sky and impart unusual clarity to the atmosphere. A drive to the top of one of the hills scattered throughout the region reveals a breathtaking view. A broad, flat plain stretches from the ocean northward, ending abruptly at the base of towering mountains with snowcapped peaks. The curving coastline is broken by the silvery reflections of numerous bays and inlets, while across the slate-gray Pacific the dark mass of Santa Catalina Island rises out of the ocean mist.

As sunset approaches, the western horizon glows with brilliant hues of yellow, orange, and red, while in the east the sky is darkened by the Earth's rising shadow. In the brief moments before street lamps break the darkness, roads and buildings fade from view, and two centuries of history seem to disappear. At such moments it is easy to imagine that porpoises guard the world and powerful shamans transform themselves into grizzly bears, while *Chengiichngech* watches over and protects his people in the land of the First Angelinos.

REFERENCES

Alliot, Hector
1916   Burial Methods of the Southern California Islanders. *Bulletin of the Southern California Academy of Sciences* 15(1). (Reprinted, *The Masterkey* 43(4):125-131.)
1917   Pre-Historic Use of Bitumen in Southern California. *Bulletin of the Southern California Academy of Sciences* 16(2). (Reprinted, *The Masterkey* 44(3):96-102.)

Applegate, Richard B.
1978   *'Atishwin: the Dream Helper in South-Central California.* BP-AP No. 13, Lowell John Bean and Thomas C. Blackburn, series editors. Ballena Press, Socorro, New Mexico.

Armstrong, Wayne P.
1986   The Deadly Datura. *Pacific Discovery* 39(4):34-41.

Ashby, G. E., and J. W. Winterbourne
1966   A Study of Primitive Man in Orange County and Some of Its Coastal Areas. *Pacific Coast Archaeological Society Quarterly* 2(1):5-52.

Balls, Edward
1962   *Early Uses of California Plants.* University of California Press, Berkeley.

Bancroft, Hubert Howe
1886   *The Works of Hubert Howe Bancroft, Vol. XIX: History of California Vol. II, 1801-1824.* The History Company, San Francisco. (Facsimile reprint, Wallace Hebberd, Santa Barbara, 1966.)

Bates, Eleanor
1972   Los Altos, (Lan-270): A Late Horizon Site in Long Beach, California. *Pacific Coast Archaeological Society Quarterly* 8(2):1-56.

Bean, Lowell John
1972a   *Mukat's People: The Cahuilla Indians of Southern California.* University of California Press, Berkeley.
1972b   Introduction. In *Aboriginal Society in Southern California,* by William Duncan Strong, pp. xi-xxiv. Malki Museum Press, Banning, California.
1974   Social Organization in Native California. In *'Antap: California Indian Political and Economic Organization,* edited by Lowell John Bean and Thomas King, pp. 13-34. BP-AP No.2, Lowell John Bean, series editor. Ballena Press, Ramona, California.
1975   Power and Its Applications in Native California. *The Journal of California Anthropology* 2(1):25-33.
1976   California Indian Shamanism and Folk Curing. In *American Folk Medicine: A Symposium,* edited by Wayland D. Hand, pp. 109-121. University of California Press, Berkeley.

1978   Cahuilla. In *California,* edited by Robert F. Heizer, pp. 575-587. Handbook of North American Indians, vol. 8, W. C. Sturtevant, general editor. Smithsonian Institution, Washington, D.C.

Bean, Lowell John and Thomas C. Blackburn (editors)
1976   *Native Californians: A Theoretical Retrospective.* Ballena Press, Menlo Park, California.

Bean, Lowell John, and Thomas F. King (editors)
1974   *'Antap: California Indian Political and Economic Organization.* BP-AP No. 2, Lowell John Bean, series editor. Ballena Press, Ramona, California.

Bean, Lowell John, and Katherine Siva Saubel
1972   *Temalpakh: Cahuilla Indian Knowledge and Usage of Plants.* Malki Museum Press, Banning, California.

Bean, Lowell John, and Charles R. Smith
1978   Gabrielino. In *California,* edited by Robert F. Heizer, pp. 538-549. Handbook of North American Indians, vol. 8, W. C. Sturtevant, general editor. Smithsonian Institution, Washington, D.C.

Bean, Walton
1968   *California: An Interpretive History.* McGraw-Hill, New York. (Reprinted, McGraw-Hill, New York, 1973.)

Beck, Warren A., and Ynez D. Haase
1974   *Historical Atlas of California.* University of Oklahoma Press, Norman.

Benson, Arlene
1980   California Sun-Watching Site. *Archaeoastronomy: The Bulletin of the Center for Archaeoastronomy* 3(1):16-19.

Bickford, Virginia, and Patricia Martz
1980   Test Excavations at Cottonwood Creek, Catalina Island, California. *Pacific Coast Archaeological Society Quarterly* 16(1/2):107-124.

Black, Esther Boulton
1975   *Rancho Cucamonga and Doña Merced.* San Bernardino County Museum Association, Redlands, California.

Blackburn, Thomas
1963   Ethnohistoric Descriptions of Gabrielino Material Culture. *University of California Archaeological Survey Annual Report* 1962-1963:1-50. Los Angeles.
1975   *December's Child: A Book of Chumash Oral Narratives.* University of California Press, Berkeley.
1976   A Query Regarding the Possible Hallucinogenic Effects of Ant Ingestion in South-Central California. *The Journal of California Anthropology* 3(2):78-81.

Blackburn, Thomas C., and Lowell John Bean
1978   Kitanemuk. In *California,* edited by Robert F. Heizer, pp. 564-569. Handbook of North American Indians, vol.

8, W. C. Sturtevant, general editor. Smithsonian Institution, Washington, D.C.

Bolton, Herbert Eugene
1908 *Spanish Exploration in the Southwest, 1542-1706.* Charles Scribner's Sons, New York. (Reprinted, Barnes and Noble, New York, 1952.)
1926 *Historical Memoirs of New California by Fray Francisco Palou, O.F.M.* University of California Press, Berkeley. (Reprinted, Russell and Russell, New York, 1966.)
1927 *Fray Juan Crespi: Missionary Explorer on the Pacific Coast, 1769-1771.* University of California Press, Berkeley. (Reprinted, AMS Press, New York, 1971.)
1930 *Anza's California Expeditions, Vol. IV: Font's Complete Diary of the Second Anza Expedition.* University of California Press, Berkeley.

Boscana, Father Gerónimo
1933 *Chinigchinich: A Revised and Annotated Version of Alfred Robinson's Translation of Father Gerónimo Boscana's Historical Account of the Belief, Usages, Customs and Extravagancies of the Indians of this Mission of San Juan Capistrano Called the Acagchemem Tribe.* Fine Arts Press, Santa Ana. (Reprinted, Malki Museum Press, Banning, California, 1978.)

Bright, William
1978 Preface. In *Chinigchinich: A Revised and Annotated Version of Alfred Robinson's Translation of Father Gerónimo Boscana's Historical Account of the Belief, Usages, Customs and Extravagancies of the Indians of this Mission of San Juan Capistrano Called the Acagchemem Tribe*, by Father Gerónimo Boscana, pp iii-vii. Malki Museum Press, Banning, California.

Brown, Alan K.
1967 The Aboriginal Population of the Santa Barbara Channel. *University of California Archaeological Survey Report 69.* Berkeley.

Bryan, Bruce
1970a Archaeological Explorations on San Nicolas Island. *Southwest Museum Papers 22.* Southwest Museum, Los Angeles.
1970b The Manufacture of Stone Mortars. *Southwest Museum Leaflets No. 34.* Southwest Museum, Los Angeles.

Buschmann, Johann Karl Eduard
1855 *Die Sprachen Kizh und Netela von Neu-Californien.* Konigliche Akademie der Wissenschaften, Abhandlungen:501-531. Berlin.

Butler, William B.
1974 The San Pedro Harbor Site: A Primary Subsistence Village on the Southern California Coast. *Pacific Coast Archaeological Society Quarterly* 10(3/4):1-98.

California Private Land Claims
n.d.a *Docket 414, Rancho Sausal Redondo.* Microfilm Publication T910, Rolls 50/51. On file, National Archives, Laguna Niguel.
n.d.b *Docket 578, Rancho Santiago de Santa Ana.* Microfilm Publication T910, Roll 107. On file, National Archives, Laguna Niguel.

Cameron, Constance
1983 Birdstones of Orange Country. *The Masterkey* 57(2):63-67.
1988 Birdstones and their Associations. *Pacific Coast Archaeological Society Quarterly* 24(4):54-62.
1990 Tablets from the Murphy Collection, San Clemente Island. *Pacific Coast Archaeological Society Quarterly* 26(2/3):114-121.

Castillo, Edward B.
1978 The Impact of Euro-American Exploration and Settlement. In *California*, edited by Robert F. Heizer, pp. 99-127. Handbook of North American Indians, vol. 8, W. C. Sturtevant, general editor. Smithsonian Institution, Washington, D.C.
1991 California Indian Women and the Missions of Alta-California. Paper presented at An International Symposium: The Spanish Beginnings in California, 1542-1822, University of California, Santa Barbara.

Chace, Paul
1965 The History of Archaeology in Orange County. *Pacific Coast Archaeological Society Quarterly* 1(3):3-23.
1966 An Archaeological Survey in the Northwestern San Joaquin Hills, Orange County, California. *Pacific Coast Archaeological Society Quarterly* 2(2):3-48.
1969 Biological Archaeology of Some Coastal Middens, Orange County, California. *Pacific Coast Archaeological Society Quarterly* 5(2):65-77.

Cheetham, Francis T.
1940 San Clemente Fifty-two Years Ago. *The Quarterly* 22(1):32-46.

Cleland, Robert
1941 *The Cattle on a Thousand Hills.* The Henry E. Huntington Library and Art Gallery, San Marino, California. (Reprinted, 1951.)

Cleveland, Richard J.
n.d. *In the Forecastle, or 25 Years a Sailor.* Hurst and Company, New York.

Cohen, Chester G.
1989 *El Escorpión: From Indian Village to Los Angeles Park.* Periday Co., Woodland Hills.

Cook, Sherburne
1943 The Conflict Between the California Indian and White Civilization, I: The Indian versus the Spanish Mission. *Ibero-Americana* 21:1-194. (Reprinted, University of California Press, Berkeley, 1976).
1962 Expeditions to the Interior of California, Central Valley, 1820-1840. *University of California Anthropological Records* 20(5):151-213.

Cottrell, Marie G.
1985 Ethnohistoric and Ethnographic Review of the Inland Foothill Region of Orange County, California. *Pacific Coast Archaeological Society Quarterly* 21(3):37-43.

Cottrell, Marie, Constance Cameron, Vada Drummy-Chapel, Theodore Cooley, and Adella Schroth
1985 Archaeological Investigations Conducted at the Newland House Site (CA-Ora-183), Huntington Beach, California. *Pacific Coast Archaeological Society Quarterly* 21(1):1-74.

Cottrell, Marie G., Joyce H. Clevenger, and Theodore G. Cooley
1980 Investigation of CA-SCaI-l37, Bulrush Canyon, Catalina Island, California. *Pacific Coast Archaeological Society Quarterly* 16(1/2):5-25.

Cowan, Robert G.
1956 *Ranchos of California: A List of Spanish Concessions, 1775-1822, and Mexican Grants, 1822-1846.* Academy

Library Guild, Fresno, California. (Reprinted, Historical Society of Southern California, Los Angeles, 1977.)

Craib, John L.
1982 The Archaeology of a Late Horizon Midden (CA-Ora-197) on Newport Bay. *Pacific Coast Archaeological Society Quarterly* 18(2/3):1-86.

Dakin, Susanna Bryant
1939 *A Scotch Paisano in Old Los Angeles: Hugo Reid's Life in California, 1832-1852, Derived from His Correspondence.* University of California Press, Berkeley.

Dana, Richard Henry
1840 *Two Years Before the Mast: A Personal Narrative.* Harper & Bros., New York.

Davis, James T.
1961 Trade Routes and Economic Exchange Among the Indians of California. *University of California Archaeological Survey Report* 54:1-71. Berkeley.

Decker, Dean A.
1969 Early Archaeology on Catalina Island: Potential and Problems. *University of California Archaeological Survey Annual Report* 11:69-84. Los Angeles.

Dittman, Carl
1961 Narrative of a Seafaring Life on the Coast of California [1878]. In *Original Accounts of the Lone Woman of San Nicolas Island*, edited by Robert F. Heizer and Albert B. Elsasser, pp. 5-12. University of California Archaeological Survey Report 55. Berkeley.

Dixon, Keith A.
1968 Cogged Stones and Other Ceremonial Cache Artifacts in Stratigraphic Context at Ora-58, a Site in the Lower Santa Ana River Drainage, Orange County. *Pacific Coast Archaeological Society Quarterly* 4(3):57-65.
1970 A Brief Report on Radiocarbon and Obsidian Hydration Measurements from Ora-58 (the Banning-Norris or Fairview Hospital Site), Orange County, California. *Pacific Coast Archaeological Society Quarterly* 6(4):61-67.
1971 Archaeological Site Preservation: A Neglected Alternative to Destruction. *Pacific Coast Archaeological Society Quarterly* 7(4):51-70.
1972 Reviving Puvunga: An Archaeological Project at Rancho Los Alamitos. *The Masterkey* 46(3):84-92.
1974 *Environmental Management Element of the General Plan: Archaeological Resources and Policy Recommendation, City of Long Beach.* Copley International Corporation, La Jolla, California.

DuBois, Constance Goddard
1908 The Religion of the Luiseño Indians of Southern California. *University of California Publications in American Archaeology and Ethnology* 8(3):69-186.

Edberg, Bob
1985 Shamans and Chiefs: Visions of the Future. In *Earth and Sky: Papers from the Northridge Conference on Archaeoastronomy*, edited by Arlene Benson and Tom Hoskinson, pp. 65-92. Slo'w Press, Thousand Oaks, California.

Eisentraut, Phyllisa J.
1990 Investigations of Prehistoric Seed Caches from Site CA-SCII-1542, San Clemente Island. *Pacific Coast Archaeological Society Quarterly* 26(2/3):93-113.

Eliade, Mircea
1951 *Shamanism: Archaic Techniques of Ecstacy.* Translated by Willard R. Trask. Librairie Payot, Paris. (Reprinted, Bollingen Series No. 76, Princeton University Press, Princeton, 1972.)
1957 *The Sacred and the Profane: The Nature of Religion.* Translated by Willard R. Trask. Rowohlt Taschenbuch Verlag GmbH. (Reprinted, Harcourt Brace Jovanovich, New York, 1959.)

Elsasser, Albert B.
1978 Development of Regional Prehistoric Cultures. In *California*, edited by Robert F. Heizer, pp. 37-57. Handbook of North American Indians, vol. 8, W. C. Sturtevant, general editor. Smithsonian Institution, Washington, D.C.

Elsasser, Albert B., and Robert F. Heizer
1963 The Archaeology of Bowers Cave, Los Angeles County, California. *University of California Archaeological Survey Report* 59:1-45. Berkeley.

Engelhardt, Fr. Zephyrin, O.F.M.
1913 *The Missions and Missionaries of California, Vol. 3: Upper California.* The James H. Barry Company, San Francisco.
1922 *San Juan Capistrano Mission.* The Standard Printing Company, Los Angeles.
1927a *San Gabriel Mission and the Beginnings of Los Angeles.* Franciscan Herald Press, Chicago.
1927b *San Fernando Rey: The Mission of the Valley.* Franciscan Herald Press, Chicago.

Essig, E. O.
1934 The Value of Insects to the California Indians. *Scientific Monthly* 38:181-186. (Reprinted in *The California Indians: A Source Book*, edited by R. F. Heizer and M. A. Whipple, pp. 315-318. University of California Press, Berkeley, 1971.)

Fages, Pedro
1937 *A Historical, Political, and Natural Description of California by Pedro Fages, Soldier of Spain, Dutifully Made for the Viceroy in the Year 1775.* Translated by Herbert Ingram Priestley. University of California Press, Berkeley.

Farmer, Malcom F.
1935 The Mojave Trade Route. *The Masterkey* 9(5):155-157.

Finnerty, W. Patrick, Dean Decker, N. Nelson Leonard III, Thomas F. King, Chester King, and Linda B. King
1970 Community Structure and Trade at Isthmus Cove: A Salvage Excavation on Catalina Island. *Pacific Coast Archaeological Society Occasional Paper* No. 1.

Follett, W. I.
1966 Fish Remains From Archaeological Sites at Irvine, Orange County, California. *University of California Archaeological Survey Annual Report* 8:189-195. Los Angeles.

Forbes, Jack D.
1959 Indians of Southern California in 1888. *The Masterkey* 33(3):71-76.
1961 Pueblo Pottery in the San Fernando Valley. *The Masterkey* 35(1):36-38.
1966 The Tongva of Tujunga to 1801. In *University of*

California Archaeological Survey Annual Report No. 8:95-135. Los Angeles.

Frazer, Sir James George
1922   *The Golden Bough: A Study in Magic and Religion.* MacMillan Publishing Co., Inc. (Reprinted, Abridged Edition, MacMillan Publishing, New York, 1963.)

Galdikas-Brindamour, Birute
1970   Trade and Subsistence at Mulholland: A Site Report on Lan-246. *University of California Archaeological Survey Annual Report* 1970:124-161. Los Angeles.

Garcés, Francisco
1900   *On the Trail of a Spanish Pioneer, The Diary and Itinerary of Francisco Garcés (Missionary Priest) In His Travels Through Sonora, Arizona, and California, 1775-1776.* Translated by Elliott Coues. Francis P. Harper, New York.

Gatschet, Albert S.
1879   Linguistics. In *Report Upon United States Geographical Surveys West of the One Hundredth Meridian, Vol. VII, Archaeology*, pp. 399-485. Government Printing Office, Washington, D.C.

Geiger, Maynard
1968   The Buildings of Mission San Gabriel: 1771-1828. *Southern California Historical Society Quarterly* 50:33-36.
1976   Historical Introduction. In *As the Padres Saw Them: California Indian Life and Customs as Reported by the Franciscan Missionaries, 1813-1815*, by Maynard Geiger and Clement W. Meighan. Santa Barbara Mission Archive Library, Santa Barbara.
n.d.   *Juana Maria: The Lone Woman of San Nicolas Island, 1835-1853.* The Serra Shop, Old Mission, Santa Barbara.

Geiger, Maynard, O.F.M., and Clement W. Meighan
1976   *As the Padres Saw Them: California Indian Life and Customs as Reported by the Franciscan Missionaries, 1813-1815.* Santa Barbara Mission Archive Library, Santa Barbara.

Gifford, E. W.
1936   California Balanophagy. In *Essays Presented to A. L. Kroeber*, pp. 87-98. University of California Press, Berkeley. (Reprinted in *The California Indians: A Source Book*, edited by R. F. Heizer and M. A. Whipple, pp. 301-305. University of California Press, Berkeley, 1971.)

Gillingham, Robert Cameron
1961   *The Rancho San Pedro: The Story of a Famous Rancho in Los Angeles County and of Its Owners, the Dominguez Family.* The Dominguez Properties. (Revised edition compiled and edited by Judson Grenier, Museum Reproductions, 1983.)
n.d.   File No. 37, Special Collections and Archives, California State University, Dominguez Hills.

Glassow, Michael A.
1980   *Archaeological Overview of the Northern Channel Islands (Including Santa Barbara Island).* Western Archaeological Center, National Park Service, Tucson.

Gleason, Duncan
1958   *The Islands and Ports of California.* The Devin-Adair Company, New York.

Grant, Campbell
1965   *The Rock Paintings of the Chumash: A Study of a California Indian Culture.* University of California Press, Berkeley.
1967   Rock Art in California. In *Rock Art of the North American Indians*, ch. 14. Thomas Y. Crowell, New York. (Reprinted in *The California Indians: A Source Book*, edited by R. F. Heizer and M. A. Whipple, pp. 231-243. University of California Press, Berkeley.)
1978   Island Chumash. In *California*, edited by Robert F. Heizer, pp. 524-529. Handbook of North American Indians, vol. 8, W. C. Sturtevant, general editor. Smithsonian Institution, Washington D.C.

Greenwood, Roberta S. and John S. Foster
1989   *Context and Evaluation of Historical Sites in the Prado Basin.* U.S. Army Corps of Engineers, Los Angeles.

Gudde, Edwin G.
1949   *California Place Names: The Origin and Etymology of Current Geographical Names.* University of California Press, Berkeley. (Reprinted, 3rd ed., University of California Press, Berkeley, 1969.)

Guest, Francis, O.F.M.
1978   Mission Colonization and Political Control in Spanish California. *The Journal of San Diego History* 24(1):97-116.
1979   An Examination of the Thesis of S. F. Cook on the Forced Conversion of Indians in the California Missions. *Southern California Quarterly* 61:1-77.
1985   Junípero Serra and His Approach to the Indians. *Southern California Quarterly* 67:223-261.

Hafner, Duane H.
1971   The Buck Gully #2 Site (Ora-189): The Archaeology of a Late Horizon Coastal Site in Orange County, California. *Pacific Coast Archaeological Society Quarterly* 7(4):1-44.

Hale, Horatio
1846   *United States Exploring Expedition During the Years 1838, 1839, 1840, 1841, 1842. Under the Command of Charles Wilkes, U.S.N. Vol. VI: Ethnology & Philology.* C. Sherman, Philadelphia.

Hancock, Henry
1859   Plat of the Rancho Los Palos Verdes. On file, The Henry E. Huntington Library and Art Gallery, San Marino, California.

Hanna, Phil Townsend
1946   *The Dictionary of California Land Names.* The Automobile Club of Southern California. (Reprinted, 2nd ed., Automobile Club of Southern California, 1951.)

Hardacre, Emma
1880   Eighteen Years Alone: A Tale of the Pacific. *Scribners Monthly* 20:657-664. (Reprinted in *Original Accounts of the Lone Woman of San Nicolas Island*, edited by Robert F. Heizer and Albert B. Elsasser, pp. 23-37. University of California Archaeological Survey Report 55. Berkeley, 1961.)

Harner, Michael
1973   *Hallucinogens and Shamanism.* Oxford University Press, New York.

Harrington, John P.
1933   Annotations. In *Chinigchinich: A Revised and Annotated Version of Alfred Robinson's Translation of Father Ger-*

ónimo Boscana's Historical Account of the Belief, Usages, Customs and Extravagancies of the Indians of this Mission of San Juan Capistrano Called the Acagchemem Tribe. Fine Arts Press, Santa Ana. (Reprinted, Malki Museum Press, Banning, California, 1978.)

1934 A New Original Version of Boscana's Historical Account of the San Juan Capistrano Indians of Southern California. *Smithsonian Miscellaneous Collections* 92(4):1-42. Smithsonian Institution, Washington, D.C.

1942 Culture Element Distributions: XIX Central California Coast. *University of California Anthropological Records* 7(1):1-46.

1962 Introduction. In *California's Gabrielino Indians.* Southwest Museum, Los Angeles.

1986 *John Harrington Papers, Vol. 3: Southern California/Basin.* Smithsonian Institution, National Anthropological Archives, Washington. Microfilm edition, Kraus International Publications, Millwood, New York.

Harrington, M. R.
1934 Once in a Lifetime-Perhaps! *The Masterkey* 8(6):177-178.

Hatheway, Roger G., and Roberta S. Greenwood
1981 An Overview of History and Historical Archaeology, San Clemente Island. In *The Cultural Resources of San Clemente Island.* Chambers Consultants and Planners, Stanton, California.

Hayes, Benjamin
1929 *Pioneer Notes from the Diaries of Judge Benjamin Hayes 1849-1875.* Privately Printed, Los Angeles.

Hedges, Ken
1973 Rock Art in Southern California. *Pacific Coast Archaeological Society Quarterly* 9(4):1-28.

Heidsick, Ralph G.
1966 *Music of the Luiseño Indians of Southern California—A Study of Music in Indian Culture with Relation to a Program in Music Education.* Ph.D. dissertation, University of California, Los Angeles. University Microfilms International, Ann Arbor, 1984.

Heizer, Robert F.
1941 Aboriginal Trade Between the Southwest and California. *The Masterkey* 15(5):185-188.

1941b Alexander Taylor's Map of California Indian Tribes, 1864. *California Historical Society Quarterly* 20(2):171-180.

1955 California Indian Linguistic Records: The Mission Indian Vocabularies of H.W. Henshaw. *University of California Anthropological Records* 15(2):85-202. Berkeley.

1957 A Steatite Whale Figure from San Nicolas Island. *University of California Archaeological Survey Report* 38:10. Berkeley.

1960 A San Nicolas Island Twined Basketry Water Bottle. *University of California Archaeological Survey Report* 50:1-3. Berkeley.

1968 Introduction and Notes. In *The Indians of Los Angeles County: Hugo Reid's Letters of 1852*, edited and annotated by Robert F. Heizer. Southwest Museum, Los Angeles.

1976 A Note on Boscana's Posthumous Relacion. *The Masterkey* 50(3):99-102.

1978a Impact of Colonization on the Native California Societies. *The Journal of San Diego History* 24(l):121-139.

1978b Introduction. In *California*, edited by Robert F. Heizer, pp. 1-5. Handbook of North American Indians, vol. 8, W. C. Sturtevant, general editor. Smithsonian Institution, Washington, D.C.

Heizer, Robert F., and Albert B. Elsasser (editors)
1961 Original Accounts of the Lone Woman of San Nicolas Island. *University of California Archaeological Survey Report* 55:1-55. Berkeley.

1980 *The Natural World of the California Indians.* University of California Press, Berkeley.

Heizer, Robert F., and A. E. Treganza
1944 Mines and Quarries of the Indians of California. *California Journal of Mines and Geology* 40:291-359. (Reprinted in *The California Indians: A Source Book*, edited by R. F. Heizer and M. A. Whipple, pp. 346-359. University of California Press, Berkeley 1971.)

Heizer, Robert F., and M.A. Whipple (editors)
1951 *The California Indians: A Source Book.* University of California Press, Berkeley. (Reprinted, 1971.)

Henshaw, H. W.
n.d. Gabrielino Vocabulary Collected Near Banning on December 24, 1884. Accession Nos. 787a, 787b. Ms. on file, National Anthropological Archives, Smithsonian Institution, Washington, D.C.

Hoffman, W. J.
1885 Hugo Reid's Account of the Indians of Los Angeles County, California. *Bulletin of the Essex Institute* 17:1-33.

1886 Azusa Canyon Pictographs. *4th Annual Report of the Bureau of Ethnology, 1882-1883.* Government Printing Office, Washington, D.C.

n.d. Extracts from Letters by P. H. Ried [sic] to Hon. A. F. Coronel, Los Angeles, Calif., 1852, made by W. J. Hoffman, Oct., 1884, through the courtesy of A. F. Coronel. Accession No. 2489. Ms. on file, National Anthropological Archives, Smithsonian Institution, Washington, D.C.

Holder, Charles Frederick
1889 *All About Pasadena and Its Vicinity: Its Climate, Missions, Trails and Cañons, Fruits, Flowers and Game.* Lee and Shepard, Boston.

1910 *The Channel Islands of California: A Book for the Angler, Sportsman, and Tourist.* A. C. McClurg & Co., Chicago.

Hoover, Robert L.
1973 Incised Steatite Tablets from the Catalina Museum. *The Masterkey* 47(3):106-109.

1974 Some Observations on Chumash Prehistoric Stone Effigies. *The Journal of California Anthropology* 1(1):33-40.

Howard, Jerry
1977 Seasonality and Settlement Patterns in the Orange County Coastal Foothills. *Pacific Coast Archaeological Society Quarterly* 13(2):11-21.

Howard, William J. and L. Mark Raab
1993 Olivella Grooved Rectangle Beads as Evidence of a Mid-Holocene Southern Channel Islands Interaction Sphere.

Pacific Coast Archaeological Society Quarterly 29(3):1-11.

Howorth, Peter C.
1988   San Nicolas Island: The Elusive Source of the Chumash Magic Stones. *The Magazine of Santa Barbara County* 14(4):38-43.

Hudson, Dee Travis
1969   The Archaeological Investigations During 1935 and 1937 at ORA-237, ORA-238, and ORA-239, Santiago Canyon, Orange County, California. *Pacific Coast Archaeological Society Quarterly* 5(1):1-68.

1971   Proto-Gabrielino Patterns of Territorial Organization in South Coastal California. *Pacific Coast Archaeological Society Quarterly* 7(2):51-76.

1979a   A Rare Account of Gabrielino Shamanism from the Notes of John P. Harrington. *Journal of California and Great Basin Anthropology* 1:356-362.

1981   Recently Discovered Accounts Concerning the "Lone Woman of San Nicolas Island." *Journal of California and Great Basin Anthropology* 3:187-199.

1988   The "Classical Assumption" In Light of Chumash Astronomy. In *Visions of the Sky: Archaeological and Ethnological Studies of California Indian Astronomy*, edited by Robert A. Schiffman, pp. 97-108. Coyote Press, Salinas, California.

Hudson, Dee Travis, and Thomas C. Blackburn
1978   The Integration of Myth and Ritual in South-Central California: The "Northern Complex." *The Journal of California Anthropology* 5:225-250.

1982   *The Material Culture of the Chumash Interaction Sphere, Vol. I: Food Procurement and Transportation*. BP-AP No. 25, Thomas C. Blackburn, series editor. Ballena Press, Menlo Park, California.

1983   *The Material Culture of the Chumash Interaction Sphere, Vol. II: Food Preparation and Shelter*. BP-AP No. 27, Thomas C. Blackburn, series editor. Ballena Press, Menlo Park, California.

1985   *The Material Culture of the Chumash Interaction Sphere, Vol. III: Clothing, Ornamentation, and Grooming*. BP-AP No. 28, Thomas C. Blackburn, series editor. Ballena Press, Menlo Park, California.

1986   *The Material Culture of the Chumash Interaction Sphere, Vol. IV: Ceremonial Paraphernalia, Games, and Amusements*. BP-AP No. 30, Thomas C. Blackburn, series editor. Ballena Press, Menlo Park, California.

1987   *The Material Culture of the Chumash Interaction Sphere, Vol. V: Manufacturing Processes, Metrology, and Trade*. BP-AP No. 31, Thomas C. Blackburn, series editor. Ballena Press, Menlo Park, California.

Hudson, Dee Travis, Janice Timbrook, and Melissa Rempe (editors)
1978   *Tomol: Chumash Watercraft as Described in the Ethnographic Notes of John P. Harrington*. BP-AP No. 9, Lowell John Bean and Thomas C. Blackburn, series editors. Ballena Press, Socorro, New Mexico.

Hudson, Dee Travis, and Ernest Underhay
1978   *Crystals in the Sky: An Intellectual Odyssey Involving Chumash Astronomy, Cosmology and Rock Art*. BP-AP No. 10, Lowell John Bean and Thomas C. Blackburn, series editors. Ballena Press, Menlo Park, California.

Hudson, J. W.
n.d.   Typescripts of unpublished Gabrielino fieldnotes recorded at Tejon, Accession No. A 11-2. Ms. on file, Grace Hudson Museum and the Sun House, Ukiah, California. Copies on file, Field Museum of Natural History, Chicago.

Jackson, Robert
1991   The Economy and Demography of San Gabriel Mission, 1771-1834: A Structural Analysis. Paper presented at An International Symposium: The Spanish Beginnings in California, 1542-1822, University of California, Santa Barbara.

Johnson, John R.
1988   The People of *Quinquina*: San Clemente Island's Original Inhabitants as Described in Ethnohistoric Documents. Report prepared for the Natural Resource Office, Naval Air Station, North Island, San Diego.

Johnston, Bernice Eastman
1962   *California's Gabrielino Indians*. Southwest Museum, Los Angeles.

Jones, Philip Mills
1969   San Nicolas Island Archaeology in 1901. *The Masterkey* 43(3):84-98.

Kelsey, Harry
1986   *Juan Rodriguez Cabrillo*. The Henry E. Huntington Library and Art Gallery, San Marino, California.

King, Laura Evertson
1899   Hugo Reid and His Indian Wife. *Annual Publication of the Historical Society of Southern California and Pioneer Register* 4(2):111-113. Los Angeles.

King, Chester
1971   Chumash Inter-village Economic Exchange. *The Indian Historian* 4(1):30-43. (Reprinted in *Native Californians: A Theoretical Retrospective*, edited by Lowell John Bean and Thomas C. Blackburn, pp. 289-318. Ballena Press, Menlo Park, California, 1976.)

1978   Protohistoric and Historic Archeology. In *California*, edited by R. F. Heizer, pp. 58-68. Handbook of North American Indians, vol. 8, W. C. Sturtevant general editor. Smithsonian Institution, Washington, D.C.

1993   Native American Placenames in the Santa Monica Mountains. Draft Submitted to the Santa Monica Mountains National Recreation Area, Agoura Hills. Ms. on file, Topanga Anthropological Consultants.

King, Chester, and Thomas C. Blackburn
1978   Tataviam. In *California*, edited by Robert F. Heizer, pp. 535-537. Handbook of North American Indians, vol. 8, W. C. Sturtevant, general editor. Smithsonian Institution, Washington, D.C.

Knight, Lavinia C.
1979   Bell Rock and Indian Maze Rock of Orange County. *Pacific Coast Archaeological Society Quarterly* 15(2):25-32.

Koerper, H. C.
1979   On the Question of the Chronological Placement of Shoshonean Presence in Orange County California. *Pacific Coast Archaeological Society Quarterly* 15(3):69-84.

1981   *Prehistoric Subsistence and Settlement in the Newport Bay Area and Environs, Orange County, California*. Ph.D. dissertation, University of California, Riverside.

University Microfilms International, Ann Arbor, Michigan, 1988.

1988 *Memoirs of the Natural History Foundation of Orange County, Vol. 2: The Natural and Social Sciences of Orange County.* Natural History Foundation of Orange County, Newport Beach, California.

Koerper, H. C., and Joseph Cramer

1988 Archaeological Evidence of Visual Aesthetic Expression in Prehistoric Orange County. In *Memoirs of the Natural History Foundation of Orange County, Vol. 2: The Natural and Social Sciences of Orange County*, edited by Henry C. Koerper, pp. 93-105. Natural History Foundation of Orange County, Newport Beach, California.

Koerper, Henry C., Christopher E. Drover, Arthur E. Flint, and Gary Hurd

1978 Gabrielino Tizon Brown Pottery. *Pacific Coast Archaeological Society Quarterly* 14(3):43-58.

Koerper, H. C., J. E. Ericson, C. E. Drover, and P. E. Langenwalter II

1986 Obsidian Exchange in Prehistoric Orange County. *Pacific Coast Archaeological Society Quarterly* 22(1):33-69.

Koerper, Henry C., and E. Bonita Fouste

1977 An Interesting Late Prehistoric Burial from CA-Ora-119-A. *Pacific Coast Archaeological Society Quarterly* 13(2):39-61.

Koerper, Henry C., and Arthur E. Flint

1978 Some Comments on "Cerritos Brown" Pottery. *Pacific Coast Archaeological Society Quarterly* 14(2):19-25.

Koerper, Henry C., and Armand J. Labbe

1987 A Birdstone from San Diego County California: A Possible Example of Dimorphic Sexual Symbolism in Luiseño Iconography. *Journal of California and Great Basin Anthropology* 9(1):110-120.

Kroeber, A. L.

1907 Shoshonean Dialects of California. *University of California Publications in American Archaeology and Ethnology* 4(3):65-166. Berkeley. (Reprinted, Kraus Reprint Corporation, New York, 1964.)

1909 Notes on Shoshonean Dialects of Southern California. *University of California Publications in American Archaeology and Ethnology* 8(5):235-269. Berkeley.

1925 *Handbook of the Indians of California.* Bureau of American Ethnology Bulletin 78, Smithsonian Institution, Washington, D.C. (Reprinted, Dover Publications, New York, 1976.)

1959 Ethnographic Interpretations 7-11: Problems on Boscana. *University of California Publications in American Archaeology and Ethnology* 47:282-293. Berkeley.

LaLone, Mary

1980 Gabrielino Indians of Southern California: An Annotated Ethnohistoric Bibliography. *University of California Institute of Archaeology Occasional Paper* 6. Los Angeles.

Landberg, Leif C. W.

1965 The Chumash Indians of Southern California. *Southwest Museum Papers* 19. Southwest Museum, Los Angeles.

Langenwalter II, Paul E.

1986 Ritual Animal Burials from the Encino Village Site. *Pacific Coast Archaeological Society Quarterly* 22(3):63-97.

Latta, Frank F.

1976 *Saga of Rancho El Tejón.* Bear State Books, Santa Cruz, California.

Lauter, Gloria A.

1977 The Harper Site: Ora-302. *Pacific Coast Archaeological Society Quarterly* 13(2):23-38.

Lee, Georgia

1979 The San Emigdio Rock Art Site. *Journal of California and Great Basin Anthropology* 1(2):295-305.

1981 *The Portable Cosmos: Effigies, Ornaments, and Incised Stone from the Chumash Area.* BP-AP No. 21, Lowell John Bean and Thomas C. Blackburn, series editors. Ballena Press, Socorro, New Mexico.

1993 Fake Effigies from the California Coast? Robert Heizer and the Effigy Controversy. *Journal of California and Great Basin Anthropology* 15(2):195-215.

Librado, Fernando, and John P. Harrington

1977 *The Eye of the Flute: Chumash Traditional History and Ritual as Told by Fernando Librado Kitsepawit to John P. Harrington.* Santa Barbara Museum of Natural History, Santa Barbara, California.

Librado, Fernando, John P. Harrington and Travis Hudson

1979 *Breath of the Sun: Life in Early California as Told by A Chumash Indian, Fernando Librado to John P. Harrington.* Malki Museum Press, Banning, California.

Los Angeles Star

1851 Article, 24 May. Los Angeles, California.

1859 Article, 12 December. Los Angeles, Calfornia.

Los Angeles Times

1921 [Race Vanishes as Junco Dies.] 10 February. Los Angeles, California.

Martínez, José Longinos

1938 *California in 1792: The Expedition of José Longinos Martinez.* Translated by Leslie Byrd Simpson. The Henry E. Huntington Library and Art Gallery, San Marino, California.

Mason, Roger D.

1986 Summary of Work Carried Out at CA-Lan-43, The Encino Village Site. *Pacific Coast Archaeological Society Quarterly* 22(3):9-17.

Mason, William Marvin

1975 Fage's Code of Conduct Toward Indians, 1787. *The Journal of California Anthropology* 2(1):90-100.

1984 Indian-Mexican Cultural Exchange In the Los Angeles Area, 1781-1834. *International Journal of Chicano Studies Research* 15(l):l23-144.

1986 Alta California During the Mission Period, 1769-1835. *The Masterkey* 60(2/3):4-13.

McKusick, M. B., and C. N. Warren

1959 Introduction to San Clemente Island Archaeology. *University of California Archaeological Survey Annual Report* 1958-1959 1:106-185.

Mead, George R.

1969 Redigging the WPA: The Bonita Sheep Corral Site. *Pacific Coast Archaeological Society Quarterly* 5(4):1-13.

Meighan, Clement W.

1954 The Nicoleño. *Pacific Discovery* 7(l):22-27.

1959 The Little Harbor Site, Catalina Island: An Example of

Ecological Interpretation in Archaeology. *American Antiquity* 24(4):383-405.

1976a   Stone Effigies in Southern California. *The Masterkey* 50(1):25-29.

1976b   An Anthropological Commentary on the Mission Questionnaires. In *As the Padres Saw Them: California Indian Life and Customs as Reported by the Franciscan Missionaries, 1813-1815*, by Maynard Geiger and Clement W. Meighan. Santa Barbara Mission Archive Library, Santa Barbara.

1983   New Findings at the Ledge Site, San Clemente Island. *The Masterkey* 57(4):164-168.

Meighan, Clement W., and Hal Eberhart
1953   Archaeological Resources of San Nicolas Island, California. *American Antiquity* 19(2):109-125.

Meighan, Clement W., and Keith L. Johnson
1957   Isle of Mines: Catalina's Ancient Indian Quarries. *Pacific Discovery* 10(2):24-29.

Meighan, Clement W., and Sheldon Rootenberg
1957   A Prehistoric Miner's Camp on Catalina Island. *The Masterkey* 31(6):176-184.

Merriam, C. Hart
1918   The Acorn, A Possibly Neglected Source of Food. *National Geographic* 34:129-137.

1955   *Studies of California Indians*. University of California Press, Berkeley.

1968   Village Names in Twelve California Mission Records. *University of California Archaeological Survey Report* 74. Berkeley.

1979   *Indian Names for Plants and Animals among Californian and other Western North American Tribes*. Assembled and annotated by Robert F. Heizer. BP-PAEH No. 14, Robert F. Heizer, series editor. Ballena Press, Socorro, New Mexico.

n.d.a   Unpublished fieldnotes of Interviews with Gabrielino Informant Jose Zalvidea, May-June 1933, "California Journal" Box 17, pp. 52, 63, 64. Ms. on file, Library of Congress, Washington, D.C.

n.d.b   Interviews with Mrs. James Rosemyre at Tejon. Accession No. 32698. Box 10, Folder 1903, Vol. 5, pp. 396-405, October 11-15, 1903. Box 10, folder 1905, Vol. 1, pp. 12-13, July 7-14, 1905. Ms. on file, Library of Congress, Washington, D.C.

n.d.c   Vocabularies and miscellaneous notes and clippings on the Tongva from the C. Hart Merriam Collection. Call No. 80/18. Carton 2, folder "Misc./N18," and folder "Y/24a/N1." Carton 6, folder "Y/24a/E77." Carton 13, folder "Y/24a/NH129." Carton 19, envelope "Tongva." The Bancroft Library, Berkeley.

Mills, Elaine L., and Ann J. Brickfield
1986   *The Papers of John P. Harrington in the Smithsonian Institution, 1907-1957, Vol. 3: A Guide to the Fieldnotes: Native American History, Language and Culture of Southern California/Basin*. Kraus International Publications, White Plains, New York.

Minor, Rick
1973   Known Origins of Rock Paintings of Southwestern California. *Pacific Coast Archaeological Society Quarterly* 9(4):29-36.

Morgan, Ron
1979   An Account of the Discovery of a Whale-Bone House on San Nicolas Island. *Journal of California and Great Basin Anthropology* 1(1):171-177.

Moriarty III, James Robert
1982   Ritual Plaques from Southern California. *The Masterkey* 56(3):85-93.

Moratto, Michael J.
1984   *California Archaeology*. Academic Press, Orlando, Florida.

Muñoz, Jeanne
1982   *A Partial Index to the Mission San Gabriel Baptism, Marriage, and Death Registers*. Archaeological Resource Management Corporation, Garden Grove, California.

Munro, Pam
1994   *Takic Foundations of Nicoleño Vocabulary*. Ms. in files of William McCawley.

n.d.   *Gabrielino: A Grammar and Dictionary*. Ms. in preparation.

Murbarger, Nell
1947   California's Vanished Islanders. *Grizzly Bear* 81(481):4-5.

Newmark, Harris
1930   *My Sixty Years in Southern California*. Houghton Mifflin Company, New York.

Nidever, George
1937   *The Life and Adventures of George Nidiver [1802-1883], The Life Story of a Remarkable California Pioneer Told in His Own Words, and None Wasted*, edited by William Henry Ellison. University of California Press, Berkeley. (Reprinted, McNally & Loftin, Santa Barbara, 1984.)

O'Dell, Scott
1960   *Island of the Blue Dolphins*. The Houghton Mifflin Company and The Riverside Press, Boston.

Ogden, Adele
1941   The California Sea Otter Trade, 1784-1848. *University of California Publications in History* 26:i-251. Berkeley. (Reprinted, Kraus Reprint Co., Millwood, New York, 1974.)

O'Neil, Stephen
1988   Their Mark Upon the Land: Native American Place Names in Orange County and Adjacent Areas. In *Memoirs of the Natural History Foundation of Orange County, Vol. 2: The Natural and Social Sciences of Orange County*, edited by Henry C. Koerper, pp. 106-122. Natural History Foundation of Orange County, Newport Beach.

n.d.   *Historic Gabrielino Villages Associated with the Original Site of Mission San Gabriel de Arcángel*. Ms. in files of William McCawley.

O'Neil, Stephen, and Nancy H. Evans
1980   Notes on Historical Juaneño Villages and Geographical Features. *Journal of California and Great Basin Anthropology* 2(2):226-232.

Oxendine, Joan
1983   *The Luiseño Village During the Late Prehistoric Era*. Ph.D. dissertation, University of California, Riverside.

Palmer, Dr. Frank M.
1905   Nucleus of Southwestern Museum. *Out West* 22:23-34.

Phelps, William D.
1961   Logbook of the Alert [1841]. In *Original Accounts of the Lone Woman of San Nicolas Island*, edited by Robert F.

Heizer and Albert B. Elsasser, University of California Archaeological Survey Report 55:22-23. Berkeley.

Phillips, George Harwood
1975 *Chiefs and Challengers: Indian Resistance and Cooperation in Southern California.* University of California Press, Berkeley.

Polhemus, H. D., and E. F. Northam
n.d. *Map of a Portion of Los Angeles County.* Copy on file, Rancho Los Alamitos Historic Ranch and Gardens, Long Beach, California.

Pond, Gordon G.
1968 Steatite Tablets from Malaga Cove. *The Masterkey* 42(4):124-131.

Prebble, Donna
1940 *Yamino Kwiti: A Story of Indian Life in the Los Angeles Area.* Caxton Printers. (Reprinted, Heyday Books, Berkeley, 1983.)

Priestley, Herbert Ingram
1937 Introduction. In *A Historical, Political, and Natural Description of California by Pedro Fages, Soldier of Spain, Dutifully Made for the Viceroy in the Year 1775.* Translated by Hebert Ingram Priestly. University of California Press.

Queenan, Charles F.
1986 *Long Beach and Los Angeles: A Tale of Two Ports.* Windsor Publications, Northridge, California.

Quist, Richard
1978 Channel Island Pictographs. *Journal of New World Archaeology* 2(4):40-45.

Rabb, L. Mark and Andrew Yatsko
1990 Prehistoric Human Ecology of *Quinquina*, A Research Design for Archaeological Studies on San Clemente Island, Southern California. *Pacific Coast Archaeological Society Quarterly* 26(2/3):10-37.

Reichlen, H. and R. F. Heizer
1963 La Mission de Léon de Cessac en Californie, 1877-1879. Objets et Mondes III:17-34. Paris. (Translated and reprinted in *University of California Archaeological Survey Reports* 61:1-23, Berkeley, 1964.)

Reid, Hugo
1852 Los Angeles County Indians. *Los Angeles Star* 1(41)-2(11) 21 February-24 July. (Reprinted, *The Indians of Los Angeles County: Hugo Reid's Letters of 1852*, edited and annotated by Robert F. Heizer. Southwest Museum, Los Angeles, 1968.)

Reinman, Fred M.
1962 New Sites on San Nicolas Island, California. *University of California Archaeological Survey Annual Report* 1961-1962:11-19. Los Angeles.

Reinman, Fred M., and Hal Eberhart
1980 Test Excavations at the Ripper's Cove Site (SCaI-26). *Pacific Coast Archaeological Society Quarterly* 16(1/2):61-105.

Reinman, Fred M., and Sam-Joe Townsend
1960 Six Burial Sites on San Nicolas Island, California. *University of California Archaeological Survey Annual Report* 1959-1960:1-134. Los Angeles.

Roberts, Helen H.
1933 *Form in Primitive Music: An Analytical and Comparative Study of the Melodic Form of Some Ancient Southern California Indian Songs.* W. W. Norton and Company, Inc., New York.

Robinson, John W.
1977 *The San Gabriels: Southern California Mountain Country.* Golden West Books, San Marino, California.
1983 *The San Gabriels II: The Mountains from Monrovia Canyon to Lytle Creek.* Big Santa Anita Historical Society, Arcadia, California.

Robinson, W. W.
1952 *The Indians of Los Angeles: Story of the Liquidation of a People.* Glen Dawson, Los Angeles.
1966 The Spanish and Mexican Ranchos of San Fernando Valley. *The Masterkey* 40(3):84-95.

Rogers, David Banks
1929 *Prehistoric Man of the Santa Barbara Coast.* Santa Barbara Museum of Natural History, Santa Barbara, California.

Rogers, Harrison G.
1918 The Second Journal of Harrison G. Rogers. In *The Ashley-Smith Explorations and the Discovery of a Central Route to the Pacific, 1822-1828*, edited by H. C. Dale, pp. 237-271. Arthur H. Clark, Cleveland.

Rogers, Malcom J.
1993 Report of Archaeological Investigations on San Nicolas Island in 1930. *Pacific Coast Archaeological Society Quarterly* 29(3):16-21.

Romani, John, Gwen Romani and Dan Larson
1985 Astronomical Investigations at Burro Flats: Aspects of Ceremonialism at a Chumash/Gabrielino Rock Art and Habitation Site. In *Earth and Sky: Papers from the Northridge Conference on Archaeoastronomy*, edited by Arlene Benson and Tom Hoskinson, pp.93-108. Slo'w Press, Thousand Oaks, California.

Romani, John, Dan Larson, Gwen Romani, and Arlene Benson
1988 Astronomy, Myth, and Ritual in the West San Fernando Valley. In *Visions of the Sky: Archaeological and Ethnological Studies of California Indian Astronomy*, edited by Robert A. Schiffman, pp. 109-134. Coyote Press, Salinas, California.

Rose, L. J., Jr.
1959 *L. J. Rose of Sunny Slope, 1827-1899: California Pioneer, Fruit Grower, Wine Maker, Horse Breeder.* The Henry E. Huntington Library and Art Gallery, San Marino, California.

Rosen, Martin D.
1980 Archaeological Investigations at Two Prehistoric Santa Catalina Island Sites: Rosski (SCaI-45) and Miner's Camp (SCaI-118). *Pacific Coast Archaeological Society Quarterly* 16(1/2):27-60.

Rosenthal, E. Jane
1981 Prehistoric Traders on Santa Catalina Island. *Archaeology* 34(5):60-61.

Rosenthal, E. Jane, Steven L. Williams, Mark Roeder, Wayne Bonner, and Ivan Strudwick
1988 The Bulrush Canyon Project: Excavations at Bulrush Canyon Site (SCaI-137) and Camp Cactus Road Site, Santa Catalina Island. *Pacific Coast Archaeological Society Quarterly* 24(2/3):1-120.

Ross, Lester A.
1970 4-ORA-190: A Descriptive Site Report of a Late Prehistoric Horizon Site in Orange County, California.

Pacific Coast Archaeological Society Quarterly 6(2/3):1-135.

Rozaire, Charles E.
1959   Archaeological Investigations at Two Sites on San Nicolas Island, California. *The Masterkey* 33(4):129-152.

Rozaire, Charles E., and George Kritzman
1960   A Petroglyph Cave on San Nicolas Island. *The Masterkey* 34(4):147-151.

Ruby, Jay
1966   Archaeological Investigations of the Big Tujunga Site (LAn-167). *University of California Archaeological Survey Annual Report* 8:95-135. Los Angeles.
1970   *Culture Contact Between Aboriginal Southern California and the Southwest.* Ph.D. dissertation, University of California, Los Angeles.

Ruby, Jay, and Thomas Blackburn
1964   Occurrence of Southwestern Pottery in Los Angeles County, California. *American Antiquity* 30:209-210.

Rudkin, Charles N. (editor)
1956   *Observations on California 1772-1790, by Fr. Luis Sales, O.P.* Glen Dawson, Los Angeles.

Rust, H. N.
1904   Rogerio's Theological School. *Out West* 21:243-248. (Reprinted, in *A Collection of Ethnographic Articles on the California Indians*, pp. 63-68. BP-PAEH No. 7, Robert F. Heizer, series editor. Ballena Press, Ramona, California, 1976.)

Salls, Roy A.
1990a   Return to Big Dog Cave: The Last Evidence of a Prehistoric Fishery on the Southern California Bight. *Pacific Coast Archaeological Society Quarterly* 26(2/3):38-60.
1990b   The Ancient Mariners: Ten Thousand Years of Marine Exploitation at Eel Point, San Clemente Island, California. *Pacific Coast Archaeological Society Quarterly* 26(2/3):61-92.

Sanburg, Delmer E., Jr.
1972   A Pictograph Site Near Los Angeles. *The Masterkey* 46(1):18-26.

Sanburg, Delmer E., Jr., Dana Bleitz Sanburg, Frank Bleitz, and Edith Bleitz
1978   Two Rock Art Sites in the San Fernando Valley: Ven-149 and LAn-357. *Journal of New World Archaeology* 2(4):28-39.

Sánchez, Nellie Van de Grift (translator)
1929   Keeper of the Keys: The Recollections of Senora Eulalia Perez, Oldest Woman in the World, of Life at Mission San Gabriel. *Touring Topics* 21(1):24-53.

San Gabriel Mission Registers
n.d.   Marriage, baptismal, and death registers for Mission San Gabriel. Registers on file, Chancery Archives of the Archdiocese of Los Angeles at Mission San Fernando. Copies on file, Santa Barbara Mission Archive Library.

Saunders, Charles Francis, and Father St. John O'Sullivan
1930   *Capistrano Nights: Tales of a California Mission Town.* Robert M. McBride and Company, New York.

Schiffman, Robert A. (editor)
1988   Visions of the Sky: Archaeological and Ethnological Studies of California Indian Astronomy. *Coyote Press*

Archives of California Prehistory, No. 16. Coyote Press, Salinas, California.

Schumacher, Paul
1875   The Manufacture of Shell Fish-hooks by the Early Inhabitants of the Santa Barbara Channel Islands. *Archiv für Anthropologie* 8:223-224. Braunschweig. (Reprinted, *University of California Archaeological Survey Report* 50:23-24, Berkeley, 1960.)
1876   Beobachtungen in den verfallen Dörfern de pacifischen Küste in Nord-Amerika [Observations Made in the Ruins of the Villages of the Original Inhabitants of the Pacific Coast of North America]. *Mitteilunger der Anthropologischen Gesellschaft in Wien* 7:287-293. Vienna. (Reprinted and translated in *University of California Archaeological Survey Report* 50:19-23, Berkeley, 1960.)
1878a   The Method of Manufacture of Several Articles by the Former Indians of Southern California. *Eleventh Annual Report of the Peabody Museum of Archaeology and Ethnology*, pp. 258-268. Peabody Museum, Cambridge. (Reprinted, *University of California Archaeological Survey Report* 59:77-81, Berkeley, 1963.)
1878b   Ancient Olla Manufactory on Santa Catalina Island, California. *The American Naturalist* 12(9):629.

Shaler, William
1935   *Journal of a Voyage Between China and the North Western Coast of America, Made in 1804 by William Shaler.* Saunders Studio Press, Claremont, California.

Sheridan, Sol
1926   *History of Ventura County, California.* 2 vols. S. J. Clarke Publishing, Chicago.

Shiner, Joel L.
1949   A Fernandeño Site in Simi Valley, California. *The Masterkey* 23(3):79-81.

Shinn, G. Hazen
1941   *Shoshonean Days: Recollections of a Residence of Five Years Among the Indians of Southern California, 1885-1889.* The Arthur Clark Company, Glendale, California.

Silka, Henry P.
1984   *San Pedro: A Pictorial History.* San Pedro Bay Historical Society, San Pedro, California.

Simpson, Ruth D.
1953   Shoshonean Burial Ground Excavated. *The Masterkey* 27(2):69.

Smith, Donald Eugene, and Frederick J. Teggart (editors)
1909   Diary of Gaspar de Portola During the California Expedition of 1769-1770. *Publications of the Academy of Pacific Coast History* 1(3). University of California, Berkeley.

Sparkman, Philip Stedman
1908   The Culture of the Luiseño Indians. *University of California Publications in American Archaeology and Ethnology* 8(4):187-234. Berkeley.

Spier, Robert F. G.
1970   *From the Hand of Man: Primitive and Preindustrial Technologies.* Houghton Mifflin Company, Boston.

Splitter, Henry Winfred
1956   The Development of Science in Los Angeles and the Southern California Area (1850-1900). *The Historical Society of Southern California Quarterly* 38:99-140.

Stephenson, Terry E.
1931 *Shadows of Old Saddleback: Tales of the Santa Ana Mountains.* Fine Arts Press, Santa Ana. (Reprinted, The Rasmussen Press, Orange, California, 1974.)

Strong, William Duncan
1929 Aboriginal Society in Southern California. *University of California Publications in American Archaeology and Ethnology* 26(1):1-358. Berkeley. (Reprinted, Malki Museum Press, Banning, California, 1972.)

Strudwick, Ivan
1985 The Single-Piece Circular Fishhook: Classification and Chronology. *Pacific Coast Archaeological Society Quarterly* 21(2):32-69.

Sugranes, Rev. Eugene, C.M.F.
1909 *The Old San Gabriel Mission.* San Gabriel.

Schwartz, Steven J. and Patricia Martz
1992 An Overview of the Archaeology of San Nicolas Island, Southern California. *Pacific Coast Archaeological Society Quarterly* 28(4):46-73.

Swanton, John R.
1953 *The Indian Tribes of North America.* Smithsonian Institution Bureau of American Ethnology Bulletin 145. United States Government Printing Office, Washington, D.C.

Swartz, B. K., Jr.
1960 Evidence for the Indian Occupation of Santa Barbara Island. *The Kiva* 26(1):7-9.

Tac, Pablo
1952 Indian Life and Customs at Mission San Luis Rey: A Record of California Mission Life Written by Pablo Tac, An Indian Neophyte (Rome ca. 1835), edited by Minna and Gordon Hewes. *The Americas: A Quarterly Review of Inter-American Cultural History* 9:87-106. The Academy of American Franciscan History, Washington, D.C.

Taylor, Alexander S.
1860a The Indianology of California: No. 9, Indians of the Mission of San Gabriel, etc. *The California Farmer and Journal of Useful Sciences* 13(12), 11 May.
1860b A Report of the Indian Woman of San Nicolas Island. *The California Farmer and Journal of Useful Sciences* 8 June. (Reprinted in *Original Accounts of the Lone Woman of San Nicolas Island,* edited by Robert F. Heizer and Albert B. Elsasser, University of California Archaeological Survey Report No. 55:52, Berkeley, 1961.)
n.d. Handwritten Gabrielino Vocabulary and Ethnographic Notes. Accession No. 4719 CALIF. Ms. on file, National Anthropological Archives, Smithsonian Institution, Washington, D.C.

Taylor, Thomas T., and Ronald D. Douglas
1982 Archaeological Investigations at CA-Ora-681, A Ceramic Site on the Irvine Coast, Orange County, California. *Pacific Coast Archaeological Society Quarterly* 18(2/3):87-102.

Teggart, Frederick J. (editor)
1911 The Portola Expedition of 1769-1770, Diary of Miguel Costanso. *Publications of the Academy of Pacific Coast History* 2(4). University of California, Berkeley.

Temple II, Thomas Workman
1958 Toypurina the Witch and the Indian Uprising at San Gabriel. *The Masterkey* 32(6):136-152.
1959 The Founding of Misión San Gabriel Arcángel. *The Masterkey* 33(4):103-112.
1960 The Founding of Misión San Gabriel Arcángel Part II: Padre Cambon's Contemporary Report of the Founding. *The Masterkey* 34(1):153-161.
n.d.a Extracts from Mission San Fernando Baptismal, Marriage and Burial Registers. The Thomas Workman Temple Collection. Registers on file, Chancery Archives of the Archdiocese of Los Angeles, Mission San Fernando.
n.d.b The Thomas Workman Temple II Collection of Baptismal Records from the San Gabriel Mission and the Plaza Church in Los Angeles. [Copied by the State Daughters of the American Revolution Genealogical Records Committee in 1944, indexed in 1945 by the State Chairman.] On file, Special Collections, University of California, Los Angeles.

Thompson, Thomas, and Albert West
1883 *History of Santa Barbara County, California.* Thompson and West, Oakland. (Reprinted as *History of Santa Barbara and Ventura Counties, California,* Howell-North, Berkeley, 1961.)

Timbrook, Jan
1987 Virtuous Herbs: Plants in Chumash Medicine. *Journal of Ethnobiology* 7(2):171-180.
1990 Ethnobotany of Chumash Indians, California, Based on Collections by John P. Harrington. *Economic Botany* 44(2):236-253.

Timbrook, Jan, John R. Johnson, and David Earle
1982 Vegetation Burning by the Chumash. *Journal of California and Great Basin Anthropology* 4(2):163-186.

United States Geological Survey
1966 El Monte Quadrangle, 7.5 minute topographic series, photorevised in 1981. Denver.
1967 Riverside West Quadrangle, 7.5 minute topographic series, photorevised in 1980. Denver.

Vane, Sylvia Brakke, and Lowell John Bean
1990 *California Indians: Primary Resources. A Guide to Manuscripts, Artifacts, Documents, Serials, Music and Illustrations.* Revised Edition. BP-AP No. 36, Sylvia Brakke Vane, series editor. Ballena Press, Menlo Park, California.

Van Valkenburgh, Richard
1952 We Found the Lost Indian Cave of the San Martíns. *The Desert Magazine* 15(1):5-8.

Vernon, Charles Clark
1956 A History of the San Gabriel Mountains. *The Historical Society of Southern California Quarterly* 38(4):39-60; (2):141-166; (3):263-288; (4):373-384.

Venegas, Miguel
1759 *A Natural and Civil History of California.* 2 vols. Translated from the original Spanish published in Madrid, 1758. James Rivington and James Fletcher, London. (Reprinted, University Microfilms, Inc., Ann Arbor, 1966.)

Vizcaino, Fr. Juan
1959 *The Sea Diary of Fr. Juan Vizcaino to Alta California 1769.* Glen Dawson, Los Angeles.

Wagner, Henry R.
1929 *Spanish Voyages to the Northwest Coast of America in*

the Sixteenth Century. California Historical Society, San Francisco. (Reprinted, N. Israel, Amsterdam, 1966.)

1941   *Juan Rodríguez Cabrillo: Discoverer of the Coast of California*. California Historical Society, San Francisco.

Walker, Edwin Francis

1952   *Five Prehistoric Archaeological Sites in Los Angeles County, California*. Publications of the Frederick Webb Hodge Anniversary Publication Fund, Volume VI. Southwest Museum, Los Angeles.

Wallace, William J.

1955   A Suggested Chronology for Southern California Coastal Archaeology. *Southwestern Journal of Anthropology* 11(3):214-230. (Reprinted in *The California Indians: A Source Book*, edited by R. F. Heizer and M. A. Whipple, pp. 186-201. University of California Press, Berkeley, 1971.)

1978   Post-Pleistocene Archaeology, 9000 to 2000 B.C. In *California*, edited by Robert F. Heizer, pp. 25-36. Handbook of North American Indians, vol. 8, W. C. Sturtevant, general editor. Smithsonian Institution, Washington, D.C.

1980   A Turtle Shell Rattle from Long Beach. *The Masterkey* 54(3):102-107.

1984   Prehistoric Cultural Development in the South Bay District, Los Angeles County, California. *Pacific Coast Archaeological Society Quarterly* 20(3):1-4.

1987   A Remarkable Group of Carved Stone Objects from Pacific Palisades. *Pacific Coast Archaeological Society Quarterly* 23(1):47-58.

Wallace, William J., and Edith Taylor Wallace

1974   Palos Verdes Carved Stone Figures. *The Masterkey* 48(2):59-66.

Walsh, Jane MacLaren

1976   *John Peabody Harrington: The Man and His California Indian Fieldnotes*. BP-AP No. 6, Lowell John Bean, series editor. Ballena Press, Ramona, California.

Warner, J. J.

1856   Lost Woman of the Island. *Los Angeles Star* 13 December.

Warner, Col. J. J., Judge Benjamin Hayes, and Dr. J. P. Widney

1876   *An Historical Sketch of Los Angeles County, California from the Spanish Occupancy, by the Founding of Mission San Gabriel Archangel, September 8, 1771, to July 4, 1876*. Louis Lewin & Co., Los Angeles. (Reprinted, O. W. Smith Publishers, Los Angeles, 1936.)

Webb, Edith Buckland

1952   *Indian Life at the Old Missions*. W. F. Lewis, Los Angeles. (Reprinted, University of Nebraska Press, Lincoln, 1982.)

Weinman, Dr. Lois J., and Dr. E. Gary Stickel

1978   *Los Angeles-Long Beach Harbor Areas Cultural Resource Survey*. U.S. Army Engineer District, Los Angeles.

Wheeler, George M., First Lieut.

1879   *Report Upon United States Geographical Surveys West of the One Hundredth Meridian, Vol. 7: Archaeology*. Government Printing Office, Washington, D.C.

White, Raymond C.

1963   Luiseño Social Organization. *University of California Publications in American Archaeology and Ethnology* 48(2):91-194.

Whitney-DeSautels, Nancy

1986   Encino Village: The Three Faces of Cultural Resource Management: A Unique Cultural Resource Management Challenge Interspersed with Application of Present Laws vs. A Changing Political Climate. *Pacific Coast Archaeological Society Quarterly* 22(3):1-8.

Wilbur, Marguerite Eyer (editor and translator)

1937   *Duflot de Mofras' Travels on the Pacific Coast*. The Fine Arts Press, Santa Ana, California.

Willey, Gordon R.

1966   *An Introduction to American Archaeology, Vol. I: Middle and North America*. Prentice-Hall, Englewood Cliffs, New Jersey.

Williams, Stephen L., and E. Jane Rosenthal

1993   Soapstone Craft Specialization at the Upper Buffalo Springs Quarry, Santa Catalina Island. *Pacific Coast Archaeological Society Quarterly* 29(3):22-50.

Williamson, Mrs. M. Burton

1903   History of Santa Catalina Island. *Annual Publication of the Historical Society of Southern California and of the Pioneers of Los Angeles County* 6(1):14-31. Los Angeles.

1904   Catalogue of Indian Relics Found on Santa Catalina Island; In the Museums of Los Angeles Chamber of Commerce, the Smithsonian Institute, and Peabody Museum of Archaeology and Ethnology, Harvard University, Cambridge, Mass. *Bulletin of the Southern California Academy of Sciences* 3(3):38-41; 3(4):60-63; 3(9):149-152. Los Angeles.

Winterbourne, J. W.

1967   Report of the Goff's Island Site Excavation. *Pacific Coast Archaeological Society Quarterly* 3(2/3):1-156.

1968a Orange County California Historical Research Project: Newland Hillside Excavation 5/27/35-5/31/35 and 6/3/35-6/24/35. *Pacific Coast Archaeological Society Quarterly* 4(2):1-9.

1968b Orange County California Historical Research Project: Report of Banning estate Excavation (Norris Property), 6/25/35-6/27/35, 7/1/35-7/31/35, and 8/1/35-8/22/35. *Pacific Coast Archaeological Society Quarterly* 4(2):10-17.

1968c Orange County California Anthropological Project: Report of the Excavation of the Grisset Site at Costa Mesa, Orange County, January 21-March 8, 1938. *Pacific Coast Archaeological Society Quarterly* 4(2):18-68.

1969   Orange County California Anthropological Project: Report of the Excavation of the Bonita Site in the San Joaquin Hills, Irvine Ranch, Orange County, March 9-April 25, 1938. *Pacific Coast Archaeological Society Quarterly* 5(4)17-42.

Wlodarski, Robert J.

1978   Ralph Glidden: His Museum and Collection. *The Masterkey* 52(1):4-10.

1979a Catalina Island Soapstone Manufacture. *Journal of California and Great Basin Anthropology* 1(2):331-355.

1979b Ralph Glidden's Catalina Investigations. *The Masterkey* 53(2):55-61.

1982   A Bibliography of Catalina Island Investigations and Excavations (1850-1980). *University of California*

Institute of Archaeology Occasional Paper 9. Los Angeles.

Wlodarski, Robert J., and Daniel Larson
1976 Soapstone and Indian Missionization: Part II. In *The Changing Faces of Main Street: Ventura Mission Plaza Archaeological Project*, edited by Roberta S. Greenwood, pp. 39-62. Redevelopment Agency, City of San Buenaventura.

Wlodarski, Robert J., John F. Romani, and Dan A. Larson
1985 Archaeological Investigations at CA-Ora-1054, A Late Period Site in Laguna Canyon, Orange County, California. *Pacific Coast Archaeological Society Quarterly* 21(3):1-24.

Wlodarski, Robert J., John F. Romani, Gwen R. Romani, and Dan A. Larson
1984 Preliminary Evidence of Metal Tool Use in Soapstone Quarry-Mining on Catalina Island: Jane Russell Quarry. *Pacific Coast Archaeological Society Quarterly* 20(3):35-66.

Woodward, Arthur
1934 An Early Account of the Chumash. *The Masterkey* 8(4):118-123.
1941 Archaeological Notes and Domestic Fowl as Ceremonial Offerings. *American Antiquity* 6(2):284-285.

1944 Gabrielino Indian Language. *The Masterkey* 18(5):145-149.
1957 Juana Maria: Sidelights on the Indian Occupation of San Nicolas Island. *The Westerners Brand Book, The Los Angeles Corral, Book No.* 7:245-270.
1959 Introduction. In *The Sea Diary of Fr. Juan Vizcaino to Alta California 1769*. Glen Dawson, Los Angeles.

Yatsko, Andrew
1989 Reassessing Archaeological Site Density at San Clemente Island. In *Proceedings of the Society for California Archaeology, Vol. 2: Papers Presented at the Annual Meeting of the Society for California Archaeology*, edited by Susan M. Hector, Martin D. Rosen, Lynne E. Christenson, and G. Timothy Gross, pp. 187-204. San Diego.
1990 San Clemente Island Archaeology: An Introduction. *Pacific Coast Archaeological Society Quarterly* 26 (2/3):1-9.

Zahniser, Jack L.
1981 The Prehistory of San Clemente Island: Prolegomena. In *The Cultural Resources of San Clemente Island, California*. Chambers Consultants and Planners, Stanton, California.

INDEX

APPENDIX I

INDIAN VOCABULARIES COLLECTED BY
C. HART MERRIAM

Name of tribe: Tong-vā
Home of tribe: San Gabriel Valley, Calif.
Vocabulary Obtained from: Mrs. J.V. Rosemyre
At (place): Bakersfield, Calif.
Date: Oct. 1903

THE ALPHABET

My vocabularies are written, so far as possible, in simple phonetic English. The words are divided into syllables separated by hyphens. The accented syllable is marked with the acute accent (´).

1. Sounds that have fixed and definite value in English, like our words pin, peg, hat, not, and so on, are pronouced exactly as in English. In such syllables diacritical marks are unnecessary and as a rule are omitted.

2. Sounds represented in English by a double consonant, or by a syllable the pronunciation of which is not phonetic, are always spelled phonetically. Thus the sounds represented by our words *all* and *who* are written *awl* and *hoo*.

3. Unmarked vowels, except in syllables having a fixed value like those mentioned in section 1, have the usual long or pure sound given them in the English alphabet.

4. An unmarked vowel standing alone (as a syllable or word) always takes its long or pure alphabetic sound.

Key to vowel sounds, diacritical marks, and so on.

ā	as in acorn, date, late, mane.
ă	as in fat, bat, hat, have, man.
ah	as in far, father, what.
aw	as in awl, awful.
ē	(or **e** unmarked) as in eject, eternal, meat.
ĕ	as in end, met, net, check, peg, pen, her.
ī	(or **i** unmarked) as in ice, iron, pine, file.
ĭ	as in it, ill, pin, fin, fit, pick, admit.
ō	(or **o** unmarked) as in note, poke.
ŏ	as in not, pot, odd, frog.
oo	as in ooze, spoon.
oi	as in oil, boil, join.
ow	as in how, plow, out.
ū	(or **u** unmarked) as in mule, mute, acute. If the **u** sound forms a syllable by itself, it is commonly spelled *yu*, pronounced *you*.
ŭ	as in tub, mud, us.
û	for a somewhat uncertain or obscure vowel sound, as in but and sun, known as 'the neutral vowel.'

Prolonged vowels are indicated by doubling the letter (as aa, ee, &c.)

Prolonged or trilled consonants are indicated by a double acute accent (˝).

The consonants, except **c**, **g**, and **q**, have their ordinary English values; **c** and **g** having in English both hard and soft sounds, require special treatment; **q** is not used. The **q** sound occurs only before **u**, and is better represented by **kw** (*kween* instead of *queen*).

c is never used except before **h**, as in chin, chum, chap, church. It is commonly preceded by **t** to render the pronunciation more correct. Hence the usual combined is *tch*, as in *hatch*.

g is always hard, as in get, give, grind.

j is always soft, as in jet, jam, jelly, judge.

k has its usual value, as in kill, keep, king. It is also used instead of **c** for the hard sound of **c** in our words cat, cow, come, cold, cream, clinic, and the like.

s has its usual sound, as in see, sink, soft, &c., and is also used instead of **c** for the soft sound of **c** in our words cent, cinder, nice.

^{ch} (super) has the soft sound as in german *ach, büch*, &c. (In MS written $\underset{\smile}{ch}$).

^{n} (super) is nasalized, and follows a nasalized vowel, as o^n. (In MS written $\underset{\smile}{n}$).

An apostrophe (') after a vowel followed by another letter gives the long sound to the vowel, and may also indicate an omitted or silent letter.

An apostrophe (') at either end of a syllable calls for an exploded sound.

An exclamation (!) after a letter indicates that the letter is stressed.

* = Compares with Buschmann vocab. of 1856

1. NUMERALS

1.	Po-koo	23.	
2.	Wĕh-hā	24.	
3.	Paĥ-hā	25.	Wā'-hās wā-haś mah-hahr
4.	Wah-chaĥ	26.	
5.	Mah-haŕ	27.	
6.	Pah-vaĥ-hā	28.	
7.	Wah-chaĥ-kaν́-e-ah	29.	
8.	Wā-hā's-wah-chah	30.	Pah-hās wā-hās mah-har
9.	Mah-ha'hr-kaν́-e-ah	35.	
10.	Wā-hāś-mah-hah'r	40.	Wah-chaĥ hās wā-hā's mah-haŕ
11.	Wā-hā's-mah-hah'r-koi-po-koo	45.	
12.	Wā-hā's-mah-hah'r-koi-wĕh-hā	50.	Mah-haŕ-is-wā-hās mah-haŕ
13.		55.	
14.		60.	Pah-vaĥ-hās wā-hāś mah-har
15.	Wā-hās-mah-hak'r-koi-mah-har	65.	
16.		70.	Wah-chaĥ kav-e-ah wā-hās mah-har
17.		75.	
18.		80.	
19.		85.	
20.	Wā-hās-wa-hās-mah-hah'r	90.	
21.		95.	
22.		100.	

2. PERSONS

People (Indian):	Tah-raĥ-hat
Crowd or lot of people:	Tar-raĥ$\underset{\smile}{^{ch}}$-um
The old people:	Tah-tah-row'm
The young people:	E-mé-mōt tah-raĥ-hat
People (White men):	Rah-waĥ-nat
Man:	Wahr-raw-ē't; Wah-roi-ē't; Wah- roit*

Woman:	Tō-kō'r*
My father:	Ne-nŏk
Your father:	Mo-noḱ
His father:	Ah-nok
Father:	(his) Ah-nŏ'k*
Father (addressed):	Ne-noḱ
Mother:	(his) Ah-ō'k (my mother Ne-ō'k)*
Mother (addressed):	Mō'k
Son:	(his) Ah-ā´-kok, Ē-kok=son*
My son:	Nā-e-kok*
Daughter:	(his) Ah-ā-aŕ-ro*
My daughter:	Nā-aŕ-ro*
Brother:	(his) Ah́-pah*
My brother:	Ne-pah*
Sister:	Ah-ŏh-hŏ
Elder brother (my):	Ne-e-kok wor-roit
Elder sister (my):	Nā-aŕ-ro to-kōn
Younger brother (my):	Ne-e-kok che-noo-e
Younger sister (my):	Nā-aŕ-ro tah-hí͡ch
Grandfather (father's father):	Ah-kah-kah, Ne͡ch-howk
Grandfather (mother's father):	(my) Ne-kah́-kah
Grandmother (father's mother):	(my) Ne-sook
Grandmother (mother's mother):	(my) Ne-sook
Uncle (father's brother):	Ne-tah́-is
Uncle (mother's brother):	Ne-tah-is
Aunt (father's sister):	Ne-pow'k
Aunt (mother's sister):	Ne-nah́-tso
Old man:	Er-ra͡ch´-po
Old woman:	Tah-hoo˝
Young man:	Koo-vah́-cho
Young woman:	Kah-vó-che
Little boy (4 to 12 years):	Kwé-te
Little girl (4 to 12 years):	Tah-hí-e͡ch
Children (4 to 12 years):	Tah-rah́-hí͡ch
Boy baby:	Koo-ar˝
Girl baby:	Ta͡ch-hi
Married man:	Nah-ō´t
Married woman:	Nah-ō´t
Widow:	Hah-vach́-mē͡ch
Widower:	Hah-vach́-mē͡ch
Old maid:	Hí-nah-oot´
Old bachelor:	Hí-nah-oot´
Barren woman:	Tō-ō'r
My husband:	Ne-ah́-sung
Your husband:	Mo-ah́-sung
Husband:	Ah-ah-sung
My wife:	Ne-toó-ho
Wife:	Ah-too-ho
Mother-in-law (husband's mother):	Ne-ahś
Mother-in-law (wife's mother):	Ne-ahś
Your wife's mother:	Mo-waś
Wife's sister:	Ne koos-nah
Husband's sister:	Ne-pe-hah
Husband's brother:	Ne-kooź-nah
Somebody:	Hah-ké-ke
Anybody:	Too-mah-hah́-ké

Nobody:	Hí-hah-ke
Companion:	Ne-ā´-he-ah
Stranger:	Tah́-haht
Friend:	Ne-ā´-yah*
Enemy:	Né-kit*
Adopted person:	Ā-rah́-ho-ē̱ᶜʰ
Orphan:	Yah-hí-hah-ke
Artist (man who makes drawings):	Ā-sí-nē̱ᶜʰ
Dandy:	Che-too˝
Thief:	Po-kē´̱ᶜʰ
Trader:	Nah-hwahń-nahᶜʰ
Runner:	Hah-vah́-veet
Hunter:	Hah́-chā-nar
A dancer (both men and women):	Yah-kā´-nar
A singer (both men and women):	Che-eń-nar˝
Man singer:	Che-eń-nar war-roit
Woman singer:	Che-eń-nar tō-koŕ

3. PARTS OF BODY

My head:	Ne-poo-ań
Your head:	Mo-poo-ań
His head:	Ah-po-ań
Head:	Ah-] po-ań*
Top of head:	Ah-hé-kī´n
Forehead:	Ah-kon-nin
Temple:	Ah-yah́-rin
Eye:	Ah-tso-chōn
Eyelid:	Ah-tso-chon
Eyelash:	Ah-pe-ve-se-ro
Nose:	Ah-mŭẃ-pin // Ah-meŕ-pin*
Nostril:	a-soon-gnah
Ear:	Ah-nahń-naᶜʰ
Cheek:	Ah-hŏ´-hŏ
Chin:	Ah-ohń
Mouth:	Ah-tō’ng-in*
Lips:	Re-vo-tōng-ē̱ᶜʰ
Tongue:	Ah-noń-in*
Back of neck:	Ah-koo-tchan
Throat:	Ang-on*
Shoulder:	Ah-sō’k
Arm:	Ah-mahn*
Elbow:	Ah-ché-eń
Hand:	Ah-mah́-mahn*
Right hand:	Ah-té-ve
Left hand:	Ah-kah́-no
Fist (closed hand):	Ah-teŕ-min
Palm of hand:	Ah-mahń
Back of hand:	Ah-té-vĕh
Fingers:	Ah-mah́-mahn
Thumb (=big finger):	Yo-o-ē’t-tah́-mahn
Index finger (=pointer finger):	Ah-hooch́-ket ah-mahn
Middle finger (=middle finger):	Nah-mah́-kit ah-mahn
Fourth finger (=4th finger):	Wah-chah́ ah-mahn
Little finger (=10th finger):	Wā-hās-mah-hahr ah-mahn
Knuckles:	Ah-ā-en

Whole body:	Ah-tah́-tah^ch*
Back:	Ah-tsah́^ch
Side:	Ah-ní-krin
Chest:	Ah-too-nō'n
Female breasts:	Ah-peeṕ-cho
Belly:	Ah-hō-nan
Hip:	Ah-o
Thigh:	Ah-kah́-chin
Knee:	Ah-tong-un
Lower leg:	Ah-hook
Foot:	Ah-nā'v
Sole:	Ah-nā'v
Heel:	Ah-toó-mon
Toes (same as fingers):	Ah-mah-man
Nails:	Ah-choo-choos
Skin:	Tach́-tah-ho-hutch
Hair:	Ap-po-wań/Ap-pă-han*
Beard:	Ah-pā´-har-rōt
Mustache:	Ah-pā´-han
Bone:	Ah-eń*
Skull:	Ah-pwah́-nah-ā'n
Jaw:	Ah-o'n
Cheek bone (malar):	Ah-eń
Back bone (vertebræ):	Ah-chah́^ch
A single vertebra:	Nah-veets-ko ah-en
Shoulderblade:	Ah-poó-mōn
Ribs:	Ah-ah́-man
Tendon or sinew:	Ah-tahń
Teeth:	Ah-tah́-tum*
Incisor tooth:	Ah-tah́-tum
Canine tooth:	Ah-tah́-tum
Molar tooth:	Ah-tah'ḿ
Brain:	Ī'^ch-cheek
Heart:	Ah-hōń*
Pulse:	Ah-he-kī'n
Lungs:	Ah-poop-mon
Windpipe:	Ah-he-kī'n ah-mó-nin
Stomach:	Ah-heŕ-nan
Liver:	Ah-sahŕ
Gall Bladder:	Ah^ch-ahń
Intestines:	Ah-seen
Kidneys:	Ah-poo-von
Bladder:	Ah-se-seets ah-hah́-vin
Uterus:	Ak ké-hahn
Blood:	Ah-hī´'n*
Milk:	Ah-hah^ch-ī'n
Excrement:	Yi-yi-tah
Saliva:	Ah-hah́-ran
Sweat:	Ah-tonǵ
Fat:	We-tah́
Oil:	Ah-wé-u

4. HEALTH, DISEASE, AND PHYSICAL CONDITION

Well:	Te-heŕ-vit
Sick:	Tsí-ē't
A sick man:	Tsi't-wor-ro-it
Strong:	Mo-ti-e
Weak:	Ah-pooś-too-e-ve
Alive:	Yí-ē't
Dead:	Ah-mŭ´-yah
Death:	Moi-yuḱ-mē͞eᶜʰ
Dying:	Moi-yuḿ-yen mōk
Awake:	Yí-ē't
Asleep:	Yah-tahḿ-kōk*
Sleepy:	Yah-tō´-arr˝
Drowned:	O-mé-nō'k
Burned:	Taẃ-ke
Lame:	No-meé
Blind:	Tō'-ah-vōr
A blind man:	Tō-ah-vōr war-ro-e't
Deaf:	Tō-mōnᶜʰah
A cut:	Gni-kā͞ᶜʰ
A scar:	U-pe-hah-híᶜʰ
A sore:	Ah-chí-in
A cold:	Ho-hahí (Hro-hahí)
Fever:	O-ró-ah-tań
Pain:	Mo-tí-e͞ᶜʰ
Headache:	Mo-tí-ne ne-poo-ahń
Toothache:	Mo-tí-ne tahm
Rheumatism:	Nā-nā´-ver
Diarrhoea:	Wé-vaht
Vomiting:	Yo-é
Consumption (tuberculosis):	Hŏ-haht
Puberty:	Wo-sō'-ḱ-mōk
Menstruation:	Ah-moó-sin
Pregnant:	To-ī't
Miscarriage:	Yo-seé-nōk
Insane:	Hah-mah́-pe
Drunk:	Pi-yaŕ
Fat (corpulent):	We-tań
Slim:	Yah-rŏ-re
Old:	Too-ho
Young:	E-mōt
Tired:	Yah-pahk-mō'k
Quick:	Mah-hé-ko
Slow:	Wah-wahnǵ-e
Hungry:	Ko-vé
Thirsty:	Pah-rhar

5. DISPOSITION, ATTRIBUTES, AND EMOTIONS

Happy:	Ah-wā´-es-ko
Unhappy:	Ah-hoẃ-oo-soon
Glad:	Ah-wā´-es-ko
Sorry:	Ne-o-mah-re
Good:	Te-hŏ´-vit* [or Te-her-vit]

Better:	Me-nā te-her-vit
Bad:	Mŭh-hí-itch * [or Mŭh-hi´-e̲ch]
Worse:	Mĕh-hí me-eí-te
Kind:	Te-hŏv´-so-nar
Unkind:	Mĕh-hí soo-nar [same word as below]
Cruel:	Mŭ-hí-soo-nar [same word as above]
Cross:	É-tah-ko
Angry:	Ā-tok-koí
Quarrelsome:	Noẃ-om-so
Honest:	Mah-né-sar
Dull (stupid):	Nah-noẃ-re
Smart:	I-yaí-kā-rō't
Proud:	Che-toó
Afraid:	Kwah-e-ō'k
Scared:	Whań-hā-o-so / Kwań-ā-o-so
Surprised:	Hā-rā´k-muk
Jealous:	Ní-hes-so
Ashamed:	E-poo-ye
Inquisitive:	He-owń-sah-mit he-tań
Intelligent:	Yah-rah-vī't
Mistaken:	Hí-ne-yah-rah-ko-mă
Lonesome:	Ah-hoẃ-so-kwah-ań
Lucky:	Te-heí-kwe i-yań-rin
Unlucky:	Ah-hoẃ-so ni-yań-rin
Clothed:	Ah-hań-wo-me
Naked:	Mah-man-vah
Clean:	Kwi-ā̲ch
Dirty:	Yĕh-mah-hĕ
Pretty:	Tā-hó-vit
Homely (plain):	Mĕh-hí-ē̲ch
Poor:	Mo-ré-vātch
Rich (wealthy):	Ah-hé-rō't
Right:	Hí-yah-yań-re
Wrong:	Hi-haht-e-hŏv́-ko
Revenge:	Í-e-kit
Mischief:	Mer-hí-ke-hań
Busy:	I-yó-e-nin-ny mí-kan
Idle:	Yah-hi-ne mi-kan
Lazy:	Choo-ē't
Present:	Har-rō't-e
Absent:	Hi̲ch-hah
Disappointed:	Choo-choo-ē'k
Hate:	Ne-ī's-min
Love:	Yŏ-yum-mē̲ch
Married:	Nah-oó

6. CLOTHING AND ORNAMENTS

Rabbit-skin blanket:	Tŏ-saẃ-tah-ah-pā´-han
Buckskin (tanned):	Soo-kah´-tah ah-pā´-han
Toga or blanket:	Hah-vō't
Belt worn by men:	Ah-mań-che
Belt worn by women:	Ah-mań-che
Ceremonial belt:	Ah-mań-che
Breech-cloth:	Ah-tah-par-ră-bo

Shirt (formerly worn by men):   Ah-ko-ton
Skirt (formerly worn by women):   Ah-now-wah
Moccasins for men (winter):   Ah-nā´-nāv-sah<u>ch</u>
Hat (basket) worn by women: Ah-maḣ-kah
Necklace of bear claws: Hooń-rah ah-choó-chov
Necklace of shells: Ah-hoó-no<u>ch</u>
Headband: Pah-vahḿ-ut
Headdress of feathers: Pah-vahḿ-ut
Bracelet: Maḣ-mo-nah
Beads: To-koó-par
Wampum (long string of it):   Ow-vā-rōt
Wampum (of small shells, worth more than big):   Ho-pe-hah
A shell: E-cheé<u>ch</u>
Abalone shell: E-che-ē´<u>ch</u>
Ear pendant (of small shells):   Toó-e-kā<u>ch</u>
Amulet ('lucky stone,'&c.):   To-sow˝t
Red paint: O-ye˝
Black paint: Nō´-ve-ō't
White paint: Tó-vē<u>ch</u>
Tattoo marks: Ah-ā´-sin
Face tattooing: Ah-ā´-sin
Body tattooing: Ah-ā´-sin

7. DWELLINGS (INCLUDING FIRE)

Village or town: Ke-kē´<u>ch</u>
Village ground (plaza or court):   Hahr-ró-chō't
House (permanent):   Kē<u>ch</u>*
Home: Né-ké-in
Ceremonial house (covered with earth):   Ke-hí-e, Nah-tōr-rē´<u>ch</u>
Sweat house: Se-hi-ē<u>ch</u>
Brush wikiup: Mah-maḣ-har-kē<u>ch</u> // O-ró-vā-ve ke<u>ch</u>
Brush roof-canopy or arbor: Mah-maḣ-har-kē<u>ch</u> // O-ró-vā-ve ke<u>ch</u>
Brush blind (for hunting):   Hoo-wē´<u>ch</u>
Doorway: Ah-hó-non
Floor: Ă´-hor
Bed: O-kaw´-chō't
Fireplace: Hó-mā-chō't
Fire: Tsaḣ-bō't
Flame or blaze: Ah-vāŕ-ko-min // Bā-rā´k-mut
Live coals or embers: Ah-too-ahń
Dead coals: Ah-troó-hin ah-too-ahń
Ashes: Koo-see˝
Smoke: Ah´-che-ahń
Smoke hole: Ah-heŕ-pă-ké
Poker: Kwe-che-ahí
Firewood: Koo-taḣ
Light from fire: Pah-hahí-ko-min
Light from torch or lamp: Ah-paḣ-haht ko-meeń
Steps: Ep-pā<u>ch</u>-mī´<u>ch</u>
Ladder (pole with sticks tied on):   Ā-pāk-mo-tsoot
Pole: Ko-toó-mut
Seat: Sā-haí
Tule mat: Sā-hé
Fence of brush: Mah-maḣ-rat-tar

Footbridge: Nahm̀-ko-mots-ōt

Deserted: Ah-nít ké-ē<u>^{ch}</u>

8. WEAPONS, IMPLEMENTS, AND UTENSILS
(Except baskets)

Bow (common bow):	Pí-tro-ar
War bow (for bears etc., sinew on back):	Chah-kah́-mar*
Bow string:	Wé-vōr
Arrow, blunt pointed:	Choó-ar*
Arrow, stone pointed:	Hoo-pā´-kah, Choó-rah hoo-pā-kah
Stone arrow-point:	Hoór
Arrowstone (for polishing):	O-roó-sar
Quiver:	Ap-pŭ<u>^{ch}</u>
Spear (for fish):	Ah-nah́<u>^{ch}</u>
Snare:	Ho-ah-chō´t
Knife (of stone):	Pah<u>^{ch}</u>-hō't
Hunting (belt) knife:	Ah-tanǵ-an
Pocket knife:	Ah-tanǵ-an ah-pach́ hun
Skin scraper or dressing knife:	Kō'ng-ar
Rabbit stick (=hunting stick):	Koo-tah́ hoo-koov́-chōt
Fire drill:	To-tah-chah́-vō't (Wahn-ne-kit=the tree)
Stone mortar, portable:	Tō-kwé-is
Pestle of stone:	Ah-pah́-ho
Hand stone for rubbing:	Ah-mahń
Acorn leach:	Wah́<u>^{ch}</u>
Cache for acorns:	Tso-ah́-kah
Earthenware vessel:	Kwe-nahŕ
Earthenware oja (water jar):	O-roó-sar
Kettle or vessel for cooking:	Kwe-nahŕ
Cooking hole in ground:	Nah-hē´<u>^{ch}</u>
Hot stones for cooking in basket:	To-tah́
Stirring stick (to stir hot stones in basket):	Wā-ah́-ho
Digging stick:	Ah-nah́<u>^{ch}</u>
A stick:	Koo-tah́
Pipe:	Wee'k-chot (straight)
Tobacco bag:	Pā´s-pe-vaht ah-ah-wah<u>^{ch}</u>-han
Tobacco:	Pāś-pe-baht
Pine resin or pitch:	Ah-sah́-nah
Glue of a kind of stuff comes on limbs of high branches, for arrow points & other purposes:	Hoo-oot
Bone awl used in basketry:	E-vē't
Needle:	E-vē't
Thread of sinew:	Ah-tahń = sinew
Thread of:	We-vor
Gourd cup or dipper (inside of gourd used for soapsuds in washing. Good to take stains out and make clothes white):	Wahnǵ-ar
A kind of pointed instrument:	Hoo-pā´-kah (a point) tar-rī'n-hah
Soaproot brush:	Să-pā´cho-hah
Cord or rope:	Wé-vor˝
Carrying band for head:	Wé-vor
Carrying net:	Hoẃ-oo-kut

Rabbit net:	Had none
Fish net:	Wé-vor
Boat (bundles of tules):	Tah-rī'ng-hah
Paddle:	Koo-taḣ
Saddle:	Yaḣ-ko-mōts-hōt
Riata or lariat:	Ne-wé-vor
Circular tray or shallow bowl of wood for serving food (made of al-é-sah [aliso?] wood):	Koo-tah-mí-ē^{ch}

9. BASKETS

The baskets:

Basket (general term):	Ko-mé-me
Burden basket:	Paḣ-tsah-ah^{ch}
Seed paddle:	Ho-kov́-chōt
Large cooking bowl (coiled, also for carrying in net on back):	Choo-aḣ-kah
Small mush or soup bowl (coiled):	Ko-mé-me
Circular winnower (flat; coiled):	No-vor
Coarse scoop-shape tray of open work:	Choo-ooŕ / Chah-aŕ
Hat (coiled):	Ah-mah-kah
Baby or papoose basket:	Tahr-raḣ-hoor
Water bottle (large):	Se-aḣ-mo / Pí-ro-aŕ
Urn or bottleneck:	Mo-tooṁ-hah
Subglobular choke-mouth bowl:	Toó-moó-hah
Mortar or winnowing basket:	To-kweeś
Gambling tray:	Re-vaḣ-hah
Storehouse basket (large subglobular, for acorns, pine nuts, &c.):	Choo-moó-hah

The kinds of weave:

Coarse open-rod work:	Choo-or
Coiled weave:	Swahr

The body materials:

Rods of willow (*Salix*):	Mo-ār
Rush (*Juncus textilis*):	So-ar"
Root of tree yucca (*Yucca brevifolia*):	Ah-wé-win
Plume of California Quail (*Lophortyx*):	Kah-kaŕ-ah-aḣ-poo-ahn

10. FOOD AND DRINK

Food:	Kwah-ē´^{ch}
Drink:	Pah-ē^{ch} // Pah^{ch}
Meat:	Hoong-é-vit
Dried meat:	Ah-hó-kin hoong-é-vit
Tallow:	Ah-wé-yu
Marrow:	Ah-paḣ-nah
Deer tongue:	Ah-nō'ṅg-in
Fish:	Kū'r Ke-ūr
Dried fish:	Ah-hó-kin ke-yū'r
Meat soup:	Ah-saḣ-hin

Egg:	Ah-hah^{ch}-ne-he
A feast:	Ke-hi-e
Acorn feast:	Ke-hí-e^{ch}
An acorn (of *Q.lobata*):	Shev-vé
Acorn meats:	Che-me^{ch}-kwahr
Acorn meal before leaching:	Kwar pā'r-ē^{ch}
Acorn meal after leaching:	Wō-ē^{ch}′
Acorn mush:	We$^{\prime ch}$
Acorn soup:	Wé^{ch}
Cakes of mush hardened in water:	Pē^{ch}-kā-e
Bread (tortilla):	Sang-ah-he
Pine nut (of *Pinus monophylla*):	Tō-vah-aht
Pine nut (of *P. sabiniana*):	Wah^{ch}-huí
Pine nut soup:	O-rooś-ko-mi^{ch}
Tule root (*Scirpus lacustris*):	Sā-é-ă ah-wé-win
Mush of wild oats:	Pee'r-kā^{ch}
Beans (cultivated):	Pe-tó-nat
Blackberries (*Rubus sp.*):	Mō-aŕ
Cherry stones:	Chah-mē^{ch}
Pinole seed (*Madia elegans* [*Linum*?]):	Pah-sé-e
Edible mushrooms (toad-stool):	Sé-so-ah-mah-kah
Honey:	Ah-wā
Sourberry cider:	Pi-ē′^{ch}
Sourberry brush:	Tsah-mē^{ch}
Intoxicant drink of *Datura*:	Mah-neek
Whisky:	Pí-e-vet
Indian tobacco (*Nicotiana attenuata* and other species):	Pāś-pe-baht
Indian tobacco made into cakes (boiled and evaporated till dry):	Pāś-pe-baht
Medicine:	Ah-no-vēn
Salt:	Ung-er$^{\prime\prime}$*
Salt from saltgrass (used for fever):	Sé-e-mōt
Raw:	Sow't
Cooked:	Ah-kwah-sin
Ripe:	Kwah-sō'k
Unripe:	Sow't (or Soẃ-wut)
Sweet:	Ah-wā
Sour:	Ché-kwah
Bitter:	Te-pă
Chewing gum (of milk of milkweed, the milk is boiled to convert it to gum):	To-haŕ-che-ar

11. MORTUARY, CEREMONIAL, AND RELIGIOUS TERMS

Corpse:	Ah-mŭ′-yah
Grave in ground:	Nah-he^{ch}′; Nah-hah-met-sut
Burial place, cemetery:	Koo-nas-gnă
Cremation:	Nah-hah-ming-ah
The funeral pyre:	Ah-tō′ch-gnah
The ashes and burnt bones of the dead:	Koo-seé-rō'k
Mourning ceremony (at time of burial or burning):	Yū-im-kah-too-ē^{ch}
Mourning ceremony (at a later period; named for the effigy [Chí-e-vōr] which is burned):	Chí-vor (Chí-e-vor)
The presents burned at the Chi-e-vor:	Se-ō^{ch}-he
Spirit or soul while in body:	Pe-sah-gah-soon

After leaving body:	Pe-sah́-gah hé-ki'n
Direction taken on leaving body (down):	Tó-rah o^{ch}-ah-rah (=going down)
Final abode (future world, above, name used before priests came-place above):	To-koop-nah-af-ro
God or spirit:	Te-huv-soo-nar (kind-hearted); To-me-ar [(Chief) Probably had no such word.]
The Devil or bad spirit:	She-soo
A ghost:	Ah-ní't
A witch:	Ah-hoov́-war-rā-rō't
Magic:	Ah-hoov́-war-rā-rō't
A dream:	Hoó-hoo-waf-ră-wē͇^{ch}
A poison:	Nah-vā-haf́
Medicine or healing dance:	Nah-mí-ē´^{ch}͇ // Nah-mí-nōk
A dance:	Yah-kā-ē͇^{ch}
Medicine or healing song:	Che-ā´-ē͇^{ch} (any song)
A song:	Che-ā´-ā͇^{ch} [or Che-ā´-ē´^{ch}͇]
Rattle (made of bladder of mountain sheep; stones):	Ah-pah́-an
Mask:	No

12. SOCIAL ORGANIZATION, GOVERNMENT, WAR

Hugo Reid (1852) gives To-me-ar, as chief's eldest son.
" " " " Man-i-sar, " " " daughter.

Chief:	Tō´-me-r*
Tribe:	Hah-ké-vet
Family:	Ah-taf́-hi-rot
Head of family:	P-mō't́-me-ah-wah́
Doctor or shaman:	Ah-hoó-var-e-doot
A council:	Pe-ō'ts-ko-me
Signal fire:	Che-wā-et chah́-wot
War:	Noẃ-mē͇^{ch}
A fight (between several people):	Now-mem-mō'k
A fight (of 2):	Now-mach-moi
A Witch:	Ā-hoó-war-roo-e-ruit
A fiesta:	Ke-hí-yah́

13. AMUSEMENTS

Rabbit hunt:	Hah́-chā-ro
Game of lacrosse:	Pe-ah-kā-e
The ball:	Hah-bo-ve
The bat:	Pe-ah-kā-e
Game of ball:	
The ball:	Hah-bŭ´-ve
Game of throwing pole:	Ne-yah́-kā´-e͇^{ch}
Game of 10 sticks:	Chah-chahń-kā
Guessing game of 2 sticks (or other objects):	Choo-chooch́-kā͇^{ch}
A doll:	Mā-hah́-ar
A popgun:	Pī't́-ho-ar

14. PHYSIOGRAPHIC TERMS

Water:	Pahr˝*
Lake:	Mo-mŭt
Ocean:	Mo-mŭt*
River:	Pah-hī´t*
Creek:	Hur-rin-nah
Spring:	Pahŕ-rah-tsó-tsōn
Waterfall:	Po-ré-no-ke-pahŕ to-sowt˝-gnă
Rapids:	To-sowt˝-gnă
Salt water:	Ché-kwah́ pahr
Alkaline water:	Té-pû-paŕ
Running water:	Yah-mé-nō'k-ā-paŕ
Stagnant water:	Too-roo-ke-hah-paŕ
Shallow:	Che-wé-ve
Wet:	Pah-vaŕ
Dry:	Ah-hó-kin
Land:	Ŏ-hŭr*
Island:	Nah-mah́-king mōń-tah ĕh-hur
Mountain:	Hí-ē̲ᶜʰ
A bald mt.:	Re-ó-pe hi-ē̲ᶜʰ
Cliff:	Nah́-har
Bank:	Nah́-har
Canyon:	Ah-huŕ-rin
Cave:	Hŭ-ró-pe
Forest (woods):	We-se-ah́ᶜʰ̲ nah
Chaparral:	Pah-sah́-kit
Meadow (moist cienega):	Kwe-nah́-vet
Swamp (tule):	I-yō´-in-se-e
Valley:	Ā-wāḱ-gnah-ar-ro
Plain or flat:	Yow-wé-hah
Desert:	Wah-wah́-wē't
Trail or road:	Pet˝
Footprint:	Ah-me-ach
The whole world:	Yŭh-oo-et-ur-hur [Yŭh-oo-et = big]
An earthquake:	Yí-tok-ah́-hor [or Yi´-tok-ŭ-hor]
Earth (ground):	Ŏ-hŏr*
Dust:	Ah-kó-yah-kin
Sand:	O-hā't́
Sandy:	O-hā'ting-ah
Mud:	Kwe-naŕ
Muddy:	Kwe-nahńg-ah
Rock:	To-tah́*
Rocky:	To-tó-ting-ah
Big rock:	To-tah́ yo-o-ē't
Small rock (stone):	Che-noó-e to-tah́
Flat rock:	Te-hŭ-ve to-tah́
Salt:	Ung-ar˝*
A salt lick:	Che-kwanǵ-ah
Asphalt:	Sah˝-naht
Shade:	Ah-too-she
Shadow:	Ah-too-she
Reflection in water:	Ne-ā´-sah pah'ng-ah
An echo:	Ah-nah́-hahr-ră-se

15. POINTS OF COMPASS, CELESTIAL BODIES, WEATHER

North:	Pí-e-me
South:	Ke-tah́-me
East:	Tah́-ming- af́-ro
West:	Toó-ŏ-mé
Sun:	Tah́-met*
Moon:	Mwaŕ*
New moon:	E-mooí mwaŕ
Full moon:	Yă-o-ē't-mwar
Star:	So-sō't*
North star:	E-ū´-ko soo-se-ō't
Shooting star:	Po-ré-no-ke soo-se-ō'ţ
Great Dipper:	Nah-ví-ū-e soo-se-ō't
Milky way:	Nah-ví-ū-e̱ch to-koó-prah
Sky:	Too-koó-par
Air:	Ah-he-kī´n
Sunshine:	Ah-pah́-haht-ko-min-tah́-met
Moonlight:	Ah-pah́-haht ko-min-mwaŕ-rah
Daylight:	Ah-yoẃ-ko-min
Dark:	Ah́-o-me
Clear:	Er-re-ō'p-ko
Cloudy:	E-yūm-ko
A cloud:	Nah-vah́-kit
Clouds:	
Light:	Tah́-ur
Dark (storm clouds):	Ow'm kō-no-vah́-kit [Ow'm pronounced Yoom]
Fog:	Koo-teeí
Rain:	Ah-kwah́-kin*
Wind:	He-kí-o-kre (windy) // Ah-he-kī'n*
North wind:	Tooḿ-kah-ve ah-hé-ki'n
South wind:	Kee-tah-ne ah-he-ki'n
East wind:	Kŏ-meek-vă ah-he-ki'n
West wind:	Pím kah-vā ah-hé-ki'n
Storm:	Ah-kó-yah-ko-miń
Thunder:	Tah́-arr˝
Lightning:	Kwi-yah́-ko-muk
Rainbow:	Ah-soo-in to-koo-per-ah
Earthquake:	Yí-tōk-e-ŭr-hur
Snow:	Yow-ahí*
Ice:	Yow-ahí
Frost:	Po-tōś-kă muk-e-paŕ
Cold:	O-tsé*
Hot:	O-ró*

16. SEASONS AND PERIODS

A year:	Po-koo-tah-mā-ving-e̱ch
This year:	Me-tā'mt-tah-mā-ving-e̱ch
Last year:	Po-nah-me
Next year:	Mahm-por-ā-ke tah-mā-ving-e̱ch
Summer:	Aw-ró-re-vā*
Winter:	Ah-chó-ché-vā*
Spring:	Hā-ah-mo pah-ko o-ró-re-ve
Fall:	Hā-ah-mo pah-ko o-cho-che-vě

A month or moon:	Po-koo-mahr
A day (24 hours):	Po-koó-taĥ-met
Today:	Me-tā´-mah
Yesterday:	Po-ahń-nah
Tomorrow:	He-yahń-tā
Tonight:	Yoẃ-ke
Day:	Tah-raĥ-me
Night:	Yoẃ-ke
Morning:	He-aĥ-me
Evening:	Ah-se-ahnǵ-ah
Noon:	Ah-ni-kah-rin-tah-mit (=sun up above)
Midnight:	Ah-naĥ-mah ke-ă-mă
Sunrise:	Pe-saĥ-ke taĥ-mit
Sunset:	Pah-kó-ke taĥ-mit

17. FREQUENCY, TIME, AND QUANTITY

Once:	Poo-koó-se-mah-nā'm tow
Twice:	Wā-hās mah-nā²m-tow
Three times:	Pah-hās mah-nā²m-tow
Four times:	Wah-chah-hās mah-nā²m-tow
Five times:	Mah-haĥ-ris mah-nā²m-tow
Ten times:	Wā-hās mah-har mah-nā'm-tow
First:	Mo-pé-vā
Second:	Í-he-an
Third:	Ah-paĥ-he-an
Fourth:	Ah-wah˝-chan
Fifth:	Ah-maĥ-her-re-ań
Tenth:	Ah-wā´-hes mah haŕ
Last:	Ah-weet́-ko-min
Often:	Hoo-roó-rah
Seldom:	Mahm-hutś-ko
Sometimes:	Po-vo-me
Usually:	Mahm-hutcĥ-ko
Always:	Hoo-roó-rah
Never:	Hí-hah-miń-kah-pe
Time:	He-ahḿ-ō-ē-fe-mé
Early:	Hoo-noó-ko
Late:	Ah-se anǵ-ah
Now:	Ah-nahng-e
Not yet:	Hí-po
By and by:	Me-nā´-per-ro
Before:	Ho-noo-ko
After:	Sé-vé
Soon:	Mah-he-ko
Nearly:	He-ă´-moo-too-maĥ
Recently:	Pó-me
Next time:	Wā-ā´-kā-pro
Long ago:	Ho-nó-ko
Common:	Wé-ŏ-chōt
Rare:	Yah-hí-he-tah
Plenty:	He-yaĥ-mo i-yó-in
Scarce:	Hí-yah-yó-in
Enough:	I-yó-in
Not enough:	Mé-che

Full:	Poo-e˝-nōk
Empty:	Tah-kweé-nōk
Something:	He-tahḿ-nĕh
Nothing:	Yah-hí-e
All:	O-wā´-ē⁀ᶜʰ
Some:	Po-me-che
Another:	Wă´-haʰ-ké
Many (or much):	I-yó-in
Few (or not much):	Mé-che
More:	Hah-maṅ
Less:	Ah-ní-krīn
None:	Yah-hí-he-taṅ
The whole:	O-wā´
Half (in length):	Ah-ní-krin
Half (in quantity):	Ah-ní-krin
A quarter:	Mé-che ă-ní-kar-in
Single:	Ah-níkrin hah-vahᶜʰ
Double:	Nōḿ-num-kaw
Unit (measure) of length [about inches 4], tip of middle finger to around wrist twice:	Nah-wi/Nah-wi-u-ē⁀ᶜʰ
Unit of value [string of wampum], (8 strings used to be worth one Mexican dollar!):	Pō´nk

18. SIZE, FORM, AND PROPERTIES

Large:	Yŭh-oo-et
Small:	Che-noó-e
Heavy:	Po-tŏ´
Light:	Hoẃ-me
Tall:	Kah-hŏ
Short:	Kah-moo-é
Long:	Kah-hŏ
High:	Kah-hŏ
Low:	Kwet-ches-ko
Narrow:	Che-noó-e
Broad:	Yah-oo-ē't
Flat:	Mă-taṅ-pe
Thick (by measure):	Po-ré-hah
Thick (like mush):	Pē'r-kā
Thin (by measure):	Ho-mo-kah
Thin (like water):	Pah-var˝
Shape:	Ah-vaṅ-hah
Round (like a ball):	Hrah-boo-be
Round (like a stick):	Re-kwaṅ-hah
A circle or hoop:	Ter-rah-re
A crescent:	Chah-kaṅ-mar
A triangle:	Paṅ-he-ah ché-en
A square:	Wahts-saṅ-ah-che-eń
A rectangle:	Wahts-saṅ-ah-che-eń haṅ-wŏ-hi-kah-hur
A point:	Hoo-pā´-kah
A corner or angle:	Nah-raṅ-ko & Che-eń
Diamond shape ◇:	Só-tah-ă-ā-sin
Zigzag:	Ke-mahŕ
Crooked:	Kwe-ōs-pe
Slanting:	Tsă-hah'k koo-tan

Straight:	Re-kwah-nah
A straight line:	Wah-rahḱ
A horizontal line:	To-pōk war-rok wah-rok
A vertical line:	Hah-hoot́-ko wah-rok
Sharp:	Hoo-pā´-kah
Dull (knife &c):	Yah-hí-ah-nó-mah (=has no edge)
Blunt (point):	Pe-mŏ-hah
Rough:	Să-ro-re
Smooth:	Kwā-ah-te
Hard:	Pŭt-tah
Soft:	Bo-ah-te
Coarse:	Ah-tahḿ-chin
Fine:	Mā-ah́-ne
Bald:	Re-o-pe

19. POSITION AND DISTANCE

Up:	Het-tek-ko / hā-tā-ko
Down:	Tó-bah
Above (or over):	Hā-tā-kó
Below (or under):	Tó-ro / Toŕ kwah-po
Up stream:	Hā-tā-ko
Down stream:	Tō'ng-ō'k-gnah-aŕ-ro
In:	Ah-soo'ng-ah
Out:	Oẃ-ă-wah'ng-ah
Inside:	Ah-soo'ng ah
Outside:	Ah-o-wahng
Opposite:	Mo-moi-ne-kó-hah
Across:	Nahḿ-ko-mok [or Nahḿ-ko-muk]
Top:	Pah-i-e-vah
Bottom:	Tó-ro-mi-et-te
Center:	Nah-mah́-king
Middle:	Nah-mah-king
End:	Ah-tsoó-ing-ah
Side:	Tsah-hah́-koo
In front:	Ā-wā'ḱ-ne-koo
Behind:	Ne-chah-vā ne-koo-hah
Between:	Nah-mah́-king e-yuḿ-ko
Beyond:	Mo-ro-me-che
Right:	Ah-té-ving-ar-ro
Left:	Ah-kah́-nung-ar-ro
Alone:	Ah-noó-no
Together:	Hah-rā-mok
Separated:	Yah^{ch}-hi-e
Joined together:	Po-koó-roí-ā-mok
One on top of another:	Pah-vah́-e-vah
A day's journey:	Me-ah́-em roi^{ch}
A moon's journey:	Me-ah́-em-ró-re po-koo mwahr [mwahr = moon]
A step:	Tahń-ko-mōk
Near:	Mo-mo-wah // Mo-mwah
Nearer:	Mo-mwah-mi-et-te
Far:	Po-ahń-nā
Farther:	Po-ahń mi-et-te
Way off:	Po-ahń-nā

Close to: Mo-mwi-hah́
Fallen: Po-ré-nōk

20. COLORS AND MARKINGS

Red: Kwah-ho-<u>ᶜʰ</u>ah
Yellow: Yah-taht́-ko
Green: Tah-kah́-pe
Blue: Too-koó-par
Black: Yo-pé-haᶜʰ*
White: Raŕ-ŏ-rŏh
Gray: To-sé-hah
A stripe: Wah-hŏ-hah
Striped: Wah-hŏ-hah
A spot: Tó-e-ko-muk
Spotted with very small spots: Tō-e-to-e-ko
Spotted with large spots: Tā-vā´-ve // Ah-ā´-se-rōt
A drawing or picture: E-shí-nē<u>ᶜʰ</u>
A sign or symbol: E-si-nōk
A mark: Nah-ví-ū-ah
A cairn: Mah-aht-kāᵉᶜʰ to-tōt
A cross or crossmark: To-pōḱ-tah-vē´<u>ᶜʰ</u>

21. UNCLASSIFIED NOUNS

A question: Nah-mí-e<u>ᶜʰ</u>
An answer: Aŕ-rok
A story (tale):   Yah́-oo-wē´<u>ᶜʰ</u>
A name: Aí-to-ahń yan
A word: Po-kó-se roẃ-wē<u>ᶜʰ</u>
A dream: Ho-ho-văr-ă-wē<u>ᶜʰ</u>
A noise: Yi-look-e
A smell: Ah-hin
A mystery: Tŭ-mŏ-e
A secret: Yah-rah-ko
A mistake: Ah-kó-nah<u>ᶜʰ</u>-noi<u>ᶜʰ</u>
A quarrel: Ní-e-keeᶜʰ
An accident: Nah-ah́-kō-ē<u>ᶜʰ</u>
A journey: Me-yah́-ro-ne Me-aŕ-ro-ne
Invitation: Kŏ-ē<u>ᶜʰ</u>
Truth: Oẃ-te
Falsehood: Yah-yah-re
Good luck: Te-hōv́-ko ne-pen
Bad luck: Mă-hi'k-nĕ-me
A joke: To-mah́ hō<u>ᶜʰ</u>-rē<u>ᶜʰ</u>
Ridicule: Nah-hah́-vi-ē<u>ᶜʰ</u>

22. NEW WORDS

Cattle: Ah-ah́-ah-rōt (horned, means horns)
Bull: Ah-ah́-ah-rōt wor-roit
Cow: Ah-ah́-ah-rōt to kōr
Calf: Ah-ah́-ah-rōt ah-tah-hin

Sheep:	Paẖ-aht
Cat:	To-koot
Scissors:	Gnoi˝-kā-chōt´
Hammer:	Che-che nav́-ro-mī't
Money:	Too-raẖ-nat
Gold:	Kwah-ho-naht too-raẖ-nat
Silver:	Rah-o-ro too-rah-nat
Glass beads:	To-koo-par
Watch:	Nah-ví-u-ar
Pants:	Ah-kaẖ-so-han
Shoes:	Ah-nā´-nāv-sah<u>ch</u>
Pencil:	Es-sí-ne-choot
Paper:	Ā's-tsoot

23. PARTICLES AND DESCRIPTIVES

Yes:	Ā´-hā
No:	Hí-e<u>ch</u>
Not (general negative):	Hí-hé
Why:	Hah-meeń-ko-mah
When:	Hah-meeń-ko-pă
Then:	Yé-kaẃ
What:	He-tah
Which:	He-tah
How:	Me-yé
Where:	Ham-mé-ro
Here:	E-kwaẖ
There:	Moó-ro
This:	Me-nĕ
That:	Pā-ĕ
Other:	Pā-ā´-mah
Part:	Pā-eḿ
With:	Hah-kee˝
And:	We'k-chot
Also:	E-kwaẖ-hă-mah
Or:	Pā-ă
If:	Oẃ-te
Perhaps:	Mah-reeḿ-pah
Because:	Hah-meen-ko
At:	Ahńg-en-ah
Till (until):	Mah-tā´-pō'm
But:	He-wí-pā-mah
Again:	Wā-ā-ky
On (or upon):	Taẖ-wō'k-ni<u>ch</u>
Around:	Ter-raŕ-ko
Open:	Av́-ve-ă
Shut:	Hrat-tā´-yah
Tight:	Nah-hahḱ-nā<u>ch</u>
Loose:	Hi-yí-ko
Lost:	Tah-sō'k
Found:	Yā-ō'k
New:	E-moot
Old:	Too-ho
Like:	Mah-ré ho-roó-rah
Alike:	Man-nā´-hoo-roó-rah

Different:	So-woŕ-ko
Begun:	Chah-tahḱ-mōk
Finished:	Weeŕ-ko-mōk
Easy:	Ah-woó-ē´t
Difficult:	Tŭ-moí-e
Abandoned:	Tŭr-mé͡ch
Bent:	Nō'm-ko
Broken:	No-mé-nō'k
Mended:	Nah-vēch-kā͡ch
Marked:	A-shi-ni͡ch
Funny:	Nah-haʹ-ko
Mysterious:	Tŭ-mŭ-ē´͡ch
Careful:	Yah-rahḱ
If possible:	Wah-kí-nip-no͡ch-mé
Impossible:	Hí-ni-wah-ki-ne
Necessary:	Veʺ-chah͡ch
Safe:	Te-hov-ko
Dangerous:	Kwaḱ-e-ó-ē͡ch
Horrible (dreadful):	Mar-hí-ē͡ch / Mŭ-hí-ē͡ch
Wild:	Hah-hí-vet
Tame:	Nang-é-pe-yot
Animate:	Ah-ni'ʺt [does not include plants, rocks, ground, etc.]
Inanimate:	Ah-naḱ-ni't [does not include plants, rocks, ground, etc.]
Intentional (purposely):	Ah-he-ro'ng-ah
Accidental:	Mahm-hutch-ko po-ré-nok
Secretly:	Mo-nó-no he-ó-wah

24. PRONOUNS AND POSSESSIVES

I (or me):	Nó-mah
My (or mine):	Ne-hiń
You (singular):	Ó-mah
You (dual):	O-mó-mah
You (plural):	O-mó-mah
Your or yours (singular):	Mo-hin
Your or yours (dual):	O-mo-hin
Your or yours (plural):	O-mo-hin
He (him, she, or her):	Mon-nā'm
Him:	Pā-ā
His (or hers):	Ah-heem
We (dual):	E-yó-mo-mah
We (plural):	O-e-yó-mo-mah
Ours (dual):	E-yō'm-heen
Ours (plural):	O-ā´-e-yo'm hin
They or them (dual):	Paḱ-mo-mah
They or them (plural):	Pah-mo-mah
Theirs (dual):	Po-mó-heen-e
Theirs (plural):	Po-mo-heen-e
Who?:	Hah-keé-e
Whose?:	Hah-kee-ah mah-heen
My mother:	Ne-ō'k
Your (singular) mother:	Mō'k
Your (dual) mother:	O-mó-yō'k
Your (plural) mother:	O-mo-yō'k
His mother:	Mō'ḱ pā-mah

Our (dual) mother:	E-yō'm̀-yō'k
Their (plural) mother:	Po-mó-yō'k
My dog:	Ne-hin wo-sé //Ne-uń-chin wo-sé
Your (singular) dog:	Mo-hin e-pem-wo-sé // Mo-ah́-chin e-pem-wo-se
His dog:	Ah-heen e-pem wo-sé
Our (dual) dog:	E-yō'm-heen e-pem wo-sé
Their (plural) dog:	Po-mó-heen e-pem wo-sé
Bow:	Choó-ar
My Arrow:	Né-pi-tŏ$^{ch}_{=}$
Your (singular) arrow:	Mo-pi-tŏ$^{ch}_{=}$
His arrow:	Ah-pi-to$^{ch}_{=}$
Our (dual) arrow:	E-yo-pi-to$^{ch}_{=}$
Their (plural) arrow:	O-mo-pi-tō$^{ch}_{=}$
My basket:	Ne-koó-me e-pā´-mah
Your (singular) basket:	Mo-koo-me-e-pā-mah
Your (dual) basket:	Ó-mó-koo-me-e-pā-mah
His basket:	Ah-koo-me e-pā-mah
Our (dual) basket:	E-yō'm ko-ko-me e pā mah$^{ch}_{=}$
Their (dual) basket:	Po-mo-koó-me e-pā-mah
Their (plural) basket:	Koo-koo-me-me e-pā-mah$^{ch}_{=}$

25. PLURALS

One dog:	Po-koó Wo-sé
Two dogs:	Wǎ-hā´ Wó-se
Many dogs:	I-yó-in Wó-se
One man:	Po-koo Woŕ-rah-ē't
Two men:	Wǎ-hā Woŕ-rah-ē't
Many men:	I-yó-in Wor-rah́-rōt
One woman:	Po-koo to-kō'r
Many women:	I-yo-in To-to-kō'r
A child:	Tah-hí-e$^{ch}_{=}$
Many children:	Tah-rah-hí-e$^{ch}_{=}$
A boy:	Kwe-té
Many boys:	Ko-kwé-té
A girl:	Tah-hi-e$^{ch}_{=}$
Many girls:	Tah-rah́-hi-ē$^{ch}_{=}$
A mountain:	Hi-ē$^{ch}_{=}$
Many mountains:	Hah$^{ch}_{=}$-hí-ē$^{ch}_{=}$
A star:	Sé-ō't
Many stars:	Só-se-ō't
A tree:	Koo-tah
Many trees:	Koo-koo-tah
Cottonwood:	Too-vaŕ
Many cottonwoods:	Too-toó-var
A fish:	Ke-ū'ŕ (Ke-yūŕ)
Many fishes:	Ke-ke-ū'r
A bird:	Ah-mah́-sah-rot // Che-e-yú
Many birds:	Ah-mom-sah-rot // Che-ré-yú
An arrow:	Choo-ar
Many arrows:	Choo-roo-ar
A house or wickiup:	Kée$^{ch}_{=}$
Basket:	Koo-mé me
Baskets:	Koo-koo-me-me
Many houses or wickiups:	Ke-ké-e$^{ch}_{=}$

Word:	Se-rơw-wā̱ch-e
Words:	I-yo-in se-row-e̱ch
Egg:	Ah-haẖch´-ne-he

26. VERBS

See:	Hoó-too-ah
I see:	Hoó-tuk-ni
I see you (singular):	Hoó-tin-poo-re
I see you (dual):	Hoó-took-re̱ch
I see you (plural):	Hoó-took-re̱ch
You (singular) see me:	Hoó-took-nā´-i
You (dual) see me:	Hoó-took-né-av-e
I see him:	Hoo-took-ní-e-pam
He sees me:	Hoó-took-nā-pem
I see them (dual):	Hoo-took-moi-pam
I saw you (singular):	Hoó-tuk-re̱ch / Hoo-tuk-ree̱ch / He-wi-rē̱ch
I saw you (dual):	He-ah́-mo-re-ve-hoó-took
I saw you (plural):	He-ah́-mo-re-ve-hoó-took
You (singular) saw me:	He-ah́-ne-ah hoo-tuk // Hoó-took hah́-ne-ah
He saw me:	Hoo-took nā´-pā-mah
I shall see:	Hoó-tin-pŏ-rā
Go out!:	Pe-sah ơw-wang-ah
I am going out:	Pe-saẖch no-yow wang-ah
I have gone out:	Hā-ah ne-pe-saẖch
Stay!:	Ha-ah́-me
I am staying:	Har-ro-rōn e-kwah
Give!:	Mah-hah́-ó-mah
I'm giving:	Mah-hah́ch-rē̱ch
I shall give:	Mah-hah́ ro-rē̱ch (Mah-hah-ro-ni = same)
I have given:	He-ah́-ni-ē̱ch mah-hah́
Eat:	Kwah-ah
I am eating:	?He-ah́-mon he-kwah-aẖch?
I shall eat:	Kwah-ah ro-ne
I have eaten:	He-ah-ne kwah-ah
GO!:	Me-ah́
I am going (present):	He-ah́-mon-he-me-ah́-ro
I shall go:	Mē'p-no-ho-roó-ră
I have gone:	He-ah́-ne̱ch-me-at
He is going (present):	Mah-nā-me [or Man-nĕ-me]
has gone:	Mah-nā-me-at́
You (singular) are going:	O-ah-me
You (dual) are going:	O-mo-ah-vēm-me
We (you and I) are going:	E-yó-mo-rē'm me
COME!:	Ke-mah́
Coming:	He-yah́-mŭr-rā-ke?
He is coming:	Mah-nā-rā-ké
They are coming:	Mah-ró-re mem-ké
I am coming:	Ne-ah́-mon he-ké
I shall come:	Me ar-rōn-e
I have come:	He-ah́-e̱ch-ké
KILL! (a man):	Mo-kah́n-naẖch
Kill! (an animal):	Mo-kah́-ah
I am killing:	Mo-kah́n-naẖch-nī̱ch
I shall kill:	Mo-kah́p-nah

I have killed:	He-yah́-ni-e mo-kah́-nah
I may kill:	Ser-rō'ḱ po-nah-mo-kah́
He is killing:	Pā-ā´-choo-mā-nah
will kill:	Pā-ā´-pro-mo-kah́
has killed:	He-ah́-re mo-kah́-nah
LIE DOWN!:	O-kŏh́ / Uḱ-kŏ
I am lying down:	O-kō'ḱ-ni
I shall lie down:	O-kō'p-naw
I have lain down:	He-ah́-ne o-kō'k
STAND UP!:	Kar-ooḱ-moó-ah
I am standing up:	Kar-ooḱ noi-hah
I shall stand up:	Kar-rook mo-ro-ne
I have stood up:	He-ah-ne Kah-rōk-mōk
RUN!:	Yah-mé-no
I am running:	Yah-mé-nō'k-noi
I shall run:	Yah-mé-po-no
I have run:	He-yah́-ne yah-me-nō'k
FETCH!:	Mah^ch͇-ah-ne? / Ke-mah́-hé oo-ah
I shall fetch:	He-oo-ră-ni
I have fetched:	He-ah́mo nah-he-ook
TAKE AWAY!:	He-o-moó rah-mah
STOP!:	Kah-rooḱ-mwah
I am stopping:	Kah-rooḱ mo-ro
I shall stop:	Kah-roḱ-pŏ-naw
I have stopped:	He-ah-ne Kah-rōk-mōk
HURRY!:	Mah-hé-ko
I am hurrying:	Mah́-he-ōḱ-noi
I shall hurry:	Mah-heeḱ-po-no
I have hurried:	He-ah́-mon-him mah́-he-ō'k
DANCE!:	Yah-kā´-ah
A dance:	Yah-kā-ē^ch͇
I am dancing:	Yah-kā´nah^ch͇-noi^ch͇
I shall dance:	Yah-kā'ṕ-nŏh
I have danced:	He-ah́-ne ah-kā-nah
SING!:	Che-ā´-ah
I am singing:	Che-ā-nah^ch͇-noi
I shall sing:	Che-ā-rō-ne
I have sung:	He-ah́-ne-che-ā´-nah
I am suffering:	Wah-wanǵ-in mōk-noi^ch͇
I shall suffer:	Mō-ti-ŭ ro-nā´^ch͇
I have suffered:	Wahng-ă nah^ch͇-noi
He is suffering:	Mo-ti-yo e ker-oi
You shall suffer:	Op-me mo-ti-u
A laugh:	Ā-yē^ch͇
LAUGH!:	Á-ye-ah́
I am laughing:	Ā-yā´-yin mō^ch͇-noi^ch͇´
I shall laugh:	Ā-yā ro-ne
I have laughed:	He-ah́-ne ắ-yā-nah^ch
CRY!:	Yū-ah
I am crying:	Yo-yū'n mō^ch͇-noi
I shall cry:	Yū-´rō'n-né
I have cried:	He-ah́-ne yū'k
WEAVE A BASKET!:	No-hah́-ah
I am weaving a basket:	No-hah^ch͇-noi^ch͇
I shall weave a basket:	No-hać-ro-ne
I have woven a basket:	He-ah́-ne no-hah^ch͇

I AM WELL!:	Te-hoṽkah ne-haṅ
You are well:	Ah-vaṅ-ah-haṅ
He is well:	Te-hoṽ koi-pem-haṅ
Are you well:	Te-hoṽ kah-ah-hah
I AM SICK:	Mah-sé yū'k-noi$^{ch}_=$
strong:	Te-hoṽ-ko e-haṅne taṅ tah
weak:	Hí-haht-te hoṽ-ko-ne-tah-tah
alive:	Yi'-ē't nó-e-haṅ
dead:	Ah-mŭṅ-yah-naw-ē^{ch}
awake:	Yi-ē't nŏ́-e-hah
asleep:	Yah-tahṅ ko-kan-noi
sleepy:	Yah-tō'r-nā̄$^{ch}_=$
lame:	No-mē't-naw-e
blind:	To-ah vor-noi$^{ch}_=$
deaf:	To-mon-hah-naw-e
drunk:	Hah-mahḱ-muk-noi
insane:	Hah-maṅ pe-noi
fat:	We-tah-noi
slim:	Yah-ró-re-noi$^{ch}_=$
old (woman speaking):	Too-hoo-noi
old (man speaking):	Ā-ră̄$^{ch}_=$-po-noi
young:	Ā-moot-noi
tired:	Yah-pahḱ-muk-noi$^{ch}_=$
busy:	To-mahṅ ko-ne-hah
lazy:	Tsoo-ē't-noi$^{ch}_=$
hungry:	Ko-vé-nok-noi$^{ch}_=$
thirsty:	Pah-raht-nā-ē$^{ch}_=$
happy:	Ah-wā̄'ś ko-ne-hah
unhappy:	Ah-haṅ so-kwah-ah-noi$^{ch}_=$
Mark (or make a mark):	Woẃ-kă
I am marking:	Woẃ-ken nah$^{ch}_=$-ni
I shall mark:	Woẃ-kep-nah
I have marked:	He-aṅ-nah e woẃ-ken-nah
Mourn (or grieve):	
I am mourning:	Ah-hoẃ-sah-kwaṅ ah$^{ch}_=$-noi
I shall mourn:	Ah-hoẃ-sah-kwaṅ ă-rōn-ē$^{ch}_=$
I have mourned:	He-ah-ne ah-hoẃ-sah nā̄$^{ch}_=$

27. SHORT SENTENCES

I am hot:	O-ro-nā̄$^{ch}_=$
I am cold:	O-tso-nā̄$^{ch}_=$
It is too hot:	O-ró-ah$^{ch}_=$ ă-rā̄$^{ch}_=$
it is too cold:	O-tsó ah$^{ch}_=$ ă-rā̄$^{ch}_=$
You are cold:	O-tsó-mē̄^{ch}
Are you cold?:	O-tsó-ham-me
Yes, I am cold and wet:	Ā-hā,o-tso nā-par-rahr-noi
I am going to warm myself:	Mă-hō'p-no
Make a fire:	Hó-mĕ-ah / Hó-mā-ah
He made a fire:	Hā-ah-a-ho men-nah
Put out the fire:	Tsoo-hā-choṽ˝-tah
He put out the fire:	Hā-aŕ-re-tsoo hā́-nah chav-tah
The rain put out the fire:	Ah-kwah-kin roi^{ch}-tsoo-ha-nah chav-tah

The fire went out:	Hā-ah ē^{ch} tsoo-he-nō^{ch}-chav-tah
Go away:	He-rē'ḱ-mo me-tah́
Go home:	Mā-ah́
I am going home:	He-ah mon he-me ne-kē'ng-aŕ-ro
I'm in a hurry:	Mah́-he-o^{ch}-noi
Get out of the way:	He-re'k mo-me-tah
Don't cry:	Hah-ah́-yū´
Come here:	Ké-mah́
Come with me:	Ke-mah́-ne-koó-kar-ro
I go with you:	Mē'n-ē-mo-koó kar-ro [or Me-ne-mo-koo´ kar-ro]
Let's go:	Kow'm-é^{ch}
Are you ready?:	Hā-ah́-ă-hah
No, I am not ready:	Hí-pō'n-ē^{ch}-hah
Run away:	Yah-mé-no
Run quick:	Mah-keeḱ yah-mé-no
Try again:	Nah-wi˝ wā-ā´-kā
Catch him!:	Yoẃ-wah
All right:	Te-hov-koi
Where is he?:	Har-re-e
Over there:	Pā-ā-yah^{ch}-moó-ro
On the ground:	Pā-yah^{ch} o ^{ch}´-nah
How many?:	Hin-né-ke
Only one:	Po-koo-o
All gone:	Hā-ah-e-wee't-ko-muk
I am sorry:	Mo-tí-e-nā^{ch}
Look at that!:	Yo-hoó-to-mó-ro
I lost my knife:	Tah-sōk-ē-ne-pah́-hōn
He found my knife:	Yā-ō'k-roi mo-pah-hōn
I don't know:	Hí-ne-he-ó-nah^{ch}
Go get water:	Mā-ah-o-par˝
Give me a drink:	Pah-ví-nań-e-par
I feel better:	Te-hov́-ki-ne-sōn
It is mine:	Ne-heeń-ne
He is smoking:	Wé-kō'k-e
Give me something to eat:	Mah-hah́-ne né-kwah́-kah
The fire is smoking:	Che-aŕ-rōk-e-chah wō't
Hear the dog bark!:	Nah-hah-kwan wi-no-ke wo-sé
All the dogs are barking:	Wí-ne mo-ke wo-sé
The dog bit the man:	Ko-kōk-roi wo-sé wah-roi-tah
The man hit the dog:	Mo-kahn-nah hroi wah-roi-ē't wo-se´-ah
An old dog:	Ā-rah-po-e wo-sé
An old man:	Ā-rah-po-wah-roi-ēt
Go to bed!:	Mā-i-ah-tahḿ-ko-ah
Come to bed:	Ke-mí-ah tahḿ-ko-ah
Go to sleep:	Yah-tahm-ko-ah
Get up!:	Wo-vé-no
Sit down!:	Tó-vah-haŕ-ro
I'm afraid:	Kwah-e-ō'k-noi^{ch}
I'm ashamed:	E-poó-yuk-noi
I'm sick:	Chi-nōk-noi
So are you:	Ó-ah-hah-mah chí-nōk
My belly aches:	Mo-tí-ne ne-hŏ´-nan
You are sick:	Ó-ah-chí-nōk
He is sick:	Me-nā´-chí-nōk
We all are sick:	O-wār-re-choo-me-nōk
He is a bad man:	Me-nā mah hi-ē^{ch} war-roit

He killed my dog:	Mo-kah-nah^{ch} roi^{ch}-ne-aht́s-no-wo- sé-ah
Where did he go?:	Hă-mé-ro-me
He went home:	He-ah-e-me-ah-kē'ng ar-ro
He struck me:	Ti-yahb́-kă-nah^{ch}-nā^{ch}
I struck him:	Ti-yahb́-kă-pre & No-nok ti-yahb́-kin-hah-mah
He is picking berries:	Ah^{ch}́ ā-pe-hó-an-r
He is dead:	Moi-yuk mah-kah́
Is he dead?:	Ah-moi yah-hah
Yes, he is dead:	Ā´-he-ah-moi-yah-e
Yes, he died:	Ă-hĕ' moi-yuk mo-ké
I killed him yesterday:	Pwah-nah mah-e-mo-kah-nah^{ch}
I am killing him now:	Mo-kah-nah^{ch} ní-ē^{ch}
No he is not dead:	Hí mo-yoḱ mok
He is dying:	Mă-yăm-yin mō'k-e
He loves her:	Oo-wis-me-no-kro-e
He married her:	Hā-ah-ē^{ch} nah-ō'k
She married him:	Nah-ō'k-moi
She had a baby:	Hé-ah-mo ní-e-vē^{ch}
Somebody is coming:	Kwah́-ra-ké hah-ké
A white man is coming:	Rah-wah́-te rā-ké
An Indian is coming:	Ke-rā´ hah-ké
Who are you?:	Ah-ké-ah-ó-mah
What is your name?:	Hah^{ch}-keem-mo-toi-yam
Where did you come from?:	Hah-mé pah-ké
Where are you going?:	Hah-mé ro-ah-mé
I love you:	Yŏ-mah^{ch}-ha-rē^{ch}
Do you understand?:	He-o-nah^{ch} hah-ah́
I understand:	Ā-hā-he-o-nah^{ch}-noi
Hold up your hand:	Het-kah-mo-man-no
I caught a fish:	Hah-tsa-no^{ch} ni-kŭ́-rah
I killed a deer:	Mō-kah-nah^{ch}-ni soo-kah-tah
He shot a coyote:	Pā-ā-rim mo-kah-nah-e-trah
I killed a rattlesnake:	Mo-kah́-nah^{ch} ă-ni-só-tah
He killed a rattlesnake:	Pā-ā-rim mo-kah-nah so-tah
A rattlesnake killed him:	Só-troi ko-kō'k
He was seized by a bear:	Hoon-nah-roi-mo kah-nah
A bear seized him:	Hoon-nah roi yow'k
He killed a bear:	Mo-kah-nah^{ch} roi-hoón-rah?
A bear killed him:	Hoon-rah roi mo-kah-nah^{ch}
The snake is crawling:	Sō´t-e-me
The fish is swimming:	Ke-yū'r-e-yar-rah^{ch}
The meadowlark is flying:	E-sar-re e vah^{ch} mōk
The duck is diving:	Sah't-e-har-rooṕ-ko-mōk
The owl is hooting:	Yōḱ-e-mo-hut
The dog is barking:	Wah-wí-nah-ah e wo-sé
The coyote is howling:	Wah-wí nah-e-e-tah
The sun is not yet up:	Hi-pó-e-pe sah́^{ch} tah-mēt
The sun is rising:	Ah-koo-yah^{ch} ko-min-rā-ke-tah- met
The sun is up:	Pe-sah́^{ch} e-tah met
The sun is going down:	He-ah-mo pah ko-ro-tah-met
The night is dark:	Ah-ah́-ŏ-me ah-ŏ-meet
Is it going to rain?:	Wah-kwó-rah rā-ē^{ch}
It's raining now:	Wah-kōk rah^{ch}
The bird is singing:	Towí-che-ā-ne-muk
Greeting:	Ah-vah́-ah-hah
Farewell (I am going):	Yah́-mon-hēne

Answer; go:	Me-ah́
It's there:	Hah-re or Hahr-re
Handing a person something with the exclamation 'take it or here':	Oó-ah
With me:	No-mah
With him:	ah-koó-kă-ră
He shot me:	Moo-hoo-roo-e
He shot many arrows:	Choo-ar moo-hooḱ
Exclamation of surprise:	Ne-o-mar-re
Let him tell:	Tā-ah-nó-po
Tell me a story:	Yah-ó-ah

28. GEOGRAPHIC OR PLACE NAMES

Bakersfield Plain:	Pah-vah-vet-tum
Los Angeles:	Yah́-vit
San Bernardino Plain & Gabriel:	Yo-wé-hah
San Bernardino Mts.:	Kó-kam-o-vit
San Bernardino Peak:	Yu-aht-hi-e$\frac{ch}{=}$
Kern River:	Pah-hī´t
Mohave Desert:	Mah-mah́-ve-ă-tah
Mts. just north of San Gabriel:	Ah-sooḱ-să-vit
Peak south of San Gabriel (Santa Ana?):	Har-wo-vē't

29. PERSONAL NAMES

Of men and boys:	Of women and girls:
Mō'ng-ah	Loo-soo: Mrs. Rosemyre's own name
Tean-re	Ah-chah́n-chah

30. NAMES OF OTHER INDIAN TRIBES

Tong-vā (name for themselves)	San Gabriel Valley
Ko-kó-em-kam (=Ham-me-nat or Serranos) Ke-tah́-nă-mwah-kan (name for themselves)	San Bernardino Mts.
Pan-vah-sā-kwum	San Fernando Valley (related to Tong-vā)
To-tó-vah-vit (=Tŭ-vah-te-lob-e-lā [or tŭ-bah-te-lob-e-lā])	Valley of South Fork of Kern
Ahk-koó-toos (Ah-koó-toos)	Tehachapi Serrano
Que-Que-nă-vit Kwe-kwe-nă-vit (Kwe-nar-mud)	San Buenaventura

The tong-vā or San Gabriel Indians were called mi-yah́-hik-tchal-lop (=long arms) by the Buena Vista Lake Ham-met-wel-le. They (the Tong-vā) were called Pah-pi-nă-mo-nam by the Ke-tah́-nă-mwah-kan (Ko-kōm-kam in Tong-vā) of the San Bernardino Mts.

Hugo Reid in Los Angeles Star of 1852 (quoted by Taylor in Calif. Farmer, Jan. 11, 1861) says that the name of the rancheria at San Gabriel was <u>Sibagna</u>.

Taylor, (Calif. Farmer, May 11, 1860) says that the mission site of San Gabriel was called <u>Toviskanga</u> [or Toviscanga]. He spells it <u>Tobiscanga</u> in another reference (Ibid, Feb. 22, 1860).

APPENDIX II

U.S. DEPARTMENT OF AGRICULTURE BIOLOGICAL SURVEY
C. HART MERRIAM, Chief

FIELD CHECK LISTS
PACIFIC COAST REGION

<u>Tong-vā</u> or San Gabriel = GABRIELIÑO

LOCALITY: San Gabriel Valley, Calif.
RECORDED BY: C. Hart Merriam

FIELD CHECK LISTS

MAMMALS

Grizzly bear (*Ursus horribilis*):	Hoó-nahr
Black bear (*Ursus americanus*):	Pí-yah́-hó-naht
Whale:	Pan-nah<u>ch</u>´-har
Mountain lion (*Felis hippolestes*):	To-koó-rō't
Bob-cat (*Lynx californicus*):	To-koóut
Desert fox (*Vulpes macrotis* group):	E-roẃ
Coyote (*Canis lestes* or *ochropus*):	É-taŕ
Big wolf (*Canis*):	E-soẃt
Big skunk (*Mephitis*):	Po-né-vo
Little spotted skunk (*Spilogale*):	Che-noó-e po-né-vo ("small skunk")
Badger (*Taxidea*):	Hoo-naŕ (same as Bear!)
Weasel (*Putorius*):	Se-raŕ
Mole (*Scapanus*):	Hoó-po
Bat:	Po-vah́-kaht
Elk (*Cervus*):	Paŕ-soo-kaht
Deer, mule (*Odocoileus hemionus* group):	Soo-kaht˝
Antelope (*Antilocapra*):	To-naŕ˝
Bighorn (*Ovis*):	Pah́-aht
Beaver (*Castor*):	To-le-vah́-che
Gray ground squirrel (*Citellus beecheyi* group):	Hung-ē't
Gray tree squirrel (*Sciurus fossor*):	Se-sé-kot
Chipmunk (*Eutamias*):	Se-sé-kōt
Pocket gopher (*Thomomys*):	Mhwat
Kangaroo rat (*Dipodomys* or *Perodipus*):	'Har˝

Wood rat, round-tail (*Neotoma*):	Har˝
Cottontail rabbit (*Lepus auduboni*):	*Tŏ-só-hut*
Black-tail jackrabbit (*Lepus texianus* group):	Soo-ē't
Horse:	Ah-chah́-che
Dog:	Wo-sé
Bark of dog:	Wí-nōk
Tail:	Ah-pŭ-kin
Horns:	Ah-ah́-ahn
Hoofs:	Ah-choó-choor̂
Claws:	Hooń-rah-choor̂
Hide:	Ta^ch˝-tah-ho-hutch
Hair:	Ap-pā´-han
Dung:	Yi-yi-tah ah-wa-rin
Tracks:	Ah-me-atch
Animal's burrow:	Ah-hŭr̂-rin
Spotted:	Tā-vā´-ve

BIRD LIST

Golden eagle (*Aquila*):	Ah-sоẃt
Bald eagle (*Haliæetus*):	Yŭ-ă-weeí-ah-mah́-sah-rō't
Red-tailed hawk (*Buteoborealis*):	Pah-ké-sar
Marsh hawk (*Circus hudsonius*):	Hah́-chet
Duck hawk (*Falco anatum*) or Prairie falcon (*F. mexicanus*):	Pah-ké-sar
Fishhawk (*Pandion*):	Hahtś ă-nar ke-kūr̂
Sparrow hawk (*Falco sparverius*):	Koó-neets
California condor (*Gymnogyps*):	Wé-soo-yŭ-roo-it
Turkey buzzard (*Cathartes*):	Wé-sŏ
Great horned owl (*Bubo*):	Mŏ-hoot
Barn owl (*Strix*):	Chah-mār
Screech owl (*Megascops*):	Po-pó-o
Burrowing owl (*Speotyto*):	Koo-koó-oo
Pigmy owl (*Glaucidium*):	Po-pó-o
Crow (*Corvus americanus*):	Oẃ-koots
Crested jay (*Cyanocitta*):	Ah-oó-so-rōt
California jay (*Aphelocoma*):	Tsí-e
Pinyon jay (*Cyanocephalus*):	Hí-inǵ che-ū
Blue grouse (*Dendragapus*):	Hoó-e
Mountain quail (*Oreortyx*):	Man-né-sar kah-kahŕ
Valley quail (*Lophortyx*):	Kah-kahŕ
Band-tail pigeon (*Columba fasciata*):	We-ahnǵ-ar˝
Dove (*Zenaidura*):	Mah-kah-ho
Road runner (*Geococcyx*):	Poó-he-awt
Kingfisher (*Ceryle*):	Hah́-tsā-nar-kū'r
Night hawk (*Chordeiles*):	Pah́-ké-sar che-noó-ē^ch
Flicker (*Colaptes*):	Ké-mar˝
Lewis woodpecker (*Asyndesmus torquatus*):	Pah^ch̲ hah́
California woodpecker (*Melanerpes formicivorus bairdi*):	Pe-var˝
Pygmy nuthatch (*Sitta pygmæa*):	To-mah́-hah-ming che-ū´
Brewer blackbird (*Euphagus cyanocephalus*):	Hoonǵ-ē^ch̲
Red-shouldered blackbird (*Agelaius*):	Hoó-re-ō't
Meadowlark (*Sturnella*):	E-sahŕ
Oriole (*Icterus*):	Tsah-hatś-har

Shrike (*Lanius*):   Tah́-ō't-ne-keet
Mountain tanager (*Piranga ludoviciana*):   Tsé-re-u pi'm-kah-ve (=bird from north)
Kingbird (*Tyrannus verticalis*):   Tsǎ´-kwé-ū
Horned lark (*Otocoris*):   Yū-wé-ahng-che-ú
Barn swallow (*Hirundo*):   Mah-wā-ō't
Cliff swallow (*Petrochelidon*):   E-vē´´ng-aŕ
Bluebird (*Sialia*):   Ché-ū-tah-kah́-pe [or Tse-ū-tah-kah´-pe]
Water ouzel (*Cinclus*):   Hoo-vā-koo-me-ar
Lazuli finch (*Cyanospiza*):   Tah-kah́-pe che-ū
Purple finch (*Carpodacus*):   Ché-ū´
Yellowbird (*Astragalinus*):   Pah́-har-ring-r che-u (=sunflower bird)
Larch finch (*Chondestes*):   Ah-ā´-sin ah-poo'ang che-u (striped)
Junco (*Junco*):   O-cho-che-vā che-ū (winter bird)
Towhee (*Pipilo maculatus*):   Yū-pé-e
Brown towhee (*Pipilo crissalis*):   To-seé hatch-e-yu
Robin (*Merula*):   Tah́-ma-vā kwah-ē´ch̲
Mockingbird (*Mimus*):   Tow't
Thrasher (*Toxostoma*):   Ko-kó-ar kwah-é-ar
Canyon wren (*Catherpes*):   To-tō't-gnah che-u (=rock bird)
Wren tit (*Chamæa*):   Hi-e-vā che-u
Mountain chickadee (*Parus gambeli*):   Wé-pen-ar
Bushtit (*Psaltriparus*):   Tsō˝t (chō˝t)
Yellow warbler (*Dendroica æstiva*):   Tsah-hats-haŕ
Humming bird: Pé-nor
White pelican (*Pelecanus erythrorhynchos*):   Ah'ng-ŭ´-root-sah́t
Merganser (*Merganser*):   Kwah-e-ar-kū'r saht [kū'r = fish]
Mallard (*Anas boschas*):   Te-hoo-vits saht [or Te-ŭ-vits saht] (=pretty duck)
Shoveler (*Spatula clypeata*):   Ah-mer-per-rōt saht
Pintail (*Dafila acuta*):   Hoo-pā-kah a-per-kin-saht
Redhead (*Aythya americana*):   Kwah-hó-hah pó-an saht (=red head)
Ruddy duck (*Erismatura*):   Ah-ā's-rōt-saht
Duck: Che-ē´ch̲
Lesser snow goose (*Chen hyperborea*):   Row-roo-saht (=white goose)
White-fronted goose (*Anser gambeli*):   To-seé-hah-saht
Western Canada goose (*Branta canadensis occidentalis*):   Ta-vā-ve-saht
Swan (*Olor buccinator*):   Kah-hŭ-ang-ung-sah́t (long neck)
Bittern (*Botaurus*):   Se-ē'ng saht
Great blue heron (*Ardea herodias*):   Kah-hŭŕ-ahang
Night heron (*Nycticorax*):   Wah́-ah-kah
Sand-hill crane (*Grus mexicanus*):   Ni-yí-so
Coot (*Fulica*):   Kwah-e-ar kwe-nar saht (mud eater)
Avocet (*Recurvirostra*):   Ah-ā's-rōt ah-mah-san
Black-neck stilt (*Himantopus*):   Roẃ-rah ah-toó-nun
Killdeer (*Oxyechus vocifera*):   Too-é-rǎ-roo
Spotted sandpiper (*Actitis macularia*):   Hah-rooṕ koo-me aŕ
A bird: Chē´-ū
A small bird: Tsé-ū
An egg: Ah-hah́-ne-hi
A nest: Ah́-hoo-ah́n
Wing: Ah-mah́-san
Feather: Ah-pe-ah́n
Plume (Quail):   Kah-kaŕ-ah-poo-ahn
Bill: Pah-ŭ´
Claw: Ah-choo-chōr
Crop: Ang-ung wē'r-ko

REPTILES AND BATRACHIANS

Snake (any):	Taĥ-hoor
Rattlesnake (*Crotalus*):	Sō't
Water snake (*Eutænia*):	Seˮ-ro
King or milk snake (*Ophibolus boyli*):	Ah-ā
Gopher or bull snake (*Pityophis*):	Yŭ-ē't tah-hoor [or Yŭ-ē't tah-hŭr]
Whip snake (*Bascanion*):	Wahᶜʰ-hó-hut
Small brown lizard (*Uta*):	Che-roó-ko
Scaly lizard (*Sceloporus*):	" ?
Horned toad (*Phrynosoma*):	Chaŕ-roẃ-ă-hoᶜʰ
Turtle:	Paĥ-arˮ
Frog (*Rana*):	Kwaŕ-ro
Toad (*Bufo*):	Kwaŕ-ro

FISHES

Fish (any):	Kēk-ū'ˊr

INSECTS

Grasshopper:	Wā-ĕt́
Beetle:	Tsoo-ré-ar
Butterfly:	Aĥ-tab-bah
Butterfly (a small pale butterfly):	E-yah-aĥ-tab-bah
Moth:	Aĥ-tab-bah
Dragon fly:	Sho-pāˊ-rā
Mosquito:	Arrˮ
Fly:	Pé-tso-kwaŕ
Black ant:	Yoᶜʰ-harˮ
Red ant:	Aĥ-nahí
Ant's nest:	To'ng-ah-ah-naht
Yellow jacket:	Haĥng-ar
Yellow jacket's nest:	Ah-ké-mī'n hahng-ar
Bumblebee:	Ró-rung-aht
Flea:	Mŭ-too-che
Spider:	Wer-rā-cheᶜʰ
Spider's web:	Ah-hwan
Tarantula:	Yŭ-ŭ-et wā-rā-che Ŭ-rŭ-it wā-rā-ch [or wer-rā-ch]
Worm, hairy caterpillar:	Ah-ker-ran-mah-mah-her-rah
Worm, smooth caterpillar:	Ker-ker-aŕ (Kă-kŭ-aŕ)

TREES AND SHRUBS

Digger pine (*Pinus sabiniana*):	Wahᶜʰ-oí
Piñon or nut pine (*Pinus monophylla*):	Tŏ-vaht
Juniper (*Juniperus*):	Waĥ-aht
Valley oak (*Quercus lobata*):	Sa-vēᶜʰ (Spanish Robles)
Valley live oak (*Quercus agrifolia*):	Weí (Spanish Encinos)
Sycamore (*Platanus racemosa*):	Shăˊ-var' Sā-vār
Cottonwood (*Populus*):	Too-warˮ (Spanish alamo)
Willow (*Salix lasiolepis*):	Sahᶜʰ-haht (Plural Sah-saĥ-haht)

Elder (*Sambucus glauca*):   Hoo-kaht
The flower, Hook-tah-swim
The leaf, Hook-tah-nan-nah^{ch}
The berry, Hook-tah-ah^{ch}-an
A tea made from the pitch is used as a cathartic and is called Hook-tah-ah-shoon.

Manzanita (*Arctostaphylos*):   Soo-boó-che^{ch}
Blackberry (*Rubus vitifolius*):   Pe-kwahŕ
Wild rose (*Rosa* sp.):   O-chooŕ (make arrows of the straight stems)
Gooseberry (*Ribes* sp.):   Ko-chaŕ
Yerba Santa (*Eriodiction glutinosum*):   Hŭ-hěŕ-hetch-ō't (medicine)
Sour berry; Aromatic sumac (*Rhus trilobata*):   So-rah́ ? Tsah́-mē^{ch} ?
Poison oak (*Rhus diversiloba*):   O-ar˝
Sage herb (*Artemisia ludoviciana*):   Soś-maht (used for medicine)
Tree yucca (*Hesperoyucca arborescens*):   Ah-wé-win
Foothills yucca (*Yucca whipplei*):   Ah-kó
The tree or wood the fire drill is made of: Wahn-ne-kit

MISCELLANEOUS PLANTS

Milkweed, broad leaf (*Asclepias*):   To-hah́-che-aŕ
Milkweed, narrow leaf (*Asclepias*):   To-hah́-che-aŕ
Milkweed pod: Ché-o-hut
Milkweed string: Wé-vor
Milkweed gum (boiled milk):   To-hah́-che-aŕ
Soaproot (*Chlorogalum pomeridianum*):   Să-pā´-cho-hah
Big round tule (*Scirpus lacustris*):   Sé-e
Mission tule (*Juncus textilis*):   So-ar˝ Swăr
Wild oats (*Avena sativa*):   Ă-vā´-har
Grass (any):   Mah-mah́-har
Salt grass (*Distichlis spicata*):   Se-mut (the salt used as remedy for chills & fevers & other fevers)

Wild sunflower (*Helianthus annuus*):   Pah^{ch}´-har (seeds used for food)
Indian tobacco: Pā-eś-pe-vot
Indian whisky (*Datura*):   Mah́-neet
Wild grapevine (*Vitis californica*):   Pah-vahś kā-veet

PARTS OF PLANTS

Flower: Ah-soo-iń
Leaf: Ah-nań-nah^{ch}
Stem: Tse-noó-e-ah-kó
Thorn: I-hahn
Seed: Ah-pootś
Berry: Ah^{ch}-hah́n
Cherry pit: Chah-mē^{ch}
Acorn: Kwahŕ / Kwaŕ
Acorn shell: Ah-hă´-huts
Acorn cup: Ah-koó-ro
A bush: Mah-mah-har
Brush or chaparral: Pah-sah́-kit
A tree: We-she-ă-har˝ (a pine tree) / Sah-hah́ng
Trunk: Ah-mŭh́-pitch koo-tah

Branches: Ah-mah́-man
Bark: A$^{ch}_{=}$-ho-hutch
Pine cone: A^{ch}nań to-vah´tah
Pine needles: Ah-nań-nah to-vah́-tah
Log: Ah-mŭ-pitch

APPENDIX III

THE INDIANOLOGY OF CALIFORNIA
by Alexander Taylor

Vol. XIII No. 12, May 11th 1860
No. 9 Indians of the Mission of San Gabriel, etc.

Vocabulary of the Indians living near the Mission of San Gabriel, in Los Angeles county, taken by the Author, in November, 1856.

ENGLISH	INDIAN
God	Aykoa-tam-o-ribko
wicked spirit	chee-sho
man	wo
father	nin-na
mother	neo
husband	neashon
wife	neashon
son	ni-skum
daughter	ne-arro
head	ne-peann
hair	caba-yo
face	ne-cho-cho
forehead	ne-cre-nin
ear	ne-nanak
eye	ne-cho-chon
nose	ne-mur-pin
mouth	ne-tung-in
tongue	ne-nong-in
tooth	ne-tatum
beard	ne-pay-an
neck	ne-neuñg
arm	ne-shokk-nemann
hand	ne-mann
Indian shoes of deer-skin	ne-na-nepsha
bread	wo-anin
pipe, calumet	wickocha
tobacco	shu-ke
sky, heaven	tu-kupña
sun	ta-mit
moon	mo-ar
fingers	nemann
nails	ne-chur

belly	ne-han
leg	ne hook-uk
feet	ne-nunich
toes	ne-chu-chur
bone	ne-tan
grasshopper	way-et
vulture, condor	lo-wo
whale	que-hote, or ka-hote
heart	a-hun
blood	a-hin
town, village	yang-a
chief	to-mayre
warrior	ma-hay
friend	pay-a-yan
house, hut	wa-pa-enga
arrow	ne-hun
bow	ne-pik-ha
knife	pa-hut
canoe, boat	ta-rin-ha
star	so-sho-ot
day	ow-rong-a
light	pa-ha-ha
it is night	yamarawo-howke
darkness	aul-me
morning	yañr-ne
evening	a-she-anga
wind	a-he-kin
lightning	a-we-rin
thunder	arr-en
hail	che-nar
fire	cha-wat
crow	ow-kutch
bear	hoo-nar
water	par
ice	yo-at
earth, land	urx-her
sea	mo-mot
river	pa-hyt
lake	mo-mot
great valley	yo-wik-ha
hill	ca-wo-nat
Sierra	hy-e-cur-h
stone, rock	to-ta
copper	cobro (same as Spanish)
iron	hierro (same as Spanish)
gold	oro (same as Spanish)
maize	maiz (same as Spanish)
wood	ko-tar
bark	ar-hierk-kutch
grass	ma-ma-har
oak	tome-char
pine-tree	wish-ye-arker
flesh, meat	yo-hung-ing
deer	shoo-kat
wolf	e-shot
elk	pa-at

dog	woo-she
antelope	to-nar
fox	pone-wo
coyote	etar
ground squirrel	hern-eek
rabbit	tu-shur-kut
hare	shu-eet
rattlesnake	shote
bird	po-hi-yot
egg	a-hak-ne
goose	we-shara
duck	che-ee
pigeon	ma-kau-oo
Cal. quail	ka-kar
hawk	ashout
small hawk	pakisha
sea-museles	achin-ka-hi
avelones [abalones]	apow
fish	que-ur
white	ara-wat-i
black	upei-ka
red	qua-ho-ka
blue	yu-pe-ka
yellow	takapi
green	the same
great, big	ca-ruhl
small, little	chi-noo
strong	hurr-ka
old	er-ha-po
young	how-miy
good	te-hur-wy
bad	ma-hy
handsome	caboche
ugly	mahy
alive, life	yahitiha
dead, death	am-riya
cold	yamonyocho
warm, hot	yamanyhust-koino
I	no-ma
thou	oma
he	parama
we	yomomaw
you	omono-awiwin
west	yamopocoratamit
north	ro-mee
one	po-koo
two	wa-hay
three	pa-hey
four	wat-sa
five	mahar
six	pawahe
seven	wat-sa-kabiya
eight	wa-hish-watchsa
nine	mahar-cabearka
ten	wa-hish-mar
(they do not count farther than ten.)	

their tobacco pipes were made of reeds
the rainy season was called yamorewacore
the spring-time was called yamore-takap-comock-urker
the summer-time was called yamokino-urker
the fall-time was called ymoquoshok-qui-ivet
it is raining was called yamarawoksk

none of the Indians of California seems to have a name for buffalo
the site of the Mission was called Toviscanga, and near by was a large rancheria
the site of Los Angeles town was called Yang-ha
the beach or playa of San Pedro was called Sow-vingt-ha

The vocabulary of San Gabriel was taken down from an old Christian-Indian about sixty years old, and his appearance and features similar to our other Indians. He says, San Gabriel was first built by Padre Miguel Cruzado, and he was born near the mission.

The Indians of San Fernando spoke nearly the same language as those of San Gabriel. The site of San Fernando was a rancheria called Pasheckna, and was more populous than any other rancheria of the Fernandinos. Other clans were Okowvin-jha, Kowanga, and Saway Yanga. The Ahapchingas were a clan or rancheria between Los Angeles and San Juan Capistrano, and enemies of the Gabrielenos, or those of San Gabriel.

APPENDIX IV

VOCABULARY OF THE TOBIKHAR INDIANS OF SAN GABRIEL

**The following vocabulary was recorded by Dr. Oscar Loew in
June, 1875 and published in Gatschet (1879:401-475).**

ORTHOGRAPHY BY GEORGE GIBBS

a	as long in *father*, and short in German *hat* (nearly as in English *what*).
e	as long in *they* ("long *a*" in *face*), short in *met*.
i	as long in *marine*, short in *pin*.
o	as long in *go*, short in *home, whole* (as generally pronounced in the Northern States).
u	as long in *rule* (*oo* in *fool*), short in *full* (*oo* in *good*). *u* as in *union, pure*, &c., to be written *yu*.
â	as in *all* (*aw, au* in *bawl, taught*).
<u>a</u>	as in *fat*.
<u>u</u>	as in *but* (*o* in *love, oo* in *blood*).
ai	in *aisle* ("long *i*" in *pine*).
au	as *ow* in *now, ou* in *loud*.

The distinction of long and short vowels to be noted, as far as possible, by the division into syllables, joining a following consonant to a short vowel, and leaving the vowel open if long. Where this is insufficient, or where greater distinctness is desirable, a horizontal mark above, to indicate a long vowel, a curved mark a short one, thus: ā, ă, ē, ĕ, &c. A nasal syllable, like those found so commonly in French, to be marked by an index, *n*, at the upper right-hand corner of the vowel; thus o^n, $â^n$, a^n, u^n, will represent the sounds of the French *on, an* or *en, in,* and *un*, respectively.

CONSONANTS

b	as in English *blab*.
c	not to be used excepting in the compound *ch*; write *k* for the hard sound, *s* for the soft.
d	as in English *did*.
f	as in English *fife*.
g	as in English *gig*, never for the soft sound, as in *ginger*; for this use always *j*.
h	as in English *how, hoe, handle*.
j	as in English *judge*.
k	as in English *kick*.
l	as in English *lull*.
m	as in English *mimic*.
n	as in English *noon*.
p	as in English *pipe*.
q	not to be used: for *qu* write *kw*.
r	as in English rear.
s	as in English *sauce*.
t	as in English *tight*.
v	as in English *vow*.

w	as in English *wayward*.
x	not to be used: write *ks* or *gz*, according to the sound, in *wax, example*.
y	as in English *you, year*.
z	as in English *zeal, buzz*.
ñ	as *ng* in English *singing*.
sh	as in English *shall, shoe*.
zh	as *z* in *azure*, *s* in *fusion*.
ch	as in English *church*.
th	as in English *thin, truth*.
dh	as *th* in *the, with*.
kh	a surd gutteral aspirate, the German *ch* in *ach, Loch, Buch*, and sometimes approaching that in *ich, recht, Bücher*.
gh	a sonant gutteral aspirate (Arabic *ghain*); other compounds, like the clucks occurring in Chinook, &c., to be represented by *kl, tkl, tlk*, &c., according to their analysis.

VOCABULARY COLLECTED BY DR. OSCAR LOEW
AT SAN GABRIEL MISSION IN 1875

1.	Man:	voro´y
2.	Woman:	to-kor
3.	Boy:	ui-ti
4.	Girl:	tak-ha´ikh
5:	Infant:	ko-ar
6.	My father (said by son):	ni-nak
7.	My father (said by daughter):	....
8.	My mother (said by son):	ni-o´-ok
9.	My mother (said by daughter):	....
10.	My husband:	ni-a´shun
11.	My wife:	....
12.	My son (said by father):	ni-ikok
13.	My son (said by mother):	....
14.	My daughter (said by father):	ni-a´rur
15.	My daughter (said by mother):	....
16.	My elder brother:	ni-pa
17.	My younger brother:	ni-pe´-ets
18.	My elder sister:	ni-okho
19.	My younger sister:	ni-pi-its
20.	An Indian:	takhat
21.	People:	....
22.	Head:	apo-a´n
23.	Hair:	po-ar
24.	Face:	a-ho´ho
25.	Forehead:	a-konin
26.	Ear:	ana´nakh
27.	Eye:	atso´tchon
28.	Nose:	amo´rpin
29.	Mouth:	ato´nin
30.	Tongue:	ano´nin
31.	Teeth:	ata´tam
32.	Beard:	ape´han
33.	Neck:	aku´tchan
34.	Arm:	ama´mam
35.	Hand:	aman
36.	Fingers:	....
37.	Thumb:	....
38.	Nails:	atchu´tchur

39.	Body:	atcho-on
40.	Chest:	atu´nun
41.	Belly:	akho´nan
42.	Female breasts:	api-pi´tchu
43.	Leg:	ahorkuk
44.	Foot:	aneb
45.	Toes:	....
46.	Bone:	a-e´n
47.	Heart:	ahu´n
48.	Blood:	akhain
49.	Town, village:	....
50.	Chief:	tomear
51.	Warrior:	....
52.	Friend:	ni-e´ya
53.	House:	gigh
54.	Skin lodge:	....
55.	Kettle:	....
56.	Bow:	ni-pay-tulkh
57.	Arrow:	tchu-ar
58.	Ax, hatchet:	....
59.	Knife:	pakhut
60.	Canoe:	....
61.	Moccasins:	....
62.	Pipe:	....
63.	Tobacco:	....
64.	Sky:	tu-gu-pan
65.	Sun:	tamet, tame-at
66.	Moon:	mo-ar
67.	Star:	sosiot
68.	Day:	poku-tamet
69.	Night:	yauke
70.	Morning:	yamden
71.	Evening:	asi-ama
72.	Spring:	....
73.	Summer:	ororibe
74.	Autumn:	....
75.	Winter:	otcho´tchibe
76.	Wind:	ahi´kain
77.	Thunder:	ta-er
78.	Lightning:	....
79.	Rain:	akva´-kin
80.	Snow:	yua´t
81.	Fire:	tchabo
82.	Water:	p´ar
83.	Ice:	yuat
84.	Earth, land:	o´lkhor
85.	Sea:	mo´mot
86.	River:	otcho´-o
87.	Lake:	....
88.	Valley:	....
89.	Prairie:	....
90.	Hill, mountain:	khaikh
91.	Island:	....
92.	Stone, rock:	to-ta´
93.	Salt:	ung-o´r
94.	Iron:	....

95.	Forest:	....
96.	Tree:	basha´kit
97.	Wood:	....
98.	Leaf:	....
99.	Bark:	....
100.	Grass:	mama´-har
101.	Pine:	ushi-a´gar
102.	Maize:	mais
103.	Squash:	....
104.	Flesh, meat:	....
105.	Dog:	voshi´
106.	Buffalo:	....
107.	Bear:	unar
108.	Wolf:	i-shot
109.	Fox:	khau´rat
110.	Deer:	shugat
111.	Elk:	bashgat
112.	Beaver:	....
113.	Rabbit, hare:	toshokhot
114.	Tortoise:	pa-ar
115.	Horse:	kavay
116.	Fly:	pi´tchukvar
117.	Mosquito:	....
118.	Snake:	vakhorkhat
119.	Rattlesnake:	sho´-ot
120.	Bird:	khu´nikh
121.	Egg:	akha´khni-et
122.	Feathers:	amamshan
123.	Wings:	....
124.	Goose:	....
125.	Duck (mallard):	tchi-ikh
126.	Turkey:	....
127.	Pigeon:	veangar
128.	Fish:	ki-ur
129.	Salmon:	....
130.	Sturgeon:	....
131.	Name:	....
132.	White:	ra´uro
133.	Black:	yu-bi´kha
134.	Red:	kvaho´kha
135.	Light blue:	ta-ka´pi
136.	Yellow:	....
137.	Light green:	taka´pi
138.	Great, large:	yu-uit
139.	Small:	tchi-nuigh
140.	Strong:	hu-u´rka
141.	Old:	era´kh-bu
142.	Young:	pu-vatchun
143.	Good:	ti-hurko
144.	Bad:	ma-ha´ikh
145.	Dead:	....
146.	Alive:	yait
147.	Cold:	otso´-o
148.	Warm, hot:	oro´-o
149.	I:	noma
150.	Thou:	o´ma

151.	He:	mane´ma
152.	We:	yo´muma
153.	Ye:	mamum-omo´ma
154.	They:	mamum-urura-omo´ma
155.	This:	mine´
156.	That:	pe-e´
157.	All:	o´-e
158.	Many, much:	a-yoin
159.	Who:	akim-be´ma
160.	Far:	po-a´ne
161.	Near:	mo-moa´
162.	Here:	i-kva´
163.	There:	mu´ru
164.	To-day:	yamde
165.	Yesterday:	po-a´na
166.	To-morrow:	hi-amne
167.	Yes:	e´-he
168.	No:	khai
169.	One:	pu-gu´
170.	Two:	ve-he´
171.	Three:	pa´-hi
172.	Four:	va-tcha´
173.	Five:	maha´r
174.	Six:	pa-va´he
175.	Seven:	vatcha´-kabya´
176.	Eight:	vehesh-vatcha´
177.	Nine:	mahar-kabya´
178.	Ten:	vehes-mahar
179.	Eleven:	puku-hurura
180.	Twelve:	vehe-hurura
181.	Twenty:	hurura-vehe´
182.	Thirty:	hurura-pahi´
183.	Forty:	....
184.	Fifty:	....
185.	Sixty:	....
186.	Seventy:	....
187.	Eighty:	....
188.	Ninety:	....
189.	One hundred:	....
190.	One thousand:	....
191.	To eat:	kva-akh
192.	To drink:	bakh
193.	To run:	yamino
194.	To dance:	ya-ke´a
195.	To sing:	tche-e´a
196.	To sleep:	ya-ta´m-kuan
197.	To speak:	si-ra´ua
198.	To see:	u´-toa
199.	To love:	....
200.	To kill:	muka´nakh
201.	To sit:	to´ba
202.	To stand:	to-bakh-aro´
203.	To go:	ma^e, mĕa
204.	To come:	mahikima´
205.	To walk:	yungino
206.	To work:	me-hue´khvua

207.	To steal:	pu-kitcha´
208.	To tell lies:	ya-ga´re
209.	To give:	....
210.	To laugh:	mea
211.	To cry:	pau-e´nakh

ADDITIONS

When Dr. O. Loew visited the country around San Gabriel Mission in June, 1875, he was told that only two old men able to speak their paternal language were living, the rest of the Indians having exchanged their vernacular for Spanish. He visited them both, and from one of them, Fernando Quinto, a nonagenarian chief, who seemed to be near his dissolution, he obtained the vocabulary with additions. This old man remembered having seen one of Colonel J.C. Frémont's expeditions.

I eat:	nonim kva-a´kh
Thou eatest:	oa kva-a´kh
He eats:	pe-es kva-a´kh
I do not eat:	khai ni kva-a´kh
I shall eat:	nonim kva-a´ron
I shall not eat:	khai ni kva-a´ron
I have eaten:	yamo ni kva-a´kh
I have not eaten:	khaipo ni kva-a´kh
My hand:	onam aman
Thy hand:	aman para
His hand:	aman hurura
Our hands:	iyo´m ama´n ue´
Your hands:	ue´ nuperko iyom aman
Their hands:	ue´ nuperko iyom aman
My first son:	mu piar varake
My second son:	ayan ni ikok
My third son:	apayan ni ikok
The water is good:	tiribit par
I have two burros (mules):	nona vauhe eni-in buroa´
I have bought a burro:	no nahuat buroa´
I shall buy a burro:	ne hua´ron naik buroa´
My burros are white:	raua´nat nihin buro

APPENDIX V

UNITED STATES EXPLORING EXPEDITION

DURING THE YEARS
1838, 1839, 1840, 1841, 1842
UNDER THE COMMAND OF CHARLES WILKES, U.S.N.
VOL. VI
ETHNOLOGY AND PHILOLOGY
BY HORATIO HALE
PHILOLOGIST OF THE EXPEDITION

ALPHABET

A	a	as in *mart, mat.*
Å	α	as *a* in *hall, what.*
B	b	
Ç	ç	as *sh* in *shine.*
D	d	
Δ	δ	as the soft *th* in *thy.*
E	e	as *a* in *fate,* and *e* in *met.*
F	f	
G	g	always hard, as in *go, give.*
Γ	γ	soft guttural, as in the German *Tage*
H	h	
I	i	as in *machine, pin.*
J	j	as *z* in *glazier.*
K	k	
X	χ	hard guttural, as *ch* in the German *lock.*
L	l	
M	m	
N	n	
Π	η	nasal *ng,* as in *singing, hanger.*
O	o	
P	p	
Q	q	very harsh guttural.
R	r	
S	s	
T	t	
Θ	θ	the hard or hissing *th,* as in *thin.*
U	u	as in rule, pull.
Ʊ	υ	as *u* in *burn, but.*
V	v	
W	η	
Y	y	
Z	z	

Man	*worōit*
Woman	*tokór*
Boy	*kwitī*
Girl	*taχaí*
Infant; child	.....
Father	*anāk*
Mother	*āök*
Husband	.....
Wife	.....
Son	*äíkok*
Daughter	*aiárok*
Brother	*nipēëts*
Sister	*nipīïts*
Indian; People	.....
Head	*apoān*
Hair	.....
Face	.....
Forehead	.....
Ear	*anāna, nājas*
Eye	*atçōtçon, tsōtson*
Nose	*amēpin, mūpin*
Mouth	*atóŋin*
Tongue	*anóŋin*
Teeth	*atátʋm*
Beard	*aóŋ, péhen*
Neck	*aŋén, paχon*
Arm	*amān, mān*
Hand	*amān*
Fingers	.....
Nails	.....
Body	.....
Leg	*anēf, nēneʋ*
Foot	.....
Toes	.....
Bone	*aént, ēan*
Heart	*ahúŋ, sūn*
Blood	*aχain*
Town; Village	.....
Chief	*tomēr, tomiár*
Warrior	.....
Friend	.....
House	*kītç, kīn*
Kettle	.....
Bow	*paítχʋar, paítōχ*
Arrow	*tçūar, nihún*
Axe; Hatchet	.....
Knife	.....
Canoe; Boat	*traínχe, nikín*
Shoes	.....
Pipe	.....
Tobacco	.....
Sky; Heaven	.....
Sun	*tāmet*
Moon	*mōár*
Star	*suōt*
Day	*oróŋa*

Night	*yauket*
Light	.....
Darkness	.....
Morning	.....
Evening	.....
Spring	.....
Summer	*orōrive*
Autumn	.....
Winter	*otçōtçive*
Wind	*ahīkain, ahōken*
Thunder	.....
Lightning	.....
Rain	*akwākit, wakóro*
Snow	*yoāt, toíit*
Hail	.....
Fire	*tçāwot, tōina*
Water	*bar, akwāken*
Ice	.....
Earth; land	*továŋa*
Sea	.....
River	.....
Lake	.....
Valley	.....
Hill; Mountain	*haiχ*
Island	.....
Stone	*totā*
Salt	.....
Iron	.....
Tree	.....
Wood	*kutā*
Leaf	.....
Bark	.....
Grass	.....
Pine	.....
Flesh; meat	.....
Dog	*wausī, wasī*
Buffalo	.....
Bear	*hunār*
Wolf	*īçot, īsot*
Deer	*çukāt*
Elk	.....
Beaver	.....
Tortoise	.....
Fly	.....
Musquito	.....
Snake	.....
Bird	*amāçarot*
Egg	*ahāχnehe, akākan*
Feathers	*amāçan, apēhan*
Wings	.....
Duck	.....
Pigeon	.....
Fish	*kwaiīŋ*
Salmon	.....
Sturgeon	.....
Name	*toāian*

Affection	.....
White	*ārawātai, χosīeχa*
Black	*yupīχa, yomāχpe*
Red	*kwauŏχa, rāure*
Blue	*saçāsça*
Yellow	*payū-uwi*
Green	.....
Great	*yŏit, warīajeren*
Small	*tçīnūi*
Strong	*apūsterot*
Old	*erāχpo*
Young	*morīvaits*
Good	*tihūrvet, tihūrwait*
Bad	*mohvrāi, mōhai*
Handsome	.....
Ugly	.....
Alive	*yait*
Dead	*amēya*
Cold	*otçō*
Warm	*orō*
I	*noma*
Thou	*oma*
He	*ahē, paēma*
We	*ayōhin, eyōmoma*
Ye	*asōin, omōma*
They	*pāmŭmŏe*
This	.....
That	.....
All	*oē*
Many (Much)	*ayōin, aiōen*
Who	*hakī*
Near	*momoa*
To-day	*mitēma*
Yesterday	*poāna*
To-morrow	*hiámte*
Yes	.....
No	.....
One	*pukū*
Two	*wehē*
Three	*pāhe*
Four	*watsā*
Five	.....
Six	.....
Seven	.....
Eight	.....
Nine	.....
Ten	.....
Eleven	.....
Twelve	.....
Twenty	.....
Thirty	.....
One Hundred	.....
One Thousand	.....
To Eat	*kwāχ, kwaa*
To Drink	*pāχ, paa*
To Run	.....

To Dance	.....
To Sing	.....
To Sleep	*yatámkoa*
To Speak	.....
To See	.....
To Love	.....
To Kill	.....
To Sit	.....
To Stand	.....
To Go	*mea, tankomōko*
To Come	*kima, kemā*

In the languages of Kīj and Netēla a few examples of the plural and pronominal forms were obtained, which may be worth preserving.

worōit, man	pl. *wororōt*
kītç, house	pl. *kīkitç*
haiχ, mountain	pl. *hahaiχ*
içot, wolf	pl. *içīçot*
tihúrwait, good	pl. *tiríwait*
tçínui, small	pl. *tçitçínui*
yupīχa, black	pl. *yupīnʋt*
tokór, woman	pl. *totókor*
paítχuar, bow	pl. *papaítχuar*
wasi, dog	pl. *wausi* (qu. *wáwasi ?*)
mohai, bad	pl. *momohai*
arawātai, white	pl. *rawānʋt*
kwauōχa, red	pl. *kwauχōnʋt*
nīnak, my father	pl. *ayōinak*, our father
mōnak, thy father	
anak, his father	
asōinak, your father	
nikīn, my house	
mukīn, thy house	
akīŋa, his house	
eyōkŋa, our house	
asokŋa (?), your house	
pomokŋa, their house	

APPENDIX VI

FAMILY: Shoshonean

LANGUAGE: San Gabriel Mission

PLACE OF RECORD: Near Banning, Cala.

RECORDED BY: H.W. Henshaw

DATE OF RECORD: Dec. 24, 1884

Vocabulary taken from a very old and decrepit Indian now living in an Indian rancheria near the town of Banning. He formerly lived at the San Gabriel Mission. His wife and children speak the Serrano ("Mountaineer") language. His granddaughter, a school girl, understands English and she acted as interpreter.

Schedule 1.

Man	Wö-râít
Woman	Tûk-kâś
Old Man	E-rák-pau
Old Woman	Tû-hó
Young Man	Ku-vá-tcu
Boy	Kwi-tí
Girl	Tă-hai-i
Thief	Po-kí

Schedule 2.

Head	A-pwân
Hair	"
Eye	A-tcaú-tcûn
Ear	A-ná-nă
Nose	A-mö´-pĭn
Beard	A-pé-hûn
Mouth	A-loñǵ-ĭn
Tooth	A-tá-tûm
Saliva	A-nó-niñg
Chin	No-âí-ĭ-tam
Neck	Niñg-öń
Arm	A-má-ho
Hand	A-mám
Thumb	A-má-mam
First finger	Ní-mam

Second finger	Nĭ-man-nu-ma-kit
Third finger	Nĭ-man-tci-nu-ĭ
Small finger	A-háv-ku-mĭn
Finger nail	A-tcú-tcu
Leg	A-tcú-tcü
Foot	A-név
Blood	A-pén
Brain	A-wil-kut
Heart	A-hún
Spine	A-tcarrh'
Skin	A-hö-hutc
Bone	A-ö´-ĭn
Paint (black)	Tú-hut
Paint (red)	U-yí
Barehead	Ma-ka-yû-hai

Schedule 4.

Village	Tci-nú-ĭ
Fire	Tcá-wŏt
Fire wood	Ku-tá
Living coals	A-tú-an
Ashes	Ku-cít
Smoke	Tcĭ-aŕrh

Schedule 5.

Bow of wood	Pait-ho-as
Arrow	Ni-tcú
Arrowhead of stone	A-whán
Food	Nĭ-nĭ
Black	Yo-pí-h'a
Blue	Ta-ká-pĭ
Red	Kwa-hań-ha
White	Raú-rau

There are no Schedules 6 and 7.

Schedule 8.

One	Pu-kú-u
Two	Wĕ-hé
Three	Pa-hĕ
Four	Wu-tcá
Five	Ma-harrh
Six	Pa-wá-hĭ
Ten	We-heś-wa-tca
Twenty	We-hes-ma-ha
Thirty	Pá-hĭc